ECONOMIC
REPORT
OF THE
PRESIDENT

JANUARY 2017

TOGETHER WITH
THE ANNUAL REPORT
OF THE
COUNCIL OF ECONOMIC ADVISERS

C O N T E N T S

*For a detailed table of contents of the Council's Report, see page 11.

ECONOMIC REPORT
OF THE
PRESIDENT

ECONOMIC REPORT OF THE PRESIDENT

To the Congress of the United States:

Eight years ago when I took office, our economy was in crisis. We were just months into the worst recession since the Great Depression, with unemployment rising rapidly toward a peak of 10 percent. Nearly 800,000 Americans were losing their jobs each month, and home prices and the stock market had plummeted. The auto industry was on the verge of collapse. Many American families struggled to pay their bills, and millions had lost their homes.

Faced with this crisis, my Administration acted quickly, taking steps to shore up the financial system; cut taxes for working families; invest in infrastructure, clean energy, and teacher jobs; help families refinance their homes; and rescue the auto industry. These actions stemmed the tide of the crisis and laid the foundation for a stronger economy over the long term.

Today, thanks to the resilience of the American people, our economy has emerged as the strongest and most durable in the world. By nearly every economic measure, America is better off than when I took office. We are in the midst of the longest streak of job growth on record. U.S. businesses have added 15.6 million jobs since early 2010. The unemployment rate has been cut by more than half from its peak, falling much faster than economists expected. Rising home prices have brought millions of homeowners back above water, we are less reliant on foreign oil than we have been in nearly three decades, and we have cut our budget deficit by two-thirds as a share of the economy.

Most importantly, wages have begun to rise again for working families. In 2015, median household income rose at the fastest rate on record, with the typical family earning an additional $2,800. The poverty rate fell by more than any year since 1968. And data indicate that these gains have continued in 2016, with wages rising over 2.7 percent at an annual rate so far this year, much faster than inflation.

While American families have made remarkable progress during the recovery, my Administration has also strengthened the long-term foundation of our economy and worked to ensure that every American has a fair chance to succeed if they work hard. We enacted the Affordable Care Act (ACA) and reshaped our healthcare system, expanded opportunity by making education more affordable and our tax code fairer, and increased our economy's resilience by strengthening the financial system and addressing climate change. These efforts have yielded undeniable results.

Today, 20 million more American adults have health insurance. On top of that, more than 3 million additional children have health insurance today than in 2008, thanks in large part to the ACA and other actions under my Administration. Our uninsured rate has hit its lowest level ever, and insurance companies can no longer discriminate against those with pre-existing conditions. At the same time, we have slowed the growth of health costs dramatically. The average premium for a family who gets coverage on the job is $3,600 lower today than it would be if premium growth had matched the decade before the ACA. All of these changes pay dividends for our economy.

We have also worked to ensure that all American families can share in the benefits of the economy, not just those at the top, and we have succeeded in rolling back some of the rise in inequality since the 1970s. Tax changes since 2009 have increased the share of income going to the bottom 99 percent of families by more than any Administration since at least 1960. These tax changes and the ACA will boost incomes for our lowest-income families by 18 percent, or $2,200.

Over the long term, education provides the surest path to increasing economic opportunity. During my Administration, we have increased access to early childhood education, lifted high school graduation rates to record highs, and encouraged States to adopt higher standards and provide better training for teachers. And to help make college more affordable, we have doubled investments in Pell Grants and college tax credits; simplified the application for Federal student aid; and helped more than 5 million borrowers cap their monthly student loan payments.

Finally, we have made our economy more resilient against future challenges. After the financial crisis, we passed the toughest Wall Street reforms in history. Banks have sharply increased the size of their capital buffers, there are new tough limits on risky behavior by banks, and we have brought dark corners of the shadow banking industry under the regulatory umbrella, all of which make another crisis less likely. We have new tools to guard against another "too big to fail" scenario and a new consumer watchdog to hold financial institutions accountable.

Sustainable economic growth also requires addressing climate change, and since 2008, we have seen U.S. emissions fall even as our economy has grown. America's economy is becoming more energy efficient and less carbon intensive. Our policies helped to catalyze this change: In 2009, the Recovery Act made a historic investment in clean energy, and we have since increased incentives for renewable energy like wind and solar, improved energy efficiency, and implemented the first-ever greenhouse gas standards for power plants, cars, and trucks. And America's leadership on climate issues helped pave the way for the Paris Agreement, in which almost 200 countries committed to take concrete steps to reduce emissions.

Our economic progress over the past eight years has been nothing short of remarkable, and I am proud of everything my Administration has accomplished. But I have always acknowledged that the work of perfecting our union, and making our economy work for every American, would take far longer than my time in office.

As I pass the baton to my successor, much work remains to continue strengthening our economy and, most importantly, lifting wages for working families. It is no secret that our openness to new ideas and inclusivity are part of what make the United States the most resilient economy in the world. Continuing our technological progress and innovation, engaging with the world economy through trade, and welcoming immigrants and new American families will create shared growth and help define our economy for the coming decades.

The first step is to make smart, long-term investments that raise productivity, like boosting funding for infrastructure and research and development. We must also promote competition and innovation in the economy and open new markets for American businesses through high-standards trade agreements.

But strengthening economic growth is only half of the equation. We must also make sure that workers can share in that prosperity by creating new, well-paid jobs and preparing workers for them. That means investing in education from Pre-K all the way through college and increasing access to apprenticeships and other career pathways. It means giving workers a bigger voice and setting fair rules of the road by strengthening collective bargaining, raising the Federal minimum wage, expanding access to paid leave, and supporting retirement savings. And it means making our tax system fairer so that those at the top pay their fair share.

Finally, we must ensure that growth is sustainable by continuing to address the global risk of climate change, by increasing the safety and accountability of our financial system, and by making responsible fiscal decisions.

Over the past eight years, our country has come back from a once-in-a-lifetime economic crisis and emerged even stronger. For all the work that remains, a new foundation has been laid. A new future is ours to write. I have never been more optimistic about America's future, and I am confident that this incredible journey that we are on as Americans will continue.

THE WHITE HOUSE
DECEMBER 2016

THE ANNUAL REPORT
OF THE
COUNCIL OF ECONOMIC ADVISERS

LETTER OF TRANSMITTAL

COUNCIL OF ECONOMIC ADVISERS

Washington, D.C., December 15, 2016

MR. PRESIDENT:

The Council of Economic Advisers herewith submits its 2017 Annual Report in accordance of the Employment Act of 1946 as amended by the Full Employment and Balanced Growth Act of 1978.

Sincerely yours,

Jason Furman
Chairman

Sandra E. Black
Member

Jay C. Shambaugh
Member

CONTENTS

APPENDIXES

FIGURES

TABLES

BOXES

C H A P T E R   1

EIGHT YEARS OF RECOVERY AND REINVESTMENT

As the 2017 *Economic Report of the President* goes to press, the United States is eight years removed from the onset of the worst economic crisis since the Great Depression. Over the two terms of the Obama Administration, the U.S. economy has made a remarkable recovery from the Great Recession. After peaking at 10.0 percent in October 2009, the unemployment rate has been cut by more than half to 4.6 percent as of November 2016, below its pre-recession average. Real gross domestic product (GDP) per capita recovered fully to its pre-crisis peak in the fourth quarter of 2013, faster than what would have been expected after such a severe financial crisis based on historical precedents. As of the third quarter of 2016, the U.S. economy was 11.5 percent larger than at its peak before the crisis. As of November 2016, the economy has added 14.8 million jobs over 74 months, the longest streak of total job growth on record. Since private-sector job growth turned positive in March 2010, U.S. businesses have added 15.6 million jobs. Real wage growth has been faster in the current business cycle than in any since the early 1970s. Meanwhile, from 2014 to 2015, median real household income grew by 5.2 percent, the fastest annual growth on record, and the United States saw its largest one-year drop in the poverty rate since the 1960s.

Other indicators at the end of 2016 also show substantial progress. Rising home prices have helped bring millions of homeowners back from negative equity. Real, or inflation-adjusted, household net worth exceeds its pre-recession peak by 16 percent. Since 2008, the United States has tripled the amount of energy harnessed from wind and increased solar generation thirtyfold. The United States is less reliant on foreign oil than it has been in nearly three decades. Since the Affordable Care Act (ACA) became law in 2010, health care prices have risen at the slowest rate in 50 years. Measured as a share of the economy, the Federal budget deficit has been cut by about two-thirds since 2009.

The forceful response of the Federal Government to the crisis in 2008 and 2009 helped stave off a potential second Great Depression, setting the U.S. economy on track to rebuild, reinvest, and recover. Recovery from the crisis alone, though, was never the President's sole aim. The Administration has also addressed the structural barriers to sustained, shared prosperity that middle-class families had faced for decades—rising health care costs, limited access to higher education, slow growth in incomes, high levels of inequality, a reliance on oil and other sources of carbon pollution, and more—so that the U.S. economy would work for all Americans. Thanks to these policy efforts, eight years later, the American economy is stronger, more resilient, and better positioned for the 21st century than ever before.

The 2017 *Economic Report of the President* reviews the economic record of the Obama Administration, focusing both on how its policies have promoted economic growth that is robust and widely shared and on the challenges the U.S. economy still faces in the years ahead.

THE RECOVERY IN REVIEW

Across a broad range of macroeconomic measures, the U.S. economy has made remarkable progress in the eight years since one of the most tumultuous and uncertain periods in its history.

Employment and Wages

The Great Recession was well underway when President Obama took office in January 2009. In that month, the unemployment rate stood at 7.8 percent, already elevated from its average of 5.3 percent in the 2001-07 expansion period. The unemployment rate would continue to increase until it peaked at 10.0 percent in October 2009. The long-term unemployment rate—the share of the labor force unemployed for 27 weeks or more—rose to an all-time high of 4.4 percent, as did the share of Americans working part-time for economic reasons (that is, those working part-time who would prefer a full-time position), which doubled to 6.0 percent from its pre-recession average.

From its peak, the unemployment rate recovered to its pre-recession average in mid-2015 and continued to fall, standing at 4.6 percent as of November 2016. This rapid decline came far more quickly than most economists predicted: as recently as March 2014, private forecasters expected the unemployment rate to remain above 5.0 percent until at least 2020 (Figure 1-1). All but one of the broader measures of labor underutilization published by the Bureau of Labor Statistics (BLS) have recovered fully to their respective pre-recession averages. Further, the labor force participation rate, which

Figure 1-1
Actual and Consensus Forecast Unemployment Rate, 2008–2020

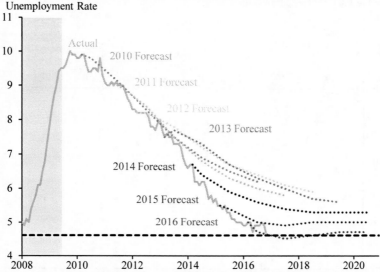

Unemployment Rate

Note: Annual forecasts are current as of March of the stated year. Black dashed line represents November 2016 value (4.6 percent). Shading denotes recession.
Source: Bureau of Labor Statistics, Current Population Survey; Blue Chip Economic Indicators.

has been subject to downward pressure due to the aging of the U.S. population, has been broadly stable since the end of 2013, as the strengthening labor market recovery has led workers to enter (or reenter) the workforce, offsetting downward pressure from demographic trends.

Total nonfarm employment peaked in January 2008 before falling by 8.7 million jobs, or 6.3 percent, to its trough in February 2010; over the same period, private-sector employment fell by 8.8 million jobs, or 7.6 percent. In the first quarter of 2009 alone, total job losses averaged 772,000 a month, larger than the populations of a number of U.S. States. While job losses were broad-based across industries, several sectors were particularly hard-hit. From January 2008 to February 2010, employment in the manufacturing sector declined by 16.6 percent, while employment in the construction sector declined by 26.4 percent.

Nonfarm job growth turned consistently positive beginning in October 2010. Since then, the U.S. economy has added jobs for 74 straight months, the longest streak of total job growth on record; over this period, nonfarm employment growth has averaged 199,000 jobs a month. Total nonfarm employment recovered to its pre-recession peak in 2014—the best year for job creation since the 1990s—and, as of November 2016, exceeded its pre-recession peak by 6.7 million jobs. Since private-sector job growth

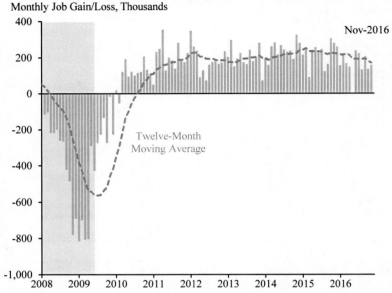

Figure 1-2
Private-Sector Payroll Employment Growth, 2008–2016

Monthly Job Gain/Loss, Thousands

Nov-2016

Twelve-Month
Moving Average

Note: Shading denotes recession.
Source: Bureau of Labor Statistics, Current Employment Statistics; CEA calculations.

turned positive in March 2010, U.S. businesses have added 15.6 million jobs (Figure 1-2). The manufacturing sector has added over 800,000 jobs since February 2010, the industry's fastest growth since the 1990s (see Box 1-2). And since June 2009, when Chrysler and General Motors (GM) emerged from bankruptcy, the automobile industry (manufacturing and retail) has added nearly 700,000 jobs, the industry's strongest growth on record.

As the labor market has strengthened, the recovery has translated into real wage gains for American workers. Due to both an acceleration in nominal wage growth and low inflation, since the end of 2012 private production and nonsupervisory workers, who comprise about 80 percent of private-sector employment, have seen their real hourly earnings increase by 5.3 percent, more than the total cumulative real wage gains for these workers from 1980 to 2007. Overall, real hourly wage growth since the business cycle peak in December 2007 has averaged 0.8 percent a year for these workers, the fastest growth of any business cycle (measured peak-to-peak) since the 1970s (Figure 1-3).

The combination of robust employment growth and accelerating real wage growth has translated into strong growth in household incomes. From 2014 to 2015, real median household income grew 5.2 percent, or $2,800, the fastest growth on record. Moreover, these income gains have been widely

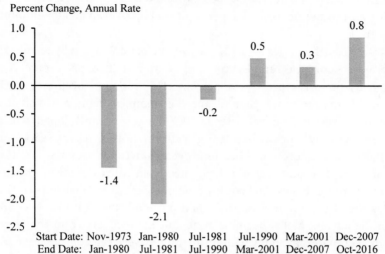

Figure 1-3
**Real Hourly Wage Growth Over Business Cycles,
Cycle Peak to Cycle Peak**

Percent Change, Annual Rate

| Start Date: | Nov-1973 | Jan-1980 | Jul-1981 | Jul-1990 | Mar-2001 | Dec-2007 |
| End Date: | Jan-1980 | Jul-1981 | Jul-1990 | Mar-2001 | Dec-2007 | Oct-2016 |

Note: Wages for private production and nonsupervisory workers.
Source: National Bureau of Economic Research; Bureau of Labor Statistics, Real Earnings;
CEA calculations.

shared: households at the bottom and middle of the income distribution saw faster real income gains from 2014 to 2015 than did households at the top of the income distribution.

While the labor market has made major improvements, some challenges still remain. The share of employees working part-time for economic reasons, and, accordingly, the broadest measure of underemployment, the U-6 rate (of which this share is a component), remain modestly elevated relative to their respective pre-recession averages. As discussed below, labor force participation, particularly for many workers in their prime working years, has been declining for decades, a key challenge for the U.S. labor market in the years ahead. And while real wage growth has picked up in recent years, more work remains to reverse decades of limited income growth for many middle-class families.

Output and Economic Growth

Like employment, economic output contracted sharply in the Great Recession. Real GDP peaked in the fourth quarter of 2007 before falling rapidly over the following year. In the fourth quarter of 2008 alone, real GDP contracted at an annualized rate of 8.2 percent. As discussed in Box 1-1, this drop was more severe than initially estimated: the first estimate of GDP growth in the fourth quarter of 2008 was a contraction of 3.8 percent. All told, real GDP fell 4.2 percent, from its peak in the fourth quarter of 2007 to its trough in the second quarter of 2009. Since the U.S. population continued to grow over this period, real GDP per capita fell by an even greater amount, 5.5 percent.

By the fourth quarter of 2013, per-capita real GDP had fully recovered to its pre-recession peak, and by the third quarter of 2016, per-capita GDP exceeded its pre-crisis peak by 4 percent. This rebound occurred much more quickly than in most other advanced economies, many of which also experienced systemic financial crises in 2007-08. For example, Japan, which recovered relatively quickly, has seen growth level off in recent years, and while the euro area economy has improved noticeably over the last two years, the area is on the verge of missing nearly an entire decade of growth, as it still has not attained 2008 levels of income per capita (Figure 1-4). Not only has the U.S. economy outperformed those of other advanced economies in the current global business cycle, but the recovery from the Great Recession compares favorably with historical recoveries in countries experiencing systemic financial crises (Reinhart and Rogoff 2014). Still, a number of trends—including demographic changes resulting in slower workforce growth and a slowdown in productivity growth—have presented headwinds to U.S. output growth over the recovery.

Equity Markets, House Prices, Household Wealth, and Other Measures

The collapse of the housing bubble and the financial crisis of 2007-08 manifested in steep declines in both house and equity prices. From their peak in February 2007 to their trough in January 2012, house prices (as measured by the S&P CoreLogic Case-Shiller Home Price Index) fell by 26 percent. The S&P 500 index, meanwhile, fell by more than half between August 2007 and March 2009. These steep declines in asset prices caused stark drops in overall household wealth: real household net worth—the assets of U.S. households minus their liabilities, net of inflation—fell 21 percent from its peak in 2007 to its trough in 2009.

By the end of 2016, the landscape was much improved. From March 2009 to November 2016, the S&P 500 index increased 186 percent. Since their January 2012 trough, home prices have increased 34 percent as of September 2016, and have nearly recovered to their February 2007 nominal peak (Figure 1-5). As of the second quarter of 2016, rising home prices since the end of 2012 have helped to lift almost 7.9 million households out of negative equity, and the number of homes in foreclosure has declined dramatically. The combination of rising employment and wages, rebounding asset prices,

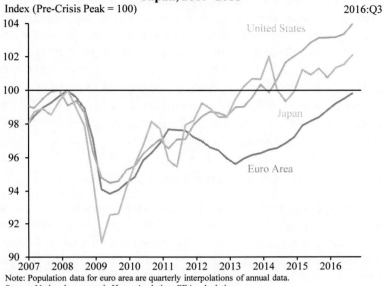

Figure 1-4
Real GDP per Capita: Euro Area, United States, and Japan, 2007–2016

Index (Pre-Crisis Peak = 100)   2016:Q3

Note: Population data for euro area are quarterly interpolations of annual data.
Source: National sources via Haver Analytics; CEA calculations.

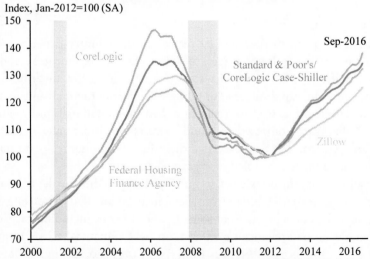

Figure 1-5
National House Price Indexes, 2000–2016

Index, Jan-2012=100 (SA)

Sep-2016

Note: Shading denotes recession. The Standard & Poor's/CoreLogic Case-Shiller, Federal Housing Finance Agency, and CoreLogic indexes all adjust for the quality of homes sold but only cover homes that are bought or sold, whereas Zillow reflects prices for all homes on the market. All indexes are seasonally adjusted.
Source: Zillow; CoreLogic; Federal Housing Finance Agency; Standard & Poor's.

and diligent efforts to pay down debts has left American households with their strongest net worth position on record: as of the third quarter of 2016, real household net worth exceeded its pre-recession peak by 16 percent.

Other indicators show a similar pattern of strong progress. Since the ACA was signed into law in 2010, health care prices have risen at the slowest pace in 50 years. Since 2008, the United States has tripled the amount of energy harnessed from wind and has increased solar generation thirtyfold. Today, the United States is less reliant on foreign oil than it has been in nearly three decades. The Federal budget deficit in fiscal year (FY) 2016 was 3.2 percent of GDP, about a third of the 9.8 percent of GDP deficit recorded in 2009 and equal to the average over the last 40 years.

The Crisis and the Response

After eight years of recovery, it is easy to forget how close the U.S. economy came to an outright depression during the crisis. Indeed, by a number of macroeconomic measures, the first year of the Great Recession in the United States saw larger declines than at the outset of the Great Depression in 1929-30. However, the forceful policy response by the Federal Government—including the efforts of the Bush Administration, the Obama Administration, the Federal Reserve, Congress, and others—combined with the resilience of American businesses and families and coordination with our international partners to help stave off a second Great Depression.

A Once-in-a-Lifetime Crisis

In the run-up to the 2007-09 recession, the country experienced a dramatic escalation in home prices, fueled in part by lax mortgage underwriting standards and a financial system that channeled too much funding into housing. The rapid increase in home prices came to an abrupt halt in late 2006. Home prices stopped rising and then started falling rapidly within a year. Millions of homeowners found themselves "underwater"—that is, their mortgage loan balances exceeded the value of their homes—and many were unable to make scheduled mortgage payments.

Fallout from the housing crisis quickly spread to the broader economy through a complex web of opaque financial instruments tied to housing and questionable business practices of some financial firms, including excessive leverage and an overreliance on short-term debt (Financial Crisis Inquiry Report 2011). Investors pulled back from risky assets and, during one fateful week in September 2008, the investment bank Lehman Brothers went out of business, a prominent money market fund "broke the buck" (meaning that depositors could no longer count on getting their money back in its entirety,

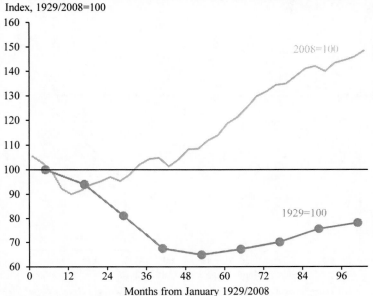

Figure 1-6
Household Net Worth in the Great Depression and Great Recession
Index, 1929/2008=100

Months from January 1929/2008
Note: Orange markers represent annual averages.
Source: Federal Reserve Board of Governors; Mishkin (1978).

an almost unprecedented event), and the large insurance firm American International Group (AIG) teetered on the edge of bankruptcy until the U.S. Government provided $85 billion in financial support.

The dramatic fall of asset prices—due to both the collapse of the housing bubble and the resulting financial turmoil—was, by many measures, deeper than at the outset of the Great Depression in 1929-30. Home prices in the United States fell 5.6 percent between 2008 and 2009, outpacing the 4.3-percent decline from 1929 to 1930. Between 2008 and 2009, the S&P 500 Index declined 23 percent on an annual average basis, exceeding the 1929-30 decline of 19 percent. As a result of these steep declines in asset prices, nominal household net worth declined by a total of $13 trillion, or 19 percent of total U.S. household wealth, from its peak in 2007 to its trough in 2009. The decline in wealth in the early stages of the Great Recession was far larger than the reduction experienced at the onset of the Great Depression (Figure 1-6).

Faced with a drop in demand for their goods and services and extraordinary uncertainty about their economic futures, businesses stopped hiring and laid off workers: employment declined 4 percent from 2008 to 2009, nearly the same rate as from 1929 to 1930 (Figure 1-7). Businesses also

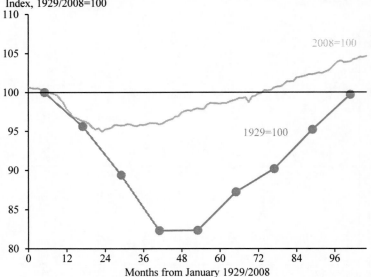

Figure 1-7
Civilian Employment in the Great Depression and Great Recession
Index, 1929/2008=100

Months from January 1929/2008

Note: Civilian employment of those ages 16 and older for 2008 series; ages 14 and older for 1929 series. Orange markers represent annual averages.
Source: Bureau of Labor Statistics,; CEA calculations.

shelved investment plans and consumers cut back on spending. The financial crisis also had wide-ranging effects abroad, and global trade suffered a much more drastic fall between 2008 and 2009 than during the first year of the Great Depression (Figure 1-8). In short, as the Obama Administration began, the United States faced an economic crisis of historic proportions.

The Policy Response

The short-term policy response in the United States to the global financial crisis in 2008-09 was aggressive, swift, and—by the preponderance of evidence from many private-sector, academic, and government analyses—effective. It included a combination of aggressive aggregate demand management driven by expansionary fiscal and monetary policy and short-term financial stability measures that prevented the risks of the crisis from compounding further.

Fiscal Policy

The fiscal response began in early 2008, well before the height of the financial crisis, as the economy began to slide into recession. Congress and the Bush Administration enacted the Economic Stimulus Act in February 2008, cutting taxes for low- and middle-income households while providing

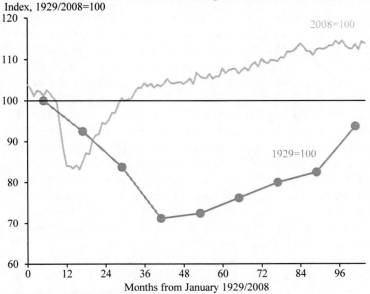

Figure 1-8
Global Trade Flows in the Great Depression and Great Recession
Index, 1929/2008=100

Months from January 1929/2008

Note: Orange markers represent annual averages.
Source: CPB World Trade Monitor; Statistical Office of the United Nations; CEA calculations.

tax incentives to encourage business investment. The value of the cuts in the Act totaled $124 billion over 11 years, with nearly all of the cuts concentrated in FY 2008. The Act was designed to counteract a short recession by providing brief, temporary support to consumer spending—including electronic payments to households that began less than three months after passage of the Act—but it was insufficient to reverse the emerging distress and, by design, did not have long-lasting effects.

In December 2008, then-President-elect Obama proposed an outline of what would become the American Recovery and Reinvestment Act of 2009, also known as the Recovery Act or "ARRA." The Recovery Act was the first bill introduced in the House of Representatives just days after the President's inauguration, and the President signed it into law less than a month after he took office. As the name of the Act suggests, the intention was for the bill to both generate recovery from the crisis and to be an important investment in the future of the economy.

Several principles guided the new Administration's fiscal policy. First, the fiscal effort was to be implemented quickly. Second, it should be large, given the scope of the economic problem. Finally, it should be a sustained effort that would not only provide immediate fiscal support over the first two years, but would also provide smaller levels of temporary support

Box 1-1: Revisions to Crisis-Era Data

Policymakers face a number of challenges in assessing the state of the economy in real time. First, macroeconomic indicators are only available on a lagged basis, since it takes time for the Federal statistical agencies—such as the Census Bureau, the Bureau of Economic Analysis (BEA), and the Bureau of Labor Statistics (BLS)—to collect and analyze the data underlying their estimates. Initial estimates of gross domestic product (GDP) for a given quarter, for example, are released several weeks after that quarter ends. Second, more timely data generally tend to be incomplete and can only present a partial snapshot of the economy. Third, and perhaps most importantly, though subsequent revisions to macroeconomic data—particularly estimates of employment and output—often do not receive the same attention as initial estimates, they can often be large and economically meaningful, especially around turning points in the business cycle (when extrapolations and assumptions underlying some initial estimates can turn out badly wrong).

These challenges confronted the Obama Administration in determining the response to the 2008 crisis. When President Obama took office on January 20, 2009, BEA had not yet released its advance estimate of GDP growth in the fourth quarter of 2008, a critical measure for understanding how much the financial crisis had affected real economic activity. Yet what data were available at that point showed an economy facing a substantial and protracted decline in economic output, and the incoming Administration had proposed the contours of what would become the American Recovery and Reinvestment Act in December 2008. When BEA released its advance estimate of GDP growth for the fourth quarter of 2008 in late January 2009—a contraction of 3.8 percent at an annual rate, the largest quarterly decline since 1982—it confirmed the need for a vigorous response from the Federal Government.

Table 1-i

Revisions to Crisis-Era Output Data

Estimate Date	Real GDP Growth, 2008:Q4 (Percent, Annual Rate)
January 2009 (Advance Estimate)	-3.8
February 2009 (Second Estimate)	-6.2
March 2009 (Third Estimate)	-6.3
July 2009	-5.4
July 2010	-6.8
July 2011	-8.9
July 2013	-8.3
July 2014	-8.2

Source: Bureau of Economic Analysis, National Income and Product Accounts.

Subsequent revisions to fourth-quarter GDP growth, however, have revealed that early estimates greatly *underestimated* the extent of output losses in the immediate aftermath of the financial crisis. As shown in Table 1-i, BEA's most recent estimate is that real GDP decreased by 8.2 percent at an annual rate in the fourth quarter of 2008, the largest one-quarter drop since 1958.

Labor market data show a similar pattern, with initial estimates of job losses in the fourth quarter of 2008 subsequently revised further downward, as shown in Table 1-ii. In January 2009, contemporary estimates of nonfarm employment losses from September to December 2008 totaled 1.5 million jobs. As of 2016, BLS estimates that 1.9 million Americans lost their jobs during those months.

All told, subsequent revisions to crisis-era data have revealed that the state of the U.S. economy in early 2009 was even worse than initial data indicated. The revisions have also helped to confirm both the historic nature of the economic downturn that policymakers faced in the early months of 2009 and the role that policy played in helping to avert a second Great Depression.

Table 1-ii
Revisions to Crisis-Era Employment Data

Estimate Date	Change in Total Nonfarm Employment, September 2008 to December 2008 (Thousands)
January 2009	-1,531
February 2009	-1,554
March 2009	-1,658
February 2010	-1,955
February 2011	-1,930
February 2012	-1,953
February 2013	-1,952
February 2014	-1,936
February 2015	-1,937

Source: Bureau of Labor Statistics, Current Employment Statistics.

thereafter. The new approach would require a mix of policy instruments such as tax cuts and other temporary assistance that put cash in the hands of households who needed it immediately and who were likely to spend it, boosting aggregate demand. Other measures provided States with funding to continue providing necessary services and to help them avoid cutting their own budgets drastically in the face of fiscal shortfalls. Additional components, such as investments in infrastructure and innovation, would be more lagged but would be more likely to have larger cumulative counter-cyclical impacts and greater longer-run benefits. In all cases, however, the measures would end and would not have long-term impacts on the Federal Government's primary budget deficit.

To ensure that the fiscal stimulus would be as effective as possible, the Recovery Act utilized a variety of spending, tax, and incentive channels. Recovery Act policies were fairly evenly distributed across individual tax cuts and business tax incentives (29 percent), aid to directly impacted individuals and State fiscal relief (34 percent), and public investments in infrastructure, education, job training, energy, and health information technology (37 percent).

When passed, the Congressional Budget Office (CBO) estimated that the Recovery Act would cost $787 billion, though that estimate would increase as the full impact of the recession became apparent (CBO 2009). The most recent CBO estimate shows that the fiscal support from the Recovery Act will total $836 billion through 2019 (CBO 2015). Between calendar years 2009 and 2012, the period for which the Recovery Act had the largest impact, the Act provided a total fiscal impulse of approximately $700 billion.[1]

Importantly, while the Recovery Act provided a considerable short-term boost to aggregate demand, its investments were targeted for their long-term growth potential, helping ensure that the United States climbed out of the crisis stronger than before. The provisions of the Recovery Act were tailored to deepen the United States' stock of private physical capital (through business tax incentives), public physical capital (through investments in transportation infrastructure), human capital (through extensive education investments), and intellectual capital (through research and development investments).

More than a dozen subsequent fiscal measures extended certain Recovery Act provisions and introduced additional countercyclical policies, such as the temporary payroll tax cut in effect during 2011 and 2012. In total, discretionary fiscal stimulus from 2009 through 2012 totaled $1.4 trillion and averaged around 2 percent of GDP. Together with automatic stabilizers, the total fiscal stimulus over these four years averaged 4 percent of GDP (Figure 1-9). The initial U.S. fiscal response exceeded the response by the euro area or Japan, one of the reasons the United States recovered sooner and more strongly (Furman 2016a).

Monetary Policy

The Federal Reserve's independent decision to take a vigorous approach to monetary stabilization was another major driver of the United

---

[1] This figure excludes a routine set of patches for the Alternative Minimum Tax (AMT). This part of the Recovery Act, a continuation of a longstanding practice, is best thought of as ongoing fiscal policy, not as a temporary fiscal impulse designed specifically to counter the effects of an economic recession.

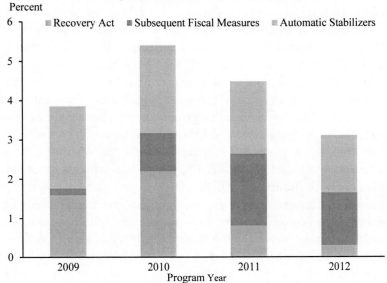

Figure 1-9
Fiscal Expansion as Share of GDP, 2009–2012

Percent

■ Recovery Act   ■ Subsequent Fiscal Measures   ■ Automatic Stabilizers

Program Year

Source: Congressional Budget Office (2016); Bureau of Economic Analysis, National Income and Product Accounts; CEA calculations.

States' recovery. The traditional tool of monetary policy—the Federal Funds target rate—was reduced to nearly zero by the end of 2008, after which the Federal Reserve turned to a program of unconventional policy in an effort to reduce long-term interest rates. The Federal Reserve used two principal mechanisms to achieve this end: forward guidance, by which it provided an indication of its plan for the future path of short-term interest rates, and asset purchases (commonly known as "quantitative easing"). As part of its forward guidance, the Federal Reserve assured market participants that it would maintain its near-zero interest rate policy for an extended period of time. As part of its quantitative easing program, the Federal Reserve purchased long-term debt instruments, including mortgage-backed securities and U.S. Treasury bonds, expanding its balance sheet from $900 billion to $4.5 trillion between 2008 and 2014. In contrast, the European Central Bank initially did not cut rates to zero, raised rates in 2011, and did not undertake nearly as large a balance sheet expansion as the Federal Reserve.

Stabilizing Financial Markets

In addition to expansionary fiscal and monetary policy, the Bush and Obama Administrations and the Federal Reserve implemented a package of short-term measures to stabilize financial markets. In late 2008, the Treasury

Department established a temporary guarantee program for money market mutual funds while the Federal Deposit Insurance Corporation (FDIC) expanded its guarantee on bank deposits and debt to avoid runs on banks and other financial institutions. The Bush Administration also proposed, and Congress approved, the Troubled Asset Relief Program (TARP), providing up to $700 billion to stabilize troubled banks. Meanwhile, the Federal Reserve instituted a number of programs designed to provide liquidity to borrowers, investors, and financial market participants. These early policy responses helped stem a plunge in consumer confidence, credit flows, and corporate balance sheets that could have been much worse.

Within three weeks of President Obama taking office, the new Administration released its Financial Stability Plan. Building on the initial action of the Bush Administration, the plan included a host of new measures designed to continue to shore up financial markets and increase credit flows. Ultimately, over 700 banks received capital through TARP, and the Obama Administration also expanded the use of TARP funds to help millions of families affected by the housing crisis, restructure the automobile industry, and support small businesses. It is important to note, however, that TARP gave the Federal Government authority to recoup any returns on asset purchases or equity investments made under the program. To date, the Federal Government has collected 103 percent of the $412.1 billion spent on investment programs, as well as an additional $17.5 billion from Treasury's equity stake in AIG, for a total return of about $28 billion.

In addition to expanding and effectively managing the TARP program, the Administration established comprehensive stress tests of the Nation's 19 largest financial institutions to reduce uncertainty regarding their solvency, stabilize the financial system, and ensure the banks were able to continue lending. By using TARP funding as a backstop for firms unable to raise necessary capital, the Administration moved the financial system rapidly toward a better-capitalized system where financial institutions and investors knew that institutions were solvent, so normal financial activity could resume.

Rescuing the Automobile Sector

In addition to stabilizing the financial market, the Administration provided substantial support to automobile companies to keep them from failing during the Great Recession. At the height of the financial crisis, capital markets would have been unable to oversee the orderly restructuring of the automobile companies necessary to preserve their viable assets. The ensuing job losses and the concentrated, severe impact on specific communities would also have resulted in large economic hardship as well as substantial costs to the Federal Government for Medicaid, unemployment insurance, and other social assistance programs. In these circumstances, the Federal Government took extraordinary steps to avoid the unmanaged bankruptcy of the largest automobile manufacturers, failures that likely would have cascaded through supply chains, threatening even more firms.

The Administration guided two of America's largest automobile manufacturers—GM and Chrysler—through a targeted bankruptcy and comprehensive restructuring. In the spring of 2009, the Administration's Auto Task Force worked with these two firms to produce plans for viability. For both companies, a quick, targeted bankruptcy was judged to be the most efficient and successful way to restructure. Chrysler filed for bankruptcy on April 30, 2009; GM, on June 1. In addition to concessions by all stakeholders, including workers, retirees, creditors, and suppliers, the Federal Government invested funds to bring about an orderly restructuring. By the end of 2013, the Federal Government had disposed of all of its investments in Chrysler and GM. To date, American taxpayers have recovered $71 billion of the $80 billion invested in the automobile industry, and the Federal Government continues to receive proceeds from the bankruptcy liquidations of Old Chrysler and Old GM.

Supporting the Housing Market

The loss in household wealth from the collapse in housing prices was a significant factor slowing the economy in the recession, and financial products linked to real estate valuations were central to many aspects of the global financial crisis. The short-term policy response did not lose sight of this key fact. By establishing the Home Affordable Refinance Program (HARP), the Obama Administration helped more than 3 million borrowers refinance their loans and save hundreds of dollars each month. The Administration also eliminated additional barriers to refinancing and proposed reforms so that all responsible borrowers with loans insured by Fannie Mae and Freddie Mac would have access to simple, low-cost refinancing.

In addition to helping millions of Americans refinance, the Administration created the Home Affordable Mortgage Program (HAMP) to provide millions of homeowners who are behind on their payments an opportunity to modify their mortgages in order to reduce their monthly payments and avoid foreclosure. The Administration also provided over $7 billion in targeted support to the hardest-hit communities who experienced the sharpest declines in home prices. These funds were intended to help manage vacant and foreclosed properties that bring down local home values, support unemployed and underwater homeowners, and convert foreclosed properties into rentals.

Box 1-2: The Manufacturing Sector

A robust manufacturing sector acts as a galvanizing force for America's economic well-being, as it is linked to productivity growth, innovative capacity, and high-quality jobs. The average worker employed in the domestic manufacturing sector earns an hourly wage that is 2 to 9 percent higher than the overall average worker (Nicholson and Powers 2015). Further, the manufacturing sector houses a great deal of innovation, accounting for nearly 80 percent of private-sector research and development (R&D) and the vast majority of patents issued in the United States. The high-quality jobs and innovative capacity of the manufacturing industry, supported by the Administration, serve as investments in a strong macroeconomy and broad-based growth. In the last two decades of the 20th century, manufacturing employment followed a slight downward trend, while manufacturing output rose quickly (Figure 1-i). However, throughout the first decade of the 21st century, employment fell sharply. By the time that the Great Recession hit, the manufacturing sector had already lost 3.5 million jobs relative to January 2000. By the beginning of 2010, the sector had shed another 2.3 million jobs.

Given the importance of the manufacturing sector to the U.S. economy, the Obama Administration made revitalizing domestic performance in this sector a central component of its economic agenda and

Figure 1-i
Manufacturing Output and Employment, 1980–2016

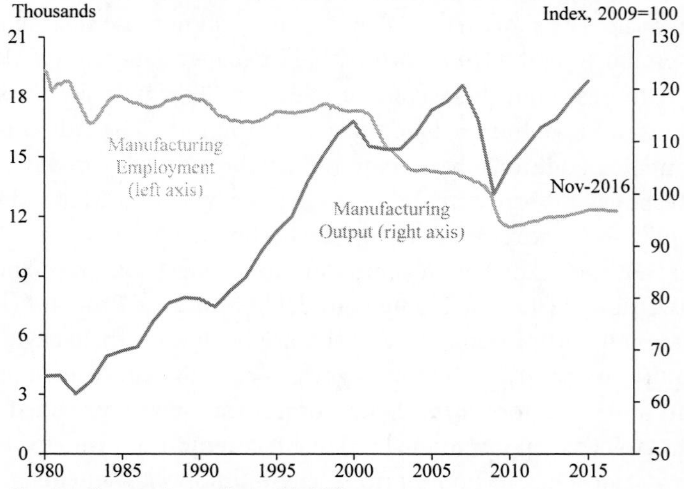

Note: Data for output is annual and ends in 2015.
Source: Bureau of Economic Analysis, National Income and Product Accounts; Bureau of Labor Statistics, Current Employment Statistics; CEA calculations.

worked to promote innovation and invest in manufacturing workforce skills.

The Administration's commitment to manufacturing was manifested in its decision to save the automobile industry. The President made the crucial, early decision to not only rescue, but to also restructure and rebuild American automobile manufacturing and its many connected industries. Yet, support for manufacturing went beyond this rescue. Creating the Manufacturing USA initiative in 2012 marked another significant action taken to support manufacturing. The Federal Government has committed over $600 million—which has been matched by over $1.3 billion in non-Federal investment—to fund the development of world-leading manufacturing capabilities with technologies such as 3D printing, integrated photonics, and smart sensors. In the four years since its establishment, Manufacturing USA has grown from one institute with 65 members to a network of nine institutes and over 1,300 members.

Further, the Administration has taken steps to reinvest in our manufacturing workforce to prepare it for a more competitive, global economy. First, the Administration awarded nearly $2 billion in Trade Adjustment Assistance Community College Career Training grants to help community colleges expand and improve programs that prepare workers for high-paying, high-skill occupations. To date, nearly 300,000 participants have enrolled in retraining programs through these grants, and 160,000 credentials have been awarded. Second, the Administration has prioritized apprenticeships. Research shows that apprenticeships tend to lead to high-paying jobs and provide a strong return on investment for employers. Recent Department of Labor data indicate that after completing her programs, the average registered apprentice earns a starting wage above $60,000, and 89 percent of registered apprenticeship program completers enter employment after exiting. To these ends, the Administration has allocated $265 million toward grants aimed at expanding apprenticeships in the United States. Since 2014, active apprenticeships have increased 31 percent, with an estimated 20,000 new apprentices in the manufacturing industry.

Ultimately, U.S. manufacturing output since the Great Recession has recovered at twice the pace of the overall economy since the third quarter of 2009. This marks the longest period in which manufacturing has outpaced U.S. economic output in 50 years. Contrary to the pattern in all other U.S. expansions since 1982, the current expansion has seen an increase in manufacturing output as a share of U.S. value-added. Notably, the U.S. manufacturing sector's job growth since the Great Recession is a marked departure from last decade, when the sector struggled to recover the jobs lost in the 2001 recession. Since February 2010, U.S. manufacturing has added over 800,000 new jobs.

Following the strong manufacturing recovery in the expansion after the Great Recession, the manufacturing sector has seen lackluster output and employment growth since 2014. The sector is inextricably tied to the global economy, and as global demand has slowed and energy-related capital expenditure has fallen, U.S. manufacturing has suffered. Global economic output, as one of the key drivers of export demand, is particularly important to manufacturing, as it is a far more trade-exposed sector than other parts of the economy. For example, while manufacturing represents roughly 12 percent of value added in the economy, manufactured exports have maintained a share of more than 60 percent of U.S. exports. Real exports rebounded swiftly after the crisis, helping the manufacturing sector. But recently, real exports of goods and services have fallen slightly, tied in large part to slower foreign GDP growth and a strong U.S. dollar. Moreover, recent declines in energy prices have affected many manufacturing industries that serve as significant upstream suppliers for the energy sector, such as steel manufacturers that supply oil producers.

Yet, even despite these headwinds, manufacturing job growth over the last two years is comparable with its *best* two years in the previous

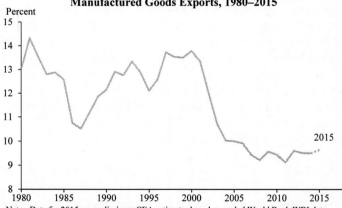

Figure 1-ii
U.S. Manufactured Goods Exports as a Share of World Manufactured Goods Exports, 1980–2015

Note: Data for 2015 are preliminary CEA estimates based on scaled World Bank WDI data. Manufactured exports are defined by SITC sections 5, 6, 7, and 8 (which includes iron and steel, chemicals, machinary and transport vehicles, and textiles), but exclude division 68 (non-ferrous metals) and group 891 (arms and amunition). This differs from the Census definition of manufacturing, which is based on NAICS codes 31-33.
Source: World Trade Organization; IMF International Financial Statistics; Eurostat Comext; World Bank.

expansion, a period of low production and negative employment growth in the sector. Further, the underlying structure of the sector is robust. One clear piece of evidence regarding the continued resilience of the U.S. manufacturing industry is that the United States has stabilized its market share in global manufacturing exports (Figure 1-ii). This stabilization is all the more notable given that the U.S. share of world manufacturing exports fell precipitously in the first half of the 2000s. These are signs that the headwinds that the U.S. manufacturing sector is facing are likely temporary and will subside as the underlying strength of the sector continues to support the U.S. macroeconomy.

The Impact of the Policy Response

A number of studies adopting a wide range of approaches to measuring the effect of the Recovery Act and subsequent fiscal measures find a large positive impact on output and employment (CEA 2014). Overall, CEA estimates that the Recovery Act saved or created about 6 million job-years (where a job-year is the equivalent of one full-time job for one year) through 2012 and raised the level of GDP by between 2 and 2.5 percent in FY 2010 and part of FY 2011. Combining effects of the Recovery Act and additional countercyclical fiscal legislation that followed, CEA estimates that the cumulative gain in employment was about 9 million job-years through the end of 2012 (Figure 1-10a). The cumulative boost to GDP from 2009 to 2012 was equivalent to about 9.5 percent of the level of GDP in the fourth quarter of 2008 (Figure 1-10b).

CEA's results are consistent with outside estimates, including those from CBO and academic researchers. These include studies that focus on portions of the Recovery Act that provided relief to States in ways that were not tied to current conditions (Feyrer and Sacerdote 2011; Chodorow-Reich et al. 2012), as well as those taking a broader view of the Federal policy response to the crisis and recession. Blinder and Zandi (2015) find that in the absence of policy actions by the Bush and Obama Administrations, Congress, and the Federal Reserve, the peak-to-trough decline in real GDP would have been nearly 14 percent (instead of 4 percent), the unemployment rate would have risen to nearly 16 percent (instead of 10 percent), and real output would have contracted for 13 quarters (instead of six).[2]

---

[2] For a more comprehensive discussion of methods of estimating the impact of the Recovery Act and subsequent fiscal measures, see Chapter 3 of the 2014 *Economic Report of the President*.

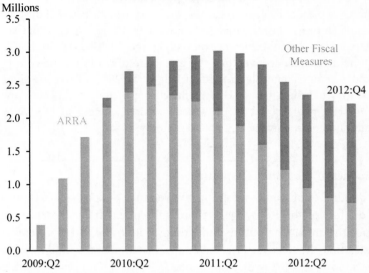

Figure 1-10a
**Quarterly Effect of the Recovery Act and Subsequent Fiscal
Measures on Employment, 2009–2012**

Millions

Source: Bureau of Economic Analysis, National Income and Product Accounts; Congressional
Budget Office; CEA calculations.

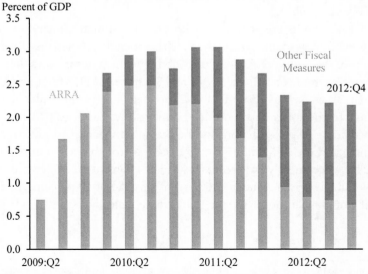

Figure 1-10b
**Quarterly Effect of the Recovery Act and Subsequent Fiscal
Measures on GDP, 2009–2012**

Percent of GDP

Source: Bureau of Economic Analysis, National Income and Product Accounts; Congressional
Budget Office; CEA calculations.

THE 2017 *ECONOMIC REPORT OF THE PRESIDENT*: PROMOTING STRONGER, MORE INCLUSIVE, AND MORE SUSTAINABLE GROWTH

The response of the Federal Government to the crisis averted a sharper and more prolonged downturn and put the U.S. economy back on a path to growth. Even so, a number of decades-long trends that preceded the crisis—rising inequality, insufficient health insurance coverage, high health care costs, and growing costs for higher education—still remained, preventing middle-class Americans from seeing gains in their incomes, economic security, and standards of living. Addressing these barriers to inclusive growth has been the cornerstone of the Obama Administration's economic policy, which has been focused not only on returning the U.S. economy back to stability, but on setting it on a firmer path to sustained growth that is broadly shared among all American families.

The Administration's reforms—and their effects on the U.S. economy and American families—are the main topic of this year's *Economic Report of the President*. Following a summary of macroeconomic developments in the last year (Chapter 2), each subsequent chapter focuses on a different aspect of the Obama Administration's economic record, describing the great strides that the Nation has made in building a stronger foundation for future prosperity.

Chapter 3: Reducing Inequality

The legislation President Obama fought for and signed into law represents a historic accomplishment in reducing inequality. The Administration has achieved its most substantial and immediate success in this respect in three areas: restoring economic growth, expanding health insurance coverage, and enacting a fairer tax code.

The policy response to the Great Recession served a dual role in reducing inequality. It reduced inequality in after-tax incomes directly through progressive tax and spending policies, such as temporary tax cuts for working and middle-class families and extensions of unemployment insurance, and it reduced wage inequality indirectly by boosting employment. By reducing unemployment, these policies offset roughly half of the increase in wage inequality that would otherwise have occurred if more workers lost their jobs and saw their wages fall to zero.

In addition to providing substantial gains in health insurance coverage (see below), the ACA also led to a large reduction in inequality in after-tax incomes. Meanwhile, progressive changes in tax policy have increased

Figure 1-11
**Change in Share of After-Tax Income by Income Percentile: Changes
in Tax Policy Since 2009
and ACA Coverage Provisions, 2017**

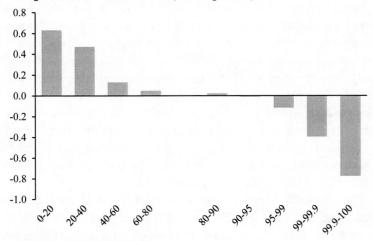

Change in Share of After-Tax Income (Percentage Points)

Source: U.S. Treasury, Office of Tax Analysis.

tax rates for the highest-income Americans and increased the generosity of tax credits for working families, reducing inequality in after-tax incomes.

Together, changes in tax policy and the ACA coverage provisions will increase the share of after-tax income received by the bottom quintile of households in 2017 by 0.6 percentage point, or 18 percent—equivalent to more than a decade of average income gains—and the share received by the second quintile by 0.5 percentage point, or 6 percent. At the same time, they will reduce the share received by the top 1 percent by 1.2 percentage points, or 7 percent (Figure 1-11). These changes will increase average tax rates for the top 0.1 percent of families, a group projected to have average pre-tax incomes over $8 million, by nearly 7 percentage points.

The impacts of these policies are large relative to previous Federal policy actions. Tax changes enacted since 2009 have boosted the share of after-tax income received by the bottom 99 percent of families by more than the tax changes of any previous administration since at least 1960. President Obama has overseen the largest increase in Federal investment to reduce inequality since the Great Society programs of the Johnson Administration. However, while these accomplishments are historically large, they have offset only a fraction of the decades-long increase in inequality, and much more work remains to be done.

Chapter 4: Reforming the Health Care System

The Obama Administration has made dramatic progress in ensuring that all Americans have access to affordable, high-quality health care by expanding and improving health insurance coverage and reforming the health care delivery system.

In his first month in office, President Obama signed legislation improving the Children's Health Insurance Program (CHIP). Slightly more than a year later, the President signed into law the ACA, which reformed the individual health insurance market to ensure that all Americans, including people with pre-existing health conditions, could find affordable, high-quality coverage; provided generous financial support to States that expand their Medicaid programs to cover more low-income Americans; and allowed young adults to remain on a parent's plan until age 26, among other reforms. The ACA also improved financial security and access to care for those already insured, including by ensuring that everyone with private insurance has an annual limit on out-of-pocket spending and closing the Medicare Part D coverage gap.

Together, these actions have led to a historic expansion of health insurance coverage. Because of the ACA, an estimated 20 million additional adults now have health insurance. In addition, thanks in large part to the ACA and improvements to CHIP, the uninsured rate among children has fallen by almost half since the President took office, providing health insurance to more than 3 million additional children. As of 2016, the uninsured rate stands at its lowest level ever. Evidence demonstrates that broader insurance coverage is improving access to care, health, and financial security for the newly insured, while reducing the burden of uncompensated care for the health care system as a whole, without the adverse effects on the labor market that critics of the ACA had predicted.

The ACA and related legislation have also implemented comprehensive reforms to make the health care delivery system more efficient and improve the quality of care. The ACA achieved significant near-term savings by better aligning payments to medical providers and private insurers in Medicare with the costs of providing services. The law also began a long-term process of deploying alternative payment models (APMs) that, unlike existing fee-for-service payment systems, reward providers who deliver efficient, high-quality care, rather than just a high quantity of services. As of early 2016, more than 30 percent of traditional Medicare payments were associated with APMs, up from virtually none in 2010. The tools provided by the ACA, enhanced by the bipartisan physician payment reform legislation enacted in 2015, will enable further progress in deploying APMs in the years ahead.

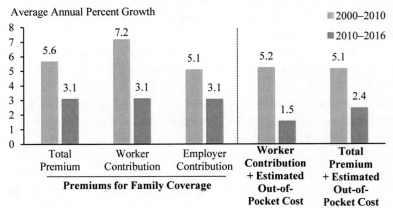

Figure 1-12

**Growth in Real Costs for Employer-Based
Family Coverage, 2000–2016**

Average Annual Percent Growth

■ 2000–2010

■ 2010–2016

Note: Out-of-pocket costs were estimated by first using the Medical Expenditure Panel Survey to
estimate the out-of-pocket share in employer coverage for 2000–2014 and then applying that
amount to the premium for each year to infer out-of-pocket spending. The out-of-pocket share for
2015 and 2016 was assumed to match 2014. Inflation adjustments use the GDP price index. GDP
price index for 2016 is a CBO projection.
Source: Kaiser Family Foundation/Health Research and Educational Trust Employer Health
Benefits Survey; Medical Expenditure Panel Survey, Household Component; CEA calculations.

Health care costs have grown exceptionally slowly since the ACA
became law. Prices of health care goods and services have grown at a slower
rate under the ACA than during any comparable period since these data
began in 1959, and recent years have also seen exceptionally slow growth in
per-enrollee spending in both public programs and private insurance. The
reforms implemented in the ACA have made an important contribution to
these trends. CBO estimates imply that the ACA has reduced the growth rate
of per-beneficiary Medicare spending by 1.3 percentage points per year from
2010 through 2016, and "spillover" effects of these reforms have subtracted
an estimated 0.6 to 0.9 percentage points per year from the growth rate of
per-enrollee private insurance spending over the same period. Moreover,
there is reason to believe that the ACA has had systemic effects on trends in
costs and quality that go beyond these estimates.

Because of slow growth in costs in employer coverage, illustrated in
Figure 1-12, the average costs for a family with employer-based coverage
in 2016 were $4,400 below where they would have been had costs grown at
their pace over the decade before the ACA became law. Similarly, the premium and cost sharing amounts incurred by the typical beneficiary enrolled
in traditional Medicare in 2016 are about $700 below 2009 projections, even
before accounting for reductions in cost sharing for prescription drugs due

to the ACA and other factors. The ACA and the accompanying slow growth in health costs have also driven dramatic improvements in the Nation's long-term fiscal outlook, while at the same time adding 11 years to the life of the Medicare Trust Fund.

In parallel, the ACA's reforms have helped drive major improvements in health care quality. Since 2010, the rate at which patients are harmed while seeking hospital care has fallen by 21 percent, which is estimated to have led to approximately 125,000 avoided deaths through 2015. Payment incentives created in the ACA have also driven a substantial decline in the rate at which patients return to hospital after discharge, corresponding to an estimated 565,000 avoided readmissions from April 2010 through May 2015.

Chapter 5: Investing in Higher Education

The Obama Administration made great strides to help students make more effective investments in higher education. To help expand college opportunity, the President doubled investments in higher education affordability through Pell Grants and the American Opportunity Tax Credit (AOTC). To help more students choose a college that provides a worthwhile investment, the Administration provided more comprehensive and accessible information about college costs and outcomes through the College Scorecard, simplified the Free Application for Federal Student Aid (FAFSA), and protected students from low-quality schools through a package of important consumer protection regulations including the landmark Gainful Employment regulations. To help borrowers manage debt after college, income-driven repayment options like the President's Pay as You Earn (PAYE) plan have allowed borrowers to cap their monthly student loan payments at as little as 10 percent of discretionary income to better align the timing of student loan payments with the timing of earnings benefits from attending college (Figure 1-13).

Moreover, Administration efforts to improve PreK-12 outcomes have helped to better prepare students for success in college and in their careers. The wide-ranging set of policies have included increasing funding for educators in the Recovery Act; expanding funding for high-quality early education programs; improving the research evidence base with Investing in Innovation (i3) grants and better data systems; closing gaps in opportunity with School Improvement Grants and other programs at disadvantaged schools; and encouraging excellence for all students with higher standards and stronger teaching.

The benefits of some of these policies are already evident, while many more will be realized over the coming decades. For example, CEA analysis finds that the Pell Grant expansions since 2008-09 enabled at least 250,000

Box 1-3: The Administration's Record in the Technology Sector

The technological advancements of the 21st century, like cloud computing, personalized medicine, and advanced materials, not only improve our daily lives, but also have the potential to increase productivity growth, one of the most important factors in raising standards of living and incomes. The Obama Administration has been dedicated to laying the groundwork for technology to improve the lives of all Americans. It has created and updated essential infrastructure for providing more equitable access to technology and worked to modernize America's institutions so that they support, rather than inhibit, innovation. The Administration has also placed a large emphasis on preparing Americans for the 21st century economy. (For a discussion of the economic impact of a number of these policies, see Chapter 5 of the 2014 *Economic Report of the President* and Chapter 5 of the 2016 *Economic Report of the President*.)

The Administration has worked to ensure that the technological infrastructure is in place, and the rules of the road are set, so that all Americans can benefit from technology. The American Recovery and Reinvestment Act provided funding to deploy or upgrade more than 114,000 miles of new broadband infrastructure, consistent with the President's goal of enhancing consumer welfare, civic participation, education, entrepreneurial activity, and economic growth through greater access to broadband. The Recovery Act financed additional broadband projects totaling $2.9 billion, bringing high-speed Internet access to 260,000 more rural households, 17,500 businesses, and 1,900 community facilities. Indeed, average home Internet speed in the United States has tripled over the past four years.

In addition, the Administration has taken unprecedented action to free up spectrum—the airwaves that carry our wireless communications—with Presidential Memoranda directing the Department of Commerce, through the National Telecommunication and Information Administration, to collaborate with the Federal Communications Commission (FCC) to make available 500 MHz of spectrum for mobile broadband use by 2020 and to accelerate spectrum sharing efforts. The Nation is halfway to the 500 MHz goal, thanks to the hard work of nearly two dozen Federal agencies to free up spectrum for auction and innovative new plans to share the airwaves. The FCC's 2015 spectrum auction was its most successful ever, raising more than $40 billion in revenue for the Federal Government while spurring the deployment of faster wireless and mobile broadband. Thanks in large part to these efforts, we have achieved the President's 2011 State of the Union goal that more than 98 percent of Americans should have access to fast 4G/LTE mobile broadband.

Further, the President supported FCC rules to protect net neutrality—the concept that Internet providers must treat all Internet traffic equally. By putting into effect strong net neutrality rules, the FCC has helped ensure that the Internet remains open, fair, and free.

In addition to updating physical infrastructure, the Administration set about making sure that America's institutions better support innovation. For example, the Administration recognized that the U.S. patent system needed to be updated to address the needs of America's entrepreneurs. From excessive wait times, to decreasing patent quality, to overly aggressive Patent Assertion Entities, the patent system was doing more to stifle innovation than promote it. The America Invents Act (AIA) of 2011 helped reform the patent system, leading to a 20 percent reduction in patent wait times from 2011 to 2016 and establishing a tribunal-based process for patent disputes, leading to an increase in patent quality. These reforms help ensure that all entrepreneurs will have fair and easy access to the patent system and increased incentives to innovate, supporting a roughly 30 percent increase in U.S. patents granted from 2011 to 2015 (Figure 1-iii).

Finally, President Obama prioritized education and training to ensure that everyone is able to fully enjoy the benefits of today's technological progress. Over half a million of today's open jobs are in technology fields such as software development and cybersecurity—many of which did not even exist a decade ago. The average salary in a job that requires technology skills is 50 percent more than the average private-sector job. For this reason, the Administration has prioritized investing in America's youngest generation so that they have the necessary skills to succeed in science, technology, engineering, and math (STEM) fields.

The U.S. technology sector has thrived since 2009, with rapidly growing new sectors like the "app economy," rising valuations and venture capital for technology firms, robust growth in technology employment, and the positioning of major U.S. technology firms as global leaders. And technology employment and investment are not limited to the computer hardware, software, and Internet industries. Advanced manufacturing, health care, and many other industries increasingly employ software engineers and data specialists, and have seen parallel improvements. These successes are due to the innovation and skills of American businesses and workers, and the Administration has worked to ensure that government has played its role to enable these successes.

Administration efforts have secured more than $1 billion in private investment in STEM education and, since 2008, STEM degrees as a

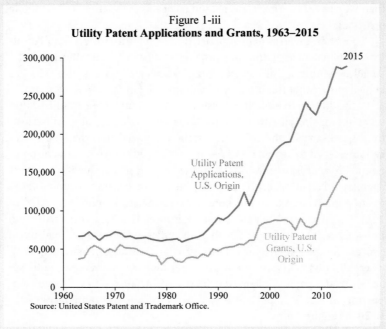

Figure 1-iii
Utility Patent Applications and Grants, 1963–2015

Source: United States Patent and Trademark Office.

share of total degrees awarded have grown 12.4 percent overall, and 20.3 percent for women. More than 100,000 engineers are graduating from American schools every year, a new record, and the Nation is 30 percent of the way to achieving the President's goal of training 100,000 new STEM educators. Further, the Administration has helped workers get the skills and training they need for jobs in the 21st century. The TechHire initiative—which works to expand local tech sectors by providing training assistance through grants and public-private partnerships and has now been rolled out to 50 communities with 600 employers participating—is actively drawing on people from all backgrounds, including young adults who are disconnected from school and work, the long-term unemployed, and those living in rural areas where access to technology training is scarce. In support of TechHire, the Department of Labor awarded 39 grants—totaling $150 million—for programs in 25 States and Washington, DC to support innovative ways to get more than 18,000 participants on the fastest paths to well-paying jobs in in-demand sectors such as information technology (IT), healthcare, advanced manufacturing, and financial services.

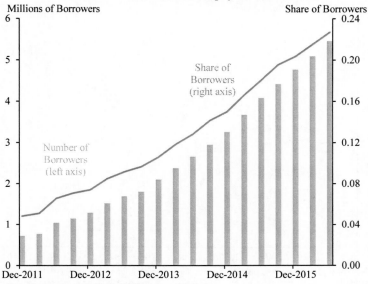

Figure 1-13
Borrowers in Income Driven Repayment Over Time

Note: Data are restricted to Federally-managed debt.
Source: Department of Education

students to access or complete a college degree in 2014-15, leading to an additional $20 billion in aggregate earnings. This represents a nearly two-to-one return on the investment. While more work remains, these policies taken together represent a significant step forward in building an educational system that supports and encourages all Americans who wish to invest in an affordable, high-quality college education to do so.

Chapter 6: Strengthening the Financial System

The 2007-08 financial crisis revealed a number of fault lines in the U.S. financial system. Many banks were inadequately capitalized, did not have enough liquidity, and took too many risks. Many non-bank financial firms faced the same risks as banks, but lacked the same regulatory supervision or protection against runs. In addition, gaps in the regulatory architecture meant that financial regulators lacked a holistic view of the risks in the system.

Responding quickly, the Obama Administration, Congress, and Federal regulators addressed these failures by adopting necessary reforms to the financial system. Financial reform included measures aimed to improve the safety and soundness of individual financial institutions by not only increasing their capital and liquidity but also decreasing risky behavior.

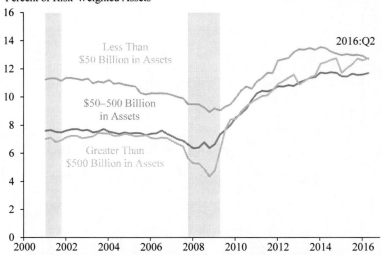

Figure 1-14

Tier 1 Common Equity Ratios for U.S. Banks by Bank Size, 2001–2016

Percent of Risk-Weighted Assets

Note: Shading denotes recession. Includes data for U.S. bank holding companies (BHCs) and "stand-alone" banks not controlled by a BHC, but not savings bank holding companies, branches and agencies of foreign banks, or nonbanks that are not held by a U.S. BHC.
Source: Federal Reserve Bank of New York; Haver Analytics.

These reforms should increase the banking sector's ability to absorb shocks arising from financial and economic stress. Other reforms included measures aimed at reducing systemic risk in the financial system by bringing more of the financial system under a regulatory umbrella, improving financial regulatory coordination, and ensuring that individual financial institutions can fail without derailing the system. Also included were specific measures designed to increase transparency and accountability in financial markets in addition to providing additional consumer and investor protections.

Financial reform has helped make the financial system more secure by requiring financial firms to have less unstable funding, more liquid assets, higher capital levels (Figure 1-14), and reduced risk-taking. The recovering economy and implementation of financial reform have been accompanied by strong performance of a wide variety of financial market indicators. Not only have financial markets recovered from the losses suffered during the crisis, but banks are healthier and stronger, regulators are on the lookout for systemic risk, once-opaque derivatives markets are safer and more transparent, credit ratings agencies are subject to more effective oversight and increased transparency, and investor protections have been strengthened. The recovery of markets—particularly those that serve a core role in the economy, such as equity and housing markets—is also an indicator of the success of the financial rescue and reform efforts in this Administration. Banks and other financial institutions now face different rules designed to make them safer and less of a threat to the overall system. In many ways, these longer-run reforms have reshaped and ensured greater resilience in the financial regulatory system of the United States.

Chapter 7: Addressing Climate Change

The Obama Administration has also demonstrated a commitment to fighting climate change through a diverse set of policy approaches. In 2009, the Administration made a historic investment of more than $90 billion in clean energy in the Recovery Act, helping to spur both a dramatic increase in clean energy capacity and advances in clean energy technology. The President's 2013 Climate Action Plan mapped out a new framework for the transformation to a more energy-efficient economy with lower greenhouse gas emissions. Related policies and initiatives included the first-ever Federal greenhouse gas pollution standards for power plants, light-duty cars and trucks, and commercial trucks, buses, and vans; investments in research and development to support innovative clean energy technologies; enhanced incentives for renewable energy and improvements in the energy efficiency of homes and appliances; and stronger international cooperation to drive down greenhouse gas emissions and limit increases in global temperatures. The Administration has worked to ensure that environmental regulations are undertaken in an efficient and cost-effective manner, as documented by rigorous regulatory impact analysis.

The Administration's policies have supported a considerable shift toward clean energy resources. From 2008 to 2015, energy intensity, energy consumed per dollar of real GDP, fell by 11 percent; carbon intensity, the amount of carbon dioxide emitted per unit of energy consumed, declined by 8 percent; and, as a result, carbon dioxide emitted per dollar of GDP declined by 18 percent. In fact, U.S. carbon dioxide emissions from the energy sector fell by 9.5 percent from 2008 to 2015, and in the first six months of 2016 they were at their lowest level in 25 years. This encouraging drop in carbon intensity was not anticipated, even as recently as 2010, and was driven both by an increase in renewable energy and increased use of cleaner fossil fuels like natural gas. CEA analysis shows that more than two-thirds of the decline in emissions relative to 2008 can be attributed to decreased energy intensity (40 percent) and carbon intensity (29 percent), with the remaining 31 percent of the emissions decline due to the lower-than-expected level of GDP after unanticipated shocks such as the Great Recession (Figure 1-15).

Figure 1-15
Decomposition of Total CO$_2$ Emission Reductions, 2008–2015

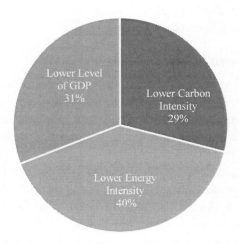

Source: Bureau of Economic Analysis, National Income and Product Accounts; Energy
Information Administration, Monthly Energy Review (August 2016) and Annual Energy
Outlook (2008); CEA Calculations.

Box 1-4: Administration Actions in the International Economy

The Obama Administration moved on several international fronts
to promote America's prosperity and security. These include: global
policy leadership and cooperation; expanding opportunities for U.S.
businesses, farmers, entrepreneurs, and consumers through trade; and,
advocating for more inclusive global economic growth, development and
health, including in the most vulnerable areas of the world.

Global economic cooperation. Elevating the G-20 to be the pre-
mier forum for international economic cooperation was a critical part
of the Obama Administration's economic strategy. The elevation of the
G-20 has advanced the goal of a more representative and inclusive global
economic governance, allowing leaders representing approximately 85
percent of global economic output to work together towards the shared
objective of strong, sustainable, balanced, and inclusive global growth.
The G-20 in turn worked to launch reforms that modernized and
strengthened the international financial architecture, including historic
recapitalization and reform across multilateral development banks
and commitment to reform of the quota and governance system of the
International Monetary Fund (IMF). Taken together, these steps have

reinforced U.S. leadership in the rules-based global economic system that has prevailed since the end of World War II.

Within months of taking office, in April 2009, the President joined the second-ever summit meeting of the G-20 leaders. At that time, the global economy was shrinking for the first time in half a century as the world dealt with the financial crisis and its aftershocks. Together, the G-20 countries mobilized trillions of dollars in fiscal stimulus and expanded the resources of the IMF and Multilateral Development Banks by $1 trillion. The G-20 created the Financial Stability Board, which has helped to coordinate the G-20's financial reform agenda and to put in place international policies to end "too-big-to-fail." This has made the global economy better able to weather financial shocks and to prevent these shocks from causing broader economic damage on Main Street and across borders. The G-20 countries agreed to refrain from beggar-thy-neighbor competitive devaluation of currencies and to take actions against tax havens and profit shifting. By 2016, both the U.S. and global economies are substantially stronger than they were—though more work remains to be done.

In addition to immediate crisis response, the G-20 is taking steps to build a framework for strong, sustainable, balanced, and inclusive growth in the long term. These have included commitments to increase female labor force participation, phasing-out of fossil fuel subsidies, implementing strategies to create jobs and boost investment, and commitments to promote sustainable development. In 2010, the Obama Administration hosted the first meeting of G-20 labor and employment ministers in Washington and committed to spur action to create quality jobs, lift living standards, and promote broadly shared prosperity. Since then, G-20 member nations have committed to bring more women into the labor force, reduce income inequality, address youth unemployment, and invest in workforce sustainable development, including through quality apprenticeships and other measures. They have also improved financial transparency and made significant progress to address corruption around the world.

Expanding opportunities for U.S. businesses, farmers, entrepreneurs, and consumers through trade. The United States has initiated and strengthened high-standards trade agreements with countries across the world, seeking to open foreign markets to U.S. goods and services and ensure a level playing field for workers and businesses. At the same time, U.S. consumers enjoy opportunities to shop from the world, expanding their choices and stretching their budgets further.

• Free Trade Agreements (FTAs) with Korea, Panama, and Colombia were signed, approved by Congress, and entered into force in

2012. From 2009 to 2015, U.S. export growth was substantially higher to FTA partners than to non-FTA partners.

- President Obama called for global free trade in environmental goods in his Climate Action Plan in 2013 and, the following year, the Administration commenced negotiations on the Environmental Goods Agreement with a group of countries that accounts for more than 85 percent of global trade in environmental goods.

- The Obama Administration lifted sanctions on Cuba and Myanmar (formerly known as Burma), laying the path for increased economic engagement and U.S. investment.

- The Trans-Pacific Partnership (TPP) agreement would eliminate over 18,000 tariffs, establish the highest labor and environmental standards of any trade agreement in history, enhance opportunities for small and medium enterprises, promote Internet-based commerce, protect American workers and businesses from unfair competition from foreign state-owned enterprises, and strengthen transparency and anti-corruption.

Global development and health. President Obama has also worked intensively to elevate global development as a central pillar of our national security policy, on par with diplomacy and defense, as articulated in Presidential Policy Directive 6 on U.S. Global Development Policy. In 2015, the United States joined the rest of the world in adopting the 2030 Agenda for Sustainable Development, which sets out an ambitious global development vision and priorities for the next 15 years that strive to end extreme poverty and to prioritize policies and investments that have long-term, transformative impact. The Administration has harnessed donor assistance, domestic resource mobilization, and private-sector capital to promote the development agenda in health, livelihoods, food security, and energy.

Programs building domestic resources have taken a variety of forms. The Addis Tax Initiative, launched by the United States in July 2015, is an example of how the Administration has worked to help developing countries mobilize and effectively use their own domestic resources for sustainable development. In a similar vein, the U.S. Government's Feed the Future program helped over 9 million smallholder farmers, food producers, and rural families adopt innovations and new practices to improve domestic agricultural productivity in 2015 alone. Also in 2015, the President and the First Lady launched Let Girls Learn to address the challenges preventing adolescent girls from obtaining a quality education and to empower them to reach their full potential, building crucial human capital in vulnerable communities. In 2011, President Obama joined with seven other heads of state to launch the Open Government

Partnership (OGP), a global partnership between governments and civil society to advance transparency and accountability, bolster citizen engagement, and leverage new technologies to strengthen governance.

The Administration also has promoted new public- and private-sector efforts to harness cutting-edge technologies, including to accelerate research and scale innovations to support sustainable development. In 2015 alone, USAID maintained over 360 active public-private partnerships that, over their active lifetimes, have leveraged over $5.9 billion from the private sector and other partners. Through FY 2014, the Overseas Private Investment Corporation (OPIC) supported more than $35 billion in private investment in developing and emerging markets. The Administration's Power Africa initiative has successfully built a broad coalition of more than 130 bilateral, multilateral, and private-sector partners who have collectively committed to invest more than $52 billion in the energy sector in sub-Saharan Africa, where two-thirds of the population lack access to electricity.

The Administration also has fought aggressively for global health by building on successful existing programs and launching new initiatives. President Obama built on the President's Emergency Program for AIDS Relief (PEPFAR) launched by President George W. Bush, bringing the prospect of an AIDS-free generation within sight. Over the past 15 years, investments in the President's Malaria Initiative, the Global Fund to Fight AIDS, Tuberculosis, and Malaria, and other partnerships have averted an estimated 6.2 million malaria deaths. In addition, the Obama Administration has challenged the world to end preventable child and maternal deaths, and, since 2008, efforts by USAID have helped save the lives of 4.6 million children and 200,000 mothers.

FOUR CONTINUED STRUCTURAL CHALLENGES: PRODUCTIVITY, INEQUALITY, PARTICIPATION, AND SUSTAINABILITY

The Obama Administration has taken great strides in addressing many structural barriers to inclusive growth over the last eight years, working to ensure both that growth is stronger in the future and that the benefits of this growth are more widely shared among American households. However, these efforts have only started to address the structural obstacles to future prosperity for middle-class families. Many of these barriers have been decades in the making, and many are shared across a wide range of advanced economies. Addressing four of these structural challenges—boosting productivity growth, combatting rising inequality, raising labor force participation, and building a resilient economy that does not grow today at the expense of the future—will be critical in the years ahead.

Productivity Growth

The single most important determinant of living standards, across countries and over time, is labor productivity—the amount of output a worker can produce in an hour of work. The evolution of labor productivity growth in the United States since World War II can be roughly partitioned into four regimes. Labor productivity in the nonfarm business sector rose by an average of 2.8 percent a year between 1948 and 1973. Beginning in the early 1970s, though, productivity growth slowed sharply, averaging only 1.4 percent annually between 1973 and 1995. Productivity growth did not rebound meaningfully until the mid-1990s, when information technology advanced at a startling rate. Productivity growth surged, rising 3.0 percent at an annual rate between 1995 and 2005 in the nonfarm business sector. However, from 2005 to 2015, labor productivity growth averaged just 1.3 percent a year, due to slowdowns in both capital deepening and in growth in total factor productivity (a measure of how much output can be produced from a given combination of labor and capital, with increases largely representing advancements in technology, management, and institutions).

The recent slowdown in productivity growth has also been seen in other advanced economies. Average annual productivity growth in advanced economies slowed to less than 1 percent from 2005 to 2015, roughly half the rate of the previous decade—with productivity slowing in 30 of 31 advanced economies, including all of the G-7 economies, as shown in Figure 1-16. Despite its sharp slowdown, the United States has had the strongest record in terms of productivity growth in the last decade among the G-7 economies.

Productivity growth is critical to the long-run health of the U.S. economy because it is a necessary component of both potential GDP growth and real increases in household incomes, and thus living standards. A range of policies can help boost labor productivity growth. These include increasing public investment in infrastructure; providing greater funding for research and development; reforming the business tax code to better incentivize innovation and investment; promoting high-skilled immigration; continuing to improve education and worker training; and expanding trade, which can boost innovation through the spread of ideas across borders, greater specialization in innovative activities, access to larger markets by high-productivity firms, and expanded competition.

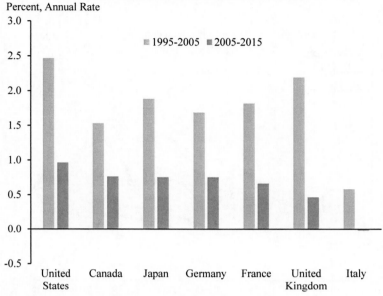

Figure 1-16
Labor Productivity Growth, G-7 Countries

Percent, Annual Rate

1995-2005   2005-2015

United States   Canada   Japan   Germany   France   United Kingdom   Italy

Source: Conference Board, Total Economy Database; CEA calculations.

Income Inequality

In the long run, productivity growth is the most important factor in increasing earnings. But income growth for households across much of the distribution also depends on the degree to which economic gains are shared, or, in other words, on the degree of income inequality. Here, too, the trend among advanced economies has been unfortunately similar, with the majority seeing increased inequality in recent decades. However, the United States has the highest levels of inequality, and has seen a faster increase in inequality, than any of the G-7 economies, as shown in Figure 1-17.

As discussed in Chapter 1 of the 2016 *Economic Report of the President*, traditional economic explanations of inequality are grounded in competitive markets, wherein workers receive wages commensurate with their productivity. According to this explanation, a combination of skill-biased technological change, a slowdown in the increase in educational attainment, and globalization have increased the demand for highly skilled workers at the same time that their relative supply has not kept pace—resulting in higher wages for these workers and greater inequality. However, a growing body of evidence has pointed to economic rents as a potential additional source of inequality. Rents occur whenever capital owners or workers receive more income than they would require to undertake their production or work.

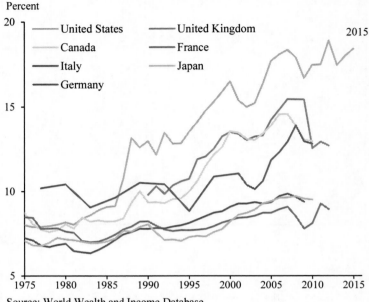

Figure 1-17
Share of Income Earned by Top 1 Percent, 1975–2015

Source: World Wealth and Income Database.

Rents could play a role in rising inequality either to the degree that the division of rents is becoming increasingly unequal or to the degree that they are increasing and being captured by capital or by high earners (Furman and Orszag 2015).

Despite the historic progress in rolling back rising inequality over the last eight years described above, more work remains to combat high levels of inequality in the United States in both pre-tax-and-transfer and after-tax-and-transfer incomes. Policies like expanded access to quality education, increasing the minimum wage, providing greater support for collective bargaining and other forms of worker voice, and reforming barriers to mobility like occupational licensing requirements and land-use restrictions to reduce rents can all play a role in reducing inequality. Meanwhile, making the fiscal system more progressive by, for example, expanding tax credits for low-income workers financed by higher tax rates on high-income households would reduce inequality in after-tax incomes. A growing body of evidence has also found that a more progressive fiscal system does not just increase after-tax incomes for low- and moderate-income households; when fiscal transfers (such as programs for health, nutrition, cash assistance, and housing support) are focused on children, they can also increase future earnings and educational outcomes (Furman and Ruffini 2015).

Labor Force Participation

Household incomes also depend on the labor force participation rate: the share of the adult population working or actively in search of work. In recent years, the participation rate has faced substantial downward pressure from the aging of the U.S. population as members of the baby-boom generation begin to retire. This demographic trend implies a decrease in the overall participation rate of about a quarter of a percentage point a year. However, the participation rate has been broadly stable since the end of 2013, as the strong recovery of the U.S. labor market has pulled workers into the labor force and offset the downward pressure from the aging of the population.

But the United States faces an additional long-run challenge of declining participation among "prime-age" workers, those between the ages of 25 and 54. This troubling pattern in labor force participation goes back for more than a half-century for men and about a decade and a half for women. In 1953, 3 percent of prime-age men did not participate in the labor force. In November 2016, the fraction stood at 12 percent (Figure 1-18a). Nonparticipation has been even higher in recent years for men with less educational attainment: in 2015, 17 percent of prime-age men with a high school degree or less did not participate in the workforce. Meanwhile, 25 percent of prime-age women do not participate in the labor force today, compared to 23 percent in 1999 (Figure 1-18b). Over the second half of the 20th century, the decline in prime-age male labor force participation was largely obscured in aggregate data by rising female participation and favorable demographics. But as the trend for prime-age women plateaued and then reversed, the impact of declining prime-age participation on the overall labor force participation rate has been far clearer in recent years. (For an expanded discussion of the decline in prime-age labor force participation, see Box 2-3.)

The reduced participation rate for prime-age workers in the United States presents a number of challenges, both for these workers' long-term employment prospects and well-being and for the U.S. macroeconomy. Policies to help boost participation include strengthening the "connective tissue" in the U.S. labor markets by, for example, modernizing the unemployment insurance system and expanding wage insurance; promoting work by expanding tax credits for low-income workers and raising the minimum wage; and increasing workplace flexibility by increasing access to paid leave and affordable child care.

Economic Sustainability

Even as work remains to boost productivity growth and labor force participation and to combat rising inequality, the Nation must take a

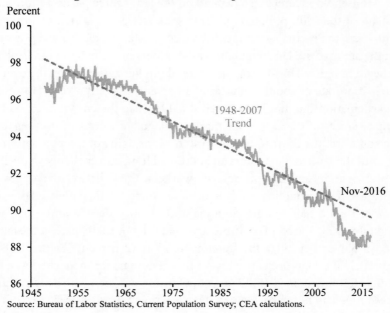

Figure 1-18a
Prime-Age Male Labor Force Participation Rate, 1948–2016

Percent

Source: Bureau of Labor Statistics, Current Population Survey; CEA calculations.

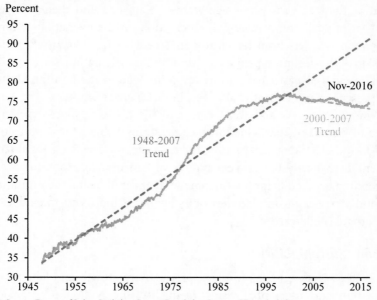

Figure 1-18b
Prime-Age Female Labor Force Participation Rate, 1948–2016

Percent

Source: Bureau of Labor Statistics, Current Population Survey; CEA calculations.

number of steps to ensure that economic growth is sustainable and does not come at the expense of future prosperity.

Given the current strong position of the U.S. economy in the business cycle, steps should be taken to protect against future recessions, helping to ensure that just as we avoided a second Great Depression, we are able to avoid a second Great Recession. In particular, modifying the design of automatic stabilizers like unemployment insurance such that they are automatically expanded or extended during downturns would provide better countercyclical support for the economy during recessions (CEA and DOL 2014; Furman 2016b). Moreover, as demonstrated by the Obama Administration's efforts, it is possible to combine short-run fiscal expansion with medium- and long-run fiscal consolidation to maintain fiscal discipline. Further curbs to the growth of entitlement costs that build on the ACA's progress in reducing health care costs, as well as limiting tax breaks for those at the top of the income distribution, can also help address our long-term fiscal challenges without sacrificing investments in growth and opportunity.

Finally, sustainable economic growth also requires addressing both the short- and long-run effects of climate change, which presents large risks not just to our environment but also to economic growth and fiscal sustainability. As discussed above, the Administration has taken ambitious steps to reduce carbon emissions and move toward a clean energy economy, including agreeing to reduce net emissions to between 26 and 28 percent of their 2005 level by 2025 in the historic Paris Agreement (Figure 1-19). But more work remains to ensure that the effects of manmade climate change do not endanger future prosperity. As President Obama has acknowledged, even as the Paris accord has established an enduring framework for confronting the climate crisis, its ambitious goals are not sufficient. More will need to be done to invent new technologies, generate energy from low-carbon sources, and reduce the energy and carbon intensity of our economy so that damage from climate change does not undermine the economy and living standards in the future. As the last eight years have demonstrated, efficient policies tailored to fight climate change can be implemented in ways that support, and do not hinder, economic growth.

CONCLUSION

The actions undertaken by the Obama Administration in the midst of the crisis not only helped prevent a second Great Depression, they set the U.S. economy on a path to becoming stronger, more resilient, and better positioned to face the economic challenges of the 21st century. In the pages that follow, the 2017 *Economic Report of the President* reviews the efforts of

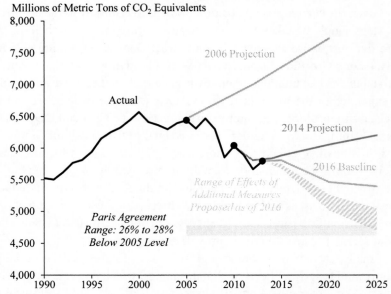

Figure 1-19
U.S. Net Emissions, 1990–2025

Millions of Metric Tons of CO_2 Equivalents

Note: Projections for 2014 and 2016 shown are the "high-sequestration" scenario for each year.
Source: Department of State (2016).

the Obama Administration to ensure economic growth that is both robust and broadly shared among all American families. As the Nation emerges from the shadow of the Great Recession, promoting inclusive, sustainable growth will remain the key objective in the years ahead. While several structural challenges for shared growth remain, the experience of the past eight years shows that, by acting decisively and by choosing the right policies, the United States can build a stronger and more prosperous economy for generations to come.

CHAPTER 2

THE YEAR IN REVIEW AND
THE YEARS AHEAD

The U.S. economy continued to grow in 2016, as the recovery extended into its seventh year with strong gains in employment and real wages, low inflation, and moderate output growth. Robust employment growth and moderate output growth imply low labor productivity growth, an important challenge in the years ahead. Strong employment gains along with rising real wages in 2016 were a continuation of the trends in 2015 that helped contribute to the fastest real median income growth on record and, in conjunction, a falling poverty rate.

Real gross domestic product (GDP) increased at an annual rate of 1.8 percent during the first three quarters of 2016 (the latest data available as this *Report* goes to press), down slightly from the 1.9-percent growth during the four quarters of 2015.[1] During the first three quarters of 2016, real consumer spending, which grew at an annual rate of 2.9 percent, exceeded real GDP growth as personal saving rates fell. Residential investment contributed positively to overall real GDP growth in the last quarter of 2015 and the first quarter of 2016, but subtracted from growth in the second and third quarters of 2016. The weakness in residential investment is surprising given the solid fundamentals: low mortgage interest rates, favorable demographic trends, rising real wages, and rising house prices. Business fixed investment contracted in the last quarter of 2015 and the first quarter of 2016, but has since returned to contributing positively, though weakly, to overall growth. Inventory investment—one of the most volatile components of GDP—subtracted from GDP during the five quarters prior to 2016:Q3, in particular in 2016:Q2, before rebounding in the third quarter. Net exports contributed positively to growth in each of the first three quarters of 2016 after subtracting from growth in in the four quarters of 2014 and 2015. Government

---

[1] The *2017 Economic Report of the President* only discusses the first three quarters of GDP and employment gains through November. It was finalized in December: only the second estimate of 2016:Q3 GDP and the November employment report had been released. Previous *Economic Reports of the President* were finalized in February.

purchases have been roughly neutral in their effect on overall GDP during the first three quarters of 2016.

The economy added 2.3 million jobs during the 12 months ended in November 2016, extending the streak of consecutive months of positive nonfarm employment growth to 74 months. During the 12 months ended in November 2016, nonfarm job growth has averaged 188,000 a month, a somewhat more moderate pace than during 2014 and 2015, but similar to the strong pace during 2011-13. The unemployment rate was down 0.4 percentage point during the 12 months ended in November to 4.6 percent (Figure 2-1). The labor force participation rate during the 12 months ended in November 2016 averaged 0.14 percentage point higher than its 2015 average as the labor market continued to strengthen. The labor force participation rate had been falling since 2008 due to the aging of the population into retirement, cyclical factors, and other long-term trends, but it has rebounded slightly to its 2014 level as the strengthening labor market offset some demographic trends.

Inflation remained low with consumer price inflation, as measured by the consumer price index (CPI), at only 1.6 percent over the 12 months ended in October 2016. Low energy prices continue to restrain overall inflation. The core CPI, which excludes food and energy, increased 2.1 percent over the 12 months ended in October. Over the same period, core personal consumption expenditure (PCE) inflation increased 1.7 percent, remaining below the Federal Reserve's 2-percent target for overall PCE inflation. Real average hourly earnings of production and nonsupervisory workers rose 0.9 percent over the 12 months ended in October, as nominal wage growth continued to exceed the subdued pace of price inflation, building upon the 2.2-percent gain experienced during 2015 (Figure 2-2). Real median household income increased 5.2 percent in 2015, the fastest growth on record. Households at all income percentiles reported by the Census Bureau saw real gains in income, with the largest gains among households at the bottom of the income distribution.

Challenges remain for 2017 and the longer term, including uncertain prospects for global growth, the low rate of productivity growth, and constraints posed by slowing trend growth in the labor force due to demographic shifts.

The economic recovery that continued in 2016 has been characterized by a robust labor market but modest output growth. The labor market continued to strengthen and, by November 2016, the unemployment rate had fallen to half its peak in October 2009, but the 1.6-percent real output growth during the four quarters ended in 2016:Q3, was slower than its pace in recent years. The dissonance between the robust labor market and moderate output

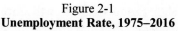

Figure 2-1
Unemployment Rate, 1975–2016

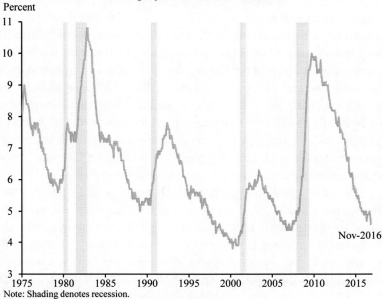

Note: Shading denotes recession.
Source: Bureau of Labor Statistics, Current Population Survey.

Figure 2-2
Real Hourly Wages, 1980–2016

Note: Shading denotes recession. Nominal wages are deflated using the CPI for urban wage
earners and clerical workers (CPI-W).
Source: Bureau of Labor Statistics; CEA calculations.

growth reflects slow labor productivity growth during this business cycle relative to its long-term average. Foreign growth showed signs of stabilizing, with the International Monetary Fund (IMF) expecting real output growth over the four quarters of 2016 to be 3.1 percent, the same pace as in 2015 (IMF 2016b). However, the 3.1-percent pace of global growth in 2016 is below the year-earlier expectations (3.6 percent), with slower-than-forecasted growth in both advanced and emerging markets (IMF 2015b). Slow global growth has been a headwind for U.S. exports in recent years (continuing through 2016), especially for U.S. manufacturing, which constitutes 60 percent of U.S. exports, as well as for global trade. However, the outlook is improving in emerging markets with India's growth continuing at a fast pace and with Brazil and Russia likely to return to positive growth in 2017.

The Administration expects real GDP to grow at 2.4 percent during the four quarters of 2017, and 2.2 percent in the long-term, a forecast based on a baseline that assumes enactment of the President's policy proposals. In 2017, consumer spending is expected to continue to support solid growth, along with a pickup in foreign demand. The unemployment rate is projected to fall slightly from its projected fourth-quarter rate of 4.9 percent. Inflation, as measured by the price index for GDP and which was only 1.3 percent during the four quarters through 2016:Q3, is forecasted to creep up gradually to 2 percent, and then to remain at that pace thereafter. The yield on ten-year Treasury notes is projected to edge up from its third quarter level of 1.6 percent toward 3.7 percent in the mid-2020s, partly due to inflation increasing and term premiums returning to more-normal levels.

POLICY DEVELOPMENTS

Fiscal Policy

Fiscal restraint in the United States continued in fiscal year (FY) 2016 with the Federal Budget deficit (expressed as a share of nominal GDP) rising a moderate 0.7 percentage point to 3.2 percent. The deficit-to-GDP ratio is about equal to the average over the past 40 years, and has fallen by 67 percent since FY 2009. The Federal deficit-to-GDP ratio had declined 1.9 percentage points a year from FY 2012 to FY 2014, but has flattened out in the 2-to-3 percent of GDP range in FY 2015 and FY 2016 under Administration policies.

The President signed three pieces of significant fiscal legislation in 2015. The first was the Bipartisan Budget Act (BBA) of 2015, signed in October, which set discretionary spending limits for the FY 2016 and FY 2017, providing a moderate $80 billion in total sequestration relief, thus allowing for additional investments in education, job training, research, and health care, as well as postponing reaching the statutory limit on the Federal debt (Somanader 2015). Second, the Fixing America's Surface Transportation (FAST) Act signed into law in December 2015 funded surface transportation including roads, bridges, and rail for five years, authorizing $306 billion in spending—or an increase of roughly 4 percent in highway investment and 7 percent in transit investment in real terms—while increasing predictability of funding (CEA 2016b). Third, the Protecting Americans from Tax Hikes (PATH) Act signed into law in December 2015 ensured that the expansions enacted in 2009 of the Earned Income Tax Credit and Child Tax Credit, and the American Opportunity Tax Credit (which provides a tax credit for students in higher education) are permanent features of the tax code. These tax credits now provide tax cuts of about $1,000 for about 24 million families each year (Leibenluft 2015). The PATH Act also made permanent tax incentives for investment in research and experimentation and small business investment (through expensing capital purchases). In addition, in September 2016, Congress approved a spending bill funding the government through December 9 and provided $1.1 billion in the fight against Zika, as well as additional funding for military infrastructure and housing.

Federal

Over the four quarters ended in 2016:Q3, real Federal purchases grew 1.1 percent. At the Federal level, government purchases—including consumption and gross investment—contributed weakly, but positively, to four-quarter GDP growth (0.1 percentage point), approximately the same as during the four quarters of 2015. This modest contribution is accounted for by decreases in other spending which partly offset the sequester relief under the BBA. On a quarterly basis, real Federal purchases can be volatile (Figure 2-3). Federal purchases picked up in the third quarter after falling in the first two quarters of 2016.

State and Local

After strong contributions to real GDP during the four quarters of 2015, State and local government purchases—consumption plus gross investment—are on track to have a negligible impact in 2016. Real State and local government purchases contracted 0.2 percent in the four-quarters ended in 2016:Q3, after growing 2.5 percent during the four-quarters of 2015 (Figure 2-3).

The State and local share of nominal GDP fell from its historical peak of 13.0 percent in 2009 to 11.0 percent in 2016, a level not seen since the late 1980s, as State and local governments cut their purchases in the face of budget pressures (Box 2-1).[2] In 2016, State and local government purchases were about 60-percent larger than Federal purchases and three-times larger than Federal nondefense purchases (Figure 2-4). The roughly 90,000 state and local governments employ roughly 13 percent of nonfarm workers, and added about 159 thousand jobs in the twelve months ended November 2016. Changes in State and local purchases can be as important as changes in Federal purchases.

Monetary Policy

In December 2015, the Federal Open Market Committee (FOMC) increased the target range for the federal funds rate by 0.25 percentage point, ending seven years with the effective federal funds rate maintained at a level just above the zero lower bound. The FOMC's decision to tighten monetary policy was based on its judgment that labor markets had improved considerably and that it was reasonably confident that inflation would move up over the medium term to its 2-percent objective. Through the first 11 months of 2016, the FOMC did not raise the target range for the federal funds rate.

As was the case in previous years, the Federal Reserve's realized pace of raising rates in 2016 was below the median forecasted pace of FOMC participants at the close of the previous year. In December 2015, the median of FOMC participant projections was four 25-basis point rate hikes in 2016. In March 2016, the median forecast of the federal funds rate from FOMC participants for the end of 2016 fell to 0.9 percent, implying just two hikes in 2016. Throughout 2016, the FOMC continued to maintain the target range for the federal funds rate at between 0.25 and 0.50 percent, as inflation remained below target, U.S. economic growth was subdued, global growth prospects remained weak, and some financial market turmoil emerged in early 2016. Britain's vote to leave the European Union in June introduced more uncertainty about global growth and financial conditions. Throughout the year, the market-implied federal funds rate for the end of 2016 was below the median forecast of FOMC participants at the time. Importantly, the FOMC emphasized throughout the year that monetary policy is not on a "preset path"[3] and that the projections of FOMC participants are only an indication of what they view as the most likely path of interest rates given beliefs on the future path of the economy.

---

[2] Forty-nine out of fifty states have constitutions or statutes mandating a balanced budget and many local governments have similar provisions (National Conference of State Legislatures 2010). This does not prevent them from running deficits. Many of those balanced budget statutes apply only to the operating budget, while deficits may be allowed on their capital accounts. Also, spending from "rainy day funds" appears as a deficit on the government balance sheet in the national income and product accounts.

[3] See Transcript of Chair Yellen's Press Conference, September 21, 2016 (Yellen 2016a).

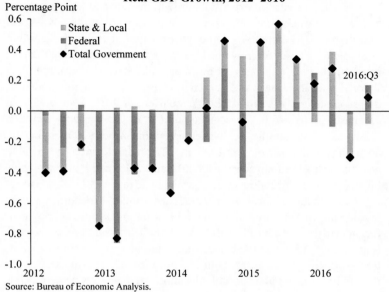

Figure 2-3
**Quarterly Contribution of Government Purchases to
Real GDP Growth, 2012–2016**

Percentage Point

■ State & Local
■ Federal
◆ Total Government

2016:Q3

Source: Bureau of Economic Analysis.

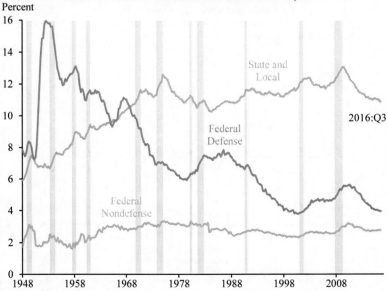

Figure 2-4
Government Purchases as Share of Nominal GDP, 1948–2016

Percent

State and
Local

Federal
Defense

2016:Q3

Federal
Nondefense

Note: Shading denotes recession.
Source: Bureau of Economic Analysis.

Box 2-1: Challenges in the State and Local Sector

During the current expansion, growth in State and local purchases has been the weakest of any business-cycle recovery in the post-World War II period (Figure 2-i). Although in a typical recovery State and local spending tends to grow quickly and at a similar pace as in the pre-recession period, in the current business cycle, State and local spending sharply contracted and, after seven years, has still not rebounded to its pre-crisis levels. During the four quarters of 2010, State and local purchases subtracted 0.5 percentage point from GDP growth, and then subtracted about another 0.3 percentage point in both 2011 and 2012. Spending in this sector stabilized in 2013, added modestly to GDP growth during the four quarters of 2014 and 2015, and had a negligible impact on GDP during the three quarters of 2016.

Real State and local government consumption expenditures, gross investment (particularly investment in structures), and employment (particularly in the education sector) remain below their pre-crisis levels (Figure 2-ii). Real State and local government consumption expenditures—which consists of spending to produce and provide services to the public, largely public school education—remains 2.8 percent below its peak in 2009:Q3. Real State and local government gross investment—which consists of spending for fixed assets that directly benefit the

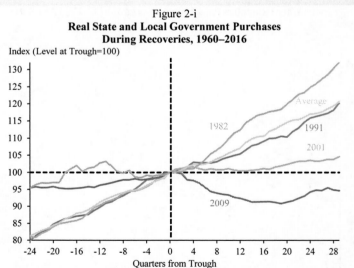

Figure 2-i
**Real State and Local Government Purchases
During Recoveries, 1960–2016**
Index (Level at Trough=100)

Note: "Average" indicates average across recessionary periods from 1960–2007, excluding the 1980 recession due to overlap with the 1981–1982 recession.
Source: Bureau of Economic Analysis, National Income and Product Accounts; National Bureau of Economic Research; CEA calculations.

public, largely highway construction and maintenance—remains 17.3 percent below its peak in 2009:Q2.

As of November 2016, the roughly 90,000 State and local governments have added 371 thousand jobs since January 2013. Even so, employment in this sector remains 367 thousand below its previous high in July 2008, with almost half of this net job loss in educational services. The 1.7-percent decline in education employment exceeded the 1.0-percent decline in the school-age population (ages 5 to 19) over the 2008-15 period. This disparity implies a rising student-teacher ratio.

Despite some recovery in 2016, there are still factors likely to restrain State and local spending growth. State and local governments continue to spend more than they collect in revenues, and their aggregate deficit during the first three quarters of 2016 amounted to about 1 percent of GDP. This deficit has shrunk, however, during the recovery (Figure 2-iii). During 2016, State and local expenditures (including transfers and interest payments, as well as purchases) were roughly flat at about 14 percent of GDP, and revenues held at about 13 percent of GDP. Until 1990, State and local governments only ran deficits during recessions. Since then, State and local governments have frequently run deficits.

Unfunded pension obligations—the shortfall between benefits promised to government workers and the savings available to meet those

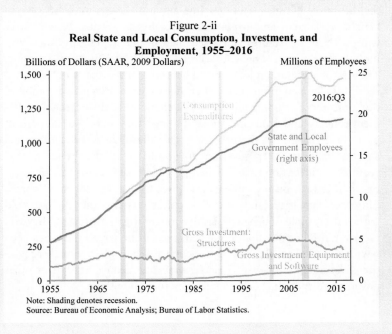

Figure 2-ii
Real State and Local Consumption, Investment, and Employment, 1955–2016

Note: Shading denotes recession.
Source: Bureau of Economic Analysis; Bureau of Labor Statistics.

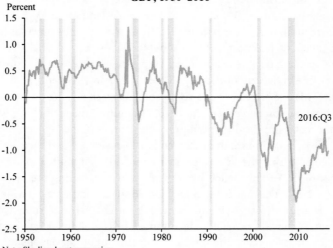

Figure 2-iii
State and Local Government Surplus as Percent of Nominal GDP, 1950–2016

Note: Shading denotes recession.
Source: Bureau of Economic Analysis.

obligations—place a burden on finances for many State and local governments. Unfunded liabilities, measured on a net-present value basis, equal the difference between liabilities (the amount the governments owe in benefits to current employees who have already accrued benefits they will collect in the future) and assets held in public pension funds, and indicate the amount of benefits accrued for which no money is set aside. The size of these unfunded pension liabilities relative to State and local receipts ballooned immediately after the recession driven by a combination of factors, including underfunding and lower-than-expected investment returns, and remain elevated at a level that was about 80 percent of a year's revenue in the first three quarters of 2016. Assets may fall short of liabilities when governments do not contribute the full annual required contribution (ARC), when they increase benefits retroactively, or when returns on investments are lower than assumed. Additionally, unfunded liabilities can grow if actuaries' assumptions do not hold true. For example, if beneficiaries live longer than anticipated, they will receive more benefits than predicted, even if the government has been paying the ARC consistently. Unfunded liabilities will eventually require the government employer to increase revenue, reduce benefits or other government spending, or do some combination of these.

The size of the Federal Reserve's balance sheet at the end of November 2016 was $4.45 trillion—over five times its size at the end of 2006, largely reflecting several large-scale asset purchase programs (quantitative easing) from 2008 to 2014, which are estimated to have lowered long-term interest rates by about a percentage point (Ihrig et al. 2012; D'Amico et al. 2012; Engen, Laubach, and Reifschneider 2015).[4] Since the conclusion of its large-scale asset purchase program in 2014, however, the Federal Reserve's asset holdings have remained at $4.4 trillion as maturing bonds were replaced with purchases of new issues.

In recent years, FOMC participants have tended to lower their estimates of the longer-run level for the federal funds rate. As of September, the median of FOMC participants' projections of the long-run federal funds rate was 2.9 percent, down from 3.5 percent in December 2015. The downward revisions are consistent with downward trends in long-term interest rates in U.S. and global financial markets.

The natural rate of interest is the real interest rate that should prevail when the economy is producing at its long-run potential level and has attained full employment. Both cyclical factors (such as unconventional monetary policies, fiscal austerity measures, and private sector deleveraging) and structural factors (such as slowing productivity growth, changing demographics) could be contributing to the decline in the natural rate of interest.[5] An interest-rate decline implies that monetary policy may now have less room to provide accommodation during recessions than in the past because it has less room to lower rates.[6] In light of this, some have argued that stabilization policy could benefit from greater use of countercyclical fiscal policy and perhaps changes in the approach to monetary policy such as targeting nominal GDP or adopting a higher inflation target.[7]

---

[4] See Ihrig et al. (2012) for a discussion of how interest rates paid on excess reserves and overnight reverse repurchase agreement have replaced open market operations—the buying and selling of Treasury securities—as the way in which the Federal Reserve achieves its target policy rate.

[5] See CEA 2015d for a survey on the nature and sources of the decline in long-term interest rates.

[6] Yellen (2016b) has argued that a low equilibrium federal funds rate does not mean that the Federal Reserve's current toolkit will be ineffective. She points out that a recent paper using simulations from a Federal Reserve model finds that forward guidance and asset purchases should be sufficient to combat most recessions "even if the average level of the federal funds rate in the future is only 3 percent."

[7] See Williams (2016), Summers (2014), Yellen (2016b), Fischer (2016), Bernanke (2013), Goodfriend (2016).

LABOR MARKET

The labor market continued to improve in 2016, with many measures of labor-market performance having recovered to, or near to, their pre-recession levels. From November 2015 to November 2016, the economy added 2.3 million jobs, continuing the longest streak of total job growth on record. American businesses have now added 15.6 million jobs since private-sector job growth turned positive in March 2010, and the unemployment rate has fallen to 4.6 percent, cut by more than half from its peak in October 2009. Moreover, the pace of nominal earnings growth picked up in 2016, with average hourly earnings up at a 2.7 percent annual rate through November 2016. This progress has translated into broad-based gains, but some slack likely remains in the labor market, including a somewhat elevated rate of those who are working part-time but would like to work full time.

Private employment increased by 2.0 million jobs from November 2015 to November 2016, after rising by 2.7 million jobs in 2015 (Figure 2-5). Over the 12 months through November 2016, more than half of private-sector job gains came from "professional and business services" and "education and health services," both of which have been major drivers of job growth in this recovery. These sectors account for a large part of growth despite making up only about 35 percent of private-sector jobs in the economy. Education and health services added 581,000 jobs in the 12 months through November 2016 and professional and business services added 571,000 jobs, consistent with its growth over the course of this recovery.

Despite overall strength, particularly in the services sector, some industries faced specific headwinds that held down growth in 2016. Mining, which includes oil and gas extraction, lost 87,300 jobs in the 12 months through November 2016, largely due to industry cutbacks in the face of the sharp fall in oil prices, and reverted to its employment level at the beginning of the labor market recovery in early 2010 (Box 2-2). Manufacturing also experienced a weak year, losing 54,000 jobs or 0.44 percent, likely reflecting dampened demand for U.S. exports, which are disproportionately composed of manufactured goods, amid slow and declining growth among our trading partners. In fact, after excluding the mining and manufacturing sectors, job growth since 2014 has been at its strongest since the late 1990s.

The labor market's improvement was apparent in the continued decline of the unemployment rate. By November 2016, the unemployment rate had fallen to 4.6 percent, declining an average of 0.9 percentage point a year from 2010 to 2016, and dropping below its pre-recession average

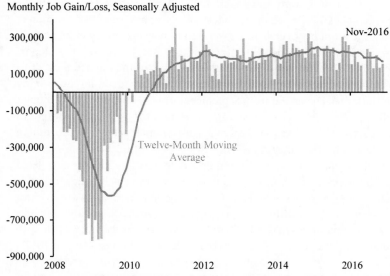

Figure 2-5
Private-Sector Payroll Employment, 2008–2016

Monthly Job Gain/Loss, Seasonally Adjusted

Source: Bureau of Labor Statistics, Current Employment Statistics; CEA calculations.

of 5.3 percent earlier than most forecasters expected.[8] As of March 2014, economists generally expected the unemployment rate to remain above 5.0 percent until at least 2020 (Figure 2-6). Many economists have revised down their estimates of the "natural" rate of unemployment as unemployment fell to low levels without an accompanying increase in the inflation rate. Still, given today's low unemployment rate, further declines are expected to moderate during 2017.

Although the overall unemployment rate was below its pre-recession average and mirrored other indicators of labor-market strength in November 2016, some indicators of labor-market slack remained above their pre-recession levels. For example, the long-term unemployment rate, or the share of those unemployed for 27 weeks or more, was 1.2 percent in November 2016, roughly its lowest point since 2008 but above its pre-recession average of 1.0 percent (Figure 2-7). If the long-term unemployment rate continues to fall at the same pace as it has over the past year, it will reach its pre-recession average in 2017. Looking historically across recoveries, the long-term unemployment rate is typically among the last labor-market indicators to return to normal (CEA 2010).

Similarly, the share of the labor force working part-time for economic reasons (those working part-time but who would prefer full-time

---

[8] Throughout this section, pre-recession average refers to the average from December 2001 to December 2007.

Box 2-2: Oil Prices and Employment in Related Industries

Oil prices were more than 100 dollars-per-barrel as recently as September 2014. While the decline in oil prices has benefitted consumers and the economy overall, it has weighed heavily on mining employment, which includes oil and gas extraction. (See Box 2-1 of the 2016 Report or CEA 2015c for a more in-depth discussion of the impact of oil price declines on spending and production). Employment in the mining industry fell 26 percent from September 2014 to November 2016, though the pace of decline has slowed in recent months as the price of oil has stabilized. Oil and gas workers make up about 60 percent of the mining industry; though, they represent just 0.3 percent of total U.S. nonfarm employment. The level of mining employment is closely correlated with the price of oil, with shifts in employment usually following price changes (Figure 2-iv). Since 2000, mining employment has been most closely correlated with the lagged price of oil, suggesting that the stabilization in oil prices in the 40-50 dollar-per-barrel range since April 2016 may translate into a stabilization of employment in this sector in 2017.

Employment in the mining sector is more directly correlated with the oil and gas rig count—a measure that reflects the rate of drilling for new oil and natural gas—which also tend to lag oil prices. The rig count

Figure 2-iv

Oil Prices and Mining Employment, 2000–2016

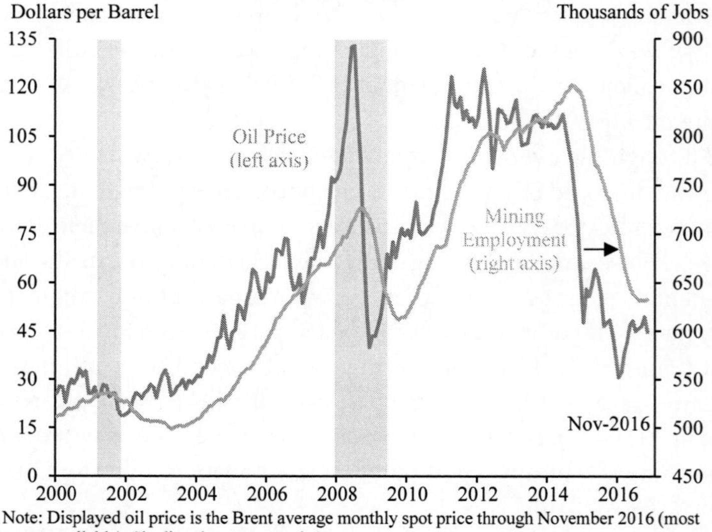

Note: Displayed oil price is the Brent average monthly spot price through November 2016 (most recent available). Shading denotes recession.
Source: Energy Information Administration; Bureau of Labor Statistics.

fell 80 percent from September 2014 to May 2016, but has grown since May. The partial rebound in the rig count has moderated the decline in mining employment, which has edged down 0.9 percent from June to November. The Energy Information Agency (EIA) forecasted in November that U.S. natural gas production during 2016 will fall 1.9 percent below its 2015 pace, which would be the first decline in average annual production since 2005 (EIA 2016). However, the EIA expects U.S. natural gas production to increase 3.8 percent in 2017.

employment), while falling steadily, remained above its pre-recession average through November 2016 and could indicate continued underutilization of labor. Between December 2007 and December 2009, the share of the labor force working part-time rose from 15.7 to 18.0 percent, driven by a large rise in the share of people working part-time for economic reasons. As the recovery progressed, the share of the labor force working part-time for economic reasons began to recede and, in 2016, fell a further 0.3 percentage point (Figure 2-8)[9]. As of November, the rate stood at 3.6 percent, 2.4 percentage points below its peak in 2010, but still above its pre-recession average of 3.0 percent.

The persistence in the rate of part-time work for economic reasons, especially relative to other measures of slack, is largely responsible for the continued elevation of the U-6 "underemployment" rate. The underemployment rate uses a broader concept of labor market slack than the official unemployment rate (also known as U-3), by including discouraged workers who have given up looking for a job, others who are marginally attached to the labor force, and those employed part-time for economic reasons. In November 2016, the U-6 rate was 9.3 percent, 7.8 percentage points below its recession peak, but still 0.2 percentage points above its pre-recession average. In the 12 months through November 2016, the U-6 rate declined 0.6 percentage point (Figure 2-9).

The labor force participation rate has been roughly stable since October 2013. By CEA estimates, demographic pressure from the aging of

---

[9] Care must be taken when comparing the share of workers who are part-time for economic reasons before and after the 1994 redesign of the Current Population Survey. CEA used the multiplicative adjustment factors reported by Polivka and Miller (1998) in order to place the pre-1994 estimates of the part-time for economic reasons rate on a comparable basis with post-redesign estimates. For the part-time series for which Polivka and Miller do not report suitable adjustment factors, the pre- and post-redesign series were spliced by multiplying the pre-1994 estimates by the ratio of the January 1994 rate to the December 1993 rate. This procedure generates similar results to the Polivka and Miller factors for series for which multiplicative factors are available.

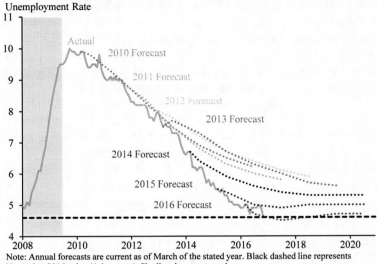

Figure 2-6
Actual and Consensus Forecast Unemployment Rate, 2008–2020

Unemployment Rate

Note: Annual forecasts are current as of March of the stated year. Black dashed line represents
November 2016 value (4.6 percent). Shading denotes recession.
Source: Bureau of Labor Statistics, Current Population Survey; and Blue Chip Forecasts

Figure 2-7
Unemployment Rate by Duration, 1990–2016

Percent of Labor Force

Note: Shading denotes recession. Dashed lines represent averages over 2001–2007.
Source: Bureau of Labor Statistics, Current Population Survey.

Figure 2-8
Rates of Part-Time Work, 1960–2016

Percent of Labor Force

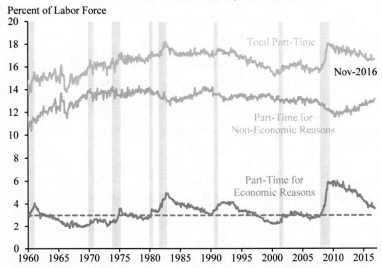

Note: Shading denotes recession. Dashed line represents pre-recession average. See footnote 5 for details on comparability over time.
Source: Bureau of Labor Statistics, Current Population Survey; Polivka and Miller (1998); CEA calculations.

Figure 2-9
Alternative Measures of Labor Force Underutilization, 2007–2016

Percent of Labor Force

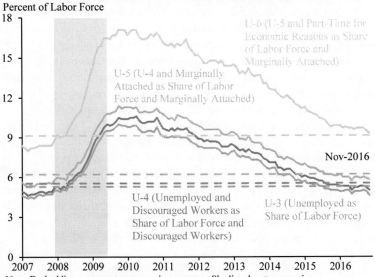

Note: Dashed lines represent pre-recession averages. Shading denotes recession.
Source: Bureau of Labor Statistics, Current Population Survey.

Box 2-3: Male Prime-Age Labor Force Participation[1]

Labor force participation among American men between the ages of 25 and 54, or "prime-age men," has been declining for more than 60 years, from a peak of 98 percent in 1954 to 89 percent today. More recently, over the last 15 years, labor force participation has also declined among prime-age women. These trends have troubling implications not only for overall economic growth, but also for individuals, as prolonged joblessness is linked to worse economic prospects, lower overall well-being and happiness, and higher mortality, as well as negative consequences for families and communities.

The United States has had the second largest decrease in prime-age male participation rates among the Organisation for Economic Cooperation and Development (OECD) countries since 1990. Today, the United States has the third lowest labor force participation rate in that group. Participation has fallen among every birth cohort of prime-age men over time, and the decline has been steeper among less-educated men and among black men. Three classes of explanations for this decline—supply driven, demand driven, and institutional—are explored in turn below.

Reductions in labor supply—in other words, prime-age men choosing not to work for a given set of labor market conditions—explain relatively little of the long-run trend. Data show that nonparticipating prime-age men are actually less reliant than in the past on income from spouses or from government assistance. Among prime-age men who are not in the labor force, the share receiving government assistance (excluding Social Security benefits) peaked at about 50 percent in 1975 and has since halved to roughly 25 percent in 2015. In addition, nearly 36 percent of these men lived in poverty in 2014—up from 28 percent in 1968. These patterns cast doubt on the hypothesis that nonparticipation represents a choice enabled by other personal means or income sources.

In contrast, reductions in the demand for labor, especially for lower-skilled men, appear to be an important driver of the decline in prime-age male labor force participation. Consistent with a decline in demand for the labor of less-educated men, the drop in participation has been particularly steep for this group (Figure 2-v) and has coincided with a fall in their wages relative to more-educated men. CEA analysis suggests that when the returns to work for those at the bottom of the wage distribution are particularly low, more prime-age men choose not to participate in the labor force. These relative wage declines are likely due to multiple factors, including a broader evolution of technology,

[1] Analysis in this section is from CEA (2016e). See the report for further discussion on this topic.

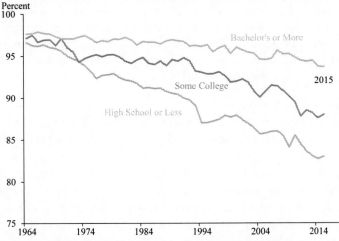

Figure 2-v

Prime-Age Male Labor Force Participation by Educational Attainment

Percent

Bachelor's or More

Some College

2015

High School or Less

Source: Bureau of Labor Statistics, Current Population Survey Annual Social and Economic
Supplement; CEA calculations.

automation, and globalization in the U.S. economy and, possibly, also an
increase in the wage-setting power of firms (CEA 2016d).

Institutional factors also appear to be important—and may help
explain some of the differences in the U.S. experience both over time
and compared with other countries. For example, the United States
spends only 0.1 percent of GDP on "active labor market policies" such
as job-search assistance and job training that help keep unemployed
workers connected to the labor force. This is less than nearly every other
OECD country and much less than the OECD average of 0.6 percent
of GDP. The rapid rise in incarceration may have also played a role,
disproportionately affecting low-skilled men and men of color. Although
incarcerated men are not counted in the labor force, formerly incarcerated men are in the labor force and they are more likely to experience
joblessness after they are released from prison and, in many states, are
legally barred from a large number of jobs. For example, according to
the American Bar Association, over 1,000 mandatory exclusions bar
individuals with records of misdemeanors from professions requiring
licenses and nearly 3,000 exclusions barring those with felony records
(American Bar Association 2016).

A number of policies proposed by the Administration would help
to boost prime-age male labor force participation. These include, but are
not limited to, creating new job opportunities for less-educated prime-

age men; reforming unemployment insurance to provide better search assistance and give workers more flexibility to use benefits to integrate into a new job; insuring workers against earnings losses; reforming the U.S. tax system to make participation in the workforce easier; investing in education and reforming the criminal justice and immigration systems; and increasing wages for workers by raising the minimum wage, supporting collective bargaining, and ensuring that workers have a strong voice in the labor market.

the baby-boom cohorts into retirement would have been expected to lower the participation rate by roughly 0.25 percentage point a year, and so this stabilization is consistent with a strengthening economy that has brought people into, and kept people attached to, the workforce. Between 2007 and November 2016, the labor force participation rate fell 3.3 percentage points. CEA analysis finds that nearly three-quarters of this decline was due to the aging of the baby-boom generation into retirement. These demographic-related declines will become steeper in the near term, as the peak of the baby-boom generation retires. Cyclical factors, including the lingering effects of high long-term unemployment rates in the wake of the Great Recession, also played a role in reducing the labor force participation rate and may still be having a small impact. The remaining decline of the labor force participation rate beyond what can be accounted for by demographics likely reflects structural factors, including the longstanding downward trend in participation among prime-age workers, particularly among males but also among females for the past decade-and-a-half (Box 2-3). As demographic shifts and longer-term trends continue to be offset by further cyclical recovery, the participation rate is expected to remain flat in 2017 before resuming its downward trend in 2018.

The Administration has proposed policies to support labor force participation through a range of measures that include promoting more flexible workplaces and paid leave, expanded high-quality pre-school, increased subsidies for child care, and a new proposal for a wage insurance system that would encourage reentry into work. As the recovery in the labor market progresses, the pace of job growth is likely to fall as the unemployment rate begins to plateau, particularly in light of increased retirements of an aging population.

OUTPUT

Real GDP grew 1.6 percent over the four quarters ended in 2016:Q3, somewhat below its pace in recent years. Real GDP grew somewhat slower than the 1.8 percent annual rate posted by gross domestic output (GDO)—an average of GDP and gross domestic income that is generally a more accurate measure of output than GDP—during the four quarters through 2016:Q3.[10]

The overall composition of demand during the first three quarters of 2016 shows that most of the growth was accounted for by strong growth in consumer spending, which was partially offset by declines in inventory investment. Contributions from other sectors were generally small. Real consumer spending growth outpaced overall growth, expanding 2.7 percent during the four quarters ended 2016:Q3.

Business fixed investment (non-residential fixed investment) was sluggish, declining 1.4 percent in the four quarters through 2016:Q3. Growth in business investment was hurt by the sharp declines in oil-related investment, which fell 45 percent in the four quarters ended 2016:Q3. Overall, despite weakness in equipment and structures spending, business investment was supported by growth in intellectual property products. Indeed, research and development spending as a share of GDP grew to over 2.6 percent, its highest share since 1992.

Growth in domestic demand was resilient in 2016, while diminishing foreign growth was a headwind. The aggregate of consumption and private fixed investment, known as private domestic final purchases (PDFP), rose faster than overall output at 2.0 percent in the four quarters ended 2016:Q3 (Figure 2-10). The solid pace of PDFP growth in 2016, which is typically a better predictor of future output growth than GDP growth, suggests that near-term U.S. growth prospects are positive. Nevertheless, CEA expects that the components of real GDP that are not in PDFP, such as net exports, will hold back overall real GDP growth in 2017. Despite weak foreign growth and a strong dollar, net exports contributed positively to growth over the four quarters ended in 2016:Q3.

Consumer Spending

Real consumer spending increased 2.7 percent during the four quarters through 2016:Q3. Stronger growth in real disposable income, due in part to rising nominal wages and to the direct impact of lower oil prices, as well as upbeat consumer sentiment and earlier gains in household wealth

---

[10] Research has shown that GDO can be especially helpful in predicting future revisions to GDP (CEA 2015a). GDO growth is initially estimated to be faster than GDP growth, GDP growth tends to revise up and vice versa (Box 2-4, CEA 2016a).

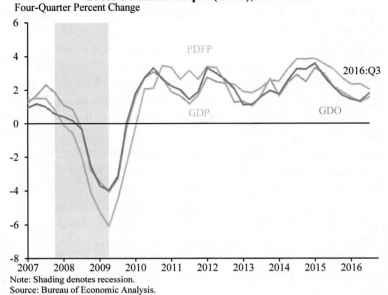

Figure 2-10
Real Growth in GDP, Private Domestic Final Purchases (PDFP), and Gross Domestic Output (GDO), 2007–2016
Four-Quarter Percent Change

Note: Shading denotes recession.
Source: Bureau of Economic Analysis.

all contributed to the solid pace of consumer spending growth. Low interest rates and improving access to credit, particularly automobile loans, also supported consumer spending. In general, real consumption growth and the wages and salaries component of real income growth tend to track one another well, as has been the case in 2016 (Figure 2-11). Overall, the personal saving rate has been fairly stable at around 5.6 percent of disposable personal income since the beginning of 2013, implying that real consumer spending growth has largely tracked real income growth (Figure 2-12).

During the past four quarters, growth was strong for real household purchases of durable goods (6.1 percent), nondurable (2.1 percent), and services (2.4 percent). Light motor vehicles sold at a 17. 4 million unit annual rate during the 11 months through November, roughly the same pace as the 17.4 million units during 2015, which was the strongest selling pace on record (CEA 2016a). Mirroring the strong selling pace, domestic automakers assembled light motor vehicles at an 11.8 million-unit annual pace during the first 10 months of 2016, while capacity utilization at the automakers was at its highest level since 2000. The inventory-to-sales ratios for domestically produced light motor vehicles were slightly elevated by the end of the third quarter. Consumer sentiment has remained at high levels through 2016, likely due in part to a strong labor market and low inflation. In 2016, the Reuters/University of Michigan's Index of Consumer Sentiment remained

Figure 2-11
Compensation and Consumer Spending, 1975–2016

Four-Quarter Percent Change

2016:Q3

Real Personal
Consumption
Expenditures

Real Wages and
Salaries,
Domestic
Employers

Note: Shading denotes recession. Wages and salaries of domestic employers is deflated using the
personal consumption expenditure price index.
Source: Bureau of Economic Analysis. CEA calculations.

Figure 2-12
Personal Saving Rate, 2000–2016

Percent

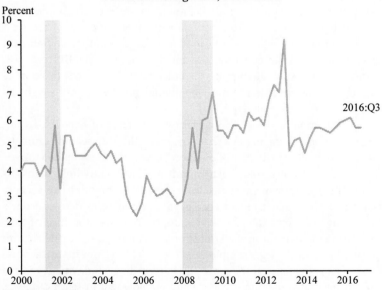

2016:Q3

Note: Shading denotes recession.
Source: Bureau of Economic Analysis.

Box 2-4: Optimal Weighting for Combining Measures of Economic Activity

The U.S. economy is large, dynamic, and complex; measuring it in real time can be extremely difficult at best. Data on the strength of the economy depend on extensive surveys of households and businesses and administrative data that are necessarily imperfect and incomplete, and the Federal statistical agencies—the Bureau of Economic Analysis (BEA), the Bureau of Labor Statistics (BLS), and the Census Bureau—frequently revise their estimates as newer and better underlying data become available. Given both the uncertainty inherent in any statistical measure and the standard practice of revising estimates, it is often better to look at multiple sources of data when assessing the state of the U.S. economy in real time. For example, as noted in Box 2-4 of the 2016 *Economic Report of the President*, growth in the average of estimates of real gross domestic product (GDP) and real gross domestic income (GDI)—which CEA refers to as real gross domestic output (GDO)—is a better predictor of one-quarter-ahead real GDP growth than are estimates of real GDP growth itself.

However, policymakers must often make decisions in real time, and may not have the ability to wait for multiple rounds of revisions to assess current economic conditions. (See Box 1-1 for a specific example.) As such, they may need to rely on early (incomplete) economic data on employment and output. It is important to note, though, that not all measures contain the same amount of uncertainty: some first-reported estimates come from surveys with large sample sizes and tend to be revised less, while others contain a larger number of statistical assumptions and consequently may undergo more substantial revisions. Consequently, when attempting to understand the current position of the U.S. economy in real time, one should not necessarily weight all current measures equally.

Each month, the BLS reports two estimates of over-the-month changes in employment. The first, known as the "household" estimate, is derived from the Current Population Survey, which samples approximately 60,000 households each month and asks household members about their employment status in the previous month. The second, known as the "establishment" or "payroll" estimate, is derived from a survey of more than 400,000 worksites covering about a third of total nonfarm employment in the United States. Although the establishment survey has a much larger sample size, it suffers both from statistical noise and some systematic errors, especially in recording employment gains at new firms that come into existence and employment losses at old firms that have closed. Moreover, monthly jobs estimates are revised multiple

Table 2-i

Optimal Weighting for Household Employment vs. Payroll Employment

Measure Predicted	Optimal Weight on First-Reported Household	Optimal Weight on First-Reported Payroll	Standard Deviation of Error Using Optimal Weight	Standard Deviation of Error Using Only Payroll
Final Payroll	0.000	1.000	92.303	92.303
State-Space Model	0.084	0.916	135.205	137.826

Note: Data from Jan-1994 to Dec-2014. Excludes data for January in each year.
Source: Bureau of Labor Statistics; CEA calculations.

times following their initial release. In principle, then, both the household and establishment measures of job growth contain some information about the true underlying path of U.S. employment (ignoring some conceptual differences in how employment is defined in each survey).

However, in practice the household survey is so volatile that it contains almost no additional information about monthly changes in employment beyond that contained in the establishment survey. Table 2-i shows the results of CEA analysis of the optimal weighting to put on first-reported employment growth from the household and payroll surveys when attempting to accurately predict "true" monthly employment growth using a weighted average of the two first-reported measures. The difficulty in such an exercise is in defining truth. When using the final-reported figure from the establishment survey—which is based in part on a near-complete census of nonfarm employment in the United States—as the measure of true employment growth, one should optimally put 100 percent of weight on the payroll survey. An alternative is to use a statistical model called a state space model to estimate the truth. This model extracts an unobserved component that is common to, and explains as much as possible of movements in, all variables in the model. When using a state-space model that combines the final-reported household and payroll estimates to derive an estimate of the common movements in employment, one should still place approximately 92 percent of weight on the payroll estimate—with very little difference in error compared with using the payroll survey alone.

More generally, it is possible to combine real-time measures of economic output (GDP, GDI, and their average, GDO) with real-time measures of employment growth to gain a more accurate assessment of broad economic conditions on a quarterly basis. This is particularly important given that quarterly estimates of output growth can see extensive revisions across multiple years as new and more complete data on real economic activity become available to BEA. Table 2-ii repeats the exercise of Table 2-i, this time predicting several final-reported measures

Table 2-ii

Optimal Weighting for Payroll Employment vs. Gross Domestic Output

Measure Predicted	Optimal Weight on 3rd Estimate GDO[1]	Optimal Weight on Preliminary Payroll Employment[2]	Standard Deviation of Error Using Optimal Weight
Final Payroll Employment	0.012	0.988	0.406
Final GDO	0.697	0.303	1.243
State-Space Model	0.000	1.000	0.831
Chicago Fed National Activity Index	0.379	0.621	0.373
Philadelphia Fed Current Economic Activity Index	0.053	0.947	0.543
Conference Board Current Economic Indicators	0.214	0.786	1.176

Note: Data from 1994:Q1 to 2014:Q4. [1] The 3rd estimate GDO is the release of GDO that is published with the 3rd estimate of GDP. [2] Preliminary payroll employment is the release of payroll employment that is published contemporaneous with the 3rd estimate of GDO.
Source: Bureau of Economic Analysis; Bureau of Labor Statistics; Federal Reserve Bank of Chicago; Federal Reserve Bank of Philadelphia; Conference Board; CEA calculations.

of quarterly economic activity: the payroll survey estimate of nonfarm employment growth, growth in real GDO, a state-space model combining payroll employment growth and real GDO growth, and three indexes of economic indicators from the Federal Reserve Bank of Chicago, the Federal Reserve Bank of Philadelphia, and the Conference Board that are designed to measure the state of the economy. In each case, the third estimate of real GDO growth is combined in a weighted average with the payroll-survey estimate of employment growth available at the time of the GDO estimate's release.

Here, too, optimal weighting places a substantial emphasis on the information contained in the early payroll estimates of employment growth. This is particularly true when predicting post-revision employment growth—where early output estimates contribute no information beyond that contained in early payroll estimates—but is true even when assessing output growth. Even when predicting post-revision real GDO growth, one should still place approximately one-third weight on contemporaneous measures of nonfarm employment growth. Optimal weighting for predicting the broader measures of economic activity vary somewhat from index to index, but in all cases more emphasis is placed on early estimates of employment growth than on early estimates of output growth. (CEA (2016f) contains a more extensive table with additional variables and details of these computations.)

No single measure of the economy is perfect, and all measures are subject to measurement error and conceptual challenges. But these results suggest that, to a first approximation, more emphasis should be placed on contemporaneous estimates of employment growth than on contemporaneous estimates of output growth when attempting to assess the overall current state of the U.S. economy.

Box 2-5: The Economics of Aging

The growth of the working-age population (15-64 year olds) in the United States has been slowing notably, which puts downward pressure on labor force participation, productivity, and real GDP growth. The working-age population grew 1.4 percent at an annual rate in the 1960s through the 1980s, but just 0.6 percent during this recovery. The decline in the growth rate of the working-age population is expected to continue through 2028 (Figure 2-vi). As the working-age population growth rate falls relative to the growth rate of other age groups, it follows that the working-age share of the population should fall as well. Between 2008 and 2015, the share declined from 67.3 percent to 66.3 percent (averaging -0.15 percentage point per year). The working-age share is expected to fall at an increasing rate through 2029, reflecting a growing share of the elderly population (65+). The only age group that is projected to

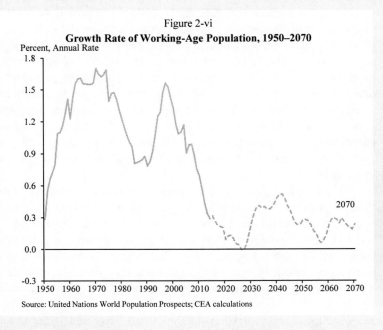

Figure 2-vi
Growth Rate of Working-Age Population, 1950–2070
Percent, Annual Rate

Source: United Nations World Population Prospects; CEA calculations

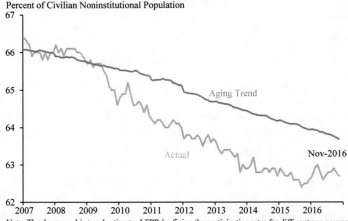

Figure 2-vii
Labor Force Participation Rate (LFPR) – Actual vs. Aging Trend, 2007–2016

Percent of Civilian Noninstitutional Population

Aging Trend

Actual

Nov-2016

Note: The demographic trend estimates LFPR by fixing the participation rates for different age groups at their 2007 annual average and updates the LFPR solely based on changes in the distribution of the population across those age groups.
Source: Bureau of Labor Statistics; CEA calculations

grow as a share of the population over the next 10 years is the 65+ age group.

Much of the recent decline in the labor force participation rate can be explained by the aging of the population. Of the 3.3 percentage points drop in the labor force participation rate between its 2007 average and November 2016, 2.3 percentage points can be explained by a simple demographic trend that only accounts for the aging of the population over this period (Figure 2-vii). Because older workers are less likely to work, the LFPR should decline as the population ages. The remaining 1.0 percentage point gap reflects other long-term trends, such as a declining participation rate among prime-age men (Box 2-3), as well as possibly a cyclical effect from the extraordinarily long duration of unemployment in the aftermath of the recession.

Real GDP has grown more slowly in the current economic recovery than in other cycles, but after taking into account demographic and workforce changes the current recovery looks more typical. Peak to peak, real GDP growth averaged 3.1 percent at an annual rate in prior cycles compared with just 1.2 percent so far this cycle, but comparing across business cycles can be misleading unless one considers demographics. The working-age population (ages 16-64) grew 1.4 percent at an annual rate in the 1960s through the 1980s, but just 0.6 percent during this recovery. In addition, previous recoveries had faster underlying trend

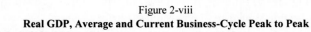

Figure 2-viii
Real GDP, Average and Current Business-Cycle Peak to Peak

Percent, Annual Rate

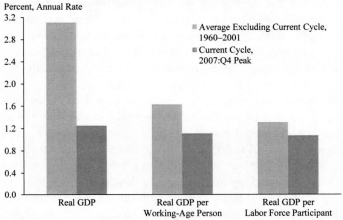

Note: Peak start dates: 1960:Q2, 1969:Q4, 1973:Q4, 1980:Q1, 1981:Q3, 1990:Q3, 2001:Q1, 2007:Q4.
Source: Bureau of Economic Analysis; National Bureau of Economic Research; Bureau of Labor
Statistics; Haver Analytics; CEA Calculations.

Figure 2-ix
Actual and Projected Labor Force by Age, 2000–2040

Percent of Labor Force, Projected After 2015

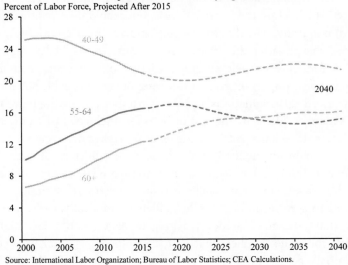

Source: International Labor Organization; Bureau of Labor Statistics; CEA Calculations.

growth in part driven by the rapid shift of women into the labor force. Controlling for the number of people in the labor force, growth in this recovery is quite similar to previous ones (Figure 2-viii).

Beyond the downward pressure on GDP caused by a slower working-age population growth rate, another economic impact of demographic shifts in the United States is that they may have reduced productivity growth. A range of papers finds that higher proportions of certain age groups are correlated with higher productivity growth (Feyrer 2007; Aiyar, Ebeke, and Shao 2016; Maestas, Mullen, and Powell 2016). As the share of these age groups employed in the labor force changes, productivity is affected. In particular, studies find the 40-49 cohort to be correlated with higher productivity (due to a bigger pool of managerial talent) and 55 and older to be less so. Estimates based on these papers suggest that somewhere from 0.2 to 0.8 percentage point of the 1.5 percentage points productivity slowdown from 1995-2005 to 2005-15 could be due to demography. Projections of the composition of the labor force suggest that the drag on productivity from demographics may soon be abating (Figure 2-ix).

around its pre-recession levels, oscillating between 87 and 95, driving the strong consumption growth (Figure 2-13). The Conference Board index hit its highest level since 2007 in November 2016, although the 2016 average was only somewhat higher than pre-recession levels.

Meanwhile, U.S. household debt relative to income continued to fall (Figure 2-14). Before the financial crisis, household debt relative to income rose dramatically, largely due to net mortgage originations, and then declined sharply after the crisis, a pattern known as "deleveraging." (See Box 2-6 for more on deleveraging.) Charge–offs of delinquent mortgage debt played an important role in lowering household debt, but the decline in new mortgage originations and less consumer borrowing played roles as well (Vidangos 2015). By the end of 2016:Q2, the debt-to-income ratio was at its lowest level since 2002. The level of mortgage debt relative to income continued to decline in 2016, while consumer credit (including credit cards, automobiles, and student loans) relative to income increased slightly.

Moreover, with historically low interest rates, the amount of income required to service these debts has fallen dramatically. Still, it should be noted that estimates based on aggregate data could mask higher debt burdens for some families; that is, the health of personal finances varies substantially across households. Nonetheless, in aggregate, there is evidence of deleveraging as discussed in Box 2-6.

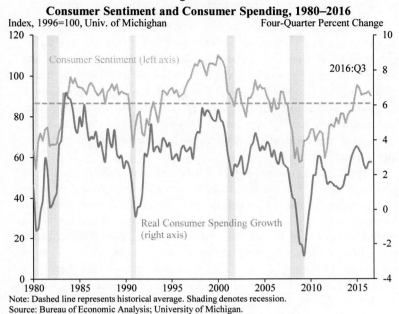

Figure 2-13
Consumer Sentiment and Consumer Spending, 1980–2016
Index, 1996=100, Univ. of Michigan   Four-Quarter Percent Change

Note: Dashed line represents historical average. Shading denotes recession.
Source: Bureau of Economic Analysis; University of Michigan.

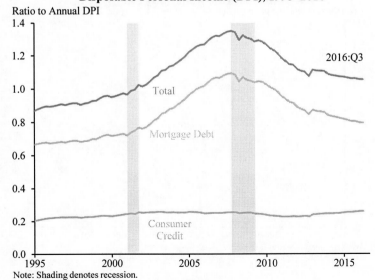

Figure 2-14
**Household Debt Relative to
Disposable Personal Income (DPI), 1995–2016**
Ratio to Annual DPI

Note: Shading denotes recession.
Source: Federal Reserve Board; Bureau of Economic Analysis.

Box 2-6: Household Deleveraging and Consumption Growth

Household balance sheets have continued to recover from the damage wrought during the recession, helping to support the strong consumption growth seen in recent years. Real household net worth—the difference between the market value of household assets and the value of outstanding liabilities, adjusted for inflation using the price index for personal consumption expenditures—did not regain the pre-crisis high reached in 2007:Q1 until 2013:Q3. Growth has continued and, as of 2016:Q3, real household net worth is 16 percent above the pre-crisis high (Figure 2-x).

The improvement of household balance sheets reflects a number of positive factors. First, households have increased their saving, with the saving rate moving up to 5.9 percent post-recession compared with the 3.8 percent average from 2001:Q4 to 2007:Q4. Second, the strong stock market growth seen in 2012-14 and substantial (roughly 6 percent a year) increases in house prices during the past four years have increased the value of household assets. Third, mortgage debt—by far the largest component of household liabilities—has fallen substantially, especially relative to income gains since the crisis, far outstripping small increases in other categories of debt. Household debt as a share of disposable income is at 106 percent as of 2016:Q3, far below the 2007:Q4 peak of 135 percent.

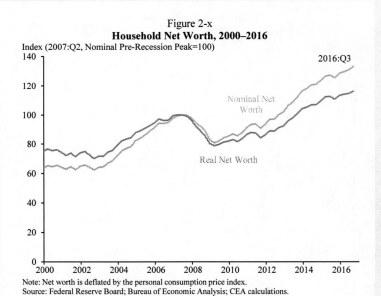

Figure 2-x
Household Net Worth, 2000–2016
Index (2007:Q2, Nominal Pre-Recession Peak=100)

Note: Net worth is deflated by the personal consumption price index.
Source: Federal Reserve Board; Bureau of Economic Analysis; CEA calculations.

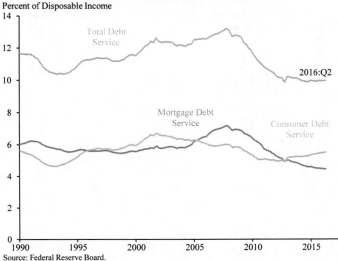

Figure 2-xi
Household Debt Service, 1990–2016

Percent of Disposable Income

Total Debt Service

2016:Q2

Mortgage Debt Service

Consumer Debt Service

Source: Federal Reserve Board.

In addition to lower debt balances and strong asset returns, low interest rates have further supported household finances. Debt service costs as a fraction of disposable personal income, which reflects the current burden of carrying debt including interest and principal payments, fell from 13 percent in 2007 to only 10 percent in 2013. This leaves households with more cash to spend. As shown in Figure 2-xi, the debt service-to-income ratio has held steady at this new lower level since 2013, with mortgage expenses continuing to decline while servicing costs for consumer debt—which includes automobile, student, and credit card debt—having increased somewhat.

Strong household balance sheets, together with low debt servicing costs, help to support consumption growth. As shown in Figure 2-xii, though household debt has begun to grow once more it is still growing very slowly—on a four-quarter basis, growth is still lower than in any period between 1971 and 2007. These developments, along with strong growth in employment and wages, have allowed households to increase their consumption. In particular, spending on durable goods—which are more likely to be paid for with borrowing and thus sensitive to balance sheet and interest rate considerations—accounted for 26 percent of personal consumption growth from 2014 through 2016:Q3, despite making up only 11 percent of expenditures. A large portion of this growth in durable goods spending comes from sales of motor vehicles, which fell sharply in the Great Recessions and were slow to recover until more recently.

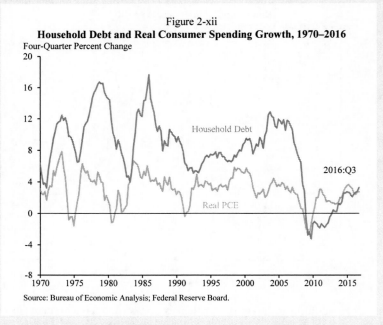

Figure 2-xii
Household Debt and Real Consumer Spending Growth, 1970–2016
Four-Quarter Percent Change

Household Debt

2016:Q3

Real PCE

Source: Bureau of Economic Analysis; Federal Reserve Board.

Earlier gains in household net worth (that is, assets less debts, also referred to as household wealth), such as the moderate increases in equity wealth so far in 2016, also supported consumer-spending growth in 2016 (Figure 2-15). The wealth-to-income ratio remained elevated in 2016, following a marked increase during 2013. Changes in net worth have been spread unevenly across households, though, and these disparities may have implications for families and macroeconomic activity.

Housing Markets

The housing market recovery continued in the first quarter of 2016, but residential investment was a drag on economic growth in the second and third quarters. In 2016, sales of newly constructed single-family homes and single-family housing starts, bolstered by strong labor market conditions and low mortgage interest rates, averaged their highest annual level through the first 10 months of a year since 2007. However, growth in new construction slowed from its 2015 pace: total housing starts and permits zig-zagged around their 2015 level. Real residential investment decreased 1.7 percent

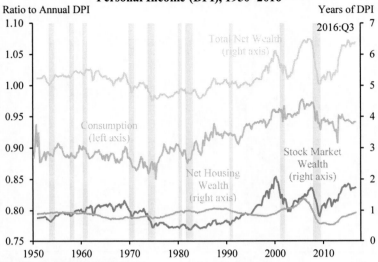

Figure 2-15
**Consumption and Wealth Relative to Disposable
Personal Income (DPI), 1950–2016**

Ratio to Annual DPI

Years of DPI

2016:Q3

Total Net Wealth
(right axis)

Consumption
(left axis)

Stock Market
Wealth
(right axis)

Net Housing
Wealth
(right axis)

Note: Shading denotes recession.
Source: Bureau of Economic Analysis, National Income and Product Accounts; Federal Reserve
Board, Financial Accounts of the United States; CEA calculations.

at an annual rate through the first three quarters of 2016, down from 13.1 percent positive growth in the four quarters of 2015.

While the housing market has continued its recovery since the recession, several structural challenges remain, including a constrained housing supply, low affordability in some areas of the country, and persistently muted household formation for 18-34 year olds. Housing supply is constrained: the inventory of homes available for sale is below its historical average and vacancy rates (for both renter and owner occupied) have fallen to levels that had prevailed before the boom, particularly in metropolitan areas, indicating that there is no longer excess supply (Figure 2-16). Sale volumes of the most affordable new single-family homes, particularly those less than $200 thousand, are lower than before the crisis. The share of young adults living with their parents remains above its long-run historical average, stifling household formation. These challenges may explain why housing starts still seem to be below their long-run steady state level.

House prices continued to rise in 2016, similar to the pace in 2015. National home prices increased between 5.5 and 6.1 percent (depending on the index) during the 12 months ended September 2016 compared with

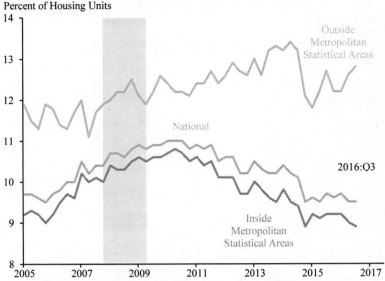

Figure 2-16
Year-Round Vacant Housing Units, 2005–2016

Percent of Housing Units

Outside
Metropolitan
Statistical Areas

National

2016:Q3

Inside
Metropolitan
Statistical Areas

Note: Shading denotes recession. Covers housing units that are vacant all year.
Source: Census Bureau, Housing Vacancy Survey.

4.7-to-6.2 percent in the year earlier period.[11] While price increases are above estimates for long-run steady state house price increases, they are not as rapid as the 6-to-11-percent increase in 2013. Nominal house prices are between 25 and 39 percent above their recessionary trough and between 6 percent below and 6 percent above their pre-recession peak (Figure 2-17). However, in real terms (adjusting for inflation with the CPI), house prices remain roughly 17 percent below their pre-recession peak.

Continued house price increases have improved owners' equity relative to the debt they owe on their houses. Homeowners' equity as of 2016:Q3 equaled slightly more than half of the total value of household real estate (57 percent), 20 percentage points higher than the recessionary trough and near the historical average of roughly 60 percent. Rising home prices since 2012 also helped lift more than 9 million households out of a negative equity position from 2012:Q2 to 2016:Q2, reducing the overall share of single-family homeowners with an underwater mortgage (when mortgage debt exceeds the value of their house) to 12.1 percent in the second quarter, down from 14.4 percent a year earlier. In addition, the number of delinquent home mortgages (when the homeowner misses at least one monthly payment) has fallen to its lowest level since 2007, though the share of mortgages that are

---

[11] Seasonally-adjusted national home price indexes from Zillow, CoreLogic, FHFA Purchase-Only, and S&P CoreLogic Case-Shiller are used.

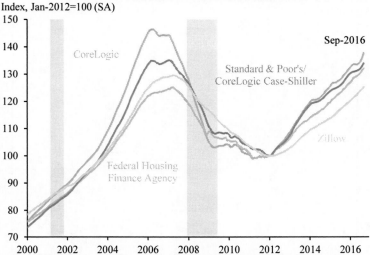

Figure 2-17
National House Price Indexes, 2000–2016

Index, Jan-2012=100 (SA)

Note: Shading denotes recession. The Standard & Poor's/CoreLogic Case-Shiller, Federal Housing
Finance Agency, and CoreLogic indexes all adjust for the quality of homes sold but only cover
homes that are bought or sold, whereas Zillow reflects prices for all homes on the market. All
indexes are seasonally adjusted.
Source: Zillow; CoreLogic; Federal Housing Finance Agency; Standard & Poor's.

seriously delinquent (payment more than 90 days overdue, with the bank
considering the mortgages to be in danger of default) remains somewhat
elevated (Figure 2-18). Falling delinquencies support overall economic
growth because homeowners with underwater or delinquent mortgages
are less likely to spend or relocate in search of better-paying jobs (Ferreira,
Gyourko, and Tracy 2012).

Single-family homes were still more affordable in 2016 than the
historical average, as rising incomes and low and steady mortgage rates
partially offset the effect of rising house prices on the cost of homeownership
(Figure 2-19). Nevertheless, affordability decreased somewhat over the past
three years because median existing home prices grew roughly 4 percentage
points faster than median family incomes on average each year.

The national homeownership rate was 63.5 percent in the third quarter of 2016, much lower than the historical average due to a variety of trends
in the housing market. The decline has been concentrated among young
households. The homeownership rate of those aged 18-34 was 35.2 percent
in 2016:Q3, roughly 8-percentage points lower than its all-time high in 2004.
The major reason for this decline is that young adults are waiting longer to
get married or form households, and first-time homebuyers are older, on
average, than they were in the 1980s. Second, credit availability remains

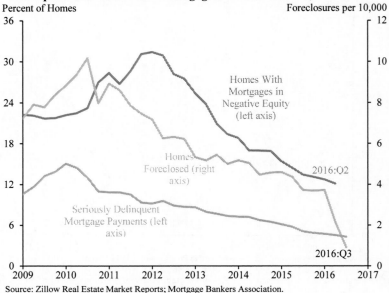

Figure 2-18
Delinquent and Underwater Mortgages and Foreclosures, 2009–2016

Percent of Homes   Foreclosures per 10,000

Source: Zillow Real Estate Market Reports; Mortgage Bankers Association.

tight for borrowers with credit scores below 620. Third, it can be difficult for prospective buyers, especially those living in urban areas, to save for a down payment.

Overall household formation has showed some tentative signs of picking up in recent years, after having been weak since the recession. The number of households increased by 1.2 million in 2016 after rising 0.7 million in 2015. This uptick in household formation contributed to a 5.5 percent rise in overall housing starts during the first ten months 2016 relative to 2015 as a whole and a solid 9.2 percent rise in single-family housing starts during the first ten months of 2016 relative to 2015 as a whole (Figure 2-20). Nevertheless, starts remained well below the roughly 1.5 million rate that is consistent with long-term demographics and the replacement of the existing housing stock.[12] Further, because the rates of homebuilding have been below that pace since the recession, pent-up demand for housing may play a role in supporting further recovery in the housing market. However, an increase in housing demand, if not accompanied by an increase in housing supply, would not bring about a full recovery in the housing market. The accumulation of State and local barriers to housing development—including

---

[12] Demographics and historical trends would have predicted 1.2 to 1.4 million new households formed each year requiring housing (Joint Center for Housing Studies 2015). Together with the assumption that about 0.25 percent of the existing homes deteriorate and need to be replaced a given year, yields an underlying trend of roughly 1.5 million housing starts.

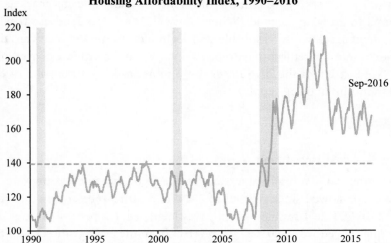

Figure 2-19
Housing Affordability Index, 1990–2016

Index

Note: Index is 100 when the median income family can exactly qualify for a mortgage on a median-priced home. An index over 100 means that the median income family has more than enough income to qualify for a mortgage on a median-priced home. Dashed line represents average over 1990–2016. Shading denotes recession.
Source: National Association of Realtors.

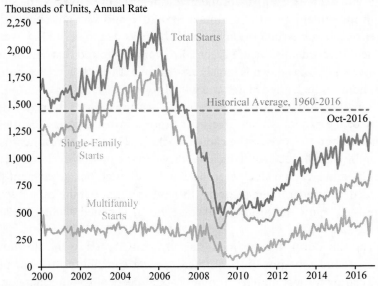

Figure 2-20
Single-Family and Multifamily Housing Starts, 2000–2016

Thousands of Units, Annual Rate

Note: Shading denotes recession.
Source: Census Bureau.

zoning, other land use regulations, and unnecessarily lengthy development approval processes—have reduced the ability of many housing markets to respond to growing demand (White House 2016). While land use regulations sometimes serve reasonable and legitimate purposes, they can also give extra-normal returns to entrenched interests at the expense of everyone else (see Box 2-6 of the 2016 *Report* for a more in-depth discussion of the constraints on housing supply).

Investment

Business Fixed Investment

After being a bright spot early in the recovery, business investment growth has slowed since the end of 2014, and turned negative in 2015:Q4 and 2016:Q1. Real business fixed investment fell 1.4 percent during the four quarters ended in 2016:Q3, a reversal from the average increase of 5.0 percent at an annual rate during the twelve quarters of 2012-14, and much slower that the average of 8.5 percent annual rate increase during the eight quarters of 2010-11. Not all components of investment were weak in 2016. The rate of investment growth remained strong for intellectual property products, which grew 4.5 percent at an annual rate during the first three quarters of 2016, and has now been positive for 13 consecutive quarters. However, the strong gains in intellectual property products were more than offset by larger declines in equipment investment (Figure 2-21). While oil price declines can explain part of the investment decline in 2015, the slowdown in investment growth continued into 2016 and was not simply due to lower oil and gas structures investment, but was due to shrinking overall equipment investment as well. Recent CEA work has found that this broad-based investment slowdown is largely associated with the low rate of output growth both in the United States and globally (Box 2-7).

Slower investment growth is a concern because it limits the productive capacity of the economy. Net investment (gross investment less depreciation) is required to increase the capital stock. In 2009, net investment as a share of the capital stock fell to its lowest level in the post-World War II era and the nominal capital stock even declined. Although net investment has rebounded somewhat in the recovery, its level as a share of the capital stock remains well below the historical average and it declined slightly in 2015 (Figure 2-22).

The slowdown in investment has also contributed to the slowdown in labor productivity growth. Investment growth contributes to labor productivity growth most directly through capital deepening—the increase in capital services per hour worked—that had added nearly 1 percentage point

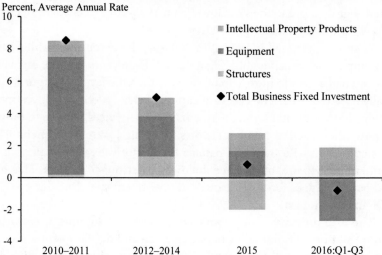

Figure 2-21
Composition of Growth in Real Business Fixed Investment (BFI)

Percent, Average Annual Rate

Note: Components may not sum to total due to rounding. Growth rate computed using Q4-to-Q4 changes
Source: Bureau of Economic Analysis; CEA calculations.

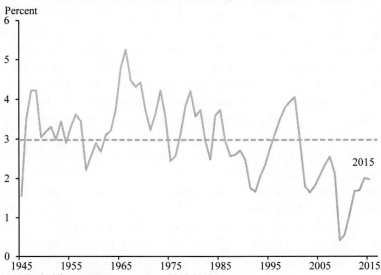

Figure 2-22
Net Investment as a Share of the Capital Stock, 1945–2015

Percent

Note: Dashed line represents average over 1945–2015.
Source: Bureau of Economic Analysis.

a year to labor productivity growth in the post-war period to 2010. But since 2010, capital deepening has subtracted from productivity growth and contributed slightly more to the slowdown from 1948-2010 to 2010-15 than did the slowdown in total factor productivity growth.

With the sharp fall in output in 2008-09, the amount of capital relative to output rose considerably (Figure 2-23). Even years into the recovery, businesses had access to more capital services than the level of output would typically have required. The excess of capital likely reduced new investment and helped lower capital services growth. Capital services relative to output have now fallen back to trend, a factor supporting future investment. This view is consistent with the usual pattern that historically weaker periods of investment growth are, on average, followed by stronger periods. This historical pattern argues for faster growth in investment spending during 2017 than in the recent past.

The Administration has pursued policies to support investment, including additional funding for public research and development and public infrastructure as well as the Trans-Pacific Partnership, all of which can stimulate private sector investment. In addition, the President has proposed business tax reform that would directly spur private investment (see Box 2-9 and Chapter 5 of the 2015 *Report* for a more in-depth discussion of the economic benefits of business tax reform (CEA 2015b)).

Inventory Investment

Inventory investment continued to weaken during the first half of 2016, a continuation of the pattern during the last three quarters of 2015. The inventory-to-sales ratio in manufacturing and trade had crept up over the past few years, and by 2016:Q1 had reached 1.41 months' supply, substantially above its post-2000 non-recessionary average of 1.32 months' supply (Figure 2-24).Given the higher-than-average ratio, it was not surprising that inventories fell relative to sales in the second and third quarters of 2016. As of September, the latest data available as this *Report* goes to press, the ratio was 1.38, still somewhat elevated relative to recent history.

Real inventory investment—the change in the inventory stock—has subtracted from output growth thus far in 2016, especially in the second quarter. Although inventory investment is volatile, and can greatly affect quarterly GDP growth rates, its contribution to output growth generally averages close to zero over 4- or 8-quarter horizons outside of recessions and their immediate aftermath (Figure 2-25). After inventory-to-sales ratios had risen to relatively high levels in 2015:Q1, though, the change in inventory investment was negative for five consecutive quarters, a string of negative changes that is unusual in non-recessionary conditions. By the second

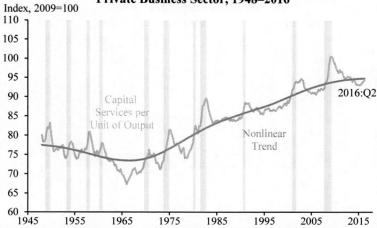

Figure 2-23
**Capital Services per Unit of Real Output,
Private Business Sector, 1948–2016**

Index, 2009=100

Note: Shading denotes recession. Post-1964 data interpolated quarterly using Macroeconomic Advisers quarterly data. Pre-1965 data interpolated by moving average. Nonlinear trend is a bi-weight filter using a 60-quarter window. Shading denotes recession.
Source: Bureau of Labor Statistics, Labor Productivity and Costs; Macroeconomic Advisers; CEA calculations.

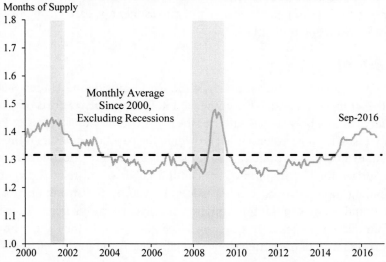

Figure 2-24
Inventory-to-Sales Ratio: Manufacturing and Trade, 2000–2016

Months of Supply

Note: Manufacturing and trade inventories at book value. Shading denotes recession.

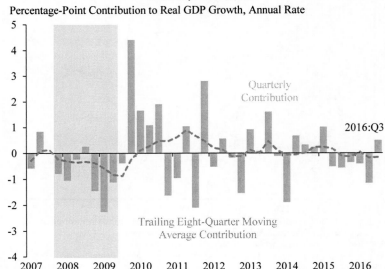

Figure 2-25
Contribution of Inventory Investment to Real GDP Growth, 2007–2016

Percentage-Point Contribution to Real GDP Growth, Annual Rate

Note: Shading denotes recession.
Source: Bureau of Economic Analysis, National Income and Product Accounts; CEA calculations.

quarter, the level of inventory investment itself was negative, and the third quarter's positive contribution of inventory investment to real GDP growth reflects the swing from negative inventory investment in 2016:Q2 to positive inventory investment in 2016:Q3.

Net Exports

With weak demand in much of the world outside the United States and the stronger dollar that has come with it, U.S. nominal exports of goods and services rose only 0.8 percent over the four quarters ended 2016:Q3. Part of the reason for the weak nominal growth in the past four quarters is the 1.2 percent drop in export prices, as lower oil and commodity prices have meant lower prices for U.S. exports of agricultural goods or oil-related products and falling input costs have other prices. Driven by the strong growth in agricultural exports in the third quarter, real exports rose 2 percent during the four quarters ended 2016:Q3, shown in Figure 2-26. As the Figure shows, real exports tend to trace trade-weighted global growth rates[13], and as global

[13] Trade-weighted global growth is calculated as a weighted average of real GDP growth for 25 foreign economies and the Euro area, using those economies' share of U.S. goods exports as weights.

**Box 2-7: Explanations for the Recent Performance
of Business Fixed Investment**

Business fixed investment comprises business spending on structures and equipment, as well as expenditures on intellectual property
products such as software and research and development (R&D). While
it constitutes only 12 percent of GDP, business fixed investment affects
short-run growth disproportionately, as it accounts for about 20 percent
of the quarterly volatility in real GDP growth. Moreover, business fixed
investment is crucial to long-run growth because it supports future output (and income) and thereby consumption and is a major contributor
to productivity growth. Business fixed investment has weakened since
2014:Q4; for the first time since it began recovering after the recession,
its four-quarter growth rate was negative in 2016:Q1 (Figure 2-xiii).
Although oil-related investment has dragged on investment growth due
to low oil prices, non-oil related investment growth has also slowed over
the period. Finding the sources of this broad-based slowdown in investment spending is an ongoing discussion and empirical effort among
economists. CEA has found that slow U.S. and global growth provides
a partial quantitative explanation for the recent slowdown, while CEA's
analysis indicates that other factors such as business confidence, policy
uncertainty, or financial conditions do not seem to explain the recent

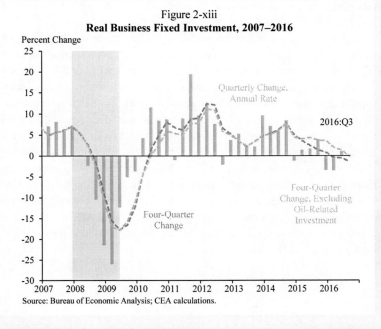

Figure 2-xiii
Real Business Fixed Investment, 2007–2016

Source: Bureau of Economic Analysis; CEA calculations.

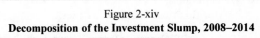

Figure 2-xiv
Decomposition of the Investment Slump, 2008–2014

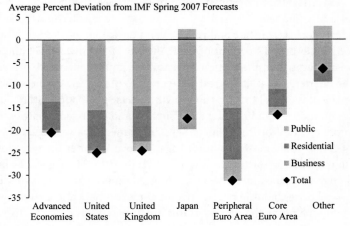

Note: Peripheral Euro Area refers to economies (Greece, Ireland, Italy, Portugal, Spain) with high borrowing spreads during the 2010–2011 sovereign debt crisis.
Source: Consensus Economics; IMF, Fiscal Monitor database; national authorities; IMF staff estimates.

data. While this implies that headwinds to investment are coming from the broader economy, it also suggests that investment spending should rebound if and when consensus forecasts for stronger global growth are realized.

The slowdown in investment in the United States is not an isolated trend; in recent years, investment spending in advanced economies has fallen short of forecasts made by the IMF in the spring of 2007 (Figure 2-xiv). Emerging market economies, which have been accumulating capital at higher rates than advanced economies, have also seen a slowdown. The global nature of the investment slowdown sheds doubt on the theory that any particular factor specific to the United States, such as government policy, is behind the current U.S. investment slowdown.

A standard model that economists employ to explain investment theoretically and empirically is called the "accelerator model." This model assumes that businesses invest if they expect rising demand growth for their products, so rising GDP growth rates will lead to higher investment growth. CEA research has found that this accelerator model explains much of the recent fluctuation in investment, as shown in Figure

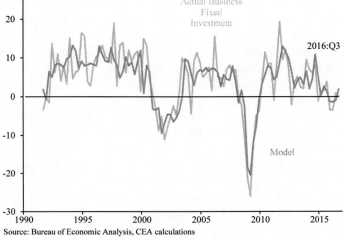

Figure 2-xv
Business Fixed Investment - Actual vs. Accelerator Model, 1991–2016
Percent Change, Annual Rate

Actual Business Fixed Investment

2016:Q3

Model

Source: Bureau of Economic Analysis, CEA calculations

2-xv.[1] The uptick in output growth after the crisis spurred faster investment growth in 2011 but the slowdown in growth in 2015-16 contributed to a slowdown in investment growth more recently, though investment growth is still somewhat weaker than this model would predict over this past year. Importantly, the model shows that changes in global growth—not just domestic growth—affect business investment, consistent with findings from the IMF and the Organisation for Economic Cooperation and Development (OECD) (IMF 2015a; OECD 2015).

Several factors that have historically mattered for investment growth have little explanatory power in the recent slowdown. These include two main financial stress measures, the credit spread (the gap between treasury yields and corporate bond yields that is sometimes seen as a measure of concerns for financial risk in the economy) and an index of tightness of loan conditions. Both of these increased recently, but not enough to have any explanatory power in the investment slowdown. Therefore, constraints on credit or in the financial system cannot explain on their own the slowdown in business investment over the last year and

---

[1] The standard "accelerator" model assumes that investment growth is a function of the change in the growth of real GDP because firms target a level of the capital stock that moves with the overall level of GDP. The accelerator model can be estimated using first or second differences of the relevant series. CEA ran both specifications – Figure 2-xv shows the results using the model where changes in investment are driven by lags of itself as well as the second difference of US and a foreign trade-weighted GDP aggregate. As Figure 2-xv shows, this specification closely matches investment growth.

a half, consistent with the observation that, even as the financial sector has healed, business investment growth has actually slowed further.

Another possibility is that declining profits have held back investments in the last two years. Real corporate profits rebounded after the recession but have been declining since 2014, leaving fewer funds for internal funding of investment projects. But this theory also does not match the data. Firms still have a high level of profits relative to history, and have been taking the profits they do have and increasing payouts to shareholders instead of investing in structures or equipment. This suggests firms could invest if they wanted to, but do not see adequately attractive uses of investment funds.

While evidence shows that weak global growth explains weak business investment growth, this does not suggest that it is the only explanation. Investment, like any other macroeconomic variable, is affected by both short- and long-run trends. There is evidence to suggest that the recent slowdown is also connected to a longer-run downward trend in investment as a share of GDP over the last few decades. Part of this decline can be attributed to secular shifts in the U.S. economy. U.S. output is increasingly produced by services industries that require less capital. For example, from 2010 to 2015, average investment-to-output ratio for services industries was 15.6 percent, while it was 21.9 percent for all non-service industries.

The accelerator model predicts a rebound in investment in the future. A key feature of the model is that investment depends on changes in GDP growth (in other words, the acceleration of GDP). The deceleration in GDP, both in the United States and abroad, has already had its negative impact on investment growth. Moving forward, more normal investment growth should occur if—as expected—world output growth stabilizes. Further, a rebound in global growth should also contribute to a rebound in overall U.S. GDP growth.

growth seems to be stabilizing, real export growth rates have begun to rise as well.

At the same time, real U.S. imports increased just 0.6 percent in the four quarters ended 2016:Q3, slower than did exports. Taken together, Figure 2-27 shows net exports contributed 0.4 percentage point to real GDP growth during the first three quarters of 2016, after subtracting 0.7 percentage point from overall growth during the four quarters of 2015.

Figure 2-26
Foreign Real GDP and U.S. Real Export Growth

Four-Quarter Percent Change

Four-Quarter Percent Change

Trade-Weighted Foreign Real GDP Growth (left axis)

U.S. Real Export Growth (right axis)

2016:Q3

Source: Bureau of Economic Analysis; National Sources; Haver Analytics; CEA Calculation.

PRODUCTIVITY

Labor productivity, defined as nonfarm output per hour worked, has grown slower in the past decade and in particular over the past few years. Productivity growth slowed first around 2005 and then even more after 2011, averaging just 0.5 percent over the five years ending 2015:Q4—the slowest five years during an expansion in the postwar data and well below its 2.0-percent average since 1953 (Figure 2-28). This low productivity growth reflects rapid growth in employment while GDP has grown more slowly. Over longer periods of time, growth in real output and real wages depend on rising productivity, so this slowdown is a cause for concern.

Similar to trends in business fixed investment, the slowdown in productivity growth is shared across the advanced economies: 34 of the 35 OECD member countries saw slowdowns labor productivity per hour worked from 2005 to 2015 relative to the prior 10-year period.[14] In fact, despite its own slowdown, the United States has had higher productivity growth than any other G-7 economy over the past 10 years (Figure 2-xvi). The sources of the productivity slowdown are shared across advanced economies to some extent, so the approaches to address these problems are

---

[14] The calculation uses data from The Conference Board: Labor productivity per hour worked in 2015 US$ (converted to 2015 price level with updated 2011 PPPs).

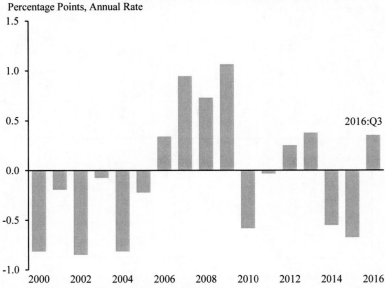

Figure 2-27
Contribution of Net Exports to U.S. Real GDP Growth, 2000–2016

Percentage Points, Annual Rate

Note: Contributions are computed using Q4-to-Q4 changes.
Source: Bureau of Economic Analysis.

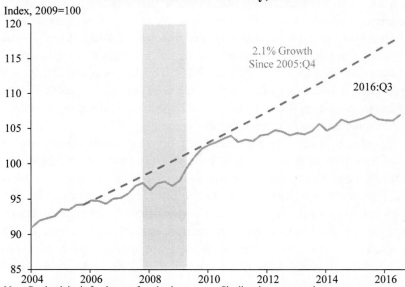

Figure 2-28
Nonfarm Business Productivity, 2004-2016

Index, 2009=100

2.1% Growth
Since 2005:Q4

2016:Q3

Note: Productivity is for the non-farm business sector. Shading denotes recession.
Source: Bureau of Labor Statistics.

somewhat generalizable (Box 2-8), but the U.S. productivity slowdown has several of its own specific causes.

A useful way to analyze labor productivity is to decompose its growth into three factors: increased capital services per hour worked (capital deepening), increased skills per worker (labor composition), and increased technology or efficiency (technically termed "total factor productivity" and measured as a residual). While the contribution of all three decreased in the post-recessionary period compared with their long-run averages, the slowdown in capital deepening has been the largest factor subtracting from productivity growth, accounting for more than half the decline in total productivity growth, although the slowdown in total factor productivity (TFP) was substantial as well (Figure 2-29).

In the period from 1953 to 2010, about 0.92 percentage points (41 percent) of productivity growth was attributable to additional capital services per worker. Even as the recovery was underway during 2010 to 2015, the capital-deepening contribution to labor productivity growth was actually negative; in 2014 and 2015, a worker had less capital services at his or her disposal than five years earlier—the first time this has occurred during any five-year period since the end of World War II (Figure 2-30). These data suggest that net investment (that is, gross investment less depreciation) has not sufficed to grow capital services in line with the increase in hours worked. Indeed, business fixed investment growth has fallen short of IMF forecasts and been weak since 2014 (IMF 2014; IMF 2015a).

Another possible explanation is that we are not measuring productivity correctly in the information-driven economy. Measurement error, however, has probably always been present in the official productivity data and is therefore unlikely to explain much of the recent, productivity slowdown. CEA analysis and recent research suggests that mismeasurement has not grown in such a way to explain such a large slowdown in productivity growth from a 2.1-percent historical average to 0.0 percent during the four quarters ended 2016:Q3 (Box 2-5 in CEA 2016a). Some reasons for skepticism include: (i) productivity growth was high from 1995 to 2005 when many of the potentially underestimated information technology innovations were introduced; (ii) the slowdown in productivity has affected well-measured sectors of the economy too; and (iii) many recent innovations boost consumer surplus and the value of leisure, which GDP was not designed to measure.

Changes in industrial composition can explain some of the decrease. Since 2011, output and employment growth has been higher in lower output-per-hour sectors, such as business services, construction, and hospitality, holding back productivity growth overall. Conversely, as commodity

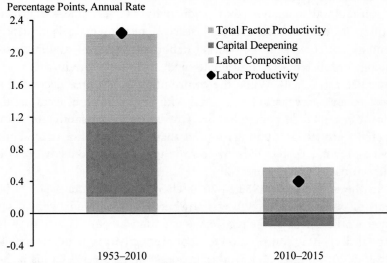

Figure 2-29
Contributions to Growth of Labor Productivity, 1953–2015

Percentage Points, Annual Rate

Note: Productivity is measured for the private non-farm business sector.
Source: Bureau of Labor Statistics; CEA calculations.

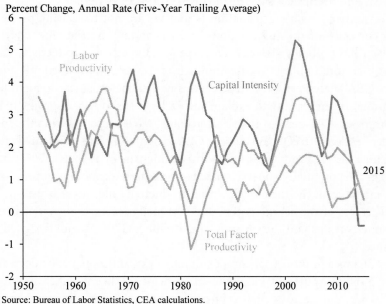

Figure 2-30
Labor Productivity and Major Components, 1953–2015

Percent Change, Annual Rate (Five-Year Trailing Average)

Source: Bureau of Labor Statistics, CEA calculations.

prices weakened and the global economy slowed during 2015 and 2016, both the energy-producing sector and manufacturing have struggled. A shrinking role for these capital- and technology-intensive sectors reduces output per hour.

In the labor market, there is some evidence that the improving economy is drawing in workers who have at least temporarily lower productivity, which also reduces measured productivity growth. Newly employed workers tend to receive lower wages, presumably because they are at least temporarily less productive than their more experienced co-workers. Partly for these reasons, it is not unusual for measured productivity growth to be higher early in a business cycle recovery and slower as a business-cycle expansion matures as workers are added back onto payrolls, though this is actually an overall positive development for the economy as long as it moves the economy towards full employment. Since 2011, newly employed workers have made up a larger-than-normal share of the workforce as employment growth has boomed. This has suppressed wage growth by 0.5 to 1.0 percentage point over this period. These newer hires may have lower skills or productivity than otherwise similar workers, or their skills may have eroded during their extended time out of work. Adding relatively more of these below-median-wage workers may have temporarily depressed productivity growth.

Longer-standing declines in the fluidity and dynamism of the economy may also be contributing to slower productivity growth. The entry of new firms has been slowing for decades and, to the extent that these firms drive both investment and productivity growth, their decline is important. A pessimistic view put forward by economist Robert Gordon is that the world economy may have simply run through the best productivity-enhancing innovations such as the steam engine, the telephone, and indoor plumbing while more recent innovations may not have the same impact on output (Gordon 2012). This pessimistic view of our future is not universally held. The world has more educated and connected people than at any time in history. Investment in intellectual property products has been strong throughout the recovery. Spending on the research and development component of investment (R&D) in particular has risen to its highest share of GDP on record, suggesting good prospects for continued innovation remain.

Of the possible explanations, it appears that more cyclical or short-term explanations explain a large portion of the slowdown. In particular, to the degree that the productivity slowdown is caused by an investment bust, that may actually be encouraging for the future outlook. It means we are not out of ideas or permanently mired in secular stagnation, but instead just need to invest more. Not only do we have policy tools to help push in that direction, but to some degree such investment busts have historically

Box 2-8: Productivity Among the Advanced Economies—Explanations and Prospects

The slow productivity growth over the last decade in the United States is hardly an exception within the advanced economies. While there is still substantial heterogeneity across the advanced economies in terms of their cyclical position, there is commonality in terms of their experience with productivity growth. Average annual productivity growth in the advanced economies slowed to 1 percent in the period from 2005 to 2015, down from 2 percent in the previous decade—with productivity slowing in 34 of the 35 OECD member countries, including all of the G-7 economies, with the United States having the fastest productivity growth in the G-7 (Figure 2-xvi).

An economy takes various inputs, such as labor and capital, and produces goods and services. Low labor productivity growth means that labor inputs are growing relatively quickly compared with output, such that growth in output per hour worked is low. This may be due to less capital for each worker or because technology or management are not using these inputs efficiently.

It is unlikely to be a mere coincidence that a substantial shortfall in aggregate demand and a large slowdown in productivity growth have occurred simultaneously. In fact, the causal relationship between the two phenomena likely runs both ways. In the period from 2008 to 2014,

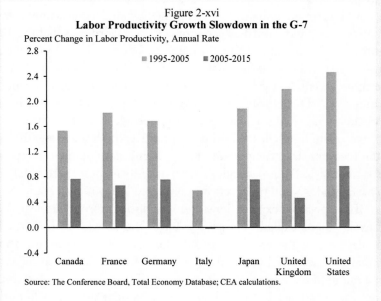

Figure 2-xvi
Labor Productivity Growth Slowdown in the G-7

Percent Change in Labor Productivity, Annual Rate

Source: The Conference Board, Total Economy Database; CEA calculations.

inadequate demand has contributed to a large shortfall of investment in both advanced and emerging markets. Moreover, CEA has found that the U.S. investment slowdown in the past 18 months can, in part, be quantitatively explained by slow global growth (Box 2-7).

In the United States, the largest contributor to the decline in labor productivity in the past five years is a reduction in capital deepening. This was not a unique experience, as all of the G-7 countries except Canada saw appreciable slowing in their rates of capital deepening between 1995-2005 and 2005-15 (Figure 2-xvii). As in the United States, the slowdown in capital deepening was even than the slowdown in total factor productivity (TFP) in Germany, Japan, and Italy. In France and the United Kingdom, however, relatively larger slowdowns in TFP growth account for the larger share of the decline in labor productivity (Figure 2-xviii).

On the supply side, slowing total factor productivity growth has also played a role in all of the G-7 economies. There is some evidence that the slowing began before the crisis, around 2004, as the impulse from the information technology revolution either did not endure or was not well measured.

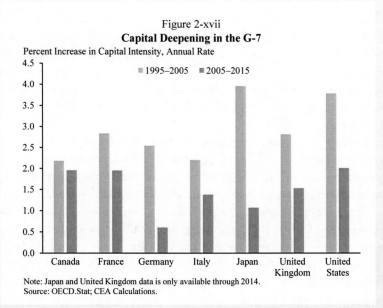

Figure 2-xvii
Capital Deepening in the G-7

Percent Increase in Capital Intensity, Annual Rate

Note: Japan and United Kingdom data is only available through 2014.
Source: OECD.Stat; CEA Calculations.

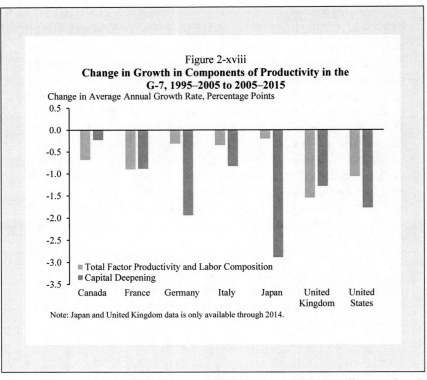

Figure 2-xviii
**Change in Growth in Components of Productivity in the
G-7, 1995–2005 to 2005–2015**

Change in Average Annual Growth Rate, Percentage Points

■ Total Factor Productivity and Labor Composition
■ Capital Deepening

Canada   France   Germany   Italy   Japan   United   United
                                                 Kingdom States

Note: Japan and United Kingdom data is only available through 2014.

been self-correcting as investment tends to be negatively serially correlated, with busts followed by booms and vice versa. Other factors holding down productivity growth—particularly shifting industry composition and new-worker entry—should fade. As the labor market normalizes over the long term, the economy will no longer be adding a disproportionate number of new workers.

Looking forward, a number of the President's proposed policies would contribute to increasing productivity growth. Infrastructure spending would lift public investment, raising effective capital per worker; investing in job training and greater access to higher education would raise labor quality; reforming innovation policy, patent reforms, expanding R&D tax credits, and supporting public R&D spending would all increase total factor productivity. Broader policies would aid as well: the Trans-Pacific Partnership (TPP) trade agreement would help better firms grow and hire more workers, increasing productivity within sectors; immigration reform would increase high-skilled immigration and improve job matching of workers and increase certainty for undocumented workers already here; supportive entrepreneurship policies would help both investment and firm dynamism; business tax reform would encourage domestic investment and innovation; and better competition policy would steer firms away from rent-seeking toward

Figure 2-31
Nominal Wage Inflation Over Past Year, 2003–2016

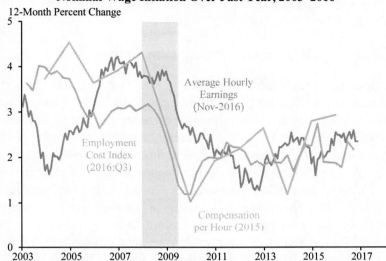

Note: Compensation per hour refers to the productivity and cost measure for nonfarm business. The Employment Cost Index ialso refers to the nonfarm sector, but uses a different survey. Aver-age hourly earnings refers to production & nonsupervisory workers. Shading denotes recession.
Source: Bureau of Labor Statistics; Department of Labor; Haver Analytics.

Figure 2-32
Consumer Price Inflation, 2012–2016

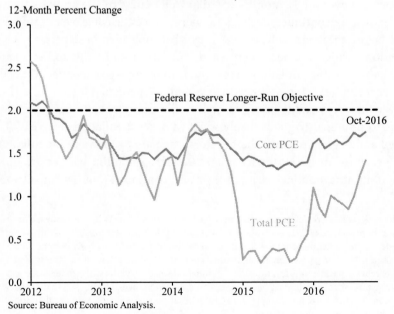

Source: Bureau of Economic Analysis.

productive innovation. There is no silver bullet for improving productivity growth, but sound policy across a range of initiatives could support it, raising real wages and living standards in the process.

WAGE AND PRICE INFLATION

Nominal wage inflation has trended up over the course of the recovery as the labor market has continued to strengthen amid robust job growth. Average nominal hourly earnings for private sector production and non-supervisory employees increased 2.4 percent during the 12–month period ended November 2016, up from 2.3 percent during the year-earlier period. Nominal hourly compensation for private-sector workers, as measured by the employment cost index, increased 2.2 percent during the four quarters through 2016:Q3, up from 1.9 percent in the four quarters of 2015. Alternatively, the more-volatile compensation per hour measure for the non-farm business sector, as measured by the labor productivity and cost dataset, increased 2.2 percent during the four quarters through 2016:Q3, below its 3.1-percent rise during the four quarters of 2015. Taken together, as shown in Figure 2-31, nominal wage inflation has increased with the strong recovery in the labor market. However, the pace remains below the pre-crisis pace.

Consumer prices, as measured by the price index for personal consumption expenditures (PCE) and shown in Figure 2-32, increased roughly 1.4 percent over the 12 months ended in October 2016. The growth rate was held down by continued declines in energy prices, leaving overall inflation well below the Federal Reserve's longer-run objective of 2 percent. Core inflation—which excludes energy and food prices and tends to be a better predictor of future inflation than overall inflation—was also less than the 2-percent target, ranging between 1.6 and 1.7 percent thus far in 2016.[15] Lower imported goods prices, as well as the pass through of lower energy costs to non-energy goods, likely weighed on core inflation this year. The speed and degree to which these factors wane are two keys to the inflationary pressures in the economy this year. While inflation has picked up in recent months, nominal earnings have also continued to grow considerably

---

[15] The Federal Reserve defines its inflation objective in terms of the PCE price index. The consumer price index (CPI) is an alternate measure of prices paid by consumers and is used to index some government transfers, such as Social Security benefits. Largely because of a different method of aggregating the individual components, PCE inflation has averaged about 0.3-percentage point a year less than the CPI inflation since 1979. Recently, though, the gap between core price inflation has been larger across the two indices. During the 12 months ended in October 2016, for example, core CPI prices increased 2.2 percent, more than the 1.7-percent increase in core PCE prices.

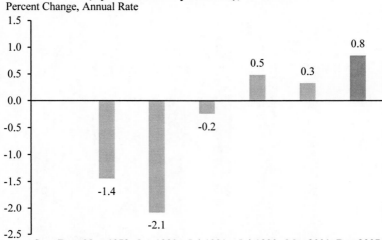

Figure 2-33
**Real Hourly Wage Growth Over Business Cycles
(Cycle Peak to Cycle Peak), 1973–2016**
Percent Change, Annual Rate

	Start Date	Nov-1973	Jan-1980	Jul-1981	Jul-1990	Mar-2001	Dec-2007
	End Date	Jan-1980	Jul-1981	Jul-1990	Mar-2001	Dec-2007	Oct-2016

Note: Wages for private production and nonsupervisory workers. Nominal wages are deflated using the CPI for urban wage earners and clerical workers (CPI-W).
Source: National Bureau of Economic Research; Bureau of Labor Statistics; CEA calculations.

Figure 2-34
Change in Real Median Household Income, 1968–2015
Percent Change from Prior Year

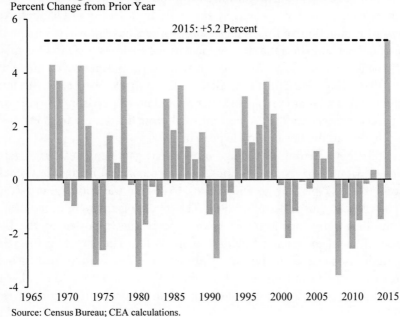

Source: Census Bureau; CEA calculations.

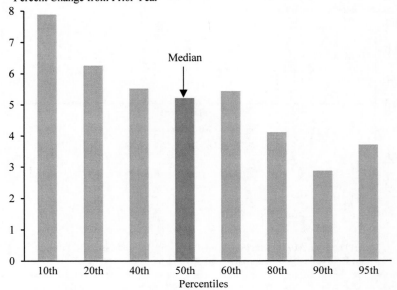

Figure 2-35
Growth in Real Household Income by Percentile, 2014–2015
Percent Change from Prior Year

Source: Census Bureau; CEA calculations.

faster than inflation, translating into sustained real wage gains for American workers.

Real average hourly earnings of production and nonsupervisory workers have grown at a relatively high rate in 2016. As of October, real wages of production and nonsupervisory workers have grown at an annual rate of 0.8 percent since the start of the current business cycle in December 2007, which is the fastest real wage growth over a business cycle since the early 1970s (Figure 2-33). From October 2012 to October 2016, the total growth of real wages of private production and nonsupervisory workers was 6.1 percent, exceeding the 2.1-percent total growth from the business cycle peak in 1980 to the business cycle peak in 2007.

The combination of strong employment gains and real wage gains have contributed to rising real household income. Real median household income rose 5.2 percent, to $56,516 in 2015. This was the largest percent increase since records began in 1967. The income gains were broad based: for the first time since 2006, all income percentiles reported by the U.S. Census Bureau experienced gains (Figure 2-34). The largest gains were among households at the bottom of the income distribution; real income growth was the fastest on record for the 10th, 20th, 40th, 50th, and 60th percentiles (Figure 2-35). In addition, all racial and ethnic groups saw

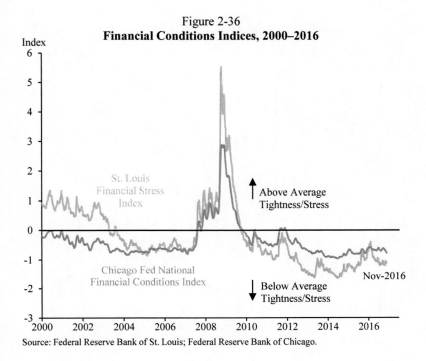

Figure 2-36
Financial Conditions Indices, 2000–2016

Source: Federal Reserve Bank of St. Louis; Federal Reserve Bank of Chicago.

income gains—6.1 percent for Hispanic households, 4.1 percent for African-American households, 3.7 percent for Asian households, and 4.4 percent for non-Hispanic White households.

FINANCIAL MARKETS

U.S. financial markets have been robust so far in 2016, with equity indexes higher, government bond yields slightly higher, credit spreads lower, and oil prices rallying from lows that were touched in January. Equity markets had been broadly down in late 2015. The level of the S&P 500 Index as of November 30 is up 3.2 percent relative to the high reached in mid-2015. Asset prices in 2016 tended to be broadly affected by central bank policy decisions and investor perceptions of domestic and global growth prospects. Financial markets were volatile and equity markets were down early in the year, but have since recovered. In general, investor sentiment has been cautiously optimistic and, as shown in Figure 2-36, financial conditions have been relatively loose. Both rising asset prices and eased financial conditions should continue to support the economic recovery.

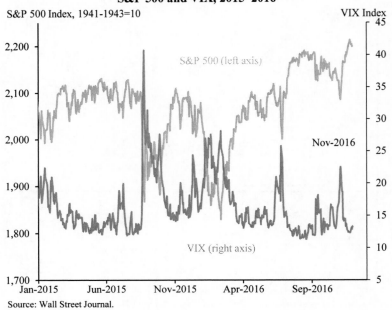

Figure 2-37
S&P 500 and VIX, 2015–2016

S&P 500 Index, 1941-1943=10

VIX Index

S&P 500 (left axis)

Nov-2016

VIX (right axis)

Source: Wall Street Journal.

Equity Markets

The S&P 500 is up 7.6 percent in 2016 as of November 30. The first two months of the year saw steep declines, reflecting investor concern about the health of the global economy. During those episodes of market declines, the Chicago Board of Options Exchange Market Volatility Index (VIX), which reflects investor expectations of future volatility for the S&P 500, spiked to almost 30 in early January and again in early February (VIX levels above 30 are generally considered high). Thereafter, equity markets recovered broadly and investor volatility expectations were generally much lower for the rest of the year.

The United Kingdom's decision to exit the European Union (popularly termed "Brexit") was followed by falling equity prices in markets around the globe, but the spike in volatility was temporary and major U.S. equity indices quickly recovered. The S&P 500 reached a record high in August, before easing back a bit in September and October. The index rose sharply in November, rising 3.4 percent and hitting a new all-time high on November 25. With the exception of early November, the VIX has closed below 20 since shortly after Brexit, as shown in Figure 2-37. As of November 30, 2016, the S&P 500 was 40 percent above its pre-recession peak in 2007.

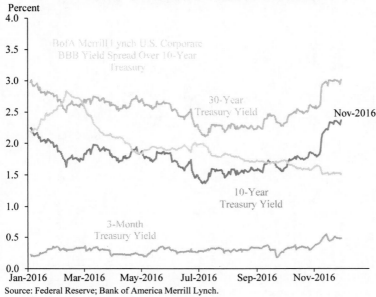

Figure 2-38
Nominal Long- and Short-Term Interest Rates, 2016

Percent

BofA Merrill Lynch U.S. Corporate BBB Yield Spread Over 10-Year Treasury

30-Year Treasury Yield

Nov-2016

10-Year Treasury Yield

3-Month Treasury Yield

Source: Federal Reserve; Bank of America Merrill Lynch.

Interest Rates and Credit Spreads

During the first half of the year, yields on government and corporate debt generally moved lower, continuing the downward trend of the past few years. However, Treasury yields rose in the second half of the year and spiked upward in November, with the 10-year yield ending the month above its end-of-2015 level. Levels of default risk, as measured by credit default swap (CDS) spreads, spiked in tandem with the equity and oil market volatility near the start of the year but, consistent with equity market volatility, have returned to relatively low levels since. At the same time, consensus forecasts of long-run U.S. interest rates have fallen over 2016. The market-implied expectation for the 10-year Treasury yield 10 years from now fell in the first half of the year but spiked upward in November and, as of November 30, is at its end-of-2015 level.

Long-term government interest rates, or yields on 10-year and 30-year U.S. Treasury notes, declined more than did yields on shorter-term debt during the first half of 2016. The 10-year U.S. Treasury yield fell below 2 percent at the beginning of the year and reached its lowest level on record (1.37 percent) on July 5, but recovered steadily throughout the third quarter and reached 1.84 percent at the end of October (Figure 2-38). In November, the 10-year yield jumped up 53 basis points (bps) to 2.37 percent, a large move shared by the 30-year Treasury yield as well as the government bond

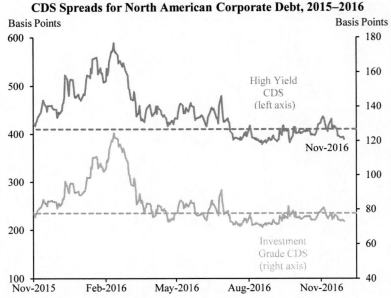

Figure 2-39
CDS Spreads for North American Corporate Debt, 2015–2016

Note: Dotted lines indicate average spreads 2015-2016 year to date.
Source: Markit; Bloomberg.

yields of other advanced economies. Despite the recent upward movements, Treasury yields are still low relative to their long-term averages. Unusually low interest rates are not unique to the United States, as relatively low interest rates were common among G7 economies in 2016.

Average borrowing costs for BBB-rated companies decreased more than 10-year U.S. Treasury yields did in 2016, with the BBB spread over 10-year U.S. Treasuries declining from 2.18 percentage points at the end of 2015 to 1.51 percentage points at the end of November. The BBB spread had widened in late 2015 and peaked at 2.84 percentage points in February before steadily narrowing to 1.61 percentage points by the end of October. In November, the spread decreased another 10 basis points, though both the 10-year Treasury yield and the average BBB yield to maturity rose. As of November 30, the BBB spread is slightly below its average post-recession level of 1.70 percentage points. Narrowing corporate credit spreads relative to Treasury notes mean the market is requiring less compensation for the credit risk of corporate debt. This is consistent with the downward movement of credit default swap (CDS) spreads for corporate debt over the year (Figure 2-39). Because CDS spreads are the cost of insurance against the default of a borrower, falling CDS spreads mean that the market perceives debt defaults as less probable now than at the start of the year. Corporate bond issuance has been proceeding at a robust pace; over the first 10 months

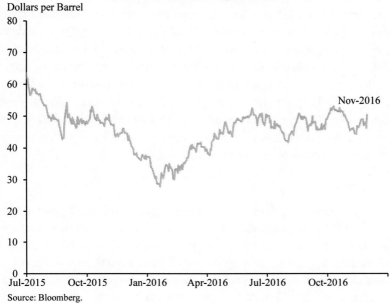

Figure 2-40
Brent Crude Oil Prices, 2015–2016

Dollars per Barrel

Nov-2016

Source: Bloomberg.

of 2016, corporate bond issuers have issued 1.4 trillion dollars of debt, on par with the pace in 2015.[16] This high rate of debt issuance, however, does not appear to reflect rising business fixed investment (Box 2-7).

North American high-yield CDS spreads increased roughly 80bps in early February due in part to the increasing credit risk of energy producers, some of which defaulted after the price of oil plummeted after the start of the year. As oil prices recovered, industry-average CDS spreads fell, reflecting the improved health of energy firms as well as improved investor sentiment. As of November 30, high-yield and investment grade CDS spreads are below their average 2015-16 levels.

Market estimates for long-term U.S. Treasury rates decreased in the first half of the year along with the current (spot) Treasury rates, signaling that markets may believe that interest rates will remain low over the long-term as well. The 10-year U.S. Treasury rate, 10 years forward, which is a function of the 20-year U.S. Treasury rate and the 10-year U.S. Treasury rate, was 3.6 percent as of November 30, same as the level at the end of 2015, but slightly lower than the 3.7-percent rate projected for 2026 by a consensus of professional forecasters. This forward interest rate may be interpreted

---

[16] This measure was provided by SIFMA and includes all non-convertible corporate debt, MTNs, and Yankee bonds, but excludes all issues with maturities of one or less and certificates of deposits.

as a market forecast of the 10-year interest rate a decade from today but may diverge from it due to liquidity and maturity risk premia. Some of the gap between the market-implied rate and the consensus forecast may be explained by a lower term premium, global flight-to-safety flows, or divergent expectations about long-term productivity and output growth. Forward rates incorporate risk premia, can be highly volatile, and their movements may reflect transitory developments as opposed to structural changes; as such, they may be poor predictors of future rates. For a more in-depth analysis into the 10-year U.S. Treasury rate, 10 years forward, and the overall shift to lower long-term rates, see the Council of Economic Advisers (2015d) report, "Long-Term Interest Rates: A Survey."

Energy Prices

Weakness in oil prices contributed to equity and credit market volatility in the first two months of the year. Brent crude oil closing prices fell to less than $30 a barrel in late January and touched $30 a barrel again in early February on data suggesting slower Chinese growth would depress oil demand, dollar appreciation would restrain price increases, and that excess supply would persist. Oil prices have rallied since then and have mostly hovered between $40 and $50 a barrel since April (Figure 2-40), exceeding $50 in the beginning of November as OPEC members agreed to an output agreement capping production at 32.5 million barrels per day, 3 percent below the 33.64 million barrels per day reported by OPEC members in October.

THE GLOBAL MACROECONOMIC SITUATION

The growth of the global economy in 2016 is expected to be the same as in 2015, but was below the year-earlier expectations of a rebound. Relatively lower growth is both a long-term phenomenon, with advanced economies repeatedly underperforming over the past six years, and the manifestation of short-term developments arising in part from uncertainty in European markets following the Brexit vote as well as recessions and continued risks in selected emerging markets. Downward revisions to growth forecasts occurred amid an environment of weak global demand and investment and disappointing global productivity growth. Compared with forecasts in October 2015, IMF forecasts for four-quarter growth in the October 2016 *World Economic Outlook* reflected downward revisions across both advanced and emerging markets, resulting in a downward revision in the global four-quarter growth forecast for 2016 from 3.6 percent to 3.1 percent (IMF 2015b; IMF 2016b).

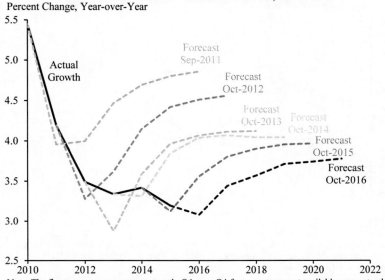

Figure 2-41
IMF World Real GDP Growth Forecast, 2010–2021
Percent Change, Year-over-Year

Note: The figure uses year-over-year growth. Q4-over-Q4 forecacasts are not available over extended horizons.
Source: International Monetary Fund (IMF) World Economic Outlook.

Some developments, especially as they relate to advanced economies, were unexpected, but the slow growth seen throughout 2016 was an extension of developments seen in 2015, namely the stabilizing but persistently slowing growth in China, the persistence of low prices for some commodities, and slower working-age population growth in many countries. Despite coming in below expectations, the pace of growth has broadly stabilized with growth projected for the four quarters of 2016 matching the pace over the four quarters of 2015. The weak global growth, particularly among U.S. trading partners, continued to be a headwind to U.S. economic growth in 2016, but the prospect that global growth has stabilized and may pick up could be a promising sign for U.S. growth.

The IMF's projected global growth rate of 3.1 percent during the four quarters of 2016 is well below both the pace earlier in the recovery and pre-crisis (between 4 and 5 percent). This longer-term slowdown was not anticipated in earlier forecasts. Figure 2-41 shows the IMF's forecast for global growth at different times. The solid line represents the actual growth outcomes while the dotted lines show the forecast. At first, as growth slowed, the IMF—along with most other forecasters—expected a near-term pickup in growth to over 4 percent. Since then, medium-term global growth has

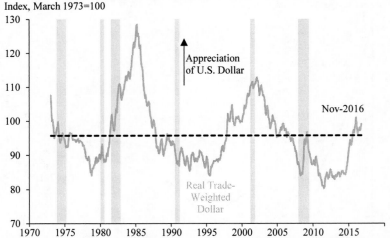

Figure 2-42
Real Broad Trade-Weighted Dollar, 1973–2016

Index, March 1973=100

Appreciation
of U.S. Dollar

Nov-2016

Real Trade-
Weighted
Dollar

Note: This index is a weighted average of the foreign exchange values of the U.S. dollar against major
U.S. trading partners. The dotted line represents the 1973-2016 average. Shading denotes recession.
Source: Federal Reserve Board.

consistently fallen short of expectations, as the long-term growth forecasts
have flattened and medium-term risks have deepened.

As discussed above, the slowdown in global growth has been a headwind for the U.S. economy, dragging on real export growth. As global growth
and the appreciation of the dollar have stabilized, however, real exports have
grown 2 percent in the four quarters ended in 2016:Q3. Still, global growth
is below expectations and there appears to be room for more growth in
many countries. That is why it is critical for economies around the world to
coordinate efforts focused on promoting growth, undertaking the necessary
steps to expand demand, increase investment, encourage trade, and manage
economic and financial developments as appropriate in different contexts.

Global Headwinds and Trade

Starting in July 2014, the dollar entered a period of sustained real
appreciation, increasing by 17 percent through December 2015, according
to the Federal Reserve's broad real dollar index. Such a major wave of dollar
appreciation has occurred only twice before since the dollar began to float
freely in 1973 following the collapse of the Bretton Woods fixed exchange
rate system. In 2016, the dollar was largely stable for most of the year but
appreciated 2.3 percent on a trade-weighted basis in November (Figure
2-42). The limited appreciation of the trade-weighted exchange rate so far
in 2016 obscures some larger bilateral moves in the dollar, with appreciation

against the Mexican peso, the Chinese renminbi (RMB) and the British pound partially offset by depreciation with respect to the Canadian dollar and the Japanese yen.

While well above the level that prevailed in the years immediately following the financial crisis, the recent appreciation leaves the dollar close to its 40-year historical average on a real, price-adjusted basis. Among the drivers of the recent dollar appreciation is the strong performance of the U.S. economy against a backdrop of relatively weak growth in the rest of the world. U.S. Federal Reserve policy is at a different juncture than monetary policy in other major economies. The Federal Reserve increased interest rates for the first time since the 2008 financial crisis at its December 2015 meeting. In the first half of 2016, however, both the pace of U.S. growth and of monetary tightening by the Federal Reserve fell behind expectations. FOMC participants consistently marked down both their interest rate and U.S. growth forecasts throughout 2016, while several other advanced economies chose to keep their policy rates unchanged. Although markets expect the Federal Reserve to reduce monetary policy accommodation over the coming year, the European Central Bank (ECB) and the Bank of Japan (BOJ) are in the midst of maintaining or expanding monetary stimulus with the aim of raising inflation from low levels toward their respective 2-percent targets.

The manufacturing sector, in particular, struggles when foreign demand for U.S. exports is low because it is a more export-oriented part of the economy. While manufacturing makes up roughly 12 percent of U.S. value added, it constitutes about one-half of U.S. exports. Within manufacturing, the more export-oriented sectors have struggled most. In the first half of the year, export-intensive manufacturing sectors lagged in terms of both output and employment growth (Figure 2-43).[17]

Weak global demand and subdued investment growth have driven a slowdown in global trade. The IMF notes that the rate of growth in the volume of world trade in goods and services has fallen to less than half its average rate of growth over the preceding three decades. Both the IMF and the OECD note that growth in real world trade has just barely kept up with growth in real global GDP since 2011, whereas it grew on average twice as fast as real global GDP during the two decades before the crisis. Various analysts attribute the slowdown to weak global growth, especially in investment, a decline in the growth of trade in both capital and intermediate goods through the "global value chain," rebalancing in China, the shift across

---

[17] The CEA defines export share as being the sum of direct export sales and "indirect" export sales, which are the input-cost weighted export sales of downstream users, using the Leontief inverse method in Johnson and Noguera (2012).

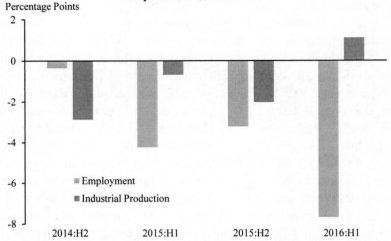

Figure 2-43
Employment and Industrial Production Relative to Trend Given High Export Share, 2014–2016

Percentage Points

Note: These values represent the average difference between the annualized monthly growth rate for June 2014-June 2016 and the annualized monthly growth rate for 2010-2014:H1, for U.S. manufacturing industries associated with a 15 percent higher total (direct + indirect) export share.
Source: Bureau of Labor Statistics; Federal Reserve; CEA calculations.

many economies toward services, and rising protectionist sentiment. The slowdown in trade may both be associated with, and contribute to, slower future economic growth. This is because both the slowdown in capital deepening through investment, which is more import-intensive than other contributors to aggregate demand, and the end to the rapid expansion of global value-chain activity, partly attributed to China's re-balancing toward consumption and services, may reduce productivity growth.

Developments in 2016

Economic growth in 2016 continued to be subdued in a number of advanced economies, but improved in emerging market and developing economies in aggregate. Though total growth for emerging markets and developing economies as a group continued to improve, it underperformed forecasts made in fall 2015 and was weighed down by continuing contraction and slowing growth in emerging European economies, Latin America and the Caribbean, and Sub-Saharan Africa. Emerging markets had been expected to grow 4.8 percent over the four quarters of 2016, but now look set to grow only 4.3 percent (IMF 2015b; IMF 2016b).

United Kingdom

It has been a turbulent year for the United Kingdom since the June referendum in which voters called for the county to leave the European Union. It remains too early to tell what the economic impact of a 'Brexit' will be for the United Kingdom and the world, as expectations for future growth evolve with the release of new data. The Bank of England originally marked down its forecast for UK growth for 2016 through 2018 in its third quarter inflation report after the referendum; in its fourth quarter inflation report, the bank revised its forecast upward for 2016 and 2017 reflecting positive GDP data in 2016:Q3, but further lowered its forecast for 2018. The central bank acted strongly to support the UK economy at its August policy meeting, lowering its key policy rate and signaling that it stood ready to provide more accommodation if needed. However, the depreciation of the pound since the referendum—it fell as much as 16 percent on a trade-weighted basis, reaching its lowest level since 2010—has sparked inflationary pressures. Citing these developments at its November meeting the bank's policy committee shifted its guidance from an easing to a neutral outlook for monetary policy.

Global equity markets initially plunged after the Brexit vote, though generally rebounded later and recovered their losses. The FTSE 250 Index—made up of the stocks of the largest 250 companies on the London Stock Exchange that are not in the top 100 stocks by market capitalization—dropped 7.5 percent in the immediate aftermath of the vote, but has since recovered these loses. Despite these developments, the real economy has proved to be remarkably resilient in the months after the vote: real GDP growth for 2016:Q3 surprised on the upside, growing at a 2-percent annual rate, similar to the pace over the preceding four quarters and meeting forecasts issued prior to the vote; the harmonized unemployment rate held steady at 4.8 percent through the end of August 2016; consumer confidence was above its long-term average; and purchasing manager surveys of manufacturing and services activity continued to indicate expansion. Growth in industrial production, however, missed expectations, and some economists assert that the negative implications of Brexit have yet to materialize given the estimated two-year exit process once formal negotiations with the European Union begin. Of particular concern is the risk to the UK's financial sector if UK-based firms lose "passporting" rights to operate on an equal footing in the EU single market. In many ways, Brexit's impact is yet to be seen as the true terms of exit are yet to be understood, and the uncertainty involved could weigh on the economy over time.

Euro area

Recovery from the financial and sovereign debt crises in the euro area remains uneven, with new uncertainties creating downward pressure on growth. Unemployment only recently edged down to 9.8 from over 10 percent, and the euro area's real GDP-per-capita has only just recovered its pre-crisis peak in 2016:Q3. The IMF expects the euro area economy as a whole to grow 1.6 percent over the four quarters of 2016, more slowly than its 2-percent growth rate in 2015, reflecting some weakness in domestic demand in the first half of 2016. The unemployment rate in the nations hardest hit by the sovereign debt crisis remains elevated, as high as 20 percent. This persistently slow economic growth and labor market slack, coupled with very low inflation (averaging 0.2 in 2016 for the euro area as a whole, and deflation in Ireland, Italy, and Spain) highlight the need for more supportive policy in Europe, including expansionary fiscal policy. Meanwhile, the euro area's current account surplus has widened since 2012, driven by Germany's growing current account surplus.

Although euro area banks are more resilient to market stress than before the financial crisis, weak profits and concerns about sufficiency of financial capital leaves euro-area banks and the financial sector vulnerable, potentially acting as a drag on growth. Burdened by high levels of legacy non-performing loans, Portuguese and Italian banks in particular are struggling to recapitalize and achieve a sustainable business model. Additionally, declines in investor confidence may signal questions about the capacity of both countries to support its banks, if necessary, given weak growth and high sovereign indebtedness. Similar vulnerabilities are also weighing on some large institutions such that the Euro Stoxx Bank Index—an aggregate of European bank equity prices—has fallen 17.8 percent since the beginning of the year. Slow growth, low interest rates, and what some observers call oversaturation of lenders in some credit markets have compressed profit opportunities.

Japan

Japan has continued to face economic challenges in 2016. Prime Minister Shinzo Abe is promoting a package of structural reforms aimed at jumpstarting growth in the Japanese economy, in addition to campaigning for monetary stimulus and advocating for "flexible" fiscal policy, renewing his signature "Abenomics." After dipping in and out of recession since its 1992 financial crisis, economic growth in 2016 continues to be sluggish, growing 0.8 percent over the four quarters ended in 2016:Q3. Slow growth is due in large part to Japan's declining working-age population. When looking at real GDP per working-age population rather than real GDP, for example, Japan has grown almost as robustly as the United States over the past 25 years. For this reason, promoting fertility while encouraging women's continued engagement in the labor force is a pillar of the second phase of Abenomics.

Deflationary pressures continue to plague Japan despite expansive monetary policy. In 2016, the Bank of Japan began an experiment using negative interest rates to complement its quantitative easing program. The objective is to put downward pressure on short-term interest rates and raise inflation by reinforcing its commitment to its inflation target and trying to encourage spending over saving. Partly as a result of these policies, the yield curve flattened, with even the 10-year benchmark yield falling below zero. More recently, the bank has announced continued asset purchases and introduced a policy of yield curve control, which sets up an interest rate target of around 0 percent on 10-year Japanese government bonds. The IMF Global Financial Stability report cautions on the increased reliance of Japanese banks on wholesale dollar funding to finance foreign asset purchases, which could make banks more sensitive to disruptions in dollar funding markets.

Emerging Markets

The situation in some emerging markets has improved relative to 2015, but growth in 2016 is still underperforming expectations compared with forecasts made in 2015, while there continues to be uncertainty surrounding major commodity exporters and China. Emerging markets are expected to account for 54 percent of world growth in 2016, compared with 53 percent in 2015, and 60 percent between 2010 and 2014. As a group, their 2016 growth is expected to come in below the 2015 forecast. The IMF estimates that growth will pick up in 2017, as growth in several oil-producing emerging markets, such as Brazil, and Russia (which are expected to recover from recession) compensates for the steady slowdown in China (IMF 2016b).

Oil-Exporting Emerging Markets. The substantial decline in oil prices from mid-2014 through 2016 has put considerable pressure on the economies of many oil exporters, especially those with undiversified economies. Oil sales remain the primary source of government revenues in several oil-exporting countries, so the drop in oil prices from over $100 a barrel in 2014 to between $25-$55 a barrel in 2016 has put tremendous pressure on government budgets. As figure 2-44 demonstrates, the oil price that guarantees a neutral fiscal balance is well above the current price of Brent in many oil-exporting countries.

Beyond the fiscal concerns, in countries where the price of extracting oil is relatively high, the strain of lower prices for oil and other commodities

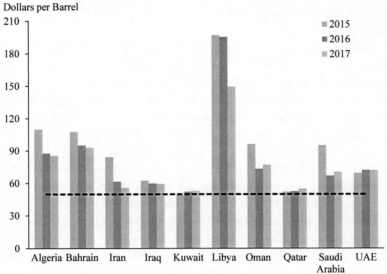

Figure 2-44
Fiscal Breakeven Oil Prices by Country, 2015–2017

Dollars per Barrel

Note: Dotted line represents the average price of Brent in October 2016.
Source: International Monetary Fund (IMF) Middle East and Central Asia Regional Outlook.

has generated recessions. For example, Brazil's economy continued to contract (partially due to oil prices) and Venezuela's economy collapsed. Unemployment in Brazil in October 2016 was at its highest level since mid-2004, though this may be due to a recent change in its computation. Recent improvements—such as real GDP contracting less than expected in the third quarter, housing prices beginning to stabilize, and the appreciation of the Brazilian real reflecting strengthening financial market sentiment—suggest Brazil's economy may be beginning to recover and see positive growth in 2017. The combination of the commodities price bust, economic sanctions following its annexation of Crimea in 2014, and reduced firm access to international capital markets have caused Russia to enter a recession since late 2014 from which the IMF expects Russia will exit in 2017 (IMF 2016b).

Other Major Emerging Markets. Among other major emerging market economies, growth has been mixed in 2016. India remains one of the fastest-growing countries in the world, with real GDP expanding at 7.3 percent in the four quarters through 2016:Q3. However, countries that typically export to China and the advanced economies have suffered due to the slowdown in those important markets.

Economic growth in China has been on a downward trend since a brief rebound after the global financial crisis. China has been attempting to rebalance from an investment- and export-driven economy to an economy

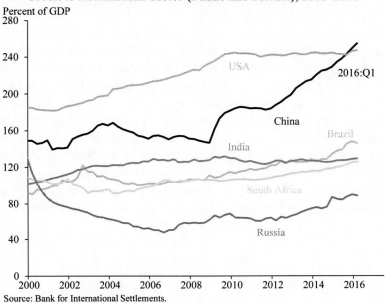

Figure 2-45
Credit to Nonfinancial Sector (Public and Private), 2000–2016

Percent of GDP

Source: Bank for International Settlements.

driven more by private consumption. However, more recently, China may be postponing its longer-term goal of rebalancing in order to stabilize growth in the near term after growth fell from 7.2 percent in the four quarters ended in 2014:Q4 to 6.7 percent in the four quarters ended in 2016:Q3. In 2016, credit growth has been rapid, increasing financial risks, with credit to the non-financial sector as a percent of GDP now exceeding that of major emerging market economies (see Figure 2-45), real estate prices hitting record highs, and distressed bank assets rising.

Against this backdrop, the Chinese renminbi (RMB) has been gradually depreciating since mid-2015 against both the dollar and a weighted basket of currencies. Net capital outflows, which had stabilized in the spring and early summer, edged up again in the third quarter and uncertainty about the course of policy in the near term may be putting downward pressure against the RMB. China's current account surplus is well below its recent peak, but has been considerably above levels the IMF assesses to be appropriate, and it still constitutes a substantial portion of the world's current account surpluses. As China's economy grew to 15 percent of global GDP in 2015, targeted industrial policies have made it the world's largest manufacturer and the dominant producer of some key goods in the global marketplace, as well as a major source of demand for an array of goods, magnifying the effects of changes in its domestic economy on global prices and growth. Delays in adjusting to changing dynamics in the world economy have led to excess capacity in some industries where China is a dominant player. Adjusting to these factors poses additional challenges for policymakers.

Economic growth in India continues at a solid pace of a projected 7.4 percent over the 4 quarters of 2016 (IMF 2016b). Private consumption has been a major driver in economic growth, contributing 4.3 percentage points to its 7.3 percent real GDP growth rate in the four quarters through 2016:Q3. Lower inflation and fiscal consolidation over the past year has created additional policy space for India to stimulate growth should a crisis occur. Macroeconomic risks revolve around inflationary pressure stemming from increasing commodity prices, which could weigh on the current account and fiscal deficit (OECD 2016). Inefficiencies remain in the public sector, with India's poor still lacking health care coverage, educational attainment, and access to financial services (IMF 2016a). Further, inequality in India remains high.

THE OUTLOOK

GDP Growth over the Next Three Years

After growing roughly 2.6 percent on average during the four quarters of 2013 and 2014, real GDP growth averaged 1.9 percent during the four quarters of 2015 and 1.8 percent at an annual rate during the first three quarters of 2016. The Administration forecast (finalized on November 9, 2016) projects an acceleration to 2.4-percent growth during the four quarters of 2017. The Administration forecast is the same as the CBO's August 2016 forecast and slightly above the Blue-Chip November consensus forecast of 2.2 percent. All forecasts implicitly or explicitly make assumptions about the future course of economic policy. The Administration's forecast is based on a baseline that assumes enactment of the President's policies, most of which were spelled out in the budget released in February 2016. In contrast, the CBO forecast assumes that current laws are unchanged while the Blue Chip implicitly reflects the expectations that private forecasters have about what policies will actually be enacted in the future.

The Administration's forecast expects that forces that influence investment and government spending point to faster growth in 2017 than in the recent past, while consumer spending will moderate somewhat and international forces will likely be a drag on growth. With a strengthening State and local sector, State and local fiscal actions will likely be somewhat expansionary in 2017.

Meanwhile, core inflation (excluding food and energy) is at 1.7 percent during the 12 months through October and remains below the Federal Reserve target of 2 percent for the PCE price index (the version of the consumer price index in the National Income and Product Accounts), partly due to declining import prices, and below-average capacity utilization. And so, though the unemployment rate is now close to the rate consistent with stable inflation, inflation is likely to remain low and unlikely to impose constraints, at least during the next four quarters. For consumers, continued growth in nominal and real wage gains in 2016—together with strong employment growth—will probably continue to boost spending in 2017. These income gains—following a multiyear period of successful deleveraging—leave consumers in an improved financial position (Box 2-6). Business investment also shows brighter prospects for growth in 2017 than in earlier years as the overhang of excess capital that suppressed investment earlier in this expansion has been reduced. As the economy continues to grow, businesses will need new facilities, equipment, and intellectual property to meet growing demand, and the expected pickup in output growth should support an uptick in investment as well (Box 2-7), though global headwinds will continue to be a concern for this sector.

Although most domestic signals are positive, the United States faces some headwinds from abroad. The available late-2016 indicators suggest that the economies of China, India, Mexico, and our euro-area trading partners are growing more slowly than in 2015, while Canada's growth is accelerating. The trade-weighted average of foreign GDP growth in the four quarters ended in 2016:Q3 has been 2.1 percent, down from the 2.3 percent average growth rate during the preceding four quarters. On the more positive side, forecasts are for a small pickup in global growth in 2017. Overall weak growth abroad not only reduces our exports and slows domestic investment, but also raises risks of adverse financial and other spillovers to the U.S. economy.

The unemployment rate in November 2016 at 4.6 percent differed little from the projected long run unemployment rate that is consistent with stable inflation in the long run, though some broader measures of labor market slack remain somewhat elevated. These facets of the labor market along with the fact that the capacity utilization rate in manufacturing, which was 74.9 percent in October, is below its long-run average (80 percent), suggest that the economy still has a bit of room to grow faster than its potential rate.

The Administration's economic forecast is presented in Table 2-1. When the Administration forecast was finalized in November 2016, real GDP growth during the four quarters of 2016 was projected at 1.9 percent. Real GDP is projected to grow 2.4, 2.3, and 2.2 percent during the four

Table 2-1

Administration Economic Forecast, 2015–2027

	Nominal GDP	Real GDP (Chain-Type)	GDP Price Index (Chain-Type)	Consumer Price Index (CPI-U)	Unemploy-ment Rate (Percent)	Interest Rate, 91-Day Treasury Bills (Percent)	Interest Rate, 10-Year Treasury Notes (Percent)
	Percent Change, Q4-to-Q4				Level, Calendar Year		
2015 (Actual)	3.0	1.9	1.1	0.4	5.3	0.1	2.1
2016	3.4	1.9	1.5	1.5	4.9	0.3	1.8
2017	4.3	2.4	1.8	2.3	4.7	0.6	2.1
2018	4.3	2.3	1.9	2.3	4.7	1.2	2.7
2019	4.2	2.2	2.0	2.3	4.7	1.8	3.1
2020	4.2	2.2	2.0	2.3	4.8	2.3	3.4
2021	4.2	2.2	2.0	2.3	4.8	2.6	3.5
2022	4.2	2.2	2.0	2.3	4.8	2.7	3.6
2023	4.2	2.2	2.0	2.3	4.8	2.8	3.7
2024	4.2	2.2	2.0	2.3	4.8	2.8	3.7
2025	4.3	2.2	2.0	2.3	4.8	2.8	3.7
2026	4.3	2.2	2.0	2.3	4.8	2.8	3.7
2027	4.3	2.2	2.0	2.3	4.8	2.8	3.7

Note: Forecast was based on data available as of November 9, 2016. The interest rate on 91-day T-bills is measured on a secondary-market discount basis.
Source: Forecast was done jointly with the Council of Economic Advisers, the Department of the Treasury, and the Office of Management and Budget.

quarters of 2017, 2018, and 2019, respectively. The growth rates slightly exceed the Administration's estimated rate of potential real GDP growth over the long run of 2.2 percent a year based on the view that some limited slack remains in the economy. As a consequence of growth being slightly above the long-run trend over the next two years, the unemployment rate is likely to temporarily fall from its 4.9 percent rate in 2016:Q3 to 4.6 percent in 2017:Q4. The unemployment rate is expected to return to the administration's estimate of 4.8 percent for the rate of unemployment consistent with stable inflation in 2019:Q4. The price index for GDP, which increased just 1.3 percent during the four quarters through 2016:Q3, is expected to slowly creep up, reaching 2.0 percent in 2019, a rate that is roughly consistent with the Federal Reserve's 2-percent target for the PCE price index.

Nominal interest rates are currently low because of forces that have led to a reduction in expected long-run interest rates and wounds that have not fully healed from the last recession, while monetary policy has kept rates low across a wide range of debt securities with long maturities. Consistent with the Federal Reserve's forward policy guidance at the time of the forecast, long-term interest rates are projected to rise. Eventually, real interest rates (that is, nominal rates less the projected rate of inflation) are predicted to move toward, but still remain well below, their historical average. These interest-rate paths are close to those projected by the consensus of professional economic forecasters. During the past several years, consensus forecasts for long-term interest rates and long-term economic growth have fallen, reflecting changes in views on productivity, demographics, the term premium, and global saving and investment behavior.

GDP Growth over the Long Term

As discussed earlier, the long-run growth rate of the economy is determined by the growth of its supply-side components, including those governed by demographics and technological change. The growth rate that characterizes the long-run trend in real U.S. GDP—or potential GDP—plays an important role in guiding the Administration's long-run forecast. After a brief period of above-trend growth in 2017 and 2018, real output growth shifts down to its long-term trend rate of 2.2 percent a year. These growth rates are slower than historical averages mostly because of the aging of the baby-boom generation into the retirement years and because of slower growth of the working-age population (Box 2-5).

The long-run potential GDP growth rate is 0.5-percentage point higher than the growth rate that would be expected if current law is unchanged. Specifically, the forecast assumes the President's policies, including substantial investments in transportation infrastructure, business tax reform, universal preschool (and other policies to boost female labor force participation), free community college, reforms to the immigration system, policies to expand cross-border trade, and approximately $2 trillion in deficit reduction (Box 2-9). A different set of policy assumptions would lead to different assumptions for potential GDP growth.

The potential real GDP projections are based on the assumption that the President's full set of policy proposals, which would boost long-run output, are enacted (Box 2-9).

Table 2-2 shows the Administration's forecast for the contribution of each supply-side factor to the growth in potential real GDP: the working-age population; the rate of labor force participation; the employed share of the labor force; the length of the workweek; labor productivity; and the difference between productivity growth for the economy as a whole and the

Box 2-9: Policy Proposals to Raise Output over the Next-Ten Years

The Administration has a wide-ranging and robust economic agenda that, if enacted, would expand the labor force and boost productivity. In line with long-standing precedent, the Administration's economic forecast incorporates the impact of the President's policy proposals. CEA estimates that, in total, these proposals would add over 5 percent to the level of output in 2027. As a result of including policy assumptions, the Administration's forecast for the level of output in 2027 is about 2 percent higher than the forecasts from both the Congressional Budget Office and the Blue Chip consensus panel, as well as about 4 percent higher than the median forecast from the Federal Open Market Committee.

Immigration reform. The policy proposal with the largest effect on output is immigration reform, as embodied in the bipartisan Border Security, Economic Opportunity, and Immigration Modernization Act that passed the U.S. Senate in June 2013. CBO (2013a) estimated that this legislation, if enacted, would raise the level of real GDP by 3.3 percent after 10 years. Immigration reform would benefit the economy by counteracting the effects of an aging native-born population, attracting highly skilled immigrants that engage in innovative or entrepreneurial activities, and enabling better job-matching for currently undocumented workers who are offered a path to citizenship. Much of the overall effect is due to an expanded workforce. However, 0.7 percentage point of the total effect from immigration reform is due to increased total factor productivity, and this is reflected in the Administration's economic forecast.

Policies to expand cross-border trade and investment. The other set of policies with a large effect on output are a number of international agreements that would boost cross-border trade and investment, including the Trans-Pacific Partnership (TPP), the Transatlantic Trade and Investment Partnership (TTIP), an expansion of the Information Technology Agreement (ITA), and a Trade in Services Agreement (TISA). A new study supported by the Peterson Institute for International Economics (Petri and Plummer 2016) finds that TPP could raise U.S. real income by 0.5 percent in 2030. The European Commission (2013) estimates a roughly similar effect of TTIP on the U.S. economy, an increase of 0.4 percent in GDP in 2027. In addition, if TPP does not pass, the United States would also face trade diversion and enjoy less market access compared with other countries such as China. The Regional Comprehensive Economic Partnership, a trade agreement that involves China, Japan, and other fast-growing Asian economies, will provide its member countries with improved market access, putting U.S. exporters at a disadvantage (CEA 2016c).

Investments in surface transportation infrastructure. The Administration recognizes that investments in infrastructure support economic growth by creating jobs, and boosting productivity, and strengthening the manufacturing sector. In December 2015, the bipartisan Fixing America's Surface Transportation Act (H.R. 22), which authorizes $226.3 billion in budget authority for Federal-aid highway programs over five years, was enacted into law. This funding is an important down payment, but the country must further transform our transportation system to achieve a cleaner, safer transportation future. The President's FY 2017 budget calls for $32 billion a year over 10 years to support innovative programs that make our communities more livable and sustainable. The IMF (2014) estimates that, given the current underutilization of resources in many advanced economies, a 1-percent-of-GDP permanent increase in public infrastructure investment could help increase output by as much as 2.5 percent after 10 years.

Policies to boost labor force participation. The Administration has pursued policies that enable all workers to participate in the labor force to their full potential by making it easier for workers to balance career and family responsibilities. The Administration's FY 2017 budget calls to triple the maximum child care tax credit to $3,000 for children younger than 5, while enabling more middle-class families to receive the maximum credit. In addition, every year since 2013, the President has proposed a Federal-State partnership that would provide all 4-year olds from low- and moderate-income families with access to high-quality preschool. Finally, the budget calls to provide technical assistance to help states implement and develop paid parental leave programs. These policies would increase labor force participation and the level of output.

Policies to make college affordable. The Administration is committed to making college affordable. The budget includes $61 billion over 10 years to make the first two years of community college tuition free for responsible students through a Federal-State cost sharing partnership. This plan would increase America's human capital and productivity by enabling 2 million people who would not have enrolled in college to earn an associate's degree.

Business tax reform. President Obama's framework for business tax reform issued in 2012 sets out a series of changes that would strengthen the economy in three main ways. First, by lowering average tax rates, the President's plan would boost investment in the United States. Second, by moving to a more neutral tax system, the proposals would result in a more efficient allocation of capital. And third, to the degree the new system better addresses externalities, for example with a more generous research and development credit, it would also increase total factor productivity and therefore growth. (See Chapter 5 of the 2015 Report for a discussion of the economic benefits of business tax reform.)

Deficit reduction. CBO's (2013b) analysis of the macroeconomic effects of alternative budgetary paths estimates that a hypothetical $2 trillion in primary deficit reduction over 10 years raises the long-term level of real GDP by 0.5 percent. This effect arises because lower Federal deficits translate into higher national saving, lower interest rates and, in turn, greater private investment. The Administration's FY 2017 budget proposal includes $2.9 trillion in primary deficit reduction relative to the Administration's plausible baseline. Results of CBO's methodology would raise the level of output in 2027 by 0.6 percent.

Other Policies. Numerous other policies—ranging from policies to increase competition to increasing innovation or spurring green energy development might also raise growth over time, but are not explicitly modeled in the budget forecast.

(Note, to be consistent with previous Administration forecasts the portion of growth due to the workforce effects of immigration reform are not incorporated in the forecast or the underlying detail, for example in Table 2.1. Excluding this component, the policies add 3 percent to the level of output in 2027.)

nonfarm business sector. The two columns of Table 2-2 show the average annual growth rate for each factor during a long period of history and over the forecast horizon. The first column shows the long-run average growth rates between the business-cycle peak of 1953 and the latest quarter available when the forecast was finalized (2016:Q3). Many of these variables show substantial fluctuations within business cycles, so that long-period growth rates must be examined to uncover underlying trends. The second column shows average projected growth rates between 2016:Q3 and 2027:Q4; that is, the entire 11¼-year interval covered by the Administration forecast.

The population is projected to grow 1.0 percent a year, on average, over the projection period (line 1, column 2), following the latest projection from the Social Security Administration. Over this same period, the labor force participation rate is projected to decline 0.4 percent a year (line 2, column 2). This projected decline in the labor force participation rate primarily reflects a negative demographic trend deriving from the aging of the baby-boom generation into retirement. During the next couple of years, however, rising labor demand due to the continuing business-cycle recovery is expected to offset some of this downward trend.

The employed share of the labor force—which is equal to one minus the unemployment rate—is expected to remain roughly constant during the

Table 2-2

**Supply-Side Components of Actual
and Potential Real Output Growth, 1953–2027**

Component	Growth rate[a]	
	History	Forecast
	1953:Q2 to 2016:Q3[b]	2016:Q3 to 2027:Q4
1 Civilian noninstitutional population aged 16+	1.4	1.0
2 Labor force participation rate	0.1	-0.4
3 Employed share of the labor force	-0.0	0.0
4 Ratio of nonfarm business employment to household employment	-0.0	0.0
5 Average weekly hours (nonfarm business)	-0.2	0.0
6 Output per hour (productivity, nonfarm business)[c]	2.0	1.9
7 Ratio of real GDO to nonfarm business output[c]	-0.2	-0.3
8 Sum: Actual real GDO[c]	3.0	2.2
Memo:		
9 Potential real GDO[d]	3.1	2.2
10 Output per worker differential: GDO vs nonfarm[e]	-0.2	-0.3

[a] All contributions are in percentage points at an annual rate, forecast finalized November 2016. Total may not add up due to rounding.

[b] 1953:Q2 was a business-cycle peak. 2016:Q3 is the latest quarter with available data.

[c] Real GDO and real nonfarm business output are measured as the average of income- and product-side measures.

[d] Computed as (line 8) - 2 * (line 3).

[e] Real output per household-survey worker less nonfarm business output per nonfarm business worker. This can be shown to equal (line 7) - (line 4).

Note: GDO is the average of GDP and GDI. Population, labor force, and household employment have been adjusted for discontinuities in the population series. Nonfarm business employment, and the workweek, come from the Labor Productivity and Costs database maintained by the Bureau of Labor Statistics.

Source: Bureau of Labor Statistics, Current Population Survey, Labor Productivity and Costs; Bureau of Economic Analysis, National Income and Product Accounts; Department of the Treasury; Office of Management and Budget; CEA calculations.

next 11 years because as the 2016:Q3 unemployment rate (4.9 percent) is only slightly higher than the 4.8 percent rate at which the rate of unemployment eventually stabilizes. The workweek is projected to be roughly flat during the forecast period, an improvement relative to its long-term historical trend growth of a 0.2-percent-a-year decline. The workweek is expected to stabilize because some of the demographic forces pushing it down are largely exhausted, and because a longer workweek is projected to compensate for the anticipated decline in the labor force participation rate in what will eventually become an economy with a tight labor supply.

Labor productivity is projected to increase 1.9 percent a year over the entire forecast interval (line 6, column 2), slightly less than the same as the average growth rate from 1953 to 2015 (line 6, column 1). Productivity tends to grow faster in the nonfarm business sector than for the economy as a whole, because productivity in the government and household sectors of the economy is presumed (by a national-income accounting convention) not to grow (that is, output in those two sectors grows only through the use of more production inputs). The difference in these growth rates is expected to subtract 0.3 percentage point a year during the 11-year projection period, similar to the 0.2-percent-a-year decline during the long-term historical interval (line 10, columns 1 and 2). This productivity differential is equal to the sum of two other growth rates in the table: the ratio of nonfarm business employment to household employment (line 4) and the ratio of real GDP to nonfarm business output (line 7).

Summing the growth rates of all of its components, real GDP is projected to rise at an average 2.2 percent a year over the projection period (line 8, column 2), the same as the annual growth rate for potential real GDP (line 9, column 2). Actual GDP is expected to grow faster than potential GDP only in 2017 and 2018, and by a small margin that is invisible in the long-term averages shown in the table.

As noted earlier, but shown in more detail in this table, real potential GDP (line 9, column 2) is projected to grow more slowly than the long-term historical growth rate of 3.1 percent a year (line 9, column 1), primarily due to the lower projected growth rate of the working-age population and the retirement of the baby-boom cohort.

Upside and Downside Forecast Risks

Like any forecast, the Administration's economic forecast comes with possible errors in either direction, and several are worth enumerating here. One upside risk is from the homebuilding sector, which has some upside potential given the current low level of homebuilding relative to historic trends and its potential for increase. Additionally, labor force participation could continue to grow as it has this year, after decades of decline in participation among prime-age workers (Box 2-3). On the downside, it appears that global growth may remain sluggish and global trade growth has slowed dramatically, which may slow the growth of exports and investment. In addition, financial market developments—either reflecting spillovers from abroad or U.S.-specific issues—also pose downside risks. Over the longer-run, there are some downside risks to the estimate of potential output growth insofar as recent low productivity growth rates might continue.

CONCLUSION

The economy continued to strengthen during 2016, especially in the labor market with robust employment gains and continued declines in unemployment. Job growth continued to exceed the pace needed to maintain a steady unemployment rate (given that labor force participation is trending down with demographics). That job growth, along with solid wage growth, combined to generate rising household incomes and improving living standards. The American economic recovery has outpaced most of the other advanced economies and left a national economy well-prepared for continued resilience. The United States has domestic strengths, especially in the household sector, that have the potential to support continued solid growth in 2017—but at the same time, we face a set of challenges associated with the slowing global economy.

Looking ahead, some of the most important decisions that we make as a Nation are the structural policies that influence long-term growth and how it is shared. The President's FY 2017 budget set forth a number of policies that could be expected to increase the level or long-term growth rate of potential GDP. As the economy has approached its long-run natural rate of unemployment, it is these long-term structural policies that could lift growth and sustain long-term prosperity for a greater share of Americans.

CHAPTER 3

PROGRESS REDUCING
INEQUALITY

In 2013, President Obama declared inequality "the defining challenge of our time." According to the Congressional Budget Office (CBO), in that year—the most recent year for which complete data are available—the 20 percent of households with the lowest incomes had an average pre-tax income of $25,000, while the 1 percent of households with the highest incomes had an average income of $1.6 million (CBO 2016b). Roughly 15 percent of Americans lived in poverty, even as mean household income reached $75,000 (Proctor, Semega, and Kollar 2016).[1] Moreover, these disparities persist across generations due to low levels of intergenerational mobility. Only 8 percent of children from the bottom 20 percent of the income distribution make it to the top 20 percent as adults, while 37 percent of children from the top 20 percent stay there (Chetty et al. 2014).

Inequality extends well beyond the distribution of income. Median wealth for non-Hispanic White families in 2013 was $142,000, compared with only $18,000 for all other families (Bricker et al. 2014). A 40-year-old man at the 95th percentile of the income distribution has a life expectancy 10 years longer than a man at the 5th percentile (Chetty et al. 2016). Students from families in the bottom 25 percent of the income distribution drop out of high school at a rate four times higher than students from families in the top 25 percent (NCES 2015).

Perhaps most troubling is the fact that rising inequality, in conjunction with slower productivity growth, has led to slow growth in inflation-adjusted incomes for the typical household for more than three decades. In previous work, the Council of Economic Advisers (CEA) found that if inequality had

---

[1] The Census Bureau and the Congressional Budget Office use different definitions of income in their estimates of the income distribution. CBO's definition is generally more comprehensive than that used by the Census Bureau. Mean income in 2013 per the Census Bureau was $75,000 while mean before-tax income in 2013 per CBO was $100,000.

not increased from 1973 to 2013, income for the typical household in 2013 would have been about 18 percent, or $9,000, higher (CEA 2015).

From his first days in office, President Obama has taken important steps to reduce inequality and make the economy work for all Americans. The policy response to the Great Recession directly reduced inequality in after-tax incomes through progressive tax and spending policies, such as temporary tax cuts for working and middle-class families and extensions of unemployment insurance; and indirectly, the response reduced earnings inequality by boosting employment. This policy response—including the American Recovery and Reinvestment Act (Recovery Act) and subsequent fiscal measures, bank stress tests, and other financial policy measures, support for the automobile industry, and the actions of the Federal Reserve—kept the unemployment rate 6 percentage points lower than it otherwise would have been between 2010 and 2012. By reducing the unemployment rate, these policies offset roughly half of the increase in earnings inequality that would have occurred as even more workers lost their jobs and saw their earnings fall to zero.

The Affordable Care Act (ACA), enacted in March 2010, provided Federal support to states to expand their Medicaid programs and financial assistance for families purchasing coverage through the Health Insurance Marketplace, leading to the largest reduction in the uninsured rate since the creation of Medicare and Medicaid and a substantial reduction in inequality in after-tax incomes. The ACA has resulted in 20 million additional American adults gaining health insurance coverage as of early 2016 and helped reduce the uninsured rate to 8.9 percent in the first half of 2016, the lowest level on record. The ACA reduced inequality in health insurance coverage by age, race, and income, with larger reductions in uninsured rates for groups with lower levels of coverage, including young adults, racial minorities, and low-income families. A growing body of research documents that expanded coverage under the ACA is greatly improving families' well-being by increasing their access to care, financial security, and health. Viewed as additions to income, expanded Medicaid eligibility and financial assistance for families purchasing health insurance through the Marketplace have dramatically reduced inequality in after-tax incomes.

Over the course of this Administration, the President has signed into law a series of progressive changes in tax policy that have increased tax rates for the highest-income Americans and increased the generosity of tax credits for working families, thereby reducing inequality in after-tax incomes. Changes in tax policy other than ACA coverage provisions will boost after-tax incomes in the bottom quintile by 2 percent in 2017 and reduce after-tax incomes for the top 0.1 percent by 9 percent relative to what incomes would have been under 2008 policies.[2,3] (The policy impacts discussed in this chapter generally compare after-tax incomes in 2017 under current policy with counterfactual after-tax incomes in 2017 under 2008 policies. After-tax incomes include the value of government transfers such as Medicare and Medicaid.)

Together, changes in tax policy and the ACA coverage provisions will increase the share of after-tax income received by the bottom quintile in 2017 by 0.6 percentage point, or 18 percent, and the share received by the second quintile by 0.5 percentage point, or 6 percent. They will reduce the share received by the top 1 percent by 1.2 percentage points, or 7 percent. Moreover, they will boost incomes in the bottom quintile by 18 percent, equivalent to more than a decade of average income gains. And they will increase average tax rates for the top 0.1 percent of families, a group projected to have average pre-tax incomes over $8 million, by nearly 7 percentage points.

The legislation President Obama has signed into law represents a historic achievement in reducing inequality. Tax changes enacted since 2009 have boosted the share of after-tax income received by the bottom 99 percent of families by more than the tax changes of any previous administration since at least 1960. The President has also overseen the largest increase in Federal investment to reduce inequality since the Great Society programs of the Johnson Administration, an increase that largely reflects the coverage provisions of the ACA and expanded tax credits for working families.

However, while these accomplishments are historically large, much more work remains to be done to reverse the decades-long increase in inequality. From the business cycle peak in 1979 to the business cycle peak in 2007, the after-tax income share of the top 1 percent more than doubled. Changes in tax policy and the coverage provisions of the ACA have rolled back one-third of the decline in the share of after-tax income accruing to the bottom quintile of households over this period and one-tenth of the increase in the share accruing to the top 1 percent of households.

As the discussion above highlights, addressing the many manifestations of inequality requires a comprehensive set of policies. Inequality is a product of economic institutions, standards, and norms; technological

---

[2] Each quintile contains 20 percent of families, ranked by their incomes (adjusted for family size). For example, the bottom quintile contains the 20 percent of families with the lowest incomes, and the second quintile contains the 20 percent of families with the next lowest incomes. However, in this analysis, families with negative incomes are excluded from the bottom quintile as these families are typically quite different from other low-income families.
[3] As used in this report, the ACA coverage provisions include expanded Medicaid eligibility, the Premium Tax Credit, cost-sharing reductions, small employer tax credits, the individual shared responsibility payment, and the employer shared responsibility payment.

developments; individual behavior; and a multitude of other factors. Some policies—such as ensuring that everyone pays their fair share in taxes, expanding access to health insurance and to high-quality child care, raising the minimum wage, and expanding tax credits for working families—address inequality directly and in the near term, in addition to their longer-run benefits. Other policies—such as improving education, reforming intellectual property laws, and reforming land use and zoning regulations—work to reduce inequality primarily over the long term. Still others address the temporary inequality that accompanies economic downturns by providing appropriate countercyclical fiscal support to reduce economic slack and unemployment.

The President's policy proposals would further reduce inequality in both pre-tax and after-tax incomes. Increasing the minimum wage, as the President has called on Congress and State and local governments to do, would immediately boost incomes for millions of low-wage workers and reduce income inequality. Expanding access to high-quality child care and early education and ending family homelessness, as the President has proposed, would reduce inequality today while also increasing mobility and improving economic outcomes in the longer term. The tax reforms proposed in the Fiscal Year 2017 Budget would increase average tax rates on the top 0.1 percent by an additional 9 percentage points and would roll back an additional 13 percent of the increase in the after-tax income share of the top 1 percent of households between 1979 and 2007. Expanding the Earned Income Tax Credit (EITC) for workers without dependent children would provide 13 million low-income workers with a tax cut averaging nearly $500 for each worker, increasing the returns to work and supporting labor force participation.

This chapter focuses on three specific areas where the Administration has achieved its most substantial and immediate success in reducing inequality: restoring economic growth, expanding health insurance coverage, and enacting a fairer tax code (Table 3-1). However, the Administration also has undertaken a much broader set of initiatives designed to address inequality and promote opportunity. Some of these efforts, such as investments in early childhood education and job training, are designed to have longer-term impacts. (See Box 3-4 for an overview of additional policies that will reduce inequality by raising wages and expanding educational opportunity, but are not examined in detail in this chapter. Also see Chapter 5 for additional discussion of the Administration's record on education policy.)

The chapter first examines each of the three major policy areas listed above. It then places the Administration's record in historical context, comparing the reductions in income inequality first with previous Federal

Table 3-1
Timeline of Select Recovery, Health, and Tax Legislation, 2009-2015

Legislation	Date of Enactment	Key Inequality-Related Provisions
American Recovery and Reinvestment Act of 2009 (Recovery Act)	02/17/2009	Provided countercyclical fiscal support for the economy. The Recovery Act: • Created the Making Work Pay credit, a refundable tax credit of up to $400 for individuals and $800 for married couples, for 2009 and 2010; • Expanded the Earned Income Tax Credit (EITC) and Child Tax Credit (CTC), refundable tax credits for working families, for 2009 and 2010; • Created the American Opportunity Tax Credit (AOTC), a refundable tax credit to help pay for higher education, for 2009 and 2010; • Temporarily extended and enhanced unemployment insurance benefits, temporarily increased Supplemental Nutrition Assistance Program benefits, expanded Pell Grants, and provided other aid to individuals; and • Provided temporary fiscal relief to States through additional Medicaid payments and education grants to spur innovation and prevent layoffs of education workers.
Patient Protection and Affordable Care Act (Affordable Care Act)	03/23/2010	Reformed the American health care system to expand health insurance coverage, reduce health care costs, and improve health care quality, financed with reforms to health and tax policy. The ACA: • Provided Federal support to States that expand their Medicaid programs to cover individuals up to 138 percent of the poverty level; • Created the Premium Tax Credit and cost-sharing reductions to help low, moderate, and middle-income Americans afford coverage; introduced insurance reforms and an individual responsibility requirement; • Increased the Medicare payroll tax rate by 0.9 percentage point for high-income families and extended the tax to the investment income of high-income families.
Tax Relief, Unemployment Insurance Reauthorization, and Job Creation Act of 2010	12/17/2010	Extended the 2001/2003 income tax cuts through 2012. Reinstated the estate tax with a $5 million exemption and 35% rate. Cut the payroll tax rate by 2 percentage points for 2011. Extended the Recovery Act EITC and CTC improvements and the AOTC through 2012.
Middle Class Tax Relief and Job Creation Act of 2012	02/22/2012	Extended the 2 percentage point reduction in the payroll tax rate through 2012.
American Taxpayer Relief Act of 2012	01/02/2013	Repealed the 2001/2003 income tax cuts for high-income families and permanently extended them for all others. Increased the estate tax rate to 40 percent. Extended the Recovery Act EITC and CTC improvements and the AOTC through 2017.
Protecting Americans from Tax Hikes Act of 2015	12/18/2015	Permanently extended the Recovery Act EITC and CTC improvements and the AOTC.

Note: For simplicity, this chapter does not distinguish between the Affordable Care Act and the Health Care and Education Reconciliation Act of 2010, enacted on March 30, 2010.

action affecting income inequality since the 1960s and then with the growth in income inequality since the late 1970s. The chapter finishes by highlighting several of the President's proposals that would further reduce inequality.

THE RECOVERY ACT: RESTORING GROWTH

When the President took office in January 2009, the country was experiencing the worst economic and financial crisis since the Great Depression. In the previous year, private employers shed 3.6 million jobs, household wealth dropped 16 percent, and the unemployment rate jumped from 5 percent to 7 percent on its way to a peak of 10 percent. One important aspect of combatting inequality is limiting macroeconomic downturns, during which unemployment rises and earnings inequality rises along with it. By taking timely, aggressive action to combat the financial crisis and economic downturn, the Administration limited the extent to which inequality rose during the Great Recession and its aftermath.

In February 2009, the President signed into law the American Recovery and Reinvestment Act (Recovery Act) to provide countercyclical fiscal support to the economy and to help boost employment, output, and wages. The Recovery Act included a mix of aid to affected individuals, support for State and local governments, public investments, and individual and business tax cuts. More than a dozen subsequent fiscal measures extended certain Recovery Act provisions and introduced additional countercyclical policies, such as the temporary payroll tax cut in effect during 2011 and 2012. In total, discretionary fiscal stimulus from 2009 through 2012 totaled $1.4 trillion and averaged around 2 percent of GDP (Furman 2015). The Recovery Act, subsequent fiscal measures, financial policy measures, support for the automobile industry, and the Federal Reserve's independent actions combined to substantially reduce the harm of the Great Recession, in part by moderating the increase in unemployment that would otherwise

---

Box 3-1: Trends in Inequality

Income, wealth, and consumption inequality have increased sharply in the United States in recent decades (Table 3-I). However, while overall inequality of income and wealth has increased, some other measures of financial inequality have decreased. For example, the gender pay gap has narrowed in recent decades, even as it remains too large (CEA 2016b). Similarly, while inequality in life expectancy at middle age has also increased, some other aspects of health inequality show signs of improvement.

Table 3-I
Measures of Inequality, 1980 and Most Recent Available

	1980	Most Recent Available
Income		
Top 1% Income Share *(CBO)*		
Market Income (Income Before Government Transfers)	10%	18%
Pre-Tax (Income Including Government Transfers)	9%	15%
After-Tax (Pre-Tax Income Less Federal Taxes)	8%	12%
Bottom 90% Income Share *(CBO)*		
Market Income (Income Before Government Transfers)	67%	57%
Pre-Tax (Income Including Government Transfers)	70%	62%
After-Tax (Pre-Tax Income Less Federal Taxes)	72%	66%
90-10 Ratio[1] *(Census)*	9.4	12.1
50-10 Ratio[1] *(Census)*	3.9	4.2
Gini Index *(CBO)*		
Market Income (Income Before Government Transfers)	0.48	0.60
Pre-Tax Income (Income Including Government Transfers)	0.40	0.48
After-Tax Income (Pre-Tax Income Less Federal Taxes)	0.36	0.44
Ratio of CEO Compensation to Worker Compensation *(EPI)*	34	276
Wealth		
Top 1% Wealth Share		
Survey of Consumer Finances[2]	30%	36%
Bricker et al. (2016)[2]	27%	33%
Saez-Zucman (2016)	24%	42%
Top 10% Wealth Share[2] *(CBO)*	68%	76%
Consumption		
Ratio of Top/Bottom Income Quintiles[3] *(Aguiar and Bils 2015)*	2.46	3.35
Gini Index *(Attanasio and Pistaferri 2014)*	0.22	0.26
Wages		
Gender Pay Gap[4] *(Census)*	0.40	0.20
Racial Pay Gap[4,5] *(Census)*		
Black-White	0.25	0.20
Hispanic-White	0.24	0.30
Health		
Percentage Point Gap Between Top and Bottom Income Quintiles at Age 50 in Probability of Reaching Age 85 *(National Academies 2015)*		
Men	18	40
Women	14	45
Ratio of Age 0-4 Mortality Rates Between Richest and Poorest Counties[6] *(Currie and Schwandt 2016)*		
Men	1.9	1.6
Women	1.9	1.6

[1]Adjusted for 1994 CPS redesign, most recent data values for 2013 (pre-2014 redesign); [2]Values for 1989 (earliest available); [3]Values for 1980-82 (closest available); [4]Pay gaps for full time workers (50-52 weeks) at least 15 years of age, 1980 value for civilian workers only, higher value represents larger gap; [5]Values for white alone, black alone, and Hispanic (any race); [6]Ratio of mortality rates for 95th and 5th percentile counties as ranked by poverty rate, value for 1990 (earliest available).

have occurred. In doing so, these policies partially offset the cyclical increase in earnings inequality associated with economic downturns. In addition, the progressive fiscal policies included in the Recovery Act and subsequent legislation, including tax cuts for working and middle-class families and extended unemployment insurance, further reduced inequality and helped families struggling to handle job loss, reduced working hours, and other consequences of the downturn.

Reducing Unemployment and Earnings Inequality

The economic suffering caused by recessions is distributed in a highly unequal manner. The unemployed, particularly the long-term unemployed, bear a disproportionate share of the burden. Countercyclical policy is thus not only essential to ensure that our economy operates at its potential, but also plays an important role in reducing inequality (Bivens 2015; Coibion et al. 2016).

The Recovery Act and other elements of the fiscal policy response to the Great Recession boosted employment and output and reduced the unemployment rate relative to what they would have been absent the policy response. According to Blinder and Zandi (2015), the fiscal policy response boosted employment by roughly 2.5 million jobs and reduced the unemployment rate by 1.5 percentage points on average each year between 2010 and 2012 (Figure 3-1). The broader policy response, including not only fiscal policy but also financial measures pursued by the Administration, independent actions by the Federal Reserve, and support for the automobile industry, boosted employment by about 9 million jobs and reduced the unemployment rate by 6 percentage points on average each year from 2010 through 2012.[4] These estimates may even understate the impact of the policy response because they do not incorporate a role for negative long-term effects of recessions. If unemployment reduces the economy's potential going forward, the true impact of the policy response may exceed the impact shown here.

One particularly stark illustration of the unequal burden created by economic downturns is the disparity in unemployment rates by race and other demographic characteristics. The unemployment rate for the population as a whole increased 5 percentage points, from 5 to 10 percent, during the Great Recession and its immediate aftermath. However, the unemployment rate for African American workers rose 8 percentage points to nearly

---

[4] In previous work, CEA estimated that the Recovery Act and subsequent fiscal measures increased employment by about 9 million job-years through the end of 2012, broadly consistent with the estimates of the impact of the fiscal policy response by Blinder and Zandi (CEA 2014a). (A job year is the equivalent of a full-time job held for one year.)

Figure 3-1

Figure 3-1

Unemployment Rate by Policy Scenario, 2007–2015

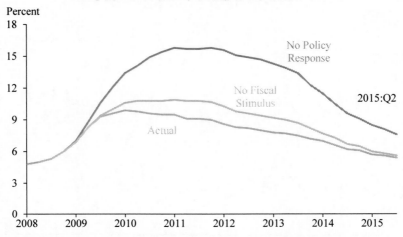

Percent

No Policy
Response

No Fiscal
Stimulus

2015:Q2

Actual

Note: The no policy reponse scenario assumes no fiscal policy response, no financial policy by the Administration or by the Federal Reserve (e.g. TARP, QE), and no support for the auto industry. The no policy response scenario assumes the Fed does conduct traditional monetary policy via management of short-term interest rates.
Source: Blinder and Zandi (2015).

17 percent, and for Hispanic workers it rose 7 percentage points to 13 percent (Figure 3-2). As the overall unemployment rate has fallen during the recovery, the unemployment rates for African American and Hispanic workers have fallen by even more, though they continue to exceed the rates of unemployment for the overall population.

Through increases in the unemployment rate, economic downturns drive increases in earnings inequality. As measured by the Gini index, changes in inequality in weekly earnings for the population ages 18-64—including those not currently employed—closely track changes in the unemployment rate over time (Figure 3-3). (The Gini index is a summary measure of inequality that ranges from 0 to 1, with higher values indicating greater inequality.) During and immediately after recessions, earnings inequality increases sharply along with the unemployment rate. As the unemployment rate recovers, earnings inequality decreases. The correlation between unemployment and the Gini index reflects both the mechanical effect of higher unemployment as well as any changes in the distribution of earnings.

While earnings inequality increases during recessions, other measures of inequality can decrease. A decrease in inequality would be expected for measures of income inequality that rely on more comprehensive definitions of income, that are more sensitive to changes in average incomes for the highest-income families, or that measure incomes over longer periods of

Figure 3-2

Unemployment Rate by Race, 1970–2016

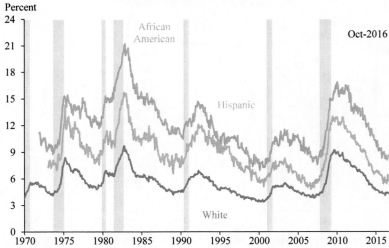

Note: Shading denotes recession.
Source: BLS.

Figure 3-3

Unemployment and Earnings Inequality, 1980–2015

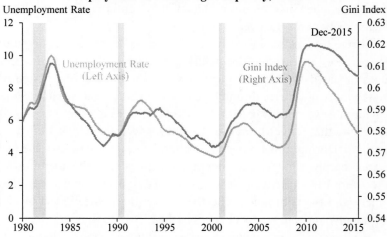

Note: Twelve-month moving average of not seasonally adjusted data. Gini index for the population ages 18-64, including those not currently employed. Unemployment rate for labor force participants ages 18-64. Shading denotes recession.
Source: BLS; CEA calculations.

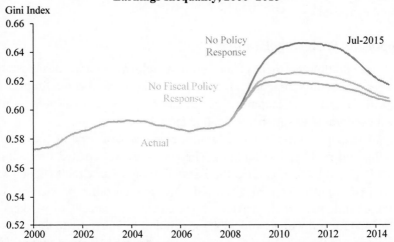

Figure 3-4
Earnings Inequality, 2000–2015

Gini Index

Note: Twelve-month moving average of not seasonally adjusted data. Gini index for the population ages 18-64, including those not currently employed.
Source: BLS; Blinder and Zandi (2015); CEA calculations.

time. Investment income is concentrated among high-income families and generally falls sharply during recessions, which reduces the income share of these families when using broader measures of income or measures of inequality that are particularly sensitive to high incomes. Similarly, safety-net policies provide partial protection against income losses that result from unemployment even though earnings fall to zero, thus reducing the recessionary increase in inequality in broader measures of income. The different behavior of these inequality measures provides important insights into how different parts of the economy vary with the business cycle. Earnings inequality reflects individuals' experiences in the labor market, while inequality in more comprehensive measures of income tracks the financial resources families have available. (Another important issue in evaluating inequality is distinguishing short-term cyclical developments from longer-term trends. See Box 3-2 at the end of this section for a discussion of this issue as it relates to the evolution of the income share of the top 1 percent of households since 2000.)

To quantify the impact of the policy response to the Great Recession on inequality, Figure 3-4 shows the actual Gini index for earnings since 2000 and the Gini index for two simulations reflecting what might have occurred without the policy response.[5] These calculations suggest that the policy response to the Great Recession reduced the increase in the Gini index for earnings by roughly half compared with what would have occurred absent the policy response.

Supporting Struggling Families

In addition to their effects on unemployment and earnings, the Recovery Act and subsequent fiscal measures also had a direct impact on inequality in after-tax incomes through the progressive fiscal policies that they incorporated to support struggling families.

A large portion of the fiscal policy response consisted of tax cuts for working and middle-class families. The Recovery Act created the Making Work Pay credit and expanded the Earned Income Tax Credit (EITC) and Child Tax Credit (CTC) for 2009 and 2010, among other provisions. The Making Work Pay credit provided a tax cut for 95 percent of workers of up to $400 for individuals and $800 for couples. In 2009, the Making Work Pay credit and the EITC and CTC expansions boosted after-tax incomes for families in the lowest quintile of the income distribution by 4 percent and boosted incomes in the second quintile by 2 percent (Figure 3-5). In dollar terms, these provisions provided average tax cuts of $400 and $500, respectively, for families in the first two quintiles. In 2011, the Making Work Pay credit was replaced by a 2 percentage-point reduction in the payroll tax rate, sometimes referred to as the payroll tax holiday, which was subsequently extended through 2012. All told, for a family of four making $50,000 a year, the Making Work Pay credit and payroll tax holiday provided a cumulative tax cut of $3,600 over the first four years of the Administration.

A second key plank of the fiscal policy response was enhancements to the unemployment insurance (UI) system. Both the pre-existing UI system and the enhancements enacted during the Great Recession provided essential support for hard-working American families struggling with the loss of a job during the downturn. The U.S. Census Bureau estimates that unemployment insurance kept more than 11 million people out of poverty

---

[5] Using data from the Current Population Survey, the simulation randomly re-assigns employed individuals to unemployment (and thus zero earnings) within 64 demographic cells in numbers calibrated to match the aggregate trends as estimated by Blinder and Zandi (2015), assuming proportional increases in unemployment across all cells. Two important sources of uncertainty in the estimate are the (unknown) distribution of earnings for those who would have lost their jobs absent the policy response and the earnings impacts for those who remain employed. This estimate assumes the earnings distribution for those who would have lost their jobs absent the policy response is identical to the overall earnings distribution within demographic cells and assumes no change in earnings for those who remain employed. A sensitivity exercise suggests that the conclusion is not substantially affected unless the workers who would have lost their jobs absent the policy response were selected primarily from the tails of the earnings distribution.

Figure 3-5

Percent Change in After-Tax Income by Income Percentile: MWP and Recovery Act EITC and CTC Expansion, 2009

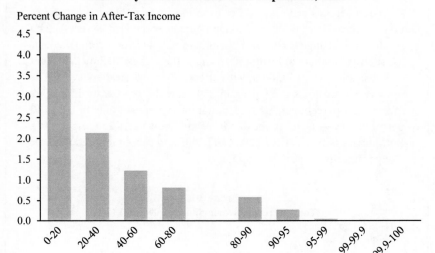

Source: Urban-Brookings Tax Policy Center; CEA calculations.

cumulatively between 2008 and 2012, according to the Supplemental Poverty Measure (CEA and DOL 2013). (This is not a causal estimate because it does not account for any changes in recipients' behavior that might occur in the absence of UI.) In 2012 alone, UI kept 2.5 million people out of poverty. Between 2008 and 2013, more than 24 million workers received extended benefits through either the Emergency Unemployment Compensation program or Extended Benefits program. Including workers' families, more than 70 million people—including 17 million children—were supported by extended UI benefits over this period (CEA and DOL 2013).

The Recovery Act also temporarily expanded benefits in the Supplemental Nutrition Assistance Program, provided emergency benefits through the Temporary Assistance for Needy Families program, and ended or prevented homelessness for over 1.3 million families through the Homelessness Prevention and Rapid Rehousing Program (CEA 2014a). It provided temporary support for States to sustain Medicaid coverage and made investments in health centers, workforce programs, prevention, and electronic health records.

In total, the pre-existing social insurance system, combined with the expansions in the Recovery Act and subsequent extensions, offset nearly 90 percent of the increase in poverty that would otherwise have occurred, even without accounting for impacts in moderating the recession itself (CEA

Box 3-2: Income Inequality and the Business Cycle

Income inequality is highly sensitive to economic conditions, and short-term trends can easily differ from longer-term developments (see Box 3-1 for a description of developments over the last 30 years). As a result, interpreting year-to-year changes in measures of income inequality, such as the share of income accruing to the highest-income 1 percent of households, must be done with attention to the business cycle. The most recent business-cycle peak in 2007 saw the pre-tax income share of the top 1 percent reach a record high of 19 percent, only to fall to 13 percent two years later in the depths of the Great Recession (Figure 3-i). Both its sharp drop between 2007 and 2009 and subsequent rebound are likely primarily cyclical developments.

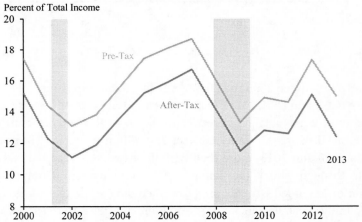

Figure 3-i
Top 1 Percent Income Shares, 2000–2013

Note: Households ranked by pre-tax income for both pre-tax and after-tax income shares. Shading denotes recession.
Source: CBO (2016b); CEA calculations.

Notwithstanding this short-term cyclical variation, income inequality has increased sharply in recent decades. This longer-term trend of rising income inequality culminated in the record-high income share of the top 1 percent in 2007. The top 1 percent income share in 2013, the most recent year for which comprehensive CBO estimates are available, was below this record level but still high by historical standards. Averaged across years, the income share of the top 1 percent has increased through each complete decade from the 1980s to the present (see Figure 3-ii).

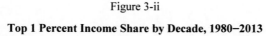

Figure 3-ii

Top 1 Percent Income Share by Decade, 1980–2013

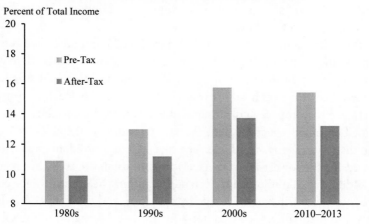

Note: Households ranked by pre-tax income for both pre-tax and after-tax income shares.
Source: CBO (2016b); CEA calculations.

Notably, however, the growth rate of inequality may have slowed or paused in recent years according to this measure. Since 2000, the income share of the top 1 percent has been highly cyclical, but relatively little-changed on net. At the same time, other measures of inequality, such as the Gini index for market incomes, have continued to increase. These data raise the possibility that the rapid increase in income inequality that the United States has experienced over recent decades may be entering a new phase. However, even if the growth in inequality has slowed, the elevated level of inequality will remain a pressing concern.

2014a). Although the economy was dealt its most severe blow since the Great Depression, the poverty rate measured to include the effects of antipoverty policy measures rose just half a percentage point. Excluding these measures, the poverty rate would have risen 4.5 percentage points—9 times greater than the actual increase.

THE AFFORDABLE CARE ACT: PROVIDING AFFORDABLE, ACCESSIBLE HEALTH INSURANCE

In 2008, 44 million Americans lacked health insurance. Individuals with pre-existing conditions were often locked out of health insurance, unable to obtain insurance at any price. For many others, health insurance was available but unaffordable. Many workers faced strong financial incentives to remain in low-quality jobs, or jobs for which they were poorly matched, because they needed the health insurance those jobs provided, even when a better job was available or they saw an opportunity to go back to school or to start a business.

The Affordable Care Act (ACA) introduced comprehensive reforms to address these and other problems in the health care system. It requires insurers to offer health insurance on the same terms to all applicants regardless of their health status. Families can use the Health Insurance Marketplace to compare and purchase policies with the certainty that they will not be denied coverage, and the law provides financial assistance to ensure that coverage is affordable. The law also supported an expansion of Medicaid for the lowest-income Americans. In total, the ACA has resulted in an additional 20 million American adults gaining health insurance coverage; reduced disparities in coverage by age, race, and income; and reduced poverty and inequality. (See Chapter 4 for further discussion of the Obama Administration's record on health care policy.)

Reducing Disparities in Health Coverage and Health Status

The ACA has substantially reduced inequality in access to health care. It has increased the number of American adults with health insurance by 20 million as of early 2016 and contributed to the largest drop in the share of the population without health insurance since the creation of Medicare and Medicaid in the 1960s (Furman and Fiedler 2014e; Uberoi, Finegold, and Gee 2016). From 2010—the year of the law's enactment—through the first half of 2016, the share of the population without health insurance (the uninsured rate) has fallen from 16.0 percent to 8.9 percent (Figure 3-6).

Uninsured rates varied markedly across different population groups in 2010 (Figures 3-7A, 3-7B, and 3-7C). Uninsured rates for African Americans, Hispanics, and Native Americans were substantially higher than those for Whites. And while nearly every American over age 65 had health coverage thanks to Medicare, more than 30 percent of those between the ages of 19 and 26 lacked health insurance. Families with incomes below 150 percent of the Federal poverty line lacked health insurance at a rate 9 times that for families with incomes above 400 percent of the poverty line.

Improvements in health insurance coverage have reduced inequality in access to health insurance along numerous dimensions, as demonstrated by the particularly large coverage gains for groups with elevated uninsured rates prior to reform. Between 2010 and 2015, coverage rates increased by 25 percentage points for Native Americans, 11 percentage points for Hispanics,

Figure 3-6

Percent of Population Without Health Insurance, 1963–2016

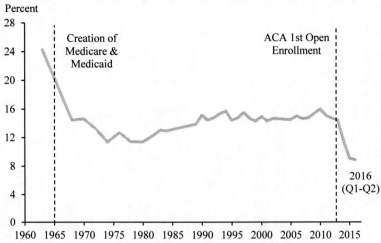

Percent

Note: For 2016, data reflect the first two quarters only. For years 1989 and later, data are annual. For prior years, data are generally but not always biannual.
Source: CEA analysis of NHIS and supplemental sources described in Furman and Fiedler (2014).

Figure 3-7A

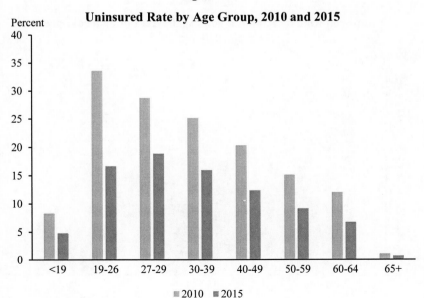

Source: NHIS; CEA calculations.

Figure 3-7B

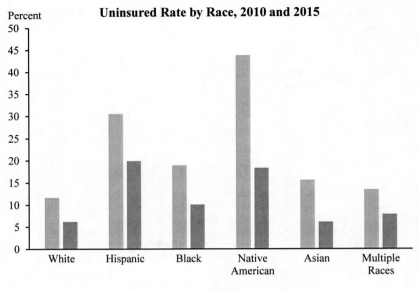

Uninsured Rate by Race, 2010 and 2015

Percent

Source: NHIS; CEA calculations.
■ 2010 ■ 2015

Figure 3-7C

Uninsured Rate by Family Income as Percent of Federal Poverty Level, 2010 and 2015

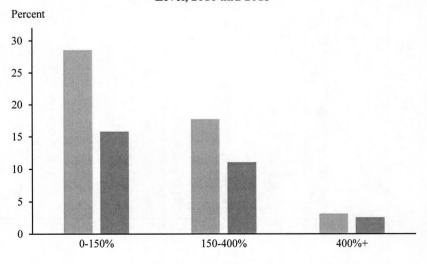

Percent

Source: NHIS; CEA calculations.
■ 2010 ■ 2015

and 9 percentage points for African Americans, compared with 7 percentage points overall. Coverage increased by 17 percentage points among those ages 19 to 26, with this age group no longer exhibiting the lowest rates of coverage, and coverage increased by 13 percentage points for families with incomes below 150 percent of the poverty line.

A growing body of research finds that the coverage expansions resulting from the ACA are generating important improvements in families' well-being. Perhaps the most visible goal of expanding health insurance coverage is improving access to care. Examining data through March 2015, Shartzer, Long, and Anderson (2015) find that the share of non-elderly adults with a usual source of care and the share who received a routine checkup in the last 12 months has risen with expanded insurance coverage, while the share reporting problems accessing care or forgoing care due to cost has fallen. Examining a similar time period, Sommers et al. (2015) report similar improvements in access to care, including reductions in the share of non-elderly adults reporting problems affording care or lacking a personal physician. The pattern of gains in these studies is consistent with the gains having been caused by the ACA. Both studies report notably larger gains in Medicaid expansion states, and Shartzer, Long, and Anderson (2015) find that the largest gains in access were realized by low- and moderate-income adults, a population that saw the largest gains in insurance coverage as a result of the ACA's coverage provisions.

This research also provides early evidence that gains in access to care are translating into better health. Sommers et al. (2015), for example, find reductions in the share of non-elderly adults reporting that they are in fair or poor health, as well as reductions in the percentage of days that respondents report having their activities limited by health problems. There is also evidence that these gains are larger in states that have expanded their Medicaid programs (Sommers et al. 2016). Further research will be required to examine the effects of the law on a broader array of health outcomes, though it is notable that studies of prior coverage expansions targeting populations similar to those targeted by the ACA's coverage provisions concluded that those expansions reduced mortality among those gaining coverage (Sommers, Baicker, and Epstein 2012; Sommers, Long, and Baicker 2014).

The coverage expansions resulting from the ACA also appear to be achieving one of the other key goals of health insurance coverage: protecting the sick from financial hardship. Survey data show substantial reductions in the share of families reporting problems paying medical bills, with particularly large reductions for low- and moderate-income adults as the law's coverage provisions have taken effect (Shartzer, Long, and Anderson 2015). Studies using data from consumer credit reports to compare states that have and have not expanded Medicaid found similar improvements in financial security, with one study estimating that Medicaid expansion reduced the amount of debt sent to collection by $600 to $1,000 per person gaining coverage (Dussault, Pinkovskiy, and Zafar 2016; Hu et al. 2016).

Reducing Poverty and Income Inequality

To facilitate this dramatic expansion in health insurance coverage, the ACA combined Federal support for states that expand their Medicaid programs with financial assistance for people purchasing coverage in the individual market so as to make health insurance more affordable for all Americans. These policies have directly reduced poverty and income inequality.

The value of the Medicaid benefits and Marketplace financial assistance made available by the ACA is substantial. Average medical expenses covered by Medicaid for adults newly eligible in 2017 as a result of the ACA will be an estimated $5,400 (CMS 2015).[6] CBO has estimated that individuals receiving subsidized coverage through the Health Insurance Marketplaces in 2017 will receive benefits of around $4,500 (CBO 2016a). For working families struggling to make ends meet, these forms of assistance can be the difference between health insurance coverage and medical bankruptcy or going without necessary care.

Analysis from the Treasury Department highlights the powerful inequality-reducing effects of the ACA coverage provisions. Treasury estimates that the ACA coverage provisions will boost incomes in the lowest decile by 25 percent and for the bottom quintile as a whole by 16 percent in 2017. They will also boost incomes for families in the second quintile by 5 percent. The average benefit for families in the first quintile from the ACA coverage provisions will be about $1,900 and for families in the second quintile about $1,400.[7]

---

[6] Different analysts compute the value of health insurance to households in different ways when measuring the income distribution. CBO (2016a) values Medicare and Medicaid at the average cost to the government of providing those benefits and the analysis here follows the same approach in valuing expanded Medicaid programs in the ACA at the cost to the government. Other approaches are also possible. For example, one recent study has argued for valuing Medicaid at less than cost because some of the care provided by Medicaid was previously being received from other sources for free (Finkelstein, Hendren, and Luttmer 2015). In this case, some of the value of the coverage expansions will accrue to whatever entities bear the cost of providing the care that goes uncompensated, a combination of medical providers themselves; privately insured individuals; and local, State, and Federal governments.

[7] After-tax incomes include the value of the Premium Tax Credit and cost-sharing reductions even if the assistance is realized as a reduction in premiums or out-of-pocket expenses rather than a direct payment.

ENACTING A FAIRER TAX CODE

In 2008, average tax rates on high-income families had fallen to their lowest levels in many years. Since then, President Obama has signed into law new tax cuts for working and middle-class families, restored Clinton-era tax rates for high-income Americans, created new tax credits to make health insurance affordable for all Americans, and fully paid for the coverage expansions of the ACA with responsible tax increases for high-income families.

These tax policies have served many purposes: restoring growth and boosting employment, expanding access to health care, helping working families get ahead, and reducing the deficit. In addition to their other purposes, the combined effect of these policies has been to reduce inequality substantially. Changes in tax policy, other than the ACA coverage provisions, will boost after-tax incomes in the bottom quintile by 2 percent in 2017 and reduce after-tax incomes for the top 0.1 percent by 9 percent relative to what incomes would have been under 2008 policies.

Cutting Taxes to Support Work, Reduce Poverty, and Strengthen Opportunity

During his first term in office, the President signed into law legislation that cut taxes for a family of four making $50,000 a year by a cumulative total of $3,600 between 2009 and 2012. As part of the Recovery Act, the President and Congress enacted the Making Work Pay credit, which provided 95 percent of workers with a tax cut of up to $400 ($800 for couples) in 2009 and 2010. In 2011 and 2012, the Making Work Pay credit was replaced with a 2 percentage-point reduction in the payroll tax rate. These policies were progressive in their own right, and also reduced inequality through their contribution to the economic recovery, as discussed earlier in this chapter. In addition, the Recovery Act expanded the Earned Income Tax Credit (EITC) and Child Tax Credit (CTC), helping 16 million working families make ends meet each year. These expansions now directly lift 1.8 million Americans out of poverty as measured by the Supplemental Poverty Measure, and reduce the severity of poverty for an additional 15 million Americans (Figure 3-8).

Research finds that refundable tax credits for working families lead to better short- and long-run outcomes for children. For example, one study finds each additional $1,000 increase in the EITC reduces the incidence of low birth weight by 2 to 3 percent, in part due to increased pre-natal care (Hoynes, Miller, and Simon 2015). Other research suggests that the EITC and refundable CTC increase test scores and college enrollment (Chetty,

Box 3-3: Safety Net Policies as Insurance

Distributional analysis can be conducted on either an annual or a lifetime basis. Annual estimates, like those presented in this chapter, provide a snapshot of the impact of policies in a particular year. Although they generally require richer data and stronger assumptions, lifetime estimates quantify the impact of policies over an entire lifecycle. This lifecycle perspective captures an important additional aspect of safety-net and anti-inequality policies that can be lost in annual analysis: their role as periodic supports in times of economic distress. For example, a two-earner family that is not eligible for the Earned Income Tax Credit (EITC) in most years may become eligible when one earner experiences an extended period of unemployment that depresses the family's annual income. Most individuals, in fact, experience such temporary shocks over a lifetime: a recent study indicated that more than 60 percent of Americans fall into the bottom 20 percent of incomes for at least one year between ages 25 and 60 (Rank and Hirschl 2015).

For this reason, the share of Americans that benefit from safety-net and anti-inequality policies over a longer horizon substantially exceeds the share that benefit in a single year. The ACA, for example, provides financial support to states that expand their Medicaid programs and to individuals for purchasing health insurance through the Marketplaces—

Figure 3-iii

**Percent of Nonelderly Americans Uninsured
for at Least One Month, 1997–2006**

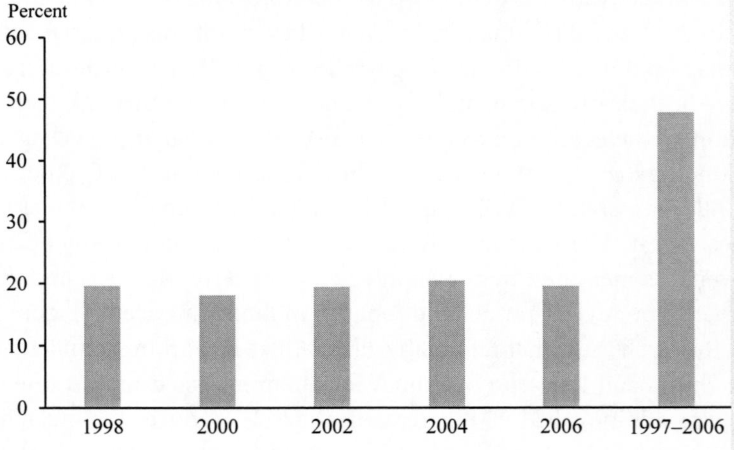

Source: U.S. Treasury, Office of Economic Policy (2009).

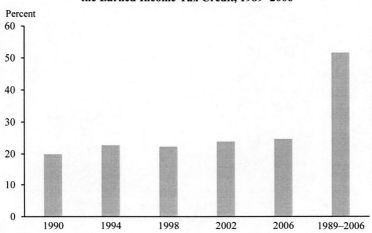

Figure 3-iv

**Percent of Families with Children Claiming
the Earned Income Tax Credit, 1989–2006**

Percent

Source: Dowd and Horowitz (2011).

provisions that provide greatest value to those who would otherwise be uninsured. In the decade prior to the enactment of the ACA, roughly 20 percent of the population was uninsured for at least one month in any particular year and thus stood to benefit from the law's coverage provisions during that year (see Figure 3-iii). However, over the course of the decade as a whole, more than twice as many people—roughly half the population—were uninsured for at least one month and thus would have had the opportunity to benefit from the law's coverage expansion. Similarly, about 25 percent of families with children claim the EITC in any given year, but 50 percent claim the EITC at some point during a 20-year period (Figure 3-iv).

In this way, the inequality-reducing tax and health care policies that the President has signed into law will ultimately benefit a much larger fraction of working and middle-class Americans than they do in a single year, as do existing policies like unemployment insurance and the Supplemental Nutrition Assistance Program.

Figure 3-8

Impact of Recovery Act EITC and CTC Improvements on Number of People in Poverty, 2018

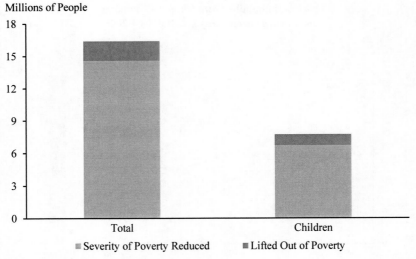

Millions of People

Source: Marr, Dasilva, and Sherman (2015).

Friedman, and Rockoff 2011; Dahl and Lochner 2012; Manoli and Turner 2016).[8]

The Recovery Act also created the American Opportunity Tax Credit (AOTC), which provides up to $10,000 over four years to help pay for college. The AOTC is the first education tax credit to be at least partially refundable. The partial refundability of the AOTC is critical because it allows low-income families with no income tax liability to claim the credit, and students who do not attend college come disproportionately from families with lower incomes. In addition, the Administration has expanded the maximum Pell Grant for low- and moderate-income college students by more than $1,000 and, for the first time, tied aid to inflation to maintain its value—an important policy that is not included in the estimates in this section, which focus solely on the tax system. (See Chapter 5 for additional discussion of changes in education policy during this Administration.)

Restoring Tax Rates to Their Level in the 1990s and Increasing Progressivity

Additional tax reforms enacted since 2009 have increased the progressivity of the tax code, helped pay for the ACA, and contributed to responsible

---

[8] For further discussion of the long-run benefits of refundable tax credits see CEA (2016a).

deficit reduction. At the beginning of 2013, the President signed into law a permanent extension of expiring tax cuts for middle-class families while also restoring Clinton-era tax rates for the highest-income families. Restoring Clinton-era tax rates for these families, along with other components of this legislation, will reduce the deficit by more than $800 billion over the next 10 years. In addition, the ACA extended Medicare taxes to cover the investment income of high-income families and modestly increased the Medicare tax rate for these same families. In combination, these reforms have restored effective tax rates on high-income Americans to the level that prevailed in the mid-1990s (Figure 3-9).

Reducing Poverty and Income Inequality

The tax policies the President has signed into law since 2009 have boosted incomes for working families, increased taxes on the highest-income families, and reduced income inequality (Figure 3-10). These policies, primarily the expansion of the CTC for low-income working families and expansion of the EITC for families with three or more children, will boost incomes in the first quintile by 2 percent in 2017 compared with what they would have been under the continuation of 2008 policies. These estimates do not take into account the additional, temporary income boosts these families saw from the temporary tax cuts enacted earlier in the Administration, including the Making Work Pay credit and the payroll tax holiday that have now expired.

The tax increases enacted by the Administration have been concentrated among the highest-income families. Families in the top 0.1 percent of the distribution, who are projected to have average pre-tax incomes of more than $8 million in 2017, will experience a tax increase of more than $500,000 on average and a reduction in after-tax incomes of 9 percent in that year. Families in the top 1 percent, but not the top 0.1 percent, will experience a tax increase of $30,000 on average and a reduction in after-tax incomes of 5 percent. In addition to their contribution to deficit reduction and to help finance the expansion of health insurance coverage made possible by the ACA, these high-income tax increases have directly reduced inequality in after-tax incomes.

The impact of these changes in tax policy are measured relative to a policy counterfactual in which 2008 tax policy remains in place. This policy counterfactual assumes the extension of the major individual and estate tax cuts scheduled to expire at the end of 2010; a set of individual, business, and energy tax provisions that have been regularly extended by Congress in the past (referred to as "extenders"); a set of provisions limiting the scope of the

Figure 3-9
**Effective Tax Rates for a Fixed Pre-Tax
Income Distribution, 1960–2017**

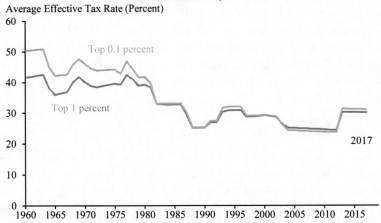

Note: Average effective Federal (individual income plus payroll) tax rates for a 2006 sample of
taxpayers augmented with non-filers constructed from the CPS. Pre-tax incomes adjusted in proportion
to changes in the National Average Wage Index.
Source: IRS, Statistics of Income Public Use File; Bureau of Labor Statics, Current Population Survey;
National Bureau of Economic Research. TAXSIM: CEA calculations.

Figure 3-10

**Percent Change in After-Tax Income by Income Percentile: Changes in Tax
Policy Since 2009
Excluding ACA Coverage Provisions, 2017**

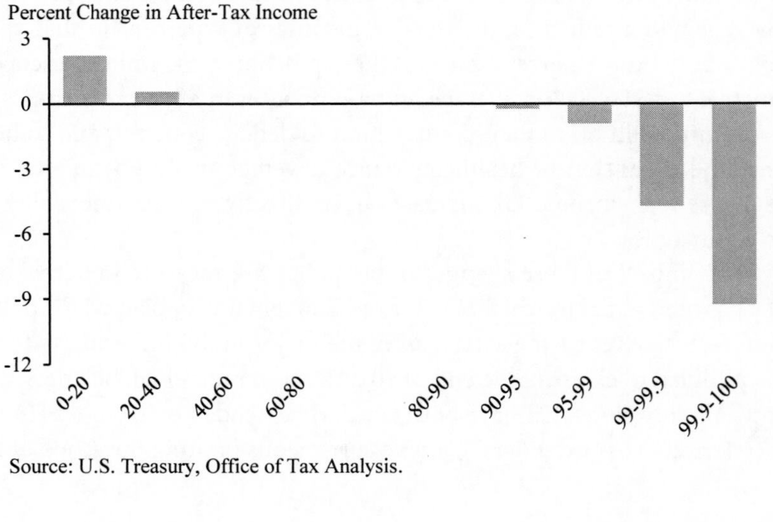

Percent Change in After-Tax Income

Source: U.S. Treasury, Office of Tax Analysis.

individual Alternative Minimum Tax; and the Federal Unemployment Tax Act surtax.

THE OBAMA ADMINISTRATION'S RECORD IN HISTORICAL CONTEXT

President Obama has overseen the largest increase in Federal invest-ment to reduce inequality since the Great Society programs of the Johnson Administration, largely reflecting the coverage provisions of the ACA and expansions of tax credits for working families. However, despite the historic nature of the Obama Administration's accomplishments, inequality remains much higher today than it was a few decades ago, and substantial work remains to continue reducing inequality and expanding economic opportu-nities for all Americans (Figure 3-11).

The Combined Impact of Changes in Tax Policy and the ACA Coverage Provisions

Earlier sections of this chapter separately examine the impact of the coverage provisions of the ACA and changes in tax policy on the distribu-tion of income. This section examines their combined impact. Changes in tax policy since 2009 and the coverage provisions of the ACA will boost 2017

Figure 3-11

Inequality in Market Income, Pre-Tax Income, and After-Tax Income, 1979–2013

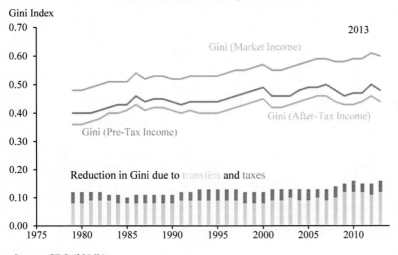

Source: CBO (2016b).

**Box 3-4: Additional Actions to Make the
Economy Work for All American**

This chapter focuses on the Administration's accomplishments in restoring growth, guaranteeing access to health insurance, and enacting a fairer tax code. However, the Administration has taken many other critical steps to reduce inequality, including both actions with more immediate effects, such as spurring State action to raise minimum wages, and actions with primarily longer-term effects, such as improving our educational system. This box describes the Administration's actions on wages and education.

Raising Wages: In his 2013 State of the Union address, the President called for an increase in the Federal minimum wage. While Congress has not acted, 18 states and the District of Columbia have enacted legislation raising their minimum wages since that time. In part due to these increases, the decline in the value of the effective minimum wage (the higher of the Federal and State minimum wage in each state weighted by worker hours) has been reversed, and the effective minimum wage has now reached roughly the same inflation-adjusted value it had in 2009 when the Federal minimum last increased (Figure 3-v). However, despite this progress, too many Americans continue to work

Figure 3-v

Real Value of Federal and State Minimum Wages, 1985–2017

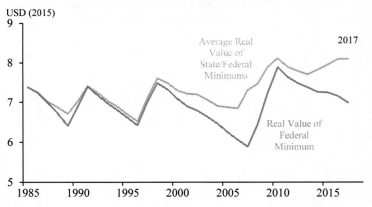

Note: Average State and Federal minimums are weighted by statewide weekly worker hours as recorded in the CPS and described further in Autor, Manning, and Smith (2016). For the combined trendline, the Federal minimum is recorded in place of State minimums where the former binds.
Source: Autor, Manning, and Smith (2016); BLS; CBO; CEA calculations.

for a minimum wage that is too low, and the President continues to call for a higher minimum wage.

The President has also worked to improve working conditions and wages by strengthening worker protections. As part of this effort, the Department of Labor completed an update to Federal overtime regulations in early 2016, extending overtime protections to more than 4 million additional workers. Unions also play an important role in supporting working conditions and wages, and the President has worked to ensure that the National Labor Relations Board is able to fulfill its role in enforcing workplace protections and upholding the rights of workers. In addition, the Administration has sought to support new approaches to enabling worker voice.

Promoting Educational Opportunity: In contrast to higher minimum wages and changes in tax and transfer policy, which generate immediate reductions in inequality, educational investments pay off over a longer time horizon. Educational investments are critical to ensure equal opportunity for children today and to reduce inequality over the long term. During the recession, the Department of Education provided over $60 billion in funding to states to support education budgets, and these resources helped prevent layoffs of education workers at a time when State and local spending was being cut. As part of the Recovery Act, the Administration encouraged states to raise educational standards, turn around the lowest-performing schools, develop effective support for teachers and leaders, and create uniform data systems to enhance instruction through the Administration's Race-to-the-Top initiative. Today, as a result of this initiative, nearly every state has adopted college and career-ready standards.

The bipartisan Every Student Succeeds Act, which the President signed into law in December 2015, codifies the requirement that every state set academic standards that prepare students for college and careers, and that the state intervene to improve both their lowest-performing 5 percent of schools as well as schools where too many students do not graduate on time—principles that were central to the funding provided under the Recovery Act. In 2014, the Administration invested $750 million in new resources to expand access to high quality early education programs, through Early Head Start-Child Care Partnership grants for infants and toddlers and Preschool Development Grants to states. Today, all but 4 States are investing in preschool, with more than 40 percent of four-year olds in the United States enrolled in publicly funded preschool. In addition, the Administration announced the availability of $135 million in competitively awarded grants to expand Early Head Start and create new Early Head Start-Child Care Partnerships in 2016, building on

$294 million in newly appropriated funds for fiscal year 2016 to ensure that more Head Start children will receive services for a full school day and full school year. The Administration has also provided new funds to support the implementation of new requirements in the reauthorized Child Care and Development Block Grant Act of 2014.

The Administration has also made progress in promoting college opportunity, affordability, and completion by expanding Pell Grants and tax credits; making student loans more affordable by cutting interest rates and allowing borrowers to cap student loan payments at 10 percent of income; making access to financial aid and college information simpler and faster; and promoting innovation and competition to bring down costs and improve college quality. Today, more students are graduating college than ever, and student loan defaults and delinquencies are trending downward.

Lastly, the Administration has worked to increase training and skills for workers during their careers. In 2015, the President signed into law the first-ever annual funding for apprenticeship grants, totaling $90 million. These investments follow earlier investments through the American Apprenticeship Grants to promote and expand job-driven apprenticeship programs in the United States. In addition, the Administration has launched a series of initiatives, partnerships, and grants to facilitate training for the American workforce. In April 2015, the White House hosted an Upskill Summit at which the President called on companies to expand education benefits and training opportunities, and employers have responded to this call—the Aspen Institute's Upskill America Initiative reports that participating companies have enhanced the skills of tens of thousands of frontline workers. The Department of Labor has also awarded a wide variety of competitive training grants. These grants have ranged from TechHire grants, which are supporting public-private partnerships to help train tomorrow's workforce in rapid-growth sectors, to America's Promise Job-Driven Training grants, which are creating and expanding innovative regional and sector partnerships between community colleges and the workforce system to create more tuition-free education and training programs for in-demand middle and high-skilled jobs across the country.

incomes in the bottom quintile by 18 percent, or $2,200, and in the second quintile by about 6 percent, or $1,500, relative to what they would have been under the continuation of 2008 policies (Figure 3-12).[9] These policies will also boost incomes in the middle quintile by 0.7 percent, or $300. In contrast, these policies will reduce the after-tax incomes of very high-income families, particularly those in the top 1 percent. Targeted tax increases will reduce after-tax incomes by 5 percent for the 99th through 99.9th percentiles and reduce after-tax incomes by 10 percent for the families in the top 0.1 percent, a group projected to have average incomes over $8 million in 2017.

Average tax rates provide an alternative perspective on the impact of these polices. Changes in tax policy since 2009 and tax-related coverage provisions of the ACA will increase the average tax rate for the top 0.1 percent by 7 percentage points in 2017, from 31 percent to 38 percent. For families in the top 1 percent but not the top 0.1 percent, these changes will increase average tax rates by 4 percentage points.

These changes in tax policy and the coverage provisions of the ACA have led to commensurate changes in the distribution of income. As a result of these policies, the share of income received by the top 1 percent will decrease by 1.2 percentage points in 2017, or 7 percent, from 16.6 percent to 15.4 percent (Figure 3-13). The share of income accruing to the bottom 99 percent of Americans will increase by a corresponding 1.2 percentage points. Income shares in the first quintile will rise by 0.6 percentage point, or 18 percent; in the second quintile by 0.5 percentage point, or 6 percent; and in the third quintile by 0.1 percentage point, or 1 percent.

The robust reduction in inequality resulting from these policies is apparent across a wide range of inequality measures (Figure 3-14). The impact of fiscal policies enacted during the Obama Administration on inequality varies by measure, ranging from a 3-percent reduction in the Gini index to a more than 20-percent reduction in the ratio of average incomes in the top 1 percent to the bottom 20 percent, but all measures show a meaningful reduction in inequality. Changes in tax policy and the coverage provisions of the ACA have had their largest effects on very high-income families, where the restoration of Clinton-era tax rates and responsible tax increases to finance the ACA are most important, and in the bottom third of the distribution, where the ACA's expansion of health insurance coverage to 20 million more Americans has had its largest impact. Thus, not surprisingly,

---

[9] The ACA coverage provisions and tax changes enacted since 2009 have offsetting effects on the 2017 deficit judged relative to a 2008 current-policy baseline, with the coverage provisions increasing the deficit and the tax changes decreasing it. Allocating an additional fiscal adjustment proportional to income to achieve zero net effect on the deficit would not substantially affect the results. Such an adjustment can be critical in assessing the ultimate distributional impact of deficit-financed policy changes.

Figure 3-12

Percent Change in After-Tax Income by Income Percentile: Changes in Tax Policy Since 2009 and ACA Coverage Provisions, 2017

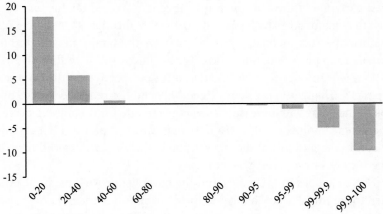

Source: U.S. Treasury, Office of Tax Analysis.

Figure 3-13

Change in Share of After-Tax Income by Income Percentile: Changes in Tax Policy Since 2009 and ACA Coverage Provisions, 2017

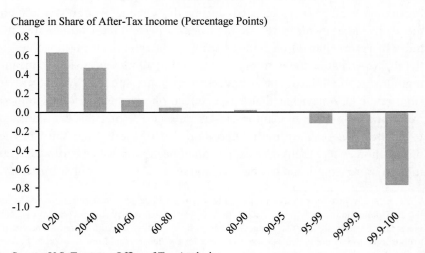

Source: U.S. Treasury, Office of Tax Analysis.

Figure 3-14

Percent Reduction in Income Inequality Due to Changes in Tax Policy and ACA Coverage Provisions, 2017

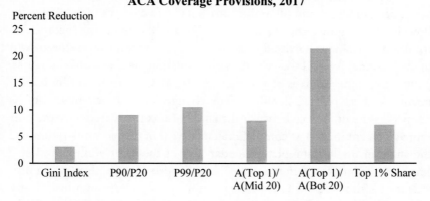

Note: P90/P20 is the ratio of the after-tax income at the 90th percentile of the distribution to the after-tax income at the 20th percentile. P99/P20 is defined similarly. A(Top 1)/A(Mid 20) is the ratio of the average after-tax income in the top 1 percent to the average after-tax income in the middle 20 percent. A(Top 1)/A(Bot 20) is defined similarly. Incomes are adjusted for family size in computing the Gini Index and percentile ratios and for purposes of ranking families in computing ratios of average incomes and income shares.
Source: U.S. Treasury, Office of Tax Analysis.

measures that are most sensitive to these points in the distribution, such as the ratio of average incomes for families in the top 1 percent to those in the bottom quintile, show the largest effects.

Obama Administration Achievements Relative to Other Federal Action in Recent Decades

The decrease in income inequality resulting from changes in tax policy since 2009 and the coverage provisions of the ACA is large not only in absolute terms but also relative to previous Federal action to reduce inequality.

There are important limitations and uncertainties in any effort to assign policy changes to particular Presidential administrations. Policies enacted in one administration may phase in through the next administration. Broader economic and demographic changes in one administration will interact with the entire history of policy changes leading up to that point. Polices may be repeatedly extended on a temporary basis and automatic adjustments may be introduced in ways that make it difficult to consistently interpret action and inaction (for instance, the introduction of automatic inflation adjustments for income tax brackets and other parameters of the tax code in the 1980s). Notwithstanding these difficulties, this section compares the anti-inequality accomplishments of the Obama

Administration with those of previous administrations, first with respect to tax policy and then with respect to spending.

Figure 3-15 shows the change in the share of after-tax income accruing to the bottom 99 percent of families attributable to changes in tax policy for Presidential administrations since 1960. The analysis holds the income distribution constant as it existed in 2006 and adjusts income levels for growth in the National Average Wage Index, thus isolating the impact of changes in policy from other sources of variation in tax rates. It focuses on individual income and payroll tax liabilities. The change for each administration is defined as the difference between the share of income received by the bottom 99 percent in the last complete calendar year of that administration and the share in the last complete calendar year of the prior administration.[10] Implicitly, tax liabilities in the final year of the previous administration provide the baseline used to assess changes in tax policy across administrations.

The tax changes enacted during the Obama Administration have had historically large effects on the distribution of income, increasing the share of income accruing to the bottom 99 percent of Americans by about 1 percentage point, an inequality-reducing shift in the tax burden more than twice as large as that achieved during the Clinton Administration, which ranks second by this measure.[11]

While the Administration's accomplishments are large by almost any measure, different measures of inequality focus on different points in the income distribution and thus can rank administrations in different ways. Under some measures, the Ford Administration, during which the Earned Income Tax Credit was created, ranks first; under others, the Clinton Administration, which substantially expanded the Earned Income Tax Credit and increased top income tax rates, ranks first.

In addition to inequality-reducing changes in tax policy, the President has also signed into law a historic investment in Federal anti-inequality programs. Figure 3-16 shows the change in Federal spending on these programs

---

[10] For purposes of these comparisons, 1963 is treated as the last complete year of the Kennedy Administration. The change for the Kennedy Administration is measured relative to 1960 because the NBER TAXSIM model (on which this analysis relies heavily) can only generate tax liabilities back to 1960.

[11] This estimate differs from other estimates presented in this chapter for four reasons. First, this estimate excludes the Medicaid expansion but includes all other ACA coverage and tax provisions, a combination of policies not reflected in other estimates. Second, Treasury estimates incorporate a more complete set of taxes, including corporate, excise, and estate taxes, which is not possible with the NBER Internet TAXSIM model. Third, the Treasury estimates apply to calendar year 2017, while these estimates are based on the distribution of income in 2006 held constant over time. And fourth, the NBER Internet TAXSIM model and CEA imputations underlying Figure 3-15 necessarily differ from Treasury's tax models on a variety of technical dimensions.

Figure 3-15

Change in Bottom 99% Share of After-Tax Income for a Fixed Pre-Tax Income Distribution, 1960–2016

Change in Share of After-Tax Income (Percentage Points)

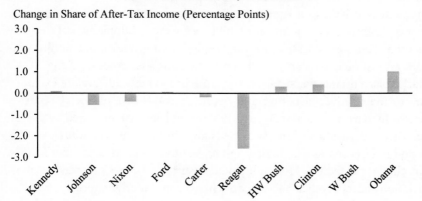

Note: Share of income received by the bottom 99% of families after Federal income and payroll taxes in the last complete year of each Administration relative to the last year of the prior Administration for a 2006 sample of taxpayers augmented with non-filers constructed from the CPS. Pre-tax incomes adjusted in proportion to changes in the National Average Wage Index.
Source: IRS, Statistics of Income Public Use File; Bureau of Labor Statics, Current Population Survey; National Bureau of Economic Research, TAXSIM; CEA calculations.

Figure 3-16

Change in Spending on Major Anti-Inequality Programs by Term, 1968–2016

Percent of Potential GDP

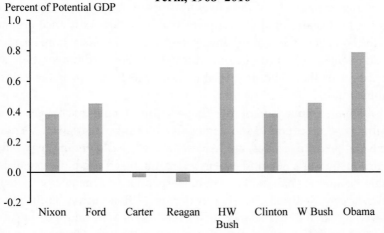

Note: Major anti-inequality programs defined as Medicaid/CHIP, SNAP, the refundable portion of the EITC and CTC, SSI, TANF and other family support, educational assistance, Pell grants, housing assistance, the refundable portion of the Premium Tax Credit, and cost-sharing reductions.
Source: OMB; CBO; CEA calculations.

as a share of potential GDP by Presidential administrations since 1968. For purposes of these comparisons, the major anti-inequality programs are defined as Medicaid and the Children's Health Insurance Program, the Supplemental Nutrition Assistance Program, the refundable portion of the Earned Income Tax Credit and Child Tax Credit, Supplemental Security Income, Temporary Assistance for Needy Families and other family support, educational assistance, Pell grants, housing assistance, and the ACA's Marketplace financial assistance. Social Security and Medicare are excluded due to their universal nature and because, in the case of Social Security, benefit increases in the last 50 years have often been accompanied by payroll tax increases. In addition, most of the change in Medicare spending over this period reflects changes in demographics, health care costs, and other factors, not changes in policy. Unemployment insurance is also excluded as most variation reflects cyclical factors, not changes in underlying policy.

Under President Obama, the Federal investment in reducing inequality has increased by about 0.8 percent of potential GDP, more than any previous President since the Great Society. Much of this increase reflects the coverage provisions of the ACA and expanded tax credits for working families first enacted as part of the Recovery Act. Federal support for states expanding their Medicaid programs, financial assistance for families purchasing health insurance through the Marketplace, and the Recovery Act's EITC and CTC expansions comprise a more than $100 billion annual investment in reducing health and income inequality in 2016, amounting to roughly 0.5 percent of potential GDP.

Earlier expansions of the safety net are also apparent in Figure 3-16, including the expansion of the Supplemental Nutrition Assistance Program (then the Food Stamp Program) during the Nixon Administration, the phase in of Supplemental Security Income through the Ford Administration, and the creation of the Children's Health Insurance Program in the Clinton Administration.

A simple comparison of spending over time combines changes in policy with broader economic and demographic changes that affect spending for existing programs. Thus, an increase in Medicaid spending may reflect the introduction of a new and expensive treatment, an eligibility expansion, or other economic changes. For example, spending on inequality-reducing policies, largely Medicaid, rose sharply during the first Bush Administration. However, research finds that most of the increase in Medicaid spending over this period reflects changes in health care prices, the early 90s recession, and other factors, not contemporaneous policy changes (Holahan et al. 1993).

An alternative comparison of each administration's policy accomplishments would focus only on those increases or decreases attributable to policy changes enacted during each administration, but the length of the historical period, the substantial changes in demographics and the economy, and the number and complexity of policy changes involved make such a comparison infeasible.

A comparison along these lines, however, would not change the conclusion that the Obama Administration's investments in reducing inequality have been historic, and it would be unlikely to change the relative ranking of the Obama Administration and previous administrations in an important way. As noted above, the increase during the Obama Administration largely reflects new programmatic investments in the form of the coverage provisions of the ACA and expanded tax credits for working families. Much of the increase in the investment in anti-inequality programs during the first Bush Administration, which ranks second by the simple change in spending over time, is attributable to factors other than changes in policy, as discussed above. And the increase in the investment in anti-inequality programs occurring during all other administrations since the Great Society is much more modest than the increase during the Obama Administration.

A Partial Reversal of Increasing Inequality

The historic investments in reducing inequality made during the Obama Administration have achieved a partial reversal of the increase in income inequality in recent decades. However much more work remains due to the sheer size of the increase in inequality between 1979 and 2007. According to CBO, the share of after-tax income received by the bottom quintile of households fell from 7.4 percent at the business cycle peak in 1979 to 5.6 percent at the business cycle peak in 2007, and the share accruing to the top 1 percent increased from 7.4 percent in 1979 to 16.7 percent in 2007 (CBO 2016b). While CBO's estimates of the income distribution and the Treasury estimates of the distribution of changes in tax policy and the ACA coverage provisions are not precisely comparable due to different methodological choices, they are sufficiently similar to make broad comparisons informative.[12]

---

[12] The comparisons presented in this chapter implement one adjustment to the Treasury analysis before comparing to CBO. Treasury percentiles are defined to contain an equal number of tax families while CBO defines percentiles to contain an equal number of people. An approximate adjustment is applied to the Treasury figures to put them on a similar equal-people basis that assumes families shifted between percentiles have the average family size of the percentile range into which they are shifted, incomes equal to the boundary between the income classes, and a tax rate equal to the simple average of the tax rate in the classes on either side of the boundary. This adjustment is applied only in determining the fraction of the increase in inequality reversed and the equivalent growth rate; the changes in shares and changes in after-tax income reported in this section are unchanged from the prior section for consistency.

Figure 3-17

Changes in the Distribution of After-Tax Income

Change in Share of After-Tax Income (Percentage Points)

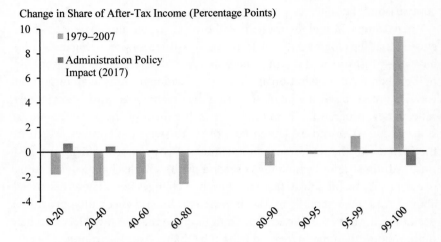

Source: CBO (2016b); U.S. Treasury, Office of Tax Analysis; CEA calculations.

The share of after-tax income received by the bottom quintile increased by roughly 0.6 percentage point as a result of laws enacted during this Administration, equivalent to a roll back of roughly a third of the deterioration in the income share for this population between 1979 and 2007 (Figure 3-17). At the top, the policy changes signed into law have reversed roughly a 10th of the increase in the share of after-tax income accruing to the top 1 percent over the last three decades.

Another way of contextualizing the impact of the policies enacted by this Administration is to compare them with the growth rate in incomes. As noted above, the laws enacted during the Obama Administration have boosted incomes in the bottom quintile by about 18 percent. Between 1979 and 2007, immediately prior to the onset of the Great Recession, cumulative growth in after-tax incomes for the bottom quintile amounted to about 45 percent. Thus, these policies provided the equivalent of more than a decade of average income growth for these families.

NEXT STEPS TO FURTHER BOOST INCOMES, EXPAND OPPORTUNITY, AND REDUCE INEQUALITY

During his eight years in office, President Obama signed into law legislation achieving a historic reduction in inequality through changes in tax policy and the coverage provisions of the ACA. However, as the preceding section makes clear, even with these accomplishments, much more work remains to be done. In the FY 2017 Federal Budget and elsewhere, the President has proposed an array of policies that would further boost incomes, expand opportunity, and reduce inequality.

Making Work Pay

Well-paying jobs are essential to reducing poverty and inequality, but too many Americans continue to work for a wage that is too low. Increasing the Federal minimum wage would be an important step in addressing the insufficient rate of wage growth in recent decades. For this reason, the President called for a minimum wage increase in his State of the Union address in February 2013. Since then, 18 states and the District of Columbia have passed increases in their minimum wages, but much more progress needs to be made.

Expanding the EITC—one of the largest and most effective anti-poverty programs—also helps make work pay. The FY 2017 budget proposes an expansion of the EITC for workers without dependent children, whose eligibility for only a very small tax credit limits the power of the EITC to reduce poverty for this population (Figure 3-18). Currently, workers without dependent children are the only group of workers taxed into poverty by the current tax code (Marr and Dasilva 2016). Expanding the EITC for workers without dependent children would provide 13 million low-income workers with a tax cut averaging nearly $500 for each worker, while also providing an additional incentive to work. This expansion would build on the success of the EITC expansions for families with three or more children and for married couples enacted as part of the Recovery Act.

Investing in Children and Families

Not only is inequality in living standards for children an immediate concern, but recent research highlights the importance of investments in children and families for future outcomes as well (CEA 2014b; CEA 2014c; Furman and Ruffini 2015). The FY 2017 budget proposes a number of inequality-reducing investments in children and families, including in child care, early education, and ending family homelessness.

First, the President has proposed a historic investment in child care to ensure that all working families from low- and moderate-income backgrounds can access safe, affordable, and high-quality care for infants and toddlers. Research finds that quality, affordable child care can promote parental employment and earnings as well as healthy child development, in addition to helping families make ends meet (CEA 2014b).

Figure 3-18

Share of Otherwise-Poor Families Lifted Out of Poverty by the EITC Based on Family Structure, 2012

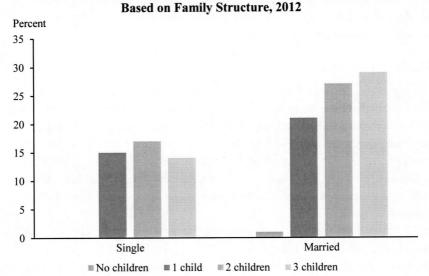

Percent

Single   Married

▓ No children ▪ 1 child ▓ 2 children ▓ 3 children

Source: Crandall-Hollick (2016).

Second, the budget proposes to further expand high-quality early education through the President's Preschool for All Initiative. This initiative would provide all four-year-old children from low- and moderate-income families with access to high-quality preschool through a new Federal-State partnership, while encouraging states to expand those programs to reach additional children from middle-class families. The President would also continue investments in high-quality learning before preschool through expansions of the Early Head Start-Child Care partnership, as well as expansions of home visitation programs for new and expecting parents. A large body of research has found that quality early education programs have high returns for both the participants and for society as a whole (CEA 2016a; CEA 2014b).

Third, the budget puts forward a package of proposals that would strengthen the Temporary Assistance for Needy Families program so it does more to help poor families get back on their feet and work toward self-sufficiency. For example, recognizing that 20 years of frozen funding has eroded the inflation-adjusted value of the block grant, the budget proposes to increase funding for TANF; the additional funds would be coupled with an increased focus on helping families prepare for and find jobs, along with new financial and programmatic accountability standards for states. The budget also includes a TANF Economic Response Fund that would provide budgetary flexibility for additional assistance when economic conditions deteriorate, so as to increase the efficacy of TANF during downturns.

Outside of TANF, the budget proposes to invest $12 billion to ensure adequate food for low-income children during the summer months, as many low-income children receive food at little or no cost during the school year but lose this support when school is not in session.

Finally, the budget proposes an $11 billion investment to prevent and end family homelessness by 2020. Reducing homelessness directly improves inequality today, and recent research suggests that moving children and their families to better neighborhoods can generate substantial earnings gains when those children become adults (Chetty and Hendren 2015; Chetty, Hendren, and Katz 2016).

In addition, an expansion of paid leave would also help reduce inequalities in childhood investment, employment, and incomes. While current law allows many workers to take time off without pay to care for a new baby or a sick family member, millions of families cannot afford to do so. Employers are not required to offer paid leave in most states even though research shows that the availability of paid maternity leave increases the likelihood that mothers return to their jobs following the birth of a child, which leads to better outcomes for infants (CEA 2014c).

As documented throughout this report, the ACA has already resulted in an additional 20 million American adults with health insurance and, in doing so, has substantially reduced income inequality. Writing in the *Journal of the American Medical Association*, the President outlined a number of suggestions as to how the country can continue making progress in expanding health insurance coverage, improving the quality of care, and reducing health care costs (Obama 2016). These suggestions include the adoption of a Medicaid expansion by all 50 states, increasing the financial assistance available to families purchasing Marketplace coverage, and considering a public option to promote additional competition in the exchanges. In addition, as the ACA covers the full cost of State Medicaid expansions only through 2016 before gradually reducing the level of Federal support to 90 percent, the budget proposes to cover the full cost of Medicaid expansion for the first three years after a state expands, regardless of when this expansion occurs, to better support states taking action to expand Medicaid.

Reforming the Tax System

The budget also proposes responsible tax increases on the most fortunate Americans to finance inequality-reducing investments in working and middle-class families and to drive down future deficits. The budget proposes to reform the taxation of capital income by increasing the top tax rate on capital gains and dividends to 28 percent and by closing a loophole that allows wealthy families to avoid ever paying tax on their capital gains if they hold assets until death. The budget would also reform tax expenditures to limit their value for high-income families and would close loopholes that allow some wealthy business owners to avoid paying Medicare taxes by classifying certain income as neither employment nor investment income. It would also increase the tax paid by the very largest estates. All told, the tax reforms in the budget would reduce the share of income received by the top 1 percent of families by 1.3 percentage points, rolling back an additional 13 percent of the increase in the after-tax income share of the top 1 percent between 1979 and 2007.

Conclusion

During his eight years in office, President Obama has overseen the largest increase in Federal investment to reduce inequality since the Great Society. The policy response to the Great Recession reduced the unemployment rate relative to what it otherwise would have been by 6 percentage points on average each year between 2010 and 2012 and offset roughly half of the increase in earnings inequality that would otherwise have occurred. The Affordable Care Act and changes in tax policy will boost incomes in the bottom quintile of families by 18 percent in 2017 and increase average tax rates for the highest-income 0.1 percent of families by nearly 7 percentage points. Together, these policies will increase the share of after-tax income received by the bottom 99 percent by 1.2 percentage points in 2017 with a corresponding reduction in the income share of the top 1 percent.

Despite this progress, income inequality remains much higher today than it was a few decades ago, and the President's Fiscal Year 2017 Budget proposes spending and tax reforms that would further reduce inequality. These steps include, among others, reforms to tax benefits for high-income Americans; an expansion of the Earned Income Tax Credit for workers without dependent children; and a landmark commitment to ensuring all low- and moderate-income families have access to quality, affordable child care that allows parents to work or pursue education and training. Taken together, the policies proposed in the budget would build on the progress made in reducing income inequality since 2009, helping to ensure that all Americans have the opportunity to succeed.

Table A1

Distribution of Changes in Tax Policy Since 2009 and ACA Coverage Provisions[1]

(2017 Income Levels under 2017 Current Law)

Adjusted Cash Income Percentile[2]	Number of Families	Distribution of Cash Income	Average Federal Tax Rate[3]		Average Transfer and Tax Change from 2008 Policy to Current Policy[4]	Change in After-Tax Income from 2008 Policy to Current Policy[4]	Distribution of After-Tax Income	
			2008 Policy	Current Policy			2008 Policy	Current Policy
	(millions)	(%)	(%)	(%)	($)	(%)	(%)	(%)
0 to 10[5]	16.4	1.0	-0.6	-10.3	-2,080	27.1	1.1	1.4
10 to 20	17.2	2.1	0.7	-4.5	-2,289	13.9	2.4	2.7
20 to 30	17.2	2.8	4.7	1.4	-2,079	9.4	3.2	3.5
30 to 40	17.2	3.7	7.4	5.5	-1,005	3.4	4.3	4.5
40 to 50	17.2	5.0	10.0	9.2	-410	1.1	5.7	5.7
50 to 60	17.2	6.6	12.7	12.3	-243	0.5	7.3	7.3
60 to 70	17.2	8.5	14.9	14.9	-7	0.0	9.2	9.2
70 to 80	17.2	11.2	17.5	17.6	70	-0.1	11.6	11.6
80 to 90	17.2	15.5	20.7	20.8	135	-0.1	15.5	15.5
90 to 100	17.2	45.1	26.4	28.9	9,710	-3.4	41.8	40.5
Total[5]	172.1	100.0	20.2	20.9	189	-0.3	100.0	100.0
90 to 95	8.6	11.2	22.9	23.2	541	-0.4	10.8	10.8
95 to 99	6.9	15.2	24.6	25.4	2,706	-1.1	14.4	14.3
99 to 99.9	1.5	9.4	29.0	32.6	31,863	-5.0	8.4	8.0
Top .1	0.2	9.4	31.0	37.7	548,941	-9.7	8.2	7.4

Notes:

[1] Both current policy and 2008 policy include a list of individual, business and energy tax provisions that are scheduled to expire at the end of 2016 but have been regularly extended by Congress (provisions referred to as "extenders"). Current policy is current law with the extenders. 2008 policy eliminates from current law a number of key provisions enacted during the Obama administration, including: the higher tax rate on tobacco enacted in CHIPRA; the AOTC and the expansions of the child tax credit and EITC enacted in ARRA; provisions in the Affordable Care Act, including expanded Medicaid eligibility, the premium tax credit, cost-sharing reductions, the additional Medicare tax, the net investment income tax, the individual shared responsibility payment, the employer shared responsibility payment, the small business tax credit, the higher floor for itemized deductions for medical expenses, the excise tax on indoor tanning services, fees on branded prescription drug manufacturers and importers, and fees on insured and self-insured plans; and the higher top ordinary and capital gains and dividend tax rates, and the reinstatement of the personal exemption phaseout (PEP) and phaseout of itemized deductions (Pease) enacted in ATRA. 2008 policy also replaces the AMT parameters enacted in ATRA with a more generous AMT "patch." In addition, 2008 policy replaces the estate tax adopted in ATRA with the carryover basis provisions provided for under EGTRRA. Finally, 2008 policy restores the 0.2% FUTA surtax that expired in 2011.

[2] Cash Income consists of wages and salaries, net income from a business or farm, taxable and tax-exempt interest, dividends, rental income, realized capital gains, cash and near-cash transfers from the government, retirement benefits, and employer-provided health insurance (and other employer benefits). Employer contributions for payroll taxes and the federal corporate income tax are added to place cash on a pre-tax basis. Families are placed into deciles based on cash income adjusted for family size, by dividing income by the square root of family size. Percentiles begin at family size-adjusted cash income of: $10,902 for 10 to 20; $16,165 for 20 to 30; $21,713 for 30 to 40; $28,753 for 40 to 50; $37,516 for 50 to 60; $48,381 for 60 to 70; $61,100 for 70 to 80; $80,449 for 80 to 90; $117,224 for 90 to 95; $165,373 for 95 to 99; $379,371 for 99 to 99.9 and $1,734,164 for Top .1.

[3] The taxes included are individual and corporate income, payroll (Social Security, Medicare and unemployment), excises, customs duties, and estate and gift taxes. Individual income taxes are assumed to be borne by payers, payroll taxes (employer and employee shares) by labor (wages and self-employment income), excises on purchases by individuals in proportion to relative consumption of the taxed good and proportionately by labor and capital income, excises on purchases by businesses and customs duties proportionately by labor and capital income, and estate and gift taxes by decedents. The share of the corporate income tax that represents cash flow is assumed to have no burden in the long run; the share of the corporate income tax that represents a tax on supernormal returns is assumed to be borne by supernormal corporate capital income as held by shareholders; and the remainder of the corporate income tax, the normal return, is assumed to be borne equally by labor and positive normal capital income. The denominator for the tax rates is cash income under 2017 current law, including ACA Medicaid expansion.

[4] Transfers (e.g. Medicaid) are treated as negative taxes for calculating total changes. The ACA coverage provisions are expanded Medicaid eligibility, the premium tax credit, cost-sharing reductions, the individual shared responsibility payment, the employer shared responsibility payment, and the small business tax credit. Pre-ACA, after-tax income under 2008 policy is the denominator used for calculating the percentage changes in after-tax income due to the transfer and tax changes.

[5] Families with negative incomes are excluded from the lowest income decile but included in the total line.

Source: Department of the Treasury, Office of Tax Analysis.

CHAPTER 4

REFORMING THE HEALTH CARE SYSTEM

INTRODUCTION

The health care system has profound effects on Americans' lives. Access to high-quality health care contributes to good health, which helps Americans meet obligations to their families, succeed in the workplace and the classroom, and enjoy an overall high quality of life. At the same time, health care is a major expense for families and governments alike, so the health care system's ability to deliver needed care at a reasonable cost is an important determinant of Americans' overall standard of living.

When President Obama took office, he confronted a health care system that was falling short both in ensuring broad access to high-quality care and in providing care at a reasonable cost. These shortcomings were the result of large gaps in our health insurance system and a health care delivery system that too often provided inefficient, low-quality care. Through the Affordable Care Act (ACA) and other legislation enacted under this Administration, as well as accompanying administrative actions, the United States has made considerable progress in addressing these two major problems.

Turning first to the health insurance system, more than one-in-seven Americans—44 million people—lacked health insurance coverage in 2008, the year before the Obama Administration began. Many uninsured individuals were simply unable to afford coverage, while many others were locked out or priced out of the individual health insurance market because they had pre-existing health conditions. Their lack of insurance coverage kept them from being able to obtain the care they needed, and left them vulnerable to financial catastrophe if they became seriously ill. Meanwhile, even many Americans with health insurance faced similar risks due to significant gaps in their coverage.

In his first month in office, President Obama took an initial step toward ensuring that all Americans had access to affordable, high-quality health insurance coverage by signing legislation improving the Children's Health Insurance Program (CHIP). Slightly more than a year later, the President signed the ACA, which reformed the individual health insurance market to ensure that all Americans could find affordable, high-quality coverage, provided generous financial support to states that wished to expand their Medicaid programs to cover more of their low-income residents, and allowed young adults to remain on a parent's plan until age 26. Together, these actions led to a historic expansion in the number of people with health insurance. Because of the coverage provisions of the ACA, an estimated 20 million additional adults now have health insurance. In addition, thanks in large part to the ACA and the improvements to CHIP that the President signed into law, the uninsured rate among children has fallen by almost half since the President took office, providing health insurance to more than 3 million additional children. Following these gains, the uninsured rate stands below 9 percent for the first time ever.

A growing body of evidence demonstrates that broader insurance coverage is generating major benefits for the newly insured and the health care system as a whole. Access to medical care has improved substantially; the share of people reporting that they have recently forgone medical care because they could not afford it has fallen by more than a third since the ACA became law. Expanded coverage has also reduced the burden of medical debt and generated corresponding reductions in the amount of uncompensated care. Nationwide, uncompensated care has fallen by more than a quarter as a share of hospital operating costs from 2013 to 2015, corresponding to a reduction of $10.4 billion. Early evidence also suggests that expanded coverage is driving improvements in health that are consistent with those observed in prior research; if experience under the ACA matches what was observed under Massachusetts health reform, an estimated 24,000 deaths are already being avoided annually. Looking beyond the health care sector, the ACA has also sharply reduced income inequality, and it has achieved this broad range of benefits without the adverse near-term effects on the labor market that the ACA's critics predicted, while also helping to lay the foundation for a stronger labor market over the long term.

The ACA also introduced reforms to improve financial security and access to care for those who were already insured. These reforms are generating important benefits. Because of the law, private insurance plans are generally required to limit enrollees' annual out-of-pocket spending. Due to the spread of out-of-pocket limits since 2010, an estimated 22 million additional people enrolled in employer-sponsored plans are protected against catastrophic costs in 2016. Similarly, because of the ACA's provision phasing out the Medicare Part D coverage gap, more than 11 million Medicare beneficiaries have received cumulative savings on prescription drugs averaging more than $2,100 a person as of the middle of 2016.

Turning next to the health care delivery system, the United States devoted roughly a sixth of its gross domestic product (GDP) to health care when President Obama took office, a far larger share than peer nations. Yet health outcomes in the United States were, at best, no better. At the same time, health care spending and health outcomes varied widely across regions of the United States, with no evidence that higher-spending areas achieved better outcomes. This and other evidence showed that there were major opportunities to reform the health care delivery system in ways that could reduce the burden that health care spending placed on the U.S. economy, while improving health outcomes.

The ACA and related legislation have implemented comprehensive reforms to make the health care delivery system more efficient and improve the quality of care. The ACA achieved significant near-term savings by better aligning payments to medical providers and private insurers in Medicare with the costs of providing services. The law also set in motion a long-term effort to develop and deploy alternative payment models (APMs) that reward providers who deliver efficient, high-quality care, unlike existing fee-for-service payment systems, which base payment chiefly on the quantity of services delivered. Using the tools provided by the ACA, the Administration has made considerable progress in deploying APMs, including accountable care, bundled payment, and medical home models. As of early 2016, more than 30 percent of traditional Medicare payments were estimated to be associated with APMs, up from virtually none in 2010. The tools provided by the ACA, which were enhanced by the bipartisan physician payment reform legislation enacted in 2015, will drive further progress in the years ahead.

Changes in Medicare's payment systems appear to be catalyzing similar changes by private payers. Indeed, at the beginning of 2016, 17 million—or roughly one in ten—private insurance enrollees are estimated to have been covered under payment arrangements similar to the account-able care contracts being deployed in Medicare, up from virtually none as recently as 2011. Similarly, one large survey found that around a quarter of provider payments made by private insurers were associated with APMs in 2015. The Administration has also taken several steps to accelerate the diffusion of APMs in the private sector by directly engaging private payers in payment reform efforts in Medicare and Medicaid, facilitating information sharing across payers, and fostering the development of common standards. The ACA's excise tax on high-cost employer-sponsored coverage, scheduled to take effect in 2020, will provide an additional impetus for private sector plans to engage in payment reform efforts over the coming years.

The six years since the ACA became law have seen very encouraging trends in both health care costs and health care quality. Prices of health care goods and services have grown at a slower rate under the ACA than during any period of the same length since these data began in 1959. Recent years have also seen exceptionally slow growth in per enrollee spending in both public programs and private insurance. In parallel, there have been promising indications that quality of care is improving. The rate at which patients are harmed while seeking hospital care has fallen by 21 percent since 2010, which is estimated to have led to approximately 125,000 avoided deaths cumulatively through 2015. Medicare beneficiaries' risk of returning to the hospital soon after discharge has also declined substantially, corresponding to an estimated 565,000 avoided readmissions from April 2010 through May 2015.

A considerable body of research has aimed to understand the causes of these encouraging trends. The Great Recession does not appear to have been an important driver of the slow growth in health care costs in recent years. The recession had little effect on Medicare spending, and, while the Great Recession did dampen private sector spending growth in the years during and immediately after the downturn, its ability to explain slow growth over the last few years is limited. Similarly, neither demographic changes nor changes in cost sharing appear to explain much of the slow growth in health care costs under the ACA.

It therefore appears that recent years' favorable trends in health care costs and quality primarily reflect structural changes in the health care delivery system. While multiple factors are likely playing a role, payment reforms introduced in the ACA have made substantial, quantifiable contributions to slowing the growth of health care costs in both Medicare and private insurance. Congressional Budget Office (CBO) estimates imply that the ACA has reduced the growth rate of per beneficiary Medicare spending by 1.3 percentage points a year from 2010 through 2016. "Spillover" effects of the ACA's Medicare reforms on the prices that private insurers pay for care have likely subtracted between 0.6 and 0.9 percentage point a year from the growth rate of per enrollee private insurance spending over the same period. Moreover, there is reason to believe that the ACA has had systemic effects on trends in health care costs and quality that go beyond what can be directly quantified.

Recent positive developments in the health care delivery system are generating major benefits to families and the economy. The average premium for people who hold employer-based family coverage was nearly $3,600 lower in 2016 than if premium growth since the ACA became law had matched the preceding decade, savings families will receive directly in the form of lower premium costs and indirectly in the form of higher wages. Far from offsetting the slowdown in premium growth, growth in out-of-pocket costs has slowed as well, and accounting for out-of-pocket costs increases these savings to $4,400 in 2016.

People who get coverage outside the workplace have also realized important savings on premiums and cost sharing. The typical Medicare beneficiary enrolled in traditional Medicare will incur around $700 less in premiums and cost sharing in 2016 than if Medicare spending trends had matched what was projected in 2009 under the policies then in place. This figure does not include reductions in cost sharing on prescription drugs due to the combination of the ACA's provision closing the Medicare Part D coverage gap and slower-than-expected growth in prescription drug spending, so it actually understates the total savings to Medicare beneficiaries.

Because State and Federal governments finance a substantial share of health care spending, slower growth in health care costs has also greatly improved the fiscal outlook. Due in large part to the ACA's provisions slowing the growth of health care costs, CBO projects that the law will reduce deficits by increasing amounts in the years ahead, rising to an average of 1 percent of GDP over the decade starting in 2026. Over the next two decades as a whole, the law is projected to reduce deficits by more than $3 trillion. In addition, since just after the ACA became law, CBO has reduced its projections of Medicare spending under current policies by an additional $125 billion in 2020 or around 0.6 percent of GDP in that year, further improving the fiscal outlook. The combination of the ACA and broader trends in the health care sector have also added 11 years to the life of the Medicare Trust Fund relative to 2009 projections.

The remainder of this chapter provides additional detail on the challenges the United States health care system faced when the President took office, the actions this Administration has taken to meet those challenges, and the progress that has been achieved to date. The first section of this chapter focuses on progress in expanding and improving health insurance coverage, and the second focuses on improvements in the health care delivery system. The final section concludes.

EXPANDING AND IMPROVING HEALTH INSURANCE COVERAGE

Prior to the Obama Administration, the United States last made substantial progress in expanding health insurance coverage in the years after

Medicare and Medicaid were created in 1965, as illustrated in Figure 4-1.[1] Over the decade that followed, the United States uninsured rate fell by more than half, from 24 percent in 1963 to 11 percent in 1974, driven by the ramp-up of Medicare and Medicaid, legislative improvements that expanded those programs to people with serious disabilities, and the continued spread of employer-based health insurance. But progress stalled by the mid-1970s, and the uninsured rate rose steadily through the 1980s before stabilizing in the 1990s. In 2008, the year before President Obama took office, 44 million people—nearly 15 percent of the U.S. population—lacked health insurance.

This section of the chapter reviews the progress that has been made under this Administration in expanding and improving health insurance coverage. The section begins by describing the features of the pre-ACA health insurance landscape that caused so many Americans to go without coverage. It then discusses the actions taken under this Administration to increase health insurance coverage and presents evidence that those actions have been highly effective. It closes by surveying early evidence demonstrating that expanded coverage is improving access to care, health, and financial security for the newly insured, reducing the burden of uncompensated care for the health care system, and reducing income inequality, all without the adverse effects on labor markets that the law's critics predicted.

Barriers to Obtaining Health Insurance Coverage Before the Obama Administration

Prior to the reforms introduced during this Administration, uninsured Americans faced a pair of often-insurmountable barriers to obtaining coverage. The first was the high cost of health insurance, which made coverage unaffordable for many. The second was the dysfunction of the pre-ACA individual health insurance market, which caused many people to be locked out or priced out of the market due to pre-existing health conditions and kept many others from finding high-quality coverage. The role of each of these factors is discussed in greater detail below.

Cost Barriers to Obtaining Health Insurance Coverage

Health insurance has long been one of the most costly products that most families purchase. In 2008, the average premium for a policy offered in the employer market was $4,700 for single coverage and $12,700 for

---

[1] This discussion draws upon the historical health insurance series described in CEA (2014). The series is based primarily on analysis of data from the National Health Interview Survey. The methods described by Cohen et al. (2009) and Cohen (2012) were used to construct a consistent series over time. For 1980 and earlier, data from the NHIS were supplemented with information from other survey data sources and administrative data on enrollment in Medicare and Medicaid.

Figure 4-1

Uninsured Rate, 1963–2016

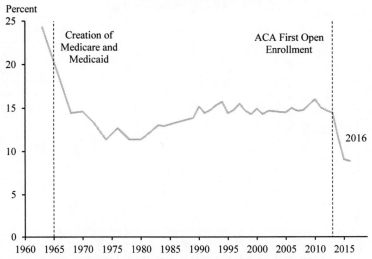

Note: Estimate for 2016 reflects only the first two quarters. Other estimates are full-year.
Source: National Health Interview Survey and supplemental sources described in CEA (2014).

family coverage (KFF/HRET 2016). These amounts would have been a major expense for most families, but they represented a particularly heavy burden for low- and moderate-income families already struggling to meet other basic needs. As illustrated in Figure 4-2, for a family of four with an income below 200 percent of the Federal Poverty Level, the average premium for an employer-sponsored family policy would have consumed 30 percent or more of family income. For a family below the poverty line, it would have consumed 60 percent or more of family income, an essentially insurmountable barrier.[2]

Public policy played an important role in helping families meet these affordability challenges, but the adequacy of these efforts varied widely by age. For people age 65 and older, Medicare had succeeded in achieving nearly universal coverage at all income levels, as illustrated in Panel C of Figure 4-3. But individuals under age 65 were served by a patchwork of programs and incentives that left significant gaps.

For people with access to coverage through an employer, the tax code provided a large implicit subsidy for purchasing coverage. Unlike cash compensation, the compensation employers provide in the form of health

---

[2] Families bore these burdens whether they purchased coverage directly or, as was typically the case, obtained it through an employer. While employers typically pay around three-quarters of the total premium, economic theory and evidence indicate that employees ultimately bear the cost of that subsidy in the form of lower wages and salaries (for example, Summers 1989; Baicker and Chandra 2006).

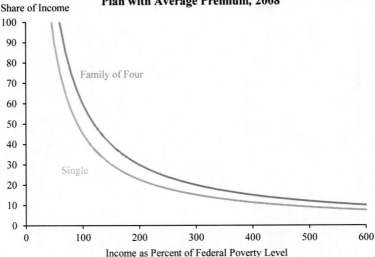

Figure 4-2

Share of Income Required to Purchase Employer-Sponsored Plan with Average Premium, 2008

Share of Income

Family of Four

Single

Income as Percent of Federal Poverty Level

Source: KFF/HRET Employer Health Benefits Survey; CEA calculations.

insurance is excluded from payroll and income taxation. The Federal marginal tax rate on labor income averages around 35 percent, so for each dollar of compensation a family received in the form of health insurance instead of wages, the family saved 35 cents in Federal taxes, reducing the effective cost of that dollar of health insurance coverage to just 65 cents.[3] This favorable tax treatment played a central role in making coverage affordable for many middle- and upper-middle class families.[4]

However, the tax benefit for employer-sponsored coverage was inadequate to make coverage affordable for many low- and moderate-income families. As depicted in Panels A and B of Figure 4-3, the likelihood of having private insurance from any source fell sharply with income. Bipartisan efforts during the 1980s and 1990s had made significant progress in filling these gaps for low- and moderate-income children by broadening eligibility for Medicaid and creating the Children's Health Insurance Program (CHIP).

---

[3] The Federal marginal tax rate reported here was estimated using data from Urban-Brookings Tax Policy Center Tables T13-0253 and T14-0091. States also generally exclude employer-provided health insurance coverage from taxation, so the value of the tax subsidy is somewhat larger than reported here.

[4] While this favorable tax treatment played an important role in making coverage affordable for many families, its unlimited nature also encouraged some employers to offer inefficient and overly generous plans. The ACA introduced a tax reform that maintains this tax benefit, but mitigates the inefficiencies created by its unlimited nature; this reform is discussed in the second half of the chapter.

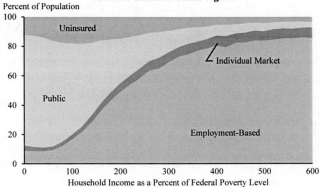

Figure 4-3
Health Insurance Coverage Status by Household Income, 2008
Panel A: Children Under Age 19

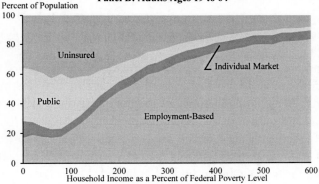

Panel B: Adults Ages 19 to 64

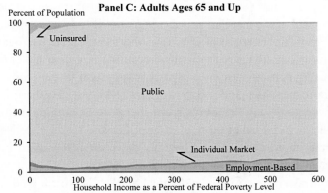

Panel C: Adults Ages 65 and Up

Note: Employment-based coverage is defined as coverage from a current or former employer, including military and VA coverage. Public coverage is defined as Medicare, Medicaid, and other government coverage for people with low-incomes or a disability. Individuals reporting multiple sources of coverage were assigned to a single insurance type using the following hierarchy: Medicare; military health coverage; VA health coverage; Medicaid and other government coverage for people with low-incomes or disabilities; coverage through a current or former employer; and coverage purchased directly from an insurance company. This hierarchy was applied prior to categorizing individuals into the coverage groups described above.
Source: American Community Survey; CEA calculations.

But these efforts left significant gaps even for children. They left even larger gaps for adults. Prior to the ACA, most state Medicaid programs did not cover adults without children, no matter how low their incomes, and the median state only covered working parents with incomes below 61 percent of the Federal Poverty Level (Heberlein, Brooks, and Alker 2013). As a result, low- and moderate-income non-elderly adults were by far the age and income group most likely to lack health insurance, as illustrated in Panel B of Figure 4-3.

Failures of the Individual Health Insurance Market

In addition to the affordability challenges described above, many uninsured Americans faced an additional barrier: the dysfunction of the individual health insurance market. While most non-elderly individuals had access to coverage through an employer, it was far from universal, even at relatively high income levels, as depicted in Figure 4-4. Retirees, many students, the self-employed, people working part-time due to family or other obligations, and the unemployed were all particularly likely to lack access to coverage through the workplace, as were individuals who happened to work at smaller firms or in industries where insurance coverage was not commonly offered. These individuals, if they did not qualify for public programs, had no choice but to turn to the individual market.

The fundamental flaw of the pre-ACA individual health insurance market was that, unlike the employer market, the individual market lacked a mechanism for forming broad pools that included both relatively healthy and relatively sick individuals. The employer market forms broad pools by taking advantage of the fact that people are matched to employers based on a wide variety of factors, many of which are only loosely related to health status. In addition, employers typically cover around three-quarters of the premium, ensuring participation by a broad cross-section of their workforces, including both healthier and sicker workers (KFF/HRET 2016). Insurers offering coverage through employers can therefore be confident that their products will attract a balanced pool of healthier and sicker enrollees. As a result, their economic incentives generally drive them to design products that maximize the well-being of the pool as a whole.

By contrast, insurers in the individual market had to contend with the possibility of "adverse selection," the tendency of people with greater health care needs—and thus higher costs to insurers—to prefer more generous insurance coverage. Insurers' concerns that they would attract an adversely selected pool drove them to engage in a wide range of practices aimed at discouraging enrollment by sicker individuals. These practices kept the individual market from performing the core functions of a health insurance

Figure 4-4

Share of Non-Elderly Individuals With an Offer of Employer-Sponsored Health Insurance in the Family, 2008

Percent with Offer of Employer-Sponsored Health Insurance

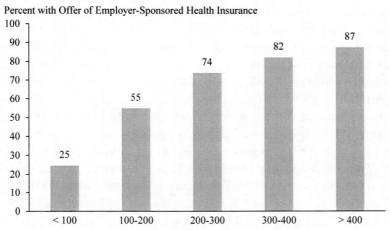

Family Income as Percent of Federal Poverty Level

Source: National Health Interview Survey; CEA calculations.

market: sharing risk between the healthy and the sick; providing robust financial protection against unexpected health shocks; and facilitating access to needed health care.

Most destructively, insurers typically offered coverage on worse terms or not at all to people with pre-existing health conditions, a group estimated to include between 50 million and 129 million non-elderly Americans, depending on the definitions used (ASPE 2011). Before issuing a policy, insurers generally required applicants to submit information about their health history. Individuals with a pre-existing condition might then be charged a higher premium, offered a policy that excluded care related to the condition, or denied coverage entirely. While estimates of the frequency of these practices vary, they were clearly quite common. An industry survey found that 34 percent of individual applicants were charged higher-than-standard rates based on demographic characteristics or medical history (AHIP 2009). Similarly, a report by the Government Accountability Office (2011) estimated that, as of early 2010, the denial rate among individual market applications was 19 percent, and the most common reason for denial was health status. A 2009 survey found that, among adults who had individual market coverage or shopped for it in the previous three years, 36 percent were denied coverage, charged more, or had exclusions placed on their policy due to pre-existing conditions (Doty et al. 2009).

Insurers' desire to discourage enrollment by individuals with significant health care needs also led them to limit coverage in ways that undermined enrollees' access to care and financial security. For example, plans offered on the individual market frequently excluded or charged a high premium for services like maternity care, prescription drugs, and mental health care (Whitmore et al. 2011). One study estimated that, in 2011, 62 percent of individual market enrollees lacked coverage for maternity services, 34 percent lacked coverage for substance abuse services, 18 percent lacked coverage for mental health services, and 9 percent lacked prescription drug coverage (ASPE 2011). Individual market policies also frequently imposed very high cost-sharing requirements or placed annual, lifetime, or other limits on the amount they would cover. Half of individual market enrollees were estimated to be in policies that covered less than 60 percent of their total medical spending (Gabel et al. 2012). Similarly, an estimated 89 percent of those purchasing individual health coverage had a lifetime limit on their benefits (Musco and Sommers 2012).

Reforms to Expand Health Insurance Coverage

The Obama Administration has implemented a series of reforms designed to overcome the barriers described above and ensure that all Americans can access high-quality, affordable health insurance coverage. This work began in February 2009 with the enactment of legislation improving CHIP and continued with the enactment and implementation of the ACA, which made broader reforms to the health insurance system in the United States. These reforms, as well as the evidence that they have dramatically expanded access to health insurance coverage, are described in detail below.

Strengthening the Children's Health Insurance Program

The Children's Health Insurance Program (CHIP) was created in 1997 and provides financial support beyond what is available through the existing Medicaid program to states wishing to cover additional low- and moderate-income children. Research has found that CHIP was highly effective in increasing insurance coverage among children and implies that CHIP was likely the main reason that the uninsured rate among children declined almost without interruption from the late 1990s through the mid-2000s, as

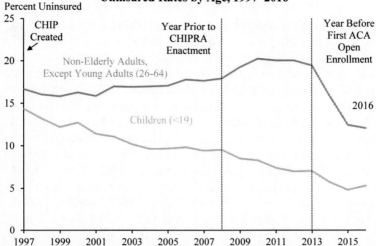

Figure 4-5
Uninsured Rates by Age, 1997–2016

Percent Uninsured

Note: Estimates for 2016 reflect only the first two quarters. See footnote in the main text for additional detail on calculation of the 2016 estimates.
Source: National Health Interview Survey; CEA calculations.

illustrated in Figure 4-5 (Howell and Kenney 2012).[5] Progress stalled after the mid-2000s, however, and 9.5 percent of children still lacked health insurance coverage in 2008.

In February 2009, just weeks after taking office, President Obama signed the Children's Health Insurance Program Reauthorization Act (CHIPRA). CHIPRA aimed to further reduce the uninsured rate among children by making a range of improvements to CHIP. Notably, the law: provided new options for states that wanted to simplify enrollment, improve outreach, or expand eligibility; created financial incentives for states to adopt best practices; and extended the program's funding.

In the years after CHIPRA's enactment, the children's uninsured rate resumed its rapid decline. From 2008 through 2013, the uninsured rate among children declined by around a quarter, equivalent to 1.9 million children gaining coverage. The timing of these gains, combined with the fact that uninsured rates actually rose during this period for adults—likely due to the Great Recession and its aftermath—suggests that policy changes introduced by CHIPRA played an important role in reducing the uninsured

---

[5] Estimates of the uninsured rate for 0-18 year olds have not yet been reported for 2016, so the uninsured rate for 0-18 year olds reported in Figure 4-5 was calculated by extrapolating the 2015 estimate using the percentage point change for 0-17 year olds, which has been reported. Similarly, estimates of the uninsured rate for 26-64 year olds were extrapolated using the percentage point change for the larger group consisting of 18 year olds and 26-64 year olds.

Box 4-1: Public Health Benefits of CHIPRA

In addition to extending and improving CHIP, CHIPRA also raised the Federal cigarette tax from $0.39 per pack to approximately $1.01 per pack. By increasing cigarette prices, cigarette taxes substantially reduce smoking rates and generate large improvements in public health. Research examining the impact of Federal cigarette tax increases on the number of teen or young-adult smokers imply that the 2009 Federal cigarette tax increase will reduce youth smoking by between 3 and 15 percentage points (van Hasselt et al. 2015; Huang and Chaloupka 2012; CBO 2012b; Carpenter and Cook 2008). Assuming that roughly a third of youth smokers die prematurely due to smoking (U.S. Surgeon General 2014), these estimates suggest that the 2009 cigarette tax increase plausibly reduced the number of premature deaths due to smoking in each cohort by between 15,000 and 70,000, as illustrated in Figure 4-i.

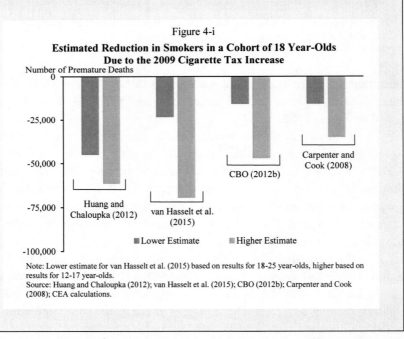

Figure 4-i
Estimated Reduction in Smokers in a Cohort of 18 Year-Olds Due to the 2009 Cigarette Tax Increase

Note: Lower estimate for van Hasselt et al. (2015) based on results for 18-25 year-olds, higher based on results for 12-17 year-olds.
Source: Huang and Chaloupka (2012); van Hasselt et al. (2015); CBO (2012b); Carpenter and Cook (2008); CEA calculations.

rate among children.[6] Consistent with this time-series evidence, research examining specific changes in state CHIP and Medicaid programs enabled by CHIPRA has concluded these changes were effective in expanding coverage for children (Blavin, Kenney, and Huntress 2014; Goldstein et al. 2014).

---

[6] Figure 4-5 uses adults ages 26-64 (rather than all non-elderly adults) as a comparison group in order to exclude any effects of the Affordable Care Act's dependent coverage expansion, which took effect in late 2010. That coverage expansion is discussed in greater detail below.

Legislative actions subsequent to CHIPRA have ensured that CHIP can continue to be a source of affordable coverage for low- and moderate-income children. The ACA extended funding for CHIP through fiscal year 2015 and increased the share of CHIP costs paid by the Federal Government, making the program even more financially attractive for states. In 2015, the Medicare Access and CHIP Reauthorization Act (MACRA) extended funding for CHIP, as well as many of the policy improvements introduced in CHIPRA and the ACA, through fiscal year 2017.

Expanding Access to Coverage for Young Adults

The ACA's comprehensive reforms to ensure access to health insurance coverage are described below, but the law also included a targeted provision to reduce the particularly high uninsured rate among young adults, which is illustrated in Figure 4-6. Young adults' uninsured rates exceeded those for older adults for a number of reasons. Because many young adults are still in school, and those who have already joined the labor force are less likely to be offered health insurance through work, they were much less likely to have employer coverage. They also were much less likely to have Medicaid coverage than children, reflecting the stricter eligibility rules that apply to adults.

To address the unique challenges faced by young adults, the ACA required private insurance plans to allow young adults to remain on a parent's policy until age 26. Immediately after this policy took effect during September 2010, the uninsured rate among young adults ages 19-25 started declining rapidly, as shown in Figure 4-7.[7] The uninsured rate fell from 34.1 percent in the four quarters ended in September 2010 to 26.7 percent in the four quarters of 2013, just before the ACA's broader coverage provisions took effect. The timing of this decline, combined with the fact that the uninsured rate for older non-elderly adults was essentially flat during this period is strong evidence that the decline was caused by the ACA provision.

On the basis of these data, the U.S. Department of Health and Human Services (HHS) estimates that 2.3 million young adults gained coverage because of this provision (ASPE 2015). The broader academic literature has also concluded that the provision generated substantial gains in young adult coverage, though estimates vary across studies, with some reporting estimates higher than ASPE's and others reporting lower estimates (Cantor et al. 2012; Antwi, Moriya, and Simon 2013; Porterfield and Huang 2016).

---

[7] The estimates of the uninsured rate for 26-64 year olds reported in Figure 4-7 were derived using the same approach described in footnote 5.

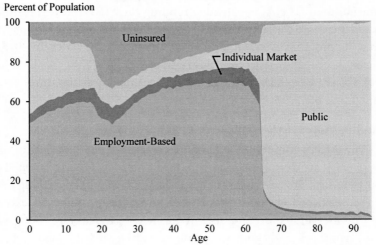

Figure 4-6
Health Insurance Coverage Status by Age, 2008

Percent of Population

Note: Individuals were categorized into coverage groupings using the procedure described in the note to Figure 4-3.
Source: American Community Survey; CEA calculations.

Comprehensive Coverage Expansions

Starting in 2014, the ACA implemented broad-based coverage expansions designed to ensure that all Americans could access affordable, high-quality health insurance coverage. These expansions consisted of two main pieces: an expansion of eligibility for Medicaid coverage and comprehensive reforms to the individual health insurance market. Each of these reforms is described in greater detail below.

To provide affordable coverage options for the lowest-income Americans, the ACA provided states with generous financial assistance to expand Medicaid coverage to all non-elderly people with incomes below 138 percent of the Federal Poverty Level (FPL), around $16,200 for an individual and $33,500 for a family of four in 2016.[8] As specified in the ACA, the Federal Government has funded 100 percent of the cost for newly eligible individuals to date, and this share gradually phases down to 90 percent in 2020 and subsequent years. This generous matching rate makes expanding Medicaid a very attractive proposition for states, particularly since research has generally concluded that states that expand Medicaid realize significant

---

[8] The base income eligibility threshold is 133 percent of the FPL. However, Medicaid program rules provide for an additional "income disregard" of 5 percent of income, which brings the effective eligibility threshold to 138 percent of the FPL. The dollar amounts reported in the text reflect the 2015 version of the FPL because those are the amounts used to determine eligibility for coverage during 2016.

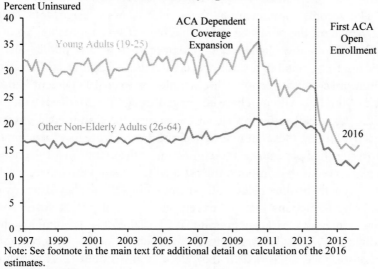

Figure 4-7
Uninsured Rates by Age, 1997–2016

Percent Uninsured

Note: See footnote in the main text for additional detail on calculation of the 2016 estimates.
Source: National Health Interview Survey; CEA calculations.

offsetting savings elsewhere in their budgets, including in existing portions of their Medicaid programs, in programs that defray the costs of uncompensated care, and in programs that provide mental health services (Buettgens, Dorn, and Carroll 2011; Dorn, McGrath, and Holahan 2014). To date, 31 states and the District of Columbia have expanded Medicaid under the ACA.

For Americans with incomes too high to qualify for Medicaid, the ACA implemented an interlocking set of reforms in the individual health insurance market. The first component of these reforms was a new set of consumer protections that guaranteed access to high-quality health insurance coverage. Most importantly, to ensure that both healthy and sick individuals could access coverage, the law required insurers to offer coverage on common terms to all enrollees, regardless of whether they had pre-existing health conditions, with premiums allowed to vary based solely on age, geography, and tobacco use. In order to ensure that the coverage available on the reformed market offered real access to medical care and financial protection, the law required all plans to cover a set of essential health benefits and provide a basic level of protection against out-of-pocket costs. As a complement to these reforms, the law created a risk adjustment program that compensates insurers that attract a sicker-than-average group of enrollees, thereby ensuring that insurers have incentives to design plans that meet the needs of all types of consumers, both healthy and sick. Finally, to foster competition, the law created the Health Insurance Marketplaces

(Marketplaces), web-based markets that help consumers comparison shop to find a plan that matches their particular preferences and needs.

The second component of these reforms was designed to ensure that coverage on the reformed individual market was affordable. To overcome the affordability challenges that kept many low- and middle-income Americans from obtaining coverage before the ACA, the law created a premium tax credit for people with incomes between 100 percent and 400 percent of the FPL who purchase coverage through the Marketplaces.[9] The premium tax credit ensures that all consumers have affordable coverage options by limiting the amount enrollees must contribute to a "benchmark" plan to a specified percentage of their income; if the premium for the benchmark plan exceeds that amount, the tax credit makes up the difference. For individuals with incomes below 250 percent of the FPL, the law also provides cost-sharing reductions that reduce enrollees' out-of-pocket costs. As an additional measure to keep premiums affordable, the law implemented an individual responsibility provision that requires people who can afford coverage to make a payment if they elect to go without it. This requirement encourages healthy individuals to enroll in coverage, which protects the individual market's ability to pool risk between the healthy and the sick, thereby helping keep premiums affordable; indeed, the Congressional Budget Office has estimated that individual market premiums would be around 20 percent higher in the absence of this provision (CBO 2015b). The provision also discourages individuals from shifting their health care costs to others in the form of uncompensated care.

The U.S. uninsured rate has declined dramatically since these reforms took effect at the beginning of 2014, falling from 14.5 percent in 2013 to 8.9 percent in the first half of 2016, as illustrated in Figure 4-1. The decline in the uninsured rate seen over this period is, by far, the largest decline since the years following the creation of Medicare and Medicaid in 1965. Consistent with the nearly unprecedented magnitude of this decline, research aimed at isolating the effect of the ACA from other trends in the health care system or the economy has concluded that the overwhelming majority of these gains are directly attributable to the ACA's reforms (Courtemanche et al. 2016; Blumberg, Garrett, and Holahan 2016). Using a methodology that controls for unrelated economic and demographic changes, HHS estimates that 17.7 million non-elderly adults have gained coverage since the end of 2013 because of the ACA's comprehensive reforms (Uberoi, Finegold, and Gee 2016). Combining these gains since 2013 with the gains for young adults

---

[9] In states that have expanded Medicaid, people with incomes between 100 and 138 percent of the FPL receive coverage through Medicaid. In non-expansion states, these people are generally eligible for subsidized coverage through the Marketplace.

because of the ACA's provision allowing young adults to remain on a parent's plan until age 26, an estimated 20 million adults have gained coverage because of the ACA.

The ACA's main coverage provisions have also driven further coverage gains among children, which are not captured in the data from the Gallup-Healthways Well-Being Index used by Uberoi, Finegold, and Gee (2016). As illustrated in Figure 4-5 above, the uninsured rate among children has seen another sharp decline as the ACA's major coverage expansions have taken effect, equivalent to an additional 1.2 million children gaining coverage.[10] Combining the gains that began in 2014 with the gains in children's coverage from 2008 through 2013 that were discussed above, an additional 3.1 million children have coverage in 2016 because of the decline in the uninsured rate among children since 2008.

Both the law's Medicaid expansion and its reforms to the individual health insurance market are contributing to this major expansion in health insurance coverage. To illustrate this, Figure 4-8 reports the decline in the uninsured rate from 2013 to 2015 by state in relation to that state's uninsured rate in 2013. While every state in the country has seen a decline in its uninsured rate since 2013, states that have taken advantage of the law's Medicaid expansion have seen markedly larger declines, with the largest declines in those states that both took up Medicaid and had high uninsured rates before the ACA's reforms took effect. However, even those states that have not taken up Medicaid expansion have made considerable progress in reducing the uninsured rate, indicating that the law's reforms to the individual health insurance market are also working to expand insurance coverage.

The pattern of coverage gains by income provides additional evidence that the law's reforms to the individual health insurance market are contributing to coverage gains, alongside Medicaid expansion. In particular, Figure 4-9 shows that the uninsured rate has declined markedly among individuals with incomes above the Medicaid eligibility threshold of 138 percent of the FPL, and these declines are similar in proportional terms to those for individuals with incomes below 138 percent of the FPL. Notably, declines have been seen both for people with incomes between 138 percent and 400 percent of the FPL, who are generally eligible for financial assistance

---

[10] The 1.2 million figure cited here reflects coverage gains for individuals ages 0 to 17 from 2013 through the first half of 2016, as reported in the National Health Interview Survey. The data reported in Figure 4-5 include individuals ages 0 to 18 because 18-year-olds are considered children for Medicaid and CHIP eligibility purposes, making this the most appropriate age range to examine when discussing CHIPRA. By contrast, 18-year-olds are already included in the estimate reported by Uberoi, Finegold, and Gee (2016) regarding the effects of the ACA, so including 18-year-olds in this estimate would double-count post-2013 gains for 18-year-olds.

Figure 4-8
**Decline in Uninsured Rate from 2013 to 2015
vs. Level of Uninsured Rate in 2013, by State**

Decline in Uninsured Rate, 2013–2015 (Percentage Points)

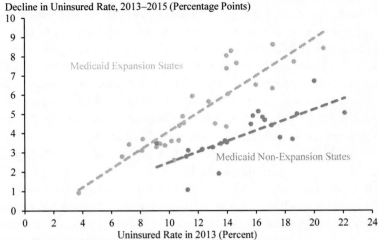

Uninsured Rate in 2013 (Percent)

Note: States are classified by Medicaid expansion status as of July 1, 2015.
Source: American Community Survey; CEA calculations.

Figure 4-9
Nonelderly Uninsured Rate by Income, 2013 and 2015

Percent Uninsured

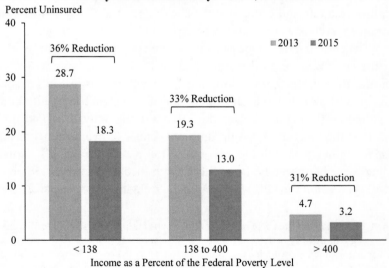

Income as a Percent of the Federal Poverty Level

Source: National Health Interview Survey; CEA calculations.

Box 4-2: Dynamics in the Individual Health Insurance Market

After two years of moderate premium growth for plans offered through the Health Insurance Marketplace, premiums are increasing at a faster pace for 2017, though experience will vary widely across states (ASPE 2016b). This box discusses the factors that are driving changes in Marketplace premiums in 2017, as well as their implications for the future of the individual market. Contrary to some recent claims, a range of evidence demonstrates that this year's premium changes are part of the ordinary process of adjustment in a new market, not a harbinger of future market instability.

Factors Driving 2017 Premium Changes

Insurers faced significant challenges in setting premiums in the years immediately following implementation of the ACA's reforms to the individual market. The ACA brought many new people into the individual market, including people with pre-existing health conditions who had previously been locked out of the market and people who could newly afford coverage because of the law's financial assistance. These major changes made predicting average medical costs in the reformed market difficult. This in turn created a significant risk that insurers would underestimate or overestimate the level of premiums required to finance those claims. In addition, some insurers may have intentionally underpriced when setting premiums in an attempt to attract the many new consumers who have entered the individual health insurance market during its first few years, accepting losses in the short run in exchange for higher market shares in the long run.

It is now clear that, on average, insurers underpriced in the early years of the new market. Insurers are estimated to have incurred losses of around 5 percent of premium revenue on ACA-compliant health insurance policies in 2014, the market's first year (McKinsey 2016). To achieve sustainable pricing in subsequent years, insurers needed to make up for these initial losses while also accommodating two additional factors. The first was the ordinary upward trend in medical costs, which averaged around 4 percent a year, though, as discussed below, this has likely been partially offset by ongoing improvements in the ACA-compliant risk pool relative to 2014. The second was the scheduled phasedown of the ACA's transitional reinsurance program, which defrayed a portion of insurers' claims spending on high-cost enrollees in 2014 through 2016. The decline in payments from this program added around 7 percent to premium growth in each of 2015, 2016, and 2017. The net effect of these various factors is that returning premiums to a sustainable level by 2017 likely required premium increases averaging a bit more than 10 percent per year in 2015, 2016, and 2017. But the premium for the second-lowest silver (or "benchmark") plan increased by just 2 percent in 2015 and 7 percent in 2016 in the states using the HealthCare.gov enrollment platform, necessitating much more significant adjustments in 2017.

The pattern of premium changes across areas strongly supports the view that Marketplace premium changes are being driven in substantial part by insurers' efforts to bring premiums in line with costs after having initially underpriced. Figure 4-ii illustrates how the annual percentage increase in the premium for the benchmark plan from 2014 to 2017 varies based on the level of the benchmark premium in 2014. In the four-fifths of the country with higher benchmark premiums in 2014, the median person has seen average annual increases in the benchmark of below 10 percent, less than what would have been needed to cover normal increases in medical costs and the gradual phasedown of the ACA's transitional reinsurance program. By contrast, the fifth of the country that had the lowest premiums in 2014 has seen much larger increases since then. This pattern is what would have been expected if insurers in some areas significantly underpriced in 2014 and have been working to bring premiums back in line with costs since then, while insurers in other areas priced appropriately or overpriced.

It is also important to note that, even after the increases seen for 2017, Marketplace premiums remain roughly in line with CBO's initial projections (ASPE 2016b). The average benchmark premium for 2014 was about 15 percent *below* what the Congressional Budget Office had

Figure 4-ii

Average Annual Change in Benchmark Premium, by Quintile of 2014 Benchmark Premium, 2014–2017

Average Annual Percent Change in Benchmark Premium, 2014–2017

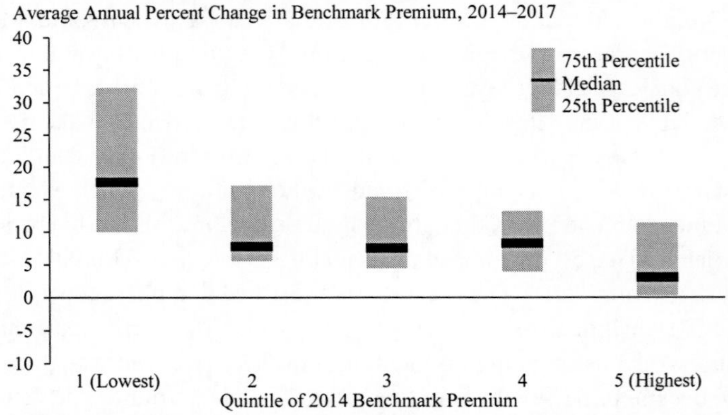

Note: Premiums analyzed at the county level. Quintiles defined to have equal non-elderly populations. Data limited to states using HealthCare.gov in all years.
Source: Department of Health and Human Services; American Community Survey; CEA calculations.

projected during the debate over the ACA (CBO 2014), and analysts have estimated that premiums remained between 12 percent and 20 percent below CBO's initial projections in 2016, depending on the methodology used (Levitt, Cox, and Claxton 2016; Adler and Ginsburg 2016). The 2017 increases are therefore taking Marketplace premiums back to their originally expected trajectory, consistent with the view that these increases are a one-time correction, not an indication of underlying problems in the individual market.

Implications of 2017 Premium Changes for the Future of the Individual Market

By bringing insurers' premium revenue back in line with their claims costs, the premium increases being implemented for 2017 help create the conditions for a more stable market in the years ahead. However, some analysts and commentators have taken a more negative view. They argue that premium increases will drive large reductions in individual market enrollment, particularly among healthy individuals. This decline in enrollment among the healthy, they argue, will increase average medical costs in the individual market, triggering further premium increases and enrollment reductions. Some observers have even speculated this feedback loop between higher premiums and falling enrollment will become so intense that it will cause a "death spiral," a scenario in which enrollment in the individual market ultimately falls nearly to zero. Some of these observers have further suggested that the premium increases seen for 2017 are evidence that this type of vicious cycle has already begun.

In fact, there is no evidence that a death spiral is underway. The defining feature of a death spiral is declining enrollment, particularly among the healthy, resulting in a deteriorating risk pool. In fact, the exact opposite is occurring. Marketplace enrollment has grown every year since the Marketplace opened in 2014, and enrollment in the individual market as a whole was estimated to be around 18 million in early 2016, up from around 11 million in 2013 (ASPE 2016a). Furthermore, it appears that the average individual market enrollee is actually getting *healthier* over time. Using data on medical spending in the individual market submitted by insurers as part of the ACA's transitional reinsurance program, the Centers for Medicare and Medicaid Services (CMS) estimate that nominal per member per month medical spending fell slightly from 2014 to 2015, and an outside analysis of a private claims database supports a similar conclusion (CMS 2016a; Avalere Health 2016). Due to the underlying upward trend in medical costs, per member per month spending would have been expected to increase if the average health status of individual market enrollees had held steady, so these data suggest that the average health status improved from 2014 to 2015.

Looking to the future, the design of the ACA's premium tax credit ensures that a death spiral can never occur in this market. The tax credit is designed so that an individual's contribution to the benchmark plan is capped at a specified percentage of income; the tax credit pays the remainder of the premium. Figure 4-iii provides a concrete example of how this works for a single person making $25,000 per year. This individual's required contribution to the benchmark plan is $143 a month in 2017. If the premium for the benchmark plan in the individual's area were $243 a month, the tax credit would then pay the remaining $100 per month, as illustrated in the left column of the Figure. If the premium for the benchmark plan were $50 a month higher, as in the right column of the Figure, the individual's contribution would remain at $143 a month, and the tax credit would increase to $150 a month. Thus, the individual is fully protected from the higher benchmark premium. Importantly, even individuals who qualify for only modest premium tax credits benefit from this protection since their required contribution, though larger, also does not depend upon the actual level of premiums.

Around 85 percent of individuals who get coverage through the Marketplace receive the premium tax credit, and about two-thirds of people in the individual market as a whole are eligible for tax credits (ASPE 2016a). The premium tax credit therefore ensures that the over-

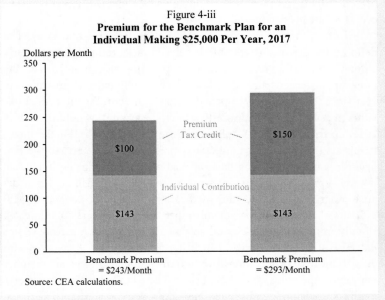

Figure 4-iii
**Premium for the Benchmark Plan for an
Individual Making $25,000 Per Year, 2017**

Source: CEA calculations.

whelming majority of Marketplace enrollees and the sizeable majority of individuals in the individual market overall are protected against premium increases and have no reason to leave the market when premiums rise. That, in turn, stabilizes the overall individual market risk pool and helps keep premiums affordable for people who are not eligible for tax credits. The result is that any negative effects of higher premiums on enrollment and the risk pool will be greatly attenuated, arresting the feedback loop of falling enrollment and higher premiums that would cause the market to unravel.

Consumers' actual behavior under the ACA to date provides no support for the view that premium increases will trigger significant market unraveling. Panel A of Figure 4-iv examines the relationship between changes in the average benchmark premium in each state from 2014 to 2015 and the corresponding changes in enrollment in the state's ACA-compliant individual market (including both on- and off-Marketplace enrollment). For there to be any risk of a death spiral, premium changes would need to have very large negative effects on enrollment, akin to the scenario illustrated by the orange dashed line. In fact, there was essentially no difference in enrollment growth across areas experiencing larger and smaller increases in the benchmark premium from to 2014 to 2015, as illustrated by the green dashed line.

Similarly, Panel B of Figure 4-iv examines the relationship between the change in the benchmark premium in each state from 2014 to 2015 and the change in average claims costs in the ACA-compliant market in that state. For there to be any risk of a death spiral, increases in premiums would have to result in substantial increases in claims costs (as a result of healthy individuals leaving the market), akin to the relationship between premium and cost changes illustrated by the orange dashed line. In fact, consistent with the evidence from Panel A that premium increases did not meaningfully affect enrollment, there is no evidence that premium increases adversely affected the risk pool. If anything, larger premium increases appeared to be associated with slightly *slower* year-over-year growth in monthly claims costs, as illustrated by the green dashed line.

Complete data on how enrollment and claims in the ACA-compliant individual market changed from 2015 to 2016 are not yet available. However, the county-level relationship between changes in benchmark premiums and changes in the number of people selecting Marketplace plans, depicted in Figure 4-v, reinforces the conclusion that the individual market is at no risk of unraveling. As above, for the individual market to be at risk of a death spiral, counties experiencing larger increases in the benchmark premium would have to see much smaller growth in plan selections, akin to the scenario illustrated by the

Figure 4-iv
Change in Benchmark Premium vs. Change in Individual Market Enrollment and Claims Costs, by State, 2014–2015

Panel A: Enrollment

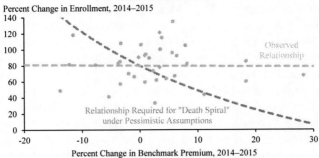

Percent Change in Enrollment, 2014–2015

Observed Relationship

Relationship Required for "Death Spiral" under Pessimistic Assumptions

Percent Change in Benchmark Premium, 2014–2015

Panel B: Monthly Claims Cost

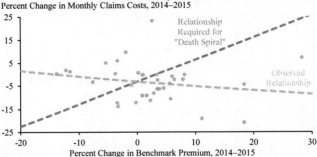

Percent Change in Monthly Claims Costs, 2014–2015

Relationship Required for "Death Spiral"

Observed Relationship

Percent Change in Benchmark Premium, 2014–2015

Note: Sample is limited to States that used HealthCare.gov in all years due to availability of data on benchmark premiums. Changes in benchmark premiums are calculated on a population-weighted basis. Enrollment and monthly claims spending for the ACA-compliant market are measured using data submitted to CMS for the risk adjustment and reinsurance programs. Enrollment is measured as the number of member months of enrollment during the year. Monthly claims spending is measured as aggregate claims in the State's individual market divided by the aggregate number of member months of enrollment. Observed relationships use a simple log-log fit. The "Relationship Required for 'Death Spiral'" lines use the same intercept coefficient estimated for the "Observed Relationship" lines, but different slope coefficients. In Panel A, the "Relationship Required for 'Death Spiral'" line reflects a slope coefficient of -2; for a demand elasticity of -2 to allow a death spiral, individuals who leave the market in response to higher premiums would need to have claims costs half as large as individuals who remain enrolled, a relatively extreme scenario. In Panel B, the "Relationship Required for 'Death Spiral'" line depicts a slope coefficient of 1, which is sufficient to ensure that additional revenue from higher premiums is fully offset by higher claims costs.
Source: Centers for Medicare and Medicaid Services; Department of Health and Human Services; Census Bureau; CEA calculations.

orange dashed line. To the contrary, counties that saw larger increases in the benchmark premium from 2015 to 2016 actually seem to have seen slightly *larger* increases in Marketplace plan selections over that period. Notably, while average premium increases were lower in 2016 than 2017, some counties saw rate increases of 30 percent or more in 2016, and even these counties show no clear evidence of slower enrollment growth.

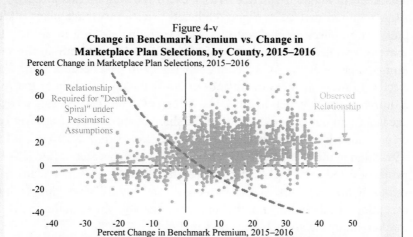

Figure 4-v
**Change in Benchmark Premium vs. Change in
Marketplace Plan Selections, by County, 2015–2016**

Note: Observed relationship reflects a simple log-log fit. The "Relationship Required for 'Death Spiral'" lines uses the same intercept coefficient estimated for the "Observed Relationship" line, but a slope coefficient of -2. For a demand elasticity of -2 to allow a death spiral, individuals who leave the market in response to higher premiums would need to have claims costs half as large as individuals who remain enrolled, a relatively extreme assumption.
Source: Centers for Medicare and Medicaid Services; Department of Health and Human Services; Census Bureau; CEA calculations.

to purchase Marketplace coverage, and people above 400 percent of the FPL, who are not eligible for financial assistance. The substantial coverage gains among the higher-income group, individuals who are not eligible for financial assistance through the Marketplaces, indicates that the combination of the ACA's consumer protections guaranteeing access to coverage and its individual responsibility requirement are also proving effective in increasing health insurance coverage.

Improvements in Existing Health Insurance Coverage

In addition to implementing reforms that have greatly increased the number of people with health insurance coverage, the ACA has also implemented reforms that are improving insurance coverage for people who were already insured, including people covered through an employer or through Medicare. Because of these reforms, tens of millions more Americans are now better protected against catastrophic out-of-pocket costs in the event of serious illness and have greater access to needed medical care.

One such set of reforms is ensuring that all private insurance plans provide real protection against catastrophic costs. When the ACA became law in 2010, 18 percent of workers enrolled in single coverage through an employer were exposed to potentially unlimited out-of-pocket spending, as illustrated in Figure 4-10 (KFF/HRET 2016). To address this problem, the ACA required that all non-grandfathered private insurance plans place a limit on enrollees' annual out-of-pocket spending starting in 2014.[11] The share of enrollees lacking an out-of-pocket limit fell modestly in the years immediately after the ACA became law (likely in part because some firms elected to make changes in advance of 2014) then fell sharply as the ACA requirement took effect. In 2016, just 2 percent of enrollees in single coverage lacked an out-of-pocket limit. If the share of enrollees in employer coverage who lack an out-of-pocket limit had remained at its 2010 level, at least 22 million additional people enrolled in employer coverage would lack this protection today.[12] The ACA also prohibits private insurance plans from imposing lifetime limits on the amount of care they will cover and, with the exception of a dwindling number of grandfathered policies in the individual market, imposing annual limits on benefits.

The ACA also strengthened protections against high out-of-pocket costs in Medicare Part D, the portion of Medicare that provides prescription drug coverage. The original Medicare Part D benefit design included a gap in coverage, commonly referred to as the "donut hole." Because of the coverage gap, Medicare beneficiaries spending more than about $2,700 on prescriptions in 2009 were required to pay the next roughly $3,500 entirely out of pocket. The ACA is phasing out the coverage gap and will close it entirely by 2020. In 2015, the most recent full year for which data are available, 5.2 million Medicare beneficiaries with high drug costs saved $5.4 billion, an average of more than $1,000 per affected beneficiary (CMS 2016d). Cumulatively through July 2016, more than 11 million beneficiaries have saved $23.5 billion, an average savings of more than $2,100 per beneficiary (CMS 2016b).

Another set of ACA reforms sought to encourage greater use of preventive services. Research prior to the ACA had documented that many preventive services—such as blood pressure screenings, mammograms, and colonoscopies—were seriously underutilized, despite strong evidence of their effectiveness (McGlynn et al. 2003; Commonwealth Fund 2008).

---

[11] The ACA specified that certain insurance policies in place prior to the law's enactment would be "grandfathered" and thus not subject to some of the insurance reforms implemented under the law. The number of grandfathered policies has fallen steadily over time (KFF/HRET 2016).

[12] Trends for those enrolled in family coverage are similar to those reported for single coverage in Figure 4-10. In 2010, 17 percent of family coverage enrollees lacked an out-of-pocket limit, and the decline in this percentage almost exactly paralleled the decline for single coverage through 2014; estimates for family coverage have not been reported for years after 2014. To be conservative, the 22 million estimate presented in the text assumes that the overall share of enrollees lacking an out-of-pocket limit declined from 17 percent in 2010 to 2 percent in 2016. It assumes that 150 million people were enrolled in employer coverage in 2016, consistent with KFF/HRET (2016).

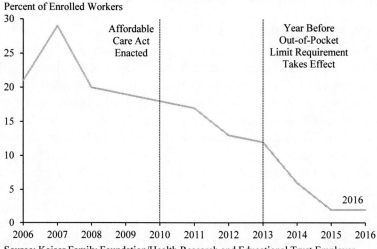

Figure 4-10
**Share of Workers in Single Coverage
Without an Out-of-Pocket Limit, 2006–2016**

Percent of Enrolled Workers

Affordable
Care Act
Enacted

Year Before
Out-of-Pocket
Limit Requirement
Takes Effect

2016

Source: Kaiser Family Foundation/Health Research and Educational Trust Employer
Health Benefits Survey.

To encourage greater utilization, the ACA required that private insurance plans and Medicare cover preventive services that are recommended by the United States Preventive Services Task Force without cost sharing. While the research literature examining the effects of this provision is still limited, one recent study examined plans that implemented this provision at different times and concluded that eliminating cost sharing had the expected effect of increasing use of the service studied, in this case contraception (Carlin, Fertig, and Dowd 2016).

Economic Consequences of Broader Health Insurance Coverage

The historic expansion in insurance coverage described in the last section is still very new, so research to evaluate its consequences is just beginning. Early evidence shows, however, that recent coverage gains are already generating major benefits similar to those documented in prior research on the effects of health insurance coverage. This evidence demonstrates that the law has already succeeded in improving access to care, health, and financial security for the newly insured and in reducing the burden of uncompensated care for the health care system as a whole. Looking beyond the health care sector, the law is helping to reduce income inequality, and it is achieving this broad range of benefits without the negative near-term effects on the labor market that many of the law's critics had predicted, while laying the foundation for a stronger labor market over the long term. This subsection of the chapter reviews this evidence base, with a particular focus on the effects of the major coverage provisions of the Affordable Care Act that took effect at the start of 2014.

Improved Access to Care

One objective of expanding insurance coverage is to ensure that individuals can access needed health care.[13] Research examining prior coverage expansions leaves little doubt that expanding insurance coverage is an effective tool for increasing access to care. For example, the Oregon Health Insurance Experiment, a randomized-controlled trial of expanding Medicaid coverage to low-income adults, found that Medicaid increased receipt of health care services, including preventive services, prescription medications, and physician visits (Baicker et al. 2013). Studies in many other contexts, including the RAND Health Insurance Experiment (Newhouse et al. 1993), studies of past Medicaid expansions targeting adults (Sommers, Baicker, and Epstein 2012) and children (Howell and Kenney 2012), studies of the effect of gaining Medicare eligibility at age 65 (McWilliams et al. 2007; Card, Dobkin, and Maestas 2009), and studies of Massachusetts health reform (Van der Wees, Zaslavsky, and Ayanian 2013; Sommers, Long, and Baicker 2014), have similarly concluded that having health insurance or having more generous health insurance enhances individuals' ability to obtain care.

A range of evidence demonstrates that recent coverage expansions are having similar effects on individuals' ability to access care. One important measure of individuals' ability to access care is the share of people reporting that they failed to obtain needed medical care due to cost during the last 12 months. As illustrated in Figure 4-11, this share rose by more than 50

---

[13] While many non-economists consider it a self-evidently good thing when expanded insurance coverage increases use of health care, a long-standing strand of economic research emphasizes the possibility that health insurance will drive overconsumption of health care by insulating enrollees from the cost of services, a phenomenon referred to as "moral hazard" (Pauly 1968). For several reasons, however, moral hazard is not the appropriate analytic lens for considering increases in the use of health care that arise from a coverage expansion. First, health insurance can increase the use of health care services by increasing the resources that individuals have available to them when seriously ill, thereby allowing them to access very expensive, but cost-effective treatments (Nyman 1999); these types of increases in use of care do not represent overconsumption. Second, in light of evidence that many effective services are persistently underused, increases in the use of care that result from reducing the cost of accessing care may, in some cases, reflect a reduction in underconsumption rather than a shift toward overconsumption (Baicker, Mullainathan, and Schwartzstein 2015). Third, the standard moral hazard analysis defines care as excessive if the individual would prefer to receive a cash payment equal to the cost of the care in lieu of that care. Because low- and moderate-income families face serious constraints on their budgets, they will often prefer a cash payment even to highly effective health care services, so care that is judged excessive by the moral hazard definition may still be quite valuable when judged using a broader social perspective.

percent during the decade preceding the ACA's passage, with particularly sharp increases coinciding with the onset of the Great Recession. By contrast, since 2010, the overall share of individuals reporting these types of affordability problems has declined by more than a third, returning to levels last seen 15 years ago.

The recovery from the Great Recession has likely played some role in reducing cost barriers to accessing care, as increased employment and rising wages have reduced financial stress on families. However, the fact that this measure is now so far below its pre-recession trend, combined with the particularly sharp declines seen after 2013, strongly suggests that recent coverage expansions are playing an important role. Consistent with that interpretation, Figure 4-12 looks across states and demonstrates that states experiencing larger reductions in their uninsured rates from 2013 to 2015 experienced larger reductions in the share of individuals reporting difficulty accessing care due to cost. State-level data show that larger coverage gains are also strongly associated with increases in the share of individuals with a personal doctor and the share of individuals with a checkup in the last 12 months, as shown in Figure 4-13.

Researchers using other survey data sources have documented similar sharp improvements in access to care as the ACA's coverage provisions have taken effect. For example, examining data through March 2015, Shartzer, Long, and Anderson (2016) report that the share of non-elderly adults with a usual source of care and the share who received a routine checkup in the last 12 months has risen alongside insurance coverage, while the share reporting problems accessing care or forgoing care due to cost has fallen. Examining a similar time period, Sommers et al. (2015) report reductions in the share of non-elderly adults reporting that they lack easy access to medicine, lack a personal physician, or are unable to afford care. As with the trends reported in Figure 4-12 and Figure 4-13, the pattern of the access gains reported in these studies is consistent with their having been caused by the ACA's coverage expansion. Both studies cited above, as well as Simon, Soni, and Cawley (2016) and Wherry and Miller (2016), document that gains in access to care have been largest in states that expanded their Medicaid programs. Similarly, Shartzer, Long, and Anderson (2016) find that low- and moderate-income adults, who saw the largest coverage gains, also saw the largest improvements in access to care.

Better Health Outcomes

The ultimate goal of expanding access to health care services is improving health. Research examining prior coverage expansions that targeted populations similar to those targeted under the ACA provides a basis

Figure 4-11

**Share of Population Not Receiving Needed Medical Care
Due to Cost in the Last 12 Months, 1997–2015**

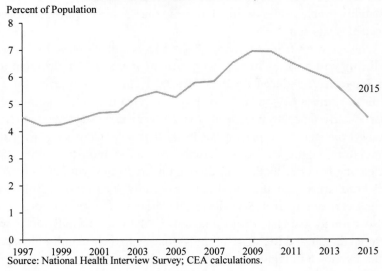

Percent of Population

2015

Source: National Health Interview Survey; CEA calculations.

Figure 4-12

**Decline in Share Not Seeing a Doctor Due to Cost vs.
Decline in Uninsured Rate, by State, 2013–2015**

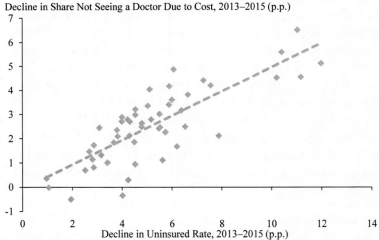

Decline in Share Not Seeing a Doctor Due to Cost, 2013–2015 (p.p.)

Decline in Uninsured Rate, 2013–2015 (p.p.)

Note: Sample limited to non-elderly adults. Percentage points denoted p.p.
Source: Behavioral Risk Factor Surveillance System; CEA calculations.

Figure 4-13
Increases in Measures of Access to Care vs.
Decline in Uninsured Rate, by State, 2013–2015

Panel A: Share with a Personal Doctor

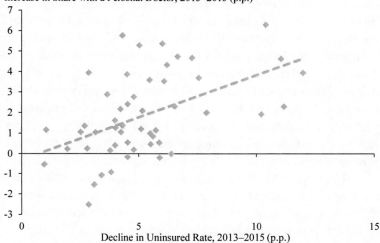
Increase in Share with a Personal Doctor, 2013–2015 (p.p.)

Decline in Uninsured Rate, 2013–2015 (p.p.)

Panel B: Share with Checkup in Last 12 Months

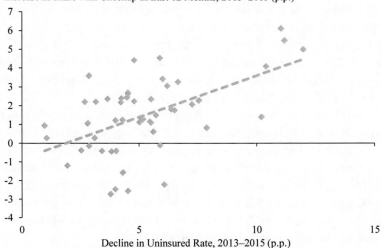
Increase in Share with Checkup in Last 12 Months, 2013–2015 (p.p.)

Decline in Uninsured Rate, 2013–2015 (p.p.)

Note: Sample limited to non-elderly adults. Percentage points denoted p.p.
Source: Behavioral Risk Factor Surveillance System; CEA calculations.

for confidence that expanded insurance coverage will translate into better health. The Oregon Health Insurance Experiment documented significant improvements in self-reported health status and mental health due to expanded Medicaid coverage (Finkelstein et al. 2012; Baicker et al. 2013). Studies of Massachusetts health reform concluded that the coverage expansion drove improvements in self-reported physical and mental health, as well as reductions in mortality (Van der Wees, Zaslavsky, and Ayanian 2013; Sommers, Long, and Baicker 2014), and a study of state Medicaid expansions targeting low-income adults during the early 2000s reached similar conclusions (Sommers, Baicker, and Epstein 2012). Studies of prior expansions of Medicaid and CHIP coverage targeting low- and moderate-income children have documented that health benefits of expanded coverage can be long-lasting, with adults who had access to coverage in childhood experiencing lower risk of death and hospitalization many years later (Wherry et al., 2015; Brown, Kowalski, and Lurie 2015; Wherry and Meyer 2016).

Early evidence on the effects of the ACA appears quite consistent with the results documented for earlier coverage expansions. Barbaresco, Courtemanche, and Qi (2015) report improvements in self-reported health status among young adults following implementation of the ACA's provision allowing young adults to remain on a parent's plan. Looking at the main ACA coverage provisions that took effect in 2014, Sommers et al. (2015) find that the share of non-elderly adults reporting that they are in fair or poor health has fallen as coverage has expanded, as has the percentage of days that respondents report having their activities limited by health problems. Research has also found evidence that gains in self-reported health status have been larger in states that have expanded their Medicaid programs (Sommers et al. 2016; Simon, Soni, and Cawley 2016).

While direct estimates of the law's effects on physical health outcomes are not yet available, largely because these data become available with longer lags, these effects are likely to be quite important. Consider, for example, one particularly important health outcome: mortality. As discussed in detail in CEA (2015), there is considerable evidence that prior coverage expansions targeting populations similar to those targeted in the ACA generated substantial reductions in mortality rates. The most relevant existing estimate of the effect of insurance coverage on mortality comes from work by Sommers, Long, and Baicker (2014) on Massachusetts health reform. By comparing experiences in Massachusetts to those in neighboring states, they estimate that one death was avoided annually for every 830 people who gained health insurance. In conjunction with the estimate cited earlier in this chapter that 20 million adult have gained coverage because of the ACA as of early 2016,

Box 4-3: Interpreting Results from the Oregon Health Insurance Experiment

The Oregon Health Insurance Experiment (OHIE) is an important recent contribution to the literature on the effects of health insurance coverage (Finkelstein et al. 2012; Baicker et al. 2013). The OHIE arose from the state of Oregon's decision in early 2008 to reopen enrollment under a pre-ACA Medicaid expansion that targeted low-income adults. Because the State could not accommodate all applicants, it allocated the opportunity to enroll in Medicaid by lottery. This decision by the State created a unique research opportunity because the only systematic difference between lottery winners and lottery losers was whether they could access Medicaid coverage. As a result, the OHIE researchers were able to estimate the effect of Medicaid coverage on a range of outcomes by comparing lottery winners to lottery losers and have confidence that those estimates represented the causal effect of Medicaid.

As discussed in the main text, the OHIE found that Medicaid coverage generated substantial benefits for those who enrolled, including greater access to health care services, improved financial security, better mental health, and better self-reported health status. The OHIE did not, however, find statistically significant evidence that Medicaid improved several objective measures of physical health, including the risk of high blood pressure, high cholesterol, uncontrolled blood sugar, and death.

The OHIE's failure to find *statistically* significant evidence that Medicaid improves physical health has sometimes been interpreted as evidence that Medicaid has no *clinically* significant effect on physical health (for example, Roy 2013; Cannon 2014). But this conclusion is incorrect. The OHIE's sample size was limited, so its estimates of how Medicaid affected physical health were quite imprecise. As a result, while the OHIE did not find statistically significant evidence of improvements in physical health, the study also could not rule out the possibility that Medicaid caused very large improvements in physical health. For this reason, the correct interpretation of the OHIE results is that they provide little insight into how Medicaid affects the objective measures of physical health examined in the OHIE, whether positively or negatively (Frakt 2013a; Frakt 2013b; Mulligan 2013; Richardson, Carroll, and Frakt 2013).

To make this point concrete, Figure 4-vi plots the OHIE estimates of the effect of Medicaid on four adverse health outcomes, death, and one outcome from each of the three physical health domains examined in Baicker et al. (2013), as well as the associated 95 percent confidence intervals. For scale, both the point estimates and confidence intervals are shown as a percentage of the risk of each outcome in the control group; the estimates reported in Figure 4-vi can therefore be interpreted as the proportional reduction in the risk of each outcome attributable to Medicaid coverage. For none of these four health outcomes can the OHIE rule out a proportional reduction in risk of more than two-fifths. For three of the outcomes, the OHIE evidence cannot rule out a risk reduction of more than a half, and for uncontrolled blood sugar and death, the OHIE evidence cannot rule out nearly complete elimination of the outcomes. Effects of this size would be clinically important and quite valuable to individuals, indicating that the OHIE simply cannot resolve the question of whether Medicaid has important effects on physical health.

Furthermore, Figure 4-vi demonstrates that the OHIE point estimates suggest that Medicaid reduced the risk of these adverse health outcomes by between 8 and 18 percent in proportional terms, depending upon the outcome. These estimates are broadly consistent with the improvements that Medicaid coverage would have been expected to achieve in light of the prior literature on the efficacy of treatment for these conditions (Frakt 2013a; Frakt 2013b; Mulligan 2013; Richardson, Carroll, and Frakt 2013). Thus, while the OHIE estimates provide little direct evidence on the effects of Medicaid on physical health of any kind, they certainly do not suggest that Medicaid generates markedly smaller improvements in physical health than would have been expected based on the pre-OHIE evidence base.

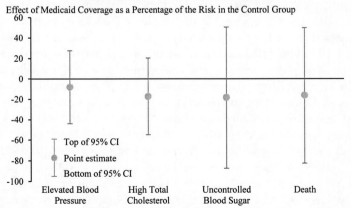

Figure 4-vi
**Estimated Proprtional Reduction in the Risk of
Adverse Health Outcomes Due to Medicaid**

Effect of Medicaid Coverage as a Percentage of the Risk in the Control Group

Note: Uncontrolled blood sugar refers to glycated hemoglobin greater than 6.5 percent.
Source: Finkelstein et al. (2012); Baicker et al. (2013); CEA calculations.

> Fortunately, the OHIE is not the only source of evidence on how health insurance affects health outcomes. Many prior studies have used "quasi-experiments" stemming from prior coverage expansions or quirks in program design to study how health insurance affects physical health outcomes. Quasi-experimental studies are more vulnerable to systematic biases than studies using randomized research designs, but they can often draw on much larger samples and, thus, deliver much more precise estimates. As discussed in the main text, well-designed studies of this type have concluded that health insurance improves physical health in a number of ways, including by reducing the risk of death.

this estimate implies that around 24,000 deaths are being avoided annually because of the ACA.

Greater Financial Security

Another function of health insurance is to protect against the medical costs associated with serious illness. As discussed above, one benefit of that protection is that it allows sick individuals to obtain needed medical care. An additional important benefit, however, is that it helps ensure that families do not experience financial hardship due to illness, ranging from having to cut back spending on other needs, to taking on debt, to failing to pay other bills and thereby impairing their ability to get a loan in the future. [14]

Research examining prior coverage expansions convincingly established that expanding health insurance coverage substantially improves financial security. The Oregon Health Insurance Experiment found that having Medicaid coverage virtually eliminated the risk of facing catastrophic out-of-pocket medical costs (defined as medical costs in excess of 30 percent of income) and sharply reduced the share of individuals reporting trouble paying bills due to medical expenses (Baicker et al. 2013). Mazumder and Miller (2016) examine the effects of Massachusetts health reform and document reductions in the amount of debt past due, the amount of debt in third-party collection, and the risk of bankruptcy, as well as improvements in credit scores. Similarly, Gross and Notowidigdo (2011) document substantial reductions in bankruptcy risk due to Medicaid expansions during the 1990s and early 2000s, and Finkelstein and McKnight (2008) demonstrate

---

[14] Medical costs are not the only financial consequence of serious illness. Dobkin et al. (2016) document that non-elderly individuals experience large earnings losses after serious health shocks, with the result that even insured individuals are at risk of financial hardship under these circumstances. A progressive tax code and the safety net, which have been strengthened by the ACA's reforms to help low- and moderate-income families afford health insurance coverage, play an important role in cushioning households against these types of shocks.

that the introduction of Medicare led to large reductions in exposure to high out-of-pocket medical costs among individuals over the age of 65.

Recent research indicates that the ACA's major coverage provisions are having similar beneficial effects on financial security. Research using survey data show that the share of families reporting problems paying medical bills has fallen substantially since 2013, with particularly large reductions for low- and moderate-income adults (Shartzer, Long, and Anderson 2016). Studies using data from consumer credit reports to compare states that have and have not expanded Medicaid found similar improvements in financial security, including reductions in the amount of debt sent to a collection agency and improvements in credit scores (Dussault, Pinkovskiy, and Zafar 2016; Hu et al. 2016). The magnitude of these improvements is substantial; Hu et al. (2016) estimate that state Medicaid expansions reduce the amount of debt sent to collection by between $600 and $1,000 per person gaining coverage under expansion.

Lower Uncompensated Care Costs

While the most salient benefits of expanded insurance coverage accrue to the newly insured, expanding insurance coverage also has implications for other participants in the health care system. Uninsured individuals still receive some medical care, and when they do so, they are often unable to pay for that care; Coughlin et al. (2014) estimated that health care providers delivered roughly $1,000 in uncompensated care per uninsured person in 2013, costs that must then be borne either by the health care provider itself or by some other entity. Correspondingly, recent research has emphasized that one important consequence of expanding insurance coverage is to reduce the amount of uncompensated care that health care providers deliver (Garthwaite, Gross, and Notowidigdo 2015; Finkelstein, Hendren, and Luttmer 2015).

Recent trends provide strong evidence that the expansion in insurance coverage driven by the Affordable Care Act is, as expected, driving substantial reductions in uncompensated care. Figure 4-14 uses data from hospitals' cost reports to the Centers for Medicare and Medicaid Services to examine trends in uncompensated care. Nationwide, these data show that uncompensated care fell by more than a quarter as a share of hospital expenses from 2013 to 2015. Had uncompensated care as a share of hospital expenses remained at its 2013 level, hospitals would have delivered an additional $10.4 billion of uncompensated care in 2015. The reductions in uncompensated care since 2013 have been concentrated in Medicaid expansion states, likely both because expansion states have seen larger coverage gains and because the low-income uninsured individuals targeted by Medicaid expansion were

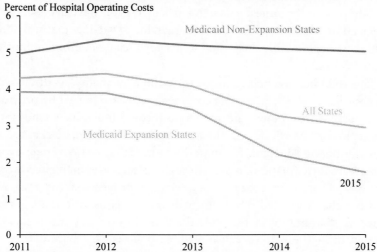

Figure 4-14
Uncompensated Care as a Share of Hospital Costs, 2011–2015

Percent of Hospital Operating Costs

Note: State Medicaid expansion status is as of July 1, 2015. Data for 2015 are incomplete.
Source: Centers for Medicare and Medicaid Services, Hospital Cost Reports; CEA calculations.

particularly likely to receive uncompensated care. In Medicaid expansion states, uncompensated care as a share of hospital operating costs has fallen by around half since 2013.

More detailed research using these hospital cost report data has provided additional evidence that the Affordable Care Act's coverage provisions, particularly Medicaid expansion, have driven substantial reductions in uncompensated care. Dranove, Garthwaite, and Ody (2016) and Blavin (2016) document similar aggregate trends in uncompensated care, including differences in trends between expansion and non-expansion states. Dranove, Garthwaite, and Ody (2016) also look at hospital-level trends in uncompensated care, finding that reductions in uncompensated care are larger for hospitals located in areas that had larger numbers of individuals likely to become eligible for Medicaid under Medicaid expansion.

Reduced Economic Disparities

The ACA's coverage expansions have also substantially reduced economic inequality, as discussed in greater detail in Chapter 3. Most directly, the law has sharply narrowed differences in uninsured rates across population groups. As illustrated in Figure 4-15 below, the coverage gains from 2010 through 2015 have been broadly shared, with the uninsured rate falling across all income, age, and race and ethnicity groups. Gains have also been seen in both urban areas, defined here as counties included in a metropolitan statistical area (MSA), and rural areas, defined as counties outside an MSA. However, the population groups that had the highest risk of being uninsured in 2010 have seen the largest gains; in particular, gains have been larger for younger adults than for older adults, larger for lower-income individuals than higher-income individuals, and larger for racial and ethnic minorities than for Whites.

The ACA has also helped to reduce income inequality. As discussed in detail above, the ACA achieved its coverage expansion in part by providing financial assistance to low- and moderate-income individuals who obtain coverage through Medicaid and the Marketplaces. That financial assistance has greatly boosted income for these households. Those coverage expansions were, in turn, financed in part through tax increases on higher-income Americans. These and other ACA coverage provisions, together with other tax policies enacted during the Obama Administration, are making the income distribution in the United States considerably more equal, as illustrated in Figure 4-16. Because of these policies, the share of after-tax income received by the bottom fifth of income distribution will rise by 0.6 percentage point (18 percent), while the share of income received by the top 1 percent will fall by 1.2 percentage points (7 percent).

Continued Labor Market Recovery

Many critics of the Affordable Care Act argued that its coverage expansions would seriously harm the labor market. While critics of the law were not always explicit about how these harms would arise, some analysts argued that the law's provisions providing low- and moderate-income people with affordable coverage options would reduce individuals' incentive to work, leading some people to leave the labor force or reduce their work hours (such as Mulligan 2014a; Mulligan 2014b). These analysts also argued that the ACA's requirement that large employers offer health insurance coverage to their full-time employees or pay a penalty would cause some employers to shift workers from full-time status to part-time status.

Other analysts noted that the law's coverage expansions had the potential to drive important positive changes in individuals' labor supply decisions. Economists have long argued that the lack of good coverage options for those who do not get coverage through the workplace can lead to "job lock," in which workers remain in a job that offers insurance coverage, despite the fact that their time and talents could be better employed elsewhere (for example, Madrian 1994). The pre-ACA research literature provided some empirical support for this view. Some research has suggested broader insurance coverage increases worker mobility and facilitates appropriate risk-taking in the labor market (for example, Farooq and Kugler

Figure 4-15
Uninsured Rate by Population Group, 2010 and 2015

Panel A: Income as a Percent of the FPL

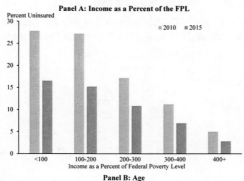

Percent Uninsured

■2010 ■2015

Income as a Percent of Federal Poverty Level

Panel B: Age

Percent Uninsured

■2010 ■2015

Age

Panel C: Race and Ethnicity

Percent Uninsured

■2010 ■2015

Race/Ethnicity

Panel D: MSA vs. non-MSA, by Expansion Status

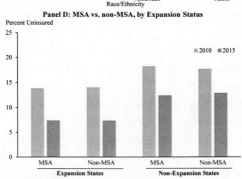

Percent Uninsured

■2010 ■2015

Expansion States   Non-Expansion States

Note: Panels A through C display estimates from the National Health Interview Survey. Panel D displays estimates from the American Community Survey, which provides more detailed geographic breakdowns.
Source: National Health Interview Survey; American Community Survey; CEA calculations.

Figure 4-16

Change in Share of After-Tax Income by Income Percentile: Changes in Tax Policy Since 2009 and ACA Coverage Provisions, 2017

Change in Share of After-Tax Income (Percentage Points)

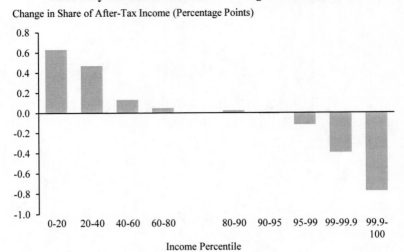

Income Percentile

Source: U.S. Treasury, Office of Tax Analysis.

2016). Providing better coverage options outside the workplace may also facilitate entrepreneurship (Fairlie, Kapur, and Gates 2011; DeCicca 2010); enable workers to invest in additional years of education (Dillender 2014); or give workers additional flexibility in structuring their work lives, such as by retiring when it makes sense for them or reducing their work hours in order to have more time to care for a family member (for example, Heim and Lin 2016).

Fully understanding how the ACA's coverage expansions have affected the labor market will require additional research, but it is already quite clear that predictions of large reductions in total employment and large increases in part-time employment have not come to pass. Implementation of the ACA has occurred alongside the steady recovery of the labor market from the Great Recession, as illustrated in Figure 4-17. The private sector started adding jobs in March 2010, the month the ACA became law, and businesses have added a cumulative 15.6 million jobs since that time. Private-sector employment has actually increased somewhat more quickly since the ACA's main coverage provisions took effect at the beginning of 2014 (around 209,000 jobs per month) than over the rest of the employment expansion (around 181,000 jobs per month).

This time series evidence, particularly the fact that private-sector job growth has actually been slightly faster after the ACA's main coverage provisions took effect than before they took effect, is sufficient to demonstrate

Figure 4-17
Monthly Gain in Private-Sector Payroll Employment, 2008–2016

Job Gain/Loss

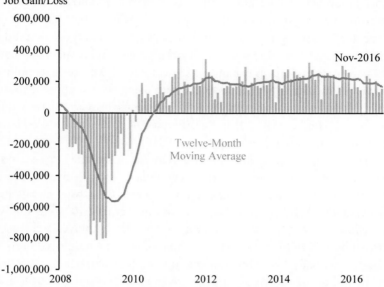

Source: Bureau of Labor Statistics, Current Employment Statistics; CEA Calculations.

that the ACA has not had the extreme negative effects on employment that many critics predicted. However, more rigorous evidence on the ACA's effects on labor markets can be obtained by comparing labor market performance between states where the ACA's coverage provisions were likely to have had larger or smaller impacts. One crude indicator of the scope of the effects of the ACA's coverage provisions is simply the state's uninsured rate in 2013; consistent with this, it is a strong predictor of the magnitude of a state's coverage gains since 2013, as demonstrated in Figure 4-8. Comparing states with higher and lower uninsured rates in 2013 can therefore provide insight into the effect of the ACA's coverage provisions on the labor market. Another useful indicator is whether the state has expanded Medicaid, which provides insight into the labor market effects of Medicaid expansion in particular.

Figure 4-18 plots each state's uninsured rate in 2013 against the change from 2013 to 2015 in the share of working-age individuals who are currently employed. [15] Contrary to what would have been expected if the ACA's coverage provisions had reduced employment, there is essentially no correlation between a state's uninsured rate in 2013 and its employment gains from 2013 to 2015. Similarly, states that expanded their Medicaid programs actually saw slightly larger employment gains than those that did not expand Medicaid (an increase in the working-age employment-population of 1.5 percentage points in expansion states versus 1.3 percentage points in non-expansion states). Several recent studies using related approaches have similarly found no evidence that the ACA's coverage provision have reduced employment (Pinkovskiy 2015; Kaestner, Gangopadhyaya, and Fleming 2015; Leung and Mas 2016; Gooptu et al. 2016).

There is also no evidence that the ACA has driven the large-scale shift to part-time work predicted by critics of the law. As with overall employment, time series evidence is sufficient to dismiss the strong claims made by many of the ACA's critics. As illustrated in Figure 4-19, since the ACA became law in March 2010, the number of workers employed full time has increased by 13.0 million, while the number of workers employed part-time has been essentially flat. This was true during the years leading up to the implementation of the ACA's major coverage provisions in 2014, and it continued to be true thereafter, contrary to claims that the ACA would usher in a major shift to part-time work.

More rigorous cross-state comparisons also provide little evidence that implementation of the ACA's coverage provisions has meaningfully reduced workers' hours. Figure 4-20 plots each state's uninsured rate in 2013 against the change in average weekly hours among workers ages 16 to 64. Contrary to what would have been expected if the ACA's coverage provisions had caused many workers to shift to part-time work or caused firms to curtail hours, there is essentially no correlation between a state's uninsured rate in 2013 and the change in average hours worked from 2013 to 2015. Similarly, average hours worked has increased by about 0.2 hours per week in both Medicaid expansion and non-expansion states, inconsistent with the view that Medicaid expansion has put substantial downward pressure on worker hours. Outside estimates using a range of methodologies similarly conclude that there is little evidence that the law has driven a major

---

[15] An alternative, simpler approach would be to compare labor market outcomes across states seeing larger and smaller declines in their uninsured rates. Comparisons of this type also support the conclusion that the ACA has not negatively affected the labor market. However, this approach has the disadvantage that improvements in labor market outcomes, whatever their cause, are likely to drive reductions in the uninsured rate since many people who gain jobs gain coverage at work. This could generate a spurious positive relationship between coverage gains and employment gains. The approach taken in Figure 4-18 and Figure 4-20 avoids this problem.

Figure 4-18

**Change in Working-Age Employment to Population Ratio
vs. Uninsured Rate in 2013, by State, 2013–2015**

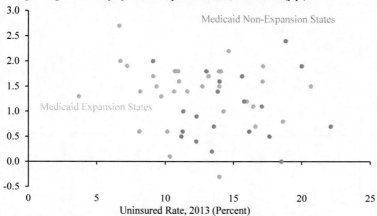

Note: Medicaid expansion status is as of July 1, 2015. Percentage points denoted p.p.
Source: American Community Survey; CEA calculations.

Figure 4-19

**Change in Number of Full-Time and
Part-Time Workers Since March 2010, 2010–2016**

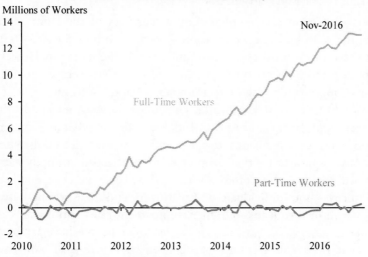

Source: Current Population Survey; CEA calculations.

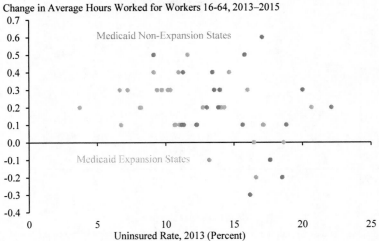

Figure 4-20
**Change in Average Weekly Hours vs. Uninsured Rate in 2013,
by State, 2013–2015**

Change in Average Hours Worked for Workers 16-64, 2013–2015

Note: Medicaid expansion status is as of July 1, 2015.

shift toward part-time work, though some studies have found evidence of small effects (Even and Macpherson 2015; Mathur, Slavov, and Strain 2016; Moriya, Selden, and Simon 2016; Dillender, Heinrich, and Houseman 2016).

Long-Term Labor Market Benefits

The discussion above—like many discussions of the labor market effects of the ACA's coverage expansions—focuses on how the ACA might directly affect the incentives of workers and firms in the short run. However, there are also mechanisms through which the ACA's coverage provisions could have longer-run positive effects on labor market outcomes.

Most directly, by making workers healthier, the ACA may boost their employment and earnings prospects. Indeed, as discussed above, evidence from prior coverage expansions, together with early evidence on the effects of the ACA, demonstrates that insurance coverage improves both mental and physical health. Furthermore, a variety of evidence indicates that better health improves both individuals' ability to work and their productivity on the job, which in turn leads to higher employment rates and higher earnings. Indeed, looking across individuals, healthier people have far higher employment rates and earnings, as depicted in Figure 4-21. Moreover, research has documented that adverse health shocks cause sharp reductions in employment and earnings, strongly implying that at least some of this cross-sectional relationship between health status and labor market outcomes reflects the effect of health status on labor market outcomes, rather than the effect of labor market outcomes on health status (Fadlon and Nielsen 2015; Dobkin et al. 2016).

There is particularly compelling evidence that coverage gains for children improve educational attainment and earnings. Identifying such effects is challenging because they are likely to appear only gradually over time. However, a pair of recent studies has examined earlier expansions in insurance coverage for children through Medicaid and CHIP, using the fact that different states expanded coverage at different times and to different extents. Because some of these coverage expansions are now decades old, the authors have been able to study their effects on long-term labor market outcomes.

These studies find important long-term labor market benefits from expanded insurance coverage. Cohodes et al. (2015) find that having Medicaid or CHIP coverage in childhood increases the likelihood of completing high school and college. Brown, Kowalski, and Lurie (2015) find that female children with greater access to Medicaid or CHIP coverage in childhood have higher educational attainment and higher earnings in early adulthood. They also find evidence that both boys and girls with greater access to Medicaid or CHIP in childhood pay more in income and payroll taxes in their young adult years, potentially offsetting a substantial fraction of the cost of providing coverage to children. These results provide direct evidence that the increases in children's insurance coverage that have occurred under this Administration will generate important long-term labor market benefits and suggest that expanded coverage for adults could generate similar benefits.

The ACA has also strengthened the U.S. system of automatic stabilizers, programs that automatically expand during hard times and contract during good ones, which will help to reduce the severity of future recessions. The ACA's coverage expansions help ensure that families facing job or income losses during a recession retain access to affordable health insurance options. Retaining access to affordable health insurance options safeguards families' ability to access health care and cushions their budgets, enabling these families to better smooth their consumption of health care and other necessities.

While these direct improvements in families' economic security in the face of recession are valuable on their own, they also have important macroeconomic benefits. By boosting consumption at the household level during recessions, the ACA will increase aggregate demand for goods and services at times when it would otherwise be impaired, increasing overall economic output and helping to mitigate the severity of the recession itself. Moreover,

Figure 4-21
Employment Outcomes for Prime Age Adults, by Health Status, 2015

Panel A: Share with Any Wage or Salary Earnings

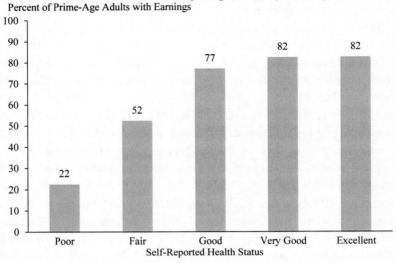

Panel B: Average Earnings, People With Earnings

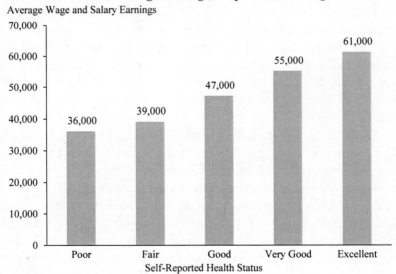

Source: Current Population Survey; CEA calculations.

recent discussions of macroeconomic policy have suggested that changes in the U.S. economy have increased the likelihood that monetary policy will be constrained by the inability to cut nominal interest rates below the zero bound in future recessions, increasing the importance of a strong system of automatic stabilizers (Furman 2016).

REFORMING THE HEALTH CARE DELIVERY SYSTEM

The United States has historically devoted a large fraction of its economic resources to delivering health care. In 2009, the year President Obama took office, the United States spent 17.3 percent of GDP—$2.5 trillion—on health care. That fraction had risen rapidly over time, having increased from 13.2 percent a decade earlier and just 5.0 percent in 1960, as illustrated in Figure 4-22. Much of that spending on health care created substantial value. Indeed, economic research has emphasized that much of the long-term rise in health care spending results from the steady advance of medical technology and that the resulting improvements in length and quality of life have historically been more than sufficient to justify the increase in spending (Newhouse 1992; Cutler 2004). Nevertheless, evidence also demonstrated that the U.S. health care delivery system suffered from serious inefficiencies that drove up spending and undermined patients' health. In light of the magnitude of the resources devoted to the health care system and the great value of better health, this evidence suggested that reform could bring large gains.

This section of the chapter reviews the progress that has been made under this Administration in reforming the health care delivery system. The section begins by summarizing the evidence that the health care delivery system has historically fallen short of its potential, and then describes the reforms implemented under this Administration to address these shortcomings. Next, the section documents the slow growth in health care costs and improvements in health care quality that have occurred as these reforms have taken effect, and presents evidence that the reforms have, in fact, played an important role in driving the positive trends of recent years. The section closes by discussing the benefits that an improved health care delivery system will have for the United States economy in the years to come.

Health Care Costs and Quality Before the Affordable Care Act

A range of evidence indicates that the U.S. health care delivery system has historically fallen short of its potential. One commonly cited piece of evidence was how health care spending and outcomes in the United States compared with those of its peer countries. The United States has historically been an extreme outlier in the share of GDP it devotes to health care,

Figure 4-22
Health Care Spending as a Share of GDP, 1960–2015

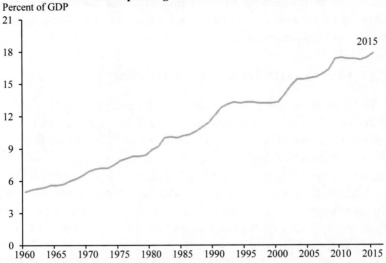

Figure 4-22
Health Care Spending as a Share of GDP, 1960–2015

Source: National Health Expenditure Accounts; National Income and Product Accounts; CEA calculations.

as illustrated in Figure 4-23. In 2009, the share of GDP that the United States devoted to health care was more than 80 percent higher than that of the median member of the Organisation for Economic Co-operation and Development (OECD) and nearly 50 percent higher than that of the next highest OECD member. Due in part to challenges in obtaining comparable data for the United States and other OECD countries, the reasons that spending was so much higher in the United States are not fully understood. However, research has generally concluded that the United States paid higher prices for health care services—potentially reflecting the greater market power held by providers and insurers in the United States' system—and made greater use of costly, but not necessarily effective, medical technologies and treatments (Anderson et al. 2003; Garber and Skinner 2008).[16]

The United States' much-higher spending could have been justified if the additional spending translated into better health care outcomes. In fact, life expectancy was almost two years shorter in the United States than in the median OECD country, and cross-county comparisons of various measures of the quality of care, such as the risk of hospital-acquired infections, found that the outcomes achieved in the United States were, at best, unremarkable

---

[16] These two drivers of higher health care spending in the United States may, to some degree, be related if providers' ability to charge higher prices facilitates investment in costly medical technologies.

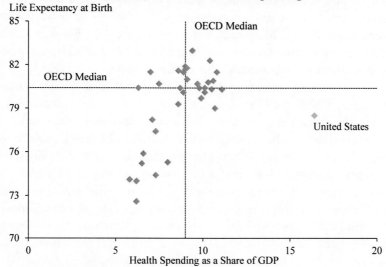

Figure 4-23
Life Expectancy at Birth vs. Health Spending, 2009

Source: OECD; CEA calculations.

(Drösler, Romano, and Wei 2009). In principle, this pattern could arise if factors outside the health care delivery system, such as the United States' high obesity rate and uniquely large share of people without health insurance, masked the large returns generated by the United States' higher health care spending. While these factors may have played some role in explaining the United States' poor performance, the sheer magnitude of the difference in spending between the United States and its OECD peers made it unlikely that this was a full explanation (Garber and Skinner 2008).

Patterns of health care spending and quality performance within the United States provided additional evidence that the United States health care delivery system suffered from serious inefficiencies. Research documented that the amount Medicare spent per enrollee varied widely in the United States, largely reflecting substantial differences in the quantity of care provided in different parts of the country (Fisher et al. 2003a). Other research has documented a similarly large variation in spending among people covered through private insurance, with those in private insurance also seeing wide variation in the *prices* paid for care in different markets in addition to the quantity of care provided (Chernew et al. 2010; Philipson et al. 2010; Cooper et al. 2015). As with cross-county comparisons, however, there was little evidence that higher-spending areas achieved better health outcomes, suggesting that the additional spending in high-spending areas was unnecessary (Fisher et al. 2003b). Moreover, this research found that there was wide variation in health outcomes among areas with similar levels of spending, suggesting that there might be major opportunities to improve patient outcomes, even while holding spending fixed. Figure 4-24 illustrates these empirical patterns using data on spending and outcomes among Medicare beneficiaries from the Dartmouth Atlas of Health Care.

One important advantage of comparing cost and quality among different areas within the United States, as opposed to across countries, is that much richer data are available. This greater data availability makes it easier for researchers to have confidence that confounding factors were not masking a positive relationship between spending and health outcomes. For example, one possible explanation for the patterns in Figure 4-24 is that people in some areas of the country were in worse health, which led those areas to spend more on health care, but masked any benefits of that additional spending for health care outcomes. However, the research cited above found that these patterns held after controlling for individual-level characteristics, casting doubt on whether this could explain the observed patterns. More recent research has examined people who move from one part of the country to another and similarly concluded that much of the variation in spending across areas reflects differences in how care is delivered in different areas, not differences in the characteristics or preferences of people in different places (Finkelstein, Gentzkow, and Williams 2016).

Aggregate data on patterns of care in the United States also suggested that the delivery system was falling short of what a well-functioning delivery system could be expected to achieve, driving up costs and leading to worse outcomes for patients. Research examining individual patient encounters with the health care system found that patients commonly failed to receive care that was recommended under clinical guidelines, while also commonly receiving care that was not recommended (McGlynn et al. 2003). Studies similarly found evidence that care was often poorly coordinated, with patients commonly receiving duplicate tests and different medical providers responsible for a patient's care often failing to communicate when a patient transitioned from one care setting to another (Commonwealth Fund 2008). Research also found that patients were often injured in avoidable ways when seeking medical care, suffering harms ranging from medication errors, to pressure sores, to infections (Institute of Medicine 1999). Others noted that patients were often readmitted to the hospital soon after discharge, despite evidence that these readmissions might be avoidable with better planning for post-discharge or other changes in medical practice (MedPAC 2007; Commonwealth Fund 2008).

Figure 4-24
**Mortality Rate vs. Medicare Spending per Beneficiary,
by Hospital Referral Region, 2009**

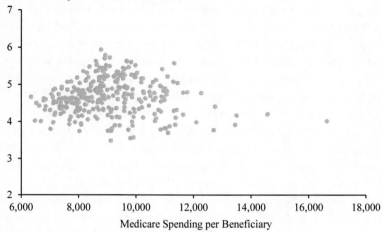

Annual Deaths per 100 Medicare Beneficiaries

Medicare Spending per Beneficiary

Note: Spending and mortality adusted for age, sex, and race.
Source: Dartmouth Atlas of Health Care.

Reforms to the Health Care Delivery System Under the Obama Administration

In light of the compelling evidence that the health care delivery system has historically fallen short of its potential, this Administration has implemented a comprehensive set of reforms, largely using tools provided by the ACA, to make the health care delivery system more efficient and improve the quality of care. These reforms fall in three main categories: better aligning payments to medical providers and insurers in public programs with actual costs; improving the structure of Medicare's provider payment systems to ensure that those systems reward providers who deliver efficient, high-quality care, rather than simply a high quantity of care; and engaging private insurers in a similar process of payment reform. Each of these reforms, as well as its underlying economic logic, is discussed in detail below.

Aligning Public Program Payment Rates with Actual Costs

One way of reducing spending on health care is to ensure that the amounts Medicare and other public programs pay for health care services match the actual cost of delivering those services. Setting Medicare payment rates at an appropriate level has at least two major benefits. Most directly, reductions in Medicare payment rates reduce costs for the Federal

Government, which pays for the majority of care Medicare beneficiaries receive, as well as for beneficiaries themselves, who pay the remaining costs through premiums and cost sharing.[17]

Recent research implies that reductions in Medicare payment rates can also generate savings for individuals enrolled in private insurance plans by enabling private insurers to secure better rates from medical providers.[18] Clemens and Gottlieb (forthcoming) study a past reform in Medicare's payments to physicians that had different effects in different parts of the country. They find that when Medicare reduces its payment rate by one dollar, private insurers reduce their payment rates for the same services by $1.12, on average. White (2013) and White and Wu (2014) undertake a similar analysis focused on Medicare payment to hospitals using variation in how earlier Medicare payment reforms affected different hospitals. White (2013) finds that when Medicare reduces its payment rates by one dollar, private payers reduce their payment rates by $0.77. White and Wu (2014) find that for each dollar Medicare saves in response to such a reform, other payers realize savings of $0.55. These results run contrary to earlier conventional wisdom that Medicare payment reductions generate offsetting "cost shifts" to private payers that drive up the costs of private insurance.

The ACA made a range of changes designed to bring payment rates in public programs more closely in line with the actual cost of delivering services. Two of these were particularly important due to their large size. First, the ACA modified Medicare's formula for updating payment rates to certain medical providers to reflect an expectation that providers will improve their productivity to a similar extent as the rest of the economy over the long run. Previously, Medicare had updated payment rates for these providers based solely on changes in the costs of the inputs they use to deliver care, without accounting for improvements in productivity, an approach that caused payment rates to rise more quickly than the providers' actual cost of delivering health care services.

Second, the law addressed long-standing deficiencies in the system used to pay Medicare Advantage plans that led to those plans being paid far

---

[17] Many Medicare beneficiaries have supplemental coverage that pays for some or all of their cost sharing. In some cases, they purchase this coverage individually and in other cases they receive it from a former employer or a state Medicaid program. In these cases, cost-sharing is ultimately financed by the entity paying for the supplemental coverage. Similarly, some Medicare beneficiaries also have all or part of their premiums paid by another entity, typically a state Medicaid program or a former employer.

[18] The mechanism by which Medicare payment rates affect private payment rates remains unclear. Clemens and Gottlieb (forthcoming) suggest that reducing Medicare's payment rate may strengthen private payers' negotiating position, perhaps because it becomes less attractive for a provider to walk away from the negotiation or because Medicare's rates serve as a benchmark for judging whether contract terms are reasonable.

more to cover Medicare patients than it would have cost to cover the same patient in traditional Medicare (MedPAC 2009). To do so, the ACA phased in changes to the "benchmarks" used to determine payments to Medicare Advantage plans. These provisions have taken effect without adverse effects on the premiums or availability of Medicare Advantage plans, consistent with the view that pre-ACA payment rates were excessive. Access to Medicare Advantage plans remains essentially universal among Medicare beneficiaries, and the share of Medicare beneficiaries enrolled in a Medicare Advantage plan has risen from 24 percent in 2010 to a projected 32 percent in 2017, while average premiums are estimated to have fallen by 13 percent from 2010 through 2017 (CMS 2016b).

Reforming the Structure of Medicare's Payment Systems

A second approach to increasing the value produced by the health care delivery system is to improve the *structure* of the payment systems that public health care programs and private insurers use to pay medical providers. Historically, the U.S. health care system has been dominated by "fee-for-service" payment systems in which medical providers are paid separately for each individual service they deliver, like an office visit, a diagnostic test, or a hospital stay.

Fee-for-service payment undermines the efficiency and quality of patient care in three important ways. First, fee-for-service payment encourages providers to deliver more services than necessary since each additional service translates into additional revenue. Second, fee-for-service payment encourages providers to deliver the wrong mix of services. In a system with payment rates for thousands of different services, payment rates for some services will inevitably end up being set too high relative to the underlying cost of some services and too low for others, biasing care toward those services that happen to be particularly profitable, whether or not those services create the most value for patients. Third, fee-for-service payment fails to reward providers who improve health outcomes because payment is completely independent of the outcomes they achieve for their patients.[19]

The perverse short-run incentives created by fee-for-service payment may also distort the long-run trajectory of medical technology. Because of the shortcomings catalogued above, fee-for-service payment tends to encourage widespread use of resource-intensive new technologies, even if they generate modest health benefits, while often failing to ensure equally widespread use of less resource-intensive new technologies that generate

---

[19] While health care professionals have other reasons to deliver high-quality care, including their concern for their patients' well-being and their desire to attract and retain patients, the evidence summarized earlier demonstrates that this was not always sufficient to ensure that all patients received high-quality care.

large health benefits. When deciding what new technologies to develop, potential innovators and investors are likely to favor technologies that they expect to have a larger market, causing them to focus more on the former type of technology than the latter. Over time, this bias may lead to larger increases in health care spending and smaller improvements in health outcomes than would occur under a payment system that rewards efficient, high-quality care.

Largely using tools provided by the ACA, the Administration has implemented two types of reforms in the Medicare program designed to address the shortcomings of fee-for-service payment. The first was targeted improvements to existing fee-for-service payment systems to encourage more efficient, higher-quality care, which have the important advantage that they can be implemented quickly at scale. The second was setting in motion a longer-term shift away from fee-for-service payment and toward alternative payment models (APMs) that pay providers based on overall cost and quality of the care they deliver, rather than the numbers and types of services they provide. In addition, to facilitate continuous learning and progress along both of these tracks, the ACA created the Center for Medicare and Medicaid Innovation (CMMI) to develop and test innovative new payment models. Importantly, the Secretary of Health and Human Services has the authority to expand a payment model tested through CMMI nationwide if the model is determined to reduce spending without harming quality of care or to improve quality of care without increasing spending.

Targeted Reforms to Fee-For-Service Payment Systems

This Administration has implemented a range of targeted improvements to existing fee-for-service payment systems. One such improvement is greater use of "value-based" payment systems, which adjust providers' fee-for-service payment amounts upward or downward according to how they perform on measures of the quality or efficiency of care. For hospitals, the ACA introduced value-based payment incentives aimed at encouraging hospitals to reduce their hospital readmission rates and their hospital-acquired infection rates. The ACA also introduced broader value-based payment programs for physicians and hospitals that reward providers that perform well across a broad array of quality and efficiency measures. More recently, CMMI began testing a value-based payment system for home health care services, and the bipartisan Medicare Access and CHIP Reauthorization Act (MACRA) introduced a new value-based payment system for physician services that will consolidate existing value-based payment programs for physicians into a single program starting in 2017.

Another type of improvement is beginning to pay providers to deliver high-value services for which payment was not previously available. For example, through CMMI, the Administration tested the Medicare Diabetes Prevention Program (MDPP), which provides coaching aimed at helping participants transition to a healthier lifestyle and lose weight. The evaluation of this initiative demonstrated that MDPP both reduced spending and improved quality of care for Medicare beneficiaries, and the Chief Actuary of the Centers for Medicare and Medicaid Services (CMS) has certified that expanding the initiative would not increase Medicare spending (RTI 2016; Spitalnic 2016; HHS 2016a). On this basis, CMS is now taking steps to begin paying providers to deliver MDPP services to eligible Medicare beneficiaries nationwide starting in 2018. The Administration has also used various pre-ACA authorities to begin covering other high-value services under Medicare in recent years, such as care management services for individuals with chronic diseases and care planning services for patients with cognitive impairments like Alzheimer's disease or dementia.

Development and Deployment of Alternative Payment Models

Most important for the long term, the Administration has also made substantial progress in deploying APMs that reorient payment to be based upon the overall cost and quality of the care providers deliver. The Administration has tested and deployed a range of different types of APMs in Medicare. Two particularly important types of APMs are bundled payment models and accountable care organization (ACO) payment models, each of which is discussed in greater detail below.

Under bundled payment models, sometimes called episode payment models, Medicare makes a single payment for all care involved in a clinical episode, rather than paying for each of those services separately.[20] Bundled payment models use a range of different approaches to define clinical episodes, but they generally start when a specified triggering event occurs and then continue for a follow-up period. For example, in a bundled payment model CMMI is currently testing for hip and knee replacement, the episode begins when the patient is admitted to the hospital for surgery and continues through 90 days after discharge. The bundled payment covers all the health care services the patient receives during that time, including the initial hospital admission, the surgeon's services, post-discharge home health services,

---

[20] Some bundled payment models literally make a single payment for the episode and rely on the providers involved in the patient's care to split that payment among themselves. However, most bundled payment models being tested by CMMI instead pay for care on a fee-for-service basis during the episode, and then "reconcile" these payments after the fact. If fee-for-service spending falls below the episode price, CMS makes a payment to the provider equal to the savings, while if the fee-for-service spending exceeds the episode price, the provider makes a corresponding payment to CMS. Either approach to bundled payment creates similar incentives.

and any other services associated with the patient's recovery, including those triggered by complications.

Making a single payment for this broad array of services associated with an episode allows providers to deliver the most appropriate combination of services to patients, without regard to how those individual services are compensated, creating opportunities to improve the efficiency and quality of care. Many bundled payment models further encourage quality improvement by providing a higher payment per episode to providers who perform well on specified measures of care quality. Medicare captures a portion of the savings generated by more efficient care by setting the bundled payment amount at a discount relative to the costs historically associated with each type of clinical episode.

CMMI is testing several different types of bundled payment models. Through the Bundled Payments for Care Improvement initiative, CMMI is testing bundled payments for 48 different clinical episodes, and this model has attracted nearly 1,500 participating provider organizations across the country as of the middle of 2016. Similarly, CMMI is testing bundled payment for the full scope of care provided to beneficiaries receiving chemotherapy through the Oncology Care Model, which has enrolled 194 oncology practices from markets across the country. CMMI has also begun tests of bundled payment models that include all providers in randomly selected metropolitan areas. Specifically, CMMI began this type of test of a bundled payment model for hip and knee replacement in 67 metropolitan statistical areas across the country in early 2016 and recently proposed a similar approach to testing bundled payment for additional orthopedic procedures and certain types of cardiac care.

Testing models on a geographic basis, as these new bundled payment models do, has two important advantages relative to other approaches. First, randomly selecting metropolitan areas to participate in the model ensures that participants will not differ systematically from non-participants, allowing the test to deliver particularly compelling evidence on how the model affects the efficiency and quality of care. Second, participation by all providers in the randomly-selected geographic areas allows the test to provide evidence on how the model would perform if it were expanded program-wide; evidence from tests that allow each individual provider to opt in or out of the model are much more challenging to generalize in this fashion. In light of these advantages, CBO recently noted that CMMI's ability to conduct geographically based tests is an important reason that CBO projects CMMI to generate substantial savings for the Medicare program (Hadley 2016).

A second major category of APM deployed under this Administration are ACO models, which go a step further than episode payment models and orient payment around the entirety of the care a patient receives during the year, rather than just the care delivered during a particular episode of care. Under an ACO model, a group of providers join together and agree to be held accountable for the overall cost and quality of the care their patients receive during a year. ACOs that reduce average per beneficiary spending below a "benchmark" level share a portion of the savings, giving providers a strong incentive to deliver care more efficiently. (Certain ACO models are "two-sided," meaning that providers also agree to repay a portion of any spending in excess of the benchmark.) ACOs that perform well on a suite of measures of the quality of the care they deliver are eligible for larger financial rewards, giving them a strong incentive to deliver high-quality care and a corresponding disincentive to limit access to necessary care.

ACOs are now widespread in the Medicare program. As of January 2016, 8.9 million traditional Medicare beneficiaries—nearly a quarter of the total—were receiving care through more than 470 ACOs, as illustrated in Figure 4-25. The substantial majority of these beneficiaries are aligned with ACOs operating under the Medicare Shared Savings Program, the permanent ACO program created under the ACA. A smaller number are participating in ACO models being tested by CMMI that aim to improve upon existing ACO models in a range of ways. These CMMI ACO models include: the Next Generation ACO; the Comprehensive ESRD Care Model, which aims to improve outcomes for patients with a particular high cost, high risk condition; and the ACO Investment Model, which supports the participation of small practices or practices in rural areas. Notably, an earlier CMMI ACO model—the Pioneer ACO model—became the first model to meet the criteria for expansion under the Secretary's expansion authority (L&M Policy Research 2015; Spitalnic 2015; HHS 2015). Features of the Pioneer ACO model have now been incorporated into the Medicare Shared Savings Program on a permanent basis.

Through CMMI, the Administration has also tested a range of other innovative payment approaches in addition to bundled payments and ACOs. For example, CMMI is testing medical home models that provide additional resources to primary care practices that agree to engage in a set of specified activities, including care management and care coordination activities, and to be held financially accountable for the cost and quality of the care their patients receive. CMMI began its first major test of medical homes through the Comprehensive Primary Care Initiative, which began operating in October 2012; currently, there are 442 participating practices in seven states. In early 2016, CMMI announced an improved medical home initiative, known as the Comprehensive Primary Care Plus model, which will begin operating in 16 states in January 2017. In collaboration with the

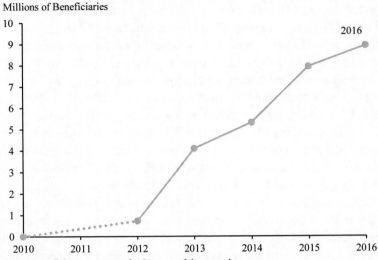

Figure 4-25
Medicare Beneficiaries Aligned to ACOs, 2010–2016

Millions of Beneficiaries

Note: Beneficiary counts are for January of the year shown.
Source: Centers for Medicare and Medicaid Services.

states of Maryland and Vermont, CMMI is also testing statewide all-payer initiatives aimed at making comprehensive changes in how providers in those states deliver care.

In light of the potential of APMs to improve the performance of the health care delivery system, the Administration set the goal of having 30 percent of traditional Medicare payments flowing through APMs by the end of 2016, up from essentially none before the ACA. As illustrated in Figure 4-26, CMS estimates that this goal was reached ahead of schedule in early 2016. The Administration has set the goal of having at least 50 percent of traditional Medicare payments flowing through APMs by the end of 2018.

Provisions included in the bipartisan MACRA will help accelerate the Administration's efforts to deploy APMs in Medicare. Under the law, physicians who provide a sufficiently large fraction of their care through "advanced" APMs will receive a bonus payment equal to 5 percent of their annual Medicare revenue. Advanced APMs are a category that includes most of CMS' most ambitious APMs, including the two-sided ACO models operating through the Medicare Shared Savings Program and CMMI, several of CMMI's bundled payment models, and the new Comprehensive Primary Care Plus medical home model. Additionally, CMS has committed

Figure 4-26

**Percentage of Traditional Medicare Payments
Tied to Alternative Payment Models, 2010–2019**

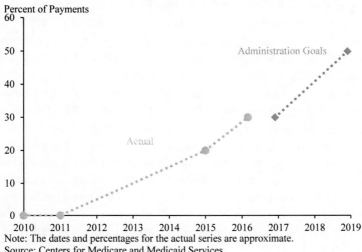

Percent of Payments

Note: The dates and percentages for the actual series are approximate.
Source: Centers for Medicare and Medicaid Services.

to developing new models that qualify as advanced APMs as well to revising some existing models to meet the advanced APM criteria.

Engaging the Private Sector in Payment Reform

Reforming payment systems in Medicare is an important step, as Medicare accounts for around a quarter of all health care spending in the United States. However, more than half of Americans receive coverage through private insurers, which have also historically relied upon fee-for-service payment systems. Ensuring that all Americans receive efficient, high-quality care therefore requires improving private insurers' provider payment systems as well. In light of the substantial shortcomings of fee-for-service payment systems, it may seem puzzling that private insurers had not already done so. But insurers faced two major barriers: a serious collective action problem and poor incentives created by the tax treatment of employer-sponsored health insurance coverage.

A collective action problem exists because developing and deploying new payment models is a costly endeavor, requiring significant investments by both payers and providers, but, as described below, many of the benefits of investments made by any individual actor accrue to its competitors. As a result, each individual payer's return to investing in new payment methods is far below the overall return to the health care sector, leading private payers to substantially underinvest in new payment approaches.

The benefits of one payer's investment in alternative approaches to provider payment spill over to other payers in two important ways. First, once new approaches to payment have been developed and providers have been induced to make the investments needed to deploy them, other payers can adopt those same payment structures at lower cost, but still realize the resulting benefits for the efficiency and quality of care. Largely for this reason, private payers have often elected to base their payment systems on Medicare's payment systems, at least in part (Ginsburg 2010). Private payers typically set payment rates for physicians by starting with the Medicare physician fee schedule rates and increasing them by a specified percentage. Consistent with this, recent research has documented that when Medicare changes the relative amount it pays for different types of physician services, private payers follow suit, at least on average (Clemens and Gottlieb forthcoming). For hospital services, there is far more diversity in the methods used, though Medicare's payment systems are a common starting point (Ginsburg 2010).

A second reason spillovers occur is that medical providers often apply a common "practice style" across all of their patients, so changes made in response to payment changes implemented by one payer often affect patients covered by other payers as well. For example, research examining the diffusion of managed care in the 1990s found that increases in the prevalence of managed care in an area led to changes in treatment patterns for patients in non-managed policies as well (Glied and Zivin 2002). Research has found similar effects for the Alternative Quality Contract (AQC), an ACO-like contract that Blue Cross Blue Shield of Massachusetts has been experimenting with since 2009. McWilliams, Landon, and Chernew (2013) report that patients who were treated by AQC-participating providers, but who were not covered by Blue Cross Blue Shield of Massachusetts, also benefited from lower costs and improved quality along some dimensions.

The Administration has taken several steps to overcome this collective action problem. The Administration's aggressive efforts to improve Medicare's payment systems, described in detail in the previous section, are one particularly important step. As discussed above, private payers often pattern their payment systems after Medicare's payment systems, so transforming payment in Medicare can facilitate improvements in private payment systems. The resulting trends in private payment approaches have been encouraging. For example, recent years have seen rapid growth in private ACO contracts alongside the growth in Medicare ACO contracts, and about 17 million—or roughly one in ten—private insurance enrollees were covered under ACO contracts at the beginning of 2016, up from virtually none as recently as 2011 (Muhlestein and McClellan 2016). Looking across all types of APMs, a recent survey of private insurers estimated that approximately one in four claims dollars paid by private insurers flowed through an APM during calendar year 2015 (HCPLAN 2016).

The Administration has also taken a range of steps to directly overcome the collective action problem described above by facilitating collaboration across payers in developing innovative payment models. The Administration created the Health Care Payment Learning and Action Network in 2015, a forum in which providers and payers can share best practices on how to design and deploy new payment methods. Similarly, in partnership with the members of the Core Quality Measure Collaborative, a group that includes representatives of payers, providers, and consumers, CMS released agreed-upon quality measures for six major medical specialties as well as for ACO and medical home models in early 2016. CMMI has also directly included private payers in many of its model tests. For example, the medical home interventions being tested through the Comprehensive Primary Care initiatives is being implemented in parallel by CMS and other payers in each of the test markets, and the all-payer models now being tested in Maryland and Vermont involve multiple payers by definition.

These steps to facilitate collaboration across payers may have benefits in addition to resolving a collective action problem. Notably, these efforts have the potential to reduce the administrative costs to providers of participating in APMs. Reducing administrative costs is valuable in their own right, but may also facilitate more rapid diffusion of these models. Aligning incentives across payers may also make APMs more effective by ensuring that providers do not face conflicting incentives from different payers.

In addition to the collective action problem discussed above, the tax treatment of employer-sponsored health insurance coverage has been a second important barrier to the adoption of better payment methods in the private sector. In particular, employees pay income and payroll taxes on compensation provided in the form of wages and salaries, but not on compensation provided in the form of health care benefits. As discussed earlier in this chapter, this treatment means that the Federal Government provides an implicit subsidy of around 35 cents on the dollar to compensation provided in the form of health benefits that it does not provide to other forms of compensation.

As also discussed earlier in this chapter, this subsidy plays a useful role in helping make coverage affordable for many families, but it also distorts employers' incentives. Because the Federal Government subsidizes each additional dollar of health benefits, employers have a strong incentive to provide excessively costly and inefficient health plans. This in turn undermines the business case for payers to make the plans they offer employers more efficient, including by adopting new approaches to provider payment developed in the public sector and making their own investments in better benefit designs and better approaches to provider payment.

The ACA addressed this problem by including an excise tax on high-cost employer-sponsored coverage. The tax, currently scheduled to take effect in 2020, will levy a 40-percent tax on employer plan costs in excess of about $29,000 for family coverage and about $10,700 for single coverage. Plans with higher costs due to factors such as the age-sex mix of their enrollment or the industry in which their enrollees work are eligible for higher thresholds. The tax applies only to the portion of plan costs in excess of the threshold; for example, a family plan with a cost of $29,100 in 2020 would pay just $40 in tax. For these very high-cost plans, this structure counteracts the perverse incentives to offer overly generous coverage that existed under pre-ACA law, while preserving strong incentives for employers to offer appropriate coverage. The Treasury Department estimates that 7 percent of enrollment in employer-sponsored coverage and around 1 percent of plan costs will be affected when the tax takes effect in 2020.

The most direct effects of the tax will be on enrollees in the high-cost plans affected by the tax. As their employers take steps to make their plans more efficient, workers at these firms will see lower premiums and correspondingly higher wages, which Congressional Budget Office and Joint Committee on Taxation estimates imply will be around $43 billion in 2026 alone.[21] However, the benefits of this reform are likely to be felt throughout the health care system, not just by enrollees in highly inefficient plans. Just as improvements in Medicare's payment systems generate spillover benefits for the rest of the health care system, payment innovations adopted by inefficient plans are likely to generate benefits for enrollees in many different types of coverage. Similarly, the excise tax on high-cost coverage will encourage plans and employers to engage in more aggressive price negotiation with medical providers. By weakening the bargaining position of providers relative to plans, the excise tax will help plans not directly affected by the tax secure lower prices for their enrollees (Baker, Bundorf, and Kessler 2015).

---

[21] This estimate was derived from an August 2016 estimate by the Congressional Budget Office (CBO) and Joint Committee on Taxation (JCT) that repealing the excise tax would increase the deficit by $20 billion in 2026 (CBO 2016a). CBO/JCT assume that roughly three-quarters of the fiscal effects of the tax arises from the increase in payroll and income tax revenue as workers' wages rise (CBO 2015a). Calculations based on tables published by the Urban-Brookings Tax Policy Center imply that the average marginal tax rate on labor income for individuals with employer coverage is around 35 percent (see Urban-Brookings Tax Policy Center Tables T13-0253 and T14-0091). Combining these estimates implies an increase in wage and salary income of $43 billion (=[$21 billion * 0.75]/0.35).

Additional Steps to Reform the Health Care Delivery System

This Administration has also taken a range of other steps to reform the health care delivery system that complement the provider payment reforms discussed in the rest of this section. One such effort aimed to accelerate the deployment of health information technology (IT). Studies of health IT adoption have found positive impacts on the quality and efficiency of patient care (Buntin et al. 2011; Shekelle et al. 2015). For example, numerous studies provide evidence that computerized physician order entry systems, which can alert doctors to possible medication allergies or dosing errors, prevent adverse drug events (Jones et al. 2014; Shamliyan et al. 2008).

To spur greater use of health IT, the Health Information Technology for Economic and Clinical Health (HITECH) Act of 2009 created financial incentives for Medicare and Medicaid providers to adopt and make "meaningful use" of electronic health records (EHR). More recently, MACRA updated the HITECH incentives for physicians to use health IT and integrated them into Medicare's core physician payment system. Providers participating in the value-based payment system for physicians established under MACRA will be scored, in part, on their use of EHRs to improve the quality of patient care. MACRA also incorporates the use of certified EHRs (EHRs that meet certain criteria for capturing and sharing patient data) into the determination of whether a payment model qualifies as an advanced APM and thereby qualifies participating physicians for the bonus payments described in the last section.

Recent years have seen substantial progress in deploying EHRs. As illustrated in Figure 4-27, 84 percent of non-Federal acute care hospitals had adopted a basic EHR (an EHR that can perform a certain set of core functions) as of 2015, up from just 16 percent in 2010. An even greater share of hospitals possessed at least a certified EHR system. EHR use has also become common among office-based physicians. In 2015, 78 percent of office-based physicians had an EHR and more than a third had used their EHR system to transmit patient health information to external providers (Jamoom and Yang 2016). Focusing on hospitals, Dranove et al. (2015) found evidence that the HITECH payment incentives had accelerated EHR adoption.

This Administration has also taken steps to improve the availability of information on how cost and quality performance vary across medical providers to help consumers, employers, and others make better-informed choices about where to obtain care. For example, the Qualified Entity program, which was created by the ACA and expanded by MACRA, allows organizations that agree to abide by rigorous privacy and security requirements to use Medicare claims data to create public reports comparing the performance of different medical providers. CMS has also improved and

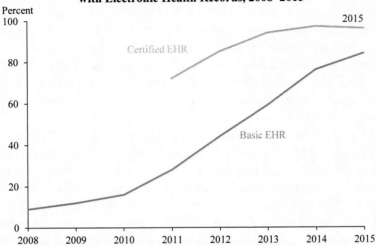

Figure 4-27
**Percent of Non-Federal Acute Care Hospitals
with Electronic Health Records, 2008–2015**

Source: American Hospital Association; Office of the National Coordinator for Health Information Technology.

expanded the websites it operates to deliver information on provider performance directly to consumers; these websites now include information on performance by hospitals, nursing homes, physicians, dialysis facilities, home health providers, and Medicare Advantage and Part D prescription drug plans. Additionally, CMS has begun releasing versions of Medicare's claims databases that have been stripped of beneficiary-identifying information as public use files. The availability of public use files can help researchers better understand patterns of care in the Medicare program in order to evaluate the effectiveness of ongoing delivery system reform efforts and develop new approaches to delivery system reform.

The ACA also created a streamlined process for implementing needed changes to Medicare's payment systems in the future. In detail, it established an Independent Payment Advisory Board (IPAB) of 15 voting members appointed by the President and confirmed by the Senate. If growth in Medicare spending per beneficiary is projected to exceed a target growth rate over a five-year period, IPAB is charged with recommending improvements in how Medicare pays providers to reduce Medicare spending growth; IPAB is not permitted to recommend changes to Medicare's benefit design, including premiums, deductibles, and coinsurance. The Secretary of Health and Human Services then implements IPAB's recommendations unless legislation that overrides the recommendations is enacted. Over the long run, the target growth rate for IPAB is the growth rate of per capita GDP plus 1 percentage point. However, a more stringent target was set for years through 2017: the average of projected growth in the overall Consumer Price Index (CPI) and the CPI for medical care. Because of the exceptionally slow growth in Medicare spending since the ACA became law, which is discussed in greater detail in the next section, IPAB has not yet been called upon to make recommendations despite this stringent target.

Recent Trends in Health Care Costs and Quality

As the reforms described in the last section have taken effect, the United States has seen exceptionally slow growth in health care costs, as well as promising improvements in the quality of care patients receive. This progress has been seen in every part of the health care system, including both public insurance programs like Medicare and Medicaid and private coverage. While the factors driving these encouraging trends are not fully understood, there is clear evidence that the reforms introduced in the ACA, together with other actions taken by this Administration, are playing an important role. This section of the chapter provides a detailed description of recent trends in health care costs and quality, as well as what is known about the causes of these trends.

Recent Trends in Health Care Costs

Economists commonly focus on three distinct measures of health care costs: unit prices; per enrollee spending; and aggregate spending. Unit prices are the amounts paid for a single unit of a health care good or service, such as a physician visit, a hospital admission, or a dose of medicine. Lower unit prices, holding quality fixed, are unambiguously good for consumers because they allow consumers to purchase the same medical care for less money, leaving more money to purchase other valued goods and services.

Per enrollee spending refers to the average health care spending per person enrolled in insurance coverage and is determined by both the unit prices of health care and the average quantity of services used by enrollees. Per enrollee spending is what ultimately determines what consumers pay in the form of premiums and cost sharing. Slower growth in per enrollee spending that reflects slower growth in health care prices is unambiguously good for consumers, for the reasons described above. Slower growth in per enrollee spending that reflects slower growth in utilization of services will often benefit consumers as well, provided that slow growth is achieved without worsening the quality of care.

Aggregate spending refers to the total amount the country spends on health care and is influenced by both spending per individual enrolled in coverage and the number of individuals enrolled in coverage. Faster growth in aggregate spending can be a negative development if it reflects faster growth in per enrollee spending that is not justified by concomitant improvements in quality. However, it can also be a positive development if, for example, it reflects improvements in access to care due to expanded health insurance coverage. Aggregate spending is not directly relevant to consumers.

Recent trends in each of these measures are examined below.

Health Care Prices

The period since the ACA became law has seen exceptionally slow growth in health care prices, as depicted in Figure 4-28. From March 2010 through October 2016, prices of health care goods and services have risen at an annual rate of 1.7 percent, far below the 3.2-percent annual rate seen over the preceding decade and even farther below the 5.4-percent annual rate over the preceding 50 years.[22] In fact, the rate of health care price inflation since the ACA became law has been slower than over any prior period of comparable length since these data began in 1959.

The slow growth in health care prices in recent years is not merely a reflection of slow inflation throughout the economy. Rather, the rate of increase in health care prices has been unusually low *relative* to the rate of increase in prices overall. Indeed, as depicted in Figure 4-29, the rate of increase in health care prices has exceeded the rate of overall inflation by just 0.2 percentage point since the ACA became law, whereas the rate of increase in health care prices exceeded overall inflation by 1 percentage point or more in both the recent and longer-term past.

Health care prices have grown slowly in both of the two largest categories of health care spending: hospital and skilled nursing facility (SNF) services and outpatient services. Real prices for outpatient services have actually *fallen* during the post-ACA period, while real prices for hospital and SNF services have barely risen. The one important exception to this pattern

---

[22] The price index for health care goods and services reported here was derived from Personal Consumption (PCE) Expenditures data produced by the Bureau of Economic Analysis. Price indices for the outpatient services, hospital and nursing home services, pharmaceutical products, other medical products, therapeutic appliances and equipment, and net health insurance categories were combined to construct a Fisher index for the aggregate. The Bureau of Labor Statistics also reports data on health care prices as part of the Consumer Price Index (CPI). This chapter relies on the PCE price indices because they endeavor to measure trends in health care prices throughout the economy, whereas the CPI encompasses a more limited set of transactions. Both series, however, show broadly similar trends in health care prices.

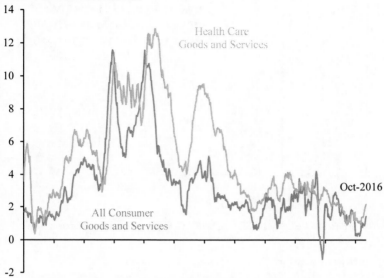

Figure 4-28
Health Care Price Inflation vs. Overall Inflation, 1960–2016
Year-Over-Year Inflation Rate

Source: National Income and Product Accounts; CEA calculations.

is pharmaceutical prices, which have grown somewhat faster post-ACA than they have historically.

For most categories of services, data limitations make it challenging to separately examine the prices paid by private insurance, Medicare, and Medicaid. One important exception, however, is services provided by general medical and surgical hospitals, which deliver the overwhelming majority of hospital services and account for around a third of total health care spending. As depicted in Figure 4-30, growth in prices paid to these hospitals has been sharply lower during the post-ACA period for all three payer categories, with a particularly large slowdown for services provided to Medicare beneficiaries.

Per Enrollee Health Care Spending
The period since the ACA became law has also seen exceptionally slow growth in overall per enrollee health care spending, as illustrated in Figure

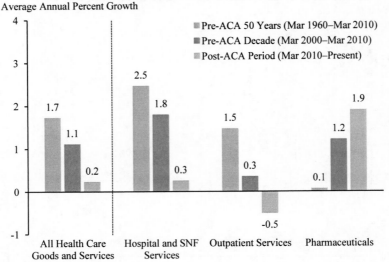

Figure 4-29
Trends in Real Health Care Prices, by Service, 1960–2016
Average Annual Percent Growth

Source: National Income and Product Accounts; CEA calculations.

4-31.[23] Real per enrollee spending in private insurance has risen at an average rate of just 1.5 percent per year during the post-ACA period, well below the pace recorded over either the five-year period that immediately preceded the ACA or the five-year period before that. Medicare spending has followed a similar pattern, with real Medicare spending per enrollee actually falling at an average annual rate of 0.3 percent per year during the post-ACA period. (Per enrollee spending growth in Medicaid has also fallen during the post-ACA period, although these trends are more complicated to interpret due to significant compositional changes in the types of individuals enrolled in Medicaid during both the pre-ACA and post-ACA periods.)

Per enrollee spending growth has slowed markedly across all major service categories, including hospital services, physician services, and prescription drugs, as illustrated in Figure 4-32. Notably, where comparable data are available, the decline in real per enrollee spending growth exceeds the decline in the growth of real health care prices described previously, indicating that much of the decline in per enrollee spending growth reflects slower growth in the utilization of health care services. For example, the

---

[23] The spending amounts attributed to each insurance type in the National Health Expenditure Accounts reflect only the payments made by the insurer. They do not include amounts borne by enrollees such as deductibles, coinsurance, or copayments. Including these amounts would not change the main conclusions reached here.

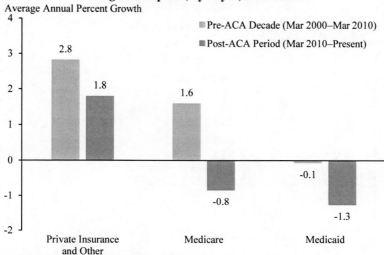

Figure 4-30

**Trends in Real Prices for General Medical and
Surgical Hospitals, by Payer, 2000–2016**

Average Annual Percent Growth

■ Pre-ACA Decade (Mar 2000–Mar 2010)

■ Post-ACA Period (Mar 2010–Present)

Source: Producer Price Indices; CEA calculations.

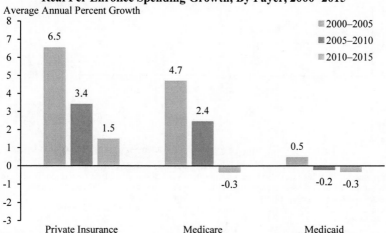

Figure 4-31

Real Per Enrollee Spending Growth, By Payer, 2000–2015

Average Annual Percent Growth

■ 2000–2005

■ 2005–2010

■ 2010–2015

Note: Medicare growth rate for 2005–2010 was calculated using the growth rate of non-drug Medicare spending in place of the growth rate of total Medicare spending for 2006 to exclude effects of the creation of Medicare Part D. Inflation adjustments use the GDP price index.
Source: National Health Expenditure Accounts; National Income and Product Accounts; CEA calculations.

Figure 4-32

**Real Per Enrollee Health Care Spending
by Service and Payer, 2000–2015**

Panel A: Private Insurance

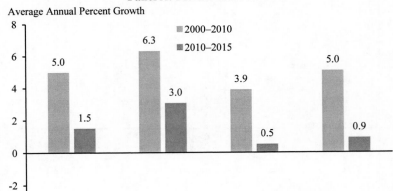

Panel B: Medicare

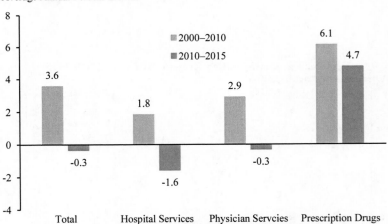

Note: To exclude effects of the creation of Medicare Part D, the average growth rate of Medicare spending for 2000–2010 was calculated using the growth rate of non-drug Medicare spending in place of the growth rate of total Medicare spending for 2006. Similarly, the average growth for Medicare prescription drug spending reflects 2006–2010 rather than 2000–2010.
Source: National Health Expenditure Accounts; National Income and Product Accounts; CEA calculations.

average growth rate of real per enrollee private insurance spending on hospital services has been 3.3 percentage points lower in the post-ACA period than over the pre-ACA decade, whereas the growth rate of the prices private insurers pay for hospital care has declined by only 0.8 percentage point over the same period.[24] Similarly, real per enrollee Medicare spending on hospital services has fallen by 3.4 percentage points from the pre-ACA decade to the post-ACA period, while the growth rate of the real prices Medicare pays for hospital services has declined by only 2.5 percentage points.

Figures 4-31 and 4-32 extend only through 2015 because they rely upon data from the National Health Expenditure Accounts, which only report annual data. However, timely indicators of per enrollee health care spending indicate that spending growth has remained low into 2016, as illustrated in Figure 4-33. CEA analysis of data on Medicare spending published by the Treasury Department indicates that growth in Medicare spending per beneficiary for the first 10 months of 2016 was roughly in line with 2015 and well below longer-term historical experience. Similarly, data from the annual Employer Health Benefits Survey conducted by the Kaiser Family Foundation and Health Research and Educational Trust's (KFF/HRET) indicate that growth in employer premiums remained near its post-2010 lows in 2016.

Trends in employer coverage merit particularly detailed attention since well more than half of non-elderly Americans get coverage through an employer. As illustrated in Figure 4-34, slow growth in underlying medical costs has translated into slow growth in the premiums of employer plans, with real premium growth dropping from an average annual rate of 5.6 percent in the pre-ACA period to an average annual rate of 3.1 percent since the ACA became law. Notably, growth in the portion of the premium paid directly by the worker has fallen by more than growth in the total premium. While economists generally believe that the total premium is the more relevant measure of the overall premium burden because workers ultimately pay for the employer's contribution to premiums indirectly through lower wages, workers' direct contributions may be particularly salient to individuals.

In principle, trends in premiums could be a misleading indicator of the overall trend in the health costs for individuals with employer coverage if the share of spending that enrollees bear in the form of out-of-pocket costs like coinsurance, copayments, and deductibles is changing over time. As

---

[24] This estimate of the slowdown in growth of real hospital prices differs modestly from what is reported in Figure 4-28. This is because, to align with the estimates reported in Figure 4-31, this calculation reflects the 2010–2015 period rather than the March 2010–March 2016 time period and uses the GDP price index, rather than the PCE price index, to adjust for inflation.

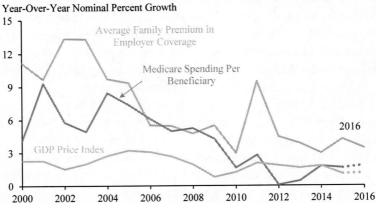

Figure 4-33
Nominal Per Enrollee Health Care Spending Growth, 2000–2016

Year-Over-Year Nominal Percent Growth

Note: Medicare estimates through 2015 are from the National Health Expenditure Accounts; the Medicare growth rate for 2006 reflects only non-drug spending to exclude effects of the creation of Medicare Part D. The Medicare estimate for 2016 reflects CEA analysis of Treasury data and covers the first ten months of the year. GDP price index for 2016 is a CBO projection.
Source: Kaiser Family Foundation/Health Research and Educational Trust Employer Health Benefits Survey; National Health Expenditure Accounts; Monthly & Daily Treasury Statements; National Income and Product Accounts; CEA calculations.

discussed in greater detail in the next subsection of this chapter, there is no evidence that out-of-pocket spending obligations have risen more quickly during the post-ACA period than the preceding years. Indeed, the rightmost columns of Figure 4-34 combine the KFF/HRET data on premiums with data on the out-of-pocket share in employer coverage from the Medical Expenditure Panel Survey's Household Component. If anything, accounting for out-of-pocket costs makes the decline in cost growth for individuals enrolled in employer coverage look slightly larger. While the extent to which incorporating data on out-of-pocket costs magnifies the slowdown in cost growth in employer coverage is somewhat sensitive to which data source is used to measure out-of-pocket costs, the core finding appears relatively robust.

Aggregate Health Care Spending

Driven by the very slow growth in per enrollee health care spending documented above, the years immediately after 2010 saw exceptionally slow growth in aggregate national health expenditures, with 2011, 2012, and 2013 seeing the slowest growth rates in real per capita national health expenditures on record, as shown in Figure 4-35. Growth in aggregate national health expenditures increased in 2014 and 2015, driven in large part by the historic expansion in health insurance coverage that began in 2014.

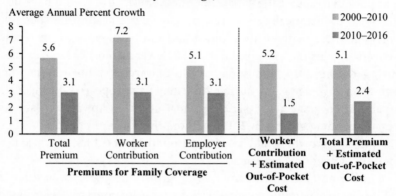

Figure 4-34
**Growth in Real Costs for Employer-Based
Family Coverage, 2000–2016**

Average Annual Percent Growth

Note: Out-of-pocket costs were estimated by first using the Medical Expenditure Panel Survey to estimate the out-of-pocket share in employer coverage for 2000–2014 and then applying that amount to the premium for each year to infer out-of-pocket spending. The out-of-pocket share for 2015 and 2016 was assumed to match 2014. Inflation adjustments use the GDP price index. GDP price index for 2016 is a CBO projection.
Source: Kaiser Family Foundation/Health Research and Educational Trust Employer Health Benefits Survey; Medical Expenditure Panel Survey, Household Component; CEA calculations.

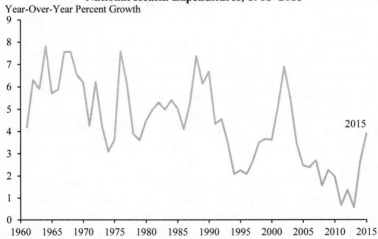

Figure 4-35
**Growth in Real Per Capita
National Health Expenditures, 1961–2015**

Year-Over-Year Percent Growth

Note: Inflation adjustment uses the GDP price index.
Source: National Health Expenditure Accounts; National Income and Product Accounts; CEA calculations.

Indeed, Holahan and McMorrow (2015) estimate that the expansion in insurance coverage added between 1.4 percentage points and 2.1 percentage points to the growth of national health expenditures in 2014. This implies that, absent the expansion in coverage, 2014 would have been another year of historically slow growth in aggregate health care spending, falling somewhere between the slowest and third-slowest year on record. The coverage gains that occurred during 2015 were almost as large as those occurring during 2014, and some of the upward pressure on spending growth from coverage gains during 2014 may have appeared during 2015, so expanding coverage likely placed a similar degree of upward pressure on aggregate spending growth in 2015. Without this upward pressure, real per capita spending growth would have been around 2 percent in 2015, also near the bottom of historical experience.

Furthermore, as noted earlier, faster growth in aggregate health care spending due to expanding coverage is not a cause for concern. Faster aggregate spending growth is the expected consequence of the major improvements in access to care that have occurred as coverage has expanded and does not indicate that costs are rising more quickly for individuals who are already covered. Moreover, faster growth in aggregate spending due to expanding coverage will be temporary, continuing only until insurance coverage stabilizes at its new higher level. Consistent with that expectation, more timely data on health care spending from the Bureau of Economic Analysis suggest that aggregate health care spending growth has begun to moderate in recent months as the pace of coverage gains has slowed.

Understanding the Recent Slow Growth in Health Care Costs

An important question is what has caused the very slow growth in health care costs under the ACA. Broader economic and demographic trends do not provide a satisfactory explanation for recent trends. The Great Recession cannot explain the slow growth in Medicare spending, nor can it explain why spending growth in the private sector remains so low years after the end of the recession. Similarly, demographic changes can explain only a small portion of the slowdown in per enrollee health care spending and actually make the slowdown in aggregate health care spending growth look slightly larger.

This evidence implies that recent trends in health care spending primarily reflect developments internal to the health care sector. Changes in the cost sharing obligations borne by individuals do not appear to explain recent trends, suggesting that the main factor has been changes in the health care delivery system. Within the delivery system, there are likely a number of factors playing a role, but the ACA's changes to provider payment have made a large, readily quantifiable contribution, and there is reason to believe that the ACA's effects on recent trends may go beyond what can be easily quantified today.

Each of these factors is discussed in greater detail below.

The Great Recession and Its Aftermath

Some analysts have pointed to the economic disruptions caused by the Great Recession as a possible explanation for the slow growth in health care costs under the ACA. However, this explanation does not fit the available data. Most fundamentally, the Great Recession does not appear to be able to explain any meaningful portion of the slow growth in Medicare spending in recent years. In addition, while it appears that the Great Recession did dampen private sector spending growth in the years during and immediately after the downturn, it is doubtful that the recession and its aftermath can explain why spending growth has remained low all the way through the present, more than seven years after the recession's end.

The fact that health care spending growth has grown slowly in Medicare, not just private insurance, is the clearest evidence that recent health care spending trends reflect much more than just the Great Recession and its aftermath. Medicare beneficiaries are generally not employed and only around a fifth live in families that get more than half of their income from earnings, so they are relatively insulated from developments in the labor market. Likewise, only around a quarter of Medicare beneficiaries have asset income in excess of $1,000 annually, suggesting that the typical beneficiary is relatively insulated from financial market developments as well.[25]

Empirical evidence strongly supports the view that the Great Recession had little effect on trends in Medicare spending. Historically, weaker macroeconomic performance has not been associated with lower growth in Medicare spending per beneficiary, either at the national level or when comparing across states experiencing stronger and weaker macroeconomic performance at a given point in time (Levine and Buntin 2013; Chandra, Holmes, and Skinner 2013; Sheiner 2014). Similarly, Dranove, Garthwaite, and Ody (2015) directly compare Medicare spending growth in areas of the country that experienced larger and smaller reductions in employment during the Great Recession. They conclude that the recession had only small effects on Medicare spending growth.

It is more plausible that the Great Recession could have affected health care spending among people under age 65. Non-elderly Americans generally depend on the labor market for their livelihoods, and those who have health insurance overwhelmingly receive coverage through an employer, as

---

[25] These estimates reflect CEA analysis of the Current Population Survey Annual Social and Economic Supplement data covering 2015.

illustrated in Figure 4-3. As a result, there many mechanisms through which the Great Recession could have affected the health care spending of people under age 65.

Most directly, an economic downturn could cause some individuals to become uninsured. For example, reduced employment could reduce access to employer coverage, and increased financial stress could cause families to conclude that premiums are unaffordable. Alternatively, financial pressure could cause employers to stop offering coverage or charge higher premiums. The uninsured rate among non-elderly adults did indeed increase sharply during and immediately after the Great Recession, as depicted in Figure 4-5. Because the uninsured are much less likely to access health care, as discussed earlier in this chapter, this development likely exerted downward pressure on aggregate health care spending growth during this period. However, the uninsured rate for non-elderly individuals peaked by 2010, so increases in the number of uninsured cannot explain why health care spending growth has remained low since that time. Furthermore, reductions in the number of people with coverage through an employer cannot explain why per enrollee health care spending, not just aggregate health care spending, has grown so slowly.

There are, however, mechanisms by which an economic downturn might affect spending by individuals who remain insured. Financial stress could cause individuals to de-prioritize spending on health care or cause employers to modify the coverage they offer in ways that reduce health care spending, such as by increasing cost sharing. Whatever the mechanism, there is empirical evidence that the Great Recession reduced the growth of per enrollee health care spending in employer coverage in its immediate aftermath. Ryu et al. (2013) find that the recession increased cost sharing in employer coverage and estimate that those increases subtracted around 1 percentage point per year from the growth of per enrollee health care spending in employer coverage in both 2010 and 2011, with smaller reductions in earlier years. Similarly, Dranove, Garthwaite, and Ody (2014) compare growth in per enrollee spending in employer coverage in metropolitan statistical areas that experienced larger and smaller reductions in employment during the Great Recession. They conclude that the Great Recession subtracted an average of 1.8 percentage points per year from growth in per enrollee spending in employer coverage in 2010 and 2011.

While this evidence demonstrates that the Great Recession exerted downward pressure on growth in private insurance spending in the years around 2010, it is doubtful that it can explain why per enrollee spending growth in private coverage has remained low through the present, as was illustrated in Figure 4-33. Research comparing health care spending growth in states experiencing weaker and stronger economic performance at a given point in time has generally concluded that, to the extent economic downturns affect health care spending growth at all, those effects fade almost completely within a few years (Chandra, Holmes, and Skinner 2013; Sheiner 2014). Because the labor market reached its trough by early 2010 and has recovered steadily since then, as illustrated in Figure 4-36, this evidence would suggest that the recession can play only a limited role in explaining why private health care spending growth has been so slow during the post-ACA period, particularly over the last few years.

One potential shortcoming of using cross-state comparisons to estimate the relationship between macroeconomic conditions and private health insurance spending is that these types of analyses cannot capture effects of economic downturns that operate at the national level, rather than state or local level. It is possible that these types of national effects might persist for a longer period of time. In an effort to capture these national effects, some researchers have examined the correlation between economic growth and growth in private health insurance spending at the national level over time.

Taken at face value, results from these "time series" analyses suggest that economic growth has large effects on private health insurance spending that emerge with a four- or five-year lag (Chandra, Holmes, and Skinner 2013; Sheiner 2014). However, analyses of this type have important methodological weaknesses. Unlike analyses that compare outcomes across different geographic areas at the same point in time, time series analyses cannot control for unobserved factors that might cause health care spending to change over time. As a result, these approaches are at much greater risk of mistaking changes in private health insurance spending growth that *coincided with* an economic downturn for change in private health insurance spending growth that were *caused by* an economic downturn.

Moreover, it is unclear whether the results from these analyses are economically plausible. In particular, the most plausible way an economic downturn could generate long-lasting effects on health care spending growth is by changing the development and diffusion of medical technology. However, as noted by Sheiner (2014), four to five years may be too soon for a downturn to have meaningful effects on the path of medical technology, given the long duration of the research and development process. Furthermore, if economic downturns change the path of medical technology in the medium term, that should affect spending growth in Medicare in addition to private insurance. However, there is little evidence that economic downturns affect spending growth in Medicare at any time horizon.

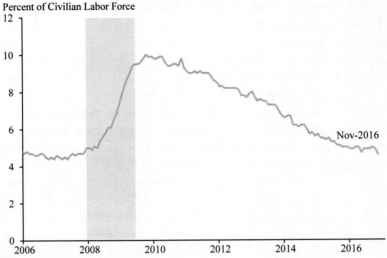

Figure 4-36
Unemployment Rate, 2006–2016

Percent of Civilian Labor Force

Nov-2016

Note: Shading denotes recession.
Source: Bureau of Labor Statistics.

Demographic Changes

Demographic changes are another factor outside the health care system that could affect health care spending trends. As illustrated in Figure 4-37, the United States population is currently aging. Because age is an important determinant of health care spending, differences in how the age distribution is changing at different points in time can cause differences in health care spending growth over time.

Figure 4-38 reports estimates of how health care spending would have changed in recent years based solely on changes in the age and sex distribution, holding fixed both spending and coverage patterns.[26] Consistent with the steady increase in the average age of the full population depicted in Figure 4-37, demographic changes have consistently added to aggregate health care spending growth in recent years. Over the decade preceding the ACA, these demographic factors added an average of 0.5 percentage point per year to growth of per capita health care spending in the full population. Those effects have been slightly larger in the years following passage of the ACA, averaging around 0.6 percentage point per year from 2010 through 2016. Thus, at the level of the population as a whole, demographic changes cannot explain why growth has slowed.

On the other hand, demographic changes can explain a small portion of the slowdown in the growth of per enrollee spending in private insurance and Medicare. As illustrated in Figure 4-37, the aging of the baby boomers drove a steady increase in the average age of the under 65 population during the decade that preceded the ACA, which essentially stopped when the first cohort of baby boomers reached age 65 in 2012. At that time, demographic factors abruptly began placing less upward pressure on per enrollee spending growth in private insurance, as illustrated in Figure 4-38. Whereas demographic changes added an average of 0.6 percentage point per year to private spending growth from 2000 through 2010, they have added an average of just 0.2 percentage point per year since 2010. Thus, demographics can explain a non-zero, but small portion of the decline in private health insurance spending growth.

Demographic changes have had a related effect in Medicare. As the early cohorts of baby boomers have turned 65, the average age among

---

[26] The first step in producing these estimates was to allocate the population across private coverage, public coverage, and uninsurance in each year, holding the age-specific propensity to be enrolled in each type of coverage fixed, but allowing population demographics to change over time. Age-specific enrollment propensities for private insurance, public coverage, and uninsurance were set at the 2000-2015 average for each age, as estimated using the National Health Interview Survey for those years. Data on the population by age and sex in each year were obtained from various Census Bureau population estimates and projections. The second step was to obtain data on spending by age and coverage type. Yamamoto (2013) reports data on relative spending by single year of age for commercial coverage and traditional Medicare coverage. Because Yamamoto (2013) reports relative spending by age within commercial and traditional Medicare coverage, additional information is required to put the commercial and traditional Medicare spending curves on the same absolute scale. To do so, CEA relied upon an estimate from Wallace and Song (2016) that spending falls by 34 percent, on average, for individuals converting from commercial coverage to traditional Medicare at age 65. The commercial age curve was used for all individuals with private coverage, while the traditional Medicare age curve was used for all Medicare enrollees. For individuals under age 65 with public coverage, spending was assumed to reflect the commercial age curve scaled down by 20 percent. For individuals under age 65 who were uninsured, spending was assumed to reflect the commercial age curve scaled down by 50 percent. The results are not particularly sensitive to the approach used for these groups.

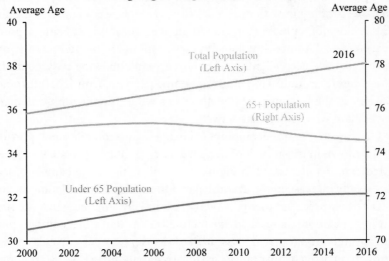

Figure 4-37
Average Age in Population, 2000–2016

Note: Age was top-coded at 100 years in the data used to calculate these averages.
Source: Census Bureau; CEA calculations.

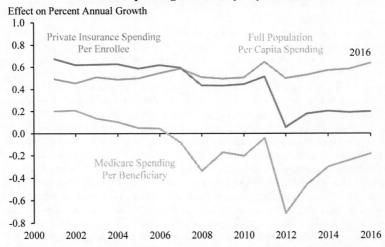

Figure 4-38
**Effects of Changes in the Age Distribution on
Health Care Spending Growth, by Payer, 2001–2016**

Source: Census Bureau; Yamamoto (2013); Wallace and Song (2016); National Health
Interview Survey; CEA calculations.

individuals among individuals 65 and older has declined, placing significant downward pressure on growth in Medicare spending per beneficiary. As reported in Figure 4-38, after having had little net effect on per beneficiary Medicare spending growth over the decade preceding the ACA, demographic changes have subtracted around 0.3 percentage point per year during the post-ACA period. As with the effects reported above, this effect is not trivial but still relatively small in relation to the overall slowdown in the growth of Medicare spending.

Changes in Enrollee Cost Sharing

Changes in cost sharing obligations, such as coinsurance, copayments, and deductibles, are another possible explanation for the slower growth in health care spending since the ACA became law. It is well-established that higher cost sharing causes individuals to use less care (for example, Newhouse et al. 1993), so if cost sharing obligations had grown more rapidly during the post-ACA period than during the pre-ACA period, this could account for slower growth in health spending after the ACA's passage. In fact, there is no evidence that this has occurred.

Focusing first on individuals who get coverage through an employer, Figure 4-39 plots out-of-pocket spending as a share of total spending in employer coverage over time derived from three different data sets: the Household Component of the Medical Expenditure Panel Survey (MEPS) and two different databases of health insurance claims.[27] The MEPS estimates suggest that the out-of-pocket share has been declining steadily since at least 2000 with, if anything, a faster pace of decline after 2010 than before 2010. The estimates from the two claims databases suggest that the out-of-pocket share has been relatively flat, with small increases in the out-of-pocket share in the years before 2010 and little net change after 2010. Thus, there is no evidence that cost sharing obligations have grown more quickly after 2010 and, therefore, no evidence that faster growth in cost sharing can explain slower growth in health care spending. If anything, these data suggest that cost sharing trends may have worked slightly *against* the slowdown in health care spending growth observed in recent years.[28]

---

[27] Each of these data series has strengths and weaknesses. The MEPS is nationally representative, whereas the claims databases are not. On the other hand, the claims databases offer larger sample sizes. They also offer more accurate information on each individual transaction since they contain the actual transaction records.

[28] This conclusion is even stronger if consumers' decisions on whether to access care depend on the *dollar amounts* they pay when they access care rather than the *share of total spending they pay*. The absolute dollar amount of cost sharing has grown more slowly in the post-ACA period than the pre-ACA period due to the combination of sharply lower overall spending growth and the relatively steady trend in the out-of-pocket share.

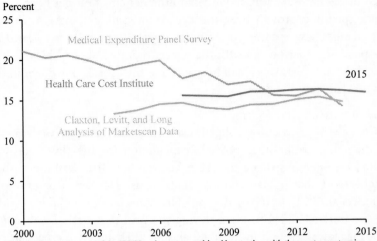

Figure 4-39
Out-of-Pocket Share in Employer Coverage, 2000–2015

Percent

Medical Expenditure Panel Survey

Health Care Cost Institute

2015

Claxton, Levitt, and Long
Analysis of Marketscan Data

Note: Different vintages of the HCCI series were combined by starting with the most recent series
and extrapolating backwards based on percentage point changes.
Source: Medical Expenditure Panel Survey, Household Component; Health Care Cost Institute and
Herrera et al. (2013); Claxton, Levitt, and Long (2016); CEA calculations.

The overall out-of-pocket share, reported in Figure 4-39, is the best metric for evaluating trends in cost sharing in employer coverage because it captures all types of cost sharing, including copayments, coinsurance, and deductibles. Focusing on individual categories of cost sharing can provide a misleading picture of the overall trend in out-of-pocket costs since different components can grow at different rates. Notably, enrollees' copayments and coinsurance obligations have grown quite slowly in recent years, while deductible spending has grown much more quickly (Claxton, Levitt, and Long 2016). This is likely in part because deductibles have simply supplanted these other types of cost sharing and in part because of the ACA's reforms requiring insurance plans to cover preventive services without cost sharing and to limit enrollees annual out-of-pocket spending, which were discussed earlier in this report.

Despite the limitations of doing so, public discussions have sometimes focused narrowly on trends in deductibles to the exclusion of other out-of-pocket costs. Even looking solely at deductibles, however, provides little support for the view that recent years' slow growth in health care spending can be explained in part by faster growth in cost sharing. Average deductibles in employer coverage have indeed risen steadily in recent years, as illustrated in Figure 4-40. However, the pace of this increase since 2010 has been similar to the increase prior to 2010, meaning it can do little to explain why growth

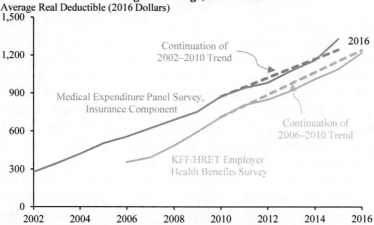

Figure 4-40
**Average Real Deductible in Employer-Based
Single Coverage, 2002–2016**

Note: Inflation adjustments use the GDP price index, including a CBO projection for 2016.
Source: Medical Expenditure Panel Survey, Insurance Component; Kaiser Family Foundation/Health
Research and Educational Trust (KFF/HRET) Employer Health Benefits Survey; National Income and
Product Accounts; CEA calculations.

in overall health spending has been slower during the post-ACA period than it was prior to the ACA.

There is also little evidence that changes in cost sharing are an important explanation for the slow cost growth in types of coverage other than employer coverage. The largest change in Medicare's benefit design in recent years was the creation of Medicare Part D in 2006. Creation of Medicare Part D did drive temporarily faster growth in drug spending by Medicare beneficiaries; however, the estimates of trends in per beneficiary Medicare spending that were presented in Figures 4-31 through 4-33 already adjusted for the large increase in drug spending associated with the creation of Medicare Part D. With respect to Medicaid and CHIP, systematic data on cost sharing obligations are not available, but both programs have historically included negligible beneficiary cost sharing, and there is no reason to believe that this has changed in recent years. Thus, it is doubtful that changes in cost sharing play a meaningful role in explaining slower spending growth in those programs in recent years.

Non-ACA Trends in the Health Care Delivery System

The inability of factors affecting the demand for medical care—including economic and demographic trends, as well as changes in cost sharing—to explain the slow growth in health care spending under the ACA suggests that changes in the health care delivery system have played the predominant role in recent years' slow health care spending growth. The next section discusses the important role that the ACA's changes in medical provider payment have played in slowing health care spending growth, but the fact that health care spending had started slowing prior to the ACA's passage, as documented in Figure 4-31, suggests that the ACA is not the only reason that health care spending growth has been slower during the post-ACA period than in the past. A pair of such factors is discussed below.

The slower growth under the ACA relative to the preceding decade may, in part, reflect the removal of factors that put upward pressure on spending growth during years preceding the ACA, particularly during the early 2000s. The late 1990s and early 2000s saw a number of states pass laws that restricted the ability of private insurers to use a range of so-called "managed care" strategies, strategies that appear to have contributed to slower health care spending growth during the 1990s (Cutler, McClellan, and Newhouse 2000; Glied 2000). Recent economic research examining these state laws has concluded that they put substantial, but temporary upward pressure on health care spending in the years after they took effect (Pinkovskiy 2014). This may partially explain why health care spending growth under the ACA has been so much slower than the first half of the 2000s, though it cannot explain why spending growth has been slower under the ACA than during the second half of the 2000s.

Another possible explanation for why health care spending has grown more slowly in recent years is that the pace at which new medical technologies are being introduced has slowed. As noted earlier in this section, economists generally believe that the development of resource-intensive new medical technologies has been the main driver of the rapid growth in health care spending over the long term (Newhouse 1992; Cutler 2004). If these types of technologies are arriving at a slower pace than in the past, then that could explain why health care spending has grown at a slower pace.

The trajectory of medical technology likely can account for much of the recent swings in prescription drug spending growth. As illustrated in Figure 4-41, per enrollee prescription drug spending in private insurance grew very slowly in the years both immediately before and after passage of the ACA after having grown quite rapidly in the early 2000s.[29] Slow growth during this period appears to have resulted from a slew of patent expirations for blockbuster drugs that allowed less expensive generic versions of these

---

[29] Figure 4-41 focuses on private insurance because Medicare generally did not cover prescription drugs before 2006 and because, as noted previously, trends in per enrollee Medicaid spending are more difficult to interpret due to changes in the composition of program enrollment.

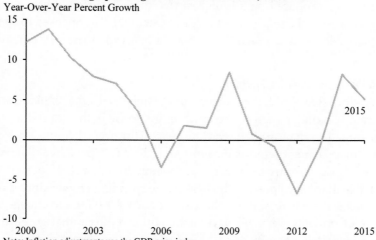

Figure 4-41
**Real Per-Enrollee Prescription
Drug Spending in Private Insurance, 2000–2015**
Year-Over-Year Percent Growth

Note: Inflation adjustments use the GDP price index.
Source: National Health Expenditure Accounts; National Income and Product Accounts; CEA caluclations.

drugs to enter the market, combined with a dearth of new drug introductions (Aitken, Berndt, and Cutler 2009; IMS 2013). This period of slow growth ended as a wave of costly new medications entered the market starting in 2014 (IMS 2016). Figure 4-41 and more-timely data from the Bureau of Economic Analysis suggest that prescription drug spending growth has begun to slow again as the effect of these new drug introductions on prescription drug spending has waned.

However, prescription drugs account for only a sixth of overall health care spending (ASPE 2016c),[30] and it is far from clear that changes in the trajectory of medical technology can account for the reductions in growth of other categories of health care spending that was documented in Figure 4-32. Chandra, Holmes, and Skinner (2013) document slower growth in utilization of certain surgical procedures in the years prior to the ACA and highlight similar evidence from Lee and Levy (2012) for certain imaging services, which they argue implies that a slower pace of technological change

---

[30] The estimate that prescription drugs account for one-sixth of total health care spending cited here incorporates both prescription drugs sold directly to consumers and prescription drugs purchased and administered by a physician or other medical provider. The other data presented in this chapter only incorporate spending on prescription drugs sold to consumers because non-retail spending on prescription drugs is not included in the prescription drug category of the National Health Expenditure Accounts.

began restraining health care spending growth in the years prior to the ACA's passage. But this evidence primarily reflects changes in how existing medical technologies were being used, not the pace at which new technologies are being introduced, so it is unclear that these data should be taken to reflect a change in the trajectory of medical technology, as opposed to some other change in medical practice that may have a wide variety of potential causes.

ACA Reforms to Provider Payment

As discussed above, the ACA is not the only factor that explains why health care spending has grown so much more slowly in the years since the ACA became law than in the preceding years. However, there is also clear evidence that payment reforms introduced in the ACA, plus the "spillover" effects of those reforms on the private sector, have exerted substantial, quantifiable downward pressure on health care spending growth since 2010. Furthermore, there is reason to believe that the ACA's efforts to change the structure of provider payment have had additional effects that go beyond what can be readily quantified.

The most direct effect of the ACA on health care spending growth has been from the ACA's provisions to better align the rates Medicare pays to medical providers and private insurers with the actual cost of services; these provisions were described in detail earlier in this chapter. CBO estimates imply that these provisions have reduced the annual growth rate of Medicare spending by 1.3 percentage points from 2010 through 2016, generating a cumulative spending reduction of close to 8 percent in 2016.[31] These provisions of the ACA, therefore, can account for around a third of the reduction in per beneficiary Medicare spending growth relative to the pre-ACA decade that was reported in Figure 4-32. Notably, more than half of this reduction in spending growth—or around 0.8 percentage point per year—comes from ACA provisions that reduce annual updates to various categories of medical providers to reflect productivity growth. These provisions will continue to

---

[31] These calculations account for the ACA's reductions to annual updates in traditional fee-for-service payment rates, reductions in Medicare Advantage benchmarks, and reductions in Medicare Disproportionate Share Hospital payments, but not other Medicare provisions included in the ACA. The magnitude of the savings from these provisions were estimated using CBO's original score of the ACA (CBO 2010c); the percentage reductions reflect CBO's March 2009 baseline projections for Medicare, which were the baseline projections used in scoring the ACA (CBO 2009). These calculations use CBO's original score of the ACA rather than its subsequent estimates of ACA repeal because those subsequent scores assume that Medicare's payment rules would not return to exactly what they would have been without the ACA if the ACA were repealed (CBO 2012a; CBO 2015a). For comparability with the other estimates included in this chapter, the CBO estimates were converted to a calendar year basis by assuming that the applicable amounts for a calendar years were three-quarters of the amount for the corresponding fiscal year and one-quarter of the amount for the subsequent fiscal year.

reduce the growth rate of Medicare spending to a similar extent in the years to come.

In addition, recent research has concluded that reductions in Medicare's payment rates lead to corresponding reductions in the payment rates that private insurers are able to secure from medical providers, as discussed earlier in this chapter. If the magnitude of these spillover savings matches the prior literature, then the ACA's provisions reducing annual payment updates have reduced growth of private insurance spending by between 0.6 and 0.9 percentage point per year from 2010 through 2016, generating a cumulative reduction in private insurance spending of between 3 and 5 percent in 2016.[32] These spillover effects on private insurance can account for half or more of the reduction in the growth of the prices private insurers pay for hospital care that was reported in Figure 4-30; they can explain between an eighth and a fifth of the reduction in the growth of private insurance spending per enrollee relative to the pre-ACA decade that was reported in Figure 4-32. Moreover, because the underlying Medicare provisions permanently reduce the growth of Medicare payment rates, these spillover effects on growth in private insurance spending would be expected to continue indefinitely as well.

While assessing the aggregate effects of the ACA's provisions to deploy alternative payment models is more challenging, early evidence is encouraging. Research examining the first three years of the Medicare Shared Savings Program, Medicare's largest ACO program, has estimated that ACOs have reduced annual spending for aligned beneficiaries by 0 to 3 percent, with early evidence suggesting that ACOs start at the bottom of that range and move toward the top as they gain experience (McWilliams et al. 2016; McWilliams 2016). Research examining the first two years of CMMI's smaller Pioneer ACO model found savings of a broadly similar magnitude (Nyweide et al. 2015; McWilliams et al. 2015), while evidence from the first two years of CMMI's Bundled Payments for Care Improvement initiative, CMMI's largest bundled payment program, found savings of around 4 percent of episode spending among participating hospitals relative to non-participating hospitals (Dummit et al. 2016).

These results are encouraging, but they also suggest that APMs have generated only modest direct savings to the Medicare program to date. Importantly, the estimates reported above reflect the gross reduction in Medicare spending under the APMs, before accounting for performance

---

[32] The lower bound of this range reflects the White (2013) estimate that each dollar reduction in Medicare payment rates reduces private payment rates by $0.77, while the upper bound reflects the Clemens and Gottlieb (forthcoming) estimate that each dollar reduction in Medicare's payment rate reduces private payment rates by $1.12.

payments made to providers. These performance payments have offset much of the gross savings reported above, at least in the Medicare Shared Savings Program (McWilliams 2016). In addition, while APMs have spread rapidly in the Medicare program since 2010, they still account for a minority of Medicare payments, so the savings estimates reported above apply to only a portion of program spending.

While the direct savings to the Medicare program may be relatively modest so far, these initiatives may be generating more substantial savings in the rest of the health care system. As discussed earlier in this chapter, research has suggested that providers use a common "practice style" with all of their patients, causing payment interventions implemented by one payer to generate savings for other payers whose enrollees see the same providers. If that evidence applies in this case, then Medicare's APM initiatives are already generating meaningful savings for private payers. Notably, unlike the savings that APM participants generate for Medicare, spillover savings are not offset by performance payments to providers. For this reason, it is conceivable that Medicare's APM initiatives have generated larger net savings for private payers than for the Medicare program itself so far.

In addition, as noted earlier in this chapter, private payers appear to have been making efforts to deploy APMs in parallel with Medicare, and it is unlikely that these efforts would have occurred in the absence of efforts to deploy these models in Medicare. While there is little systematic evidence on how successful these private sector efforts have been at reducing costs, these savings could be substantial. Furthermore, as also noted earlier in this chapter, one long-term benefit of transitioning to APMs is fostering the development of technologies and treatment approaches that generate the most value for patients, rather than the technologies and treatment approaches that are most profitable under fee-for-service payment. While changes of this type are likely to take years or even decades to reach their full effect, if even small shifts in this direction have already occurred, it would have large implications for total health care spending because these types of shifts would affect all providers, not just those participating in APMs.

Finally, whatever has happened so far, there are several reasons to believe that the savings generated by Medicare's APM initiatives will grow over time. First, as noted above, ACOs in the Medicare Shared Savings Program appear to achieve greater gross savings as they gain experience; similarly, research examining an earlier private ACO-like contract found that savings grew steadily as providers gained experience with the contract (Song et al. 2014). Second, the Administration has been making continual improvements in its APMs, such as by improving the methodologies used to align beneficiaries to ACOs and to set ACOs' spending benchmarks. These improvements will strengthen ACOs' ability to achieve savings and their incentives to do so. Third, program rules for many APMs are structured so that the performance payments earned for any given level of gross savings will shrink over time, generating larger net savings to Medicare even if gross savings remain constant. Fourth, as discussed previously, a larger share of Medicare dollars are expected to flow through APMs in the coming years.

Recent Trends in Health Care Quality

The reforms implemented under this Administration were designed to improve the quality of care, not just reduce health care costs. Reducing costs in ways that worsen the quality of care will often reduce the total value generated by the health care sector. By contrast, reducing costs while maintaining or improving the quality of care, which the evidence presented at the beginning of this section of this chapter suggested is often possible, has the potential to greatly increase the total value generated by the health care sector.

In practice, studying trends in health care quality is inherently more challenging than studying trends in health care costs. The essential information about health care costs can be captured in a few key pieces of data—the types of service used, the prices paid for those services, and the resulting total spending—and these same basic measures are applicable across all health care settings. By contrast, health care quality has many important dimensions, including a range of different aspects of patients' experiences while receiving care and myriad health outcomes. Furthermore, the most relevant dimensions vary widely from one setting to another. As a result, indicators of health care quality are unavoidably less comprehensive than indicators of health care costs. In addition, whereas health care costs are measured in dollars and so can be readily aggregated and compared across domains, different dimensions of health care quality are measured in widely varying units, which makes aggregation effectively impossible.

For both of these reasons, all-encompassing indicators of health care quality like those that exist for health care costs do not exist. However, quality measures that capture particular important dimensions of care do exist, and a few of these are discussed below. These measures indicate that recent years' slow growth in health care costs has been accompanied by important improvements in health care quality, implying that ongoing changes in health care delivery system are not just reducing health care spending, but also increasing the total value that the health care system creates. Notably, these improvements in the quality of care appear to be attributable, at least in part, to reforms introduced by the ACA.

Declines in the Rate of Hospital-Acquired Conditions

One of the most comprehensive ongoing efforts to monitor health care quality on a system-wide basis is the Agency for Healthcare Research and Quality's (AHRQ) work to track the incidence of 28 different hospital-acquired conditions, including pressure ulcers, several types of infections, and complications due to medication errors, on a nationwide basis (AHRQ 2015; HHS 2016b). The AHRQ data series combines data from a variety of sources, including reviews of medical charts, administrative hospital discharge records, and hospital reports to the Centers for Disease Control and Prevention.

The AHRQ data indicate that the rate of hospital-acquired conditions has fallen significantly since this data series began in 2010, as illustrated in Figure 4-42. The rate of hospital-acquired conditions stood at 145 per 1,000 discharges in 2010 and had fallen to 115 per 1,000 discharges in 2015, a decline of 21 percent. Using prior research on the relationship between these hospital-acquired conditions and mortality, AHRQ estimates that the reduction in the rate of hospital-acquired conditions since 2010 corresponds to approximately 125,000 avoided deaths cumulatively from 2010 through 2015. AHRQ similarly estimates that these reductions in hospital-acquired conditions have generated cost savings of around $28 billion cumulatively from 2010 through 2015.

The factors that are driving the reduction in hospital-acquired conditions have been less thoroughly studied than the factors driving recent years' slow growth in health care costs, but there is reason to believe that the ACA has played an important role here as well. Two of the value-based purchasing reforms implemented under the ACA—the Hospital Value-Based Purchasing Program and the Hospital-Acquired Condition Reduction Program—tie hospitals' Medicare payment rates to a range of quality measures, including rates of hospital-acquired conditions. The first year of incentive payments under these programs were based on performance during 2011 and 2013, respectively, and hospitals may also have begun adjusting their behavior even earlier. In addition, drawing on funding from CMMI, the Administration created the Partnership for Patients initiative, which set up mechanisms to help hospitals identify and share best practices for improving the quality of patient care. Hospital industry participants have reported that the Partnership was highly effective in achieving its goals (AHA/HRET 2014). The Partnership was recently incorporated on a permanent basis into CMS' Quality Improvement Network-Quality Improvement Organization program.

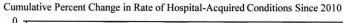

Figure 4-42

**Cumulative Percent Change in Rate of
Hospital-Acquired Conditions Since 2010, 2010–2015**

Cumulative Percent Change in Rate of Hospital-Acquired Conditions Since 2010

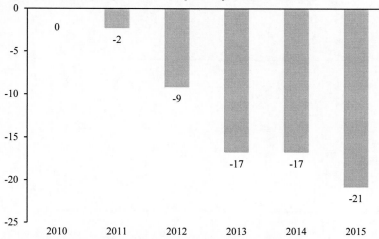

Source: Agency for Healthcare Research and Quality; CEA calculations.

Declines in the Rate of Hospital Readmissions

Another valuable indicator of health care quality is the rate of hospital readmissions, instances in which a patient returns to the hospital soon after discharge. Hospital readmissions often result from the occurrence of a serious complication after discharge, so hospital readmission rates are a useful indicator of the health outcomes patients achieve after leaving the hospital (Jencks, Williams, and Coleman 2009; Hines et al. 2014). Evidence suggests that many readmissions also reflect low-quality care during the initial hospital stay or poor planning for how a patient will receive care after discharge, which means that readmission rates are also a useful indicator of the quality of the care being provided during that initial stay (MedPAC 2007).

Hospital readmission rates have declined sharply in recent years. After several years of stability, the 30-day hospital readmission rate among Medicare patients began falling sharply starting in late 2011, as illustrated in Figure 4-43. This decline continued at a rapid pace through early 2014, with modest additional declines since then. The readmission rate for the 12 months that ended in July 2016 was 1.3 percentage points (7 percent) below the average rate recorded for 2007 through 2011. Cumulatively, the decline in hospital readmission rates from April 2010 through May 2015 corresponds to 565,000 avoided hospital readmissions (Zuckerman 2016).

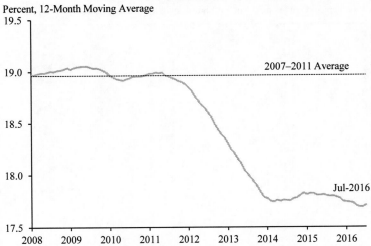

Figure 4-43

Medicare 30-Day, All-Condition
Hospital Readmission Rate, 2008–2016

Percent, 12-Month Moving Average

Source: Centers for Medicare and Medicaid Services; CEA calculations.

The ACA appears to have played a major role in reducing hospital readmission rates. The ACA's Hospital Readmissions Reduction Program (HRRP) reduces payment rates for hospitals in which a relatively large fraction of patients return to the hospital soon after discharge. Notably, the decline depicted in Figure 4-43 began around the time that the rules governing the payment reductions under the HRRP were finalized in August 2011.[33] In addition, Zuckerman et al. (2016) also document that the reduction in readmission rates has been particularly large for the specific conditions targeted under the HRRP, which is also consistent with the hypothesis that the HRRP was the main driver of this decline. Alongside the changes in financial incentives created by the HRRP, the Partnership for Patients may also have helped reduce readmissions during this period by helping hospitals identify and adopt best practices for doing so.

Importantly, recent declines in hospital readmission rates reflect real reductions in patients' risk of returning to the hospital after discharge, not mere changes in how patients who return to the hospital are being classified, as some analysts have suggested (for example, Himmelstein and

---

[33] While the first payment reductions under this program did not occur until October 2012, hospitals' incentives to reduce readmissions began as soon as the rules were finalized (or earlier, to the extent that hospitals anticipated the structure of the payment rules) because payment reductions are based on performance in prior years.

Woolhandler 2015). These analysts argued that some hospitals had tried to circumvent the HRRP's payment reductions by re-classifying some inpatient readmissions as outpatient observation stays. As a result, they argued, the observed decline in hospital readmissions rates substantially overstated the actual decline in patients' risk of returning to the hospital after discharge.

However, Zuckerman et al. (2016) demonstrate that no such shift to observation status has occurred. Although there has been a decade-long trend toward greater use of outpatient observation stays among patients who return to the hospital, there was no change in this trend after introduction of the HRRP, contrary to what would have been expected if the HRRP had caused inpatient readmissions to be re-classified as observations stays. Similarly, the authors find no correlation between the decline in a hospital's readmission rate and the increase in the share of a hospital's patients who experience an observation stay following discharge, which is also inconsistent with the re-classification hypothesis.

Quality Performance in Alternative Payment Models

Early evidence from evaluations of the APMs being deployed under the ACA also provides an encouraging picture of how these models will affect quality of care. The evaluation of the Medicare Shared Savings Program that was discussed in the last subsection found that ACOs improved quality of care along some dimensions, while not worsening it on others, at the same time as ACOs generated reductions in spending (McWilliams et al. 2016). Evaluations of the first two years of the Pioneer ACO model found broadly similar results: improvements on some measures of quality performance, with no evidence of adverse effects on others (McWilliams et al. 2015; Nyweide et al. 2015). Similarly, evidence from the first two years of CMMI's Bundled Payments for Care Improvement initiative, found that the savings achieved under that initiative came at no cost in terms of quality of care (Dummit et al. 2016). This evidence implies that APMs will be successful in improving the overall value of the care delivered, not just reducing spending.

Economic Benefits of a Better Health Care Delivery System

Recent progress in improving the health care delivery system is already having major economic benefits. Most visibly, slower growth in the cost of health care generates large savings that are then available for other valuable purposes, raising Americans' overall standard of living. Recent shifts in projections of aggregate national health expenditures illustrate the magnitude of these savings. Relative to the projections issued just before the ACA became law, national health expenditures are now projected to be 1.7 percentage points lower as a share of GDP in 2019 than projected

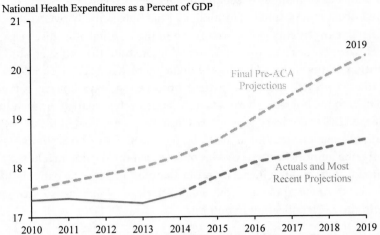

Figure 4-44
Projected National Health Expenditures, 2010–2019

National Health Expenditures as a Percent of GDP

Final Pre-ACA Projections

2019

Actuals and Most Recent Projections

Note: Pre-ACA projections have been adjusted to reflect a permanent repeal of the SGR following the methodology used by McMorrow and Holahan (2016). For consistency, actuals reflect the current estimates as of the most recent projections release.
Source: National Health Expenditures Accounts and Projections; CEA calculations.

just before the ACA became law, as illustrated in Figure 4-44, despite the fact that tens of millions more Americans are now projected to have health insurance.[34] Over the ACA's entire first decade, national health expenditures are now projected to be $2.6 trillion lower than projected before the ACA became law. The remainder of this subsection discusses the downstream consequences of lower health care costs, including increased employment in the short run, higher wages in both the short and long run, lower premiums and out-of-pocket costs, and an improved fiscal outlook for Federal and State governments.

While this subsection focuses primarily on the economic benefits of reductions in the cost of health care, it is important not to lose sight of the fact that improvements in the quality of care also have important economic benefits. Most importantly, higher-quality care ultimately allows people to live longer, healthier lives, which is immensely valuable in its own right. In addition, as noted in the discussion of the benefits of expanded insurance coverage in the first section of this chapter, better health also appears to improve the likelihood that individuals are able to work and increases their

---

[34] The pre-ACA projections have been adjusted to reflect a permanent repeal of the Sustainable Growth Rate physician payment formula following the methodology used by McMorrow and Holahan (2016).

productivity on the job. These benefits, while not as readily quantifiable as the benefits discussed below, are also important.

Higher Wages, Lower Premiums, and Lower Out-of-Pocket Costs for Workers

Roughly half of Americans see the benefits of a more efficient health care system in the form of lower costs for the coverage they get through an employer. Health care for individuals enrolled in employer coverage is financed through a combination of premiums and out-of-pocket costs, so when the underlying cost of health care falls, premiums and out-of-pocket costs fall as well. Reductions in out-of-pocket costs and the portion of premiums paid by employees accrue directly to workers. The remaining savings, which initially accrue to employers as lower premium contributions, ultimately benefits workers as well; economic theory and evidence demonstrate that reductions in the amounts employers pay toward premiums translate into higher wages in the long run (for example, Summers 1989; Baicker and Chandra 2006).

The slow growth in health costs under the ACA has generated substantial savings for workers. The average premium for employer-based family coverage was nearly $3,600 lower in 2016 than it would have been if nominal premium growth since 2010 had matched the average rate recorded over the 2000 through 2010 period, as estimated using data from the KFF/HRET Employer Health Benefits Survey and illustrated in Figure 4-45. Incorporating data on out-of-pocket costs makes these savings considerably larger. Combining these KFF/HRET data on premiums with data on out-of-pocket costs from the Household Component of the Medical Expenditure Panel Survey using the methodology described in Figure 4-34 implies that the average total spending associated with an employer-based family policy is $4,400 lower in 2016 than if trends had matched the preceding decade.[35]

As noted above, both economic theory and evidence imply that workers will receive the full amount of these savings in the long run. In practice, however, compensation packages take time to adjust, so it is conceivable that some of employers' savings on their portion of premiums have not fully translated into higher wages in the short run. To the extent that is the case, then slower growth in health care costs has had the effect of reducing employers' per-worker compensation costs in the short run, increasing their incentives to hire and potentially boosting overall employment. The empirical evidence on these effects is limited, but some studies have found evidence

---

[35] As depicted in Figure 4-39 and discussed in the main text, different data sources report somewhat different trends in the out-of-pocket share. However, this calculation is not very sensitive to which data source is used.

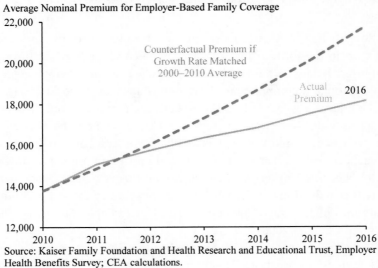

Figure 4-45
**Average Nominal Premium for
Employer-Based Family Coverage, 2010–2016**

Average Nominal Premium for Employer-Based Family Coverage

Source: Kaiser Family Foundation and Health Research and Educational Trust, Employer
Health Benefits Survey; CEA calculations.

that slower growth in health care costs is associated with faster employment
growth (Baicker and Chandra 2006; Sood, Ghosh, and Escarce 2009).

Lower Premiums and Out-of-Pocket Costs in Other Forms of Coverage

Slow growth in health care costs has also reduced premiums and
out-of-pocket costs for people who get coverage outside the workplace. For
example, due to recent years' slow health care cost growth, per beneficiary
Medicare spending has come in well below earlier projections. As discussed
in detail in the next section, this development is generating major savings
for the Federal Government. However, this development is also reducing
the premium and cost-sharing obligations borne by Medicare beneficiaries.

Focusing first on premiums, Medicare beneficiaries generally pay a
premium to enroll in Medicare Part B, which covers outpatient services,
and Medicare Part D, which coverage prescription medications.[36] The
standard Medicare Part B premium is set to cover approximately 25 percent
of program costs, while the base Medicare Part D premium is set to cover
25.5 percent of the cost of a standard plan design. Consequently, when per

---

[36] Very few beneficiaries pay a premium to enroll in Medicare Part A (which covers inpatient
hospital services and certain other services) because almost all beneficiaries are entitled to
coverage based on their prior work history.

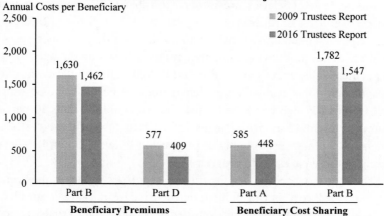

Figure 4-46
**Premiums and Cost Sharing for Medicare Beneficiaries
Under 2009 and 2016 Trustees Projections**

Annual Costs per Beneficiary

- 2009 Trustees Report
- 2016 Trustees Report

Note: Premium amounts reflect the standard Part B premium and the base Part D premium. The 2009
Trustees Projections were adjusted to reflect a scenario in which physician payment rates are held fixed
in nominal terms, rather than being reduced sharply in accordance with the Sustainable Growth Rate
formula then in law.
Source: Medicare Trustees; Centers for Medicare and Medicaid Services; CEA calculations.

beneficiary spending in those portions of the Medicare program falls, the Part B and Part D premiums fall roughly proportionally.

Indeed, 2016 premiums for both of these parts of Medicare are substantially below projections issued with the 2009 Trustees Report, the last report issued before the ACA became law, as illustrated in Figure 4-46. Whereas the standard monthly premium for Part B for 2016 was projected to be $135.80 per month under the policies then in place, the actual 2016 Part B premium was $121.80 per month, a reduction of 10 percent (Clemens, Lizonitz, and Murugesan 2009).[37,38] Similarly, the base Medicare Part D premium was projected to be $48.10 in the 2009 Trustees Report, but the actual

---

[37] This 2009 projection of the Part B premium cited here is from a scenario in which physician payment rates were assumed to remain fixed in nominal terms, rather than being cut sharply as prescribed under the Sustainable Growth Rate (SGR) formula then in law. Congress routinely blocked the SGR cuts, so this provides a more accurate picture of the spending trajectory under the policies in place in 2009. Projections for this alternative scenario are available in a supplemental memo published by the CMS Office of the Actuary alongside the 2009 Medicare Trustees Report (Clemens, Lizonitz, and Murugesan 2009).

[38] Most Medicare beneficiaries paid a lower Part B premium in 2016 because of the application of the Medicare program's "hold harmless" provision, which limits the Part B premium increases for certain beneficiaries when there is a low Social Security cost-of-living adjustment. The higher premium is used here because it is more reflective of underlying program costs. These estimates are therefore conservative.

2016 Part D premium was $34.10 per month, a reduction of 29 percent (Medicare Trustees 2009). For a typical beneficiary enrolled in both parts of the program, the annual premiums savings will total $336 in 2016.

Medicare beneficiaries are also responsible for cost sharing when they access services. Enrollees receiving Part A services through traditional Medicare pay fixed dollar cost sharing amounts when they use specified services; these dollar amounts are updated annually based on changes in provider payment rates under Part A. For Part B, traditional Medicare enrollees are responsible for a deductible, which is updated annually based on the overall trend in Part B costs, and, once the deductible is met, 20 percent coinsurance for most services. Because of the structure of these cost sharing obligations, they vary roughly in proportion to average per beneficiary spending in these parts of the program.

The rightmost columns of Figure 4-46 reports estimates of the average Part A and Part B cost sharing obligations incurred by individuals enrolled in traditional Medicare under projections issued with the 2009 Trustees Report and the most recent estimates for 2016.[39] Cost sharing obligations through Medicare Part A in 2016 are on track to be 23 percent lower than projected in 2009 and cost sharing obligations through Medicare Part B are on track to be 13 percent lower. Across both Parts A and B, the total estimated reduction in average cost-sharing obligations in 2016 is $372, bringing the combined reduction in premium and cost sharing obligations to $708.

The incidence of the cost sharing savings reported in Figure 4-46 will vary across beneficiaries depending on whether they have supplemental coverage in addition to their Medicare coverage that covers all or part of their cost sharing. Roughly a fifth of traditional Medicare beneficiaries have no supplemental coverage and will benefit directly from reduced cost sharing

---

[39] To create these estimates, projections of Medicare's average cost of providing Part A and Part B coverage through traditional Medicare in 2016 were obtained from the 2009 and 2016 Medicare Trustees Reports, as were projections of the Part B deductible (Medicare Trustees 2009; Medicare Trustees 2016). For 2009, the estimates were then adjusted to reflect a scenario in which physician payment rates remained fixed in nominal terms, rather than being cut sharply as prescribed under the Sustainable Growth Rate formula then in law; projections for this alternative scenario were published by the CMS Office of the Actuary along with the 2009 Medicare Trustees Report (Clemens, Lizonitz, and Murugesan 2009). Congress routinely blocked the SGR cuts, so this provides a more accurate picture of the spending trajectory under the policies in place in 2009. To estimate Part A cost sharing obligations, it was then assumed that beneficiary cost sharing constituted 8 percent of the total cost of Part A services. This percentage was estimated using information included in CMS' annual announcement of Part A cost sharing parameters; this approach slightly understates actual cost sharing obligations because it does not account for cost sharing for some small categories of services (CMS 2016c). To estimate Part B cost sharing liabilities, it was assumed that all beneficiaries use enough services to pay their full deductible and pay 20 percent coinsurance for all other services; this approach very slightly overstates actual cost sharing obligations.

(KFF 2016). Another fifth of traditional Medicare beneficiaries purchase individual Medigap coverage and so will see a portion of the cost sharing savings through lower cost sharing and a portion through lower premiums for their Medigap plan. Around three-fifths of traditional Medicare beneficiaries receive supplemental coverage through a State Medicaid program or a former employer. In these cases, a portion of the cost sharing savings may accrue to the sponsor of that supplemental coverage, although the extent to which that occurs will depend on each individual's particular circumstances.

Medicare beneficiaries will see savings in scenarios beyond those considered here. Beneficiaries enrolled in Part D of Medicare are seeing substantial additional cost sharing savings due to the combination of the ACA's provisions closing the coverage gap, which were discussed earlier in this chapter, and lower-than-expected prescription drugs costs. Those amounts are not included here because cost sharing obligations vary among Part D plans, which makes quantifying these savings more challenging. Similarly, this analysis does not examine cost sharing obligations for Medicare Advantage enrollees because the structure of cost sharing obligations in Medicare Advantage varies from plan to plan. In general, however, lower health care costs will tend to reduce cost sharing obligations for Medicare Advantage enrollees as well.

A Better Long-Term Fiscal Outlook

Federal and State governments finance a substantial fraction of health care spending in the United States, primarily through the Medicare and Medicaid programs, so reductions in health care costs also generate major savings in the public sector. Indeed, in large part because of the ACA's provisions reducing health care spending over the long term, the law has generated major improvements in the Federal Government's fiscal outlook, as depicted in Figure 4-47. CBO estimates imply that the ACA will reduce deficits by more than $300 billion over the 2016-25 period (CBO 2015a).[40] Those savings grow rapidly over time and average 1 percent of GDP— around $3.5 trillion—over the subsequent decade.

The slowdown in health care cost growth more broadly has led to additional large improvements in the fiscal outlook. Between August 2010 and August 2016, CBO reduced its projection of net Medicare spending

---

[40] CBO (2015a) estimates how *repealing* the ACA would affect the deficit. CBO notes that the deficit increase due to ACA repeal is not exactly equal to the deficit reduction due to the ACA's enactment. Most importantly, CBO assumes that, even if the ACA were repealed, reductions in Medicare payment rates that have already been implemented under the ACA would remain in place. CBO estimates that these payment rate reductions will generate savings of $160 billion over the 2016-2025 period. Thus, the estimates presented in Figure 4-47 likely understate the deficit reduction attributable to the ACA's enactment.

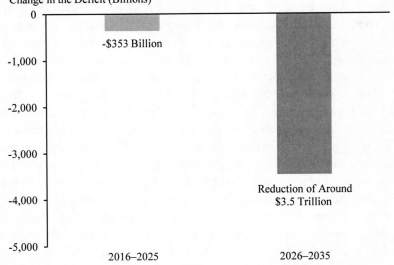

Figure 4-47
Deficit Reduction Due to the Affordable Care Act, 2016–2035
Change in the Deficit (Billions)

Note: CBO reports second-decade effects as a share of GDP. Amounts are converted to dollars using GDP projections from CBO's long-term budget projections.
Source: Congressional Budget Office; CEA calculations.

under current policy in 2020 by $125 billion or 15 percent (CBO 2010a; CBO 2016a).[41] CBO has indicated that the reductions in its projections of Medicare spending in recent years largely reflect the persistent slow growth in health care costs (Elmendorf 2013). That $125 billion reduction in projected spending constitutes 0.6 percent of CBO's current projection of 2020 GDP.

The combination of the deficit savings directly attributable to the ACA and the savings attributable to the broader slowdown in health care costs have greatly improved the United States fiscal outlook. In its most recent long-term budget projections, CBO estimated that the fiscal gap over the next 30 years—the amount of deficit reduction required to hold debt constant as a share of GDP over that period—was 1.7 percent of GDP (CBO 2016b). Without the ACA and the additional reductions in projected Medicare spending described above, the fiscal gap over this period would

---

[41] For the purposes of this comparison, CBO's August 2010 baseline projections were adjusted to reflect the continuation of routine fixes to the Sustainable Growth Rate formula used to set Medicare physician payment rates. This adjustment was based upon the nominal freeze scenario reported in CBO's April 2010 Sustainable Growth Rate menu (CBO 2010b).

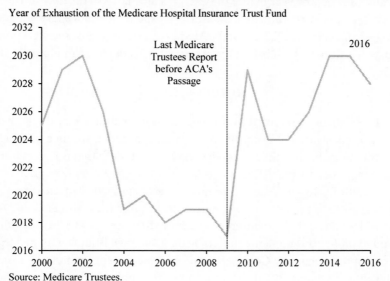

Figure 4-48
Forecasted Year of Medicare Trust Fund Exhaustion, 2000–2016

Year of Exhaustion of the Medicare Hospital Insurance Trust Fund

Last Medicare
Trustees Report
before ACA's
Passage

2016

Source: Medicare Trustees.

have been approximately 1.5 percent of GDP larger, nearly doubling the fiscal gap over that period.[42]

These improvements in the long-run fiscal outlook will have important benefits for the economy. Reductions in long-term deficits increase national saving, which increases capital accumulation and reduces foreign borrowing, and thereby increase national income and living standards over time. Alternatively, reduced spending on health care could obviate the need to take other steps that would damage overall economic performance and well-being, such as reducing spending on infrastructure, education, or scientific research or increasing taxes on low- and middle-income families.

---

[42] For this calculation, the ACA's effect on the deficit was estimated based on CBO's June 2015 estimate of ACA repeal (CBO 2015a). For 2016-2025, the year-by-year deficit effects reported in the CBO estimate were used directly. For subsequent years, the ACA was assumed to reduce the deficit by 1 percent of GDP, consistent with CBO's statement that ACA repeal would increase the deficit by around 1 percent of GDP on average over the decade starting in 2026; this assumption is conservative since the ACA's deficit reducing effects are likely to continue to grow beyond the second decade. The path of deficit savings associated with the reductions in projected Medicare spending from August 2010 to August 2016 reflects the difference in the year-by-year savings through 2020. Thereafter, these savings are assumed to grow at the rate projected for net Medicare spending in CBO's most recent long-term budget projections (CBO 2016b). All calculations reported here use the economic assumptions reported in those long-term budget projections.

The reforms included in the ACA and the broader slowdown in health care cost growth have also improved the fiscal outlook for the Medicare program. In 2009, the year before the ACA became law, Medicare's Trustees forecast that the trust fund the Medicare Hospital Insurance Trust Fund would be exhausted in 2017. As of the Medicare Trustees most recent report, that date has been pushed back 11 years, to 2028, as depicted in Figure 4-48.

CONCLUSION

The evidence presented in this chapter demonstrates that the United States has made historic progress in expanding health insurance coverage and reforming the health care delivery system and that those gains are due in large part to the ACA and other actions implemented under this Administration. Recent years' reforms have also succeeded in creating the tools needed to support further progress on both of these dimensions. As the President has noted, however, fully seizing that opportunity will require continued thoughtful implementation by the Executive Branch, targeted legislative improvements by Congress, and constructive engagement by states and localities (Obama 2016). Whether and how policymakers rise to that challenge will have profound implications for the health care system and, by extension, Americans' health and economic well-being in the years to come.

CHAPTER 5

INVESTING IN HIGHER EDUCATION

INTRODUCTION

The Obama Administration has been committed to ensuring that all students, regardless of their background, have access to a college education that prepares them for success in the workplace and in life. A high-quality education is often more than just the first step in one's career; it can be one of the most important investments young people can make in their futures. College graduates enjoy an earnings premium that is at a historical high, reflecting a trend over several decades of increasing demand for skilled workers (Figure 5-1). In 2015, the median full-time, full-year worker over age 25 with a bachelor's degree (but no higher degree) earned roughly 70 percent more than a worker with just a high school degree (CPS ASEC, CEA calculations). Moreover, people with a college degree are more likely to be employed—benefitting from both lower unemployment rates and higher rates of labor force participation.

But despite the high average returns to a college degree, Federal policy in higher education has had to confront several longer-term challenges. Research shows that college enrollments have not kept up with the rising demand for college-related skills in the workplace (Goldin and Katz 2008). This suggests that, on the whole, Americans are investing too little in higher education. At the same time, some students who attend college do not reap the high returns, especially when they attend low-quality programs or fail to complete a degree. The challenges of investing in higher education are particularly acute for students from disadvantaged backgrounds, who are less likely both to enroll in college and to complete a high-quality program. And as a growing number of students borrow to finance their education, too many struggle to manage their debt.

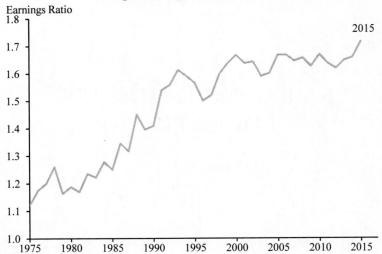

Figure 5-1
College Earnings Premium Over Time

Note: The earnings ratio compares the median full-time, full-year worker over age 25 with a
bachelor's degree only to the same type of worker with just a high school degree. Prior to 1992,
bachelor's degree is defined as four years of college.
Source: CPS ASEC

As President Obama took office, the challenges to ensuring broad access to a quality college education were intensified by the Great Recession. Rising unemployment lowered the implicit cost of forgoing earnings to attend college, and many sought to invest in higher education to improve their skills and job prospects. But at the same time, State budgets declined, exacerbating the trend of rising tuitions at public institutions and stretching funding capacity at low-cost community colleges. The changing market also fostered further expansion of the for-profit college sector, where many colleges offer low-quality programs.

Over the past eight years, the Obama Administration has met these challenges with a complementary set of evidence-based policies and reforms. These policies have been instrumental in helping students from all backgrounds finance investments in higher education and in helping to improve the quality of those investments. To help expand college opportunity, the President doubled investments in grant and scholarship aid through Pell Grants and tax credits. To help more students choose a college that provides a worthwhile investment, the Administration provided more comprehensive and accessible information about college costs and outcomes through the College Scorecard, simplified the Free Application for Federal Student Aid (FAFSA), and protected students from low-quality schools through a package of important consumer protection regulations including the landmark

Gainful Employment regulations. To help borrowers manage debt after college, income-driven repayment options like the President's Pay As You Earn (PAYE) plan have capped monthly student loan payments at as little as 10 percent of discretionary income to better align the timing of loan payments with the timing of earnings benefits.

The benefits of some of these policies are already evident today, while many more will be realized over the coming decades. For example, Council of Economic Advisers' (CEA) analysis finds that the Pell Grant expansions since 2008–09 enabled at least 250,000 students to access or complete a college degree during the 2014–15 award year, leading to an additional $20 billion in aggregate earnings (CEA 2016c). This represents a nearly 2:1 return on the investment. In addition, millions more will benefit from lower college costs and improved college quality in the future.

This chapter begins by surveying the evidence on the individual and societal returns to higher education, as well as the challenges to ensuring that all students have an opportunity to benefit from attending college regardless of their background. It then describes the many ways in which the Administration's policies have addressed these challenges, concluding with a discussion of next steps to build on this progress.

The Economic Rationale for Federal Policies and Reforms to Support Higher Education

A large body of evidence shows that, on average, college attendance yields high returns to individuals and, importantly, benefits society as well. Typically, the individual returns far exceed the costs of a degree, offering individuals a strong incentive to invest in higher education. Even in good economic times, however, individuals face many barriers that deter investment, and the potential benefits of higher education would often go unrealized in the absence of Federal policies. The barriers to finding, financing, and accessing high-quality education options are especially high for those from low-income families, first-generation college families, and other disadvantaged groups. As President Obama took office in 2009, the Great Recession intensified these challenges. Although more Americans than ever wished to enroll in college, they were stymied by financial hardship, rising tuitions, variation in program quality, lack of information to help them make good choices, and a Federal student aid system that had become so complex that many eligible students did not apply (Page and Scott-Clayton 2015). This setting called for a new set of policies and reforms to the existing system of Federal student aid.

Individual Returns to Higher Education

While research suggests that college graduates experience a wide range of non-monetary benefits such as greater health and happiness (Oreopoulos and Salvanes 2011), a primary benefit that motivates most students is the expected gain in future earnings (Eagan et al. 2014; Fishman 2015). Over a career, the median full-time, full-year worker over age 25 with a bachelor's degree earns nearly $1 million more than the same type of worker with just a high school diploma (CPS ASEC, CEA calculations). That worker with an associate degree earns about $330,000 more. The present values of these earnings premiums are also high, amounting to roughly $510,000 and $160,000 for bachelor's and associate degrees, respectively.[1] As shown in Figure 5-2 below, the present value of the additional lifetime earnings far exceeds the cost of tuition. Although tuition does not capture all of the costs of a college education—in particular, it does not capture the opportunity cost of forgone earnings while in school—even when those costs are included, the present value of added earnings typically exceeds the cumulative total cost of college by an order of magnitude (Avery and Turner 2012).

The earnings differentials shown in Figure 5-2 are caused, at least in part, by factors other than educational attainment. For example, students who attend college may have been more skilled or have better networks and, thus, would earn more regardless of their education. But a body of rigorous economic research supports the conclusion that higher education does indeed cause large increases in future earnings. Using a range of sophisticated techniques to compare individuals who differ in their educational achievement but who are otherwise similar in their earnings potential, researchers have estimated that individuals who attend college earn between 5 to 15 percent more on average per year of college than they would if they had not gone to college.[2]

Importantly, some research also suggests that the returns to college have been just as high, if not higher, for "marginal students"—that is, students who are on the border of either attending or completing college versus not doing so. These students often come from low-income families and their decisions hinge on the perceived cost or accessibility of college. Early studies used variation in college proximity to identify the returns to college and found especially large returns to students for whom proximity was a decisive factor (Kane and Rouse 1993; Card 1995). A more recent study by

---

[1] The net present value calculation here and elsewhere in the chapter uses a discount rate of 3.76 percent, corresponding with the current interest rate on undergraduate loans.
[2] See, for example, Kane and Rouse 1993; Card 1995; Zimmerman 2014; Ost, Pan, and Webber 2016; Turner 2015; Bahr et al. 2015; Belfield, Liu and Trimble 2014; Dadgar and Trimble 2014; Jacobson, LaLonde, and Sullivan 2005; Jepsen, Troske and Coomes 2012; Stevens, Kurlaender, and Grosz 2015; Gill and Leigh 1997; Grubb 2002; Marcotte et al. 2005; Marcotte 2016.

Figure 5-2
Present Value of Added Lifetime Earnings vs. Total Tuition

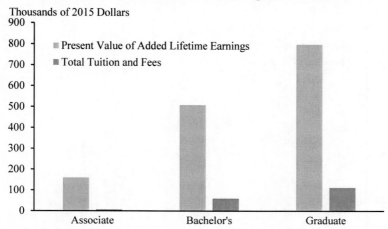

Thousands of 2015 Dollars

Note: Lifetime earnings are calculated by summing median annual earnings for full-time, full-year workers at every age between 25 and 64 by educational attainment, subtracting earnings for the same type of worker with only a high school degree, and converting to present value using a 3.76% discount rate. Tuition for associate (bachelor's) is the full-time tuition for two-(four-) year schools multiplied by two (four), and for graduate, it is the average graduate tuition multipled by three added to bachelor's tuition.
Source: CPS ASEC 2015 and 2016; NPSAS 2012; NCES 2015

Zimmerman (2014) compares students whose GPAs are either just above or just below the threshold for admission to Florida International University, a four-year school with the lowest admissions standards in the Florida State University System. This study finds that "marginal students" who are admitted to the school experience sizable earnings gains over those who just miss the cutoff and are thus unlikely to attend any four-year college, translating into meaningful returns net of costs and especially high returns for low-income students. Using a similar methodology, Ost, Pan, and Webber (2016) study the benefit of completing college among low-performing students whose GPAs are close to the cutoff for dismissal at 13 public universities in Ohio. They find substantial earnings benefits for those who just pass the cutoff and complete their degree. Turner (2015) similarly finds that women who attend college after receiving welfare benefits experience large and significant earnings gains if they complete credentials.

In addition to higher earnings, college graduates are also more likely to work than high school graduates. Data from the Bureau of Labor Statistics, summarized in Figure 5-3, show that college graduates with at least a bachelor's degree participate in the labor force at a higher rate than high school

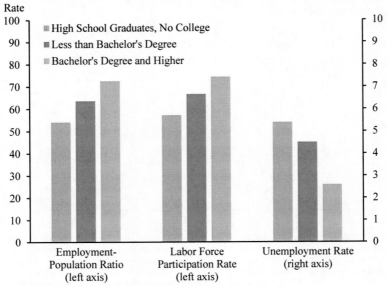

Figure 5-3
Likelihood of Working by Educational Attainment, 2015

Note: Data are for the civilian population 25 years and over.
Source: Bureau of Labor Statistics

graduates (74 vs. 57 percent in 2015)[3] and also face a lower unemployment rate among those who participate (2.6 vs. 5.4 percent in 2015). As a result, people over the age of 25 with a bachelor's degree or higher are 30 percent more likely to be working than those with only a high school degree. A somewhat smaller but still sizeable employment premium is seen for those with some college but without a bachelor's degree.[4] Consistent with college premiums in both earnings and employment, Haskins, Isaacs, and Sawhill (2008) find that individuals with college degrees have increased odds of moving up the economic ladder to achieve a higher level of income compared with their parents.

Overall, higher education helps Americans become more productive in the labor market, building the skills our economy demands and establishing a stronger foundation for the economic prosperity and security of our families and communities. Although the large individual returns to college imply that individuals have strong incentives to invest in higher education, much of the potential benefit of higher education would go unrealized in the absence of Federal policies to support these investments due to positive

---

[3] See CEA's 2014 and 2016 reports on labor force participation for a more detailed discussion about educational attainment and labor force participation (CEA 2014, 2016e).
[4] This category includes both individuals who attended college but received no degree and those who received an associate degree.

externalities, credit constraints, and information failures and procedural complexities.

Positive Externalities

An individual's postsecondary education level has spillover benefits to others in society that the individual does not capture; that is, positive "externalities." Since individuals usually do not consider the societal benefits when deciding whether to attend college, such externalities are an important motive for Federal student aid.

These societal benefits, while hard to quantify, are numerous and potentially very large (Baum, Ma, and Payea 2013; Hill, Hoffman, and Rex 2005; OECD 2013). Higher individual earnings yield higher tax revenue and lower government expenditure on transfer programs. Further, research shows that increased educational attainment can lead to higher levels of volunteering and voting (Dee 2004), lower levels of criminal behavior (Lochner and Moretti 2004), and improved health (Cutler and Lleras-Muney 2006; McCrary and Royer 2011). Individual investments in education can benefit other members of society through reduced victimization, and lower health care and law enforcement costs. Other social contributions associated with higher education—such as teaching, inventions, or public service—also are not fully captured by the individual's wages. Finally, research shows that when individuals invest in their own college education, they can actually make *other* workers more productive. A study by Moretti (2004) finds that increasing the share of college graduates in a labor market leads to significant increases in the productivity and wages of others where those college graduates live and work. Indeed, research using international comparisons suggest that the cognitive skills or "knowledge capital" of a nation are essential to long-run prosperity and growth (Hanushek and Woessmann 2015).

Credit Constraints

While the social benefits of education provide a strong justification for Federal support, equally important is the fact that, even when the private returns to a college education are high, the private market is often unwilling to supply educational loans—especially to students from low-income families. A key reason for this market failure is that the knowledge, skills, and enhanced earnings potential that a student obtains from going to college cannot be offered as collateral to secure the loan. The lack of a physical asset makes educational loans very different from mortgages or automobile loans, which provide lenders with recourse in the form of foreclosure or repossession if the borrower is unable to repay. For this reason, the private market alone would supply an inefficiently low amount of credit for the purpose of financing education.

From an individual's perspective, attending college makes financial sense whenever the present value of the benefits outweighs the present value of the costs, when both are discounted based on preferences for current outcomes versus future outcomes. But while the benefits of attending college are spread out over a long future, most of the costs—including both the direct cost of tuition and fees and the foregone earnings while in school—must be paid up front. While some students are able to finance their college educations through savings or help from their families, many need to borrow to make the investment.

A major function of the Federal student loan system is to ease the credit constraints caused by imperfections in the private loan market, thereby ensuring broad access to affordable college loans and a means to invest in one's future earnings potential.[5] However, while the student loan system has helped to alleviate credit constraints at the time of college enrollment, the traditional standard repayment plan's 10-year repayment period, with equal payments due each month, does not account for income volatility or dynamics once the student has left school. As a result, this standard plan—in which students are enrolled by default—may adversely affect some students' investment decisions and hinder others from successfully managing their debt.

The constraint imposed by the 10-year repayment plan is illustrated in Figure 5-4, which shows the lifetime earnings trajectory of a typical bachelor's degree recipient working full-time and year-round from age 25 to retirement. As the Figure shows, there is a strong positive relationship between age and earnings. This relationship is especially strong for those with a bachelor's degree and it persists for at least 15 to 20 years after many students graduate from college. In short, a college investment pays off over several decades, and a 10-year repayment window forces borrowers to pay the costs at a time when only a small share of the benefits have been realized. Indeed, the discounted values for the earnings levels used in Figure 5-4 suggest that less than a third of the earnings gains over a 40-year career are realized during the standard repayment window.

---

[5] Although a private loan market exists, the loans typically require a co-signer and often do not come with the consumer protections that Federal loans have, including discharge in instances of death or permanent disability. Today the private market constitutes only a small share of student loans—in 2012, 6 percent of undergraduates used private loans to finance their education (NPSAS 2012, CEA tabulations). In the 2000s, private student loans accounted for a larger share of student loans; see CFPB (2012) for a detailed analysis about how and why the private market for student loans has changed over the last decade.

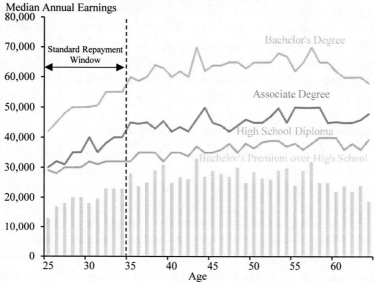

Figure 5-4
Earnings by Age and Educational Attainment

Note: Earnings are median annual earnings for full-time, full-year workers of the noted age.
Source: CPS ASEC 2015 and 2016

While many borrowers who work when they leave school earn enough to pay their student debt on the standard 10-year plan,[6] there is significant variation both in the size of student loans and in the returns to college. Further, because borrowers may face temporary unemployment or low earnings—especially at the start of their career (Abel and Deitz 2016)—some borrowers are needlessly constrained if they remain on the standard plan. Such considerations are especially pertinent to recent cohorts of students who graduated during or shortly after the Great Recession. Research shows that college graduates entering the labor market during a recession tend to experience sizeable negative income shocks, and that it can take years to recover (Kahn 2010; Oreopoulos, von Wachter, and Heisz 2012; Wozniak 2010). Young workers are often the ones affected more severely by recessions (Hoynes, Miller, and Schaller 2012; Forsythe 2016; Kroeger, Cooke, and Gould 2016). A short repayment window could therefore lead to poor loan outcomes for these students despite a longer-term ability to repay.

---

[6] CEA calculations using the CPS ASEC and NPSAS 2012 show that at age 25, the earnings premium seen by a typical bachelor's degree recipient working full-time and year-round is $16,000 a year, well above the $3,500 annual payment corresponding to a typical debt amount of about $27,000. Similarly, for an associate degree, the annual earnings premium of roughly $3,000 is above the annual payment of $1,500 associated with the typical amount of about $11,000 that students borrow for this type of degree.

The economics literature provides some evidence that credit constraints faced by students upon graduation can affect career choices. In particular, Rothstein and Rouse (2011) find that having more debt to repay reduces the probability that graduates choose lower-paid public interest jobs, especially jobs in education. Similarly, Luo and Mongey (2016) estimate that larger student debt burdens cause individuals to take higher-wage jobs at the expense of job satisfaction, likely due to credit constraints after graduating, and that this reduces their well-being.

Information Failures and Procedural Complexities

Yet another obstacle that prevents some individuals from making high-return investments in college is limited information about the associated benefits and costs, which leads to poor decisions and to underinvestment. Survey-based research yields mixed findings on whether students underestimate or overestimate the returns to college (Betts 1996; Wiswall and Zafar 2013; Baker et al. 2016) but suggests that students generally view their future earnings as uncertain (Dominitz and Manski 1996). Consistent with this view, one study estimates that only 60 percent of the variability in returns to schooling can be forecasted (Cunha, Heckman, and Navarro 2005).

Underlying this uncertainty about the return to college is the fact that, while this return is high on average, it is also quite variable. This variation is illustrated in Figure 5-5, which shows the distribution of earnings by educational attainment. For example, while workers with a bachelor's degree are far more likely to have greater earnings than those with only a high school diploma, there is a fraction whose earnings are similar to the earnings of those with only a high school diploma. Ten percent of workers age 35 to 44 with a bachelor's degree had earnings under $20,000, compared with 25 percent of workers with only a high school diploma (CPS ASEC, CEA Calculations).

The variation in the returns to college is driven by a number of factors; however, one important determinant of both the variability and student uncertainty about these returns is the large variation in the quality of schools and programs of study—which can be hard for potential students to assess. A growing body of literature shows that college quality matters both for completion and for earnings,[7] with some pointing to relatively poor returns at for-profit institutions (Cellini and Turner 2016). Studies have also estimated highly variable returns by college major for bachelor's degree recipients (for example, Altonji, Blom, and Meghir 2012), and others have

---

[7] For example, see Bound, Lovenheim, and Turner (2010); Cohodes and Goodman (2014); Goodman, Hurwitz, and Smith (2015); Hoekstra (2009).

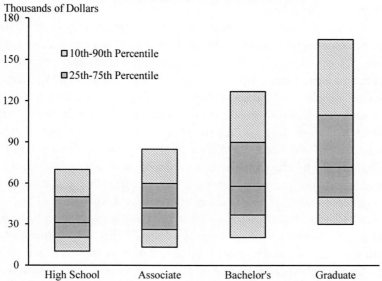

Figure 5-5
Variation in Earnings by Educational Attainment

Thousands of Dollars

Note: Data are for workers ages 35-44 with positive wage and salary income.
Source: CPS ASEC 2016, CEA calculations

found that students' forecast errors regarding earnings differences across majors can affect their major choice (Arcidiacono, Hotz, and Kang 2012).

The effects of poor information and large, difficult-to-forecast variation in earnings can be particularly detrimental since students cannot diversify their college enrollment selections. That is, students generally attend only one school at a time and focus on one or two programs. If they make a poor selection of college or major, it is costly to switch, as it can be difficult to transfer credits. This can potentially lock students into a low-quality program. For some students, the uncertainty of returns itself may prevent them from enrolling in the first place if they are sufficiently risk-averse (Heckman, Lochner, and Todd 2006). The combination of high variability and uncertainty with limited ability to diversify means that some students will realize small, or even negative returns, from college even if the expected return is high. The associated uncertainty may also cause risk-averse students to invest less than they otherwise would in their education.

Prospective students also lack good information about costs. Students often overestimate college costs—with low-income and first-generation prospective students overestimating the cost by as much as two or three times the actual amount (Avery and Kane 2004)—and parents overestimate costs as well (Grodsky and Jones 2007). Moreover, Hastings et al. (2015) find that students who overestimate costs are less likely to enroll in, and complete, a degree program, confirming that misinformation about costs can be a barrier to investing in college.

When attempting to assess the costs of college, an important obstacle for many students is the complexity of the financial-aid system (Lavecchia, Liu, and Oreopoulos 2015). Behavioral economics show that onerous processes can impact choices, especially when the individuals making decisions are young (Thaler and Mullainathan 2008; Casey, Jones, and Somerville 2011), and can therefore prevent some students who would benefit from investing in college from doing so. In a study of Boston public school students, Avery and Kane (2004) find evidence that low-income students are discouraged by the procedural complexity of applying both financial aid and admission into college, even if they are qualified and enthusiastic about going to college. These findings are consistent with those of Dynarski and Scott-Clayton (2006), who use lessons from tax theory and behavioral economics to show that the complexity of the FAFSA is a serious obstacle to both the efficiency and equity in the distribution of student aid. Page and Scott-Clayton (2015) calculate that 30 percent of college students who would qualify for a Pell Grant fail to file the FAFSA, which is required to receive a Pell Grant.

The Role of Family Income

Overall, the evidence points to a number of factors—including social externalities, credit constraints, poor information, and complexity—that cause some individuals to invest too little in their educations or to otherwise make poor education investment choices. Importantly, these factors do not affect all students equally; they are all more likely to affect disadvantaged individuals. First, students from low-income families, with lower levels of savings, are more likely to be credit constrained and, thus, in need of student loans. Further, the costs of financial-aid complexity also fall most heavily on disadvantaged students, who may have fewer resources available to help them navigate the system (Dynarski and Scott-Clayton 2006). Similarly, research shows that low-income students are less likely to accurately estimate the costs and returns to college (Avery and Kane 2004; Grodsky and Jones 2007; Horn, Chen, and Chapman 2003; Hoxby and Turner 2015). In part, this may reflect the lack of detailed information in popular sources like *U.S. News and World Report* on many colleges disproportionately attended by low-income students. In addition to the barriers they face specific to higher education, low-income students are less likely to receive a PreK-12 education that prepares them for college, making college access and success an even greater challenge for these individuals. New research shows that,

Box 5-1: Anti-Poverty Efforts and Educational Attainment

Research suggests that this Administration's anti-poverty efforts will help expand college access and success, either directly through improving college outcomes or indirectly through improved childhood health and academic performance. Clear evidence supports the expansions of Medicaid and the Children's Health Insurance Program (CHIP), the Earned Income Tax Credit (EITC), and the Supplemental Nutrition Assistance Program (SNAP).

Medicaid/CHIP improves early childhood health and protects families facing health problems from financial hardship (Currie 2000; Kaestner 2009; Kaestner, Racine, and Joyce 2000; Dave et al. 2015; Finkelstein et al. 2012), both of which are positively associated with higher educational attainment (Case, Fertig, and Paxson 2005). Cohodes et al. (2016) find that a 10 percentage-point increase in Medicaid/CHIP eligibility for children increase college enrollment by 0.5 percent and increases the four-year college attainment rate by about 2.5 percent. Brown, Kowalski, and Lurie (2015) also find that female children with more years of Medicaid/CHIP eligibility are significantly more likely to attend college. In his first month in office, President Obama signed the Children's Health Insurance Program Reauthorization Act, which provided additional tools and enhanced financial support to help states cover more children through Medicaid and CHIP, and subsequent legislation has extended funding for CHIP through fiscal year (FY) 2017. In parallel, the Affordable Care Act's comprehensive coverage expansions through Medicaid and the Health Insurance Marketplaces are helping to ensure all children and their families have access to affordable, high-quality health insurance coverage.

The EITC reduces the amount of taxes that qualified working people with low to moderate income owe and provides refunds to many of these individuals. It has been shown to raise student test scores (Dahl and Lochner 2012) and future educational attainment. Research finds that raising the maximum EITC by $1,000 increases the probability of completing one or more years of college by age 19 by 1.4 percentage points (Maxfield 2013) and of completing a bachelor's degree among 18–23 year olds by 0.3 percentage point (Michelmore 2013). For families whose household income lies near the EITC eligibility cutoff, another study provides evidence that a $1,000 increase in credits received during the spring of their senior year of high school increases college enrollment the following fall by 0.5 percentage point (Manoli and Turner 2014). Through the American Recovery and Reinvestment Act (the Recovery Act), President Obama expanded the EITC for families with more than two children and for working couples, and he made these expansions permanent in 2015; the refundable portion of the Child Tax Credit (CTC) was also expanded in parallel with these changes. Together, the EITC and CTC improvements reduce the extent or severity of poverty for about 8 million children each year.

Research has found that lower family food budgets are associated with greater discipline problems and lower test scores among school-age children (CEA 2015b). SNAP provides nutrition assistance to millions of eligible, low-income individuals and families and helps to combat these problems. A study by Almond, Hoynes, and Schanzenbach (2016) finds that early childhood access to the Food Stamp Program (as SNAP was previously known) led to higher rates of high school completion among children who grew up in disadvantaged households. By expanding SNAP benefits in the Recovery Act, President Obama prevented hundreds of thousands of families from experiencing food insecurity (Nord and Prell 2011), enabling more children to be well-nourished and prepared for school.

among individuals with similar ability, those from low socioeconomic backgrounds are less likely to complete college than their higher socioeconomic peers and, as a result, they tend not to realize their full potential in the labor market (Papageorge and Thom 2016).

In light of the evidence, many of the Administration's policies have been targeted at removing barriers to education for those who face the greatest challenges, and so represent the largest opportunities for improved efficiency and equity. The remainder of this chapter describes the set of evidence-based policies enacted and proposed by the Obama Administration to help correct market failures and to improve the investment decisions and outcomes of all students who wish to invest in higher education.

KEY ACCOMPLISHMENTS

Over the last eight years, the Obama Administration has made great strides to help students make more effective investments in higher education. These efforts have been guided by the available evidence and have addressed the challenges identified above by helping to offset the cost of college, reducing credit constraints and improving student debt outcomes, providing better information about the costs and benefits of colleges, simplifying the financial aid application process, and holding the most poorly performing colleges accountable. In addition, Administration efforts to improve PreK-12 outcomes have aimed to better prepare students for college and their careers. Some of the effects of these policies are already evident today, while many more will be realized over the coming decades. Despite these important steps, more work remains to ensure that all interested students have the opportunity to pursue higher education, and that they can do so affordably.

Helping Students Pay for College

At the onset of the Great Recession, the college earnings premium was near a historical high and the number of Americans who wished to attend college was rising. But at the same time, falling tax revenues and State budget shortfalls led to sharp declines in State funding for public institutions, which in turn contributed to rising tuitions and fees (Figure 5-6; Mitchell, Palacios, and Leachman 2014). While the costs of college were increasingly shifted to students through higher tuition, rising unemployment and financial hardship also meant more families faced credit constraints and uncertainty as to whether a college investment was feasible. With large returns at stake, reducing the cost of college became an urgent priority and an early cornerstone of this Administration's higher education policy.

Investments in Grant and Tax Aid

Since coming into office, President Obama has worked aggressively with Congress to increase the maximum Pell Grant award, the primary form of financial aid for many students. On average, Pell Grants reduced the cost of college by $3,700 for over 8 million students last year. Pell Grant funding increased by more than $12 billion from award year 2008–09 to 2014–15, a 67 percent increase, and the maximum Pell Grant award has increased by roughly $1,000 (Figure 5-7). Moreover, for the first time, Pell Grant funding has been tied to inflation to ensure the value of the aid does not fall over time.

A growing body of research confirms the potential for need-based grants to improve college access and success.[8] For example, Dynarski (2003) examines the elimination of the Social Security Student Benefit Program in 1982, and her estimates suggest that an offer of $1,000 in grant aid increases the probability of attending college by about 3.6 percentage points and appears to increase school completion. Abraham and Clark (2006) find similar impacts on college attendance in their study of the District of Columbia Tuition Assistance Grant Program instituted in 1999. A more recent study that examines the effects of a need-based program in Florida with a strict

---

[8] A few early studies focusing on the initial implementation of the Pell Grant find mixed results (Hansen 1983; Kane 1996; Seftor and Turner 2002; Bettinger 2004); however, the initial benefits of the program may have been limited by the newness of the program and the complexity of the eligibility rules and application process. These complexities have been reduced in recent years.

Figure 5-6
Annual Percent Change in State Funding for Higher Education and Public Tuition and Fees Over Time

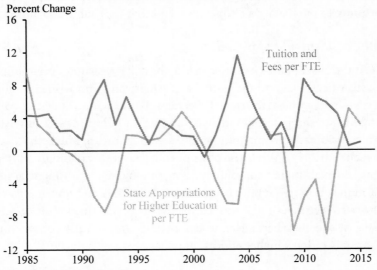

Note: Figures are inflation adjusted.
Source: College Board (2015)

Figure 5-7
Pell Expenditures Over Time

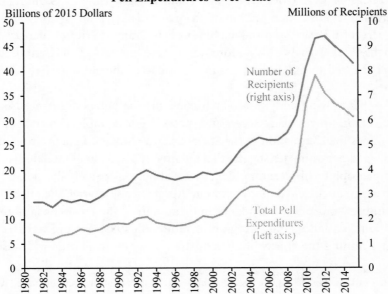

Source: College Board (2016b)

eligibility cutoff likewise finds significant increases in four-year college enrollment and completion (Castleman and Long 2013).

Using these studies to estimate the effects of this Administration's expansions of Pell Grants, CEA analysis finds that the Pell Grant expansions since the 2008–09 award year led at least 250,000 students to attend college or complete a college degree in 2014–15 who would have not otherwise done so. The increase in educational attainment among these students translates to an additional $20 billion in aggregate earnings, representing a nearly 2:1 return on the investment. However, the actual returns on the Administration's Pell Grant investments are likely even larger, as this estimate does not account for social externalities from increased educational attainment nor for other benefits to those receiving larger Pell Grants, including the opportunity to select from a broader range of options, spend more time on school instead of work, and finish sooner (see the Appendix of CEA 2016c for more details on this calculation).

The Administration has also reduced taxes for low- and middle-income families that attend college. Under the 2009 Recovery Act, the Administration established the American Opportunity Tax Credit (AOTC), which provides a maximum credit of $2,500 a year—or up to $10,000 over four years—to expand and replace the Hope higher education credit. Along with providing a more generous credit, the AOTC also is partially refundable and thus provides more benefits for low-income households that do not owe any income taxes. Before the AOTC, only 5 percent of credit and tuition deduction dollars went to filers with incomes under $25,000; by 2014, that share had risen to 23 percent (Dynarski and Scott-Clayton 2016; College Board 2016b). Although research shows that the AOTC has little impact on college enrollment (Hoxby and Bulman 2015; Bulman and Hoxby 2015), the credit lowers the costs of college for millions of students and their families; in 2016, the AOTC cut taxes by over $1,800 on average for nearly 10 million families. The bipartisan tax agreement that President Obama signed into law in 2015 made the AOTC permanent as part of a package that collectively provided about 24 million working and middle-class families a year each with a tax cut of about $1,000.

Due in part to the Administration's historic investments in grant and tax aid, the net price of college that students are responsible for paying grew far more slowly than the published cost of attendance between award years 2008–09 and 2016–17 (Figure 5-8). Although more work remains to make college more affordable, the impact of the Administration's Pell Grant and tax credit expansions have helped lower the cost of college for millions of students and their families.

Figure 5-8

Growth in the Cost of Attendance and Net Price between 2009 and 2017

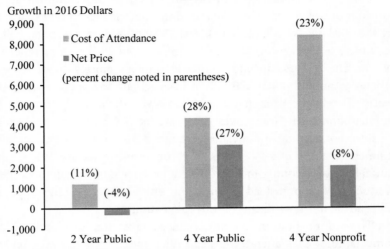

Note: Years are academic years, and prices are for undergraduate students. Public costs are for in-state students. Cost of attendance includes tuition, fees, room, and board. Net price subtracts grant and tax aid from cost of attendance.
Source: College Board (2016a)

America's College Promise

Although investments in grant and tax aid have helped make college more affordable for many students, too many families still feel as if college is out of reach. To ensure that all responsible students are able to attend college, President Obama unveiled his America's College Promise (ACP) plan in January 2015 to make two years of community college free for hard-working students. Over 1,300 American community colleges provide over 40 percent of undergraduates with educations that deepen their knowledge, make them more informed citizens, and lead to a quality, affordable degree or credential that improves their opportunities in the labor market. If all states participate in the President's ACP plan, an estimated 9 million students could benefit from such an education, and a full-time community college student could save an average of $3,800 in tuition each year.

In fewer than two years since the President challenged more states and communities to make America's College Promise a reality for their students, at least 38 Promise programs—or free community college programs—have launched in states, cities, and community colleges in all corners of the United States (Figure 5-9), increasing the total estimated number of Promise programs to more than 150 across the country. Altogether these new programs are raising more than $150 million in new public and private investments

Box 5-2: Federal Investments in K-12 Education during the Recession

As the effects of the Great Recession set in, public universities were not alone in suffering the consequences of declining State revenues; almost all states found that their projected revenues were insufficient to achieve their education plans. As a result, since State and local governments provide about 90 percent of school funding, officials were preparing for significant funding cuts for K-12 teachers, principals, and support staff, in addition to higher education personnel. Such cuts would have severely disrupted educational services for many of America's students (EOP 2009).

In response to the fiscal crisis, the Recovery Act appropriated more than $60 million to State education agencies. In doing so, it shielded schools from the worst effects of their States' budgetary shortfalls (Evans, Schwab, and Wagner 2014). While funding alone is not a panacea for solving problems in K-12 education, research suggests it is a necessary component. If invested in the most productive inputs, it can contribute to improved educational outcomes, especially for students living in poverty (Jackson, Johnson, and Persico 2016; LaFortune, Rothstein, and Schanzenbach 2016). A key way in which increased Recovery Act funding helped improve outcomes was by keeping experienced teachers in the classroom and staving off increases in class sizes. It enabled states to save or create more than 400,000 jobs, most of which were for teachers, principals, and other school staff. Research finds that students in smaller classrooms in the early grades perform higher on standardized tests, earn higher wages, and are more likely to attend college than peers in larger classrooms (Chetty et al. 2011), and that the effects may be larger for minorities and low-income students (Krueger 1999). Due to the swift action of the Obama Administration, states were provided the resources to keep teachers in the classroom and ensure that students had the educational services necessary to succeed.

In addition, the Recovery Act was able to catalyze a wave of reform through targeted investments. The Race to the Top initiative, which offered incentives to states willing to spur systemic reform to improve teaching and learning in their schools, led nearly every state to raise the bar on expectations for student learning, and an independent analysis found that Race to the Top led to significant changes in education policy across the United States (Howell 2015). Other Administration programs, such as the Investing in Innovation Fund (i3), focused funding on evidence-based interventions that could be validated by high-quality evaluations and, if proven successful, could be scaled up.

Figure 5-9
Promise Programs Across the Country

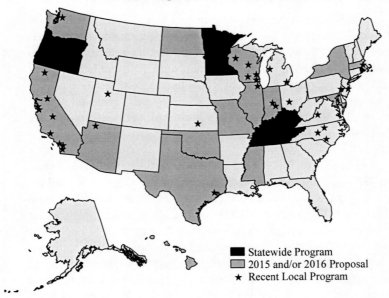

Statewide Program
2015 and/or 2016 Proposal
★ Recent Local Program

Note: Map is as of October 2016.

in community colleges to serve at least 180,000 students; and the number
of free community college programs continues to grow. Additionally, at the
Federal level, both the House and the Senate have proposed legislation to
expand Promise programs nationwide.

Free community college promotes college access not only by reducing
financial barriers,[9] but also by eliminating barriers related to misinformation
about college costs (Baum and Scott-Clayton 2015). By clearly messaging that
a post-secondary education is within reach, Promise programs help students
cross the first hurdle to applying and enrolling in college. Removing such
barriers at community colleges is especially important, as community college
students tend to be poorer than students attending four-year schools—over
half of community college students have family incomes below 185 percent
of the Federal poverty line—and are less likely to have parents who attended
college to help them navigate the student aid application process (NPSAS
2012, CEA tabulations). Indeed, research shows that Promise programs have
been highly effective, which is why the President proposed his vision for free
community college in America's College Promise.

---

[9] Researchers have found that students facing lower community college prices are more likely to
enroll in college (Denning 2016b; Martorell, McCall, and McFarlin 2014).

Evaluations of early local Promise programs show that these programs can significantly improve high school graduation, college enrollment, and college graduation rates. A number of research studies have examined the effects of Kalamazoo Promise, the first place-based Promise program. Initiated in 2005, Kalamazoo Promise offers full in-state college tuition to graduates of the Kalamazoo Public Schools in Michigan who have enrolled in the district for at least four years. Using variation in high school eligibility, length of enrollment in the school district, and/or the timing of the program's announcement and implementation, researchers have found that the program reduced suspensions in high school, improved high school credit completion, led to students sending their test scores to more selective in-state institutions, and substantially increased college enrollment and graduation (Andrews, DesJardins and Ranchhod 2010; Bartik and Lachowska 2013; Bartik, Hershbein, and Lachowska 2015; Miller-Adams 2009). Research suggests that the program has had a high rate of return, particularly for African American students (Bartik, Hershbein, and Lachowska 2016).

Carruthers and Fox (2016) likewise find large positive effects of another Promise program. Knox Achieves covered the gap between tuition and fees and grant aid from Federal, State, and institutional sources to first-year community college students making an immediate transition between high school and one of Tennessee's public community colleges or technology centers. Comparing outcomes before and after the program began between students in eligible districts and students in non-eligible districts, Carruthers and Fox find large impacts on high school graduation and college enrollment, with some shift from the four-year to two-year sector. The positive effects of high school graduation and college enrollment were strongest for lower-achieving and lower-income students. Given the success of Knox Achieves, 27 counties adopted the program to expand eligibility to nearly half of Tennessee's population in 2014, and the program became the model for the state-wide Tennessee Promise program rolled out in 2015, which guarantees free community college tuition and fees to high school seniors who sign up, apply for financial aid, and meet with a mentor. Analyses of Promise programs in New York, Pittsburgh, El Dorado, and New Haven also show sizeable effects on educational outcomes (Scrivener et al. 2015; Page and Iritri 2016; Ritter and Ash 2016; Gonzalez et al. 2014; Daugherty and Gonzelez 2016).

The economics literature suggests that program design matters, and some Promise initiatives may see less success. For example, LeGower and Walsh (2014) suggest that merit-based Promise programs may have more limited effects on college access as they disproportionately benefit wealthier and white households. An analysis of one program, which provides free

Box 5-3: Expansions of Early Education Programs

The Administration has been committed to helping students access a high-quality education at all levels of schooling, and the President's calls for universal preschool and a child care guarantee for working families with young children serve as critical complements to his other proposals. Gaps in educational achievement occur early in life and grow over time, so it is critical to ensure that all children receive the educational foundation to succeed in school and life. On nearly every measure of school readiness, from health to early human capital, children born into low-income households enter kindergarten at a substantial disadvantage relative to their higher-income peers. Indeed, disparities in physical and mental health, cognition, and socio-emotional and behavioral skills develop in children as young as 9 months (Halle et al. 2009). By the time children enter school around age 5, those in poor households are nearly four times more likely to score "very low" on assessments of math skills and over four times more likely to score "very low'" on reading skills than their peers in more well-off households (Isaacs 2012). This gap remains relatively constant through the beginning of high school, suggesting that achievement gaps in later years are established in the earliest years of childhood (CEA 2016a).

Research shows that enrollment in high-quality early childhood education accelerates cognitive and non-cognitive development during primary school years (see CEA 2016a for a review), and can lead to significantly better outcomes later in life—such as greater educational attainment and earnings and less involvement with the criminal justice system (for example, Heckman et al. 2010; Reynolds et al. 2011; Campbell et al. 2012). That is why, in addition to calling for preschool for all and high-quality care for all infants and toddlers, the Obama Administration has worked with Congress to increase investments in early childhood programs by over $6 billion from FY 2009 to FY 2016, including high-quality preschool, Head Start, early Head Start, child care subsidies, evidence-based home visiting, and programs for infants and toddlers with disabilities. Since 2009, 38 States and the District of Columbia have increased investments in preschool programs by more than $1.5 billion.

community college only to students with at least a 3.0 high school GPA who test out of remediation, found that these conditions limited eligibility to only about 15 percent of the city's high school graduates (Page and Scott-Clayton 2015; Fain 2014). Additionally, research finds that reducing the cost of lower-quality options can worsen outcomes for students, so attention to college quality in the context of lowering prices to students is essential (Peltzman 1973). A recent Department of Education report (2016a), the

America's College Promise Playbook, outlines the best evidence available to inform design features that localities creating Promise programs should consider. The report exemplifies the Administration's commitment to expanding quality free community college through Promise programs at the local, State, and National level.

Reducing Credit Constraints and Improving Student Debt Outcomes

While the Administration has worked aggressively to lower the cost of college, it has also taken important steps to ensure that students can access credit to finance their college educations. For a growing number of Americans, Federal student loans are an essential means to realizing the benefits of higher education. In fall 2013, over 20 million students enrolled in an institution eligible for Federal aid, and roughly half of these students used Federal student loans to help finance their education. Both economic theory and empirical evidence suggests that without access to Federal student loans, financially constrained students are less likely to attend college, more likely to work while in school, and less likely to complete a degree (Denning 2016a; Wiederspan 2015; Dunlop 2013; Sun and Yannelis 2016).

Key policies signed into law by the President have maintained the accessibility and affordability of student loans for borrowers. In 2010, President Obama signed student loan reform into law, which ended student loan subsidies for private financial institutions and banks and shifted over $60 billion in savings back to students. Before the reform, banks and other private financial institutions provided Federally guaranteed loans, meaning that these institutions provided the underlying loan principal and earned a profit when students paid back their loans but were compensated by the government when the students failed to repay. To remove this subsidy to financial institutions, the 2010 reform required that all new loans be financed directly by the Federal Government as Direct Loans, eliminating the middleman and saving money for taxpayers and students. In 2013, President Obama signed into law further reforms that lowered interest rates on student loans for nearly 11 million borrowers, saving them on average $1,000 over the life of their loan. To date, interest rates have remained low and currently stand at 3.76 percent for undergraduate borrowers.

As an increasing number of students have been borrowing to finance a college education, the volume of outstanding Federal debt has risen, standing at a high of $1.3 trillion dollars today. This rise in debt has made it especially important to ensure that loans serve students well and do not present a burden to borrowers once they leave college.

The evidence suggests that, on average, student loans continue to facilitate very high returns for college graduates, and most borrowers are able to make progress paying back their loans (CEA 2016d). In addition, though there has been an increase in the typical amount of debt that borrowers accumulate, most students accumulate only modest amounts of debt. Fifty-nine percent of borrowers owed less than $20,000 in debt in 2015, with undergraduate borrowers holding an average debt of $17,900. Large-volume debt remains more prevalent among graduate loans, for which loan limits are much higher, and among borrowers who completed their undergraduate degrees. Consistent with their greater educational attainment, borrowers with greater debt tend to have larger earnings and therefore tend to be well-equipped to pay back that debt (Figure 5-10; Looney and Yannelis 2015).

However, borrowers who attend low-quality schools or fail to complete their degrees face real challenges with repayment. In fact, the highest rates of student loan default occur among students with the smallest amounts of debt because these students are much less likely to have completed, having left school before paying for the full cost of a degree, as shown in Figure 5-11.[10]

The Great Recession also created some acute challenges for student loan borrowers. During the recession, many borrowers went back to school to shelter from the collapsing labor market, but a disproportionate number of these students attended schools that had relatively low graduation rates and did not provide affordable pathways to good jobs. Along with this change in the quality of schools they attended, changes in the demographics of borrowers entering repayment and the challenges they faced when entering the labor market during a deep recession contributed to rising default rates during the recession and in the period that followed. Over the last few years, the number of students attending low-quality schools has declined, labor market conditions have improved, and default rates, as measured by the official three-year Cohort Default Rate, have gone down (Figure 5-12).

In response to rising default rates, the Administration has worked to ensure that students attend high-quality schools and that borrowers who have left school and entered repayment have affordable loan payments. The following section focuses on this Administration's efforts to expand flexible repayment plans, while later sections describe efforts to improve the quality of schools that borrowers attend. In addition, the Administration has focused on strengthening loan servicing to support Americans struggling with student loan debt. In 2015, the Administration released a Student Aid

---

[10] Loans of less than $10,000 accounted for nearly two-thirds of all defaults for the 2011 cohort three years after entering repayment. Loans of less than $5,000 accounted for 35 percent of all defaults.

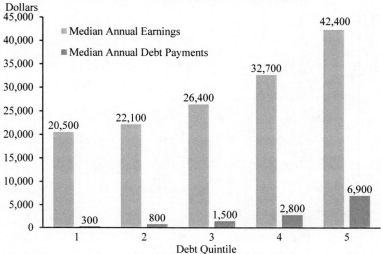

Figure 5-10
Median Annual Earnings by Debt Quintile

Note: Data are for the 2013 cohort, using the NSLDS 4 percent sample matched to de-identified tax records. Data are for both undergraduate and graduate borrowers. Debt-service figures assume a 10-year standard repayment plan and 3.76% interest.
Source: Looney and Yannelis (2015)

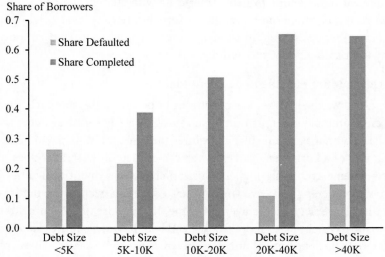

Figure 5-11
Share of Undergraduate Borrowers Who Default by Year 3 by Loan Size, 2011 Repayment Cohort

Note: Years are fiscal years. Loan size is based on balance of loan when entering repayment. Share completed refers to those who completed a credential.
Source: Department of Education

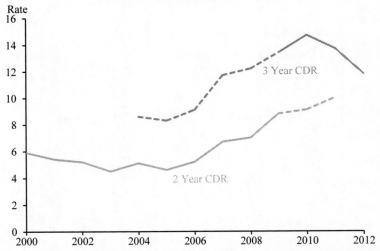

Figure 5-12
Cohort Default Rates Over Time

Note: Solid lines represent official rates while dashed lines are estimates by the Department of Education. Through the fiscal year 2008, official cohort default rates were measured after two years, after which they were measured after three years; during the transition period, estimates for both time periods were provided.
Source: Department of Education

Bill of Rights reflecting the President's vision that every borrower has the right to quality customer service, reliable information, and fair treatment, even if they struggle to repay their loans. And, in 2016, the White House announced new actions to help Americans with student loan debt understand their repayment options and to ensure they have access to high-quality customer service, strong consumer protections, and targeted support to repay their student debt successfully.

Providing More Flexible Repayment Plans

As described above, the constraint imposed by the standard 10-year student loan repayment plan (in which students are enrolled by default) can hinder debt management since it requires the same monthly payment at the beginning of a borrower's career, when earnings are lowest, as it does mid-career when earnings are higher. This can create repayment difficulties and dissuade students from investing in their education even when the investment has large net benefits over a lifetime. In response, the Administration has made payment plans more flexible and loan payments more manageable through the expansion of income-driven repayment plans. These plans increase flexibility in several ways. First, by expanding the period of repayment, they allow borrowers to spread their student loan payments over a longer period of time, while retaining the option of paying sooner with no pre-payment penalty. Second, by tying payments to borrowers' incomes, income-driven repayment plans link the timing of repayment more closely to the time path of earnings gains from higher education, and they remove needless credit constraints in times when income is temporarily low. Finally, income-driven repayment plans can serve as a form of insurance against uncertain returns to college, helping to address some barriers associated with risk.

With the new repayment plans, borrowers will never have to pay more than 10 percent of their discretionary income to repay debt. The Administration initially expanded income-driven repayment by passing into law the Pay As You Earn (PAYE) plan in 2012, which reduced monthly payments to 10 percent of borrowers' discretionary income—lower than the 15 percent required under the original Income Based Repayment plan. Under PAYE, borrowers could also have their remaining loan balances forgiven after 20 years of qualifying payments, 5 years earlier than the original Income Based Repayment plan. PAYE extended more affordable loans to 1.6 million borrowers; however, many borrowers remained ineligible. That is why, in 2015, the Administration expanded PAYE with regulation creating the Revised Pay As You Earn (REPAYE) repayment plan that provides eligibility to all Direct Loan student borrowers, including any student with a consolidated loan (excluding PLUS loans to parents). With REPAYE, these borrowers can cap their monthly payments at 10 percent of their discretionary income, regardless of when they borrowed and, after making the appropriate number of qualifying payments, will have any outstanding balance forgiven. Under REPAYE, borrowers with only undergraduate loans can have their remaining loan balances forgiven after 20 years of qualifying payments; borrowers with any graduate school loans can have their remaining balances forgiven after 25 years of qualifying payments.

Figure 5-13 below illustrates how the theoretical repayment curve for the standard 10-year plan differs from REPAYE for a typical borrower graduating with a four-year degree.[11] Data from the Baccalaureate and Beyond study show that seniors graduating college in 2008 held a median debt of $17,125 and earned a median income of $31,000 upon leaving school. The Figure assumes an interest rate of 3.76 percent consistent with the 2016 student loan rate, real earnings growth consistent with trends in Figure 5-4, 2-percent inflation, and a single-person family (for ease of REPAYE calculations). The "Standard" line corresponds to the standard 10-year repayment plan with an initial income of $31,000 and an initial debt of $17,125, consistent with the Baccalaureate and Beyond data for all students who borrowed.

---

[11] It should be noted that a number of alternative repayment plans also exist, some of which have longer payment schedules.

Figure 5-13
Repayment Distribution by Repayment Plan

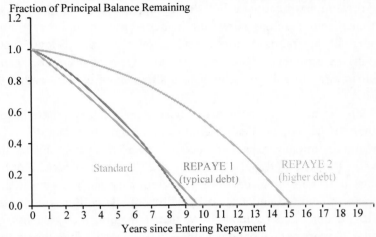

Note: Calculations assume a real interest rate of 3.76%, 2% inflation, income growth corresponding with Figure 5-4 describing earnings by age for full-time full-year workers, that borrowers are in single person families, and assumptions about income and debt from the 2008 Baccalaureate and Beyond Study. REPAYE 1 and 2 differ in their original principal debt amounts, with REPAYE 2 corresponding with a higher debt amount.
Source: CEA Calculations

The line labeled "REPAYE 1" uses the REPAYE formula with the same initial income and debt, while "REPAYE 2" uses the same initial income but an initial debt of $31,000 to show how repayment patterns differ by debt amounts. The Standard plan line is relatively flat, reflecting the constant rate at which the principal balance is paid off under this plan. In contrast, both REPAYE lines show that principal repayment is initially slow and accelerates over time. In some cases, such as in "REPAYE 1," borrowers may pay off their debt faster under REPAYE than the Standard plan if their wages are sufficiently high. Further, a comparison of the two REPAYE lines shows that the larger the debt is in comparison to income (or the smaller income is in comparison to debt), the less the REPAYE repayment curve will look like the Standard curve.

Continuing to expand enrollment in income-driven repayment plans for students who would benefit remained a key priority for this Administration. As of the third quarter of FY 2016, about 5.5 million (more than 1 in 5) borrowers with Federally managed debt were enrolled in income-driven repayment plans. The share of borrowers with Federally managed debt who are enrolled in income-driven repayment has more than quadrupled from 5 percent in the first quarter of FY 2012 to 23 percent in the third quarter of FY 2016 (Figure 5-14). To help borrowers access this debt management tool, the Administration has improved loan servicer contract requirements, pushed efforts associated with the President's Student Aid Bill of Rights, put forward a student debt challenge to gather commitments from external stakeholders, and increased and improved targeted outreach to key borrower segments who would benefit from PAYE or REPAYE. Although barriers related to recertifying income and interfacing with the income-driven repayment enrollment tools online persist, the Administration continued to explore options for how to address these remaining shortcomings.

Recent data suggest that income-driven repayment plans appear to be drawing in many of those borrowers who may most benefit (Figure 5-15). In general, the data show that income-driven repayment borrowers tend to have lower reported family incomes than borrowers on the standard repayment plan. Among borrowers with undergraduate loans who were enrolled in income-driven repayment as of the third quarter of FY 2015, the average family income (in real 2014 dollars) based on the first FAFSA filed was $45,000, compared with $57,000 for those on the standard repayment plan. For borrowers with graduate loans, the average income among those enrolled in income-driven repayment was $60,000, compared with $74,000 for borrowers on the standard plan. Even within sectors of educational institutions, borrowers enrolled in income-driven repayment tended to come from lower income backgrounds than those enrolled in the standard plan, suggesting that these plans are reaching the students who may need them the most. One factor contributing to lower incomes among undergraduate income-driven repayment enrollees was that these borrowers were more likely to be classified as independent, and independent borrowers tend to have lower reported incomes since their parents' incomes are not counted as part of their family's income. Overall, 52 percent of borrowers in income-driven repayment were classified as independent, as opposed to 42 percent of borrowers under the standard repayment plan.

Given that income-driven repayment plans tend to change repayment schedules more dramatically for borrowers whose debt is high relative to their incomes, it is perhaps unsurprising that borrowers in income-driven repayment tend to have larger loan balances outstanding (Figure 5-16). As of the third quarter of FY 2015, the median debt for these borrowers was $34,000, while the median was just $10,000 for borrowers in the standard plan. This difference partly reflects a larger share of graduate borrowers; 30 percent of income-driven repayment borrowers had graduate loans, compared with 10 percent of borrowers under the standard plan. However, substantial differences remain even among graduate and undergraduate borrowers. Differences in outstanding balances also remained when looking within sector, and data for the 2011 repayment cohort suggest they were partly driven by the fact that borrowers entering income-driven repayment

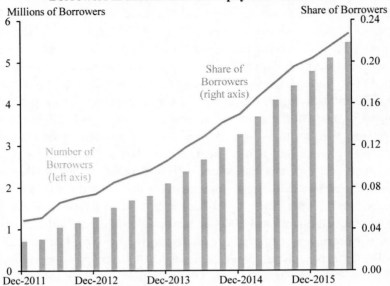

Figure 5-14
Borrowers in Income Driven Repayment Over Time

Millions of Borrowers

Share of Borrowers
(right axis)

Number of
Borrowers
(left axis)

Note: Data are restricted to Federally-managed debt.
Source: Department of Education

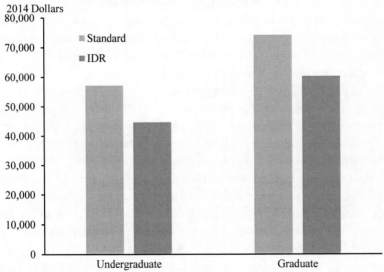

Figure 5-15
Average Family Income by Repayment Plan

2014 Dollars

■ Standard

■ IDR

Undergraduate   Graduate

Note: Data are as of the third quarter of fiscal year 2015. Income based on first FAFSA filed,
converted to 2014 dollars. Undergraduate and graduate are broken apart at the loan level.
Source: Department of Education

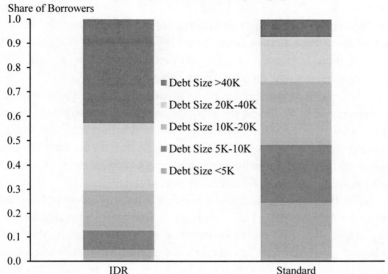

Figure 5-16
Size of Outstanding Loan Balance by Repayment Plan

Note: Data are as of the third quarter of fiscal year 2015. Debt size is based on outstanding loan balance.
Source: Department of Education

typically have larger principal loan balances than borrowers in the standard repayment plan.

Consistent with both the larger debt and the prevalence of graduate student debt among borrowers in income-driven repayment, these borrowers are more likely to have completed their undergraduate degrees than borrowers in the standard repayment plan. Among those in the 2011 repayment cohort, 64 percent of borrowers in income-driven repayment had completed, compared with only 48 percent of borrowers in the standard plan. Many of those who completed their undergraduate degree accumulated more debt because they subsequently enrolled in graduate school. But even among borrowers with no graduate school debt, those enrolled in an income-driven repayment plan were still slightly more likely to have completed a degree.

The positive relationship between completion and income-driven repayment enrollment suggests that students who enroll in income-driven repayment are more likely to have large long-run returns to their college investments and to be able to eventually pay off their loans. However, data on prior repayment behavior also show that individuals with short-run repayment difficulties are using income-driven repayment. Among borrowers entering repayment in FY 2011, a sizeable fraction that enrolled in income-driven repayment had experienced difficulty in repaying their loans before entering income-driven repayment, with slightly higher signs of distress compared with borrowers under the standard plan. Over 40 percent of these borrowers had defaulted, had an unemployment or economic hardship deferment, or had a single forbearance of more than 2 months in length before entering their first income-driven repayment plan. A much smaller fraction of these borrowers, roughly 10 percent, experienced difficulty in repayment after entering income-driven repayment.

A key way that income-driven repayment helps to improve outcomes for borrowers is by reducing monthly payments, since payment amounts are spread over a longer time period and are tied to earnings. For the 2011 repayment cohort, Figure 5-17 shows that borrowers in income-driven repayment had lower monthly payments across all sectors, despite serving borrowers who accumulated larger amounts of debt.

Some borrowers in income-driven repayment plans may have zero-dollar monthly payments. These plans allow borrowers who attended low-quality schools and subsequently experienced low earnings to stay out of default, and give borrowers who experience temporary periods of economic difficulty time to get back on their feet. Data show that the same types of borrowers who have more difficulty repaying their loans in terms of college sector, debt size, and borrower characteristics are also more likely to have zero-dollar scheduled payments, highlighting the importance of income-driven repayment in helping these borrowers manage their debt. It is important to note, however, that another factor driving the group of income-driven repayment borrowers with zero-dollar scheduled payments is that, on average, borrowers in income-driven repayment entered repayment relatively recently. As of the end of FY 2015, income-driven repayment borrowers had been in repayment for an average of about three years. As Figure 5-4 above shows, earnings increase over a career, so as borrowers progress through their careers, their scheduled payments are also likely to increase.

To further expand income-driven repayment to borrowers who could benefit from more manageable monthly payments, the Administration has announced a series of new actions to enroll 2 million more borrowers into income-driven repayment plans. Data about the characteristics of borrowers enrolled in income-driven repayment highlight the importance of these initiatives. For example, though low-balance borrowers and borrowers who did not complete school are more likely to default on their loans, they represent a relatively smaller share of borrowers in income-driven repayment. Enrolling more of these types of borrowers in flexible repayment plans like income-driven repayment will help make their debt more manageable and help them to avoid costly and unnecessary defaults.

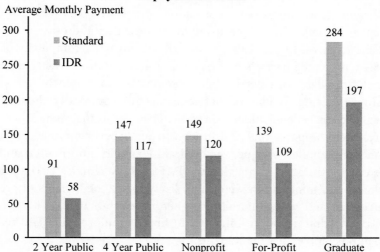

Figure 5-17
Average Monthly Payment by Sector and Repayment Plan, 2011 Repayment Cohort

Average Monthly Payment

Note: Data are for the fiscal year 2011 cohort as of fiscal year 2014. Some small sectors are excluded from this chart. Data contain some duplication across and within categories.
Source: Department of Education

At the same time, as research has shown, college choice is a crucial factor. It is critical to help borrowers avoid investing in colleges that are unlikely to increase their lifetime earnings and might leave them with high debt and low earnings. This Administration's policies have focused on strengthening the information available to students and ensuring college accountability to help students make good decisions.

Improving Information and Reducing Procedural Complexities

When students have better information, they can make better choices about their education. When choosing a college, students need information on college quality and cost to know whether their investment in higher education will pay off. Research shows that, for high-achieving low-income students, providing information about college cost and quality, like semi-customized net price and graduation rates, enables students to attend and progress at schools that better match their qualifications (Hoxby and Turner 2013). Further research shows that clear and detailed information about earnings can lead students to revise their employment expectations (Ruder and Van Noy 2014; Wiswall and Zafar 2013; Oreopoulos and Dunn 2012) and change their major choice (Ruder and Van Noy 2014; Baker et al. 2016). Accessible information about costs and economic outcomes thus plays a crucial role in encouraging students to make informed decisions about enrolling in higher education and choosing the best college for their needs.

At the same time, evidence suggests that, while prospective students can benefit from improved information, procedural complexities may prevent some individuals from using the information and other resources available to them. In particular, as described above, the complexity of the FAFSA has created barriers to efficiency and equity in the distribution of student financial aid, deterring many students who would benefit from aid from applying. It follows that reducing this complexity should help students access Federal student aid to better invest in their education, and the research supports this conclusion. In an experiment that provided low-income families with personalized aid eligibility information and, in some cases, assistance completing the FAFSA, only families who got both assistance and information were more likely to see the benefits of greater financial aid and college enrollment (Bettinger et al. 2012). This section details key Administration initiatives to improve information and reduce procedural complexities for students.

College Scorecard

In 2015, the Department of Education launched the redesigned College Scorecard to help empower Americans to select colleges based on what matters most to them. The online Scorecard provides reliable, unbiased, comprehensive, and nationally comparable data on college outcomes for all institutions. These outcomes include former students' earnings, student debt for graduates, and debt repayment rates; the data are also broken down by demographic group, which allow students to assess how well colleges are serving similar students to themselves before deciding where to apply and attend. Figure 5-18 highlights the importance of these data, showing the large variation in outcomes at two- and four-year colleges. CEA's technical report on using Federal data to measure and improve the performance of U.S. institutions of higher education provides more information about the Scorecard, including a guide to the available measures, methods for assessing college quality, and data-driven lessons for performance management (CEA 2015c).

Within its first year, the College Scorecard has reached students and families across the country (Figure 5-19), and students now have multiple opportunities to use Scorecard to make better decisions. For example, the College Scorecard data will be clearly featured in the hundreds of millions of Google searches related to colleges and universities taking place in the United States each year, and other companies like College Board are integrating the data into their college application products and programs.

Figure 5-18
Distribution of Key Outcome Measures at 2 and 4 Year Schools

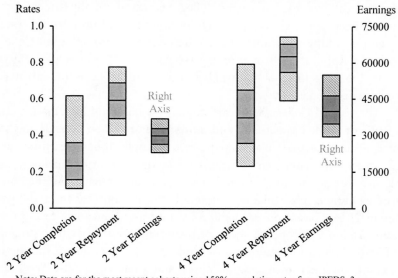

Note: Data are for the most recent cohorts using 150% completion rates from IPEDS, 3-year repayment rates, and 10-year median earnings.
Source: College Scorecard

Figure 5-19
Scorecard Usage by State

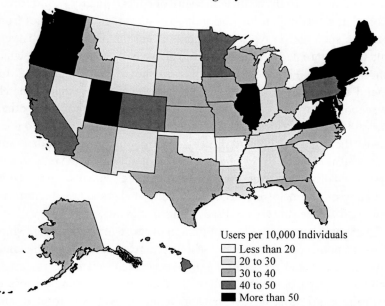

Note: Usage data are as of September 12, 2016. They only represent unique visitors to the Scorecard tool itself and exclude calls for the data through the API. The data are for individuals of all ages and are normalized with 2015 Census data.

College rankings like *Forbes, Money,* Brookings Institution, *Economist, Wall Street Journal,* and *Washington Monthly* are also using new outcomes data included in the Scorecard. Since the College Scorecard initially launched, the data have been accessed nearly 13 million times by API users and through the website. Additionally, more than 700 developers have accessed College Scorecard's Application Programming Interface (API), which allows users to create tools and insights that will help prospective college students make important decisions.

The revised College Scorecard contains a variety of information that is useful for students, parents, and administrators when considering the right college for a particular student. For example, though earnings and employment are primary motivations for students to attend college, students also care about cost, completion rates, and debt repayment outcomes, as well as broader goals like becoming a better person (Eagan et al. 2014; Fishman 2015). Based on academic literature and consumer testing, the Administration developed a series of measurable outcomes that students had identified as important. Because students value each factor differently depending on their own circumstances and preferences, the Scorecard presents each indicator independently so that students can emphasize and compare the attributes most important to them.

Additionally, because students come from a variety of backgrounds, it is helpful to provide information about how prospective institutions serve students like them. Ideally, a single measure of college quality would isolate the effect that attending an institution has on its students' outcomes from other inputs such as the types of students it enrolls. However, it is very difficult to disentangle these effects since they tend to be closely related, as demonstrated in Figure 5-20. This Figure shows that low-income students tend to have lower outcomes both because they disproportionately attend schools with poorer outcomes for all students and because of other, unobservable characteristics, such as academic preparation. In light of these challenges, the College Scorecard presents information on both student outcomes as well as characteristics of the students attending a university to help users assess quality. Moreover, the Scorecard includes data disaggregated by student subgroup to help researchers and policymakers assess institutions' successes and failures in serving disadvantaged students.

The Scorecard includes a combination of short-term measures, which are more responsive to changes in school practices, and long-term measures, which may better represent the more permanent outcomes associated with attending a particular institution. It also notes the program mix of the institution and other factors that may relate to wide variation in outcomes, and makes efforts to ensure the reliability of performance measures

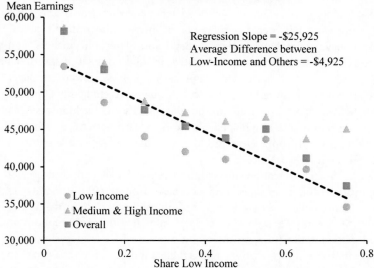

Figure 5-20
Earnings by Family Income at 4 Year Schools

Note: Data for 10 year earnings for the 2002 cohort. Low income defined as family income of less than $30,000, and medium/high income defined as greater than $30,000.
Source: College Scorecard

and information for smaller schools where small changes could lead to substantially different results. Overall, the College Scorecard—released in September 2015 and updated September 2016—represents a significant step forward in providing transparent and comprehensive data on college costs and outcomes and has encouraged the research community to focus on developing a Federal and State data agenda for postsecondary education.

The Administration has also focused on more directly getting information into the hands of students in key areas of high impact, such as when they are applying for student aid or in the form of disclosures related to accountability measures. These initiatives are discussed in further detail in the following sections.

FAFSA Simplification

In light of the evidence about the benefits of simplifying aid, the Administration has undertaken a number of administrative reforms to streamline the FAFSA process so that it can better serve students and their families. Many initiatives have focused on reducing the number of questions presented to students and families and by making it easier for applicants to directly transfer tax and income information from the Internal Revenue Service (IRS). The Administration has revamped the online form for all

Box 5-4: Improving Information to Drive Evidence-Based Policies

Building an evidence base to determine what works and what does not work has been a cornerstone of this Administration's education policy. Educational leaders, Federal and State policymakers, and researchers are increasingly interested in questions of institutional outcomes to better share and adopt best practices, steward taxpayer dollars, and determine how resources can be more efficiently allocated to benefit students. Efforts to improve data quality and facilitate research and innovation have also helped educators to learn both from their own experiences and from others and to ensure that resources are spent on the most effective practices.

In higher education, the Administration has encouraged greater innovation and a stronger evidence base around effective strategies to promote college access and success through 42 First in the World (FITW) grants. These grants support the development, replication, and dissemination of innovative and evidence-based interventions at institutions of higher learning across the Nation. Although the program has since been de-funded by Congress, the grants already made to institutions target adult learners, working students, part-time students, students from low-income backgrounds, students of color, students with disabilities, first-generation students, and other students at risk of not persisting in or completing college. In addition, through the Experimental Sites Initiative, the Administration has tested innovative practices in the delivery of Federal student aid dollars and has used the resulting evidence to inform higher education policies. Some of these experiments include, on a limited basis, making Pell Grants available to low-income high school students that dually enroll in college programs and to eligible incarcerated individuals.

Through investments in the Recovery Act, the Administration was also able to advance the use of data through three critical investments: Investing in Innovation Fund (i3); Race to the Top; and the Statewide Longitudinal Data Systems grant program. With similar goals as FITW but targeted at the K-12 level, the i3 program was designed to fund school districts and nonprofits developing and scaling innovative and evidence-based strategies that address challenges in K-12 classrooms, particularly those serving disadvantaged students. Since its establishment in 2009, more than $1.3 billion of grant money has been invested in 157 projects.

Additionally, the Administration's Race to the Top program provided support to states implementing data system improvements in four areas, including the use of data systems and technology to inform and enhance instruction. Recent research has shown that better integration of data in the classroom can help teachers tailor instruction according to student needs and improve test scores (Dobbie and Fryer 2011; Fryer 2014). Furthermore, by relying on data to inform daily instruction, researchers can compare what is and is not effective across districts and provide teachers with new insights on how to address the academic needs of their students. In addition, under this Administration, the Statewide Longitudinal Data Systems program has expanded support for states to create and link data systems across early learning, K-12, postsecondary, and labor systems so that states have better information on what works. Several states, such as Florida, North Carolina, and Texas, have collected and maintained extensive PreK-12 population-level data on public school students that have been used to study the long-term impact of schooling over time on post-secondary education, the labor market, and even the criminal justice system (Figlio, Karbownik, and Salvanes 2015).

Finally, in an effort to better understand where educational inequities currently exist, through executive action in 2011-12, the Administration changed the Department of Education Civil Rights Data Collection (CRDC) from a sample to universe collection, requiring every U.S. public school and school district to participate. The CRDC provides data on leading civil rights indicators related to access and barriers to educational opportunity at the PreK-12 levels. Having access to a full set of data helps policymakers to make more informed decisions concerning how Federal resources should be expended and to what extent schools are making progress in closing achievement and opportunity gaps.

families so they can skip questions that are not relevant to them. In addition, over 6 million students and parents took advantage of the ability to electronically retrieve their income information from the IRS when completing their 2014–15 FAFSA, an innovation that improves both speed and accuracy. These efforts have translated to a meaningfully simpler FAFSA for students.

Additionally, in 2015, the Administration announced an earlier and easier process for applying for Federal financial aid, allowing students to apply to colleges and for financial aid in tandem. Beginning in 2016, FAFSA applicants have been able to complete the form on October 1 for the following academic year, three months earlier than the original January 1 start date, and use income information from two-years prior to fill out the form. This reform benefits students in two key ways:

First, students and their families can now have a reliable understanding of their Federal aid eligibility as early as the fall—the same time that many high school students are searching for, applying to, and even selecting colleges. An earlier FAFSA helps clear an important hurdle in reducing

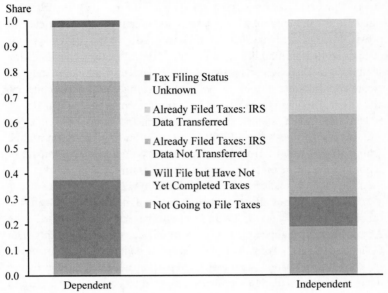

Figure 5-21
FAFSA Tax Filing Status during Initial Application, 2014–2015

Share

- Tax Filing Status Unknown
- Already Filed Taxes: IRS Data Transferred
- Already Filed Taxes: IRS Data Not Transferred
- Will File but Have Not Yet Completed Taxes
- Not Going to File Taxes

Dependent   Independent

Source: Department of Education

information barriers related to cost. Importantly, the Administration is also working with states and colleges to provide financial aid award information on this earlier timeline. Moreover, the earlier FAFSA cycle presents an opportunity to provide students with more timely information about the schools where they are applying. Starting with the 2018–19 application year, the Department of Education will present Scorecard data through the FAFSA so that students can make more informed decisions about the schools at which they plan on applying for admission and student aid based on both cost and student outcomes.

Second, more students and families can complete their FAFSAs using information retrieved electronically directly from the IRS. In past years, a significant portion of FAFSA filers were unable to electronically retrieve their income and tax information from the IRS because they had not yet filed their tax returns before completing their FAFSA forms (Figure 5-21). For example, 34 percent of parents of dependent students had not yet filed their 2013 tax returns when they were initially completing their 2014-15 FAFSA. Such applicants had to manually input their estimated income and tax information into their FAFSA, or worse, did not submit a timely FAFSA because they erroneously believed that they were not allowed to do so unless then had filed their tax returns. By utilizing tax information from two years

Box 5-5: Making Sure Students Enter College Well-Prepared

Too many students enter college unprepared to tackle college-level courses and benefit from their higher education. A recent study found that half of all undergraduate students will take at least one remedial course before enrolling in a college-level course, averaging to an annual national cost of nearly $7 billion dollars (Scott-Clayton, Crosta, and Belfield 2014). This Administration has implemented a number of policies to help ensure that all Americans graduate from high school prepared for college and their careers, and over the past 7 years, students have seen important gains. Today, high school graduation rates are at an all-time high and dropout rates at an all-time low. This Administration has also seen National test scores in reading and math for fourth and eighth graders reach new highs (NCES 2016).

Encouraging Reform with Flexibility: When President Obama entered office, No Child Left Behind (NCLB) was two years overdue for reauthorization and in serious need of repair. In the absence of congressional action, the Department of Education offered states relief from the most onerous requirements in NCLB in exchange for a commitment to engage in needed reforms. Between 2011 and 2015, more than 40 states and the District of Columbia applied for and received this flexibility while working to improve their schools using many of the policy options detailed below. Many of these reforms were codified in the bipartisan Every Student Succeeds Act (ESSA), which the President signed in December 2015.

Higher Standards: The Administration encouraged all states to adopt high standards and aligned high-quality assessments based on college- and career-ready expectations through incentives in the Recovery Act funding provided to states through the Administration's Race to the Top program. In 2016, 49 states and the District of Columbia now have higher standards than before. In the future, every state will be required to hold students to standards that prepare them for college and career as a result of ESSA. Higher standards have been linked to higher test scores (Wong, Cook, and Steiner 2011) and can help identify whether students are well-equipped with the skills and content knowledge necessary for college-level coursework.

Excellent Teachers: This Administration has supported teacher development and excellence by encouraging the expansion of high-quality educator evaluation and support systems that help equip schools to use multiple measures, which are fair and reliable, to provide timely and meaningful feedback to educators. Economics research highlights that teacher quality can be measured as a predictor of student achievement (Chetty, Friedman, and Rockoff 2014a; Bacher-Hicks, Kane, and

Staiger 2014), and feedback from evaluations can help teachers substantially improve their methods and performance (Taylor and Tyler 2012; Kane et al. 2011). The long-term impacts of improving teacher quality on outcomes such as college attendance and earnings are large (Chetty, Friedman, and Rockoff 2014b).

STEM Initiatives: The Obama Administration has made Science, Technology, Engineering, and Math (STEM) education in K-12 schools a national priority. In 2011, the President pushed to recruit 100,000 excellent STEM teachers to work in public schools over the next 10 years, and by 2016, we have exceeded in reaching 30 percent of that goal and are on track to achieve it. The future of America's workforce will require a growing number of workers with an education in STEM fields (Sargent 2014; Rothwell 2014), and research shows that exposure to and training in advanced math and science courses during high school are linked with higher earnings and later labor market outcomes in STEM fields (Rose and Betts 2004; Black et al. 2015; Levine and Zimmerman 1995).

Closing Gaps: The racial and socioeconomic gaps in educational inputs and outcomes hold back too many American students from reaching their potential, and the Administration worked to close these gaps by targeting support among those who need it most.

• The Administration issued School Improvement Grants (SIG) to more than 1,800 of the Nation's persistently lowest-achieving public schools since the program's creation in the Recovery Act. A study of California schools by Dee (2012) found that SIG contributed to closing performance gaps between on-target schools and schools considered "lowest-achieving" by 23 percent.

• In 2014, President Obama established the My Brother's Keeper (MBK) Task Force to address academic, disciplinary, and economic disparities for disadvantaged youth, particularly young men of color. CEA's 2015 analysis finds that closing these gaps would potentially yield significant economic gains, with an estimated increase in U.S. GDP of at least 1.8 percent (CEA 2015a).

• The President has also focused on developing underserved communities via the Promise Neighborhood program that was created in 2010 appropriations, building on evidence that neighborhood quality plays an important role in children's outcomes (Chetty and Hendren 2015; Chetty, Hendren, and Katz 2016). Through this program, the Administration has partnered with local public and private organizations and invested nearly $270 million in low-income communities, producing significant gains in English and math test scores (Department of Education 2016b).

prior, the early FAFSA reform helps eliminate the barrier presented to individuals who have not yet filed their taxes. This not only simplifies the aid application process for students and their families and reduces the burden on institutions, it also improves the accuracy of the information used in the determination of students' aid eligibility.

With this change, about 4 million more students and families can use this IRS Data Retrieval Tool from the start, eliminating the need to send tax information to the government twice. This enhancement can ensure that hundreds of thousands more families receive the aid for which they are eligible, that students and families save well over half a million hours in paperwork, and that schools can transfer 3 million hours from verifying information to advising students and making financial aid awards.

Protecting Students from Low-Quality Programs and Encouraging Schools to Improve

As described in the previous section, better information can help students to choose higher-quality institutions, and Administration efforts have significantly improved the information available to students. However, some colleges fail to meet baseline levels of college quality, and this Administration has targeted its more rigorous accountability efforts on those schools in order to protect students and taxpayers. In particular, it has strengthened accountability efforts in higher education by setting standards for career training programs, including many programs offered in the for-profit sector where high costs and poor outcomes are more highly concentrated.

Descriptive analysis comparing students who attended for-profit colleges to those who attended community colleges or non-selective four-year schools shows that those who attend for-profits have lower earnings on average, and hold larger amounts of debt. These students are also more likely to be unemployed, to default on their loans, and to say that their education was not worth the cost (Deming, Goldin, and Katz 2012, 2013). Loan default data presented in Figure 5-22 also show similar patterns, especially when disaggregated by completion status.

Additionally, research that compares earnings of the same students before and after attending college—including a recent analysis using individual-level administrative and tax data for Federal student aid recipients enrolled in Gainful Employment programs (Cellini and Turner 2016)—finds that for-profit colleges offer lower returns than the returns that have been estimated for other sectors (Cellini and Chaudhary 2013; Liu and Belfield 2014).[12] These lower returns are especially concerning in light of evidence

---

[12] However, one study, which focuses on the returns to for-profit colleges in the State of Ohio, finds more positive results (Jepsen, Mueser, and Jeon 2016).

Box 5-6: The Rise of the For-Profit Sector

The for-profit sector represents a small share of college enrollment, but it has grown rapidly in recent years. At its peak in 2010, for-profit enrollment reached over 2 million students, up from only 240,000 in 1995 (Figure 5-i), in part driven by funding constraints at community colleges (Deming, Goldin, and Katz 2012, 2013). Since then, for-profit enrollment has ticked down, standing at 1.6 million in 2014 and representing 8 percent of total enrollment at degree-granting institutions. The total amount of student loan dollars disbursed at for-profit colleges has also declined, standing at $15.7 billion in award year 2014–15, down from the 2009–10 peak of $24.3 billion.

Coupled with the rise in for-profit enrollment has been an increase in the number of for-profit institutions. The number of for-profit institutions, including branch campuses, increased from 345 in 1995 to 1,451 at its peak in 2012–2013 (Figure 5-ii). As with for-profit enrollment, for-profit institution counts have declined in recent years. The growth of the for-profit sector has presented a challenge to ensuring that students receive a high-quality education. A growing body of research, described in the section above, has found that outcomes for students at for-profit colleges are on average worse than at similar institutions they might otherwise attend.

Figure 5-i
College Enrollment by Sector Over Time

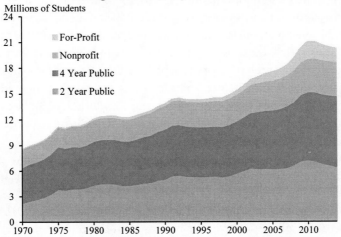

Note: Data for private enrollment in 1988 and 1989 are missing by detailed sector and are linearly interpolated. Enrollment is total fall enrollment in degree granting post-secondary institutions.
Source: NCES (2015)

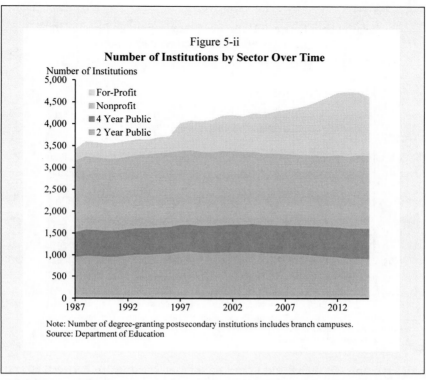

Figure 5-ii
Number of Institutions by Sector Over Time

Number of Institutions

Legend:
- For-Profit
- Nonprofit
- 4 Year Public
- 2 Year Public

Note: Number of degree-granting postsecondary institutions includes branch campuses.
Source: Department of Education

that for-profit colleges are more expensive than community colleges, even when adding in the value of the extra government support community colleges receive (Cellini 2012). Experimental evidence from resume-based audit studies further suggests that despite their relatively high cost, degrees from for-profit institutions are valued less by employers than degrees from nonselective public institutions (Deming et al. 2014; Darolia et al. 2015). Despite these poor outcomes, for-profit institutions have accounted for a large share of enrollment growth since the early 2000s.

Gainful Employment Regulations

While some career college programs are helping to prepare America's workforce for the jobs of the future, far too many students at these schools are taking on unsustainable debt in exchange for degrees and certificates that carry limited value in the job market. With the landmark Gainful Employment regulations, the Administration will eliminate Federal aid to career college programs that consistently fail accountability standards.

Under the Gainful Employment regulations, programs whose graduates have annual loan payments of less than 8 percent of total annual earnings, or less than 20 percent of discretionary annual earnings, are considered to have passed the requirements. Programs whose graduates have annual

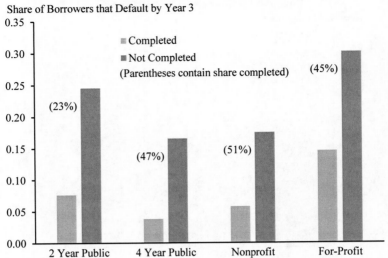

Figure 5-22

Relationship Between Undergraduate Default and Sector by Completion Status, 2011 Repayment Cohort

Share of Borrowers that Default by Year 3

Note: Years are fiscal years. Some small sectors are excluded from this chart. Data contain some duplication across and within categories.
Source: Department of Education

loan payments between 8 and 12 percent of total earnings, or between 20 and 30 percent of discretionary earnings, are considered to be "in the warning zone" and at risk of failing the requirements. Programs are deemed to have failed the requirements if their graduates have annual loan payments greater than 12 percent of total earnings and greater than 30 percent of discretionary earnings. Programs that fail in two out of any three consecutive years, or are in the zone for four consecutive years, are no longer eligible for Federal student aid for a minimum of three years.

Based on data available at the time of rulemaking in 2014, the Department of Education estimated that about 1,400 programs serving 840,000 students—of which 99 percent are at for-profit institutions—would not pass the accountability standards. Initial data for students who completed during FY 2011 and 2012 confirm that students who completed certificate programs at for-profit colleges tend to earn less than those who completed programs at public colleges (Figure 23). The data suggest that for-profit colleges have higher proportions of graduates in less lucrative programs of study than public colleges and that graduates of for-profit colleges have lower earnings compared to those who graduated from similar programs of study at public colleges. All programs will have the opportunity to make immediate changes that could help them avoid sanctions; but if

Figure 5-23
Gainful Employment Earnings Outcomes for Individuals who Completed an Undergraduate Certificate

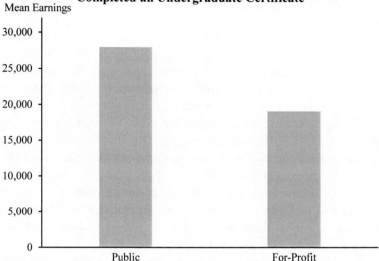

Note: Data are earnings in 2014 for students who completed an undergraduate certificate in FY 2011 or 2012 weighted by program size.
Source: Department of Education

these programs do not improve, they will ultimately become ineligible for Federal student aid—which often makes up nearly 90 percent of the revenue at for-profit institutions.

The Gainful Employment regulations also require institutions to provide disclosures to current and prospective students about their programs' performance on key metrics, like earnings of former students, graduation rates, and debt accumulation of student borrowers. This disclosure requirement complements the accountability measures in the regulation and provides additional program-level detail to the institution-level information provided in the College Scorecard.

Protecting Against Fraud and Deception

In addition to improving the information available to students, the Administration has worked to directly protect students and taxpayers from the subset of institutions of higher education who engage in fraud, deception, and other misconduct that harms students. A two-year investigation by the U.S. Senate Committee on Health, Education, Labor, and Pensions published in 2012 revealed such practices occurring in the for-profit sector. The investigation found that the 30 for-profit colleges examined spent about 30 percent more per student on marketing, advertising, recruiting, and admissions staffing than on instruction. The report also highlighted a number of tactics (consistent with a 2010 Government Accountability Office report) that misled prospective students about program costs, the availability of aid, and information about student success rates and the school's accreditation status.

In 2010, the Obama Administration released a comprehensive set of rules—known as Program Integrity and Improvement rules—to strengthen the Department of Education's authority to protect students from aggressive recruiting practices fueled by incentive compensation; to take action against colleges engaging in deceptive advertising, marketing and sales practices; and to clarify minimum requirements for states to oversee postsecondary programs and handle student complaints. The Obama Administration is also proposing new Borrower Defense to Repayment regulations to protect borrowers and taxpayers against fraud, deception, and other misconduct by postsecondary institutions. The proposed regulations would create a clear, consistent, and transparent process for borrowers who have been harmed by their school's misconduct to seek debt relief. In addition, the proposed regulations include measures that would require new warnings to help students steer clear of poorly performing for-profit schools and financially risky schools. They would also end the use of both so-called "pre-dispute, mandatory arbitration agreements" and of class action bans that prevent students from having their day in court.

These regulations build upon a record of action by this Administration that has encouraged states to step up oversight in their role as authorizers, encouraged accreditors to focus on student outcomes, and created a new Student Aid Enforcement Unit to respond more quickly and efficiently to allegations of illegal actions by higher education institutions.

NEXT STEPS

Despite the substantial progress made by the Obama Administration to expand a high-quality college education to all Americans, some challenges remain.

First, the costs of college remain too high for too many individuals, especially those from disadvantaged backgrounds. Expanding this Administration's work to provide free community college for responsible students will be a critical next step to make sure that all Americans can access a college education. However, at the same time, policymakers, community colleges, and other stakeholders will also have to work to improve student success at community colleges so that students who enroll receive the supports needed to complete a degree that raises their labor market prospects.

Additionally, Pell Grants can be better structured to put more low- and moderate-income students on the path to success, and the Administration's 2017 budget identifies various ways to improve the current program. To begin, the proposed budget further simplifies the FAFSA by eliminating burdensome and unnecessarily complex questions to make it easier for students and families to access Federal student aid and afford a postsecondary education. The Administration has also called upon Congress to indefinitely index Pell Grants to inflation in order to protect and sustain their value for future generations. Furthermore, it has included two key proposals to promote completion, creating incentives supported by academic research (MDRC 2016). The first would make additional Pell Grant funds available for an additional semester to full-time students, and the second would increase students' Pell Grants by $300 each year if they take at least 15 credit hours per semester, the amount typically needed to complete a two- or four-year degree on time. Finally, the Administration has requested that Pell Grants be expanded to incarcerated individuals eligible for release, with the goals of helping them complete college, get jobs, support their families, and strengthen their communities.[13]

There are also important changes to the education tax code that could reduce barriers to college access and success. In particular, the Administration has proposed streamlining and further expanding education tax benefits by: first, consolidating the Lifetime Learning Credit into an expanded AOTC, which would be available for five years and refundable up to $1,500 for students enrolled half-time or more; second, exempting Pell Grants from taxation and the AOTC calculation; and third, eliminating the tax on student loan debt forgiveness, while repealing the complicated student loan interest deduction for new borrowers.

Work is also needed to make sure that all borrowers can pay back their debt with an affordable repayment plan. Income-driven repayment plans are helping millions of borrowers stay on track with their payments, but too many borrowers do not take advantage of these plans, as described above. Complexities related to repayment plan selection, income verification, and recertification all present barriers to enrollment. In its 2017 budget, the Administration called upon Congress to improve and streamline PAYE and other income-driven repayment plans to create a single simple and better-targeted plan for borrowers. Academics have also proposed innovative ways to reduce the complexity of income-driven repayment plans (for example, Dynarski and Kreisman 2013). Such improvements will be critical to help borrowers manage their debt and stay out of default.

---

[13] See CEA's 2016 criminal justice report for a more detailed overview of the importance of this policy (CEA 2016b).

Better information and regulation of low-quality schools will also help students attend colleges that serve them well and enable them to pay back the debt they incur. The College Scorecard was a significant achievement, but additional efforts to improve the data's usage, the consumer tool, and the underlying data will help to expand the impact of the Scorecard. The Administration's efforts to protect students from low-quality schools have likewise been important accomplishments, and future policymakers must continue to be responsive to an ever-changing higher education landscape.

Lastly, work remains to continue strengthening outcomes at earlier levels of education to help ensure that students enter college well prepared to benefit from their investment in higher education. Despite this Administration's accomplishments, racial and socioeconomic gaps in PreK-12 educational inputs and outcomes remain, and these disparities must be addressed in tandem with the inequities in higher education access. ESSA has codified into law many initiatives created and championed by the Obama Administration to set the stage for this future policy, but further progress will require additional effort by policymakers.

CONCLUSION

The Obama Administration has enacted policies over its two terms to lower college costs, improve information, simplify student aid, and cap monthly student debt payments at a manageable portion of borrowers' incomes. The Administration has also promoted excellence and equity in PreK-12 education to better prepare students for college and their careers. Together, these policies represent a significant step forward in building an educational system that supports and encourages all Americans who wish to invest in an affordable, high quality college education to do so. Still, more work is needed to address the challenges that remain.

C H A P T E R   6

STRENGTHENING THE FINANCIAL SYSTEM

Introduction

The financial system plays an important role in any modern economy, providing key services that not only match savers with borrowers but also provide services that facilitate such economic activity as safekeeping of financial assets and payment processing. While the markets for financial services generally succeed in providing these services, there are situations in which financial markets do not function well; referred to as market failures. Due to the existence of market failures, regulation plays an important role in helping to ensure that financial service providers continue to effectively provide necessary services to the economy.

The 2008-09 financial crisis highlighted several such market failures. Responding quickly, the President, Congress, and regulators addressed these failures by adopting necessary reforms to the financial system. These measures were designed to address three areas of concern: (1) increasing the safety and soundness of individual financial institutions; (2) identifying and mitigating sources of systemic risk – the risk that a threat to one firm or small number of firms could incite widespread panic in financial markets and threaten the entire financial system; and (3) improving transparency, accountability, and protections for consumers and investors.

During the Obama Administration, the passage and implementation of financial reform has worked to address these issues with measurable impact on the safety and soundness of financial markets. Although there is still work to be done, considerable progress is evident. The financial system in 2016 is more durable and able to perform its necessary and important functions without undue risk.

The reforms involved a substantial reshaping of the financial regulatory landscape in the United States. Rules were changed to make banks hold more capital and have better access to liquidity. The ability of banks to engage in risky trading was reduced. Over-the-counter (OTC) derivatives trading is now better regulated and more transparent. The rules governing credit ratings agencies that many investors rely on were substantially reformed. Importantly, two new institutional structures were created: the Financial Stability Oversight Council (FSOC) that brings together different regulators to consider and respond to systemic risks and the Consumer Financial Protection Bureau aimed at making sure financial institutions interact in a fair manner with their clients.

This chapter focuses on the steps taken during the Obama Administration to reform the financial system, starting with a discussion of the economic rationale for regulation, particularly as it applies to financial market failures. The state of financial markets just prior to, and during, the financial crisis is detailed, followed by an outline of specific financial reforms undertaken in response to the crisis and the measurable impact of those reforms. A final section provides a snapshot of the state of financial markets in the fall of 2016 after the implementation of most of the financial reforms discussed below.

Economic Rationale for Regulating Financial Markets

The financial system —commercial banks, along with insurance companies, investment banks, mutual funds, and all the other institutions where individuals and firms put their savings or borrow funds—plays an integral role in any modern economy. Providers of financial services stand between savers who seek a return on their savings and borrowers who are willing to pay to use those savings to start a company or buy their first home. The U.S. financial system, among other things, provides financial intermediation between savers and borrowers; yet the infrastructure to perform that function is necessarily complex and costly. While the markets for financial services generally succeed in facilitating the matching of those wishing to lend or invest their savings with those wishing to borrow or invest those savings, there are situations in which financial markets do not function well — often referred to as market failures — or may not achieve the desired outcome from society's point of view. Due to the existence of market failures, regulation plays an important role in helping to ensure that financial service providers continue to effectively intermediate between savers and borrowers.

Without a financial system, the modern economy could not function. In the short run, people could keep their savings in their homes, and the only apparent losses would be the forgone interest and dividends. But with no easy way to get the funds from savers into productive investment, the economy would face bigger problems very quickly. Entrepreneurs with ideas would find it difficult to get capital, large companies in need of money to restructure their operations would have no way to borrow against their future earnings. Young families would have no way to buy a house until they had personally saved enough to afford the whole thing. Workers saving for retirement, and firms and individuals attempting to insure against risk, would find it hard to do so.

As part of collecting savings and making them available to borrowers, financial firms perform several important functions. The first is to evaluate the potential borrower and the reasons they wish to borrow, and to make reasonably sure that the loan will be repaid and that the investment will perform as promised. This includes the continued monitoring of the borrower to ensure the money is being used as promised. When the system works well, the financial service provider acts on behalf of the saver – and in the process helps ensure that capital is allocated more efficiently in the economy. Savers or investors may lack information about the quality of a firm looking to borrow money. Figuring out the creditworthiness of potential borrowers and supervising the borrower after a loan is made is costly. By specializing in making loans or providing funds, the financial service provider typically has better information than savers about potential and actual borrowers as well as the likelihood that loans will be repaid and investments will perform as expected. Problems may develop, however, if or when the financial service provider puts its interests ahead of the saver. Economists refer to this as an example of the principal-agent problem.

Another important function of financial service providers is to supply liquidity and maturity transformation. Borrowers often wish to borrow for a long period of time to invest in a home or a new business. However, savers may wish to have the ability to cash out of their investment should they desire to use their funds for other purposes. An example of maturity transformation is when a credit union that aggregates the savings deposits of many customers to make a mortgage loan that will be repaid over 30 years.

Financial service providers also facilitate diversification. Savers who invest through an intermediary typically have a small investment in many large projects rather than having "all their eggs in one basket." The financial system allows investors not only to have ready access to their funds if needed, but also to spread a relatively small amount of money across a wide range of investments.

Finally, the financial system plays a key role in the way payments are made in our economy. While people can always use cash for their purchases, it is not always the most convenient method. Checks, transfers, credit cards, and other non-cash payment methods offer effective alternatives. People depend on the financial system to make these alternatives possible.

"Financial institution" often means a commercial bank, but there are many other types of financial institution. Investment banks help firms sell stakes in the company directly to investors as well as borrow money directly from investors. Rather than taking a loan from a bank, a firm could issue stock to build a new factory. Brokers allow investors to access equity and bond markets to make it possible to buy and sell stocks and bonds. Rather than rely on a bank, investors can access liquidity through secondary markets. Over time, financial firms have learned to pool various types of individual loans or debt obligations and combine them into different securities that they can sell, a process known as securitization, allowing further diversification. Derivative contracts allow hedging, or other types of investing behavior. Various insurance products on real life or financial events can also play an important role by allowing for hedging of many different types of risk.

Financial institutions effectively provide services to their customers much of the time; however, fragility, instability, or disruption in financial markets can cause those institutions to fail. Individuals or firms, acting independently, may not be able to effectively address these market failures because there is often a conflict between the individual's or firm's best interest and the aggregate best interest of all market participants. Economists refer to this as a collective action problem. In such cases, it may be efficient for government to step in to regulate, including the monitoring and supervision of financial firms.

An example of fragility in the financial system that can lead to a market failure involves liquidity and maturity transformation. A financial service provider that offers liquidity and maturity transformation may have illiquid long-term assets and liquid short-term liabilities. If creditors all call these liabilities at the same time, the financial service provider may find itself unable to raise the cash to meet those calls. The classic example is a bank run, where depositors all "run" at the same time to withdraw their funds, leaving banks unable to sell the illiquid business loans and mortgages quickly enough to meet those demands. So-called "run-risk" can occur in a wide variety of nonbank institutions as well.

Runs can occur when all individuals are acting in their own best interests. The fact that they lack full information about a financial institution's investments means that if they believe the institution may be in trouble, the rational response may be to withdraw their funds. Once the run starts, it makes even more sense for others to try to withdraw their funds before the institution runs out of liquidity (Diamond and Dybvig 1983). Because the public has limited information, runs on an individual institution may spread to other institutions. People could worry that whatever problem afflicts the first institution may also affect others, or they could worry that the failure of the first institution may cause problems in others with which it does business. These other institutions, even though solvent, may not have sufficient liquid assets on-hand to meet the demands of depositors. In the absence of a mechanism that either stops the initial run or the contagion effects, a run on a single institution can become a run on the broader financial system.

One lesson driven home by the financial crisis is that actions taken by a single systemically important financial institution can negatively impact the stability of the entire system, particularly if the financial system is already threatened. Threats to the systemic stability can pose costs on society, and such societal costs are typically not considered in the decision-making of the firm. Thus, regulations that seek to limit the risk that the failure of a single institution can pose to the financial system are warranted when the social costs of the failure of a financial institution exceeds the private costs.

Systemic risk issues have traditionally been central to the regulation of banks due in part to the danger banks face from runs. A bank run has the potential to cause significant harm to the economy because of the pivotal position of banks in the financial system, including in clearing and payment systems, and because a run on one bank has the potential to impact the health of other banks. The dangers resulting from bank runs and issues of adverse selection and moral hazard associated with safety-net arrangements designed to lower the risk of a run, such as deposit insurance and access to the central banks as a lender-of-last resort, are common justifications for bank regulation.[1] However, run-risk can occur in financial institutions other than banks if there is a liquidity and maturity mismatch between assets and liabilities.

Run risk may be mitigated through government insurance schemes, regulations that limit the ability of financial institutions to engage in liquidity and maturity transformation, regulations that limit the ability of financial institutions to take risks, or by requiring financial institutions to keep enough loss-absorbing capital to lower the chance of a run. The government or central bank could also act as a lender of last resort — providing loans to financial firms that have good, but illiquid assets during a crisis. Each of

---

[1] Adverse selection occurs when one party to a transaction has better information than the other and will participate in trades which benefit it the most, typically at the expense of the other party. A bank that takes advantage of a lender-of-last-resort arrangement may be a much less creditworthy borrower than a typical bank.

Moral hazard occurs when the one party is more likely to take risks when another party bears part or all of the cost of a bad outcome. For example, a bank may be more likely to make loans to risky borrowers at high interest rates if deposits are insured.

Box 6-1: Financialization of the U.S. Economy

Since the late 1970s, financial deregulation, innovation, and advances in information technology have fueled an expansion of the financial services industry. The growth of the financial services industry relative to the economy, referred to as "financialization," accelerated since the 1980s, peaking before the global financial crisis that began in 2007. Most industrial countries have experienced financialization, joined more recently by emerging market economies as they liberalize their domestic capital markets.

Expanded financial markets bring many potential benefits. For example, households today have more access to financial services which, in turn, gives them greater ability to finance the purchase of homes and automobiles, and to save at low cost in diversified portfolios. Increased trading activities can enhance market liquidity and aid in price discovery. These gains may be magnified when financial activity occurs across larger and more inclusive markets.

However, there are a number of reasons to be concerned that, past a certain point, a larger financial sector could be economically costly. First, a larger financial sector may threaten the overall economy if its size is coupled with fragility as, the larger the sector, the more problematic the spillovers may be to the broader economy if a crisis does hit. Second, financial services may have expanded beyond their social value, effectively capitalizing on information asymmetries to oversell unneeded services to an unwitting population. Finally, if the financial sector is earning excess profits and some of that is used to raise the pay of those who work in the sector, the higher pay could draw talent away from alternative activities that would provide social value.

Size of the Financial Sector

A common measure of financial-sector size is the share of GDP contributed by financial services – consisting of (1) insurance, (2) securities trading, and (3) credit intermediation.[1] This measure does not capture asset *stocks*, such as outstanding mortgage credit; rather, it gives the flow of value added (the flow of compensation, depreciation, profits, rent, and other income streams) from the financial service activities. Financial services comprised 4.5 percent of GDP in 1977, crested above 7.5 percent in the mid 2000's, before crashing in the financial crisis. The

---

[1] In what follows, "Insurance" is defined as the NAICS code 524, which includes insurance carriers, agencies, brokerages, and related activities; "Securities Trading" as NAICS codes 523 and 525, which include securities and commodity contracts intermediation and brokerage, as well as funds, trusts, and other financial vehicles; "Credit Intermediation" as NAICS code 521 which includes monetary authorities, depository credit intermediation, non-depository credit intermediation, and related activities.

value added of the sector has gradually climbed since then to approximately 7 percent in 2015 (Figure 6-i).

Note that this measure may inflate financial sector growth. For example, the shift from defined benefit pension funds, often managed by the pension sponsor, to defined contribution pension plans, typically managed by a financial services firm, could result in activity shifting from the sector of the sponsor to financial services.

As the financial sector grows, any associated risks may generate larger risks to society as a whole. This is not purely a function of size, but a question of size combined with fragility. In some countries where financialization has far outpaced that of the United States, the burden of a failing financial system has been quite large. In Ireland, for example, cleaning up the financial sector following the global financial crisis required a sizable government intervention, contributing to fiscal deficits as high as 30 percent of GDP in 2010. The U.S. financial sector, though smaller relative to GDP, was still able to generate large economic costs, helping propel the economy into a protracted recession. When well-regulated and smoothly functioning, the raw size may be unimportant, but when problems strike, the size can matter.

The Value of Financial Services

Almost half of the growth in financial services as a share of GDP from 1980 to its peak in 2006 has been in the securities trading category. The asset management subcomponent of the securities trading category

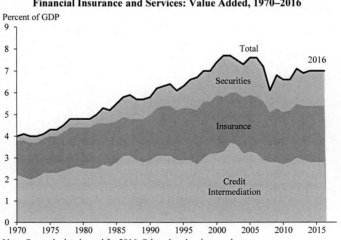

Figure 6-i
Financial Insurance and Services: Value Added, 1970–2016

Note: Quarterly data is used for 2016. Otherwise, data is annual.
Source: Bureau of Economic Analysis, National Income and Product Accounts.

accounted for half of the industry's gross output by 2007. The Credit Intermediation subcomponent that includes many traditional banking services has grown as well but more slowly. Transactional services, particularly fees related to consumer and mortgage credit, account for nearly all the growth in Credit Intermediation, approximately a quarter of the financial industry's growth. Thus, in many ways, the question of the value of this growth rests on the value of the asset management services and the expansion of credit to households.

Professional Asset-Management

Management fees account for most of the growth in professional asset management. Greenwood and Scharfstein (2013) estimate these fees to be relatively flat as a percent of assets under management, fluctuating between 1.1 and 1.6 percent. The growth in the total dollar amount of these fees is due to the growth in both the value of assets and the share of these assets that are professionally managed. Figure 6-ii below illustrates the growth in the value of total U.S. financial assets, relative to both GDP and U.S. nonfinancial (tangible) assets.

Greenwood and Scharfstein find the growth in the share of assets under professional management puzzling because there is considerable evidence that active managers tend to underperform when compared with passively managed funds, after controlling for risk. For example, Fama and French (2010) find little evidence of skill in fund management, particularly when examining returns net of fees charged by fund

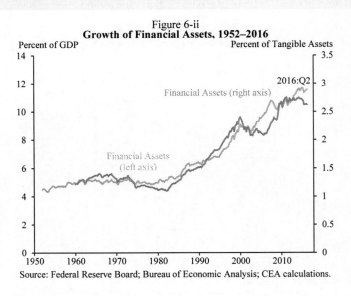

Figure 6-ii
Growth of Financial Assets, 1952–2016

Source: Federal Reserve Board; Bureau of Economic Analysis; CEA calculations.

managers. Thus, after fees, savers on average earn less when they invest in actively managed funds vs. passively managed funds. Households often misunderstand the pricing of the financial products they purchase, which could mean individuals do not recognize the overpricing of active management. Index funds, automated investment advice, and substantially less trading and lower fees might leave people better off.

Cochrane (2013) notes that financially sophisticated managers of endowments typically invest in actively managed funds. He argues that basing an explanation of the growth of active management on investor naïveté ignores the behavior of such sophisticated investors, though it is also possible that sophisticated institutional investors simply have access to better fund managers than regular investors. Further, he points to academic literature (see, for instance, Berk and Green 2004) that proposes explanations for both rational investors pursuing an active investing strategy and the observed absence of evidence in support of superior performance of active managers highlighted by Greenwood and Scharfstein.

The growth of professional asset management may also provide benefits to ordinary Americans as mutual funds or employer-sponsored retirement plans have made it easier for households to participate in securities markets and diversify their wealth. The share of households between the 20th and 80th income percentiles owning stock (including through retirement accounts) rose from 29 percent in 1989 to 49 percent in 2013, having peaked at 55 percent in 2001 (Figure 6-iii).

Credit Intermediation

Fees associated with consumer and mortgage credit largely have driven the growth in credit intermediation. Jorda, Schularick and Taylor (2016) point out this is a trend across 17 advanced economies where the bulk of credit growth over the second half of the 20th century came in the form of bank financed mortgages, not business investment.

Household credit, mainly in the form of mortgage debt, grew dramatically from 48 percent of GDP in 1980 to 99 percent in 2007. Meanwhile, household debt held by banks as a share of GDP was stable at 40 percent, meaning the broader financial market, not just banks, held the assets that were generated by this expansion of mortgage debt. Household credit that was not held by traditional banks was packaged into asset-backed securities. The expansion of the securitization market, and the plentiful assets associated with it, helped increase the supply of credit available in the housing market. However, this form of credit expansion also increased the vulnerability of the financial system to the housing collapse by creating highly-rated securities backed by portfolios of mortgages supposedly protected by equity tranches that would absorb losses in the event some mortgages in the portfolio defaulted. This loss

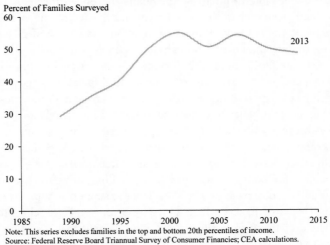

Figure 6-iii

Families with Direct or Indirect Holdings of Stock, 1989–2013

Percent of Families Surveyed

2013

Note: This series excludes families in the top and bottom 20th percentiles of income.
Source: Federal Reserve Board Triannual Survey of Consumer Financies; CEA calculations.

absorbing layer proved inadequate when it became clear the mortgages in the portfolio were of questionable quality.

Greenwood and Scharfstein provide evidence that mortgage securitization extended the number of intermediaries between initial borrowers and investors who ultimately assumed the risk of the mortgage defaults. The increase in credit intermediaries resulted in information asymmetries, where intermediate investors knew less about the original borrowers than the initial lender who created the loans. In this market, there was an incentive for original lender to grant loans to sub-optimal borrowers, knowing intermediaries would purchase the loan. When individuals began defaulting on loans, intermediaries were unable to distinguish between low-risk loans and loans at risk of default. Several studies note that this mechanism is at the core of what made the financial sector fragile.

As Cochrane points out, the problem was not strictly with the size of this market as a function of GDP but with its fragility. He also points out that this financial innovation has potentially large social benefits. Securitization of mortgage debt allows loan originators to create portfolios of loans and sell them to investors with greater ability and willingness to bear the associated risk. Securitization thus could increase risk in the market by making the credit chain longer and more opaque, but may also spread that risk in possibly efficient ways and make funds available for lending to homeowners, possibly at a lower price.

Too Many Resources in Finance?

Beyond the question of the size of the financial sector or the value it creates is the question of whether the United States dedicates too many resources—such as talent and capital—to reallocating funds from savers to borrowers. On the income side, there is concern that financialization is driving up financial sector wages relative to other industries. Philippon and Reshef (2012) find that between 1950 and 1980 wage profiles of finance and other sectors were similar. However, in 2006, the average finance worker earned 50 percent more than the average private-sector worker, adjusted for education. In high management, executives in finance earned 250 percent more than other private-sector executives in 2005. According to Benaubou and Tirole (2016), high wages in financial services may be luring talent (highly-educated individuals) away from more productive industries, which can be costly in terms of economic growth. However, Philippon and Reshef finds evidence that the high-skill high-compensation nature of our current financial system is not inherent to finance. They suggest instead that financial deregulation "may increase the scope for skilled workers to operate freely and to use their creativity to produce new complex products." Philippon and Reshef find that periods of financial deregulation in the United States see talent inflows to the financial sector, while periods of regulation see talent outflows.

The financial sector attracts not only talent, but huge, arguably excessive, amounts of capital in activities whose social benefits are unclear. For example, companies have spent billions of dollars creating slightly faster trading platforms to beat competing trades to the market by milliseconds. The returns of imperceptibly faster trading to the fastest trader may be immense, but the social value is difficult to discern. As some traders become faster, the cost of adverse selection increases for all traders, increasing incentives for investing in faster technology. Ultimately, trading becomes more expensive for all traders, with little evidence of substantially increasing benefits to society (Biais, Foucault, and Moinas 2015). Liquidity provision, price discovery, and opportunities for diversification have benefits; however, the important questions for policymakers are whether financialization implies too much talent is being drawn into the creation and sale of these new products and whether these products generate benefits broadly or just allow the accumulation of excess profits for the most successful financial firms.

While the financial sector has indeed grown and the global financial crisis exposed distortions in financial markets, not all financial market distortions are associated with financialization. As the country has seen, distortions caused by the growth of securitization of mortgages are due in part to information asymmetries, which are not necessarily characteristics of a large financial sector. Distortions stemming from inefficient consumer behavior may be due to a lack of information or insufficient consumer protection. Thus, carefully considered regulation that focuses on eliminating distortions will improve the overall system. The goals of such reforms should not necessarily focus on the size of the financial system or individual institutions *per se*. Reforms should instead focus on the reduction of market distortions so that resources find their most productive use, which may or may not impact the size of the financial sector.

these methods has benefits and drawbacks and may be used in combination to lower the systemic risk posed by run risk.

One notable risk of insurance schemes, lenders-of-last-resort, or the widespread belief that the government will not allow a particular financial firm to fail is the moral hazard it introduces into the behavior of both consumers and firms. Consumers may be less careful in the selection of financial institutions or even seek high-risk firms that offer higher returns because, if the firm fails they will be compensated by a government-backed insurance scheme. The firm is incentivized to take more risk because resulting profits may be retained while losses are born by the insurance provider. The incentive to engage in such behavior becomes stronger the closer the firm comes to failing. This is similar to what occurred during the savings and loan (S&L) crisis of the 1980s and 1990s that resulted in the failure of almost one-in-three S&L institutions. Depositors were unconcerned about risky loans and investments made by S&Ls because the Federal Savings and Loan Insurance Corporation insured their deposits. Such insurance schemes protect against bank runs and may also reduce the problem of a single firm's failure posing significant risk to the larger financial system; however, deposit insurance also requires rules to reduce incentives to take on too much risk and continual monitoring for compliance.

Financial regulation can also be necessary to correct for specific market imperfections or failures that reduce consumer welfare. These include consumers having inadequate information available to make well-informed decisions, agency costs, and the difficulties consumers face in assessing the safety and soundness of financial institutions. Many of these problems arise because of the information advantage held by financial institutions and because financial contracts are long-term in nature. This results in the inability of the consumer to ascertain the quality of a contract at the time of purchase, potential moral hazard that may emerge in that the behavior of the firm after the purchase affects the value of the contract, and the firm may have incentives to behave opportunistically. The purpose of required information disclosures is to reduce the information advantage of financial institutions, to make consumers more confident that they possess the information necessary to make well-informed decisions, and to reduce costs of making poor decisions.

Information asymmetries may reduce demand for financial services. If consumers know there are good and bad firms and products but are unable to distinguish between them, a cautious consumer may simply not purchase such products. This means families may make poor investment choices leaving them with less wealth for retirement or may not purchase products such as life insurance that may protect the family's future should tragedy strike. Similarly, firms may not take advantage of opportunities to hedge business risks or reduce financing costs, putting their financial health, and therefore the jobs of their employees, at risk.

The financial system plays a key role in the economy, but because of these various market failures, it cannot be relied upon to do so safely without regulation. The next section summarizes the state of U.S. financial markets leading up to the crisis.

U.S. FINANCIAL MARKETS IN 2007-08

Financial crises result from the collapse or serious disruption of financial intermediation. In a crisis, the ability of the financial system to move savings into investment is severely impaired with far reaching repercussions for the economy. The 2007-08 crisis and the recession that followed resulted in millions of lost jobs, trillions in lost output, and hardship for many who lost homes, savings, or financial security. As a result of declining asset prices, U.S. households lost a total of $13 trillion in wealth, 19 percent of total U.S. household wealth from its peak in 2007 to its trough in 2009. The decline in wealth was far more than the reduction in wealth experienced at the onset of the Great Depression (Figure 6-1).

While the vulnerabilities that created the potential for crisis were years in the making, the collapse of housing prices ignited a string of events that led to a full-blown crisis in the fall of 2008.[2] Banks took advantage of securitization opportunities to institute relaxed lending standards that drove a boom in mortgage lending. In particular, as seen in Figure 6-2, there was significant growth in mortgage loan types — Alt-A and subprime — that were typically made to riskier borrowers during the pre-crisis period.

---

[2] See FCIC (2011) for more complete discussion of the causes of the financial crisis.

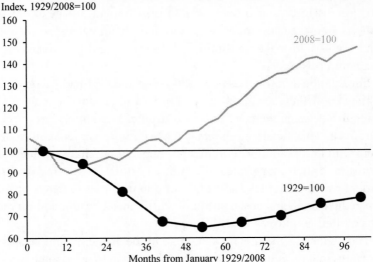

Figure 6-1
Household Net Worth in the Great Depression and Great Recession
Index, 1929/2008=100

Note: Red markers represent annual averages.
Source: Federal Reserve Board of Governors: Mishkin (1978).

This expansion of lending, and the financial system behavior that encouraged it, both fueled an unsustainable rise in housing prices and filled the financial system with risky assets that left financial firms over-leveraged and vulnerable. Publicly traded government-sponsored enterprises (GSEs) including Fannie Mae and Freddie Mac used leverage as high as 75-to-1 to build a $5 trillion mortgage exposure. This included the purchase of a growing fraction non-GSE subprime mortgage-backed securities, rising from 10.5 percent in 2001 to 40 percent in 2004. Trillions of dollars in mortgages were held directly and indirectly by many different types of market participants as mortgage-related securities were packaged, repackaged, and sold to investors around the world. When housing prices collapsed, hundreds of billions of dollars in losses in mortgages and mortgage-related securities caused problems for financial institutions that had significant exposures to those mortgages and had borrowed heavily against them. What had been excessively loose lending quickly became tight, and impacts started spilling into other sectors of the economy.

Uncertainty about exposure to losses from mortgage-related securities as well as derivatives based on those securities led to uncertainty about the creditworthiness of major financial institutions. Short-term wholesale funding became more challenging. The crisis intensified in September 2008 with

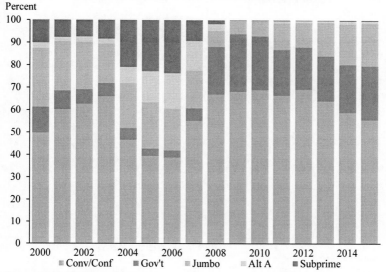

Figure 6-2
Mortgage Originations by Product Type, 2000–2015

Percent

Source: Inside Mortgage Finance.

the failure of Lehman Brothers and the near collapse of the insurance giant American International Group (AIG) shortly thereafter.

A particularly noteworthy event occurred in money markets during the crisis. The net asset value of the Reserve Primary Fund, a money market mutual fund with significant holdings of commercial paper issued by Lehman Brothers, declined below $1, the usual share price of this type of fund. In industry jargon, the fund "broke the buck." Investors in money market funds often thought of them as safe and risk-free as a bank account and, while they did in fact provide investors with immediate access to their funds, they were not in fact regulated banks with insured deposits. When a major money market fund returned less than what investors had deposited, it stood as a stark reminder that such seemingly low-risk investments could decline in value and this caused investors effectively to stage a run on this portion of the financial system. This further drove down the prices of assets as funds sold their holdings to meet investor redemption requests. These events highlighted the risks of non-banks conducting the traditional banking functions of credit, maturity, and liquidity transformation without the safety-net of the banking sector.

Additional uncertainty about the exposures of surviving financial institutions to those that had either already failed or were thought to be close to failure, and the lack of transparency of the balance sheets of those

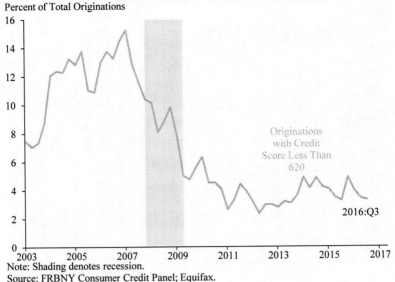

Figure 6-3
Subprime Mortgage Originations, 2003–2016

Percent of Total Originations

Originations with Credit Score Less Than 620

2016:Q3

Note: Shading denotes recession.
Source: FRBNY Consumer Credit Panel; Equifax.

financial institutions coupled with a tangle of interconnections among financial institutions caused credit markets to seize up. Trading in many securities ground to a halt, the S&P 500 stock market index lost more than half its value between early December 2007 and March 2009, and as the financial collapse disrupted the functioning of the real economy, the nation plunged into a deep recession.

There were many signs of potential instability in financial markets in the years leading up to the crisis. As shown in Figure 6-3, the fraction of mortgages that were subprime rose rapidly in the years directly preceding the financial crisis. This was accompanied by widespread reports of egregious and predatory lending practices. Easy access to credit contributed to a near doubling of housing prices in the eight years ending in February 2007 (see Figure 6-4). The rise in housing finance activity resulted in a dramatic increase in household mortgage debt as a percentage of disposable personal income, as shown in Figure 6-5.

There were also warning signs within the financial services sector. The relatively less regulated shadow banking sector was growing considerably faster than the traditional banking sector. Shadow banks are financial intermediaries that conduct maturity, credit, and liquidity transformation without explicit access to central bank liquidity or public sector credit guarantees. Examples of shadow banks include finance companies, asset-backed commercial paper (ABCP) conduits, structured investment vehicles

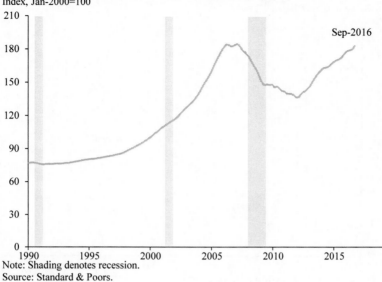

Figure 6-4
Case-Shiller Home Price Index, Seasonally Adjusted, 1990–2016
Index, Jan-2000=100

Note: Shading denotes recession.
Source: Standard & Poors.

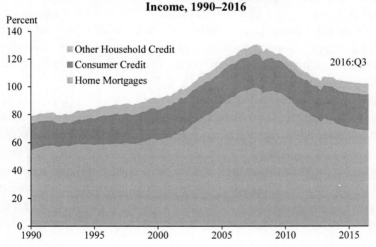

Figure 6-5
**Household Credit as a Percent of Disposable Personal
Income, 1990–2016**
Percent

Note: Other household credit includes loans to both households and nonprofit organizations.
Source: Federal Reserve; Bureau of Economic Analysis.

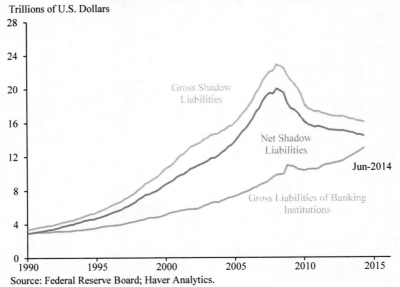

Figure 6-6
Growth of Shadow Banking, 1990–2014

Trillions of U.S. Dollars

Source: Federal Reserve Board; Haver Analytics.

(SIVs), credit hedge funds, money market mutual funds, securities lenders, limited-purpose finance companies (LPFCs), and government-sponsored enterprises (GSEs). Pozsar et al. (2012) estimate the size of the shadow-banking sector over time using flow-of-funds data.[3] Figure 6-6 uses the same methodology and shows that net liabilities of the shadow-banking sector grew at almost 1.5 times the growth rate of traditional banking sector liabilities in the decade preceding the financial crisis. By 2007, the net liabilities of the shadow-banking sector were substantially larger than the gross liabilities of banking institutions.

As shown in Figure 6-7, there was rapid growth in financial firms' trading in unregulated over-the-counter (OTC) derivatives. Many institutions took on too much risk with, as it is now known, with too little capital and with too much dependence on short-term financing. Although the rise in trading volume in these markets may have been a rational response to financial and technological innovations, the financial crisis made clear that there was a lack of transparency and market oversight that required carefully considered regulatory solutions.

---

[3] The gross measure sums all liabilities recorded in the flow of funds that relate to securitization activity (MBS, ABS, and other GSE liabilities), as well as all short term money market transactions that are not backstopped by deposit insurance (repos, commercial paper, and other money market mutual fund liabilities). The net measure attempts to remove double counting.

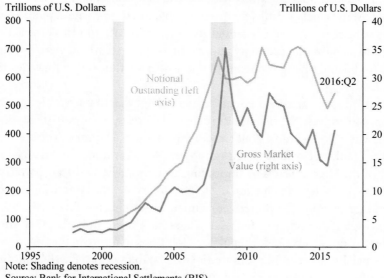

Figure 6-7
Global OTC Derivative Market, 1998–2016

Trillions of U.S. Dollars   Trillions of U.S. Dollars

Notional Outstanding (left axis)

Gross Market Value (right axis)

2016:Q2

Note: Shading denotes recession.
Source: Bank for International Settlements (BIS).

IMPACT OF REFORMS TO ESTABLISH A MORE SUSTAINABLE FINANCIAL SYSTEM

The new Administration's highest priorities were (1) to cushion the blow to the economy, (2) stabilize the financial system, and (3) get the economy growing again. The American Recovery and Reinvestment Act of 2009 provided substantial fiscal stimulus in the form of tax cuts, direct aid to states or affected individuals, along with important investments in transportation, clean energy, and other long-term priorities.[4] (For a more detailed discussion of the Administration's response to the crisis, including the Recovery Act, see Chapter 1.) At the same time, the Federal Reserve used its authority to provide monetary accommodation to support the broad economy and to provide liquidity in particular financial markets where private markets were frozen.

Congress had passed the Emergency Economic Stabilization Act of 2008, creating the Troubled Asset Relief Program (TARP), and the Bush and Obama Administrations used the authorities in TARP to provide capital injections to banks, aid to homeowners, as well as support for the automobile industry. The financial rescue was followed by stress tests of the largest banks that revealed information to the markets about the health of

---

[4] See 2014 *Economic Report of the President*, Chapter 3 "The Economic Impact of the American Recovery and Reinvestment Act Five Years Later."

these financial institutions and the magnitude of their capital needs. Banks with shortfalls under the stress tests were able to subsequently raise private capital. Many smaller banks that were unable to raise private capital, as well as many large banks, were recapitalized through TARP funds. These actions aimed to stabilize the economy and the financial system, but were not solutions to the underlying problems in the regulatory framework that the crisis revealed.

At the same time, President Obama did not wait to push for longer-run changes to address the risk of future financial crises; in July 2010, he signed into law the Dodd-Frank Wall Street Reform and Consumer Protection Act (Dodd-Frank Act) whose stated purpose was "to promote the financial stability of the United States by improving accountability and transparency in the financial system, to end 'too big to fail,' to protect the American taxpayer by ending bailouts, to protect consumers from abusive financial services practices, and for other purposes."[5] There have been multiple other efforts to identify opportunities for regulatory solutions to improve the functioning of financial markets and promote financial stability. The Basel Committee on Banking Supervision, for example, recommended a set of international banking regulations, Basel III, to strengthen the regulation, supervision, and risk management of the banking sector.

In many ways these longer-run reforms have reshaped the financial regulatory system of the United States. Banks and other financial institutions now face different rules designed to make them safer and less of a threat to the overall system. With the creation of FSOC, regulators now have a way to pool knowledge and insights about risks to the financial system. With the creation of the Consumer Financial Protection Bureau (CFPB), consumers now have a regulator whose sole job is to look out for the interests of consumers in the financial system.

The many individual components of financial reform over the past eight years can be classified into three broad overlapping categories. The first includes measures aimed to improve the safety and soundness of individual financial institutions by not only increasing their capital and liquidity but also decreasing risky behavior. These reforms should increase the banking sector's ability to absorb shocks arising from financial and economic stress. The second category of reforms includes measures aimed at reducing systemic risk in the financial system by bringing more of the financial system under a regulatory umbrella, improving financial regulatory coordination, and ensuring that individual financial institutions can fail without derailing the system. The third includes measures designed to increase transparency and accountability in financial markets as well as provide additional

---

[5] Dodd-Frank Act preamble

consumer and investor protections. These include reforms designed to improve risk management, governance and transparency of the financial system by strengthening banks' transparency and disclosures, improving consumer protections, and better regulating credit rating agencies. These three categories of longer-run reforms are the focus of this section.

Increasing the Safety and Soundness of Individual Financial Institutions

The crisis revealed clear fault lines in the financial system. Many financial firms lacked the ability to absorb losses because they had inadequate levels of capital or lacked the ability to survive runs because they lacked sufficient liquid assets. In fact, these two issues are related because fears about solvency or insufficient liquidity can lead to runs. Moreover, many firms engaged in excessively risky trading and lending activity while at the same time enjoying the benefits of federally insured deposits and access to borrowing at the Federal Reserve. Financial reform has helped make the financial system more secure by requiring financial firms to have less unstable funding, more liquid assets, higher capital levels, and reduced risk-taking.

Capital Levels

An important step toward increasing the safety and soundness of individual financial institutions was the publishing of the Basel III recommended reforms in December 2010. These reforms recommended both higher minimum capital ratios and capital buffers for banks and a stronger definition of what counts as regulatory capital. In July 2013, the Federal Reserve implemented important parts of the Basel III recommendations by finalizing rules that strengthened the definition of regulatory capital, mandated that common equity tier 1 capital must be 4.5 percent of risk-weighted assets, and introduced a capital conservation buffer of 2.5 percent of risk-weighted assets.[6] The Federal Reserve's final rules implementing Basel III also usefully constrained the role of bank internal models in the bank regulatory capital framework.

Dodd-Frank-required stress testing is a means for regulators to assess whether the largest bank holding companies (BHCs) have enough capital to weather another financial crisis. The Federal Reserve uses the results of the

---

[6] Tier 1 capital consists primarily of common stock and retained earnings, but may also include certain types of preferred stock. Risk-weighted assets are the bank's assets or off-balance-sheet exposures weighted according to risk. For example, a corporate bond would typically have a higher risk weight than a government bond reflecting the higher risk of default. A capital conservation buffer is extra capital built up when business conditions are good so that minimum capital levels are less likely to be breached when business conditions are bad.

Box 6-2: A Cross-Country Comparison of Bank Size

The financial crisis refocused attention on the challenges posed by large financial institutions that could threaten the financial system should they become insolvent, otherwise known as "too-big-to-fail" (TBTF), (see Box 6-4). Because increases in size may bring additional risk and managerial challenges, some argue that certain U.S. banks are so large that, in the event of another financial crisis, there is still a significant risk that investor uncertainty may force governments to intervene to prevent another financial crisis.

There may be certain advantages associated with bank size that help balance the potential risks. For example, large banks enjoy economies of scale in both operations and in the management of credit and liquidity risks by holding diversified portfolios of these risks (Hughes and Mester 2013). Beck, Demirguc-Kunt, and Levine (2006) also provide evidence suggesting that concentrated banking systems tend to be more stable and better able to withstand a financial crisis because banks in concentrated banking systems are more diversified and easier to monitor. However, healthy large banks may threaten competition and, when near failure, may threaten the stability of the financial system. One approach to evaluating whether large U.S. banks are "too large" and subsequently "too risky" is to compare them with the size, concentration, and systemic risk of banks of other advanced economies.

How Big is "Big?"

The five largest U.S. banks account for a large share of the U.S. banking sector's total assets, market capitalization, and revenue. In a Bloomberg ranking of the largest banks by total assets as of December 2015, four of the top 20 are based in the United States, with the largest U.S. bank ranked sixth in the world. However, these U.S. banks do not appear as large when scaled by measures of the size of the economy. For example, in Switzerland, Sweden, France, the United Kingdom, and Belgium, total assets of the top five banks were about two to four times as large as their home country's GDP, while in the United States, they were about half the size of GDP in 2015 (Figure 6-iv). Even if scaled to the aggregated Eurozone GDP (though this is not the approach used in Figure 6-iv because the repercussions of these banks' failure likely would predominantly fall on the individual country), the top five Eurozone banks still make up a greater share of their economy than do the top five U.S. banks (nearly 80 percent of GDP for the former and about 50 percent for the latter).

Beyond the traditional measures of total assets, a number of other benchmarks may be used to assess the size of banks. Across these mea-

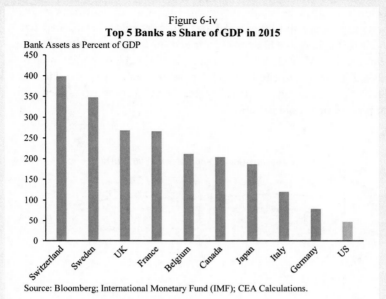

Figure 6-iv
Top 5 Banks as Share of GDP in 2015

Bank Assets as Percent of GDP

Source: Bloomberg; International Monetary Fund (IMF); CEA Calculations.

sures, U.S. banks also do not appear to be particularly large compared with those of other advanced economies.

When is "Big" Bad?

Large banks pose several potential risks to the economy. First, large banks have the potential to engage in monopolistic and rent-seeking behavior, crowding out smaller institutions. Economists often measure the potential for such behavior by the concentration of large firms within a sector. Several studies show that in the run-up and immediate aftermath of the financial crisis, large banks increasingly dominated the global financial sector. For example, International Financial Services London Research found that the share of assets of the 10 largest global banks compared with the largest 1000 rose from 14 percent in 1999 to 26 percent in 2009 (Goldstein and Veron 2011). However, there is some evidence that this trend may have changed in recent years in the United States. World Bank data shows that bank concentration (assets of the five largest banks as a share of total banking assets) in the United States rose until 2010 before stabilizing at about 47 percent. In the United Kingdom, Eurozone, and Switzerland, bank concentration has been considerably higher than in the United States and increased sharply between 2013 and 2014 (Figure 6-v).

Second, the failure of a large financial institution could cause the failure of other financial institutions with which it has business relationships. Economists refer to the risk that the failure of one bank may pose to the larger financial system as systemic risk. For example, though Lehman Brothers was only the fourth largest investment bank in 2008 and only about a third the size of the largest, its failure created repercussions throughout the financial sector and the larger economy (Wiggins, Piontek, and Metrick 2014). Recognizing that large or highly interconnected financial institutions may pose systemic risk, the Financial Stability Board designates firms that meet certain criteria as "systemically important financial institutions."

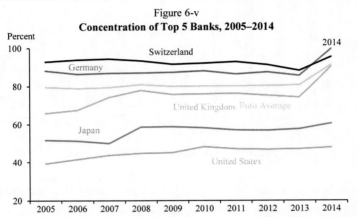

Figure 6-v
Concentration of Top 5 Banks, 2005–2014

Note: Assets of five largest banks as a share of total commercial banking assets shown. Euro Area includes Austria, Finland, France, Germany, Italy, Latvia, Lithuania, and Spain where data is available from 2005 to 2014. Total assets include total earning assets, cash and due from banks, foreclosed real estate, fixed assets, goodwill, other intangibles, current tax assets, deferred tax, discontinued operations, and other assets.
Source: World Bank Global Financial Development Database.

Glasserman and Loudis (2015) evaluate the risk of large banks using the five factors employed by the Basel Committee on Banking Supervision for designating global systemically important banks (G-SIBs): size, cross-jurisdictional activity, interconnectedness, substitutability, and complexity.[1] The methodology assumes that the distress or failure of banks that are larger, operate in more countries, do more business with other financial institutions, provide services that are diffi-

---

[1] G-SIBs are designated based on a cut-off score determined based on the scores of a sample of banks. Banks in the sample include: the 75 largest global banks based on financial year-end Basel III leverage ratio exposure, banks designated as G-SIBs in the year before, and banks added by national supervisors using "supervisory judgement." The cutoff score is then used to allocate banks to four buckets with different level of loss absorbency requirements, determined on an annual basis. There were about 90 banks in the sample in the end of 2014 exercise. See: http://www.bis.org/bcbs/gsib/gsibs_dislosures_end2014.htm.

cult to replace with services from other providers (for example, payment processing), and have more complex operations, pose greater risk to the global economy (Basel Committee on Banking Supervision 2013).[2] Figure 6-vi shows that when this overall score is decomposed into its five components, U.S. banks stand below those of several other countries in size and cross-jurisdictional activity and above those in many other countries in substitutability and complexity (particularly in the operation of payment systems), suggesting that size is not the decisive factor contributing to the systemic risk of the largest U.S. banks. This does not mean the largest U.S. banks pose no risks, but it suggests their size may not be the main issue.

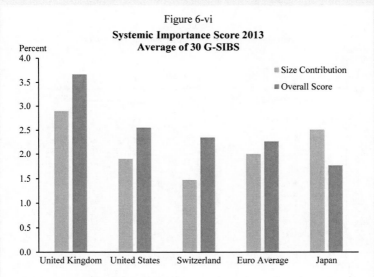

Figure 6-vi
Systemic Importance Score 2013
Average of 30 G-SIBS

Source: Glasserman and Loudis (2015).

New York University's Volatility Laboratory offers an alternative measure of the systemic risk of individual financial institutions

---

[2] Glasserman and Loudis' (2015) G-SIB score show the mean score for the top thirty banks on the G-SIB ranking scale, grouped by country. The score is calculated as the average of (1) Cross-jurisdictional activity: foreign claims, cross-jurisdictional liabilities; (2) Size: Total exposure, a more comprehensive indicator than total assets because it maintains a consistent measure across jurisdictions while assets are specific to national accounting standards; (3) Interconnectedness: intra-financial system assets, intra-financial system liabilities, total securities outstanding; (4) Substitutability: assets under custody, payments activity, underwriting activity; (5) Complexity: over-the-counter derivatives, level 3 assets, trading and available for sale value.

by scoring banks based on their percent contribution to the aggregate capital shortfall in the event of a financial crisis (SRISK%) (Engle 2012, Glasserman and Loudis 2015).[3] Firms with a high SRISK% in a crisis are not only the biggest losers in a crisis but also are the firms that create or extend the crisis. The measure, plotted in Figure 6-vii, shows that the top four U.S. financial institutions with the highest SRISK% average less than 16 percent contribution consistently from 2005 to 2016, which is well below the average percent contribution of the top four banks of France, Germany, and Switzerland over this same time period (Acharya, Engle, and Richardson 2012; Acharya et al. 2016).

The Dodd-Frank Act takes many steps to try to limit the risks posed by the largest financial institutions in the United States as well as

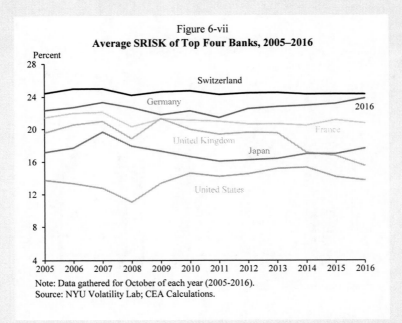

Figure 6-vii
Average SRISK of Top Four Banks, 2005–2016

Note: Data gathered for October of each year (2005-2016).
Source: NYU Volatility Lab; CEA Calculations.

limiting the ability of very large financial institutions to grow through acquisition. In addition, the President has proposed a financial fee on the liabilities of the largest financial institutions, which would reduce the incentive for such institutions to leverage, reducing the cost of externalities arising from financial firm default as a result of high leverage (Department of Treasury 2016).

---

[3] The Volatility lab samples 1,200 global financial firms. https://www.unige.ch/gsem/iee/files/7613/9574/8572/Solari_2012_slides.pdf.

> **Are U.S. Banks Too Big?**
>
> The question of whether individual banks are too big is separate from the question of whether the financial system as a whole is too large relative to the economy that could come about, for example, with many smaller firms. This issue is discussed in Box 6-1. Viewed individually, large U.S. banks do not appear disproportionate to the scale of the economy when compared with those in other advanced economies. However, their interconnection highlights the importance of global cooperation in regulating these large institutions, ensuring that the comparative benefits of large banks outweigh their risks, and enhancing the resiliency of the financial sector in the face of an economic downturn. Moreover, it is important that the size of banks reflects the underlying economics, including any external risks posed by size, and that there not exist any implicit subsidies related to size.

stress tests as a complement to its annual Comprehensive Capital Analysis and Review, a thorough qualitative and quantitative assessment of each BHC's capital plan. Within the quantitative assessment, the Federal Reserve examines the effects of various simulated financial stress scenarios on a BHC's capital ratios. The Federal Reserve also examines qualitatively the BHC's internal controls, contingency planning, governance, and the overall robustness of its capital planning process. Those banks that do not pass the annual review may not make any capital distributions such as dividend payments and common stock repurchases unless expressly permitted by the Federal Reserve.

The overall quantity and quality of capital has increased at BHCs since the crisis. As seen in Figure 6-8, from March 2009 to June 2016, aggregate tier 1 common equity capital for the largest banks and the BHCs increased from 4.8 percent to 12.7 percent of risk-weighted assets, well above the minimum required total capital ratio of 8 percent that the Federal Reserve adopted in 2013. In the most recent annual review, completed in June 2016, 30 of the 33 BHCs passed the Federal Reserve's test. The Federal Reserve objected to the capital plans of two banks, and did not object to the plan of a third, but required it to resubmit its plan with revisions by the end of 2016.

Liquidity

Federal banking regulatory agencies have also instituted reforms that help banks survive periods of financial stress by improving their ability to withstand acute short-term liquidity stress and improve their long-term funding positions. To better manage short-term liquidity stress, regulators have raised the quality and stability of the assets that banks hold to ensure

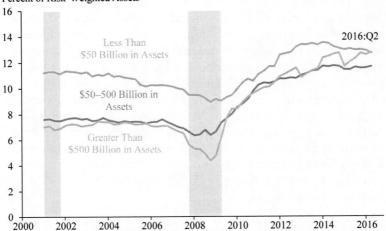

Figure 6-8
Tier 1 Common Equity Ratios for U.S. Banks by Bank Size, 2001–2016
Percent of Risk-Weighted Assets

Note: Shading denotes recession. Includes data for U.S. bank holding companies (BHCs) and "stand-alone" banks not controlled by a BHC, but not savings bank holding companies, branches and agencies of foreign banks, or nonbanks that are not held by a U.S. BHC.
Source: Federal Reserve Bank of New York; Haver Analytics.

that they will not run out of cash, or liquidity, during times of financial stress. In September 2014, the Office of the Comptroller of the Currency (OCC), the Federal Reserve, and the Federal Deposit Insurance Corporation (FDIC) finalized a rule that mandates minimum Liquidity Coverage Ratios (LCR) to be consistent with Basel III for large banks and BHCs. LCR is the ratio of a bank's high-quality liquid assets to its projected cash outflows during a 30-day stress period. The Federal Reserve defines high quality liquid assets as assets that a bank can easily convert into cash within 30 days such as central bank reserves and government or corporate debt. Mandating a higher LCR will reduce the likelihood that banks face a short-term liquidity crisis.

To improve the longer-term funding resilience of banks, the three regulatory agencies proposed a rule in May 2016 to require large banks and BHCs to have a Net Stable Funding Ratio of at least 1. This ratio is calculated by assigning scores to each type of funding based on the price "stability" of the funding source. Equity capital and long-term deposits earn higher scores, while very short-term funding (such a repurchase agreements) earn the lowest score. They then calculate the bank's required amount of stable funding based on the quality and stability of its assets. Banks must maintain the ratio of their available stable funding to required level of stable funding at a specified level, thus lowering their liquidity risk profiles.

The three federal banking agencies have tailored both the LCR and the Net Stable Funding Ratio rules to a bank's riskiness and complexity. The full requirements of each rule would apply to BHCs with $250 billion or more in total assets while less stringent versions of these rules would apply to BHCs with more than $50 billion but less than $250 billion in assets. These rules do not apply to community banking institutions.[7] The LCR rule became effective on January 1, 2015, starting with an LCR of 80 percent and increasing to 100 percent by January 1, 2017. The Net Stable Funding Ratio requirement will not become effective until January 1, 2018. Despite criticism of the expected negative impact of Net Stable Funding Ratio requirements, the Federal Reserve Board found that, as of the end of 2015, nearly all covered companies were already in compliance with the standard. The Federal Reserve Board also found that because the aggregated stable funding shortfall amount would be small relative to the size of these companies, the costs connected to making changes to funding structures to comply with the NSFR requirement would not be significant.

The result of the new bank liquidity requirements has been a general improvement in the liquidity positions of U.S. banks. The liquidity ratio reported in Figure 6-9 is similar to LCR but calculated using only publicly available data.[8] Figure 6.9 shows the average liquidity ratio of the largest one percent of U.S. BHCs has risen from its trough at the beginning of the financial crisis to well above levels observed before the crisis. Further, Figure 6-10 shows that BHCs reporting LCR using either the standard or modified methods of calculating the LCR show marked improvement in the liquidity available to them.

Thus, banks appear to be in a better position to weather a crisis or liquidity event than they were on the eve of Lehman's collapse. They have more stable funding and more liquid assets than before, and hence the risks that runs could cause an institution to seize up have been moderated.

---

[7] The LCR rules apply to all banking organizations with $250 billion or more in total consolidated assets or $10 billion or more in on-balance sheet foreign exposure and to these banking organizations' subsidiary depository institutions that have assets of $10 billion or more. The rule also will apply a less stringent, modified LCR to bank holding companies and savings and loan holding companies that do not meet these thresholds, but have $50 billion or more in total assets.

[8] This figure is reproduced from Choi and Choi (2016) with permission. The liquidity ratio is similar to LCR, which is the ratio of the stock of high quality liquid assets (HQLA) to potential net cash outflow over a 30 calendar day liquidity stress scenario. However, there are differences in the liquidity adjustments for certain assets and liability classes from those used in the LCR because the liquidity ratio uses only publicly-available data. Derivative exposures are ignored due to data limitations.

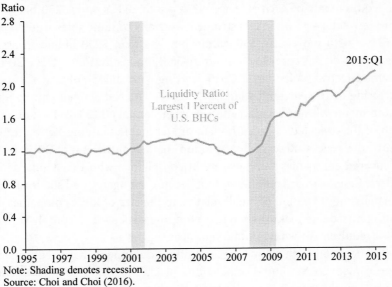

Figure 6-9
Liquidity Ratio for Largest U.S. Bank Holding Companies, 1995–2015

Ratio

Liquidity Ratio:
Largest 1 Percent of
U.S. BHCs

2015:Q1

Note: Shading denotes recession.
Source: Choi and Choi (2016).

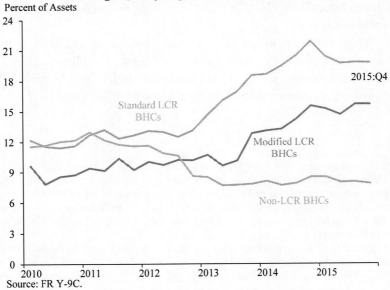

Figure 6-10
Selected High-Quality Liquid Assets at BHCs, 2010–2015

Percent of Assets

Standard LCR
BHCs

2015:Q4

Modified LCR
BHCs

Non-LCR BHCs

Source: FR Y-9C.

Risk Taking

The Dodd-Frank Act took a number of steps to limit risky behavior by financial firms. One component dubbed "the Volcker Rule" is named for Former Federal Reserve Chair Paul Volcker. As required by Dodd-Frank, the SEC, CFTC and banking regulators finalized the Volcker Rule in 2013 to restrict federally insured banking entities from engaging in proprietary trading or investing in or sponsoring private equity or hedge funds. As seen in Figure 6-11, activities related to trading and securities contributed to significant losses during the crisis. The Volcker Rule is meant to mitigate the moral hazard inherent in access to federally insured deposits by limiting high-risk-taking activities. Banks have until July 2017 to conform investments in, and relationships with, covered funds. In the meantime, banks are recording and reporting certain quantitative measurements to regulators, and divesting their proprietary positions, including those in hedge funds.

Banking regulations typically require firms to meet a minimum ratio of capital to risk-weighted assets. A risk-weighting system assigns a weight to each asset or category of assets that reflects its relative risk. Figure 6-12 shows a general decline in risk-weighted assets as a fraction of total assets, reflecting declining relative risk of bank assets over time. Both Basel 2.5, effective in January 2013, and Basel III, effective in January 2016, revised the risk-weighting methodology and are reflected in the Figure as discrete increases on these dates.

The Dodd-Frank Act included several reforms of the Federal Deposit Insurance Corporation (FDIC) to better protect depositors and stabilize the financial system. First, it permanently raised the level of deposits insured for each depositor from $100,000 to $250,000 for each insured bank. Second, it altered the operation of deposit insurance. Since its founding in 1934, the FDIC has maintained a Deposit Insurance Fund, a pool of assets meant to prevent bank runs by insuring the deposits of member banks and finance the resolution of failed banks. The FDIC maintains funds in the Deposit Insurance Fund by charging insurance premiums, or assessments, to banks whose depositors it insures. Specifically, Dodd-Frank required two changes in the methodology for calculating these premiums that provided direct relief to small banks with more traditional business models by making large banks bear more of the costs of deposit insurance.

The first change required by the Dodd-Frank Act expanded the deposit insurance assessment base. When this change took effect in spring 2011, total assessments for small banks with less than $10 billion in assets fell by a third — an annualized decrease of almost $1.4 billion. The second change required by Dodd-Frank raised the minimum Designated Reserve Ratio—the Deposit Insurance Fund balance over total estimated insured

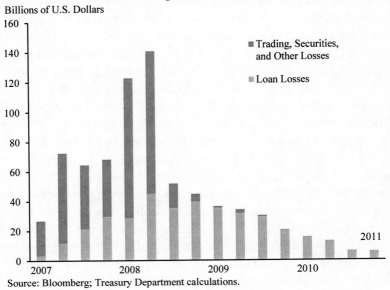

Figure 6-11
Losses for Large U.S. Banks, 2007–2011

Billions of U.S. Dollars

Source: Bloomberg; Treasury Department calculations.

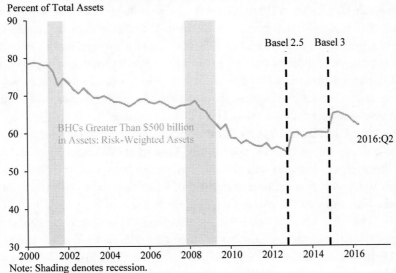

Figure 6-12
Average Risk-Weighted Assets, Largest U.S. BHCs, 2000–2016

Percent of Total Assets

Note: Shading denotes recession.
Source: Federal Reserve Bank of New York; Haver Analytics.

Box 6-3: The Performance of Community Banks[1]

Community banks, defined generally here as banks with less than $10 billion in assets, are an important part of the U.S. banking landscape, providing access to banking services for millions of Americans and serving as the only local source of brick-and-mortar traditional banking services for many counties, as well as key sources of credit for rural communities and small business loans.[2] The number of community bank institutions has declined steadily over the last two decades, yet the passage of Dodd-Frank in 2010 does not appear to have affected this long-term trend. Community banks face a challenging competitive and macroeconomic environment, but since Dodd-Frank was passed, the growth rate of lending has rebounded, market share has stabilized for some important types of community bank lending, profitability (measured by return on assets) has returned to pre-crisis levels for the smallest community banks, geographic coverage across counties has remained stable, and the largest community banks have been expanding their geographic reach.

The Dodd-Frank Act is designed to prevent excessive risk-taking and protect consumers from exploitative bank lending practices. It also distinguishes between banks on the basis of size—many rules include exemptions and tailoring for financial institutions with less than $10 billion in assets—to help keep it from being an undue burden on small banks.

Economic evidence shows that community banks remain healthy and have recovered together with big banks since 2008. The annual growth rates of lending by community banks in each asset range have returned to levels seen prior to the crisis and are well above the negative rates seen following the crisis (see Figure 6-viii). Since 2008, community banks' market share of total loans has held steady at around 20 percent.

Access to community banks has remained steady since 1994 at the county level. About 99 percent of counties have a community bank office (either a main office or a brick-and-mortar branch office), something that has not materially changed since 2010. About 1 in 4 counties rely exclusively on community banks for brick-and-mortar services within county lines. The steady decline in the number of community bank institutions over the past two decades has largely been offset by an increase in the number of brick-and-mortar branch offices per main office. The

---

[1] For more information on Box 6-3, as well as other statistics on the health of community banks over the last two decades, please see CEA's (2016) issue brief "The Performance of Community Banks over Time."

[2] Asset size is computed in constant 2009 dollars.

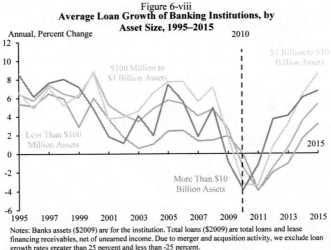

Figure 6-viii
Average Loan Growth of Banking Institutions, by Asset Size, 1995–2015

Notes: Banks assets ($2009) are for the institution. Total loans ($2009) are total loans and lease financing receivables, net of unearned income. Due to merger and acqusition activity, we exclude loan growth rates greater than 25 percent and less than -25 percent.
Source: FDIC (June, Qtr 2) Call Report Data. CEA Calculations

number of brick-and-mortar branch offices per main office has also increased slightly since 2010.

The decline in the number of community bank institutions in recent years reflects decreased entry rather than increased exit. The number of exits each year has been roughly steady since 2004. In most years, mergers with other community banks are the most common reason for exit. These merged banks are living on as community banks, but as part of a larger parent group. Entry began falling in 2006 and has been nearly zero since 2010.

Recent research suggests that macroeconomic conditions likely explain much of the drop in bank entry in recent years (Adams and Gramlich 2016). All new bank entry (both *de novo* and branch expansion by incumbent banks) has fallen considerably since 2006. The profitability of new entrants is typically lower on average than an established bank of comparable size. For younger banks, a larger proportion of their loans were originated in the current macroeconomic environment, which includes low equilibrium interest rates.[3] This depresses profit margins on traditional lending activity. The profitability of the youngest community banks fell precipitously relative to incumbent banks between 2001 and 2009, but by 2015 all cohorts have achieved a level of profitability roughly equal to or exceeding what they earned prior to the financial crisis (see Figure 6-ix). Although not shown here, the same holds true for community banks with assets between $100 million and $1 billion.

---

[3] See CEA (2015b) report "Long-Term Interest Rates: A Survey" for a discussion of factors contributing to the decline of the equilibrium interest rate.

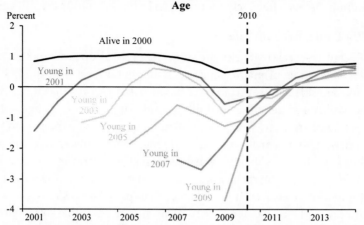

Figure 6-ix

Return on Assets of Banking Institutions with Less than $100M Assets, by Age

Notes: A bank is "Young in 2001" if it received a charter in 2000 or 2001. A bank is alive in 2000 if it had a charter in 2000. Top 1%, bottom 1% ROA for all banks excluded from average.
Source: FDIC (June, Qtr 2) Call Reports; CEA Calculations.

The Dodd-Frank Act has helped to remove some cost disadvantages for community banks. Dodd-Frank has forced large and complex banks and BHCs to better internalize the costs that their failure may have upon the broader financial system, and therefore has helped to reduce any funding cost advantages that such banks may have held in the past. Moreover, banking agencies continue to take steps to lessen and simplify the regulatory burden on community banks, while directing the burden on those banks whose riskiness Dodd-Frank has sought to reduce.

In implementing the provisions of Dodd-Frank, the Administration has taken important steps to ensure that regulatory requirements are implemented in an efficient manner. The banking agencies have begun and are continuing to tailor regulatory requirements to reflect the different level of financial risk that community banks pose. Some steps include allowing for longer exam cycles for smaller banks that are well capitalized, streamlining the regulatory reports that community banks must file, and continuing to develop a simpler and shorter regulatory reporting procedure for community banks. Furthermore, the banking agencies continue to consider the written and oral comments made by community banks in the banking agencies' nationwide meetings, working to reduce unnecessary regulatory burden under the Economic Growth and Regulatory Paperwork Reduction Act. The Administration strongly supports these ongoing efforts by the banking agencies to fairly tailor the regulatory requirements for community banks and avoid any unnecessary and inefficient burdens.

deposits—from 1.15 percent to 1.35 percent. The FDIC issued a final rule increasing the reserve ratio in March 2016 and paid for the increase by levying a surcharge on top of regular assessment fees for banks with more than $10 billion in assets, effectively requiring large banks to bear the full cost.

Have Big Banks Become Safer?

Recent research by Sarin and Summers (2016) documents that most regulatory measures of major banks such as capital levels or liquidity suggest banks are safer; however, market-based risk measures that reflect bank equity volatility and default probability seem to suggest that, though risk has decreased since its crisis peak, it is not in fact lower than the period prior to the crisis. This is consistent with evidence from sources like the NYU Volatility Lab, discussed below, that use market measures of risk and finds that, while risk in the financial system is down considerably from the crisis, based on market measures, it is not lower than prior to the crisis.

It may be the case that either risk was mispriced or markets lacked the information necessary to price the risk of individual banks before the crisis. If either is the case, better information concerning the risks the banks face could make them appear riskier today relative to the pre-crisis period, when we had a poorer understanding of banks' risk. Another explanation for this finding is that banks may simply be worth less because of the present macroeconomic environment, regulations that limit banks' ability to take risky positions, and loss of the implicit TBTF guarantee.

A central argument of the Sarin and Summers paper, and work like it, is that the franchise value of banks has fallen. Markets value bank assets and their business models as being worth less over the past few years than they were before the crisis. Consequently, one would expect the bank to appear riskier based on market metrics. Hence, a comparison of market-based measures pre- and post-crisis reflects the impact of financial reform on bank safety and soundness and the impact on banks' profitability. The rules that made banks better capitalized almost certainly made banks safer and better able to withstand future crises; however, constant vigilance is necessary to make sure that, in a changing environment, risks are adequately managed.

Systemic Risk and Identifying Sources of Risk in the System

The crisis revealed the impact that the failure, or threatened failure, of even a single financial institution can pose to the larger financial system. Financial reform has helped make the financial system more secure by identifying firms that pose such a risk and subjecting them to additional regulatory oversight and other mitigation strategies. In part, it has accomplished this by improving the coordination of regulatory oversight such that regulators can take a more holistic view of the financial system and properly identify and act on sources of risk to the system.

Individual bank failures can have negative impacts on their customers and the communities that they serve. Deposit insurance is meant to protect depositors and mitigate run-risk while FDIC resolution is meant to mitigate the impact of a bank failure on customers and communities. Regulation also seeks to minimize the impact of a bank failure on the financial system more broadly.

Promoting financial stability requires identifying potential sources of risk to the financial system. One issue the crisis revealed was the patchwork nature of U.S. financial supervision. While regulators may have been able to consider the safety of a particular institution, they often lacked the perspective to consider systemic issues.[9] The Dodd-Frank Act established a new body to fill this regulatory gap, the Financial Stability Oversight Council (FSOC). The FSOC has a clear mandate that creates for the first time collective accountability for identifying risks and responding to emerging threats to financial stability. It is a collaborative body chaired by the Secretary of the Treasury that brings together the expertise of the Federal financial regulators, an independent insurance expert appointed by the President, and state regulators. Dodd-Frank also established the Office of Financial Research (OFR) to support the FSOC by looking across the financial system to measure and analyze risk, perform essential research, and collect and standardize financial data.

Shadow Banking and Regulatory Gaps

Since its establishment by the Dodd-Frank Act, the FSOC has worked to identify non-bank financial institutions that are systemically risky to

---

[9] The U.S. financial regulatory apparatus consists of numerous agencies, each of which has a distinct, though quite closely related, jurisdiction. A useful way to organize these agencies is to categorize them into prudential bank regulators and market regulators. Prudential bank regulators focus on specific financial institutions and ensure compliance with applicable risk management and prudential rules. Within this category, the Federal Reserve Board regulates all banks that are part of the Federal Reserve System and regulated BHCs. It also sets reserve requirements, serves as the lender of last resort to banks, and assesses the overall soundness of bank and BHC balance sheets, often in concert with other regulators. The Federal Deposit Insurance Corporation (FDIC) provides deposit insurance for depositors and regulates state banks that are not Federal Reserve System members. The Office of the Comptroller of the Currency (part of the Treasury Department) regulates national banking institutions and seeks to foster both safety and competition within the national banking system. The main market regulators are the Securities and Exchange Commission (SEC) and the Commodity Futures Trading Commission (CFTC). The SEC regulates securities exchanges, brokers, dealers, mutual funds and investment advisers among other market participants. It enforces securities laws and regulates the buying and selling of securities and securities-based derivatives. The CFTC specifically regulates futures, commodity, options, and swap markets, including the exchanges, dealers, and other intermediaries that constitute these markets.

U.S. financial stability, subjecting each designated company to enhanced prudential standards and supervision by the Federal Reserve. While any financial institution that performs maturity transformation faces run-risk, in traditional banking the risk is mitigated through the use of deposit insurance and the Federal Reserve's availability as a lender of last resort. On the other hand, many non-bank financial institutions engage in financial intermediation and therefore maturity and liquidity transformation, without explicit public-sector guarantees, access to liquidity from the Federal Reserve, or regulatory oversight.

Such non-bank financial institutions gather funds from those wishing to invest, typically by issuing commercial paper, engaging in repurchase agreements (repo), or issuing debt instruments.[10] Money market mutual funds (MMFs) or other types of investment funds, often purchase these debt instruments on behalf of investors. Institutions engaged in such activities include large securities dealers, finance companies, and asset managers who use such funds to invest in other assets that have longer maturity, less liquidity, or both.

As discussed above, the size of the shadow-banking sector grew much faster than the traditional banking sector in the decade leading up to the financial crisis. Following the crisis, the sector shrank to the level seen earlier in the 2000s and continued to decrease in the following years. Two other important components of the shadow-banking sector, repo and commercial paper, grew rapidly in the years prior to the crisis before falling in the years following the crisis and ensuing recession. Figure 6-13 shows the repo market is well below its size in the years immediately preceding the crisis. As Figure 6-14 shows, the commercial paper market has stabilized at a level well below its peak in recent years. By adding additional oversight of the sector, Dodd-Frank has reduced the likelihood of shadow-banking entities being the source of financial instability.

As part of its mandate to identify risks to financial stability, in July 2013 the FSOC designated four non-bank firms as Non-Bank Systemically Important Financial Institutions. These firms became subject to heightened prudential requirements and supervision by the Federal Reserve Board. This additional regulatory scrutiny, along with pressure from investors and analysts, has led some firms to consider actions that will reduce their

---

[10] A repurchase agreement, or repo, is a type of short-term loan where the "borrower" sells securities to the "lender" with an agreement to buy them back at a future date at a slightly higher price. This is similar to a collateralized loan except ownership of the collateral passes between the borrower and lender. The difference in the selling price and the buyback price represents the interest on the loan and is referred to as the 'repo rate'.

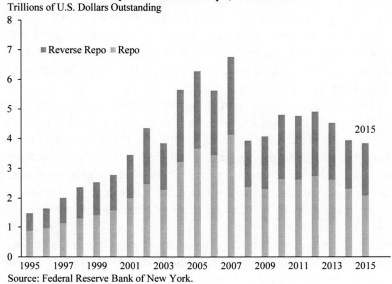

Figure 6-13
Repo and Reverse Repo, 1995–2015
Trillions of U.S. Dollars Outstanding

Source: Federal Reserve Bank of New York.

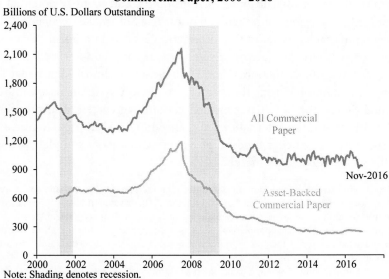

Figure 6-14
Commercial Paper, 2000–2016
Billions of U.S. Dollars Outstanding

Note: Shading denotes recession.
Source: Federal Reserve Board.

systemic footprint. In April 2015, one of these firms, General Electric Capital Corporation (GE Capital), announced that it would be selling off most of its financing arm to "create a simpler, more valuable company," and committed to working with the FSOC and the Federal Reserve to "take the actions necessary to de-designate GE Capital as a Systemically Important Financial Institution" (General Electric 2015). These actions resulted in the FSOC rescinding the "systemically important financial institution" designation for GE Capital on June 28, 2016.

Private funds can contribute to systemic risk in similar ways to other large financial institutions.[11] Losses at a large private fund may result in default to creditors and the financial institutions with which the fund does business. In addition, private funds often employ high levels of leverage. Although leverage is not a perfect proxy for risk, there is ample evidence that the use of leverage, in combination with other factors, can contribute to risks to financial stability. These risks are likely to be greater if an elevated level of leverage is employed; borrowing counterparties are large, highly interconnected financial institutions; counterparty margining requirements are limited or lax and positions are infrequently marked to market; the underlying assets are less liquid and price discovery is poor; or other financial institutions with large positions are involved in similar trading strategies.[12]

In 2011, the Securities and Exchange Commission (SEC) and the Commodities Futures Trading Commission (CFTC) adopted new Form PF, required by the Dodd-Frank Act to help the SEC, CFTC, and the FSOC monitor hedge funds and other private funds, and identify potential systemic risks associated with their activities. The SEC makes available a summary report each quarter of the information reported on Form PF. As seen in Figure 6-15, the number of private funds reported on Form PF has risen from just over 20,000 to more than 26,000 including almost 9,000 hedge fund filings. In addition to using these reports to identify systemic risks within the United States, the SEC has provided certain aggregated, non-proprietary Form PF data to the International Organization of Securities Commissions (IOSCO) on large hedge funds to provide it with a more complete overview of the global hedge fund market.

---

[11] Private Funds are excluded from the definition of an investment company and are, therefore, not registered under the Investment Company Act of 1940. Private funds may be excluded from the definition of an investment company by having fewer than 100 shareholders or only being open to "qualified purchasers" (such as institutional investors or high-net worth individuals) as defined by the SEC. Examples of private funds include hedge funds and private equity funds.

[12] See Financial Stability Oversight Council Update On Review of Asset Management Products and Activities at (https://www.treasury.gov/initiatives/fsoc/news/Documents/FSOC%20 Update%20on%20Review%20of%20Asset%20Management%20Products%20and%20Activities. pdf)

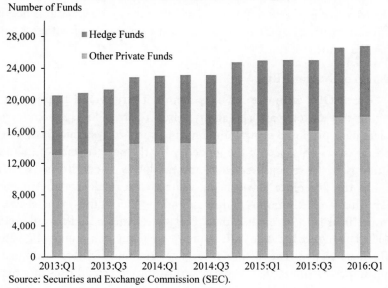

Figure 6-15
Private Funds Reporting to Form PF, 2013–2016

Number of Funds

Source: Securities and Exchange Commission (SEC).

Money market mutual funds (MMFs) are a particular type of mutual fund that invests in debt securities with short maturities and very low credit risk. These funds typically maintain a net asset value (NAV) of $1 even when the actual value is slightly above or slightly below that value. As MMF shares may be redeemed at $1 each on demand, the funds are still engaged in maturity transformation. The funds face run-risk if the value of the fund portfolio is thought to be less than $1, particularly because there is an advantage to being the first to redeem. In 2010, the SEC adopted rules that make structural and operational reforms to address risks of investor runs in money market funds, while preserving the benefits of the funds. The purpose of these rules was to reduce the interest rate, credit and liquidity risks of money market fund portfolios.

In 2012, as part of its efforts to identify and address systemic risks to financial stability, the FSOC issued proposed recommendations for how the SEC might address the risks to financial stability that money market mutual funds (MMFs) continue to present. In 2014, the SEC finalized MMF reforms that required structural and operational changes that address risks of investor runs in MMFs during times of financial stress but preserved the benefits of such funds for investors and companies. Changes included requiring a floating NAV for institutional prime money market funds, which allows the daily share prices of these funds to fluctuate along with changes in the market-based value of fund assets and provides non-government money market fund boards new tools – liquidity fees and redemption gates – to address run-risk.[13] Figure 6-16 shows the weighted-average maturity of MMFs have declined by roughly ten days since the new regulations became effective, increasing liquidity and reducing the sensitivity of net asset value to changes in interest rates.[14]

Measures of Systemic Risk

The FSOC's mandate includes identifying risks and responding to emerging threats to financial stability, often referred to as systemic risk. Scholars have proposed several different measures of systemic risk, each of which measures an aspect of the tendency for the performance of financial institutions to move together when the market is under stress. ΔCoVaR measures the difference between the value at risk (VaR) for the financial system when an institution is in distress and the VaR of the financial system when the firm is in its median or typical state (Adrian and Brunnermeier 2014).[15] The higher the ΔCoVaR, the more systemic risk is endemic within the financial system. The distress insurance premium (DIP) is calculated as the insurance premium that protects against the expected losses of a hypothetical portfolio of the liabilities of all large banks (Huang, Zhou, and Zhu 2011). Additionally, the Systemic Expected Shortfall (SES) estimates how likely a certain institution is to be undercapitalized when the financial system as a whole is undercapitalized (Acharya et al., 2016). Figure 6-17 shows the measures have receded since the financial crisis but remain above levels prior to the crisis.

SRISK, measured by the New York University Volatility Laboratory, translates systemic expected shortfall for the banking system into a dollar figure in a simulated period of financial stress. This shortfall may be interpreted as the amount of capital required to absorb a large negative shock. As shown below, the level of SRISK has come down since the financial crisis and is approaching pre-crisis levels. Similar to the systemic risk measures above,

---

[13] "Fees and redemption gates" refer to the fund board's ability to impose liquidity fees or to suspend redemptions temporarily, also known as "gate," if a fund's level of weekly liquid assets falls below a certain threshold. This provides the ability to stop temporarily a run on the mutual fund.

[14] Many institutions withdrew funds from prime MMFs as the effective date for new SEC rules that mandated a floating share price for institutional MMFs approached in October 2016. In anticipation of additional withdrawals from these prime MMFs, managers kept an unusually high portion of the portfolio in cash, reducing the weighted-average maturity. This is evident in the rapid decrease in average maturity of these funds toward the end of the period in the figure.

[15] VaR is a measure of the likelihood of a big loss. If the 1 month 1% VaR is $10 million, then there is only a 1 percent chance that there will be a loss greater than or equal to $10 million over the month.

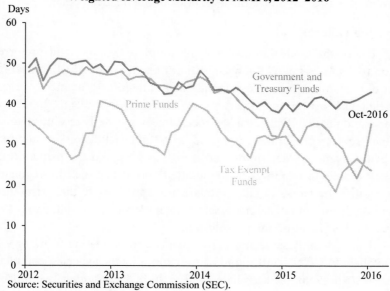

Figure 6-16
Weighted-Average Maturity of MMFs, 2012–2016

Days

Government and
Treasury Funds

Prime Funds

Oct-2016

Tax Exempt
Funds

Source: Securities and Exchange Commission (SEC).

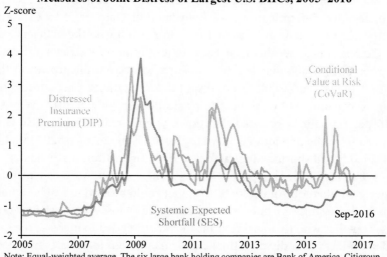

Figure 6-17
Measures of Joint Distress of Largest U.S. BHCs, 2005–2016

Z-score

Conditional
Value at Risk
(CoVaR)

Distressed
Insurance
Premium (DIP)

Systemic Expected
Shortfall (SES)

Sep-2016

Note: Equal-weighted average. The six large bank holding companies are Bank of America, Citigroup, Goldman Sachs, JPMorgan Chase, Morgan Stanley, and Wells Fargo. Z-score represents the distance from the average, expressed in standard deviations.
Source: U.S. Department of the Treasury, Office of Financial Research.

Figure 6-18 shows that the SRISK measure has receded since the financial crisis but remains just above the level prior to the financial crisis.

Resolving Failure

Under the Dodd-Frank Act, bankruptcy is the first, and preferred, option to resolve a failing financial institution and protect the financial stability of the United States. To that end, the Act requires systemically important financial institutions to periodically submit living wills to the Federal Reserve and the FDIC that detail a process for their orderly resolution under the bankruptcy code in the event of material financial distress or failure. If the banks' plans are determined not to be credible and the banks do not remedy those shortcomings in the allotted period of time, the regulators may require the banks to take certain actions to simplify their structures, including divestment of certain assets or operations. As a result, banks have increased their focus on their resolvability.

The Federal Reserve and FDIC finalized rules relating to living wills in October 2011. The latest round of evaluations by the agencies, completed in April 2016, examined each living will of the eight systemically important domestic banks. The agencies jointly determined that five of the eight institutions' living wills were "not credible or would not facilitate an orderly resolution under the U.S. Bankruptcy Code," and issued split determinations on two institutions' living wills (FRB 2016). Only one bank, Citigroup, did not fail both the Fed and FDIC's evaluations. Those banks receiving joint negative determinations were given until October 2016 to address the specified deficiencies. If these firms do not mitigate the deficiencies by the October deadline, the agencies may jointly impose stricter prudential requirements, which may include measures to restrain the growth of these firms. The two banks that received split determinations must address their plans' shortcomings by the next filing deadline of July 1, 2017. While the 2016 determinations revealed that much work remains, it was also a step forward from the previous round of feedback given in August 2014 that had identified broad shortcomings across 11 banking institutions evaluated.

The Dodd-Frank Act also created a new resolution mechanism, the Orderly Liquidation Authority (OLA), that could be used to resolve a failing firm while limiting systemic risk and imposing all losses on the firm's creditors. Together with financial reforms that are intended to increase the safety and soundness of individual financial firms, these reforms are intended to lower the risk to the broader financial system should a particular firm fail, thus lowering the necessity of a bail-out. The DFA also restricts the Federal Reserve's emergency lending powers, making it harder for the Fed to lend to a particular insolvent firm or remove toxic assets during a financial crisis.

Figure 6-18
Systemic Risk (SRISK), 2005–2016

Billions of U.S. Dollars

Source: New York University Volatility Laboratory.

Ending the Problem of Too-Big-To-Fail

Another component of systemic risk has been the view that some firms may be too large to fail without threatening the whole financial system. If these firms are indeed "too big to fail" (TBTF) it gives them a substantial advantage as their counterparties in transactions will know they are less likely to fail than similar firms without an implicit government guarantee. (See Box 6-4 on the TBTF premium.) The implicit guarantee may also make these firms more willing to take large risks as both the owners and managers of these firms do not truly face the risk of downside scenarios as they may feel they can count on the government to bail them out. The existence of TBTF firms can also be a source of risk because their counterparties may be wrong about which firms are TBTF. For example, some assumed the government would never allow a firm like Lehman Brothers to fail and were left exposed when Lehman declared bankruptcy.

The reforms of the last six years that the implementation of Basel III and Dodd-Frank Act put in place included a number of measures to address the risks posed by TBTF. First and foremost, these reforms have subjected the largest and most complex financial institutions to enhanced supervision designed to require these firms' equity and debt holders to bear the costs of the firms' failures. These enhanced supervisions increase in stringency based upon size and other risk factors. The most stringent rules apply

Box 6-4: Have We Ended "Too-Big-To-Fail"?

A financial institution that is "too-big-to-fail" (TBTF) is so large and interconnected with the financial system that market participants believe the government will intervene to prevent its failure. One of the goals of recent financial reform is to eliminate TBTF by making systemically risky banks less likely to fail, reducing the government's ability to aid insolvent firms, and reducing the damage a failure would cause so that such firms could be allowed to fail. Major credit rating agencies have cited financial reform and the reduced likelihood of a government bailout when downgrading the credit ratings of major U.S. banks. For example, in November 2013, Moody's lowered the so-called government support component of its credit ratings for global systemically important banks. In December 2015, the credit rating agency Standard & Poor's downgraded eight of the largest U.S. banks by a notch, saying it believes the banks are less likely to receive a government bailout if they find themselves in financial trouble. While ratings are not necessarily reflective of general market expectations, these actions suggest that financial reform has been successful in reducing TBTF.

A widely studied measure of TBTF is whether certain institutions are able to borrow more cheaply because of the perception that they will ultimately be bailed out if they fail. It was clear that many large financial firms were able to borrow more cheaply both shortly before and during the Financial Crisis because market participants did not believe that such institutions would be allowed to fail. Several more recent estimates of this funding advantage find it to be much reduced or eliminated. Although financial reforms have likely had an impact on TBTF, the improved macroeconomic atmosphere may make any existing funding advantage very difficult to detect, so a definitive measure of whether the TBTF advantage still exists may not be apparent until another crisis appears.

The costs of TBTF go beyond the direct costs of bail-outs. TBTF creates incentives that many consider socially harmful. Investors are willing to provide their funds to a TBTF bank without evaluating the safety and soundness of their investment because they believe that the government will bail them out should the bank get into trouble. This allows managers to engage in risky investment behavior, with the bank keeping the gains should those investments pay off but with taxpayers bearing the loss in the event of a near failure. These institutions also enjoy a TBTF discount on their funding costs, allowing them to borrow at lower interest rates than similar institutions that are not considered by investors to be TBTF. This discount is anticompetitive as it gives large or more systemically connected firms an advantage over smaller or new institutions.

In the absence of another financial crisis, it is difficult to definitively prove that financial reform has reduced or eliminated TBTF. Much has changed from the pre-crisis to the post-crisis period. First, today's macroeconomic environment is more benign than during the crisis, suggesting that the difference in the probability of default with and without an expected bail-out is small. This may make it more difficult to find evidence of changes in TBTF. Second, Sarin and Summers (2016) provide evidence that market-based measures of risk are not lower during the post-crisis period, perhaps because financial reform has lowered the franchise value of banks. This may impact funding costs in the post-crisis period making it difficult to detect a reduction in TBTF. Finally, financial reform has mandated increases in capital and liquidity that may impact funding costs. Nevertheless, one approach to evaluating the effectiveness of the reforms on reducing or eliminating TBTF is to analyze the borrowing costs of large banks. A firm's borrowing cost should reflect the firm's credit risk. A financial institution that the market views as TBTF should enjoy a lower cost of borrowing than an otherwise identical institution.

It is important to distinguish between TBTF and a bank's size. A bank that is TBTF will likely be big, but not every large bank will be TBTF. There is evidence that larger banks benefit from economies of scale (Hughes and Mester 2013, Wheelock and Wilson 2016). Large banks have global reach and more diversified services, and can provide financial products and services that small banks cannot offer (Bernanke 2016). The tradable debt of larger financial institutions tends to be more liquid. Each of these factors would likely reduce the borrowing cost of a large bank for reasons other than TBTF.

Scholars have taken several approaches to measure the TBTF premium. One approach uses a statistical technique to see if a bank's cost of borrowing varies with its size or designation of being "systemically important" after controlling for other variables related to credit risk. Examples include GAO (2014); Acharya, Anginer and Warburton (2016); and Balasubramnian and Cyree (2014). A second approach compares the market price of a contract that protects a bond holder from losses should the bond issuer default, known as a credit default swap (CDS), with the theoretical fair value of such a contract. An example of a study that uses such an approach is IMF (2014). A third approach compares the credit rating of a firm as a stand-alone enterprise with one that includes the possibility of government support. The difference between these two ratings may be interpreted as an indication of the size of the TBTF premium. Examples of studies using such an approach include IMF (2014) and Ueda and Weder di Mauro (2013).

Scholars using each of these methodologies have generally shown that the TBTF premium was positive but low in the 20 years before the crisis, illustrated by Figure 6-x (Acharya, Anginer, and Warburton 2016). During the financial crisis the TBTF subsidy spiked to approximately 100 basis points (bps). By 2012, the estimated subsidy had declined to roughly 25 bps. This illustrates an important point: the TBTF premium varies with time as market expectations change, especially regarding the likelihood of a government bailout. During a financial crisis, the probability of a financial firm's failure increases as does the probability that the government will rescue a TBTF firm, increasing the difference between the borrowing costs of a TBTF and a comparable non-TBTF financial firm.

While Acharya, Anginer, and Warburton (2016) are skeptical about the effects of post-crisis regulation on TBTF, several studies find that since the crisis, the TBTF premium either has effectively disappeared or has decreased to levels comparable with those pre-crisis. Balasubramnian and Cyree (2014) found the funding cost advantage of banks subject to the Federal Reserve's Comprehensive Capital Analysis and Review declined from 244 bps in the six-month period preceding passage of the Dodd-Frank Act to a statistically insignificant 6 bps in the six-month period following the law's passage. GAO (2014) uses 42 different econometric models to estimate the TBTF premium each year from 2006 to 2013. They find that while systemically important banks enjoyed

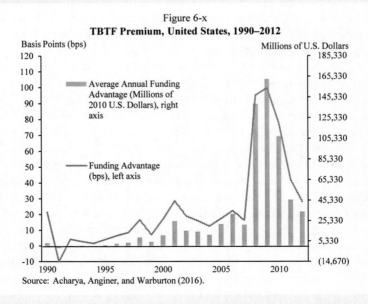

Figure 6-x
TBTF Premium, United States, 1990–2012

Source: Acharya, Anginer, and Warburton (2016).

lower funding costs in 2007-09, "such funding cost differences may have declined or reversed in recent years."

Using the CDS approach, IMF (2014) finds that the TBTF premium rose from near zero bps in 2005 to over 50 bps during the crisis. As of 2013, the premium had declined to around 15 bps, an improvement since 2009 but not yet as low as levels in 2005 through 2007 and still indicative of a funding advantage. The United States appears to have been more successful than other advanced economies in narrowing the TBTF premium, though; the advanced economy average as measured by CDS spreads is approximately 40 bps as of the start of 2014, well above the level in the U.S. (as shown in Figure 6-xi).

The credit ratings-based approach also shows that the TBTF premium for systemically important institutions fell from a high of 30 bps to 15 bps, close to but still about 9 bps above the level in 2005. The ratings approach can also decompose the TBTF premium into effects from the probability that a firm becomes distressed and the expectation of bail-out when that firm is in distress. Using ratings for systemically important firms that are sub-investment grade, IMF (2014) finds that, despite a marked decline from crisis levels, the TBTF premium in 2013 was more than 10 bps above its level in 2005. Ratings, however, are slow to adjust to market conditions and suffer from conflicting views among different credit rating agencies.

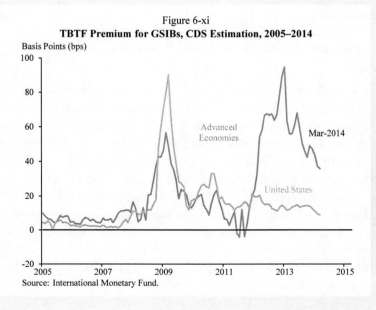

Figure 6-xi
TBTF Premium for GSIBs, CDS Estimation, 2005–2014

Source: International Monetary Fund.

Overall, the funding advantage of global systemically important banks has declined since the crisis. While measures of the TBTF premium still vary across the academic literature, several studies have found that the premium as of 2013 was either statistically insignificant or significantly narrower than the levels during, and in, the three years after the financial crisis. Further, while the benign financial and macroeconomic conditions of the post-crisis period could be partially driving this decrease in the TBTF premium, studies such as IMF (2014) and Balasubramnian and Cyree (2014) that examine changes in borrowing costs around announcements of policy reforms find that they have driven up borrowing costs for systemically important institutions, suggesting that policy changes have had at least some effect in narrowing the TBTF premium.

to systematically important financial institutions and global systemically important banks (G-SIBs), which have become designated under recent reforms. Such a designation in no way guarantees a bailout or codifies a firm as TBTF, but rather adds rules to minimize the risk that the institution will fail and adds additional responsibilities so that it is possible for the institution to fail without endangering the broader system.

These enhanced rules include significantly higher standards for capital, stress-testing, liquidity, loss-absorbing capability, and resolution. In particular, the establishment of the OLA is meant to allow such firms to be resolved without taxpayer support and without endangering the rest of the financial system.

Transparency, Accountability, and Protecting Consumers and Investors

Beyond the broad measures needed to make financial institutions safer and to limit systemic risk, the crisis highlighted a number of issues of transparency and fairness within the financial system. As noted previously, information asymmetries may mean that financial professionals and firms likely have substantial information advantages relative to their customers or investors. This may require regulation that can improve the transparency of the actions of those financial firms, and the accountability of those firms to their investors, or simply to protect consumers from bad behavior.

Protecting consumers is warranted both to preserve their confidence in the financial system and because consumers ill-informed concerning financial products may be more likely to take on inappropriate loans and increase risk in the system more broadly. The Administration took numerous steps through the Dodd-Frank Act and other measures to improve the information available in the financial system through reforms to derivatives markets, credit rating agencies, investor accountability, and through the creation of a new Consumer Financial Protection Bureau.

Improving Transparency and Oversight of Derivatives

Increased transparency in the financial system promotes investor protection and better enables market participants to price assets, risk, and other relevant inputs to financial decisions. Part of the cause of the financial crisis was a lack of critical information about counterparties. As the crisis unfolded, the potential exposures of large financial institutions to other financial institutions that were either known or suspected to be near bankruptcy led to a general unwillingness to enter into any additional transactions. This contributed to the seizing up of credit markets.

A number of measures showed how acute the problem was in late 2008. When there is fear of counter-party risk, banks will charge one another more than the safe interest rate to lend in overnight markets. One such measure of perceived credit risk in the interbank market is the TED spread, which is the difference between the three-month London Interbank Offered Rate (LIBOR)[16] and the three-month yield on U.S. Treasury bills. Figure 6-19 shows the TED spread for the years 2007 through October 2016. The TED spread jumped in the summer of 2007 when stress in the markets began to show and then again after Lehman Brothers' collapse in September 2008. An important part of making the system more stable was improving transparency among firms so that they could lend to one another more freely.[17]

One important way in which financial institutions had financial exposure to each other was through over-the-counter (OTC) derivative contracts. Just ahead of Lehman's collapse, the Federal Reserve Bank of New York was collecting information on the exposures created by Lehman's more than 900,000 derivative contracts. The volume of outstanding contracts and the

---

[16] LIBOR is an average of the rates at which large banks in London are willing to lend to each other in dollars. Collected by survey, LIBOR has been the focus of investigations of manipulation by individuals within the participating banks who were responsible for responding to the survey in cooperation with traders.

[17] The LIBOR increase in 2016 is likely due to money market reform rather than increased credit risk of large banks. New SEC rules for money market mutual funds that as of Oct. 14, 2016 mandated a floating share price for institutional MMFs that invest in commercial paper and bank CDs had driven the increase. As that date approached, many institutions withdrew from those funds in favor of those funds that only invest in government securities and whose NAV will not float. The effect was a reduction in funds that provide a source of short-term funding for banks, pushing up rates such as LIBOR.

Figure 6-19
TED Spread, 2005–2016

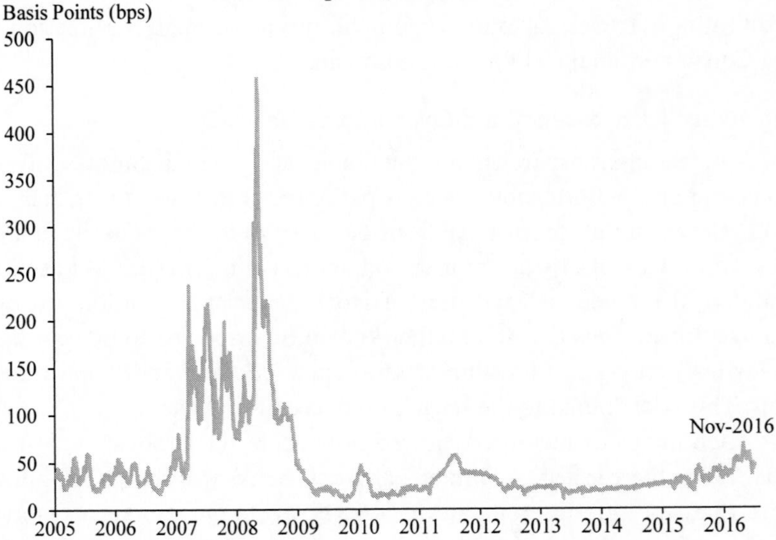

Basis Points (bps)

Source: Federal Reserve Board.

difficulty in creating a complete picture of such exposures highlighted the need for better data.

Derivatives are financial instruments whose values are determined by reference to other "underlying assets," and include forwards, futures, options, and swaps. These instruments are useful to investors and businesses seeking to hedge risks. For example, an airline may need to hedge its exposure to oil price fluctuations or a pension fund may need to hedge its exposure to interest rate changes. Derivatives often create leverage because changes in the value of the underlying asset can be magnified many times in the value of the derivative contract. Thus, while they can be used to hedge against risks, derivatives can also be used to increase exposure to risky assets and can concentrate risk rather than dispersing risk among many market participants. Many derivatives have standardized terms, are traded on exchanges, and are cleared through central counterparties (CCPs). Exchange trading and central clearing create a record of prices and transactions that can be used by the public in the price discovery process and by regulators to measure the exposures of market participants. Central clearing also helps mitigate counter-party credit risk.

Prior to the financial crisis, one category of derivatives, swaps, was not standardized and was traded over-the-counter.[18] The trading volume and outstanding notional value of these swaps, particularly the type known as a credit default swap, grew rapidly prior to the financial crisis and formed a complex network of exposures among large financial institutions.[19,20] Only the two parties to the transaction were typically aware that the transaction had occurred, resulting in an opaque market in which there was little transparency around either prices or exposures. The lack of transparency in exposures could result in a concentration of risk in particular financial institutions as occurred with AIG just prior to the financial crisis. As Figure 6-20 shows the rapid growth in several types of OTC derivatives in the years leading up to the financial crisis.[21]

The Dodd-Frank Act took a number of steps to reform the OTC market in derivatives, including the reporting of all swap trades to a trade repository, the public reporting of certain trade information, the posting of margin against possible losses resulting from counterparty default, the mandatory clearing of standardized swap contracts through registered central counterparties, trading on exchange-like trading facilities, and registration and regulation of swap dealers and certain large market participants. These steps were intended, among other purposes, to reduce the opaque nature of the derivatives market, to improve price transparency and to reduce systemic risk.

Under Dodd-Frank, swap and security-based swap dealers and major swap and security-based swap participants are required to register with and be subject to supervision by the CFTC and SEC. As of November 2016, more than 100 swap dealers were provisionally registered with the CFTC. The SEC estimates that as many as 50 security-based swap dealers, many of

---

[18] A swap is an agreement between two parties to exchange sequences of cash flows for a set period of time. Types of swaps include interest rate, foreign exchange, and credit default. For example, in an interest rate swap one party pays a fixed amount and the counterparty pays an amount determined by a variable interest rate such as LIBOR.

[19] A credit default swap (CDS) is a particular type of swap designed to transfer the credit exposure of a fixed income security from the buyer to the seller. The CDS buyer makes periodic payments to the seller, who, in the event of default, pays the buyer the difference between the face value and the defaulted value of the security. CDS are often used by buyers to hedge the credit risk of bond positions and by sellers to create positions that are similar to holding the underlying bond. Dodd-Frank reforms have ensured that most such transactions are required to have collateral posted to insure performance of the contract.

[20] The notional value of a swap contract is the nominal or face value and is used to calculate payments made on the instrument. With respect to CDS, the notional value represents the face value of the debt security whose credit risk is transferred from buyer to seller of the CDS.

[21] It is important to look at global trading activity for several reasons. These include the fact that a sizeable fraction of these transactions are between parties in different jurisdictions and many participants in these transactions, particularly dealers, have a global presence and the jurisdiction in which they book the transaction is often a matter of choice.

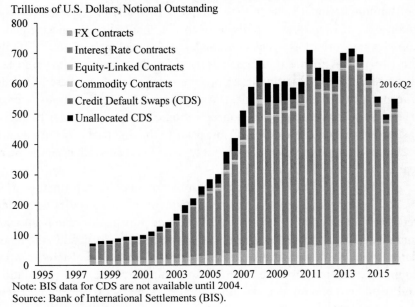

Figure 6-20
Global OTC Derivatives Market, 1998–2016

Trillions of U.S. Dollars, Notional Outstanding

- FX Contracts
- Interest Rate Contracts
- Equity-Linked Contracts
- Commodity Contracts
- Credit Default Swaps (CDS)
- Unallocated CDS

2016:Q2

Note: BIS data for CDS are not available until 2004.
Source: Bank of International Settlements (BIS).

which are already registered with the CFTC as swap dealers, and five major security-based swap participants will be required to register when the SEC's Registration Rules for Security-Based Swap Dealers and Major Security-Based Swap Participants go into effect.

Clearing through CFTC-registered derivatives clearing organizations is now required for most interest rate and index credit default swaps.[22,23] Mandatory clearing of single-name CDS and other security-based swaps through SEC-registered clearing agencies in not yet in effect, though many single-name CDS are accepted for clearing through CCPs on a voluntary

---

[22] After a trade is executed between a buyer and a seller, the CCP steps between the two counterparties and becomes the buyer to the seller and the seller to the buyer. Thus the CCP assumes the credit risk that used to be borne by the original counterparties. This can reduce risk in a number of ways including standardizing collateral requirements for all participants, allowing for the regulation of risk management practices, and promoting trade compression which reduces the total amount of trades outstanding. For example, if firm A buys a certain CDS (buys protection) from firm B on Monday and then firm A sells the same contract (sells protection) to firm C on Tuesday, because both trades have the CCP as the counterparty, they would "compress" resulting in no position for firm A.

[23] Participants in an interest rate swap exchange fixed interest rate payments for a floating rate interest payment. An index CDS is a portfolio of CDS on individual entities that comprise the index.

basis.[24] One of the advantages of central clearing is the increased ability of market participants to reduce their total exposure through trade compression – the canceling of equal and offsetting positions – that reduces the total amount of derivative positions outstanding. Figure 6-21 shows the rapid increase in trade compression in interest rate swaps as rules requiring their mandatory clearing came into effect.

Twenty-three swap execution facilities are now registered with the CFTC and the application of one additional swap execution facility is pending. The SEC estimates that as many as 20 security-based swap execution facilities will register with the SEC when its applicable rules become effective, many of which will also be registered with the CFTC. According to information compiled by the International Swaps and Derivatives Association (ISDA), in the first 10 months of 2016, 55 percent of total interest rate derivative notional value and 76 percent of total CDS notional value takes place on swap execution facilities, the exchange-like electronic trading platforms required by Dodd-Frank.

The Dodd-Frank Act improved the ability of regulators to oversee this market by requiring that all swap transactions be reported to registered swap data repositories (SDRs) and that summary information be periodically reported to the public. As of the fall of 2016, there are four SDRs provisionally registered with the CFTC and the SEC estimates that two SDRS will be registered with it when its rules become effective. In addition, there are many more trade repositories registered and operating overseas, including six registered with the European Securities and Market Authority, making a previously opaque market significantly more transparent.

Credit Rating Agencies

Credit rating agencies play an important role in the financial system. When a bank makes a loan, the bank is responsible for assessing the credit quality of the borrower and monitoring the performance of the loan. In a capital market, borrowers seek to raise funds by issuing bonds or other debt obligations to numerous investors. In this case, investors must either make their own determinations as to the borrower's creditworthiness, which is made more difficult given the information asymmetries between the borrower and the investors, or rely on third parties to perform this function. This is the role of credit rating agencies: they rate the creditworthiness of borrowers and the probability of default of bonds and other debt instruments, and provide surveillance on borrower's performance.

---

[24] A single-name CDS is a contract that pays the difference between the face value of a particular bond and the market value of that bond when the issuer defaults.

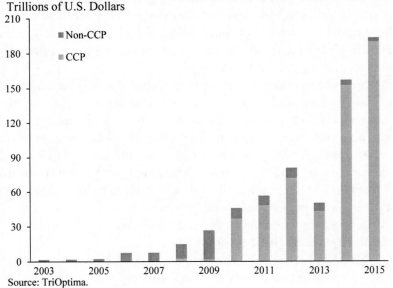

Figure 6-21
Interest Rate Derivative Compression Volume, 2003–2015

Over time, the credit rating agencies became essential parts of the financial systems. Many regulations referred to specific credit ratings, many investment funds limited themselves to holding only assets with a certain minimum rating, and ratings were a crucial part in determining what collateral was permissible in a number of transaction types, including repo transactions. In exchange for adhering to various reporting requirements, the SEC provides interested and eligible credit rating agencies with a Nationally Recognized Statistical Rating Organization (NRSRO) designation. The designation is particularly important because a variety of State and Federal laws and regulations reference NRSRO ratings.

One concern that emerged from the crisis was the problems with the incentives of the ratings agencies themselves. Although investors are the primary users of ratings, issuers hire and pay most rating agencies. The so-called issuer-pay compensation model raises conflicts of interest issues and can lead to "rating shopping." If an issuer believes a credit rating agency is likely to rate its debt lower than other agencies, the issuer would be less likely to hire that rating agency. This structure provided incentives for credit rating agencies to inflate ratings, and is compounded by the highly concentrated nature of the industry.

The Dodd-Frank Act created the Office of Credit Ratings within the SEC to oversee and conduct annual examinations of each NRSRO. The findings from the NRSRO examinations are described in annual public reports published by the SEC. The examinations have shown a number of improvements, but have also identified continuing concerns, including those about the management of conflicts of interest, internal supervisory controls, and post-employment activities of former staff of NRSROs.

To improve transparency over the ratings process, the Dodd-Frank Act required enhanced public disclosure of NRSROs' credit rating procedures and methodologies, certain business practices, and credit ratings performance. According to the SEC, in 2014, "there [was] a trend of NRSROs issuing unsolicited commentaries on solicited ratings issued by other NRSROs, which has increased the level of transparency within the credit ratings industry" (SEC 2014). The SEC reported that this trend continued in 2015. In addition, some NRSROs have issued unsolicited commentaries on an asset class, rather than a specific transaction.

The Dodd-Frank Act eliminated references to credit ratings in certain Federal laws and required all Federal agencies to remove references to credit ratings from their regulations. To that end, the financial regulators adopted rule changes that removed references and, where appropriate, substituted alternative standards of creditworthiness.

Improved Accountability to Shareholders

The financial crisis led to policy concerns about a possible link between excessive financial firm risk taking and executive compensation practices. For example, a financial executive considering a very risky investment might weigh the potential personal benefit if the investment pays off against the personal loss if the investment fails. If the benefit, say a very large bonus, is more valuable to the executive than the potential loss, perhaps the risk of getting fired, then the executive has an incentive to make the risky investment. The best interest of the shareholders or the risks to either the firm or the financial system might only be of secondary importance to the executive.

Policymakers were concerned about what economists call "misaligned incentives" in 2008, one of the motivations for the Troubled Asset Relief Program subjecting recipients to various executive pay restrictions and corporate governance requirements. Soon after, the Federal Reserve issued guidelines for reviewing banks' pay structures to identify any compensation arrangements that provide incentives to take excessive risk.

In accordance with requirements in the Dodd-Frank Act, the SEC adopted rules in 2011 that require public companies subject to the Federal proxy rules to provide shareholder advisory 'say-on-pay,' 'say-on-frequency,' and 'golden parachute' votes on executive compensation. Say-on-pay refers to a shareholder advisory vote on executive compensation, say-on-frequency refers to the frequency of say-on-pay votes, and golden parachute to advisory votes on compensation arrangements and understandings in connection with merger transactions. In 2015, 2,157 Russell 3000 companies had a say-on-pay vote, providing shareholders with the information they need to monitor potential abuses and an opportunity for shareholders to voice their opinion concerning steep increases in executive compensation packages. Sixty-one Russell 3000 companies (2.8 percent) had shareholders reject their 2015 say-on-pay vote.

In accordance with requirements in the Dodd-Frank Act, the SEC adopted rules in 2012 directing the national securities exchanges and national securities associations to prohibit the listing of any equity security of an issuer that does not comply with new compensation committee and compensation adviser requirements. To conform their rules to the new requirements, national securities exchanges that have rules providing for the listing of equity securities filed proposed rule changes with the SEC. The Commission issued final orders approving the proposed rule changes in January 2013.

Sponsors of asset-backed securities are now required to provide consistent, asset-level information to investors, improving clarity regarding the risks associated with these securities. Sponsors are also now required to retain a portion of the credit risk associated with the assets collateralizing the securities, better aligning the behavior of originators, securitizers, and investors, and addressing many of the perverse incentives that contributed to the financial crisis.

Wall Street reform recognized that markets require transparency to work properly. By shining a light on hidden business structures and increasing information for all participants, Wall Street reform has helped to realign incentives so that markets work for everyone.

Protecting Consumers

Consumers often know less about the investment or financial service they are considering than the financial industry professional with which they are doing business. Protecting consumers from this problem of asymmetric information by providing consistent and rigorous consumer protections is important to preserve consumer confidence in the financial system. If the consumer believes he or she cannot get a fair deal then the consumer is less likely to take advantage of the many beneficial financial services that are available for financing major purchases as well as saving for college or retirement.

Prior to the crisis, enforcement of laws meant to protect consumers from predatory practices was divided among multiple agencies. The Dodd-Frank Act created the Consumer Financial Protection Bureau (CFPB) "to ensure that important fair lending, debt collection, consumer credit, and other borrower protections were updated in response to quickly changing markets and consistently enforced nationwide" (U.S. House of Representatives, 2015). The financial crisis revealed that laws meant to protect consumers from predatory practices are meaningless if they are not enforced, and that consumers needed a government agency focused on their needs and experiences.

As of November 2016, the CFPB has returned $11.7 billion to more than 27 million harmed consumers —including homeowners, students, seniors, and service members. As of July 2016, millions of consumers have also taken advantage of the Bureau's financial resources at consumerfinance.gov and 930,700 complaints have been submitted to a database for collecting consumer complaints against service providers that have proved otherwise unresponsive.

The CFPB has been establishing and enforcing clear rules of the road and consumer protections to prevent the kinds of predatory behavior that contributed to the financial crisis. The CFPB protects consumers of a wide range of financial products and services, including mortgage loans, credit cards, student loans, car loans, and deposit products. The CFPB is developing landmark consumer protections for products often targeted to the unbanked and underbanked, such as prepaid accounts, payday loans, and car title loans. The CFPB also protects consumers with respect to other industry activities, such as debt collection and credit reporting.

In the lead up to the financial crisis, abusive lending practices and poor underwriting standards resulted in risky mortgages that hurt borrowers across the country. Wall Street reform addresses abusive practices in mortgage markets, including by improving disclosure requirements, curbing unfair servicing practices, restricting compensation practices that created conflicts of interest, and establishing protections for high-cost mortgage loans. In addition, mortgage lenders are required to make reasonable, good faith determinations that a borrower is able to repay her mortgage loan. More than 16 million mortgages are covered by the CFPB's Ability-to-Repay rule's protections and that number grows every month. Reforms also protect service members from deceptive mortgage advertising practices, predatory lending schemes, and hidden fees for automatic bill pay services.

Additional Investor Protections

The SEC's Whistleblower Office, created by the Dodd-Frank Act, became fully operational in 2011. In fiscal year 2014, the SEC received over 3,600 tips, covering a variety of securities law violations including those relating to corporate disclosures, financial statements, security offering fraud, market manipulation, investment adviser fraud, and broker-dealer rule compliance. Whistleblowers that provide the SEC with original information that leads to a successful enforcement action with monetary sanctions exceeding $1 million are eligible to receive an award ranging from 10 to 30 percent of the amounts collected in the action. As of November 2016, 34 whistleblowers have received awards with the total exceeding $110 million, with the highest award being over $30 million.

The Dodd-Frank Act enhanced the CFTC's ability to prosecute manipulation by prohibiting, among other things, manipulative and deceptive devices that are intentionally or recklessly employed, regardless of whether the conduct in question was intended to create, or did create, an artificial price. This authority provides the CFTC with more flexibility to go after reckless manipulation and fraud. The first case brought by the CFTC using this authority was against Panther Energy Trading LLC in 2013 for engaging in the disruptive practice of "spoofing" by using a computer algorithm to illegally place and quickly cancel bids and offers in futures contracts without ever intending to buy or sell those contracts. The CFTC also used this authority to bring charges against Navinder Singh Sarao for his role in contributing to the May 6, 2010 Flash Crash and in 2013 against JPMorgan Chase Bank in connection with its "London Whale" swaps trades.

As required by the Dodd-Frank Act, the SEC established the Office of the Investor Advocate, charged with identifying investor protection concerns and proposing to the SEC and Congress any administrative or legislative changes necessary to mitigate those concerns. Similarly, the Dodd-Frank Act also established the Investor Advisory Committee (IAC) comprised of the Investor Advocate, a representative of state securities commissions, a representative of the interests of senior citizens, and no fewer than 10 and not more than 20 members appointed by the SEC to represent the interests of various types of individual and institutional investors. The IAC may submit findings and recommendations for review and consideration by the Commission, which must promptly issue a public statement assessing those findings or recommendations and disclosing the action, if any, the SEC intends to take. Since its inception, the IAC has issued 14 recommendations covering: shortening the trade settlement cycle in U.S. financial markets, the definition of an accredited investor, impartiality in the disclosure of preliminary voting results, crowdfunding, decimalization,

Box 6-5: Addressing the Problem of Conflicted Investment Advice for Retirement Savings

In April 2016, the Department of Labor (DOL) finalized a rule that substantially expanded the number of providers of financial advice required to adhere to a fiduciary standard, which requires them to put their clients' best interest before their own profits. The rule makes considerable progress in upholding consumer protections in the retirement savings marketplace.

Individuals saving for retirement usually make use of one or more of three major types of retirement plans. First, defined benefit (DB) plans provided by many public and private employers promise specified payments to the retiree that depend on characteristics of their work history, such as age, years of service and salary of the employee. The employer that sponsors the plan is typically responsible for making contributions to the plan adequate to finance the promised payments. If investment returns are less than expected, the plan sponsor is required to make up the difference. Another type of employer-sponsored plan is the defined contribution (DC) plan, such as a 401(k), which pays a retiree an amount based on how much the beneficiary and employers have contributed in his or her working years and the investment return earned on those contributions. The beneficiary typically has several investment options to choose from within the plan but bears the risk of lower retirement income if the investment returns are less than expected. Lastly, Individual Retirement Accounts (IRA) are savings accounts composed solely of an individual's contributions during his or her working years.

IRAs require individuals to make all investment decisions. In terms of investing retirement savings, employer-sponsored defined benefit (DB) plans generally delegate retirement savings of all participants to investment professionals who must serve the best interests of their clients. Employer-sponsored defined contribution (DC) plans typically give employees a list of investment options from which to choose. While IRAs offer individuals the most freedom to invest their retirement assets, it also means they must interact directly with those who provide investment products and investment advice. This has become more important as IRA assets have grown from 2 percent to 31 percent of all retirement assets from 1978 to 2015 (Figure 6-xii) During this period, the investment landscape has become much more complex and as a result, financial advice has become increasingly important to individual's investment strategies. One survey found that roughly half of households that own a traditional IRA have a retirement strategy created with the help of an investment adviser (Holden and Schrass 2015).

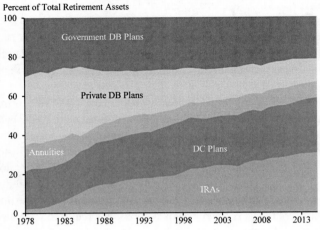

Figure 6-xii
U.S. Retirement Assets by Type, 1978–2015

Percent of Total Retirement Assets

Source: Investment Company Institute.

A growing body of academic and industry literature shows that such investment advice is not always in the best interest of clients. Table 6-i shows that savers may obtain advice from one of two main types of investment professionals: registered investment advisers (RIA), who have a fiduciary duty to clients; and broker-dealers, who are required to give only "suitable" investment advice. In addition, only registered investment advisers may give holistic advice on a client's investments, whereas broker-dealers primarily transact in financial markets and may provide only incidental advice to clients (SEC 2011).

Compensation structures for professionals who give financial advice often introduce conflicts of interest. Some investment advisers receive conflicted payments, which is compensation that depends directly on the actions taken by the advisee, such as trading shares of a company or selling shares of a fund. Certain types of mutual funds share a higher proportion of their revenues with advisers that sell them, or pay advisers relatively high fees per share that they sell to clients. These types of compensation structures incentivize advisers to steer investors into such products even if they are not optimal for a client's investment needs. Alternative compensation schemes such as an hourly rate or a yearly management fee charged as a percentage of assets provide payments that depend less on investment decisions and provide less opportunities for conflict of interest. Advisers not subject to a fiduciary standard may direct clients into funds that while meeting a "suitability" standard, are not in the best interests of the client.

Table 6-i
Sources of Investment Advice

Adviser	Description	Legal Standard
Registered Investment Advisers (RIAs)	Receives compensation in exchange for giving investment advice. May also manage a portfolio for clients.	Fiduciary duty to client, including a duty of loyalty and a duty of care. Must serve the best interest of the client.
Broker Dealers (brokers)	Makes trades for a fee or commission. A broker makes trades for a client's account, while a dealer makes trades for his or her own account.	Recommendations must be suitable for a client's investment profile taking into account factors such as age, income, net worth, and investment goals.
Other Potential Sources	Examples include friends, family, bankers, insurance agents, accountants, and lawyers.	Standards vary.

A substantial body of academic literature shows that conflicted advice leads to lower investment returns.[1] In previous work, CEA estimated that savers receiving conflicted advice earn returns roughly one percentage point lower than they would have otherwise and these losses amounted to $17 billion annually.[2]

The Employee Retirement Income Security Act (ERISA), enacted in 1974, regulates the provision of financial advice to retirement investors. Prior to the finalization of the new rule in 2016, the rules governing retirement advice had not changed meaningfully since 1975 despite the significant changes in the retirement savings marketplace. Starting in 2009, DOL started a reform effort to combat the problems stemming from conflicted investment advice. It proposed a new fiduciary rule in 2015, and after receiving stakeholder comment, adopted a revised rule in April 2016.

In its new rule, the DOL extends the fiduciary duty broadly to financial professionals giving investment advice for retirement plans subject to ERISA, including broker-dealers. The new rule requires that financial advisors who receive commissions and other transaction-based payments provide advice that is in the best interest of the client and commit to a set of policies and procedures that ensures that the advisor meets this standard. The intent of the rule is to protect retirement investors and ensure that the advice they receive is in their best interest. Though this

---

[1] See, among others, Bergstresser, Chalmers, and Tufano (2009), Del Guercio and Reuter (2014), and Christofferson, Evans, and Musto (2013).
[2] For more information on the costs of conflicted investment advice, see CEA's (2015a) report "The Effects of Conflicted Investment Advice on Retirement Savings."

rule does not ban such "conflicted payments," it does stipulate that those institutions still receiving such transaction-based compensation must have clients sign a best interest contract exemption, which pledges that the adviser will act in the client's best interest.

While the rule will only apply to transactions beginning in April 2017, the effects will become evident sooner as investment advisers adjust their business practices to comply with the new regulations. Analysts anticipate that the effects will be large. Morningstar estimates that the rule will require that accounts with more than $800 billion of defined contribution plan assets that are receiving some form of advice be checked for compliance. In addition, wealth management firms will need to justify that over $200 billion of IRA rollovers are in the clients' best interest. Commentators envision that the plan will place the highest costs on independent broker-dealers, formerly obliged only to offer suitable investment advice. Registered investment advisors (RIAs) will bear smaller costs given they are already under a fiduciary standard. The additional liability of a best interest contract exemption will likely incentivize broker-dealers to switch to fee-based compensation structures. Since fee-based compensation may make small accounts less profitable, advisers could decide either to drop small retirement accounts or shift them into automated advice accounts —so called "robo-advisors." While the results of these regulations will become more apparent in the coming year, the initial commitment of some firms toward lower fee, passive products, should then lower costs to consumers, consistent with the original intent of the DOL rule.

legislation to fund investment adviser examinations, broker-dealer fiduciary duty, data tagging, and target date mutual funds.

International Cooperation

The U.S. financial system does not exist in a vacuum. Massive volumes of capital flow between U.S. financial markets and those abroad. Over the course of a month, foreign residents buy and sell trillions of dollars' worth of U.S. assets to or from U.S. residents. European banks were major borrowers from U.S. money market funds and subsequently major investors in U.S. asset markets. Foreign domiciled financial institutions play sizable roles in many aspects of U.S. financial markets. In addition, U.S. financial firms compete for business in financial markets around the world with firms regulated by other countries' rules. Reforming the U.S. financial system and regulatory architecture alone would be insufficient to ensure the safety of the U.S. financial system if there were not important steps to ensure the global financial system and the systems of those of our partners were also better regulated.

In September 2009, the G-20 met in Pittsburgh to discuss, among other things, the measures the member nations had taken to address the global crisis and the additional steps necessary to build a stronger international financial system. The international financial reform agenda that came from the Pittsburgh and subsequent G-20 meetings aimed to ensure a "race to the top" to raise the quality of regulation and thereby the safety of the international financial system as well as level the playing field across major and emerging financial centers. To this end, G-20 leaders called for the establishment of the Financial Stability Board (FSB) to serve a key role in promoting the reform of international financial regulation and to promote financial stability and endorsed its original charter at the Pittsburg meeting. The Dodd-Frank Act is fully consistent with — and in a number of areas surpasses —the G-20 recommendations. Initiatives proposed in Pittsburgh and subsequent G-20 meetings include: 1. Strengthening bank capital and liquidity; 2. Reducing the risk posed by large systemically important financial institutions; 3. Making derivatives markets safer and more transparent; 4. Establishing higher capital margins for non-centrally cleared derivatives; and 5. Identifying parties to financial transactions.

Consistency of regulatory approach across jurisdictions is important because so much financial activity occurs between financial institutions located in different jurisdictions. To the extent that financial market activity can move to the jurisdiction with the weakest regulation and with the interconnected nature of the world economy, a financial crisis that begins in one country can quickly spread to others. A consistent regulatory approach across countries makes the financial system in every country safer.

The FSB produces a semiannual report that tracks the progress of regulatory reform around the world.[25] As seen in Figure 6-22, within the 24 FSB member jurisdictions, progress in implementing banking regulation reform has been widespread with considerable progress having been made in the reform of OTC derivative markets. Other initiatives have not yet been implemented beyond a few jurisdictions though progress continues.

---

[25] The Financial Stability Board (FSB) is an international body that monitors and makes recommendations about the global financial system. It was established after the 2009 G-20 London summit in April 2009. The FSB includes representatives from 24 countries plus The World Bank, International Monetary Fund, Bank for International Settlements, Organization for Economic Cooperation and Development, European Central Bank, European Commission, Basel Committee on Banking Supervision, International Association of Insurance Supervisors, International Organization of Securities Commissions, International Accounting Standards Board, Committee on the Global Financial System, and Committee on Payments and Market Infrastructures.

Figure 6-22
International Financial Regulation:
Implementation of G20 Financial Regulatory Reforms
Number of Countries Where Reform Implemented

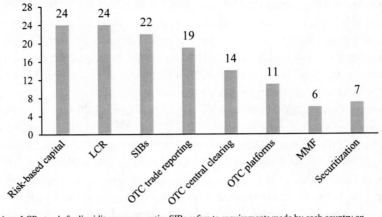

Note: LCR stands for liquidity coverage ratio. SIBs refers to requirements made by each country on domestic systemically important banks. MMF refers to money market fund reforms. MMF and securitization reform both fall under reform to the shadow banking system.
Source: Financial Stability Board 2016.

The United States has made substantial progress in implementing the priority reforms identified by the FSB. The United States has fully implemented reforms in nearly all of the priority areas and is making progress in others. Many major advanced economies with large financial systems that are highly interconnected with the U.S. financial system —in particular the United Kingdom and the euro area —are also making substantial progress.

U.S. Financial Markets in 2016

Seven years after the end of the financial crisis, the purpose of financial reform remains the same: to reduce as much as possible the likelihood of another financial crisis and the incalculable costs that it would inflict on the economy, the financial markets, and society. The recovering economy and implementation of financial reform have been accompanied by strong performance of a wide variety of financial market indicators. Not only have financial markets recovered from the losses suffered during the crisis, but banks are healthier and stronger, regulators are on the lookout for systemic risk, once-opaque derivative markets are safer and more transparent, credit ratings agencies are subject to more effective oversight and increased transparency, and investor protections have been strengthened.

A variety of measures show the renewed health of the financial markets. Equity prices and housing prices have rebounded, rebuilding

Box 6-6: The JOBS Act

While it was an imperative to correct the market failures and excesses in the pre-2008 financial system, an important aspect of financial regulatory reform is ensuring funds can be channeled to entrepreneurs who have productive uses for capital. In April of 2012, the President signed into law the Jumpstart Our Business Startups (JOBS) Act, a bipartisan bill that enacts many of the President's proposals to encourage startups and support the nation's small businesses. The Act allows for "crowdfunding", expands "mini-public offerings," and creates an "IPO on-ramp", all of which allow for easier funding of small businesses while maintaining important investor protections.

As implemented by the Securities and Exchange Commission, "crowdfunding" allows startups and small businesses to raise up to $1 million annually from many small-dollar investors through web-based platforms, democratizing access to capital. Investor protections include a requirement that crowdfunding platforms must be registered with a self-regulatory organization and regulated by the SEC. In addition, investors' annual combined investments in crowdfunded securities are limited based on an income and net worth test. SEC rules implementing the crowdfunding portion of the JOBS Act became effective in May 2016 making it possible for entrepreneurs across the country to raise small-dollar investments from ordinary Americans.

Prior to the JOBS Act, the existing "Regulation A" exemption from certain SEC requirements for small businesses seeking to raise less than $5 million in a public offering was seldom used. The JOBS Act raises this threshold to $50 million, streamlining the process for smaller innovative companies to raise capital consistent with investor protections. The SEC rules implementing this portion of the Act became effective in the summer of 2015.

The JOBS Act makes it easier for young, high-growth firms to go public by providing an incubator period for a new class of "Emerging Growth Companies." During this period, qualifying companies will have time to reach compliance with certain public company disclosure and auditing requirements after their initial public offering (IPO). Any firm that goes public already has up to two years after its IPO to comply with certain Sarbanes-Oxley auditing requirements. The JOBS Act extended that period to a maximum of five years, or less if during the on-ramp period a company achieves $1 billion in gross revenue, $700 million in public float, or issues more than $1 billion in non-convertible debt in the previous three years.

Additionally, the JOBS Act changed some existing limitations on how companies can solicit private investments from "accredited investors," tasked the SEC with ensuring that companies take reasonable steps to verify that such investors are accredited, and gave companies more flexibility to plan their access to public markets and incentivize employees.

Taken together, the components of the JOBS Act has the potential to enable entrepreneurs and small businesses to raise capital not previously available to them, increasing overall levels of capital formation in the economy.

Americans' net wealth. Measures of volatility or financial market stress are all largely contained as well. Finally, there is evidence – from firm loans to home mortgages – that capital is being channeled towards productive uses. Implementation of the Jumpstart Our Business Startups (JOBS) Act (see Box 6-6) has made it easier for entrepreneurs and small businesses to raise capital and grow. Performance in financial markets is driven by economic fundamentals as well as factors related to the markets themselves. The fact that markets have been up does not mean that the Dodd-Frank Act has been a success any more than would declining markets represent a failure of financial reform. But the recovery of markets and their ability to serve the core roles they play in the economy is an indicator of the success of the financial rescue and reform efforts in this Administration.

General Measures of Financial Sector Health

The stock market has more than recovered from the losses suffered during the financial crisis. One broad measure of U.S. stock market performance, the S&P 500 index, fell from a peak of over 1,500 in Fall 2007 to a trough below 700 in March 2009, a decline of more than 50 percent. Since then the market has recovered all of that loss and risen above 2,150 in Fall 2016 (Figure 6-23).

Forward-looking measures of equity market volatility are relatively low. Derived from options on the S&P 500 index, the VIX is a measure of expected volatility over the life of the option. The VIX, also referred to as the "fear index", is well below the crisis peak of over 60 percent (Figure 6-24). As of November 2016, the VIX was at 15.2 percent, which is below its 17-year pre-crisis average of almost 19 percent.

Measures of bond market health have also recovered from the financial crisis. The bond market analogue of the VIX, the Merrill Lynch Option Volatility Estimate (MOVE) Index, is a yield curve weighted index of the implied volatility on 1-month Treasury. The MOVE has fallen from its

Figure 6-23
S&P 500, 2003–2016

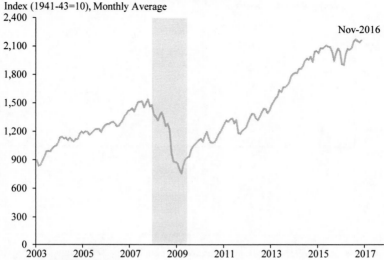

Note: Shading denotes recession.
Source: Standard & Poors.

Figure 6-24
VIX, 1990–2016

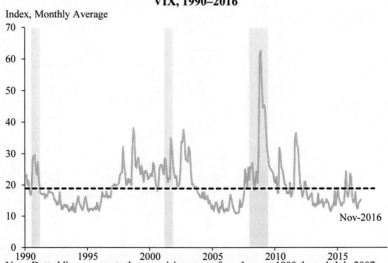

Note: Dotted line represents the pre-crisis average from January 1990 through July 2007.
Shading denotes recession.
Source: Wall Street Journal.

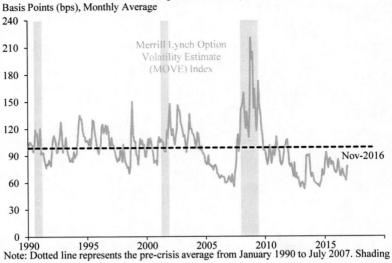

Figure 6-25
Fixed Income Implied Volatility, 1990–2016

Basis Points (bps), Monthly Average

Merrill Lynch Option Volatility Estimate (MOVE) Index

Nov-2016

Note: Dotted line represents the pre-crisis average from January 1990 to July 2007. Shading denotes recession.
Source: Bank of America Merrill Lynch.

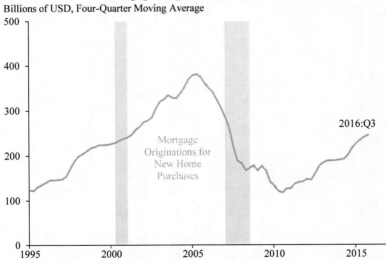

Figure 6-26
Mortgage Originations, 1995–2016

Billions of USD, Four-Quarter Moving Average

Mortgage Originations for New Home Purchases

2016:Q3

Note: Shading denotes recession.
Source: Mortgage Bankers Association.

Figure 6-27
Mortgage Delinquency and Foreclosure, 2000–2016

Percent of Total Number of Mortgages

Mortgage
Foreclosure
Inventory

Mortgages with
Payments Past Due 90+
Days

2016:Q3

Note: Shading denotes recession.
Source: Mortgage Bankers Association.

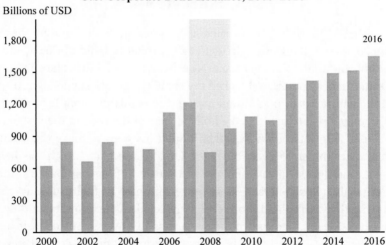

Figure 6-28
U.S. Corporate Bond Issuance, 2000–2016

Billions of USD

2016

Note: Shading denotes recession. Figures include investment grade and high yield, convertible bonds,
MTNs, and Yankee Bonds. Issuance number for 2016 is annualized based on issuance through
September 2016.
Source: SIFMA.

peak above 200 in the fall of 2008 to below 80 in Fall 2016, a level below the 17-year pre-crisis average of approximately 100 (Figure 6-25).

Measures of housing-market health, the sector in which the financial crisis began, have also improved. The Case-Shiller national index of house prices has regained almost all of the ground it lost during the crisis (Figure 6-4).

Mortgage lending has stabilized. The four-quarter moving average of mortgage originations for new home purchases fell from a pre-crisis peak of $381 billion in 2006:Q1 to a trough of $117 billion in 2011:Q2 (Figure 6-26). Since then, mortgage originations have risen steadily to $245 billion in 2016:Q3.

For existing loans, the fraction of mortgages with payments more than 90 days past due or in foreclosure continues to fall from the peak during the crisis. Mortgage payments more than 90 days past due have fallen steadily from a peak of 5.0 percent in 2010:Q1 to 1.4 percent in 2016:Q3. The fraction of mortgages in foreclosure has also fallen steadily from a peak of 4.6 percent in 2010:Q4 to 1.6 percent in 2016:Q3 (Figure 6-27). Both measures of troubled mortgages, suggest substantial progress since the crisis.

One of the most important functions of capital markets is to facilitate the formation of capital for business. Businesses have raised record amounts in the capital markets as corporate bond issuance has risen above pre-crisis levels (Figure 6-28).

Conclusion

The financial crisis revealed a number of fault lines in the U.S. financial system. Banks were inadequately capitalized, did not have enough liquidity, and took too many risks. Non-bank financial firms faced many of the same risks as banks, but lacked the same regulatory supervision or protection against runs. In addition, gaps in the regulatory architecture meant that financial regulators lacked a holistic view of the risks in the system.

The Administration has taken numerous steps to make the financial system safer, most of all through the Dodd-Frank Act, which has helped correct a number of market failures that arose in financial markets during the crisis. It helps generate safety and soundness of financial markets by requiring that banks hold more capital, have adequate liquidity, and do not take excessive risk because they have access to government deposit insurance or access to emergency liquidity provision from the Federal Reserve. Dodd-Frank takes steps to limit systemic risk by bringing unregulated parts of the financial system that were effectively performing banking functions without the necessary backstops or regulation under a regulatory umbrella.

It created the FSOC to consider risks to the overall financial system and better coordinate regulatory action. And it took steps to limit the problem of financial institutions that are too-big-to-fail by imposing additional regulatory requirements on such institutions and creating an architecture that would allow these systemically significant institutions to be unwound if they were to fail. Finally, Dodd-Frank improved the transparency, accountability, and consumer protections in our financial system. These measures will help consumers and investors engage with the financial system in a way that is beneficial to them.

Although implementation of Basel III and Dodd-Frank go a long way toward reforming the financial system, there are important issues that remain unresolved. These include reform of government sponsored enterprises Fannie (Federal National Mortgage Association) and Freddie (Federal Home Loan Mortgage Corporation) in a manner that ensures they do not return to a status as private entities that operate for profit but with implicit public guarantees, and ensuring that a sufficient resolution framework exists for systemically important insurance companies and systemically important financial companies with worldwide operations. And as the financial system evolves over time, the regulatory architecture will need to evolve as well to ensure that a financial crisis like the one from 2007 to 2009 does not wreak havoc on the economy in the future.

CHAPTER 7

ADDRESSING CLIMATE CHANGE

INTRODUCTION

Addressing climate change and transitioning to a clean energy system is one of the greatest and most urgent challenges of our time. If left unchecked, greenhouse gas (GHG) emissions threaten future national and global welfare and economic output. The impacts of climate change are real and being felt today. Fifteen of the sixteen warmest years on record globally have occurred between 2000 and 2015, and 2015 was the warmest year on record. Although it is difficult to link specific weather events to climate change, some extreme weather events have become more frequent and intense, consistent with climate model predictions. The number of weather events that have led to damages in excess of $1 billion has been increasing in recent years due to both climate change and economic development in vulnerable areas.

Without proactive steps to reduce greenhouse gas emissions and slow the climate warming already being observed, future generations will be left with—at a minimum—the costly burden of facing the impacts of a changed climate on our planet, and potentially with catastrophic climate impacts. From an economic perspective, the causes of global climate change involve a classic negative environmental externality. The prices of goods and services in our economy do not reflect their full costs because they do not incorporate the costs of the impacts of greenhouse gas emissions associated with their production and consumption. Policies that internalize these costs will improve social welfare while reducing the odds of catastrophic climate events. In addition to the costs incurred to date, delaying policy action can increase both future climate change damages and the cost of future mitigation.

Addressing the environmental externalities from climate change involves changing the long-run trajectory of our economy toward a more energy efficient and lower greenhouse gas-emitting path. Since President Obama took office, substantial strides have been made toward achieving this goal. Between 2008 and 2015, the U.S. energy system has shifted considerably toward cleaner energy resources. Energy intensity, which refers to energy consumed per dollar of real gross domestic product (GDP), declined by 11 percent from 2008 to 2015, following a pattern of steady decline over the past four decades. Carbon intensity, the amount of carbon dioxide emitted per unit of energy consumed, has declined by 8 percent from 2008 to 2015, and carbon dioxide emitted per dollar of GDP has declined by 18 percent over this period. In fact, U.S. carbon dioxide emissions from the energy sector fell by 9.5 percent from 2008 to 2015, and in the first 6 months of 2016 they were at the lowest level in 25 years. These trends, in combination, are favorable for climate change mitigation, and all have occurred while the economy recovered from the Great Recession. The economy has grown by more than 10 percent since 2008, and by more than 13 percent from its recession low point in 2009.

Since mitigating climate change serves a public good benefiting all countries, it also involves working with other countries to reduce greenhouse gas emissions worldwide. In addition to mitigation, addressing climate change involves building resilience to current and future impacts, developing adaptation plans and preparing for the changing frequency and severity of extreme events. Steps taken by the United States, along with extensive outreach to other countries, subsequently helped pave the way for the 2015 Paris Agreement in which more than 190 countries committed to take concrete steps to reduce greenhouse gas emissions. The Paris Agreement establishes a long-term, durable global framework with the aim of keeping climate warming to well below 2 degrees Celsius.

Given that the impacts of climate change are already being felt today and, that even with aggressive mitigation, impacts will continue into the future, the optimal response to climate change includes not only mitigation, but also adaptation. Building resilience to the current and future impacts of climate change is akin to insuring against the uncertain future damages from climate change. In parallel with domestic mitigation and global cooperation, Administration policies have also promoted resilience.

This chapter reviews the economic rationale for the Administration's efforts on climate change and the transformation of the energy system. It provides an overview of a selection of the most important policy efforts and then examines the key economic trends related to climate change and energy, many of which have already been influenced, and will be increasingly influenced going forward by policy measures under the Administration's 2013 Climate Action Plan. These trends include increases in electricity generation from natural gas and renewable energy resources, improvements in energy efficiency, and shifts in transportation energy use. The chapter also analyzes the sources of these trends, by decomposing emissions reductions in the power sector as attributable to lower-carbon fossil-fuel resources and renewable energy generation, as well as by decomposing emissions reductions in the entire economy as attributable to lower energy intensity, lower carbon intensity, and a lower than expected level of GDP due to economic shocks, primarily the Great Recession. Understanding the driving forces behind these trends allows for an assessment of how the multitude of policy mechanisms utilized in this Administration have helped the United States pursue a more economically efficient path that addresses environmental and other important externalities.

Consistent with long-standing policy, the Administration has worked to ensure that regulations that affect carbon emissions and other climate-related policies are undertaken in an efficient and cost effective manner. Rigorous regulatory impact analyses demonstrate that economically efficient mechanisms were used to achieve climate goals. Policies put in place since 2008 will generate substantial net benefits. The first-ever carbon pollution standards for power plants would reduce greenhouse gas emissions significantly and, depending on the methods states use to comply, could generate net benefits of $15 billion to $27 billion just in 2025. Greenhouse gas standards for light-duty cars and trucks are also estimated to have sizable net benefits. The first-ever national greenhouse gas and fuel economy standards for commercial trucks, buses, and vans should generate hundreds of billions of dollars in net benefits over the life of the vehicles affected by the rule.

Other policies will either make energy cleaner or reduce energy use. The Administration extended tax credits for wind and solar projects, first in the 2009 American Recovery and Reinvestment Act (the Recovery Act) and again in 2015. The Recovery Act included substantial funding for both energy efficiency and renewables development (CEA 2016c). In addition, stronger energy efficiency standards for residential and commercial appliances, and many others, are projected to generate substantial net economic benefits to the U.S. economy.

The long time horizons for these policies, reinforced by the Administration's substantial investments in research and development for clean energy technologies, will continue to spur innovation and ensure that recent energy-sector shifts will have a durable impact on the economy and the climate.

The Administration's climate policies go well beyond what is discussed in this chapter. Rather than provide a comprehensive review of implemented and planned policies, this chapter focuses on the economics of domestic actions to reduce greenhouse gas emissions and transition to cleaner sources of energy. Additional Federal policies and programs are assessed in other Administration documents.[1] The chapter also draws on analyses from energy and climate chapters in prior *Economic Reports of the President* (CEA 2013, 2015a).

THE ECONOMIC RATIONALE FOR CLIMATE ACTION

Climate change is not just a future problem—the costly impacts of changing weather patterns and a warming planet are being felt now (U.S. Global Change Research Program 2014). Fifteen of the sixteen warmest years on record globally have occurred between 2000 and 2015, and the 2015 average temperature was the highest on record (NOAA 2016a). Each of the first 8 months in 2016 set a record as the warmest respective month globally in the modern temperature record, dating to 1880; in fact, August 2016 marked the 16th consecutive month that the monthly global temperature record was broken, the longest such streak in 137 years of recordkeeping (NOAA 2016b). Not only are temperatures rising on average, but heat waves—which have detrimental human health impacts—have also been on the rise in Europe, Australia, and across much of Asia since 1960 (IPCC 2013). Among extreme weather events, heat waves are a phenomenon for which the scientific link with climate change is fairly robust. For example, studies suggest that climate change doubled the likelihood of heat waves like the one that occurred in Europe in 2003, which is estimated to have killed between 25,000 and 70,000 people, and that deadly heat in Europe is 10 times more likely today than it was in 2003 (Christidis et al. 2015; Stott 2004; Robine et al. 2008; D'Ippoliti et al. 2010).

Wildfires and certain types of extreme weather events such as heavy rainfall, floods, and droughts with links to climate change have also become more frequent and/or intense in recent years (Department of State 2016b; U.S. Global Change Research Program 2014). As illustrated in Figure 7-1, the annual number of U.S. weather events that cause damages exceeding $1 billion has risen dramatically since 1980, due both to climate change and to increasing economic development in vulnerable areas (NOAA 2016c).[2] An intense drought that has plagued the West Coast of the United States since 2013 led to California's first-ever statewide mandatory urban water restrictions (California Executive Department 2014).

---

[1] For discussion of clean energy investments under the American Recovery and Reinvestment Act, see CEA (2016c). For additional reviews of the Administration's climate policies, see DOE (2015), EPA (2015a), and Department of State (2016b).
[2] Regional economic development can increase the magnitude of damages from weather-related events because economic growth increases the assets (and population) at risk.

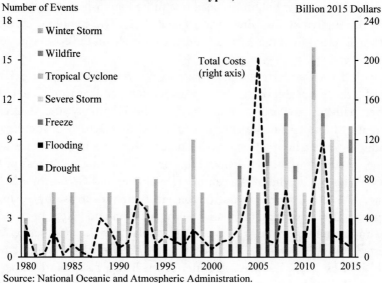

Figure 7-1
Billion-Dollar Event Types, 1980–2015

Number of Events
Billion 2015 Dollars

- Winter Storm
- Wildfire
- Tropical Cyclone
- Severe Storm
- Freeze
- Flooding
- Drought

Total Costs
(right axis)

Source: National Oceanic and Atmospheric Administration.

As atmospheric levels of carbon dioxide have increased, the amount of carbon dioxide dissolved in the ocean has risen all over the world, increasing ocean acidification and threatening marine life. Further, over the past 100 years, the average global sea level has risen by more than 8 inches, leading to greater risk of erosion, flooding, and destructive storm surges in coastal areas (U.S. Global Change Research Program 2014).

Growing research also links climate change with diminished health and labor productivity in the United States, due to both temperature and pollution increases (EPA 2015a; Crimmins 2016). For example, recent research finds that when daily maximum temperatures exceed 85 degrees Fahrenheit, U.S. labor supply is reduced by as much as one hour a day (relative to the 76- to 80-degree range) for outdoor industries such as construction and farming (Graff Zivin and Neidell 2014). Studies also suggest strong links between warming and mortality—an additional day of extreme heat (above 90 degrees Fahrenheit) can lead to an increase in annual age-adjusted U.S. mortality rates of around 0.11 percent relative to a day in the 50- to 60-degree range (Deschênes and Greenstone 2011).[3] Warmer temperatures can also lead to higher urban levels of ozone, an air pollutant that affects

---

[3]This study and the others cited here analyze inter-annual weather variation to estimate climate impacts. As such, they may overstate climate impacts, because less-costly adaptation activities may be available over longer time horizons in response to permanent climate changes than are available in response to short-term weather shocks.

people and vegetation (U.S. Global Change Research Program 2014). For example, in the California agricultural sector, a decrease in ozone concentration by 10 parts per billion can lead to a more than 5-percent increase in worker productivity (Graff Zivin and Neidell 2012). These studies represent just a small selection of the growing body of evidence on the economic costs of climate change.

Based on the current trajectory and the results of climate science research, the economic costs from warmer temperatures and changing weather patterns are expected to grow in the coming years. Increased temperatures due to climate change could lead to a 3-percent increase in age-adjusted mortality rates and an 11-percent increase in annual residential energy consumption (as demand for air conditioning increases) in the United States by the end of the century (Deschênes and Greenstone 2011). Average U.S. corn, soybean, and cotton yields may decrease by 30 to 46 percent by 2100, assuming no change in the location and extent of growing areas, and assuming that climate warming is relatively slow (Schlenker and Roberts 2009).[4] Extreme heat is also expected to affect labor productivity and health: by 2050, the average American will likely see the number of 95-degree Fahrenheit days more than double relative to the last 30 years, and labor productivity for outdoor workers may fall by as much as 3 percent by the end of the century (Risky Business Project 2014). Within the next 15 years, assuming no additional adaptation, higher sea levels and storm surges will increase the estimated damage costs from coastal storms by $2 billion to $3.5 billion annually in the United States, and these costs are projected to increase to $42 billion annually by the end of the century (Risky Business Project 2014). Based on emissions trajectories in 2014, by 2050 existing U.S. coastal property worth between $66 billion and $106 billion could be at risk of being inundated, with the Eastern and Gulf coasts particularly affected (again, assuming no additional adaptation) (Risky Business Project 2014).

The impacts of climate change will also affect the U.S. Federal Budget. For example, an increase in the frequency of catastrophic storms, along with rising seas, will require more disaster relief spending, flood insurance payments, and investments to protect, repair, and relocate Federal facilities. Changing weather patterns and extreme weather events will affect American farmers and thus expenditures on Federal crop insurance and disaster payments. Health impacts of climate change will increase Federal health care expenditures. An increase in wild-land fire frequency and intensity

---

[4] Like the studies on human health, economic estimates of the agricultural impacts of climate change are based on inter-annual weather variation and may overstate climate impacts, if less costly adaptation activities are available over long time horizons in response to permanent climate change.

will strain Federal fire suppression resources. In addition to these likely increases in expenditures, climate change is expected to reduce economic output and diminish Federal revenue. A recent report by the U.S. Office of Management and Budget projects that the combined detrimental impacts of climate change on Federal revenues and expenditures by 2100 could easily exceed $100 billion annually, when the estimates are expressed in terms of their equivalent percentage of current U.S. GDP (OMB 2016).

Addressing Externalities

The impacts of climate change present a clear economic rationale for policy as a means to both correct market failures and as a form of insurance against the increased risk of catastrophic events. Climate change reflects a classic environmental externality. When consumers or producers emit greenhouse gases, they enjoy the benefits from the services provided by the use of the fuels, while not paying the full costs of the damages from climate change. Since the price of goods and services that emit greenhouse gases during production does not reflect the economic damages associated with those gases, market forces result in a level of emissions that is too high from society's perspective. Such a market failure can be addressed by policy. The most efficient policy would respond to this market failure by putting an economy-wide price on the right to emit greenhouse gases. In the absence of a uniform carbon price to regulate emissions, however, other climate policy mechanisms can improve social welfare by pricing emissions indirectly. For example, putting in place emission limits and incentivizing low-carbon alternatives can make carbon-intensive technology relatively more expensive, shifting demand toward less carbon-intensive products, and thus reducing emissions. Energy efficiency standards can reduce energy use, implicitly addressing the external costs of emissions and resulting over-consumption of energy. Gasoline or oil taxes help to directly address the external costs due to emissions from the combustion of oil.

Correcting Other Market Failures

Some policies to address the climate change externality have an additional economic benefit from addressing other market failures. For example, reducing carbon dioxide emissions through lower carbon electricity generation often also reduces the emissions of local and regional air pollutants that cause damage to human health, a second environmental externality.

There are also innovation market failures where some of the returns from investment in innovation and new product development spill over to other firms from the firm engaged in innovation. For example, there is substantial evidence that the social returns from research and development investment are much higher than the private returns due to some of the knowledge spilling over to other firms.[5] Though in principle these positive spillovers can be good for society, they prevent the innovating firms from capturing the full returns to their investments in technological innovation, resulting in less than the efficient level of investment. While not specific to the energy area, the failure to internalize the positive spillovers to research into technologies that would reduce carbon emissions is compounded by the failure to take into account the external cost of carbon emissions.

Other market failures that may be partly addressed by climate-oriented policies include information market failures due to inadequate or poor information about new clean energy or energy-efficient consumer technologies, and network effects (such as, a situation where the value of a product is greater when there is a larger network of users of that product) that consumers do not consider in their decisions on the purchase of new clean energy technologies. While not market failures, per se, vulnerability to supply disruptions and the potential macroeconomic effects of oil price shocks provide additional reasons to invest in clean transportation technologies. These factors, taken together, can lead to an underinvestment in research, as well as underinvestment in energy efficiency and deployment of clean energy, and can provide additional economic motivations for policy. For example, energy efficiency standards may help address information market failures that hamper consumers' ability to understand the energy costs of different product choices, and policies promoting clean transportation infrastructure may reduce vulnerability to oil supply disruptions.

Insurance against Catastrophe

Despite a large body of research on how human activities are changing the climate, substantial uncertainty remains around the amount and location of damages that climate change will cause. This is because there are cascading uncertainties from the interplay of key physical parameters (such as the exact magnitude of the global temperature response to the atmospheric buildup in greenhouse gases), the local and regional manifestations of global climate change, the vulnerabilities of different economic sectors, and the adaptation measures that could decrease impacts. For example, climate scientists have developed probability distributions of the sensitivity of the climate to increases in the concentration of greenhouse gases in the atmosphere, and there is some small, but non-zero probability of very high

---

[5] See Jaffe and Stavins (1994) or Gillingham and Sweeney (2012) for more on innovation market failures in the context of clean energy.

climate sensitivity.[6] With the possibility of significant climate sensitivity, coupled with the possibility of high future greenhouse gas emissions, the risk of irreversible, large-scale changes that have wide-ranging and potentially catastrophic consequences greatly increases. The term "tipping point" is commonly used to refer to a "critical threshold at which a tiny perturbation can qualitatively alter the state of development of a system" (Lenton et al. 2008). When it comes to climate, at a tipping point, a marginal increase in emissions could make a non-marginal—and potentially irreversible—impact on damages. Hypothetical climate tipping points could lead to catastrophic events like the disappearance of Greenland ice sheets and associated sea level rise, or the destabilization of Indian summer monsoon circulation.

It is impossible to know precisely how likely or how costly these low-probability, high-impact events, or "tail risks" are, but we do know that the associated costs and impacts on human society would be very substantial and that their likelihood increases with higher atmospheric concentrations of greenhouse gases. Economists have been increasingly interested in understanding how these tail risks should be incorporated into policy choices. A series of papers by Martin Weitzman lay out an analytical framework for understanding policy under conditions with catastrophic fat tail risks (such as the risk of a catastrophe that has more probability weight than it would in a normal distribution).[7] Weitzman's analysis points out that, under certain conditions, the expected costs of climate change become infinitely large.[8] While there has been an active debate in the literature on the conditions under which Weitzman's findings may apply, his work both underscores the importance of understanding tail risks, and provides an economic rationale for taking early action to avoid future, potentially very large risks.[9] Just as individuals and businesses routinely purchase insurance to guard against risks in everyday life, like fire, theft, or a car accident, and just as conservative safety standards guard against catastrophic failures at major infrastructure like nuclear plants and highway bridges, climate policy can be seen as protection against the economic risks—small and large—associated with climate change.

---

[6] According to the IPCC, equilibrium climate sensitivity is likely in the range 1.5°C to 4.5°C (high confidence), extremely unlikely less than 1°C (high confidence), and very unlikely greater than 6°C (medium confidence) (IPCC 2013).
[7] For example, a Student's t-distribution is a fat-tailed distribution.
[8] Weitzman's "Dismal Theorem" is presented and discussed in several papers: Weitzman (2009), Weitzman (2011), and Weitzman (2014). Further analyses of the "theorem" include Newbold and Daigneault (2009), Nordhaus (2009), and Millner (2013).
[9] In fact, Weitzman's conditions are not necessary for there to be an economic motivation: there is a broader economic motivation for a precautionary policy with a sufficiently risk averse or loss averse decision-maker.

Delaying Action on Climate Change Increases Costs

When considering climate change policy from an economic perspective, it is critical to consider not just the cost of action but also the cost of inaction. Delaying climate policies may avoid or reduce expenditures in the near term, but delaying would likely increase costs substantially in the longer run. The economic literature discusses two primary mechanisms underlying the substantial increase in costs from delayed action.

First, if delay leads to an increase in the ultimate steady-state concentration of greenhouse gases, then there will be additional warming and subsequent economic damages in the long run. Using the results of a leading climate model, CEA (2014) estimates that if a delay causes the mean global temperature to stabilize at 3 degrees Celsius above preindustrial levels instead of 2 degrees, that delay will induce annual additional damages of approximately 0.9 percent of global output. (To put that percentage in perspective, 0.9 percent of output in the United States in 2015 alone was over $160 billion.) The next degree increase, from 3 degrees to 4 degrees, would incur even greater *additional* costs of approximately 1.2 percent of global output. It is critical to note that these costs would be incurred year after year.

Second, if the delayed policy aims to achieve the same carbon target as a non-delayed policy, then the delayed policy will require more stringent actions given the shorter timeframe. More stringent actions will generally be more costly, though technological innovation can make future mitigation cheaper than it is today, lowering the future cost of low-carbon technologies needed to meet the target. In addition, since investment in innovation responds to policy, taking meaningful steps now sends a long-term signal to markets that the development of low-carbon technologies will be rewarded. At the same time, this signal creates a disincentive for investing in new high-carbon infrastructure that would be expensive to replace later on. CEA (2014) estimates the costs of delaying the achievement of a specific target— by these calculations, if the world tries to hit the goal stated in Paris of less than a 2-degree increase in the global mean surface temperature relative to pre-industrial levels, but waits a decade to do so, the cost of limiting the temperature change would increase by roughly 40 percent relative to meeting the goal without the decade delay.[10]

ADMINISTRATION CLIMATE POLICIES

Since President Obama took office in 2009, the Administration has undertaken numerous steps toward both mitigating climate change and

---

[10] These estimates, as further described in CEA (2014), are developed from a meta-analysis of research on the cost of delay for hitting a specific climate target.

Figure 7-2
Greenhouse Gas Emissions by Type and Sector in 2014

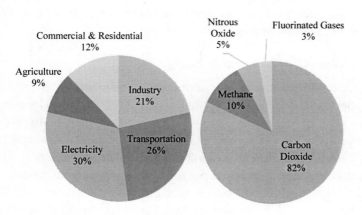

Source: Environmental Protection Agency.

responding to its effects. Greenhouse gas emissions in the United States amounted to 6,870 million metric tons of carbon dioxide equivalents in 2014 (the most recent inventory), and these emissions are spread over several sectors, as shown in the left chart of Figure 7-2.[11] In 2014, carbon dioxide emissions made up 82 percent of total greenhouse gas emissions; methane, 10 percent; nitrous oxides, 5 percent; and fluorinated gases, 3 percent (right chart of Figure 7-2) (EPA 2016a). The electricity sector in 2014 generated the largest share of emissions—nearly a third—which together with the fact that some of the least-expensive marginal emissions reductions opportunities are in the power sector (Kaufman, Obeiter and Krause 2016) motivate the Clean Power Plan and clean energy investments (discussed below). Transportation follows with 26 percent of emissions, motivating a variety of efficiency and innovation policies in the transportation sector.[12]

The Administration's steps to address greenhouse gases cover nearly all sectors and gases. These steps help reduce emissions both now and in the longer term by promoting low-carbon electricity generation, dramatically improving energy efficiency for many products, facilitating the transition to a cleaner transportation system, reducing emissions of high-potency greenhouse gases, and bolstering our land-sector sink (the capacity of land

---

[11] These are gross greenhouse gas emissions. Note that the Administration's multi-year GHG reduction targets are based on GHG emissions, net of carbon sinks.

[12] The most recent EPA GHG annual inventory is from 2014. In March 2016, the rolling 12-month average emissions estimates from the U.S. Energy Information Administration suggested that transportation emissions had exceeded those from electric power generation for the first time since 1979.

uses and land management activities to remove carbon dioxide from the atmosphere). In parallel, they have also promoted resilience, with a variety of programs focused on adapting to a changing climate. This section highlights just a few of the Administration's many climate and energy initiatives. The next section discusses outcomes.

Supporting Growth of Renewable Energy

President Obama has made substantial investments in renewable energy supported by Federal policies that promote research, development, and deployment of renewable energy. These policies help address the underinvestment in renewable energy due to environmental externalities as well as the underinvestment in R&D due to knowledge spillovers. The Administration signaled its strong support for clean energy from the beginning by making a historic $90 billion investment in clean energy in the American Recovery and Reinvestment Act. The macroeconomic demand shock of the Great Recession required a bold policy response that included stimulus spending along with tax cuts and aid to affected individuals and communities. The Administration's decision to focus an important part of that spending (about an eighth of the total) on clean energy was a vital step in pushing the economy toward a cleaner energy future, and a foundational step for supporting continued progress throughout the President's eight years in office.

The Recovery Act extended and expanded the Production Tax Credit (PTC) and the Investment Tax Credit (ITC), critical policies directly focused on renewable energy. These policies provide subsidies for renewable energy production and installation to help address the unpriced externalities that place renewable energy at a disadvantage. In December 2015, the Administration secured a five-year extension of the PTC and ITC, signaling to developers that renewable energy continues to be an area worthy of greater investment (Bailey 2015).

The Recovery Act also created two new programs to support renewable energy generation: a set of loan guarantees for renewable energy project financing (the 1705 Loan Guarantee Program) and cash grants for renewable energy projects (the 1603 Cash Grant Program). The 1705 program supported construction of the first five solar PV projects over 100 MW in the United States. The 1603 program provided $25 billion to support total installed renewable energy capacity of 33.3 GW (CEA 2016c). The Act also included funding for energy efficiency projects, clean transportation, grid modernization, advanced vehicles and fuels, carbon capture and storage, and clean energy manufacturing.[13]

Since its actions to mitigate the Great Recession, the Administration has undertaken a set of efforts to help ensure that renewable energy is accessible to all Americans and underserved communities, in particular. Launched in July 2015, the National Community Solar Partnership, part of the Administration's SunShot initiative, is fostering innovation in financing and business models and spreading best practices to facilitate adoption of solar systems in low- and moderate-income (LMI) communities.[14] The U.S. Department of Housing and Urban Development is facilitating Property Assessed Clean Energy (PACE) financing to make it easier and more affordable for households to finance investments in solar energy and energy efficiency. The Administration has set a goal to bring 1 gigawatt (GW) of solar to low- and moderate-income families by 2020, and the U.S. Department of Agriculture has awarded almost $800 million to guarantee loan financing and grant funding to agricultural producers and rural small businesses (USDA 2016). USDA programs focusing on renewable energy have resulted in support for the construction of six advanced biofuel production facilities, more than 4,000 wind and solar renewable electricity generation facilities, and more than 100 anaerobic digesters to help farm operations capture methane to product electricity (Vilsack 2016). The Administration has also set a goal for the U.S. Department of the Interior to approve 20,000 MW of renewable energy capacity on public lands by 2020, and has set ambitious annual goals for the U.S. General Services Administration to purchase minimum percentages of its electricity from renewable sources, reaching 100 percent in 2025; both of these update and expand on earlier such goals in the Energy Policy Act of 2005 (EOP 2013, EOP 2015). The Administration has also expanded opportunities to join the solar workforce with programs like the Solar Instructor Training Network, AmeriCorps funding, and Solar Ready Vets to help reach the goal of training 75,000 workers to enter the solar industry by 2020.

---

[13] See CEA (2016c) for more on the impacts of these policies and more detail on clean energy support provided by ARRA. Some funded programs were extended or had greater take-up than anticipated, so the total allocation of ARRA-related clean energy programs will be more than $90 billion; CEA calculations indicate that just under $90 billion of ARRA clean energy-related dollars had been spent by the end of 2015.

[14] The SunShot initiative in the U.S. Department of Energy, launched in 2011, has the goal of making solar electricity cost competitive with conventional forms of electricity generation by 2020.

Carbon Pollution Standards for Power Plants

In August 2015, the President and the EPA announced the finalization of the Clean Power Plan (CPP)—the first-ever national carbon pollution standards for existing power plants. This historic action by the United States to address environmental externalities from carbon dioxide emissions focuses on the power sector, the source of just under a third of all greenhouse gas emissions and the largest source of U.S. carbon dioxide emissions in 2014 (EPA 2015c).

Consistent with the framework set out in the Clean Air Act, the CPP sets emission performance rates for fossil fuel-fired power plants based on the best system of emission reduction the EPA found was available, considering cost, energy impacts, and health and environmental impacts. The CPP translates those rates into state-specific goals and provides states with broad flexibility to reach the goals. For example, a state can choose a mass-based standard, which limits the total number of tons of carbon dioxide from regulated plants and can be achieved with a cap-and-trade system or another policy approach of the state's choice. As an alternative, the state can comply with a rate-based standard, whereby the state requires regulated sources to meet a specified emissions rate (the amount of emissions generated per unit of electricity produced) through a number of policy approaches. This flexibility allows states to choose cost-effective approaches to reducing emissions that are tailored to meet the state's own policy priorities.[15] Further, for greater economic efficiency gains, the CPP permits emissions trading across states; affected electric generation units (EGUs) can trade emissions credits with EGUs in other states with compatible implementation plans (EPA 2015c).

When the CPP is fully in place,[16] CO_2 emissions from the electric power sector are projected to be 32 percent below 2005 levels by 2030, resulting in 870 million tons less carbon pollution in 2030, equivalent to the annual emissions of 166 million cars (EPA 2015b, 2015c). Not only will the CPP help mitigate climate change, but it will also protect the health of American families by reducing asthma attacks in children and preventing premature deaths and non-fatal heart attacks by reducing emissions of other harmful air pollutants, and will help to provide an incentive for further

---

[15] From an economic perspective, the mass-based approach may be preferable because it does not create incentives to expand electricity production to facilitate compliance and does not require verification of demand reductions due to energy efficiency policies and investments (Fowlie et al. 2014).

[16] Implementation of the CPP has been stayed by the Supreme Court. The Administration is confident that it will be upheld in court as it is consistent with Supreme Court decisions, EPA's statutory authority, and air pollution standards that EPA has put in place to address other air pollution problems.

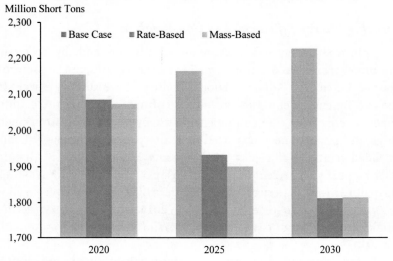

Figure 7-3
Clean Power Plan Projected Carbon Dioxide Emissions

Million Short Tons

■ Base Case   ■ Rate-Based   ■ Mass-Based

Source: Environmental Protection Agency.

innovation to lower the costs of low-carbon energy (EPA 2015b). Given the combined effects of changes in average retail electricity rates and lower electricity demand, EPA projects that average electricity bills will decline by 3-4 percent in 2025, and by 7-8 percent in 2030, due to the CPP (EPA 2015c). Figure 7-3 shows the projected emissions reductions under the CPP. The base case bars refer to a world with all other current policies, while the rate-based and mass-based bars indicate what carbon dioxide emissions from the power sector are projected to be under the CPP if all states opt for each type of plan.

The rigorous benefit-cost analysis performed for the CPP projects that it would generate substantial net benefits to the U.S. economy. Given the flexibility afforded states in compliance with the CPP's emissions guidelines, estimates of benefits and costs are not definitive—both benefits and costs will depend on the compliance approaches states actually choose. Using Federal estimates of the social cost of carbon dioxide (SC-CO2), discussed further below, along with estimates of the co-benefits from the CPP's reductions in health damages from fine particulate matter and ozone, the CPP's regulatory impact analysis projects net benefits to the U.S. economy in 2020 of $1.0 billion to $6.7 billion, depending on the compliance approaches states choose. Net benefit estimates increase significantly in later years, with a projected range of $16 billion to $27 billion in 2025, and $25 billion to $45 billion in 2030 (EPA 2015c).[17]

Improving Energy Efficiency and Conservation

Improved energy efficiency reduces emissions and, by correcting environmental externalities or information market failures, can also improve economic efficiency. Administration initiatives have already succeeded in improving energy efficiency in millions of homes around the country, reducing energy costs, and cutting energy use by the Federal Government, with greater improvements expected in future years. Technological shifts have aided greatly in efficiency improvements. For example, LED lighting has seen a nearly 90 percent decrease in cost per kilolumen since 2008. The costs of lithium-ion battery packs for electric vehicles have fallen from above $1,000/kWh in 2007 to under $410/kWh in 2014, with estimates for leading manufacturers coming in as low as $300/kWh (Nykvist and Nilsoon 2015; DOE 2015).

In the President's first term, the departments of Energy and Housing and Urban Development completed energy efficiency upgrades in over 1 million homes, saving families on average more than $400 each on their heating and cooling bills in the first year alone (EOP 2016). The President also launched the Better Buildings Challenge in 2011, a broad, multi-strategy initiative to improve energy use in commercial, industrial, residential, and public buildings by 20 percent by 2020 (DOE 2016b). More than 310 organizations have committed to the Better Buildings Challenge, and the partners have saved over 160 trillion Btus of energy from 2011 to 2015, leading to $1.3 billion in reduced energy costs (DOE 2016d).

Since 2009, the Department of Energy's Building Technologies Office has issued 42 new or updated energy efficiency standards for home appliances, which are projected to save consumers more than $540 billion on their utility bills through 2030, and to cut carbon dioxide emissions by 2.3 billion metric tons (DOE 2016a). The products covered by standards represent about 90 percent of home energy use, 60 percent of commercial

---

[17] The regulatory impact analysis for the CPP reports estimates in constant 2011 dollars. In 2015 dollars, the net benefits to the U.S. economy would be $1.1 to $7.1 billion in 2020, $17 to $27 billion in 2025, and $26 to $47 billion in 2030. The CPP applies to existing power plants. In October 2015, the EPA issued final carbon pollution standards for newly constructed, modified, or reconstructed fossil-fuel-fired power plants. Due to projected market conditions (particularly the expectation of continued low natural gas prices, which make it likely that any new plants would comply with the rule's requirements even if it were not in place), analyses performed by the EPA and the U.S. Energy Information Administration (EIA) indicate that the new source standards will have negligible impacts on emissions, as well as negligible economic benefits and costs. Should gas prices rise significantly, the rule is projected to generate significant net benefits (EPA 2015d).

Box 7-1: Quantifying the Benefits of Avoided Carbon Emissions

Benefit-cost analysis is the well-known approach to determining whether any given policy will provide net benefits to society. Benefit-cost analysis of a policy that yields reductions of greenhouse gas emissions requires an estimate of the benefits of those reductions. The question is non-trivial, as estimating the impact of marginal increases in emissions requires calculations over long time spans and distributions of climate sensitivities and socioeconomic outcomes. To take on this task, the Obama Administration established a Federal Interagency Working Group (IWG) in 2009 to develop estimates of the value of damages per ton of carbon dioxide emissions (or, conversely, the benefits per ton of emissions reductions). The resulting social cost of carbon dioxide (SC-CO2) estimates, developed in 2009-10, provide consistent values based on the best available climate science and economic modeling, so that agencies across the Federal Government could estimate the global benefits of emissions reductions. Before these estimates were available, impacts of rules on greenhouse gas emissions had been considered qualitatively, or had been monetized using values that varied across agencies and rules. Creating a single SC-CO2 was an important step in ensuring that regulatory impact analysis of Federal actions reflects the best available estimates of the benefits of reducing greenhouse gas emissions.

The IWG updated the original 2010 SC-CO2 estimates in May 2013 to incorporate refinements that researchers had made to the underlying peer-reviewed models. Since then, minor technical revisions have been issued twice—in November 2013 and in July 2015. Both of

Table 7-i

Social Cost of CO_2, 2010–2050 (in 2007 Dollars Per Metric Ton of CO_2)

Discount Rate Year	5% Average	3% Average	2.5% Average	High Impact (95th Pct at 3%)
2010	10	31	50	86
2015	11	36	56	105
2020	12	42	62	123
2025	14	46	68	138
2030	16	50	73	152
2035	18	55	78	168
2040	21	60	84	183
2045	23	64	89	197
2050	26	69	95	212

Source: Interagency Working Group (2016).

these resulted in insignificant changes to the overall estimates released in May 2013. The IWG also sought independent expert advice from the National Academies of Sciences, Engineering, and Medicine (NAS) to inform future updates of the SC-CO2 estimates. In August 2016, the IWG updated its technical support document to incorporate January 2016 feedback from the NAS by enhancing the presentation and discussion of quantified uncertainty around the current SC-CO2 estimates. The NAS Committee recommended against a near-term update of the estimates. Also in August 2016, the IWG issued new estimates of the social costs of two additional GHGs, methane (CH_4) and nitrous oxide (N_2O), applying the same methodology as that used to estimate the SC-CO2 (IWG 2016a).

To estimate the SC-CO2, SC-CH4, and SC-N2O, three integrated assessment models (IAMs) are employed. IAMs couple models of atmospheric gas cycles and climate systems with aggregate models of the global economy and human behavior to represent the impacts of GHG emissions on the climate and human welfare. Within IAMs, the equations that represent the influence of emissions on the climate are based on scientific assessments, while the equations that map climate impacts to human welfare ("damage functions") are based on economic research evaluating the effects of climate on various market and non-market sectors, including its effects on sea level rise, agricultural productivity, human health, energy-system costs, and coastal resources. Estimating the social cost of emissions for a given GHG at the margin involves perturbing the emissions of that gas in a given year and forecasting the increase in monetized climate damages relative to the baseline. These incremental damages are then discounted back to the perturbation year to represent the marginal social cost of emissions of the specific GHG in that year.

The estimates of the cost of emissions released in a given year represent the present value of the additional damages that occur from those emissions between the year in which they are emitted and the year 2300. The choice of discount rate over such a long time horizon implicates philosophical and ethical perspectives about tradeoffs in consumption across generations, and debates about the appropriate discount rate in climate change analysis persist (Goulder and Williams 2012; Arrow, et al. 2013; Arrow, et al. 2014). Thus, the IWG presents the SC-CO2 under three alternative discount rate scenarios, and, given the potential for lower-probability, but higher-impact outcomes from climate change, a fourth value is presented to represent the estimated marginal damages associated with these "tail" outcomes (IWG 2015, IWG 2016b). All four current estimates of the SC-CO2, from 2010 to 2050, are below.

Sources: IWG (2013, 2015, 2016a, 2016b), Goulder and Williams (2012), Arrow et al (2013, 2014).

building use, and 30 percent of industrial energy use, which taken cumulatively, represented around 40 percent of total primary energy use in 2015.[18] By 2030, the cumulative operating cost savings from all standards in effect since 1987 will reach nearly $2 trillion, with a cumulative reduction of about 7.3 billion tons of CO_2 emissions (DOE 2016a).

Pricing the external costs from greenhouse gas emissions would increase the likelihood of consumers adopting these options on their own, but when the greenhouse gas-emitting energy is underpriced, then programs to help move consumers toward a more energy-efficient outcome can improve economic efficiency. Each of these standards has been subject to rigorous benefit-cost analysis, and each has economic benefits in excess of costs. This demonstrates that such standards not only reduce GHG emissions, but do so in an economically efficient way. For example, new rules for commercial air conditioning and heating equipment sold between 2018 and 2048 are projected to have net economic benefits of $42 billion to $79 billion (DOE 2016c).[19]

Addressing Transportation Sector Emissions

Since 2009, President Obama has implemented policies that reduce emissions from the transportation sector—one of the largest sources of U.S. greenhouse gas emissions (EPA 2016a). Again, these policies can help internalize environmental externalities and address information market failures. Through improvements to the fuel economy of gasoline- and diesel-powered cars and trucks, and the technological progress that has been made on hybrid and electric drivetrains, the transportation sector has made substantial improvements to date, and the Administration has put policies in place to increase the likelihood that these improvements will continue for years to come. In addition, the Administration has continued to implement rules on Renewable Fuel Standards in ways that reduce the carbon intensity of our transportation sector.

Under this Administration, the EPA and the National Highway Traffic Safety Administration have issued GHG emission and fuel economy standards for light-duty passenger vehicles and the first-ever GHG and fuel economy standards for medium- and heavy-duty trucks. The latest set of standards for passenger vehicles will reduce new vehicle GHG emissions by nearly a half and approximately double the average new vehicle fuel economy

---

[18] Calculation based on total energy use by sector from the EIA's Monthly Energy Review (MER), Table 2.1.
[19] The net benefits of these new rules are represented in 2014 dollars. In 2015 dollars, these rules are expected to have slightly higher net benefits that round to the same figures ($42 to $79 billion).

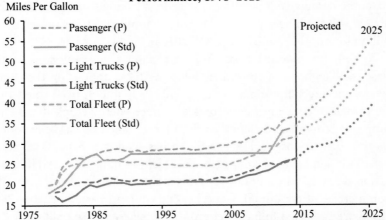

Figure 7-4
Corporate Average Fuel Economy Standards and Performance, 1978–2025

Note: Dotted lines represent actual performance (P) and solid lines represent the relevant fuel economy standard (Std). Projections are based on the CAFE MY 2017–2025 standards and assume that fuel economy performance meets the standards.
Source: National Highway Traffic Safety Administration.

(NHTSA 2012). Combined, the Phase 1 and Phase 2 GHG and fuel economy standards for light-duty vehicles are projected to reduce GHG emissions by 6 billion metric tons over the lifetime of vehicles sold from 2012 to 2025 (EPA 2012). Building on the first-ever GHG and fuel economy standards for new medium- and heavy-duty vehicles built between 2014 and 2020, issued in 2011, EPA and NHTSA finalized "Phase 2" standards in 2016 that will further raise fuel economy for these vehicles through 2027. Combined, the Phase 1 and Phase 2 heavy-duty vehicle standards are expected to reduce GHG emissions by 2.5 billion metric tons over the lifetime of vehicles sold from 2014 to 2029 (EPA and NHTSA 2016).

Achieving these goals will require a variety of innovations and investments by automobile firms that have been challenging thus far because emissions carry no price, consumers often undervalue fuel efficiency, and vehicle purchasers are not always the entities paying for the fuel.[20] These investments may unlock new technologies to further reduce transportation emissions. For example, firms with innovative low-emissions technologies may sell compliance credits or license technology to other firms, given the flexibility provisions in the vehicle emissions standards, providing an

---

[20] The lack of investment may be due to multiple market failures including from the unpriced positive externalities from innovation (Bergek, Jacobsson, and Sandén 2008).

Box 7-2: Investing in Clean Energy Research and Development

Research and development in clean energy is essential to climate change mitigation because improved technologies will reduce the cost of producing and distributing clean energy. The research and development (R&D) market failure from imperfect appropriability of innovations—in which innovations spill over to other firms and the innovative firm cannot fully capture the returns—is particularly important in early stage R&D because the private return to basic innovation is relatively low and the social return is high. The gap between social and private returns to clean energy innovations is magnified by the additional environmental externalities that private firms do not internalize (Nordhaus 2011). Since many clean energy technologies are in fledgling stages and require foundational developments, the R&D market failure leads to significant underinvestment in R&D for those technologies, suggesting a role for policy.

The Obama Administration has made significant investments in clean energy R&D. The American Recovery and Reinvestment Act directed a substantial amount of its $90 billion in clean energy funding to research and development. This included funding for the Advanced Research Projects Agency – Energy (ARPA-E) program, which funds clean energy projects that are in early innovation stages and have high potential societal value. ARPA-E's first projects were funded by the Recovery Act, and it has since sponsored over 400 energy technology projects. The Recovery Act set a precedent for continued investment in clean energy R&D; subsequent fiscal budget proposals have included significant funding to continue such programs.

The 2013 Climate Action Plan structured the Administration's continuing commitment to investment in clean energy R&D. Consistent with the goals of the Plan, the DOE's Office of Energy Efficiency and Renewable Energy (EERE) launched the SunShot Initiative, which funds solar energy R&D. The EERE Wind Program funds R&D activity in wind energy technologies, including offshore and distributed wind. EERE's Geothermal Technologies Office conducts research on geothermal systems in order to lower the risks and costs of geothermal development and exploration. Additionally, EERE supports R&D in cleaner transportation technologies through a variety of programs: the Hydrogen and Fuel Cells Program funds basic and applied research to overcome the technical barriers of hydrogen production, delivery and storage technologies as well as fuel cell technologies. The Bioenergy program supports R&D in sustainable biofuels, with a focus on advanced biofuels that are in earlier stages of development but can take advantage of existing transportation infrastructure by providing functional substitutes for crude oil, gasoline, diesel fuel and jet fuel. The Vehicles Technologies Office funds R&D to encourage deployment of electric cars by developing advanced batteries, electric drive systems and lightweight vehicles. These efforts combined represent billions of dollars invested in clean energy R&D.

Public investment in R&D helps correct for private underinvestment due to market failures and moves investment toward efficient levels, allowing for cost reductions in clean energy use. Clean energy technology costs have declined significantly since 2008, and the Administration's R&D investments supported this trend. More importantly, these investments will help to ensure that positive trends in clean energy penetration and greenhouse gas emissions reductions continue into the future, since the economic benefits of R&D—particularly in early stage innovations—accrue over a very long time horizon.

Source: Nordhaus (2011).

incentive for innovation.[21] Figure 7-4 shows fuel economy standards over time, including the major increase since 2008, and further increases projected through 2025.

In March 2012, the Administration launched "EV Everywhere," an electric vehicle Grand Challenge that seeks to make electric vehicles as affordable and convenient to own as gasoline-powered vehicles within the next decade (DOE 2012). Much of the focus of this initiative is to foster early-stage innovation, an endeavor that helps to address innovation market failures since the social return from such innovation is greater than the private return. EV Everywhere has already spurred dramatic technological and cost improvements in EV technology. In addition, since 2010, DOE investments through the Grand Challenge have contributed to a 50-percent reduction in the modeled high-volume cost of electric vehicle batteries, and DOE has invested in industry, national laboratory, and university projects that explore how to make EV batteries even more efficient and cost-effective (Brescher Shea 2014). Since the program's launch, hundreds of employers have joined the Workplace Charging Challenge pledging to provide charging access for their employees (DOE 2016f). These policies are examples of some of the incentives the Administration has implemented to support EVs; others include tax credits for purchase of electric vehicles, support for domestic electric vehicle battery manufacturing, and more than $6 billion in Recovery Act funds for programs to promote research and development of

---

[21] Economic theory and empirical evidence suggest that trading and other market-based approaches provide greater incentives for technological innovation than do prescriptive regulations that would achieve the same level of emissions reduction (Keohane 2003; Popp 2003).

advanced vehicle technologies (CEA 2016c). Much like owning a car was difficult until enough people had cars that gas stations were plentiful, the network effects of electric vehicles provide an economic case for a policy push supporting the necessary services to move the industry toward critical mass.

Reducing Emissions from High Potency Greenhouse Gases

To further help address the environmental externality from greenhouse gas emissions, the Administration has also developed policies to reduce the emissions of other potent greenhouse gases, such as hydro-fluorocarbons (HFCs) and methane. When the President launched his Climate Action Plan in June 2013, he pledged to reduce emissions of HFCs through both domestic and international leadership (EPA 2016b). Through actions like leader-level joint statements with China in 2013 and with India in 2016, the United States has led global efforts to secure an ambitious amendment to the Montreal Protocol to phase down HFCs. In October 2016, the 197 Parties to the Montreal Protocol agreed to amend the Protocol to phase down HFC use in developed countries beginning in 2019, and to freeze HFC use in developing countries in 2024, though some will wait until 2028 (UNEP 2016).

At the same time, the Administration has taken important steps to reduce HFC consumption domestically under EPA's Significant New Alternatives Policy, a Clean Air Act program under which EPA identifies and evaluates substitutes for industrial chemicals and publishes lists of acceptable and unacceptable substitutes. The Administration has also announced a suite of private-sector commitments and executive actions that are projected to reduce HFCs equivalent to more than 1 billion metric tons of carbon dioxide emissions globally through 2025.

The President has also taken steps to reduce methane emissions, which accounted for 10 percent of U.S. greenhouse gas emissions in 2014.[22] In January 2015, the Administration set a goal of reducing methane emissions from the oil and gas sector by 40 to 45 percent from 2012 levels by 2025, which would save up to 180 billion cubic feet of natural gas in 2025— enough to heat more than 2 million homes for a year. The Administration's commitment to this goal was reaffirmed and strengthened in March 2016 in a joint statement with Prime Minister Justin Trudeau of Canada, in which both countries pledged to reduce methane emissions from the oil and gas sector and to explore new opportunities for additional reductions. In May 2016, EPA finalized methane pollution standards for new and modified

---

[22] This is based on the U.S. EPA's emissions inventory, for which the most recent data are from 2014. More recent research suggests that U.S. methane emissions may be much higher than the estimates underlying EPA's 2014 inventory (Turner et al. 2016; Schwietzke et al. 2016).

Box 7-3: Building Resilience to Current and Future Climate Change Impacts

The Obama Administration has implemented many policies and actions to support and enhance climate resilience. For example, in 2013, the President signed an Executive Order that established an interagency Council on Climate Preparedness and Resilience and a State, Local, and Tribal Leaders Task Force made up of governors, mayors, county officials, and Tribal leaders from across the country. The Task Force developed recommendations on how to modernize Federal Government programs to incorporate climate change and support community resilience to its impacts. The Administration has responded to a number of these recommendations, for example, by implementing the National Disaster Resilience Competition that made nearly $1 billion available for resilient housing and infrastructure projects to states and communities that had been impacted by major disasters between 2011 and 2013. Government agencies have also provided additional support for Federal-Tribal Climate Resilience and support for reliable rural electric infrastructure. In addition, the Administration developed and launched a Climate Data Initiative and Climate Resilience Toolkit to improve access to climate data, information, and tools. A new Resilience AmeriCorps program was also established; through this program, AmeriCorps VISTA members are recruited and trained to serve low-income communities across the country by developing plans and implementing projects that increase resilience-building capacity.

The Department of Transportation (DOT) now includes improving resilience to the impacts of climate change as a primary selection criteria for its Transportation Investment Generating Economic Recovery (TIGER) grants, which provide $500 million in Federal funds to improve transportation infrastructure while generating economic recovery and enhancing resilience in communities (DOT 2016). Similarly, the newly created FASTLANE grant program includes improving resilience to climate impacts as a primary selection criterion. In 2014, USDA created Climate Hubs in partnership with universities, the private sector, and all levels of government to deliver science-based information and program support to farmers, ranchers, forest landowners, and resource managers to support decision-making in light of the increased risks and vulnerabilities associated with a changing climate.

President Obama has also used executive action to establish a clear, government-wide framework for advancing climate preparedness, adaptation, and resilience, and directed Federal agencies to integrate climate-risk considerations into their missions, operations, and cultures. As of 2016, 38 Federal agencies have developed and published climate adaptation plans, establishing a strong foundation for action (Leggett 2015). These plans will improve over time, as new data, information, and tools become available, and as lessons are learned and actions are taken to effectively adapt to climate change through agencies' missions and operations.

The Administration is developing government-wide policies to address shared challenges where a unified Federal approach is needed. For example, the Federal Government is modernizing its approach to floodplain management through the establishment of the Federal Flood Risk Management Standard (pursuant to E.O. 13690, Establishing a Federal Flood Risk Management Standard and a Process for Further Soliciting and Considering Stakeholder Input), in part to ensure that Federally funded projects remain effective even as the climate changes and flood risk increases. To promote resilience to wildfire risks, E.O. 13728, Wildland-Urban Interface Federal Risk Mitigation, directs Federal agencies to take proactive steps to enhance the resilience of Federal buildings to wildfire through the use of resilient building codes. E.O. 13677, Climate Resilient International Development, promotes sound decision making and risk management in the international development work of Federal agencies. Pursuant to E.O. 13677, the Department of the Treasury, the U.S. Agency for International Development, the Millennium Challenge Corporation, the State Department, the U.S. Department of Agriculture, and other Federal agencies with international development responsibilities have established guidelines and criteria to screen projects and investments against potential climate impacts, with a goal of making these investments more climate resilient.

In March 2016, the President signed a Presidential Memorandum: Building National Capabilities for Long-Term Drought Resilience with an accompanying Action Plan. Drought routinely affects millions of Americans and poses a serious and growing threat to the security of communities nationwide. The Memorandum lays out six drought-resilience goals and corresponding actions, and permanently establishes the National Drought Resilience Partnership (NDRP) as an interagency task force responsible for coordinating execution of these actions. These actions build on previous efforts of the Administration in responding to drought and are responsive to input received during engagement with drought stakeholders, which called for shifting focus from responding to the effects of drought toward supporting coordinated, community-level resilience and preparedness.

Sources: DOT 2016, Leggett 2015.

sources in the oil and gas sector, and the agency has taken the first steps toward addressing existing sources under forthcoming standards. EPA regulations promulgated in July 2016 will substantially reduce emissions of methane-rich gases from municipal solid waste landfills.

Promoting Climate Resilience

Even with all of the efforts to reduce emissions, the impacts of climate change are already occurring and will continue into the future. From an economic perspective, optimal responses to climate change would balance the costs of mitigation, the costs of adaptation, and the residual damages of climate change. Moreover, ideally, policies to encourage climate resilience would be informed by research on the degree of anticipated private investment in adaptation, and any anticipated gaps in such investment based on market failures or other factors. Relative to research on climate change damages and the impacts of mitigation, economic research on resilience is less developed, however, making it difficult to quantify the impacts of specific policies.

The economic literature suggests that some impacts of climate change, particularly the rise in extreme temperatures, will likely be partly offset by increased private investment in air conditioning (Deschênes 2014; Deschênes and Greenstone 2011; Barreca et al. 2016), and that movement to avoid temperature extremes, either spending more time indoors in the short run, or relocating in the long run, could also reduce climate impacts on health (Deschênes and Moretti 2009; Graff Zivin and Neidell 2014). Similarly, in the agricultural sector, farmers may switch crops, install or intensify irrigation, move cultivated areas, or make other private investments to adapt to a changing climate. Farmers are likely to make at least some investments that yield net benefits in the long run, though existing evidence is mixed regarding the likely extent and impact of private adaptive responses in agriculture (Auffhammer and Schlenker 2014; Schlenker and Roberts 2009; Fishman 2012). In terms of extreme events, countries that experience tropical cyclones more frequently appear to have slightly lower marginal damages from a storm (Hsiang and Narita 2012), suggesting some adaptive response. Recent work finds no evidence of adaptation to hurricane frequency in the United States, but significant evidence exists of adaptation for other Organization for Economic Cooperation and Development (OECD) countries (Bakkensen and Mendelsohn 2016).

Private adaptation measures are costly, and the extent to which they will mitigate climate impacts is uncertain. The costs of not enhancing resilience to climate impacts, though also uncertain, may be higher. From an economic perspective, building resilience to the current and future impacts of climate change—a critical component of the President's Climate Action Plan—is prudent planning and akin to buying insurance against the future damages from climate change and their uncertain impacts.

PROGRESS TO-DATE IN TRANSITIONING TO A CLEAN ENERGY ECONOMY

In recent years, the U.S. energy landscape has witnessed several large-scale shifts, with technological advances greatly increasing domestic production of petroleum and natural gas while renewable energy sources, particularly wind and solar energy, have concurrently seen a sharp rise in production. These shifts provide important context for the progress on decreasing greenhouse gas emissions, energy intensity, and carbon intensity. For example, renewable production provides zero carbon energy, while the rise in natural gas electricity generation, a relatively lower-carbon fossil fuel, has displaced some coal-based energy generation that had higher carbon content.

In the past decade, the United States has become the largest producer of petroleum and natural gas in the world (EIA 2016). U.S. oil production increased from 5 million barrels a day (b/d) in 2008 to a peak of 9.4 million b/d in 2015, which sizably reduced U.S. oil imports. More importantly for climate outcomes, U.S. natural gas production increased from 20 trillion cubic feet (Tcf) in 2008 to 27 Tcf in 2015. Both increases were largely due to technological advances combining horizontal drilling, hydraulic fracturing, and seismic imaging.

The U.S. energy sector has simultaneously undergone a transformation toward lower-carbon energy resources. The United States has both reduced the energy intensity of its economic activity and shifted toward cleaner energy sources, both of which have reduced emissions. This section documents the progress made to date in the transition to a clean energy economy and analyzes the contribution of different factors to that transition. The analysis considers the role of increased renewable energy production that provided additional zero carbon energy; increased energy efficiency that reduced energy consumption for a given amount of economic output; domestic natural gas production that reduced gas prices relative to coal; and shocks to the economy that affected the level of GDP, most notably the Great Recession.

Reduced Growth in Greenhouse Gas Emissions

Greenhouse gas emissions, dominated by carbon dioxide emissions, grew fairly steadily until 2008 (EPA 2016a). Since 2008, both carbon dioxide emissions and total greenhouse gas emissions have been declining (Figure 7-5). Although the economic downturn in 2008-09 certainly contributed, Figure 7-5 shows that emissions have declined since 2008, while GDP has risen after a drop in the beginning of the period. Figure 7-6 shows that the decline since 2008 in carbon dioxide emissions from the electric power sector, which made up roughly 30 percent of total emissions in 2014, has been particularly noticeable (EPA 2016a). In fact, carbon dioxide emissions from electricity generation in 2015 were the lowest since 1992, after peaking in 2007; and in the first half of 2016, carbon dioxide emissions from the U.S. energy sector were at the lowest level in 25 years (EIA 2016b).

The decline in emissions, which has continued even as the economy has recovered, largely stemmed from two major shifts in U.S. energy consumption patterns over the past decade: a decline in the amount of energy that is consumed per dollar of GDP and a shift toward cleaner energy. The amount of energy used to produce one dollar of real GDP in the United States, or the energy intensity of real GDP, has declined steadily over the past four decades and, in 2015, stood at less than half of what it was in the early 1970s (Figure 7-7). Since 2008, the energy intensity of real GDP has fallen by almost 11 percent (Figure 7-8).[23] Meanwhile, cleaner energy sources like natural gas and zero-emitting sources like renewables have increasingly displaced the use of dirtier fossil fuel sources. This shift has led to an even larger decline in carbon emissions per dollar of real GDP, which was more than 18-percent lower in 2015 than it was in 2008 (Figure 7-8).

The next subsections discuss these trends, followed by an analysis of how each trend contributed to the decline in carbon dioxide emissions.

Declining Energy Intensity

Total U.S. energy consumption has been falling—with consumption in 2015 down 1.5 percent relative to 2008. The fact that the U.S. economy is using less energy while continuing to grow reflects a decline in overall energy intensity that is due to both more efficient use of energy resources to complete the same or similar tasks and to structural shifts in the economy that have led to changes in the types of tasks that are undertaken. The continuation of these changes, which have been occurring for decades (Figure 7-7), is spurred by market forces, and the increasing efficiency in the use of energy resources is supported by energy efficiency policies.

This continual trend of declining economy-wide energy intensity was also predictable based on historical projections from the U.S. Energy

---

[23] The uptick in 2012 in Figure 7-8 is due to a number of early nuclear plant closures.

Figure 7-5

**GDP and Greenhouse Gas and Carbon Dioxide
Emissions, 2000–2015**

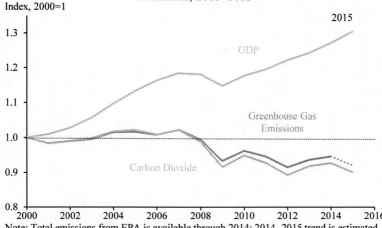

Note: Total emissions from EPA is available through 2014; 2014–2015 trend is estimated using change in CO_2 emissions from the energy sector from the EIA.
Source: Environmental Protection Agency, Energy Information Administration, and Bureau of Economic Analysis.

Figure 7-6

**Electric Power Sector Carbon Dioxide
Emissions, 1990–2015**

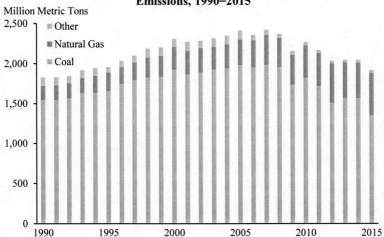

Note: Other includes emissions from the petroleum, geothermal, and non-biomass waste electric sectors.
Source: Energy Information Administration.

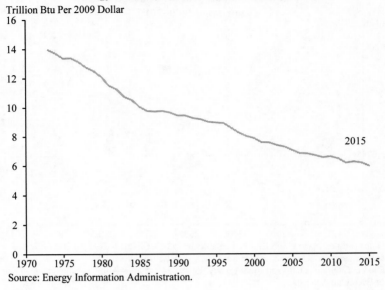

Figure 7-7
Energy Intensity of Real U.S. GDP, 1973–2015

Trillion Btu Per 2009 Dollar

2015

Source: Energy Information Administration.

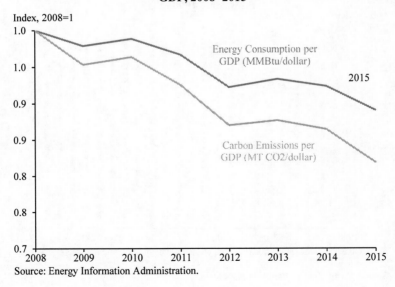

Figure 7-8
Carbon Emissions and Energy Consumption per Real U.S. GDP, 2008–2015

Index, 2008=1

Energy Consumption per GDP (MMBtu/dollar)

2015

Carbon Emissions per GDP (MT CO2/dollar)

Source: Energy Information Administration.

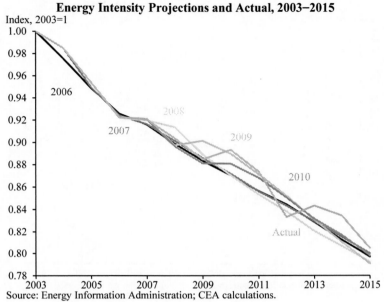

Figure 7-9
Energy Intensity Projections and Actual, 2003–2015

Index, 2003=1

Source: Energy Information Administration; CEA calculations.

Information Administration (EIA).[24] Figure 7-9 plots both the observed decline in energy intensity in the U.S. economy, as well as EIA projections of the decline in energy intensity going back to 2003.[25] Not only has the decline in energy intensity been relatively steady, but it has tracked closely with predictions. Changes in energy intensity come from policy as well as techno-logical and behavioral shifts. The fact that it has been predicted to decrease over time comes from assumptions that technology will continue to develop and policies will continue to encourage efficiency. With the extensive energy efficiency policies implemented by the Administration since 2009, EIA projects energy intensity to decline another 17 percent by 2025 (EIA 2016a).[26]

Although the aggregate energy intensity has been steadily and pre-dictably moving downward, aggregation masks differences across sectors of the economy. One notable example is the transportation sector, which has driven a decline in U.S. petroleum consumption relative to both recent levels and past projections.

---

[24] EIA forecasts do include existing policies, as well as finalized policies with impacts in the future that have been projected at the time of the forecast.

[25] Figures 7-9, 7-12, 7-13, and 7-14a to 7-14c use an index, with actual U.S. energy intensity in 2003 set equal to 1.0, and actual and projected energy intensity since 2003 expressed relative to that baseline. Projections use annual (negative) growth rates for energy intensity from the 2006, 2007, 2008, 2009, and 2010 EIA Annual Energy Outlook.

[26] Energy intensity (QBtu / GDP) metric is calculated from AEO 2016 reference case projections of annual energy use and GDP (EIA 2016a).

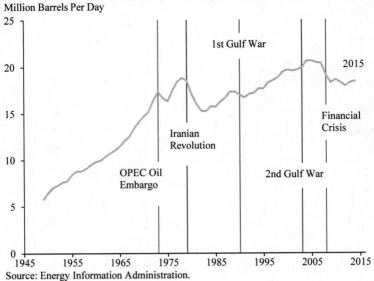

Figure 7-10
U.S. Petroleum Consumption, 1949–2015

Million Barrels Per Day

1st Gulf War

2015

Iranian
Revolution

Financial
Crisis

OPEC Oil
Embargo

2nd Gulf War

Source: Energy Information Administration.

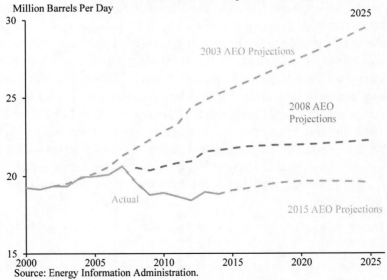

Figure 7-11
Total U.S. Petroleum Consumption, 2000–2025

Million Barrels Per Day

2025

2003 AEO Projections

2008 AEO
Projections

Actual

2015 AEO Projections

Source: Energy Information Administration.

Petroleum consumption was 2 percent lower in 2015 than it was in 2008 (EIA 2016b), while the economy grew more than 10 percent over this same period. In fact, petroleum consumption peaked in 2004, and the subsequent decline over the next several years surprised many analysts (Figure 7-10). The actual consumption of oil in 2015 was more than 25 percent below EIA projections made in 2003 for consumption that year. Moreover, the surprising decline in consumption relative to past projections is expected to grow over the next decade to 34 percent in 2025 (Figure 7-11). This trend through 2014 was primarily attributed to a population that was driving less and to rising fuel economy in the light-duty fleet.[27]

With this petroleum consumption surprise, the energy intensity in the transportation sector has declined beyond that which was projected by EIA in 2003, as seen in Figure 7-12.

In contrast, the residential sector showed less of a decline in energy intensity than was projected by EIA in 2003, and even than in some later projections (Figure 7-13). The actual residential energy intensity did decline substantially—likely due in part to energy efficiency standards—but sits above the level that was projected in most prior years for 2015. This greater-than-expected energy intensity in the residential sector may be due to factors such as new electronic appliances being plugged in, a slow-down of replacement of older appliances after the economic recession began in 2008, or a shift in preference for house size or energy consumption at home.

Energy intensity in the electric power and commercial sectors (Figures 14a and 14c, respectively) in 2015 tracked quite closely to prior projections. Actual 2015 energy intensity in the industrial sector (Figure 7-14b) was below what would have been predicted in 2003, though closer to later predictions.

Declining Carbon Intensity

While the energy intensity of the economy has continued a relatively steady downward trend, carbon intensity—carbon emissions per unit of energy consumed—has had a much more dramatic shift, relative to projections, in the past decade. Projections made in 2008 and in prior years showed carbon intensity holding relatively steady. However, since 2008, carbon intensity has fallen substantially and continues to fall—leading to revised projections nearly every single year. Figure 7-15a shows the observed carbon

---

[27] See CEA (2015b) for a more detailed analysis. In 2015-16, low gasoline prices have led to significant increases in vehicle miles travelled (VMT); VMT reached a 6-month record high in the first half of 2016. Since low oil (and thus low gasoline) prices are expected to continue at least through the end of 2016 (EIA 2016), the upward trend observed in 2015 may continue in 2016.

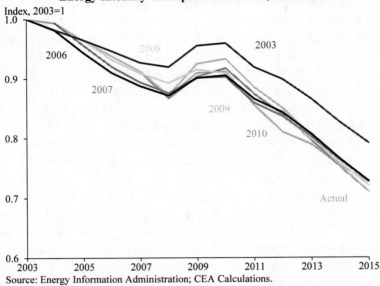

Figure 7-12
Energy Intensity Transportation Sector, 2003–2015

Source: Energy Information Administration; CEA Calculations.

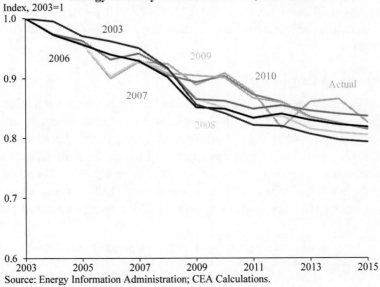

Figure 7-13
Energy Intensity Residential Sector, 2003–2015

Source: Energy Information Administration; CEA Calculations.

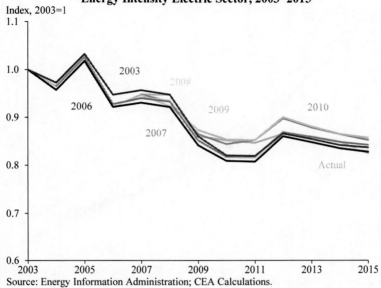

Figure 7-14a
Energy Intensity Electric Sector, 2003–2015

Index, 2003=1

Source: Energy Information Administration; CEA Calculations.

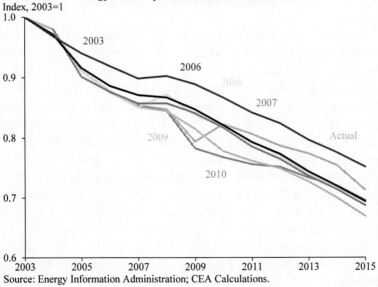

Figure 7-14b
Energy Intensity Industrial Sector, 2003–2015

Index, 2003=1

Source: Energy Information Administration; CEA Calculations.

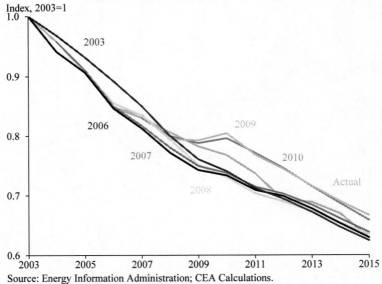

Figure 7-14c
Energy Intensity Commercial Sector, 2003–2015

Index, 2003=1

Source: Energy Information Administration; CEA Calculations.

emissions intensity of energy use in the U.S. economy, as well as several EIA projections. Beginning in 2008, these projections are all noticeably above the observed carbon intensity. Figure 7-15b shows that carbon emitted per dollar of GDP has also declined over this period, and that declines exceed predictions.

There are two primary reasons for the declining carbon intensity: a considerable shift to natural gas (a lower-carbon fossil fuel) and a remarkable growth in renewable energy, especially wind and solar.

The shift to lower carbon fossil fuels can be seen in Figure 7-16. Since 2008, coal and petroleum consumption have fallen 30 and 4 percent, respectively. Meanwhile, natural gas consumption has risen by almost 19 percent, with much of this increase displacing coal for electricity generation. This is due, in large part, to the surge in U.S. natural gas production discussed earlier. In fact, the share of electricity generation using natural gas surpassed the share produced from coal in 2015 for the first time on record (Figure 7-17). As natural gas is a much lower-carbon fuel than coal for electricity generation, this shift has contributed to lower carbon intensity.

Clean energy has undergone notable trends since 2008: electricity generation from renewable energy has increased, and costs of key clean energy technologies have fallen as there have been sizable efficiency gains in renewable energy. As seen in Figure 7-18, the share of non-hydropower renewables in U.S. electricity generation has increased from 3 percent in

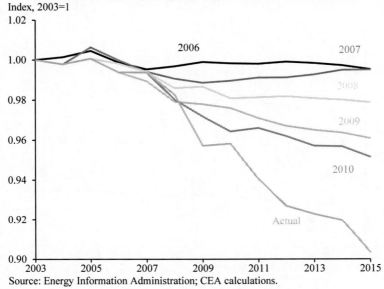

Figure 7-15a
Carbon Intensity Projections and Actual, 2003–2015

Index, 2003=1

Source: Energy Information Administration; CEA calculations.

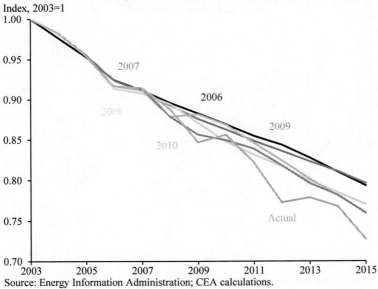

Figure 7-15b
Carbon Emissions per GDP Projections and Actual, 2003–2015

Index, 2003=1

Source: Energy Information Administration; CEA calculations.

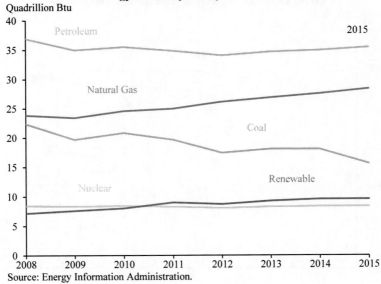

Figure 7-16
U.S. Energy Consumption by Source, 2008–2015

Quadrillion Btu

Petroleum

2015

Natural Gas

Coal

Nuclear

Renewable

2008 2009 2010 2011 2012 2013 2014 2015

Source: Energy Information Administration.

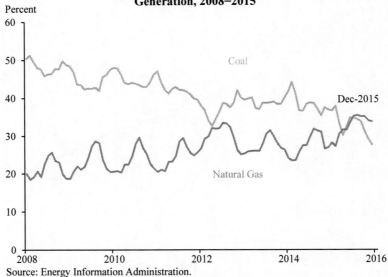

Figure 7-17
**Coal and Natural Gas Share of Total U.S. Electricity
Generation, 2008–2015**

Percent

Coal

Dec-2015

Natural Gas

2008   2010   2012   2014   2016

Source: Energy Information Administration.

Figure 7-18
**Monthly Share of Non-Hydro Renewables in Net Electric Power
Generation, 2000–2015**

Percent of Total Net Generation

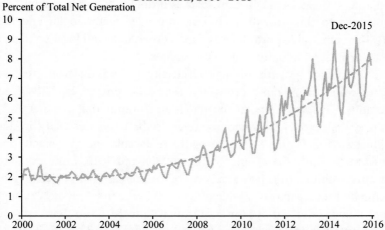

Note: Dotted line is a smoothed trend, shown to dampen the strong seasonal patterns (the
share of non-hydro renewables drops during the winter and summer-both seasons of high
power generation demand).
Source: Energy Information Administration.

Figure 7-19
Electricity Generation from Wind and Solar, 2008–2015

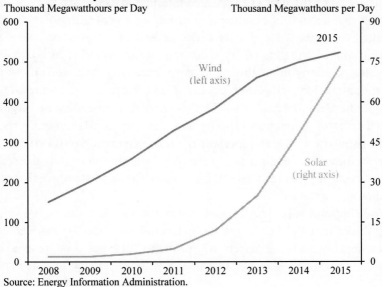

Source: Energy Information Administration.

2008 to 7 percent in 2015. Figure 7-19 shows that at the end of 2015, the United States generated more than three times as much electricity from wind and 30 times as much from solar as it did in 2008. Many factors have contributed to this growth, including improved technologies and falling costs, state renewable portfolio standards, other State and local policies, and the major Federal initiatives discussed earlier.

This rapid growth in new electricity generation from renewable sources comes from rapid growth in renewable energy capacity. Electric generation capacity refers to the maximum output that a generator can produce, while electricity generation refers to the actual electricity produced. As illustrated in Figure 7-20, non-hydro renewable energy capacity in the United States more than tripled between 2008 and 2015, from less than 30 gigawatts to almost 100 gigawatts. Most of the increase was driven by growth in wind and solar capacity, and deployments in the first half of 2016 suggest a continuing trend. From January through June 2016, no new coal capacity was installed; solar, wind and natural gas added 1,883 MW, 2,199 MW, and 6,598 MW of new installed capacity, respectively, over the same period (Federal Energy Regulatory Commission 2016).

One reason for increases in renewable electricity generation and capacity is the decline in the cost of renewable energy and other notable clean energy technologies. A common metric for comparing cost competitiveness between renewable and conventional technologies is the "levelized cost of electricity" (LCOE). The LCOE can be interpreted as the per-kilowatt-hour cost (in real dollars) of building and operating a generating plant over an assumed financial life and duty cycle. Several key inputs are taken into account when calculating LCOE, including capital costs, fuel costs, fixed and variable operations and maintenance costs, financing costs, and an assumed utilization rate for each plant type (EIA 2015). Because solar and wind technologies have no fuel costs, their LCOEs are highly dependent on estimated capital costs of generation capacity and can vary substantially by region. While using the LCOE as a measure of technology cost has drawbacks, and energy project developers may not always rely on this metric when assessing project costs, it provides a helpful benchmark for understanding changes in technology costs over time.

Wind and solar LCOEs have fallen substantially since 2008. Figure 7-21 shows that the LCOE for onshore wind technologies has decreased on average by almost 40 percent from 2008 to 2014, based on unsubsidized LCOE; that is, the cost of wind electricity without considering the benefits

Figure 7-20
U.S. Non-Hydro Renewable Energy Electric Power Sector Installed Capacity, 2008–2015

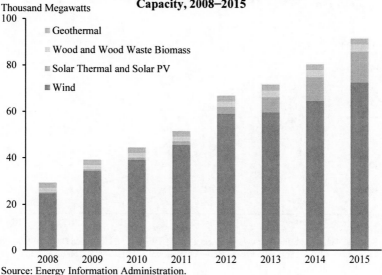

Source: Energy Information Administration.

from Federal tax incentives. Installation costs for solar PV have decreased by 60 percent, and LCOE for solar has fallen by almost 70 percent. [28]

In Figures 7-21 and 7-22, the measure of LCOE does not include local, State and Federal tax credits or other incentives for renewable energy. When these incentives are also considered, the cost declines described above mean that in many locations renewable energy costs are at or below the cost of fossil fuels. Renewables are truly reaching "grid parity," which means that the cost of renewables is on par with the cost of new fossil-generated electricity on the grid. Although wind and solar have been considered more expensive forms of new generation, current ranges of unsubsidized costs are showing some wind and solar projects coming in at lower costs than some coal generation. Further, forecasts show a trend toward increasing grid parity in the future. For example, forecasts for wind and solar PV costs from the EIA and the International Energy Agency (IEA) suggest that the unsubsidized technology cost of new wind and solar will be on par with or below that of new coal plants by 2020 (Figure 7-22).[29] Moreover, there are already places

---

[28] LCOE for wind is estimated by average power-purchase agreement (PPA) prices plus estimated value of production tax credits available for wind, and average PPA prices for solar PV.
[29] The larger bounds in costs for some renewable technologies, such as solar and off-shore wind, reflect a range of potential technology options that are being considering for future commercial deployment of these developing technologies.

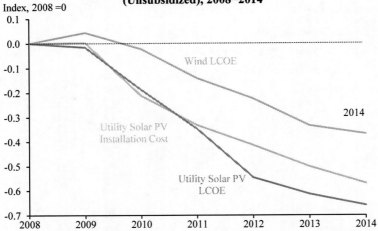

Figure 7-21
**Change in Costs for Onshore Wind and Solar
(Unsubsidized), 2008–2014**

Index, 2008 =0

Wind LCOE

2014

Utility Solar PV
Installation Cost

Utility Solar PV
LCOE

Sources: Wind: National Renewable Energy Lab, DOE (2015), Lawrence Berkeley National Laboratory (2014); Solar: Lawrence Berkeley National Laboratory (2015a), Lawrence Berkeley National Laboratory (2015b).

Figure 7-22
**Total System LCOE Comparison Across Generation Technologies
(Unsubsidized), 2020 Forecast**

2013 Dollars per Megawatthour

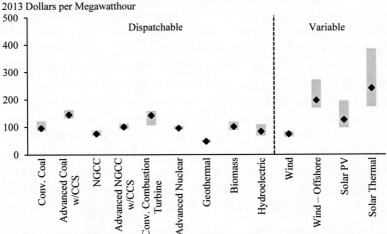

Note: Shaded region reflects minimum and maximum of range. NGCC is natural gas combined cycle. CCS is carbon capture and storage. PV is photovoltaics.
Source: Energy Information Administration.

in the United States where new wind and solar can come online at a similar or lower cost than new coal.[30] Note that EIA projections suggest that the unsubsidized LCOE for wind and solar will continue to be above that for natural gas (conventional combined cycle), on average across the United States, in 2018 and 2022 (EIA 2016a).

To better understand what is driving the declining carbon intensity, CEA estimates the portion of carbon intensity in electricity generation decline due to two factors: a reduced carbon intensity of fossil-fuel generation driven by a shift toward natural gas resources, and an increase in electric generation from renewable resources. To do so, CEA uses an analytical approach that develops estimates of counterfactual emissions holding constant the carbon intensities of the electric generating portfolio in 2008.

In particular, CEA first considers the case where the emissions factor associated with the portfolio of fossil-fuel electric generation; that is, the emissions per unit of energy generated from a fossil-fuel resource, in 2008 is held constant through 2015. As the emissions factor reflects the mix of resources in the fossil-fuel electric generating portfolio in 2008, this factor reflects the composition and efficiency of coal, natural gas, and petroleum generation resources in 2008. Applying this factor to the total electricity generated from fossil-fuel resources from 2009 to 2015 develops a counterfactual level of emissions had the portfolio of fossil-fuel resources remained constant in mix and efficiency over this time. Then, the difference between the quantity of emissions in the counterfactual and the observed emissions from electricity generated by fossil fuels during this time provides an estimate of emissions saved as a result of the reduction in carbon intensity of fossil-fuel electricity generation.[31] This reduction in carbon intensity is expected to stem primarily from increased natural gas generation, though would also include improvements in technical efficiency from fossil fuel resources. Much of the shift toward natural gas comes from rising supplies and falling prices of natural gas in the United States, though some may stem from policies that have aimed to account for and internalize some of the externalities of coal combustion.

Next, in a similar fashion, the analysis considers the emissions outcomes if the emissions factor from the entire portfolio of electricity generating resources in 2008 were held constant through 2015. The difference between these counterfactual emissions and total actual emissions from

---

[30] Wind: DOE (2015), Wiser and Bolinger (2014); Solar: Galen and Darghouth (2015), Bolinger and Seel (2015).

[31] This analytical approach holds fixed the observed kWh demand from fossil fuels and total power when estimating counterfactual emissions. To the extent that the shift to natural gas led to an increase in electricity demand, this approach would overstate the impact of coal-to-gas switching on reducing emissions.

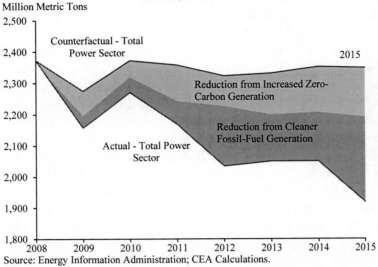

Figure 7-23
Decomposition of Emission Reductions from Power Sector, 2008–2015

Million Metric Tons

Counterfactual - Total Power Sector

2015

Reduction from Increased Zero-Carbon Generation

Reduction from Cleaner Fossil-Fuel Generation

Actual - Total Power Sector

Source: Energy Information Administration; CEA Calculations.

electricity generation would then represent the total avoided emissions from changes in the carbon intensity of the entire electricity portfolio. By subtracting total avoided emissions attributed to reduced carbon intensity from fossil fuel resources calculated as described above, the remaining difference between actual and counterfactual emissions can be attributed to an increase in resources with zero-carbon footprints; that is, an increase in the share of renewable energy resources.[32] For 2015, 284 million metric tons (MMT) (66 percent) of 428 MMT total avoided emissions was due to reduced carbon intensity from lower-carbon fossil resources, leaving 144 MMT (34 percent) attributable to increased generation from renewables. Figure 7-23 shows this decomposition from 2008 to 2015.

Decomposition of the Unexpected and Total Declines in Emissions

This section summarizes overall contributions to the observed emissions decline by decomposing reductions into those attributable to lower energy intensity, lower carbon intensity, and the difference from projections

---

[32] While this could include increased generation from nuclear power, the EIA shows that net generation from nuclear power remained fairly constant over the period, with an overall reduction in 2015 compared to 2008. Year-to-year fluctuations in nuclear or hydro power can affect annual changes in the contribution of non-carbon energy, but the overall result of significant contribution from non-hydro renewables over time is not altered by these sources, as both hydro and nuclear power saw small declines over the 2008-15 window.

Figure 7-24
**Growth Rates of GDP, Energy Intensity and Carbon
Intensity, 2008–2015**

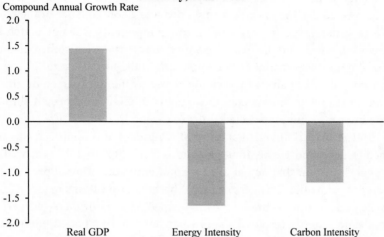

Compound Annual Growth Rate

Source: Bureau of Economic Analysis, National Income and Product Accounts; Energy
Information Administration.

on the size of the economy in 2015. The decomposition analysis follows the
methodology in CEA (2013), but with the added component of considering
emissions from both "expected" and "unexpected" trends. The emissions
considered in the analysis are energy-related carbon dioxide emissions,
which comprised 97 percent of U.S. carbon dioxide emissions and 83.6 percent of U.S. greenhouse gas emissions in 2014 (EPA 2016a).

As an initial step, one could simply look at GDP growth, energy
intensity, and the carbon intensity of energy production to see what has
influenced changes in emissions (Figure 7-24). Rising GDP, all else equal,
causes an increase in emissions, but the declining energy intensity of output (energy usage per dollar of GDP) and the declining carbon intensity
of energy (carbon emissions per energy usage) both pushed down on this
tendency of emissions to rise as the economy grows.

Alternatively, one can use expectations for the paths of these three
variables to understand what drove emissions relative to a reasonable
expectation in 2008. The general approach of this decomposition is to ask
the following: starting in a given base year, what were actual or plausible
projections of the values of GDP, energy intensity, and the carbon intensity
of energy out to the current year. These three values imply a projected value
for the current level of carbon emissions. Then, relative to this forecast,
what were the actual emissions, and what were the actual values of these

three determinants of emissions? If, hypothetically, the forecasts of energy and carbon intensity were on track, but the GDP forecast differed from projections because of the (unexpected) recession, this would suggest that the unexpected decline in carbon emissions was a consequence of the recession. In general, the forecasts of all the components will not match the realized outcomes, and the extent to which they vary—that is, the contribution of the forecast error of each component to the forecast error in carbon emissions—allows analysts to attribute shares of the unexpected decline in carbon emissions to unexpected movements in GDP, unexpected shifts in energy intensity, and unexpected shifts in carbon intensity.[33]

In the 2013 *Economic Report of the President*, this approach was performed to decompose emissions reductions from 2005 to 2012 (CEA 2013). The analysis found that actual 2012 carbon emissions were approximately 17 percent below the "business as usual" baseline projections made in 2005, with 52 percent due to the lower-than-expected level of GDP, 40 percent from cleaner energy resources, and 8 percent from increased energy efficiency improvements above the predicted trend.

CEA has completed this new decomposition approach in a similar fashion as in the 2013 *Economic Report of the President*, but over a different time frame: from 2008 to 2015 instead of from 2005 to 2012. In this decomposition, emissions in 2015 are compared to projections of emissions in 2015 made in 2008, based on the EIA's *Annual Energy Outlook* from 2008. Then, emissions reductions here can be seen as reductions above and beyond projections, or "unexpected" emissions reductions. As discussed above, energy intensity was projected to decline significantly over this time frame, and emissions reductions from energy intensity occurred largely as predicted. Thus, in this decomposition, energy intensity does not account for any of the "unexpected" emissions reductions, though it fell notably over the relevant time frame and contributed to realized declines in emissions. CEA's analysis suggests that 46 percent of unexpected emissions reductions in 2015 are attributable to a lower-than-predicted carbon intensity of energy, with the remaining 54 percent due to a lower level of GDP than projected in 2008. The role GDP plays in the decomposition largely reflects the fact that the major financial crisis and recession were not anticipated in early 2008, when EIA's projections were made. However, a larger-than-expected decline in carbon intensity also contributes substantially and reflects other

---

[33] Specifically, CO2 emissions are the product of (CO2/Btu)×(Btu/GDP)×GDP, where CO2 represents U.S. CO2 emissions in a given year, Btu represents energy consumption in that year, and GDP is that year's GDP. Taking logarithms of this expression, and then subtracting the baseline from the actual values, gives a decomposition of the CO2 reduction into contributions from each factor.

Figure 7-25
Decomposition of Total CO$_2$ Emission Reductions, 2008–2015

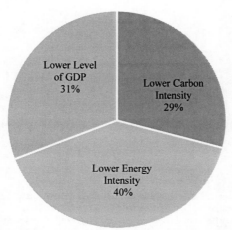

Source: Bureau of Economic Analysis, National Income and Product Accounts; Energy Information Administration, August 2016 Monthly Energy Review and 2008 Annual Energy Outlook; CEA Calculations.

developments in recent years (for example, the shifts toward natural gas and renewables discussed earlier).

Figure 7-25 takes the same decomposition approach using the forecast of 2015 GDP to determine a "GDP surprise" but considers emissions reductions in 2015 compared with observed emissions in 2008, rather than projections for 2015. That is, the projections hold energy intensity and carbon intensity in 2008 constant over the period from 2009 to 2015. In this manner, Figure 7-25 decomposes *total* emissions reductions since 2008 in a way that includes expected, as well as unexpected, movements in either energy intensity or carbon intensity.

Considering total emissions reductions compared with 2008, Figure 7-25 shows that 40 percent of total emissions reductions can be attributed to lower energy intensity, 29 percent to lower carbon intensity, and 31 percent to a lower level of GDP. The impact of lower energy intensity, while expected, was substantial.

To further understand the decline in emissions since 2008, CEA considers emission declines separately by sector—residential, commercial, industrial, and transportation—and decomposes total emission impacts from reduced energy intensity, reduced carbon intensity, and a lower level of GDP (due to unanticipated shocks, most notably the Great Recession) separately by sector. To perform the sector-by-sector analysis, CEA estimates

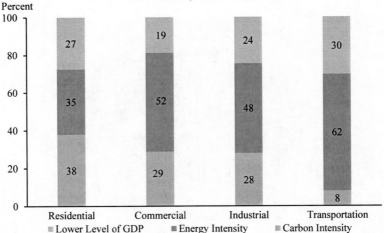

Figure 7-26
Sectoral Decompostion of Total CO$_2$ Emission Reductions, 2008–2015

Source: Bureau of Economic Analysis, National Income and Product Accounts; Energy Information Administration, August 2016 Monthly Energy Review; CEA Calculations.

the GDP contributions from each sector using data from the U.S. Bureau of Economic Analysis.[34] Then, CEA performs the same decomposition of total emissions reductions that was done for the economy as a whole in Figure 7-25.

Results of the sectoral decomposition analysis are reported in Figure 7-26. In the residential sector, a lower level of GDP, lower energy intensity, and lower carbon intensity each played a similar role in reducing emissions from 2008 to 2015. For the transportation sector, a majority of emissions reductions (more than 60 percent) were due to a decrease in energy intensity. This finding could reflect the impact of increased fuel efficiency from light-duty vehicle fuel efficiency standards implemented by the Administration over this time, though the analysis cannot establish a causal link.[35] Reductions in energy intensity also played important roles (48 to 52 percent) in emissions reductions from the commercial and industrial sectors, possibly reflecting shifts toward less energy-intensive industries. Any influence of Administration energy efficiency policies (such as, appliance standards) could also be captured here, though no causal link is established in this analysis.

---

[34] See the Appendix for more detail.
[35] Phase 1 of the first-ever medium- and heavy-duty vehicle standards, finalized in 2011, affected model years 2014-2018, so fuel economy standards for these larger vehicles could only have contributed to the energy intensity share at the very end of the period.

Lower carbon intensity also played a role in emissions reductions in the residential, commercial, and industrial sectors, responsible for 38, 29, and 28 percent of emissions reductions, respectively. In the residential sector, lower carbon intensity in regional electricity supply portfolios from shifts toward natural gas and zero-carbon energy resources would translate to reduced emissions from end-use electricity consumption. This impact would occur similarly for electricity-intensive commercial and industrial activities. Lower carbon intensity in the industrial sector could also result from substitution of lower-carbon natural gas for coal or oil in industrial processes.

How Administration Policies Meet Future Emissions Reductions Targets

In 2009, the President set a goal to cut emissions in the range of 17 percent below 2005 levels by 2020, a goal that was re-affirmed by the U.S. pledge at the 2009 United Nations Framework Convention on Climate Change (UNFCCC) Conference of the Parties in Copenhagen. Subsequently, in 2015 the United States submitted its target to the UNFCCC to reduce emissions 26 to 28 percent below 2005 levels by 2025. In the *2016 Second Biennial Report of the United States of America*, the U.S. presented results from an interagency effort to project the trajectory of GHG emissions through 2030, including the impact of U.S. policies and measures that have either been implemented or planned consistent with the Climate Action Plan. The report found that the implementation of all finalized, and planned, additional policies, including measures that at the time had been proposed but not yet finalized, would lay the foundation to meet those targets.

The estimates of U.S. GHG emissions take into account factors such as population growth, long-term economic growth, historic rates of technological change, and usual weather patterns. Projections for future emissions are modeled based on anticipated trends in technology adoption, demand-side efficiency gains, fuel switching, and implemented policies and measures. The report's estimates synthesize projected CO_2 emissions, non-CO_2 emissions, and CO_2 sequestration based on data from the Department of Energy, the Energy Information Administration, the Environmental Protection Agency, and the Department of Agriculture. The main source of uncertainty in emission projections is the range of land use, land-use change, and forestry projections, which approximate the ability of the land sector to remove CO_2 emissions from the atmosphere. The report therefore produces a range of projections using a set of modeling techniques from various agencies, which reflect differing perspectives on macroeconomic outlook, forest characteristics, and management trends. However, in part due to actions undertaken by the United States to bolster the forest carbon sink, the authors of the 2016 report believe that the United States is trending toward a more high-sequestration ("optimistic") pathway.

The report estimates two emissions projection scenarios. The first, the *Current Measures* scenario, reflects the impact of those policies and measures that have been established up to mid-2015. This includes, most notably, the Clean Power Plan, more stringent light-duty vehicle economy standards, recent appliance and equipment efficiency standards, and actions to reduce agricultural emissions and bolster our forest carbon sink. However, the *Current Measures* scenario does not include measures that were not final at the time of the publication, such as then-draft standards for oil and gas methane, phase two heavy-duty vehicle standards, and the five-year extension of tax credits for wind and solar. Therefore, the *Current Measures* scenario underestimates the full impact of policies undertaken under the President's Climate Action Plan. Under the *Current Measures* scenario, GHG emissions are projected to decline 15 percent below the 2005 level in 2020 with an optimistic land sector sink (Figure 7-27). The effects of policies implemented under the Obama Administration are clear when comparing the 2015 projections to the 2006 projections, in which emissions were expected to increase by about 20 percent above 2005 levels by 2020. Clear progress in driving down projected GHG emissions can be seen since 2010 and even since 2014. The 2016 projections mark the first time a U.S. Climate Action Report has projected GHG emissions to fall based on existing policies. This reflects the large number of policies implemented in the prior two years.

Also in the *2016 Second Biennial Report* is an *Additional Measures* scenario that includes measures consistent with the Climate Action Plan that were planned, but not implemented, when the Report was completed, such as policies to cut methane and volatile organic compound emissions from oil and gas systems, and a proposed amendment to the Montreal Protocol to phase down production and consumption of hydrofluorocarbons. The report estimates the impact of planned policies separately on emissions of carbon dioxide, hydrofluorocarbons, methane, and nitrous oxide. These estimates are synthesized and presented as a range due to uncertainty in policy implementation. The report projects that the *Additional Measures* scenario with an optimistic land sector sink will lead to emission reductions of at least 17 percent from 2005 levels in 2020, and 22 to 27 percent below 2005 levels in 2025 (Figure 7-28). Note that some of the policies included in the report as "additional measures" (for example, new GHG emissions standards for heavy-duty vehicles, and methane standards for new sources in the

Figure 7-27

U.S. Net Emissions based on Current Measures, 1990–2025

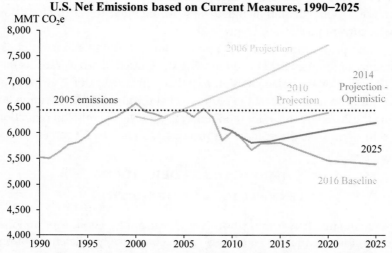

Note: The 2016 Baseline only includes policies finalized by mid-2015, so it underestimates the full impact of U.S. climate policies finalized under the Adminstration's Climate Action Plan through 2016.

Source: Department of State (2016).

Figure 7-28

U.S. Net Emissions, 1990–2025

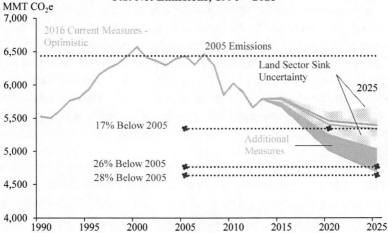

Note: Major policies included in this figure as "additional measures" such as heavy-duty vehicle standards and methane rules for oil, gas and landfills have been finalized in 2016, and would further decrease the 2016 "current measures" projection if included.

Source: U.S. Department of State (2016).

oil and gas sector) were subsequently finalized in 2016, as was an agreement by the Parties to the Montreal Protocol to phase down global hydrofluoro-carbon use (UNEP 2016). If included, these would move the 2016 projection below its current position in Figure 7-28.

These projections show that recent Administration actions on emission-reduction policies are already moving the United States toward its targets. The additional implementation of policies planned as of 2016 will put the economy on track to meet the 2020 target and will build a foundation for meeting the 2025 target. Under this scenario, this level of emission reduction will occur even while the economy is projected to grow by 50 percent.

AMERICAN LEADERSHIP IN INTERNATIONAL COOPERATION

As climate change mitigation is a global public good, international cooperation is essential for an effective and economically efficient solution. The President's ambition and dedication to addressing climate change have helped accentuate the United States' position as a global leader on this issue. On December 12, 2015, more than 190 countries agreed to the most ambitious climate change mitigation goals in history. The Paris Agreement entered into force in November 2016, 30 days after the date on which the required threshold (at least 55 Parties, accounting for at least 55 percent of global greenhouse gas emissions) was officially met. The Agreement establishes a long-term, durable global framework to reduce global greenhouse gas emissions where, for the first time ever, all participating countries commit to putting forward nationally determined contributions. The Agreement lays the foundation for countries to work together to put the world on a path to keeping climate warming well below 2 degrees Celsius, while pursuing efforts to limit the increase even more. The nationally determined contributions agreed to in Paris, though historic, will not halt climate change on their own, but the Paris Agreement provides a framework for progress toward that goal.[36]

In the lead up to the Paris Agreement in 2015, the United States worked bilaterally with many countries to build support for an ambitious agreement. Most notably, starting in 2013, the United States and China intensified their climate cooperation and, in November 2014, President

[36] Building on the historic Paris Agreement, in October 2016, 191 members of the International Civil Aviation Organization (ICAO) meeting in Montreal, Canada adopted a market-based measure to reduce carbon dioxide emissions from international aviation – aviation comprises two percent of global carbon emissions, but was not covered by the Paris Agreement. Like other aspects of climate change mitigation, reducing aviation emissions requires international cooperation.

Obama and President Xi made a surprise announcement of their countries' respective post-2020 climate targets. President Obama announced the ambitious U.S. goal to reduce emissions by 26 to 28 percent below 2005 levels by 2025, and China committed for the first time to implement policies leading to a peak in its carbon dioxide emissions around 2030 and an increase in the share of non-fossil fuels in primary energy consumption. Further, in September 2015, President Obama and President Xi reaffirmed their commitment to a successful outcome in Paris, a shared determination to move ahead decisively in implementing domestic climate policies, strengthening bilateral coordination and cooperation on climate change and promoting sustainable development. In addition to working closely with China, the United States worked hand-in-hand with a broad range of countries to increase support for international climate action and an ambitious agreement in Paris, including with Brazil, Canada, India, Indonesia, Mexico, small islands, and many others.

The United States has remained a leader in the global effort to mobilize public and private finance for mitigation and adaptation. Since the 15th Conference of the Parties (COP-15) to the United Nations Framework Convention on Climate Change in December 2009, the United States has increased its climate financing by fourfold for developing countries (Department of State 2016a). In November 2014, President Obama pledged that the United States would contribute $3 billion to the Green Climate Fund to reduce carbon pollution and strengthen resilience in developing countries, the largest pledge of any country. This strong U.S. pledge helped increase the number and ambition of other countries' contributions, and U.S. leadership helped propel initial capitalization of the fund to over $10 billion, a threshold seen by stakeholders as demonstrating serious donor commitment.

At the Paris Conference, Secretary of State John Kerry announced that the United States would double its grant-based public climate finance for adaptation by 2020. As of 2014, the United States had invested more than $400 million a year of grant-based resources for climate adaptation in developing countries, providing support to vulnerable countries to reduce climate risks in key areas including infrastructure, agriculture, health, and water services. The commitment that the United States and other countries have shown to mobilizing climate finance will help to support developing countries' transitions to low-carbon growth paths.

One of the most important components of the landmark Paris Agreement is that, by sending a strong signal to the private sector that the global economy is transitioning toward clean energy, the Agreement will foster innovation to allow the United States to achieve its climate objectives while creating new jobs and raising standards of living. The submission of ambitious national contributions in five-year cycles gives investors and technology innovators a clear indicator that the world will demand clean power plants, energy efficient factories and buildings, and low carbon transportation both in the short term and in the decades to come.

Another example of U.S. diplomatic leadership to drive global action on climate change mitigation is the Administration's work over several years toward an amendment to the 1987 Montreal Protocol to phase down the global production and consumption of hydrofluorocarbons, potent greenhouse gases. This work included the development of leader-level joint statements with China in 2013 and with India in 2015. In October 2016, the 197 Parties to the Montreal Protocol agreed to amend the Protocol to phase down HFC use in developed countries beginning in 2019, and to freeze and subsequently phase down HFC use in the vast majority of developing countries in 2024 (UNEP 2016). The agreement could avoid up to 0.5 degrees Celsius of warming by the end of the century, and it also provides financing to developing countries to help them transition to new air conditioning and refrigeration technologies that do not use HFCs.

The United States helped found the Clean Energy Ministerial, an ambitious effort among 25 governments representing around 75 percent of global greenhouse gas emissions and 90 percent of global clean energy investments. Through annual ministerial meetings (the United States hosted in 2010 and 2016), collaborative initiatives, and high-profile campaigns, the CEM is bringing together the world's largest countries, the private sector, and other stakeholders for real-world collaboration to accelerate the global clean energy transition. Twenty-one countries, the European Union, nearly 60 companies and organizations, and 10 subnational governments, made more than $1.5 billion in commitments to accelerate the deployment of clean energy and increase energy access at the June 2016 Clean Energy Ministerial.

On the first day of the Paris Conference, President Obama joined 19 other world leaders to launch Mission Innovation—a commitment to accelerate public and private global clean energy innovation. Twenty-two governments, representing well over 80 percent of the global clean energy research and development (R&D) funding base, have now agreed under Mission Innovation to seek to double their R&D investments over five years (Mission Innovation 2016). In addition, a coalition of 28 global investors committed to supporting early-stage breakthrough energy technologies in countries that have joined Mission Innovation (Bodnar and Turk 2015). The combination of ambitious commitments and broad support for innovation and technology will help ratchet up energy investments over the coming years, accelerate cost reductions for low-carbon solutions, and spur increasing greenhouse gas emissions reductions.

PLANS FOR THE FUTURE

Building on the progress discussed in this chapter in decreasing emissions and shifting toward a clean energy economy will require concerted effort over the coming years. Many of the policies and commitments begun by the President will have growing impacts over time, including several recently enacted policies mentioned above, as well as ongoing initiatives discussed below that form some of the next steps to continuing progress on climate issues. Also discussed below are some of the President's proposals for furthering clean energy goals that Congress has not yet acted upon, as well as potentially promising directions for longer-term climate policy.

On June 29, 2016 at the North American Leaders Summit in Ottawa, Canada, the President was joined by Canadian Prime Minister Justin Trudeau and Mexican President Enrique Peña Nieto in announcing the North American Climate, Energy, and Environment Partnership. The Partnership outlines several goals the three countries aim to achieve. Notably, a primary tenant of the Partnership is for North America to attain 50 percent clean power generation by 2025, including renewable, nuclear, and carbon capture, utilization and storage technologies, as well as demand reduction through energy efficiency. Each country will pursue these actions individually by establishing specific legal frameworks and clean energy national goals, tailored to each country's unique conditions. Additionally, the three countries aim to drive down short-lived climate pollutants, such as reducing methane emissions from the oil and gas sector by 40 to 45 percent by 2025. Other elements of the national methane emissions-reducing strategies could target key sectors such as waste management. To improve energy efficiency, the Partnership intends to better align and further improve appliance and equipment efficiency standards: North American neighbors plan to align six energy efficiency standards or test procedures for equipment by the end of 2017, and to align 10 standards or test procedures by the end of 2019. In order to advance integration of all clean energy sources, including renewables, the Partnership also strives to support the development of cross-border transmission projects that can play a key role in cleaning and increasing the reliability and flexibility of North America's electricity grid. At least six transmission lines currently proposed, or in permitting review, would add approximately 5,000 MW of new cross-border transmission capacity. The three economies will align approaches for evaluating the impact of direct and indirect greenhouse gas emissions of major projects, such as using similar methodologies to estimate the social cost of carbon and other greenhouse gases. In summary, the North American Climate, Clean Energy, and Environment Partnership Action Plan aims to advance clean and secure energy, drive down short-lived climate pollutants, promote clean and efficient transportation, protect nature and advance science, and show global leadership in addressing climate change.

In 2015, about 41 percent of U.S. coal was produced on Federally managed land, and this coal was responsible for about 10 percent of U.S. greenhouse gas emissions (BLM 2016a). The President's 2016 State of the Union address called to "change the way we manage our oil and coal resources, so that they better reflect the costs they impose on taxpayers and our planet." Three days later, Department of the Interior Secretary Sally Jewell announced the first comprehensive review of the Federal coal leasing program in over 30 years (DOI 2016). This announcement followed a series of listening sessions across the country in 2015, initiated by Secretary Jewell, to consider if taxpayers and local communities were getting fair returns on public resources, how the coal leasing structure could improve in transparency and competitiveness, and how the federal coal program could be managed consistently with national climate change mitigation objectives (BLM 2016b). The Department of the Interior has yet to complete its analysis of these issues. However, the current structure of the coal leasing program does not price externalities from coal combustion, and independent analysis by CEA concludes that it does not provide a fair return to taxpayers, making this review a crucial policy step from an economic perspective (CEA 2016a).

Through a Programmatic Environmental Impact Statement (PEIS) expected to be prepared over three years, the review will examine the Interior Department's current process to determine when, where, and how to provide leases and respond to feedback and concerns raised during the listening sessions as well as by the Government Accountability Office (GAO 2013). The review will inform how the Federal coal program can be reformed to ensure a fair return to American taxpayers for public resources while considering the environmental and public health impact of Federal coal production.

While the review is underway, mining will continue under existing leases, but the Department of the Interior will pause new leases, with some limited exceptions. This is consistent with practices under the previous two programmatic reviews in the 1970s and 1980s. The Department of the Interior also announced a series of reforms to improve the transparency of the Federal coal program, including the establishment of a publicly available database to monitor carbon emissions from fossil fuels on public lands and to increase transparency from Bureau of Land Management (BLM) offices regarding requests to lease coal or reduce royalties (BLM 2016b).

A transition to a clean energy economy means removing subsidies that encourage fossil fuel consumption and production, including the $4 billion in annual subsidies oil companies receive from taxpayers. The President called on Congress to end these subsidies (Slack 2012), and proposed eliminating inefficient fossil fuel subsidies in every budget he has submitted, with the Fiscal Year 2017 Federal Budget proposing to repeal $4 billion in subsidies to oil, gas, and other fossil fuel producers, as well as to expand the tax that supports the Oil Spill Liability Trust Fund to apply to oil sand crude oil. Following through on these proposals is a step toward avoiding a policy bias toward fossil fuel energy consumption and giving clean energy production a more level playing field. Given the climate externalities associated with fossil fuel use, subsidizing fossil fuel consumption or production means that not only are the externalities unpriced, but more fossil fuels are consumed than a pure market outcome even without considering the externalities. Removing the subsidies moves the incentives toward the efficient outcome.

Announced in 2016, the President's 21st Century Clean Transportation Plan seeks to improve America's transportation accessibility and convenience, while reducing the emissions intensity of travel. The President's plan includes $20 billion in additional annual investments to reduce traffic and improve accessibility for work and school trips by expanding transit systems, adding high-speed rail in major corridors, modernizing freight systems, and supporting the TIGER program, which provides grants for innovative transportation projects. The Plan also directs an additional $10 billion a year to support planning efforts by State and local governments to maximize the benefits of public investments. The funds will encourage land use planning and investments in infrastructure to support low-carbon transit options as well as the development of livable cities with resilient transit options. In addition, the Plan directs just over $2 billion a year toward the deployment of smart and clean vehicles and aircraft, supporting pilot deployments of autonomous vehicles, expanding the Diesel Emissions Reduction Act Grant Program, and investing in the safe integration of new technologies.

To fund these investments, the President proposed a $10 a barrel fee on oil, phased in gradually over five years. Revenues from the fee would provide long-term solvency for the Highway Trust Fund to maintain infrastructure, in addition to supporting new investments under the Plan. By placing a fee on oil, this policy would take a step toward ameliorating the current market failure that allows parties involved in emissions-generating activities to bear less than the full costs of that activity. Further, by directing revenues from the fee toward investments in a resilient and low-carbon transportation

Box 7-4: Supporting Increased Penetration of Variable Energy with Smart Markets and Storage

The two most rapidly growing renewable energy technologies, wind and solar, come with unique operating characteristics. The variable nature of their production profile creates new challenges for management of the electric grid, as compared to traditional generating resources with a more dispatchable output profile. For example, when considering the timing of output from wind and solar, the net electricity load, which is the demand for electricity less wind and solar generation, can exhibit a "duck curve"—where the low net load in the middle of the day ramps up quickly as the sun sets before trailing off as demand ebbs later at night—looking much like the neck, head, and bill of a duck. The figure below plots this curve for an illustrative spring day in California. We see that current levels of variable energy resource (VER) penetration begin to create this duck shape, increasingly so for future years, when VERs are projected to increase.

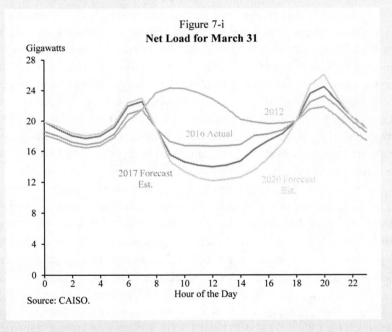

Figure 7-i
Net Load for March 31

Source: CAISO.

In addition to the unique net load profile created by variable renewable resources, wind and solar output exhibits more idiosyncratic variation as compared to traditional resources, a feature that also creates additional grid management needs.

As penetration of variable energy resources has increased across the country and the world, so too has the development of technologies and operational changes to increase the flexibility of the electricity grid. In addition to increasing transmission, larger balancing areas, and system operational changes, smarter markets and energy storage and management systems can also support the flexibility requirements created by increased use of VERs. Smart markets, which refers to communications technologies and approaches that facilitate end-user responses in the demand for electricity, can be leveraged to allow demand to adjust to the true current cost of electricity. Dynamic electricity pricing structures, as well as technology that facilitates end-user adjustment of demand such as smart appliances, support integration of VERs by increasing the incentives and ability of consumers to modify their own electricity demand. Further, the recent proliferation of smart markets infrastructure with the deployment of 16 million smart meters since 2010 (DOE 2016e), lays the necessary foundation for these resources to support grid integration.

Opportunities for energy storage to support integration are also rapidly expanding as the storage industry has seen dramatic cost reductions in the last decade from over $1,000 per KWh in 2007 to under $410 per kWh today (Nykvist and Nilsoon 2015). Storage technologies support grid integration by temporarily storing electricity for later use during times of grid stress, as well as storing variable energy produced for use later that might otherwise be discarded due to low demand.

Although analysts had previously claimed that variable energy penetration beyond 15 to 20 percent was not technically feasible (Farmer, Newman, and Ashmole 1980; Cavallo, Hock, and Smith 1993), instantaneous VER penetrations have already achieved high levels, with Texas hitting a record 45 percent of total penetration in March 2016 and Portugal running for four days straight on 100 percent renewables (wind, solar, and hydropower) (Electricity Reliability Council of Texas 2016, ZERO 2016). As more VERs increase the need and the value of grid flexibility, supporting the ability of smart markets and energy storage to provide grid integration services by ensuring that regulatory and electricity markets allow for the monetization of these resources will be critical to transition to an increasingly low-carbon grid (CEA 2016b).

Sources: CEA (2016b), DOE (2016e), Nykvist and Nilsoon (2015), Electricity Reliability Council of Texas (2016), ZERO (2016), Farmer et al. (1980), Cavallo (1993).

sector, the fee would incentivize private-sector innovation and investment in clean transportation technologies. A portion of the fee would also be directed to provide relief to vulnerable households.

In 2009, the President urged Congress to pass an energy bill that would have used market-based mechanisms to incentivize a clean energy transformation (Obama 2009). A bill with a proposed national cap-and-trade system passed in the House but was not voted on in the Senate (Walsh 2010). While over the President's terms the Administration has pursued a number of policies that indirectly price carbon-emitting activities, going forward, a widely held view across a broad spectrum of economists is that policies that put a direct, uniform price on carbon are the most efficient and comprehensive way to both meet the goals set forth in the Paris Agreement and to efficiently transition to a clean energy economy. Even with a comprehensive national carbon price, some additional Federal climate policies (such as investments in clean energy research and development) would likely still be efficient.

CONCLUSION

As discussed in this report, the costs of climate change are large, the impacts are being felt now, and they will intensify in the future. Further, delaying policy action designed to halt climate change will likely increase its costs. There is strong economic rationale for policies to address climate change based on both correcting a market failure from the negative externality produced by greenhouse gas emissions, and as a form of insurance against catastrophes caused by global warming. Since the President took office in 2009, the United States has taken numerous steps to both mitigate climate change and respond to its effects. The Administration leveraged a diverse set of policy mechanisms, from tax credits for renewable energy technologies to the first-ever greenhouse gas emission standards for vehicles and power plants, to pivot the nation toward a greener and stronger economy while recovering from the Great Recession. With the implementation of these policies, renewable energy technology costs have declined, and deployment of clean energy technologies has increased. With the implementation of Administration policies, and with a concurrent increase in supply and decrease in the cost of natural gas, the carbon intensity of our electric portfolio has decreased, and the overall energy and carbon intensity of the economy has declined. All of these changes in the U.S. energy system, favorable to climate change mitigation, have occurred while the economy has grown.

Although the progress made to date in transitioning toward a clean-energy economy since 2009 presents only a portion of the Administration's accomplishments in the clean energy and climate change space, the forward-looking policies established by this Administration, as well as proposals for further action, provide a pathway for the Nation to continue this transformation to a low-carbon economy that achieves future emissions reductions goals. Some of the progress made during the Administration's eight years is due to policy and some from technological breakthroughs and changes in natural gas production. To meet U.S. climate goals, it will be essential to build on this progress by achieving the emissions reductions projected from a number of policies that are just beginning to be implemented, and by taking further actions. The Administration's significant investments in clean energy research and development also help to ensure that the decreases in carbon intensity and energy intensity analyzed here will continue over the long run.

Finally, as climate change is global in nature, the 2015 Paris Agreement provides a critical missing link between domestic and international climate actions. Adopted by over 190 countries in December 2015, and officially entering into force in November 2016, the Agreement is the most ambitious climate change agreement in history, laying the foundation for a path to keep the global temperature rise well below 2 degrees while pursuing efforts to limit the increase even more. The United States set a goal of a 2025 emissions level in the range of 26 to 28 percent below 2005 emissions levels, and the goals set forth in the President's Climate Action Plan provide a path for the United States to uphold this commitment. However, the work is not finished. Continued efforts in upcoming years are critical to achieving these goals and transitioning to an energy system that incorporates externalities into energy production and consumption decisions, moving toward economically efficient outcomes that support the goal of global climate change mitigation.

Appendix: Detail on Sectoral Emissions Decomposition Analysis

In order to do the decomposition on a sector-by-sector basis, consider that each of the four sectors contributes to a portion of GDP. To approximate a sector's GDP contribution, each sector is matched to category in the National Income Product Accounts (NIPA), with matchings below. Then, the percent of GDP is calculated for each sector. To calculate 2008 baseline projections, this observed contribution percent is multiplied by forecasts of GDP made in 2008. This way, the difference between the actual versus the baseline of sector GDP mirrors the difference between actual and projected GDP. Performing this mapping for each sector allows for the same identity to be used to decompose emissions in the total economy as for the sector by sector decomposition.

The energy consumption and emissions included for each sector can be found in EIA glossary and documentation materials for the Monthly Energy Review (MER) Tables 2.1 and Tables 12.2 – 12.5.

Residential Sector

The account category used to approximate GDP contribution is the category for "Housing and Utilities", within Personal Consumption Expenditure - Services - Household Consumption Expenditures.

Transportation Sector

The account category used to approximate GDP contribution is the category "Transportation", within Personal Consumption Expenditures - Services - Household Consumption Expenditures.

Industrial Sector

The account category used to approximate GDP contribution is the category "Goods", within Personal Consumption Expenditures.

Commercial Sector

The account category used to approximate GDP contribution is the category "Services" within Personal Consumption Expenditures.

REFERENCES

CHAPTER 1

Blinder, Alan S., and Mark Zandi. 2015. "The Financial Crisis: Lessons for the Next One." Policy Futures Paper. Washington: Center on Budget and Policy Priorities.

Chodorow-Reich, Gabriel, et al. 2012. "Does State Fiscal Relief During Recessions Increase Employment? Evidence from the American Recovery and Reinvestment Act." *American Economic Journal: Economic Policy* 4(3): 118-45.

Congressional Budget Office (CBO). 2009. "Cost Estimate of the Conference Agreement for H.R.1 (The American Recovery and Reinvestment Act of 2009)." February.

_____. 2015. "Estimated Impact of the American Recovery and Reinvestment Act on Employment and Economic Output in 2014." February.

_____. 2016. "The Budget and Economic Outlook: 2016 to 2026." January.

Council of Economic Advisers (CEA). 2014. "Chapter 3: The Economic Impact of the American Recovery and Reinvestment Act Five Years Later." *Economic Report of the President.*

Council of Economic Advisers and Department of Labor (CEA and DOL). 2014. "The Economic Benefits of Extending Unemployment Insurance." Report.

Department of State. 2016. "Overview of the Global Climate Change Initiative: U.S. Climate Finance 2010-2015." Report.

Feyrer, James, and Bruce Sacerdote. 2011. "Did the Stimulus Stimulate? Real Time Estimates of the Effects of the American Recovery and

Reinvestment Act." NBER Working Paper 16759. Cambridge, MA: National Bureau of Economic Research.

Financial Crisis Inquiry Commission. 2011. *The Financial Crisis Inquiry Report*. Government Printing Office.

Furman, Jason. 2016a. "Demand and Supply: Learning from the United States and Japan." Speech at ESRI International Conference. Tokyo, Japan. August 2. (https://www.whitehouse.gov/sites/default/files/page/files/20160802_furman_esri_cea_0.pdf).

_____. 2016b. "The Economic Case for Strengthening Unemployment Insurance." Remarks at the Center for American Progress. Washington. July 11. (https://www.whitehouse.gov/sites/default/files/page/files/20160711_furman_uireform_cea.pdf).

Furman, Jason, and Peter Orszag. 2015. "A Firm-Level Perspective on the Role of Rents in the Rise in Inequality." Paper prepared for "A Just Society" Centennial Event in Honor of Joseph Stiglitz. New York, NY. October 16. (https://www.whitehouse.gov/sites/default/files/page/files/20151016_firm_level_perspective_on_role_of_rents_in_inequality.pdf).

Furman, Jason, and Krista Ruffini. 2015. "Six Examples of the Long-Term Benefits of Anti-Poverty Programs." Council of Economic Advisers Blog. May 11. (https://www.whitehouse.gov/blog/2015/05/11/six-examples-long-term-benefits-anti-poverty-programs).

Mishkin, Frederic S. 1978. "The Household Balance Sheet and the Great Depression." *Journal of Economic History* 38(4): 918-37.

Nicholson, Jessica R., and Regina Powers. 2015. "The Pay Premium for Manufacturing Workers as Measured by Federal Statistics." ESA Issue Brief 05-15. Department of Commerce, Economics Statistics Agency.

Reinhart, Carmen M., and Kenneth S. Rogoff. "Recovery from Financial Crises: Evidence from 100 Episodes." *American Economic Review: Papers and Proceedings* 104(5): 50-5.

CHAPTER 2

Aiyar, Shekhar, Christian Ebeke, and Xiaobo Shao. 2016. "The Impact of Workforce Aging on Euro Area Productivity." In *Euro Area Policies*,

IMF Country Report 16/220. Washington: International Monetary Fund.

American Bar Association. 2016. "National Inventory of Collateral Consequences of Conviction." Chicago. (http://www.abacollateral-consequences.org/).

Bernanke, Ben. 2013. "Semiannual Monetary Policy Report to the Congress." Testimony Before the Committee on Banking, Housing, and Urban Affairs, U.S. Senate. February 26.

Congressional Budget Office (CBO). 2013a. "The Economic Impact of S. 744, the Border Security, Economic Opportunity, and Immigration Modernization Act." June.

———. 2013b. "Macroeconomic Effects of Alternative Budgetary Paths." February.

Council of Economic Advisers (CEA). 2010. "Chapter 2: Rescuing the Economy from the Great Recession." *Economic Report of the President.*

———. 2015a. "A Better Measure of Economic Growth: Gross Domestic Output (GDO)." Issue Brief. July.

———. 2015b. "Chapter 5: Business Tax Reform and Economic Growth." *Economic Report of the President.*

———. 2015c. "Explaining the U.S. Petroleum Consumption Surprise." Report.

———. 2015d. "Long-Term Interest Rates: A Survey." Report.

———. 2016a. "Chapter 2: The Year in Review and the Years Ahead." *Economic Report of the President.*

———. 2016b. "Chapter 6: The Economic Benefits of Investing in U.S. Infrastructure." *Economic Report of the President.*

———. 2016c. "Industries and Jobs at Risk if the Trans-Pacific Partnership Does Not Pass." Issue Brief. November.

———. 2016d. "Labor Market Monopsony: Trends, Consequences, and Policy Responses." Issue Brief. October.

———. 2016e. "The Long-Term Decline in Prime-Age Male Labor Force Participation." Report.

———. 2016f (forthcoming). "Measuring the State of the Economy in Real Time." Issue Brief.

D'Amico, Stefania, et al. 2012. "The Federal Reserve's Large-Scale Asset Purchase Programs: Rationale and Effects." Finance and Economics Discussion Series 2012–85. Washington: Board of Governors of the Federal Reserve System, Divisions of Research & Statistics and Monetary Affairs.

Energy Information Agency (EIA). 2016. "Short-Term Energy Outlook." November.

Engen, Eric, Thomas Laubach, and Dave Reifschneider. 2015. "The Macroeconomic Effects of the Federal Reserve's Unconventional Monetary Policies." Finance and Economics Discussion Series 2015–05. Washington: Board of Governors of the Federal Reserve System, Divisions of Research & Statistics and Monetary Affairs.

European Commission. 2013. "Transatlantic Trade and Investment Partnership: The Economic Analysis Explained." Report. Brussels.

Ferreira, Fernando, Joseph Gyourko, and Joseph Tracy. 2012. "Housing Busts and Household Mobility: An Update." *FRBNY Economic Policy Review* November 2012. New York: Federal Reserve Bank of New York.

Feyrer, James. 2007. "Demographics and Productivity." *Review of Economics and Statistics* 89(1): 100-9.

Fischer, Stanley. 2016. "Why are Interest Rates so Low? Causes and Implications." Speech at the Economic Club of New York. New York. October 17. (https://www.federalreserve.gov/newsevents/speech/fischer20161017a.pdf).

Goodfriend, Marvin. 2016. "The Case for Unencumbering Interest Rate Policy at the Zero Bound." Paper prepared for the Federal Reserve Bank of Kansas City's 40th Economic Policy Symposium. Jackson Hole, WY. August 26. (https://www.kansascityfed.org/~/media/files/publicat/sympos/2016/econsymposium-goodfriend-paper.pdf).

Gordon, Robert J. 2012. "Is U.S. Economic Growth Over? Faltering Innovation Confronts the Six Headwinds." NBER Working Paper 18315. Cambridge, MA: National Bureau of Economic Research.

Ihrig, Jane, et al. 2012. "Expectations about the Federal Reserve's Balance Sheet and the Term Structure of Interest Rates." Finance and Economics Discussion Affairs. Series 2012–57. Washington: Board of Governors of the Federal Reserve System, Divisions of Research & Statistics and Monetary Affairs.

International Monetary Fund (IMF). 2014. "United States 2014 Article IV Consultation—Staff Report; Press Release." IMF Country Report 14/221. Washington.

_____. 2015a. "Chapter 4: Private Investment, What's the Holdup?" In *World Economic Outlook: Uneven Growth – Short- and Long-Term Factors*. Washington.

_____. 2015b. "World Economic Outlook, October 2015: Adjusting to Lower Commodity Prices." Washington.

_____. 2016a. "Regional Economic Outlook – Asia and Pacific: Building on Asia's Strengths during Turbulent Times." Washington.

_____. 2016b. "World Economic Outlook, October 2016: Subdued Demand: Symptoms and Remedies." Washington.

Johnson, Robert C., and Guillermo Noguera. 2012. "Accounting for Intermediates: Production Sharing and Trade in Value Added." *Journal of International Economics* 86(2): 224-36.

Joint Center for Housing Studies. 2015. "The State of the Nation's Housing." Report. Cambridge, MA: Joint Center for Housing Studies of Harvard University.

Leibenluft, Jacob. 2015. "The Budget Agreement Permanently Expands Important Tax Credits for Working Families." White House Blog. December 22. (https://www.whitehouse.gov/blog/2015/12/22/tax-agreement-makes-permanent-expansions-important-tax-credits-working-families).

Maestas, Nicole, Kathleen J. Mullen, and David Powell. 2016. "The Effect of Population Aging on Economic Growth, the Labor Force and Productivity." NBER Working Paper 22452. Cambridge, MA: National Bureau of Economic Research.

National Conference of State Legislatures. 2010. "NCSL Fiscal Brief: State Balanced Budget Provisions." Report. Washington.

Organisation for Economic Co-Operation and Development (OECD). 2015. "Chapter 3: Lifting Investment for Higher Sustainable Growth." In *OECD Economic Outlook 2015*. Paris: OECD Publishing.

_____. 2016. "Chapter 3: Developments in Individual OECD and Selected Non-Member Economies." In *OECD Economic Outlook 2016*, Issue 2. Paris: OECD Publishing.

Petri, Peter A., and Michael G. Plummer. 2016. "The Economic Effects of the Trans-Pacific Partnership: New Estimates." Working Paper 16–2. Washington: Peterson Institute for International Economics.

Polivka, Anne E., and Stephen M. Miller. 1998. "The CPS after the Redesign: Refocusing the Economic Lens." In *Labor Statistics Measurement Issues*, edited by John Haltiwanger, Marilyn E. Manser, and Robert Topel, pp. 249–89. Chicago: University of Chicago Press.

Somanader, Tanya. 2015. "The Bipartisan Budget Agreement: What You Need to Know." White House Blog. October 29. (https://www.whitehouse.gov/blog/2015/10/29/bipartisan-budget-agreement-what-you-need-know).

Summers, Lawrence H. 2014. "U.S. Economic Prospects: Secular Stagnation, Hysteresis, and the Zero Lower Bound." *Business Economics* 49(2): 65-73.

Vidangos, Ivan. 2015. "Deleveraging and Recent Trends in Household Debt." Finance and Economics Discussion Series Notes. April 6. Washington: Board of Governors of the Federal Reserve System. (https://www.federalreserve.gov/econresdata/notes/feds-notes/2015/deleveraging-and-recent-trends-in-household-debt-20150406.html).

White House. 2016. "Housing Development Toolkit." Report.

Williams, John C. 2016. "Monetary Policy in a Low R-Star World." *FRBSF Economic Letter*. August. San Francisco: Federal Reserve Bank of San Francisco.

Yellen, Janet. 2016a. "Transcript of Chair Yellen's Press Conference, September 21, 2016." Washington: Board of Governors of the Federal Reserve System. (https://www.federalreserve.gov/mediacenter/files/FOMCpresconf20160921.pdf).

Yellen, Janet. 2016b. "The Federal Reserve's Monetary Policy Toolkit: Past, Present, and Future." Washington: Board of Governors of the Federal Reserve System. (https://www.federalreserve.gov/newsevents/speech/yellen20160826a.htm#f20).

CHAPTER 3

Aguiar, Mark, and Mark Bils. 2015. "Has Consumption Inequality Mirrored Income Inequality?" *American Economic Review* 105(9): 2725-56.

Attanasio, Orazio, and Luigi Pistaferri. 2014. "Consumption Inequality over the Last Half Century: Some Evidence Using the New PSID Consumption Measure." *American Economic Review* 104(5): 122-6.

Autor, David H., Alan Manning, and Christopher L. Smith. 2016. "The Contribution of the Minimum Wage to US Wage Inequality over Three Decades: A Reassessment." *American Economic Journal: Applied Economics* 8(1): 58-99.

Bivens, Josh. 2015. "Gauging the Impact of the Fed on Inequality During the Great Recession." Working Paper 12. Washington: Brookings Institution Hutchins Center on Fiscal and Monetary Policy.

Blinder, Alan, and Mark Zandi. 2015. "The Financial Crisis: Lessons for the Next One." Policy Futures Paper. Washington: Center on Budget and Policy Priorities.

Bricker, Jesse, et al. 2014. "Changes in U.S. Family Finances from 2010 to 2013: Evidence from the Survey of Consumer Finances." *Federal Reserve Bulletin* 100(4): 1-41.

Centers for Medicare and Medicaid Services (CMS). 2015. "2015 Actuarial Report on the Financial Outlook for Medicaid." Report to Congress. Department of Health and Human Services.

Chetty, Raj, John N. Friedman, and Jonah E. Rockoff. 2011. "New Evidence on the Long-Term Impacts of Tax Credits." IRS Statistics of Income Paper Series. Internal Revenue Service.

Chetty, Raj, and Nathaniel Hendren. 2015. "The Impacts of Neighborhoods on Intergenerational Mobility: Childhood Exposure Effects and County-Level Estimates." Harvard University: Department of Economics. (http://www.equality-of-opportunity.org/images/nbhds_paper.pdf).

Chetty, Raj, Nathaniel Hendren, and Lawrence Katz. 2016. "The Effects of Exposure to Better Neighborhoods on Children: New Evidence from the Moving to Opportunity Experiment." *American Economic Review* 106(4): 855-902.

Chetty, Raj, et al. 2014. "Where is the land of Opportunity? The Geography of Intergenerational Mobility in the United States." *The Quarterly Journal of Economics* 129(4): 1553-1623.

Chetty, Raj, et al. 2016. "The Association Between Income and Life Expectancy in the United States, 2001-2014." *Journal of the American Medical Association* 315(16): 1750-66.

Coibion, Olivier, et al. 2016. "Innocent Bystanders? Monetary Policy and Inequality in the U.S." Working Paper. (http://eml.berkeley.edu/~ygorodni/CGKS_inequality.pdf).

Congressional Budget Office (CBO). 2016a. "Federal Subsidies for Health Insurance Coverage for People Under Age 65: 2016-2026." March.

_____. 2016b. "The Distribution of Household Income and Federal Taxes, 2013." June.

_____. 2016c. "Trends in Family Wealth, 1989 to 2013." August.

Council of Economic Advisers (CEA). 2014a. "Chapter 3: The Economic Impact of the American Recovery and Reinvestment Act Five Years Later." *Economic Report of the President.*

_____. 2014b. "The Economics of Early Childhood Investments." Report.

_____. 2014c. "The Economics of Paid and Unpaid Leave." Report.

_____. 2015. "Chapter 1: Middle-Class Economics: The Role of Productivity, Inequality, and Participation." *Economic Report of the President.*

_____. 2016a. "Chapter 4: Inequality in Early Childhood and Effective Public Policy Interventions." *Economic Report of the President.*

_____. 2016b. "The State of the Gender Pay Gap." Issue Brief. June.

Council of Economic Advisers and Department of Labor (CEA and DOL). 2013. "The Economic Benefits of Extending Unemployment Insurance." Report.

Crandall-Hollick, Margot L. 2016. "The Earned Income Tax Credit (EITC): An Economic Analysis." CRS Report prepared for Members and Committees of Congress. Congressional Research Service.

Currie, Janet, and Hannes Schwandt. 2016. "Mortality Inequality: The Good News from a County-Level Approach." *Journal of Economic Perspectives* 30(2): 29-52.

Dahl, Gordon B., and Lance Lochner. 2012. "The Impact of Family Income on Child Achievement: Evidence from the Earned Income Tax Credit." *American Economic Review* 102(5): 1927-56.

Dowd, Tim, and John B. Horowitz. 2011. "Income Mobility and the Earned Income Tax Credit: Short-Term Safety Net or Long-Term Income Support." *Public Finance Review* 39(5): 619-52.

Dussault, Nicole, Maxim Pinkovskiy, and Basit Zafar. 2016. "Is Health Insurance Good for Your Financial Health?" Liberty Street Economics Blog. Federal Reserve Bank of New York. June 6. (http://libertystreeteconomics.newyorkfed.org/2016/06/is-health-insurance-good-for-your-financial-health.html#.V8-1BvlrjX4).

Finkelstein, Amy, Nathaniel Hendren, and Erzo F.P. Luttmer. 2015. "The Value of Medicaid: Interpreting Results from the Oregon Health Insurance Experiment." NBER Working Paper 21308. Cambridge, MA: National Bureau of Economic Research.

Furman, Jason. 2015. "It Could Have Happened Here: The Policy Response That Helped Prevent a Second Great Depression." Speech at the Macroeconomic Advisers' 25th Annual Washington Policy Seminar. Washington. September 9. (https://www.whitehouse.gov/sites/default/files/page/files/jason_furman_._it_could_have_happened_here_._macro_advisers_._9_sep_2015.pdf).

Furman, Jason, and Matt Fiedler. 2014. "2014 Has Seen Largest Coverage Gains in Four Decades, Putting the Uninsured Rate at or Near Historic Lows." Council of Economic Advisers Blog. December 8. (https://www.whitehouse.gov/blog/2014/12/18/2014-has-seen-largest-coverage-gains-four-decades-putting-uninsured-rate-or-near-his).

Furman, Jason, and Krista Ruffini. 2015. "Six Examples of the Long-Term Benefits of Anti-Poverty Programs." Council of Economic Advisers Blog. May 11. (https://www.whitehouse.gov/blog/2015/05/11/six-examples-long-term-benefits-anti-poverty-programs).

Holahan, John, et al. 1993. "Explaining the Recent Growth in Medicaid Spending." *Health Affairs* 12(3): 177-93.

Hoynes, Hilary, Douglas Miller, and David Simon. 2015. "Income, the Earned Income Tax Credit, and Infant Health." *American Economic Journal: Economic Policy* 7(1): 172-211.

Hu, Luojia, et al. 2016. "The Effect of the Patient Protection and Affordable Care Act Medicaid Expansions on Financial Well-Being."

NBER Working Paper 22170. Cambridge, MA: National Bureau of Economic Research.

Manoli, Dayanand, and Nicholas Turner. 2016. "Nudges and Learning: Evidence from Informational Interventions for Low-Income Taxpayers." NBER Working Paper 20718. Cambridge, MA: National Bureau of Economic Research.

Marr, Chuck, and Bryann Dasilva. 2016. "Childless Adults Are Lone Group Taxed Into Poverty." Washington: Center on Budget and Policy Priorities. (http://www.cbpp.org/research/federal-tax/childless-adults-are-lone-group-taxed-into-poverty).

Marr, Chuck, Bryann Dasilva, and Arloc Sherman. 2015. "16 Million People Will Fall Into or Deeper Into Poverty If Key Provisions of Working-Family Tax Credits Expire." Washington: Center on Budget and Policy Priorities. (http://www.cbpp.org/research/federal-tax/16-million-people-will-fall-into-or-deeper-into-poverty-if-key-provisions-of).

Mishel, Lawrence, and Jessica Schieder (EPI). 2016. "Stock market headwinds meant less generous year for some CEOs." Report. Washington: Economic Policy Institute.

National Center for Education Statistics (NCES). 2015. "Table 219.75. Percentage of high school dropouts among persons 16 to 24 years old (status dropout rate), by income level, and percentage distribution of status dropouts, by labor force status and years of school completed: 1970 through 2014." Digest of Education Statistics. Department of Education. (http://nces.ed.gov/programs/digest/d15/tables/dt15_219.75.asp).

Obama, Barack. 2016. "United States Health Care Reform: Progress to Date and Next Steps." *Journal of the American Medical Association* 316(5): 525-32.

Proctor, Bernadette D., Jessica L. Semega, and Melissa A. Kollar. 2016. "Income, Poverty, and Health Insurance Coverage in the United States: 2015." Report P60-256. September. Census Bureau.

Rank, Mark R., and Thomas A. Hirschl. 2015. "The Likelihood of Experiencing Relative Poverty over the Life Course." *PLoS One* 10(7): 1-11.

Shartzer, Adele, Sharon K. Long, and Nathaniel Anderson. 2015. "Access To Care And Affordability Have Improved Following Affordable

Care Act Implementation; Problems Remain." *Health Affairs* 35(1): 161-8.

Sommers, Benjamin D., Katherine Baicker, and Arnold M. Epstein. 2012. "Mortality and Access to Care among Adults after State Medicaid Expansions." *New England Journal of Medicine* 367(11): 1025-34.

Sommers, Benjamin D., Sharon K. Long, and Katherine Baicker. 2014. "Changes in Mortality After Massachusetts Health Care Reform." *Annals of Internal Medicine* 160(9): 585-93.

Sommers, Benjamin D., et al. 2016. "Changes in Utilization and Health Among Low-Income Adults After Medicaid Expansion or Expanded Private Insurance." *Journal of the American Medical Association Internal Medicine* 176(10): 1501-9.

Sommers, Benjamin D., et al. 2015. "Changes in Self-reported Insurance Coverage, Access to Care, and Health Under the Affordable Care Act." *Journal of the American Medical Association* 314(4): 366-74.
Uberoi, Namrata, Kenneth Finegold, and Emily Gee. 2016. "Health Insurance Coverage and the Affordable Care Act, 2010–2016." ASPE Issue Brief. Department of Health and Human Services.

U.S. Treasury, Office of Economic Policy. 2009. "The Risk of Losing Health Insurance Over a Decade: New Findings from Longitudinal Data."

Chapter 4

Adler, Loren, and Paul B. Ginsburg. 2016. "Obamacare Premiums are Lower Than You Think." Health Affairs Blog. (http://healthaffairs.org/blog/2016/07/21/obamacare-premiums-are-lower-than-you-think/).

Agency for Healthcare Research and Quality (AHRQ). 2015. "Saving Lives and Saving Money: Hospital-Acquired Conditions Update: Interim Data From National Efforts To Make Care Safer, 2010-2014." AHRQ Publication 16-0009-EF.

AHIP Center for Policy Research (AHIP). 2009. "Individual Health Insurance 2009: A Comprehensive Survey of Premiums, Availability, and Benefits." Report. Washington.

Aitken, Murray, Ernst R. Berndt, and David M. Cutler. 2009. "Prescription Drug Spending Trends in the United States: Looking Beyond the Turning Point." *Health Affairs* 28(1): w151-w160.

American Hospital Association and Health Research & Educational Trust Hospital Engagement Network (AHA/HRET). 2014. "Partnerships for Patients Hospital Engagement Network: Final Report." Chicago. (http://www.hret-hen.org/about/hen/2014-FinalReport508.pdf).

Anderson, Gerard. F., et al. 2003. "It's the Prices, Stupid: Why the United States Is So Different from Other Countries." *Health Affairs* 22(3): 89-105.

Antwi, Yaa Akosa, Asako S. Moriya, and Kosali Simon. 2013. "Effects of Federal Policy to Insure Young Adults: Evidence from the 2010 Affordable Care Act's Dependent-Coverage Mandate." *American Economic Journal: Economic Policy* 5(4): 1-28.

Assistant Secretary for Planning and Evaluation (ASPE). 2011. "At Risk: Pre-Existing Conditions Could Affect 1 in 2 Americans: 129 Million People Could Be Denied Affordable Coverage Without Health Reform." Report. January. Department of Health and Human Services.

_____. 2015. "Health Insurance Coverage and the Affordable Care Act." Report. May. Department of Health and Human Services.

_____. 2016a. "About 2.5 Million People Who Currently Buy Coverage Off-Marketplace May be Eligible for ACA Subsidies." ASPE Data Point. October. Department of Health and Human Services.

_____. 2016b. "Health Plan Choice and Premiums in the 2017 Health Insurance Marketplace." Report. October. Department of Health and Human Services.

_____. 2016c. "Observations on Trends in Prescription Drug Spending." ASPE Issue Brief. March. Department of Health and Human Services.

Avalere Health. 2016. "The State of Exchanges: A Review of Trends and Opportunities to Grow and Stabilize the Market." Report. Washington.

Baicker, Katherine, and Amitabh Chandra. 2006. "The Labor Market Effects of Rising Health Insurance Premiums." *Journal of Labor Economics* 24(3): 463-75.

Baicker, Katherine, Sendhil Mullainathan, and Joshua Schwartzstein. 2015. "Behavioral Hazard in Health Insurance." *The Quarterly Journal of Economics* 130(4): 1623-67.

Baicker, Katherine, et al. 2013. "The Oregon Experiment – Effects of Medicaid on Clinical Outcomes." *New England Journal of Medicine* 368(18): 1713-22.

Baker, Laurence C., M. Kate Bundorf, and Daniel P. Kessler. 2015. "Does Health Plan Generosity Enhance Market Power?" NBER Working Paper 21513. Cambridge, MA: National Bureau of Economic Research.

Barbaresco, Silvia, Charles J. Courtemanche, Yanling Qi. 2015. "Impacts of the Affordable Care Act Dependent Coverage Provision on Health-Related Outcomes of Young Adults." *Journal of Health Economics* 40(C): 54-68.

Blavin, Frederic. 2016. "Association Between the 2014 Medicaid Expansion and US Hospital Finances." *Journal of the American Medical Association* 316(14): 1475-83.

Blavin, Frederic, Genevieve M. Kenney, and Michael Huntress. 2014. "The Effects of Express Lane Eligibility on Medicaid and CHIP Enrollment among Children." *Health Services Research* 49(4): 1268-89.

Blumberg, Linda J., Bowen Garret, and John Holahan. 2016. "Estimating the Counterfactual: How Many Uninsured Adults Would There Be Today Without the ACA?" *INQUIRY: The Journal of Health Care* 53: 1-13.

Brown, David W., Amanda E. Kowalski, and Ithai Z. Lurie. 2015. "Medicaid as an Investment in Children: What Is the Long-Term Impact on Tax Receipts?" NBER Working Paper 20835. Cambridge, MA: National Bureau of Economic Research.

Buettgens, Matthew, Stan Dorn, and Caitlin Carroll. 2011. "Consider Savings as Well as Cost: State Governments Would Spent at Least $90 Billion Less with the ACA than Without It from 2014 to 2019." Report. *Timely Analysis of Immediate Health Policy Issues.* Washington: Urban Institute, and Princeton: Robert Wood Johnson Foundation.

Buntin, Melinda B., et al. 2011. "The Benefits Of Health Information Technology: A Review of the Recent Literature Shows Predominantly Positive Results." *Health Affairs* 30(3): 467-71.

Cannon, Michael F. 2014. "Should Virginia Expand Medicaid?" Testimony Before the Medicaid Innovation and Reform Commission. April 7. Richmond, VA.

Cantor, Joel C., et al. 2012. "Early Impact of the Affordable Care Act on Health Insurance Coverage of Young Adults." *Health Services Research* 47(5): 1773-90.

Card, David, Carlos Dobkin, and Nicole Maestas. 2009. "Does Medicare Save Lives?" *Quarterly Journal of Economics* 124(2): 597-636.

Carlin, Caroline S., Angela R. Fertig, and Bryan E. Dowd. 2016. "Affordable Care Act's Mandate Eliminating Contraceptive Cost Sharing Influenced Choices of Women with Employer Coverage." *Health Affairs* 35(9): 1608-15.

Carpenter, Christopher, and Phillip J. Cook. 2008. "Cigarette Taxes and Youth Smoking: New Evidence from National, State and Local Youth Risk Behavior Surveys." *Journal of Health Economics* 27(2): 287-99.

Centers for Medicare and Medicaid Services (CMS). 2016a. "Changes in ACA Individual Market Costs from 2014-2015: Near-Zero Growth Suggests an Improving Risk Pool." August 11. Department of Health and Human Services.

_____. 2016b. "Medicare Advantage premiums remain stable in 2017; beneficiaries have saved over $23.5 billion on prescription drugs." Press Release. (https://www.cms.gov/Newsroom/MediaReleaseDatabase/Press-releases/2016-Press-releases-items/2016-09-22.html).

_____. 2016c. "Medicare Program; CY 2017 Inpatient Hospital Deductible and Hospital and Extended Care Services Coinsurance Amounts." *Federal Register* Nov 15, 2016, 81 FR 80060, p. 80060-3.

_____. 2016d. "More than 10 million people with Medicare have saved over $20 billion on prescription drugs since 2010." Press Release. February 8. Department of Health and Human Services. (https://www.cms.gov/Newsroom/MediaReleaseDatabase/Press-releases/2016-Press-releases-items/2016-02-08.html).

Chandra, Amitabh, Jonathan Holmes, and Jonathan Skinner. 2013. "Is this Time Different? The Slowdown in Health Care Spending." *Brookings Papers on Economic Activity*. Washington: Brookings Institution.

Chernew, Michael E., et al. 2010. "Geographic Correlation Between Large-Firm Commercial Spending and Medicare Spending." *American Journal of Managed Care* 16(2): 131-8.

Claxton, Gary, Larry Levitt, and Michelle Long. 2016. "Payments for cost sharing increasing rapidly over time." Insight Brief. April 12. Peterson-Kaiser Health System Tracker. (http://www.healthsystemtracker.org/insight/payments-for-cost-sharing-increasing-rapidly-over-time/).

Clemens, Jeffrey, and Joshua D. Gottlieb. Forthcoming. "In the Shadow of a Giant: Medicare's Influence on Private Physician Payments." Working Paper. (http://www.joshuagottlieb.ca/ShadowOfAGiant.pdf).

Clemens, M. Kent, Joseph M. Lizonitz, and Suguna M. Murugesan. 2009. "Projected Medicare Part B Expenditures Under Two Illustrative Scenarios with Alternative Physician Payment Updates." Department of Health and Human Services, Centers for Medicare and Medicaid Services.

Cohen, Robin A. 2012. "Trends in Health Care Coverage and Insurance for 1968-2011." Centers for Disease Control and Prevention, National Center for Health Statistics. (http://www.cdc.gov/nchs/health_policy/trends_hc_1968_2011.htm).

Cohen, Robin A., et al. 2009. "Health Insurance Coverage Trends, 1959-2007: Estimates from the National Health Interview Survey." National Health Statistics Report 17. Centers for Disease Control and Prevention, National Center for Health Statistics.

Cohodes, Sarah, et al. 2015. "The Effect of Child Health Insurance Access on Schooling: Evidence from Public Insurance Expansions." *Journal of Human Resources* 51(3): 727-59.

The Commonwealth Fund. 2008. "Why Not the Best? Results from the National Scorecard on U.S. Health System Performance, 2008." New York: The Commonwealth Fund Commission on a High Performance Health System.

Congressional Budget Office (CBO). 2009. "CBO's March 2009 Baseline: Medicare."

————. 2010a. "The Budget and Economic Outlook: An Update." August.

————. 2010b. "CBO Estimate of Changes in Net Federal Outlays from Alternative Proposals for Changing Physician Payment Rates in Medicare."

————. 2010c. "H.R. 4872, Reconciliation Act of 2010 (Final Health Care Legislation)." March.

_____. 2012a. "Direct Spending and Revenue Effects of H.R. 6079, the Repeal of Obamacare Act." July.

_____. 2012b. "Raising the Excise Tax on Cigarettes: Effects on Health and the Federal Budget." June.

_____. 2014. "Updated Estimates of the Effects of the Insurance Coverage Provisions of the Affordable Care Act." April.

_____. 2015a. "Budgetary and Economic Effects of Repealing the Affordable Care Act." June.

_____. 2015b. "Preliminary Estimate of Eliminating the Requirement that Individuals Purchase Health Insurance and Associated Penalties." September.

_____. 2016a. "An Update to the Budget and Economic Outlook: 2016 to 2026." August.

_____. 2016b. "The 2016 Long-Term Budget Outlook." July.

Cooper, Zack, et al. 2015. "The Price Ain't Right? Hospital Prices and Health Spending on the Privately Insured." NBER Working Paper 21815. Cambridge, MA: National Bureau of Economic Research.

Coughlin, Teresa A., et al. 2014. "An Estimated $84.9 Billion in Uncompensated Care Was Provided in 2013; ACA Payment Cuts Could Challenge Providers." *Health Affairs* 33(5): 807-14.

Council of Economic Advisers (CEA). 2014. "Methodological Appendix: Methods Used to Construct a Consistent Historical Time Series of Health Insurance Coverage." (https://www.whitehouse.gov/sites/default/files/docs/longtermhealthinsuranceseriesmethodologyfinal.pdf).

_____. 2015. "Missed Opportunities: The Consequences of State Decisions Not to Expand Medicaid." Report.

Courtemanche, Charles, et al. 2016. "Impacts of the Affordable Care Act on Health Insurance Coverage in Medicaid Expansion and Non-Expansion States." NBER Working Paper 22182. Cambridge, MA: National Bureau of Economic Research.

Cutler, David M. 2004. *Your Money or Your Life: Strong Medicine for America's Health Care System.* New York: Oxford University Press.

Cutler, David M., Mark McClellan, and Joseph P. Newhouse. 2000. "How Does Managed Care Do It?" *RAND Journal of Economics* 31(3): 526-48.

DeCicca, Philip. 2010. "Health Insurance Availability and Entrepreneurship." Upjohn Institute Working Paper 10-167. Kalamazoo, MI: W.E. Upjohn Institute for Employment Research.

Department of Health and Human Services (HHS). 2015. "Affordable Care Act payment model saves more than $384 million in two years, meets criteria for first-ever expansion." May 4. (http://www.hhs. gov/about/news/2015/05/04/affordable-care-act-payment-model-saves-more-than-384-million-in-two-years-meets-criteria-for-first-ever-expansion.html).

_____. 2016a. "Independent experts confirm that diabetes prevention model supported by the Affordable Care Act saves money and improves health." March 23. (http://www.hhs.gov/about/news/2016/03/23/independent-experts-confirm-diabetes-prevention-model-supported-affordable-care-act-saves-money.html).

_____. 2016b. "National Patient Safety Efforts Save 125,000 Lives and Nearly $28 Billion in Costs." Press Release. December. Agency for Healthcare Research and Quality.

Dillender, Marcus. 2014. "Do More Health Insurance Options Lead to Higher Wages? Evidence from States Extending Dependent Coverage." *Journal of Health Economics* 36(2016): 84-97.

Dillender, Marcus, Carolyn Heinrich, and Susan Houseman. 2016. "Effects of the Affordable Care Act on Part-Time Employment: Early Evidence." *Labour Economics* 43(2016): 151-8.

Dobkin, Carlos, et al. 2016. "The Economic Consequences of Hospital Admissions." NBER Working Paper 22288. Cambridge, MA: National Bureau of Economic Research.

Dorn, Stan, Megan McGrath, and John Holahan. 2014. "What Is the Result of States Not Expanding Medicaid?" *Timely Analysis of Immediate Health Policy Issues.* Washington: Urban Institute, and Princeton: Robert Wood Johnson Foundation.

Doty, Michelle M., et al. 2009. "Failure to Protect: Why the Individual Insurance Market Is Not a Viable Option for Most U.S. Families." Issue Brief 62(1300). New York: The Commonwealth Fund.

Dranove, David, Craig Garthwaite, and Christopher Ody. 2014. "Health Spending Slowdown is Mostly Due to Economic Factors, Not Structural Change in the Health Care Sector." *Health Affairs* 33(8): 1399-406.

_____. 2015. "The Economic Downturn and its Lingering Effects Reduced Medicare Spending Growth by $4 Billion in 2009–12." *Health Affairs* 34(8): 1368-75.

_____. 2016. "Uncompensated Care Decreased at Hospitals in Medicaid Expansion States But Not at Hospitals in Nonexpansion States." *Health Affairs* 35(8): 1471-9.

Dranove, David, et al. 2015. "Investment Subsidies and the Adoption of Electronic Medical Records in Hospitals." *Journal of Health Economics* 44(2015): 309-19.

Drösler, Saskia, Patrick Romano, and Lihan Wei. 2009. "Health Care Quality Indicators Project: Patient Safety Indicators Report 2009." OECD Health Working Paper 47. Paris: Organization for Economic Co-Operation and Development, HealthDepartment for Employment, Labour and Social Affairs, Health Committee.

Dummit, Laura, et al. 2016. "Association Between Hospital Participation in a Medicare Bundled Payment Initiative and Payments and Quality Outcomes for Lower Extremity Join Replacement Episodes." *Journal of the American Medical Association* 316(12): 1267-78.

Dussault, Nicole, Maxim Pinkovskiy, and Basit Zafar. 2016. "Is Health Insurance Good for Your Financial Health?" Liberty Street Economics Blog. Federal Reserve Bank of New York. June 6. (http://libertystreeteconomics.newyorkfed.org/2016/06/is-health-insurance-good-for-your-financial-health.html#.V8-1BvlrjX4).

Elmendorf, Douglas W. 2013. "Comment on "Is this Time Different? The Slowdown in Healthcare Spending: Presentation to the Brookings Panel on Economic Activity." September 19. Congressional Budget Office.

Even, William E., and David A. Macpherson. 2015. "The Affordable Care Act and the Growth of Involuntary Part-Time Employment." IZA Discussion Paper 9324. Bonn, Germany: Institute for the Study of Labor (IZA).

Fadlon, Itzik, and Torben Heien Nielsen. 2015. "Household Responses to Severe Health Shocks and the Design of Social Insurance."

NBER Working Paper 21352. Cambridge, MA: National Bureau of Economic Research.

Fairlie, Robert W., Kanika Kapur, and Susan Gates. 2011. "Is Employer-Based Health Insurance a Barrier to Entrepreneurship?" *Journal of Health Economics* 30(1): 146–62.

Farooq, Ammar, and Adriana Kugler. 2016. "Beyond Job Lock: Impacts of Public Health Insurance on Occupational and Industrial Mobility." NBER Working Paper 22118. Cambridge, MA: National Bureau of Economic Research.

Finkelstein, Amy, Matthew Gentzkow, and Heidi Williams. 2016. "Sources of Geographic Variation in Health Care: Evidence from Patient Migration." *The Quarterly Journal of Economics* 131(4): 1681-726.

Finkelstein, Amy, Nathaniel Hendren, and Erzo F.P. Luttmer. 2015. "The Value of Medicaid: Interpreting Results from the Oregon Health Insurance Experiment." NBER Working Paper 21308. Cambridge, MA: National Bureau of Economic Research.

Finkelstein, Amy, and Robin McKnight. 2008. "What Did Medicare Do? The Initial Impact of Medicare on Mortality and Out of Pocket Medical Spending." *Journal of Public Economics* 92(7): 1644-68.

Finkelstein, Amy, et al. 2012. "The Oregon Health Insurance Experiment: Evidence from the First Year." The *Quarterly Journal of Economics* 127(3): 1057-106.

Fisher, Elliot S., et al. 2003a. "The Implications of Regional Variations in Medicare Spending. Part 1: The Content, Quality, and Accessibility of Care." *Annals of Internal Medicine* 138(4): 273-87.

_____. 2003b. "The Implications of Regional Variations in Medicare Spending. Part 2: Health Outcomes and Satisfaction with Care." *Annals of Internal Medicine* 138(4): 288-98.

Frakt, Austin. 2013a. "My Reply to Jim Manzi." The Incidental Economist Blog. May 27. (http://theincidentaleconomist.com/wordpress/my-reply-to-jim-manzi/).

_____. 2013b. "The Oregon Medicaid Study and Cholesterol." The Incidental Economist Blog. June 6. (http://theincidentaleconomist.com/wordpress/the-oregon-medicaid-study-and-cholesterol/).

Furman, Jason. 2016. "Six Lessons from the U.S. Experience with Tobacco Taxes." Speech at the World Bank Conference: "Winning the Tax

Wars: Global Solutions for Developing Countries." Washington. May 24. (https://www.whitehouse.gov/sites/default/files/page/files/20160524_cea_tobacco_tax_speech.pdf).

Gabel, Jon R., et al. 2012. "More Than Half of Individual Health Plans Offer Coverage That Falls Short of What Can Be Sold Through Exchanges as of 2014." *Health Affairs* 31(6): 1339-48.

Garber, Alan M., and Jonathan Skinner. 2008. "Is American Health Care Uniquely Inefficient?" *Journal of Economic Perspectives* 22(4): 27-50.

Garthwaite, Craig, Tal Gross, and Matthew J. Notowidigdo. 2015. "Hospitals as Insurers of Last Report." NBER Working Paper 21290. Cambridge, MA: National Bureau of Economic Research.

Ginsburg, Paul B. 2010. "Wide Variation in Hospital and Physician Payment Rates Evidence of Provider Market Power." Research Brief 16. Washington: Center for Studying Health System Change.

Glied, Sherry. 2000. "Chapter 13: Managed Care." In *Handbook of Health Economics*, edited by Anthony J. Culyer and Joseph P. Newhouse, vol. 1A. Amsterdam: Elsevier.

Glied, Sherry, and Joshua Graff Zivin. 2002. "How Do Doctors Behave When Some (But Not All) of Their Patients Are in Managed Care?" *Journal of Health Economics* 21(2): 337-53.

Goldstein, Ian M., et al. 2014. "The Impact of Recent CHIP Eligibility Expansions on Children's Insurance Coverage 2008-12." *Health Affairs* 33(10): 1861-7.

Gooptu, Angshuman, et al. 2016. "Medicaid Expansion Did Not Result In Significant Employment Changes or Jobs Reductions in 2014." *Health Affairs* 35(1): 111-8.

Government Accountability Office. 2011. "Private Health Insurance: Data on Applications and Coverage Denials." Report to the Secretary of Health and Human Services and the Secretary of Labor. March.

Gross, Tal, and Matthew J. Notowidigdo. 2011 "Health Insurance and the Consumer Bankruptcy Decision: Evidence from Expansions of Medicaid." *Journal of Public Economics* 95(7): 767-78.

Hadley, Mark. 2016. "Testimony: CBO's Estimates of the Budgetary Effects of the Center for Medicare & Medicaid Innovation." Testimony before the Committee on the Budget, U.S. House of Representatives. September 7. Congressional Budget Office.

Health Care Payment Learning & Action Network (HCPLAN). 2016. "Measuring Progress Adoption of Alternative Payment Models in Commercial, Medicare Advantage, and State Medicaid Programs." Report.

Heberlein, Martha, Tricia Brooks, and Joan Alker. 2013. "Getting into Gear for 2014: Findings from a 50-State Survey of Eligibility, Enrollment, Renewal, and Cost-Sharing Policies in Medicaid and CHIP, 2012–2013." Report. Washington: Kaiser Family Foundation, Commission on Medicaid and the Uninsured.

Heim, Bradley T., and LeeKai Lin. 2016. "Does Health Reform Lead to an Increase in Early Retirement? Evidence from Massachusetts." *ILR Review* published online.

Herrera, Carolina-Nicole, et al. 2013. "Trends Underlying Employer-Sponsored Health Insurance Growth For Americans Younger Than Age Sixty-Five." *Health Affairs* 32(10): 1715-22.

Himmelstein, David, and Steffie Woolhandler. 2015. "The Post-Launch Problem: The Affordable Care Act's Persistently High Administrative Costs." Health Affairs Blog. May 27. (http://healthaffairs.org/blog/2015/05/27/the-post-launch-problem-the-affordable-care-acts-persistently-high-administrative-costs/).

Hines, Anika L., et al. 2014. "Conditions with the Largest Number of Adult Hospital Readmissions by Payer, 2011." Statistical Brief 172. Rockville, MD: Agency for Healthcare Research and Quality, Healthcare Cost and Utilization Project. (https://www.hcup-us.ahrq.gov/reports/statbriefs/sb172-Conditions-Readmissions-Payer.jsp).

Holahan, John, and Stacey McMorrow. 2015. "Has Faster Health Care Spending Growth Returned?" *Timely Analysis of Immediate Health Policy Issues.* Washington: Urban Institute, and Princeton: Robert Wood Johnson Foundation.

Howell, Embry M., and Genevieve M. Kenney. 2012. "The Impact of the Medicaid/CHIP Expansions on Children: A Synthesis of the Evidence." *Medical Care Research and Review* 69(4): 372-96.

Hu, Luojia, et al. 2016. "The Effect of the Patient Protection and Affordable Care Act Medicaid Expansions on Financial Well-Being." NBER Working Paper 22170. Cambridge, MA: National Bureau of Economic Research.

Huang, Jidong, and Frank J. Chaloupka IV. 2012. "The Impact of the 2009 Federal Tobacco Excise Tax Increase on Youth Tobacco Use." NBER Working Paper 18026. Cambridge, MA: National Bureau of Economic Research.

IMS Institute for Healthcare Informatics (IMS). 2013. "Impact of Patient Settlements on Drug Costs: Estimation of Savings." Report. Plymouth Meeting, PA.

_____. 2016. "Medicines Use and Spending in the U.S.: A Review of 2015 and Outlook to 2020." Report. Plymouth Meeting, PA.

Institute of Medicine. 1999. *To Err is Human: Building a Safer Health System*. Edited by Linda T. Kohn, Janet M. Corrigan, and Molla S. Donaldson. Committee on Quality of Health Care in America. Washington: National Academy Press.

Jamoom, Eric W., and Ninee Yang. 2016. "State Variation in Electronic Sharing of Information in Physician Offices: United States, 2015." NCHS Data Brief 261. October. Centers for Disease Control and Prevention, National Center for Health Statistics.

Jencks, Stephen F., Mark V. Williams, and Eric A. Coleman. 2009. "Rehospitalizations Among Patients in the Medicare Fee-for-Spending Program." *The New England Journal of Medicine* 360(14): 1418-28.

Jones, Spencer S., et al. 2014. "Health Information Technology: An Updated Systematic Review With a Focus on Meaningful Use." *Annals of Internal Medicine* 160(1): 48-54.

Kaestner, Garrett B., Anuj Gangopadhyaya, and Caitlyn Fleming. 2015. "Effects of ACA Medicaid Expansions on Health Insurance Coverage and Labor Supply." NBER Working Paper 21836. Cambridge, MA: National Bureau of Economic Research.

Kaiser Family Foundation (KFF). 2016. "An Overview of Medicare." Issue Brief. April. Menlo Park, CA.

Kaiser Family Foundation and Health Research & Educational Trust (KFF/HRET). 2016. "Employer Health Benefits: 2016 Annual Survey." Report. Menlo Park, CA and Chicago.

L&M Policy Research. 2015. "Evaluation of CMMI Accountable Care Organization Initiatives." Report. March. Washington.

Lee, David, and Frank Levy. 2012. "The Sharp Slowdown In Growth of Medical Imaging: An Early Analysis Suggests Combination of Policies Was the Cause." *Health Affairs* 38(1): 1-10.

Leung, Pauline, and Alexandre Mas. 2016. "Employment Effects of the ACA Medicaid Expansion." NBER Working Paper 22540. Cambridge, MA: National Bureau of Economic Research.

Levine, Michael, and Melinda Buntin. 2013. "Why Has Growth in Spending for Free-for-Service Medicare Slowed?" CBO Working Paper 2013-06. Congressional Budget Office.

Levitt, Larry, Cynthia Cox, and Gary Claxton. 2016. "How ACA Marketplace Premiums Measure Up to Expectations." Health Reform Policy Insight. August 1. Menlo Park, CA: Kaiser Family Foundation. (http://kff.org/health-reform/perspective/how-aca-marketplace-premiums-measure-up-to-expectations/).

Madrian, Brigitte. 1994. "Employment-Based Health Insurance and Job Mobility: Is There Evidence of Job-Lock?" *Oxford Journals* 109(1): 1-29.

Mathur, Aparna, Sita Slavov, and Michael Strain. 2016. "Has the Affordable Care Act Increased Part-time Employment?" *Applied Economic Letters* 23(3): 222-5

Mazumder, Bhashkar, and Sarah Miller. 2016. "The Effects of the Massachusetts Health Reform on Households Financial Distress." *American Economic Journal: Economic Policy* 8(3): 248-313.

McGlynn, Elizabeth A., et al. 2003. "The Quality of Health Care Delivered to Adults in the United States." *The New England Journal of Medicine* 348(26): 2635-45.

McKinsey Center for U.S. Health System Reform (McKinsey). 2016. "Exchanges Three Years In: Market Variations and Factors Affecting Performance." Intelligence Brief. McKinsey & Company.

McMorrow, Stacey, and John Holahan. 2016. "The Widespread Slowdown in Health Spending Growth Implications for Future Spending Projections and the Cost of the Affordable Care Act, An Update." Report. Washington: Urban Institute, and Princeton: Robert Wood Johnson Foundation.

McWilliams, J. Michael. 2016. "Changes in Medicare Shared Savings Program Savings from 2013 to 2014." *Journal of the American Medical Association Research Letter* 316(16): 1711-3.

McWilliams, J. Michael, Bruce E. Landon, and Michael E. Chernew. 2013. "Changes in Health Care Spending and Quality for Medicare Beneficiaries Associated With a Commercial ACO Contract." *Journal of the American Medical Association Network* 310(8): 829-36.

McWilliams, J. Michael, et al. 2007. "Health of Previously Uninsured Adults After Acquiring Medicare Coverage." *Journal of the American Medical Association Network* 298(24): 2886-94.

_____. 2015. "Performance Differences in Year 1 of Pioneer Accountable Care Organizations." *The New England Journal of Medicine* 372(20): 1927-36.

_____. 2016. "Early Performance of Accountable Care Organizations in Medicare." *The New England Journal of Medicine* 374(24): 2357-66.

Medicare Payment Advisory Commission (MedPAC). 2007. "Chapter 5: Payment Policy for Inpatient Readmissions." In *Promoting Greater Efficiency in Medicare.* Report to Congress. June.

_____. 2009. "Medicare Payment Policy." Report to Congress. March.

Medicare Trustees. 2009. "2009 Annual Report of the Boards of Trustees of the Federal Hospital Insurance and Federal Supplementary Medical Insurance Trust Funds." Washington: Boards of Trustees of the Federal Hospital Insurance and Federal Supplementary Medical Insurance Trust Funds.

_____. 2016. "2016 Annual Report of the Boards of Trustees of the Federal Hospital Insurance and Federal Supplementary Medical Insurance Trust Funds." Washington: Boards of Trustees of the Federal Hospital Insurance and Federal Supplementary Medical Insurance Trust Funds.

Moriya, Asako S., Thomas M. Selden, and Kosali I. Simon. 2016. "Little Change Seen in Part-Time Employment as a Result of The Affordable Care Act." *Health Affairs* 35(1): 119-23.

Muhlestein, David, and Mark McClellan. 2016. "Accountable Care Organizations in 2016: Private and Public-Sector Growth and Dispersion." Health Affairs Blog. April 21. (http://healthaffairs.org/blog/2016/04/21/

accountable-care-organizations-in-2016-private-and-public-sector-growth-and-dispersion/).

Mulligan, Casey. 2013. "The Perils of Significant Misunderstanding in Evaluating Medicaid." *The New York Times.* June 26. (http://economix. blogs.nytimes.com/2013/06/26/the-perils-of-significant-misunder-standings-in-evaluating-medicaid/?_r=0).

_____. 2014a. "The ACA: Some Unpleasant Welfare Arithmetic." NBER Working Paper 20020. Cambridge, MA: National Bureau of Economic Research.

_____. 2014b. "The Economics of Work Schedules under the New Hours and Employment Taxes." NBER Working Paper 19936. Cambridge, MA: National Bureau of Economic Research.

Musco, Thomas D., and Benjamin D. Sommers. 2012. "Under The Affordable Care Act, 105 Million Americans No Longer Face Lifetime Limits on Health Benefits." ASPE Issue Brief. Department of Health and Human Services, Office of the Assistant Secretary for Planning and Evaluation.

Newhouse, Joseph P. 1992. "Medical Care Costs: How Much Welfare Loss?" *The Journal of Economic Perspectives* 6(3): 3-21.

Newhouse, Joseph P, et al. 1993. *Free for All? Lessons from the RAND Health Insurance Experiment.* Cambridge, MA: Harvard University Press.

Nyman, John A. 1999. "The Value of Health Insurance: The Access Motive." *Journal of Health Economics* 18(1999): 141-52.

Nyweide, David J., et al. 2015. "Association of Pioneer Accountable Care Organizations vs Traditional Medicare Fee for Service With Spending, Utilization, and Patient Experience." *Journal of the American Medical Association* 313(21): 2152-61.

Obama, Barack. 2016. "United States Health Care Reform: Progress to Date and Next Steps." *Journal of the American Medical Association* 316(5): 525-32.

Pauly, Mark V. 1968. "The Economics of Moral Hazard: Comment." *The American Economic Review* 58(3): 531-7.

Philipson, Tomas J., et al. 2010. "Geographic Variation in Health Care: The Role of Private Markets." *Brookings Papers on Economic Activity.* Washington: Brookings Institution.

Pinkovskiy, Maxim. 2014. "The Impact of the Political Response to the Managed Care Backlash on Health Care Spending: Evidence from State Regulations of Managed Care." Working Paper. New York: Federal Reserve Bank of New York. (https://www.newyorkfed.org/medialibrary/media/research/economists/pinkovskiy/Impact_of_Political_Backlash_on_Health_Care_Costs.pdf).

———. 2015. "The Affordable Care Act and the Labor Market: A First Look." Federal Reserve Bank of New York Staff Report 746. New York: Federal Reserve Bank of New York.

Porterfield, Shirley, and Jin Huang. 2016. "Affordable Care Act Provision Had Similar Positive Impacts For Young Adults With and Without Disabilities." *Health Affairs* 35(5): 873-9.

Richardson, Sam, Aaron Carroll, and Austin Frakt. 2013. "More Medicaid Study Power Calculations." The Incidental Economist Blog. June 13. (http://theincidentaleconomist.com/wordpress/more-medicaid-study-power-calculations-our-rejected-nejm-letter/).

Roy, Avik. 2013. "The Medicaid Deniers." *National Review*. May 14. (http://www.nationalreview.com/article/348200/medicaid-deniers-avik-roy).

RTI. 2016. "Evaluation of the Health Care Innovation Awards: Community Resource Planning, Prevention, and Monitoring, Annual Report 2015, Awardee Level Findings: YMCA of the USA." Report. March. Research Triangle Park, NC.

Ryu, Alexander J., et al. 2013. "The Slowdown In Health Care Spending In 2009–11 Reflected Factors Other Than the Weak Economy and Thus May Persist." *Health Affairs* 32(5): 835-40.

Shamliyan, Tatyana A., et al. 2008. "Just What the Doctor Ordered. Review of the Evidence of the Impact of Computerized Physician Order Entry System on Medication Errors." *Health Service Research* 43(1): 32-53.

Shartzer, Adele, Sharon K. Long, and Nathaniel Anderson. 2016. "Access to Care and Affordability Have Improved Following the Affordable Care Act Implementation; Problems Remain." *Health Affairs* 35(1): published online.

Sheiner, Louise. 2014. "Perspectives on Health Care Spending Growth." Hutchins Center Working Paper 4. Washington: Brookings Institution Hutchins Center on Fiscal and Monetary Policy.

Shekelle, Paul G. 2015. "Electronic Health Record-based Interventions for Reducing Inappropriate Imaging in the Clinical Setting: A Systematic Review of the Evidence." Evidence Based Synthesis Program Report. Department of Veterans Affairs: Health Services Research & Development Service.

Simon, Kosali, Aparna Soni, and John Cawley. 2016. "The Impact of Health Insurance on Preventative Care and Health Behaviors: Evidence from the 2014 ACA Medicaid Expansions." NBER Working Paper 22265. Cambridge, MA: National Bureau of Economic Research.

Sommers, Benjamin D., Katherine Baicker, and Arnold M. Epstein. 2012. "Mortality and Access to Care Among Adults After State Medicaid Expansions." The New England Journal of Medicine 367(11): 1025-34.

Sommers, Benjamin D., Sharon K. Long, and Katherine Baicker. 2014. "Changes in Mortality After Massachusetts Health Care Reform: A Quasi-Experimental Study." Annals of Internal Medicine 160(9): 585-93.

Sommers, Benjamin D., et al. 2015. "Changes in Self-Reported Insurance Coverage, Access to Care, and Health Under the Affordable Care Act." The Journal of the American Medical Association 314(4): 366-74.

———. 2016. "Changes in Utilization and Health Among Low-Income Adults After Medicaid Expansion or Expanded Private Insurance." Journal of the American Medical Association Internal Medicine 176(10):1501-9.

Song, Zirui, et al. 2014. "Changes in Health Care Spending and Quality 4 Years into Global Payment." New England Journal of Medicine 371(18): 1704-14.

Sood, Neeraj, Arkadipta Ghosh, and José J. Escarce. 2009. "Employer-Sponsored Insurance, Health Care Cost Growth, and the Economic Performance of U.S. Industries." Health Services Research 44(5 Pt 1): 1449–64.

Spitalnic, Paul. 2015. "Certification of Pioneer Model Savings." Memorandum. April 10. Department of Health and Human Services, Centers for Medicare and Medicaid Services.

_____. 2016. "Certification of Medicare Diabetes Prevention Program." Memorandum. March 14. Department of Health and Human Services, Centers for Medicare and Medicaid Services.

Summers, Lawrence H. 1989. "Some Simple Economics of Mandated Benefits." *American Economic Review* 79(2): 177-83.

Uberoi, Namrata, Kenneth Finegold, and Emily Gee. 2016. "Health Insurance Coverage and the Affordable Care Act, 2010–2016." ASPE Issue Brief. Department of Health and Human Services.

U.S. Surgeon General. 2014. "The Health Consequences of Smoking—50 Years of Progress." Report. Department of Health and Human Services.

Van der Wees, Philip J., Alan M. Zaslavsky, and John Z. Ayanian. 2013. "Improvements in Health Status after Massachusetts Health Care Reform." *The Milbank Quarterly* 91(4): 663-89.

Van Hasselt, Martijn, et al. 2015. "The Relation between Tobacco Taxes and Youth and Young Adult Smoking: What Happened to Following the 2009 U.S. Federal Tax Increase on Cigarettes?" *Addictive Behaviors* 45(2015): 104-9.

Wallace, Jacob, and Zirui Song. 2016. "Traditional Medicare Versus Private Insurance: How Spending, Volume, And Price Change at Age Sixty-Five." *Health Affairs* 35(5): 864-72.

Wherry, Laura R., and Bruce Meyer. 2016. "Saving Teens: Using a Policy Discontinuity to Estimate the Effects of Medicaid Eligibility." *Journal of Human Resources* 51(3): 556-88.

Wherry, Laura R., and Sarah Miller. 2016. "Early Coverage, Access, Utilization, and Health Effects Associated With the Affordable Care Act Medicaid Expansions: A Quasi-experimental Study." *Annals of Internal Medicine* 164(12): 795-803.

Wherry, Laura R., et al. 2015. "Childhood Medicaid Coverage and Later Life Health Care Utilization." NBER Working Paper 20929. Cambridge, MA: National Bureau of Economic Research.

White, Chapin. 2013. "Contrary to Cost-Shift Theory, Lower Medicare Hospital Payments Rates for Inpatient Care Lead to Lower Private Payment Rates." *Health Affairs* 32(5): 935-43.

White, Chapin, and Vivian Yaling Wu. 2014. "How Do Hospitals Cope with Sustained Slow Growth in Medicare Prices?" *Health Services Research* 49(1): 11-31.

Whitmore, Heidi, et al. 2011. "The Individual Insurance Market Before Reform: Low Premiums and Low Benefits." *Medical Care Research and Review* 68(5): 594-606.

Yamamoto, Dale H. 2013. "Health Care Costs—From Birth to Death." Health Care Cost Institute Independent Report Series. Report 2013-1. Schaumburg, IL: Society of Actuaries.

Zuckerman, Rachael. 2016. "Reducing Avoidable Hospital Readmissions to Create a Better, Safer Health Care System." Blog. February 24. Department of Health and Human Services. (http://www.hhs.gov/blog/2016/02/24/reducing-avoidable-hospital-readmissions.html).

Zuckerman, Rachael, et al. 2016. "Readmissions, Observation, and the Hospital Readmissions Reduction Program." *New England Journal of Medicine* 374(16): 1543-51.

CHAPTER 5

Abel, Jaison R., and Richard Deitz. 2016. "Underemployment in the Early Careers of College Graduates following the Great Recession." NBER Working Paper 22654. Cambridge, MA: National Bureau of Economic Research.

Abraham, Katharine, and Melissa Clark. 2006. "Financial Aid and Students' College Decisions: Evidence from the District of Columbia Tuition Assistance Grant Program." *The Journal of Human Resources* 41(3): 578-610.

Almond, Douglas, Hilary Hoynes, and Diane Whitmore Schanzenbach. 2016. "Long-Run Impacts of Childhood Access to the Safety Net." *American Economic Review* 106(4): 903-34.

Altonji, Joseph G., Erica Blom, and Costas Meghir. 2012. "Heterogeneity in Human Capital Investments: High School Curriculum, College Major, and Careers." *Annual Review of Economics* 4(1): 185-223.

Andrews, Rodney J., Stephen DesJardins, and Vimal Ranchhod. 2010. "The Effects of the Kalamazoo Promise on College Choice." *Economics of Education Review* 29(5): 722-37.

Arcidiacono, Peter, V. Joseph Hotz, and Songman Kang. 2012. "Modeling College Major Choices Using Elicited Measures of Expectations and Counterfactuals." *Journal of Econometrics* 166(1): 3-16.

Avery, Christopher, and Thomas Kane. 2004. "Student Perceptions of College Opportunities: The Boston COACH Program." In *College Choices: The Economics of Where to Go, When to Go, and How to Pay For It*, edited by Caroline M. Hoxby, pp. 355-94. Chicago: University of Chicago Press.

Avery, Christopher, and Sarah Turner. 2012. "Student Loans: Do College Students Borrow Too Much—Or Not Enough?" *The Journal of Economic Perspectives* 26(1): 165-92.

Bacher-Hicks, Andrew, Thomas J. Kane, and Douglas O. Staiger. 2014. "Validating Teacher Effect Estimates Using Changes in Teacher Assignments in Los Angeles." NBER Working Paper 20657. Cambridge, MA: National Bureau of Economic Research.

Bahr, Peter, et al. 2015. "Labor Market Returns to Community College Awards: Evidence from Michigan." CAPSEE Working Paper. New York: Center for Analysis of Postsecondary Education and Employment.

Baker, Rachel, et al. 2016. "The Effect of Labor Market Information on Community College Students' Major Choice." Paper prepared for ASSA Annual Meeting: Major Choices: Students' Beliefs About Labor Market Outcomes. American Economic Association. January 8, 2017.

Bartik, Timothy J., Brad Hershbein, and Marta Lachowska. 2015. "Longer-Term Effects of the Kalamazoo Promise Scholarship on College Enrollment, Persistence, and Completion." Upjohn Institute Working Paper 15-229. Kalamazoo, MI: W.E. Upjohn Institute for Employment Research.

————. 2016. "The Merits of Universal Scholarships: Benefit-Cost Evidence from the Kalamazoo Promise." *Journal of Benefit-Cost Analysis* 7(3): 400-33.

Bartik, Timothy J., and Marta Lachowska. 2013. "The Short-Term Effects of the Kalamazoo Promise Scholarship on Student Outcomes." In *Research in Labor Economics*, vol. 38, edited by Solomon W. Polachek and Konstantinos Tatsiramos, pp. 37-76. Bingley, United Kingdom. Emerald Group Publishing.

Baum, Sandy, Jennifer Ma, and Kathleen Payea. 2013. "Education Pays: The Benefits of Higher Education for Individuals and Society." College Board Trends in Higher Education Series. New York: The College Board.

Baum, Sandy, and Judith Scott-Clayton. 2015. "Four Important Considerations Regarding the Free Community College Proposal." UrbanWire Blog. January 22. Washington: Urban Institute. (http://www.urban.org/urban-wire/four-important-considerations-regarding-free-community-college-proposal).

Belfield, Clive, Yuen Liu, and Madeline Trimble. 2014. "The Medium-Term Labor Market Returns to Community College Awards: Evidence from North Carolina." *Economics of Education Review* 44(C): 42-55.

Bettinger, Eric. 2004. "How Financial Aid Affects Persistence." In *College Choices: The Economics of Where to Go, When to Go, and How to Pay for It*, edited by Caroline M. Hoxby, pp. 207-37. University of Chicago Press.

Bettinger, Eric, et al. 2012. "The Role of Application Assistance and Information in College Decisions: Results from the H&R Block FAFSA Experiment." *The Quarterly Journal of Economics* 127(3): 1205-42.

Betts, John. 1996. "What Do Students Know About Wages? Evidence from a Survey of Undergraduates." *The Journal of Human Resources* 31(1): 27-56.

Black, Sandra E., et al. 2015. "On the Origins of STEM: The Role of High School STEM Coursework in Occupational Determination and Labor Market Success in Mid-Life." Working Paper. University of Texas at Austin: Department of Economics. (https://utexas.app.box.com/s/s6kds4q4oq1zs0z4mjcca6r1vfosg820).

Bound, John, Michael Lovenheim, and Sarah Turner. 2010. "Why Have College Completion Rates Declined? An Analysis of Changing Student Preparation and Collegiate Resources." *American Economic Journal: Applied Economics* 2(3): 129-57.

Brown, David W., Amanda E. Kowalski, and Ithai Z. Lurie. 2015. "Medicaid as an Investment in Children: What is the Long-term Impact on Tax Receipts?" NBER Working Paper 20835. Cambridge, MA: National Bureau of Economic Research.

Bulman, George, and Caroline Hoxby. 2015. "The Returns to the Federal tax Credits for Higher Education." NBER Working Paper 20833. Cambridge, MA: National Bureau of Economic Research.

Campbell, Frances A., et al. 2012. "Adult Outcomes as a Function of an Early Childhood Educational Program: An Abecedarian Project Follow-Up." *Development Psychology* 48(4): 1033-43.

Card, David. 1995. "Using Geographic Variation in College Proximity to Estimate the Return to Schooling." In *Aspects of Labor Market Behaviour: Essays in Honour of John Vanderkamp*, edited by Louis Christofides, E. Kenneth Grant, and Robert Swidinsky, pp. 201-22. University of Toronto Press.

Carruthers, Celeste K., and William F. Fox. 2016. "Aid for All: College Coaching, Financial Aid, and Post-Secondary Persistence in Tennessee." *Economics of Education Review* 51(C): 97-112.

Case, Anne, Angela Fertig, and Christina Paxson. 2005. "The Lasting Impact of Childhood Health and Circumstance." *Journal of Health Economics* 24(2): 365-89.

Casey, BJ, Rebecca Jones, and Leah Somerville. 2011. "Braking and Accelerating of the Adolescent Brain." *Journal of Research on Adolescence* 21(1): 21-33.

Castleman, Benjamin L., and Bridget Terry Long. 2013. "Looking Beyond Enrollment: The Causal Effect of Need-Based Grants on College Access, Persistence, and Graduation." NBER Working Paper 19306. Cambridge, MA: National Bureau of Economic Research.

Cellini, Stephanie. 2012. "For-Profit Higher Education: An Assessment of Costs and Benefits." *National Tax Journal* 65(1): 153-80.

Cellini, Stephanie, and Latika Chaudhary. 2013. "The Labor Market Returns to a For-Profit College Education." NBER Working Paper 18343. Cambridge, MA: National Bureau of Economic Research.

Cellini, Stephanie, and Nicholas Turner. 2016. "Gainfully Employed? Assessing the Employment and Earnings of For-Profit College Students Using Administrative Data." NBER Working Paper 22287. Cambridge, MA: National Bureau of Economic Research.

Chetty, Raj, John N. Friedman, and Jonah E. Rockoff. 2014a. "Measuring the Impacts of Teachers I: Evaluating Bias in Teacher Value-Added Estimates." *American Economic Review* 104(9): 2593-632.

_____. 2014b. "Measuring the Impacts of Teachers II: Teacher Value-Added and Students Outcomes in Adulthood." *American Economic Review* 104(9): 2633-79.

Chetty, Raj, and Nathaniel Hendren. 2015. "The Impacts of Neighborhoods on Intergenerational Mobility: Childhood Exposure Effects and County-Level Estimates." Working Paper. Harvard University: Department of Economics and NBER. (http://www.equality-of-opportunity.org/images/nbhds_paper.pdf).

Chetty, Raj, Nathaniel Hendren, and Lawrence F. Katz. 2016. "The Effects of Exposure to Better Neighborhoods on Children: New Evidence from the Moving to Opportunity Experiment." *American Economic Review* 106(4) 855-902.

Chetty, Raj, et al. 2011. "How Does your Kindergarten Classroom Affect your Earnings? Evidence from Project STAR." *The Quarterly Journal of Economics* 126(4): 1593-660.

Cohodes, Sarah, and Joshua Goodman. 2014. "Merit Aid, College Quality and College Completion: Massachusetts' Adams Scholarship as an In-Kind Subsidy." *American Economic Journal: Applied Economics* 6(4): 251-85.

Cohodes, Sarah, et al. 2016. "The Effect of Child Health Insurance Access on Schooling: Evidence from Public Insurance Expansions." *Journal of Human Resources* 51(3): 727-59.

College Board. 2015. "Trends in College Pricing: 2015." *Trends in Higher Education.* New York: The College Board.

_____. 2016a. "Trends in College Pricing: 2016." *Trends in Higher Education.* New York: The College Board.

_____. 2016b. "Trends in Student Aid: 2016." *Trends in Higher Education.* New York: The College Board.

Consumer Finance Protection Bureau. 2012. "Private Student Loans." Report to the Senate Committee on Banking, Housing, and Urban Affairs, the Senate Committee on Health, Education, Labor, and Pensions, the House of Representatives Committee on Financial Services, and the House of Representatives Committee on Education and the Workforce.

Council of Economic Advisers (CEA). 2014. "The Labor Force Participation Rate since 2007: Causes and Policy Implications." Report.

_____. 2015a. "Economic Costs of Youth Disadvantage and High-Return Opportunities for Change." Report.

_____. 2015b. "Long-Term Benefits of the Supplemental Nutrition Assistance Program." Report.

_____. 2015c. "Using Federal Data to Measure and Improve the Performance of U.S. Institutions of Higher Education." Report.

_____. 2016a. "Chapter 4: Inequality in Early Childhood and Effective Public Policy Interventions." *Economic Report of the President.*

_____. 2016b. "Economic Perspectives on Incarceration and the Criminal Justice System." Report.

_____. 2016c "The Economic Record of the Obama Administration: Investing in Higher Education." Report.

_____. 2016d. "Investing in Higher Education: Benefits, Challenges, and the State of Student Debt." Report.

_____. 2016e. "The Long-Term Decline in Prime-Age Male Labor Force-Participation." Report.

Cunha, Flavio, James J. Heckman, and Salvador Navarro. 2005. "Separating Uncertainty from Heterogeneity in Life Cycle Earnings." NBER Working Paper 11024. Cambridge, MA: National Bureau of Economic Research.

Currie, Janet. 2000. "Chapter 7: Do Children of Immigrants Make Differential Use of Public Health Insurance?" In *Issues in the Economics of Immigration, National Bureau of Economic Research Conference Report*, edited by George J. Borjas, pp. 271-308. Chicago: University of Chicago Press.

Cutler, David M., and Adriana Lleras-Muney. 2006. "Education and Health: Evaluating Theories and Evidence." NBER Working Paper 12352. Cambridge, MA: National Bureau of Economic Research.

Dadgar, Mina, and Madeline Trimble. 2014. "Labor Market Returns to Sub-Baccalaureate Credentials: How Much Does a Community College Degree or Certificate Pay?" *Educational Evaluation and Policy Analysis* 37(4): 399-418.

Dahl, Gordon B., and Lance Lochner. 2012. "The Impact of Family Income on Child Achievement: Evidence from the Earned Income Tax Credit." *American Economic Review* 102(5) 1927-56.

Darolia, Rajeev, et al. 2015. "Do Employers Prefer Workers who Attended For-Profit Colleges? Evidence from a Field Experiment." *Journal of Policy Analysis and Management* 34(4): 881–903.

Daugherty, Lindsay, and Gabriella C. Gonzalez. 2016. "The Impact of the New Haven Promise Program on College Enrollment, Choice, and Persistence." RAND Working Paper. Santa Monica, CA: RAND Corporation.

Dave, Dhaval M., et al. 2015. "The Effect of Medicaid Expansions in the Late 1980s and Early 1990s on the Labor Supply of Pregnant Women." *American Journal of Health Economics* 1(2): 165-93.

Dee, Thomas. 2004. "Are There Civic Returns to Education?" *Journal of Public Economics* 88(9-10): 1697-720.

_____. 2012. "School Turnarounds: Evidence from the 2009 Stimulus." NBER Working Paper 17990. Cambridge, MA: National Bureau of Economic Research.

Deming, David J., Claudia Goldin, and Lawrence F. Katz. 2012. "The For-Profit Postsecondary School Sector: Nimble Critters or Agile Predators?" *Journal of Economic Perspectives* 276(1): 139-64.

_____. 2013. "For-Profit Colleges." *Future of Children* 23(1): 137-63.

Deming, David J., et al. 2014. "The Value of Postsecondary Credentials in the Labor Market: An Experimental Study." NBER Working Paper 20528. Cambridge, MA: National Bureau of Economic Research.

Denning, Jeffrey. 2016a. "Born Under a Lucky Star: Financial Aid, College Completion, Labor Supply, and Credit Constraints." Working Paper. Brigham Young University: Department of Economics. (https://aefpweb.org/sites/default/files/webform/41/BornUnder-ALuckyStar.pdf).

_____. 2016b (forthcoming). "College on the Cheap: Consequences of Community College Tuition Reductions." *American Economic Association*.

Department of Education. 2016a. "The America's College Promise Playbook: Expanding the Promise of a College Education and Economic Opportunity for All Students." Report.

_____. 2016b. "Fiscal Year 2017 Budget Request."

Dobbie, Will, and Roland G. Fryer Jr. 2013. "Getting Beneath the Veil of Effective Schools: Evidence from New York City." *American Economic Journal: Applied Economics* 5(4): 228-60.

Dominitz, Jeff, and Charles F. Manski. 1996. "Eliciting Student Expectations of the Returns to Schooling." *Journal of Human Resources* 31(1): 1-25.

Dunlop, Erin. 2013. "What Do Stafford Loans Actually Buy You? The Effect of Stafford Loan Access on Community College Students." National Center for Analysis of Longitudinal Data in Education Research Working Paper. Washington: American Institutes for Research.

Dynarski, Susan. 2003. "Does Aid Matter? Measuring the Effect of Student Aid on College Attendance and Completion." *The American Economic Review* 93(1): 279-88.

Dynarski, Susan, and Daniel Kreisman. 2013. "Loans for Educational Opportunity: Making Borrowing Work for Today's Students." Discussion Paper 2013-05. Washington: Brookings Institution, The Hamilton Project.

Dynarski, Susan, and Judith Scott-Clayton. 2006. "The Cost of Complexity in Federal Student Aid: Lessons from Optimal Tax Theory and Behavioral Economics." NBER Working Paper 12227. Cambridge, MA: National Bureau of Economic Research.

_____. 2016. "Tax Benefits for College Attendance." NBER Working Paper 22127. Cambridge, MA: National Bureau of Economic Research.

Eagan, Kevin, et al. 2014. "The American Freshman: National Norms Fall 2014." Report. Los Angeles: Cooperative Institutional Research Program at UCLA.

Evans, William N., Robert S. Schwab, and Kathryn Wagner. 2014. "The Great Recession and Public Education." Working Paper. University of Notre Dame: Department of Economics. (https://www3.nd.edu/~wevans1/working_papers/Russell%20Sage%20Paper%20final.pdf).

Executive Office of the President. 2009. "Educational Impact of the American Recovery and Reinvestment Act." Report. The White House.

_____. 2016. "Giving Every Child a Fair Shot: Progress Under the Obama Administration's Education Agenda." Report. The White House.

Fain, Paul. 2014. "Benefits of Free." Inside Higher Ed. (https://www.insidehighered.com/news/2014/10/16/chicago-joins-tennessee-tuition-free-community-college-plan).

Figlio, David N., Krzysztof Karbownik, and Kjell G. Salvanes. 2015. "Education Research and Administrative Data." NBER Working Paper 21592. Cambridge, MA: National Bureau of Economic Research.

Finkelstein, Amy, et al. 2012. "The Oregon Health Insurance Experiment: Evidence from the First Year." *The Quarterly Journal of Economics* 127(3): 1057-106.

Fishman, Rachel. 2015. "2015 College Decisions Survey Part 1: Deciding to Go to College." Education Policy Program Report. Washington: New America Foundation.

Forsythe, Eliza. 2016. "Why Don't Firms Hire Young Workers During Recessions?" Working Paper. University of Illinois: School of Labor and Employment Relations and Department of Economics. (https://www.dropbox.com/s/lhq9gfksujbnk54/Youth_Hiring_2016.pdf?dl=0).

Fryer, Roland G., Jr. 2014. "Injecting Successful Charter School Strategies into Traditional Public Schools: Evidence from Field Experiments." *The Quarterly Journal of Economics* 129(3): 1335-407.

Gill, Andrew M., and Duane E. Leigh. 1997. "Labor Market Returns to Community Colleges: Evidence for Returning Adults." *Journal of Human Resources* 32(2): 334-53.

Goldin, Claudia, and Lawrence Katz. 2008. *The Race between Education and Technology.* Cambridge, MA: Harvard University Press.

Gonzalez, Gabriella, et al. 2014. "An Early Look at College Preparation, Access, and Enrollment of New Haven Public School Students (2010-2013)." RAND Research Brief. Washington: RAND Corporation.

Goodman, Joshua, Michael Hurwitz, and Jonathan Smith. 2015. "College Access, Initial College Choice and Degree Completion." NBER Working Paper 20996. Cambridge, MA: National Bureau of Economic Research.

Government Accountability Office. 2010. "For-Profit Colleges: Undercover Testing Finds Colleges Encouraged Fraud and Engaged in Deceptive and Questionable Marketing Practices." Testimony Before the

Committee on Health, Education, Labor, and Pensions, U.S. Senate. GAO-10-948T

Grodsky, Eric, and Melanie Jones. 2007. "Real and Imagined Barriers to College Entry: Perceptions of Cost." *Social Science Research* 36(2): 745-66.

Grubb, Norton. 2002. "Learning and Earning in the Middle, Part I: National Studies of Pre-baccalaureate Education." *Economics of Education Review* 21(4): 299-321.

Halle, Tamara, et al. 2009. "Disparities in Early Learning and Development: Lessons from the Early Childhood Longitudinal Study – Birth Cohort (ECLS-B)." Research Report. Washington: Child Trends.

Hansen, W. Lee. 1983. "The Impact of Student Financial Aid on Access." *Proceedings of the Academy of Political Science* 35(2): 84-96.

Hanushek, Eric, and Ludger Woessman. 2015. *The Knowledge Capital of Nations: Education and the Economics of Growth.* Cambridge, MA: MIT Press.

Haskins, Ron, Julia Isaacs, and Isabel Sawhill. 2008. "Getting Ahead or Losing Ground: Economic Mobility in America." Report. Washington: Brookings Institution.

Hastings, Justine S., et al. 2015. "(Un)informed College and Major Choice: Evidence from Linked Survey and Administrative Data." NBER Working Paper 21330. Cambridge, MA: National Bureau of Economic Research.

Heckman, James J., Lance J. Lochner, and Petra E. Todd. 2006. "Earnings Functions, Rates of Return and Treatment Effects: The Mincer Equation and Beyond." In *Handbook of the Economics of Education,* vol. 1, edited by Eric A. Hanushek and Finis Welch, pp 307-458. Amsterdam: North Holland.

Heckman, James J., et al. 2010. "The Rate of Return to the High/Scope Perry Preschool Program." *Journal of Public Economics* 94(1): 114-28.

Hill, Kent, Dennis Hoffman, and Tom R. Rex. 2005. "The Value of Higher Education: Individual and Societal Benefits." Report. Tempe, AZ: University of Arizona's Productivity and Prosperity Project (P3).

Hoekstra, Mark. 2009. "The Effect of Attending the Flagship State University on Earnings: A Discontinuity-Based Approach." *The Review of Economics and Statistics* 91(4): 717-24.

Horn, Laura, Xianlei Chen, and Chris Chapman. 2003. "Getting Ready to Pay for College: What Students and Their Parents Know About the Cost of College Tuition and What They Are Doing to Find Out." Statistical Analysis Report 2003-030. U.S. Department of Education, National Center for Education Statistics.

Howell, William G. 2015. "Results of President Obama's Race to the Top: Win or Lose, States Enacted Education Reforms." *Education Next* 15(4).

Hoxby, Caroline, and George Bulman. 2015. "The Effects of the Tax Deduction for Postsecondary Tuition: Implications for Structuring Tax-Based Aid." NBER Working Paper 21554. Cambridge, MA: National Bureau of Economic Research.

Hoxby, Caroline, and Sarah Turner. 2013. "Expanding College Opportunities for High-Achieving, Low Income Students." SIEPR Discussion Paper 12-014. Stanford, CA: Stanford Institute for Economic Policy Research.

———. 2015. "What High-Achieving Low-Income Students Know About College." NBER Working Paper 20861. Cambridge, MA: National Bureau of Economic Research.

Hoynes, Hilary, Douglas Miller, and Jessamyn Schaller. 2012. "Who Suffers During Recessions?" *Journal of Economic Perspectives* 36(3): 27-48.

Isaacs, Julia B. 2012. "Starting School at a Disadvantage: The School Readiness of Poor Children." *Brookings Social Genome Project Research* (3)5: 1-22.

Jackson, C. Kirabo, Rucker C. Johnson, and Claudia Persico. 2016. "The Effects of School Spending on Educational and Economic Outcomes: Evidence from School Finance Reforms." *The Quarterly Journal of Economics* 131(1): 157-218.

Jacobson, Louis, Robert LaLonde, and Daniel Sullivan. 2005. "The Impact of Community College Retraining on Older Displaced Workers: Should We Teach Old Dogs New Tricks?" *Industrial and Labor Relations Review* 58(3): 398-415.

Jepsen, Christopher, Peter Mueser, and Kyung-Seong Jeon. 2016. "The Benefits of Alternatives to Conventional College: Labor-Market Returns to Proprietary Schooling." IZA Discussion Paper 10007. Bonn, Germany: Institute for the Study of Labor (IZA).

Jepsen, Christopher, Kenneth Troske, and Paul Coomes. 2012. "The Labor-Market Returns to Community College Degrees, Diplomas, and Certificates." IZA Discussion Paper 6902. Bonn, Germany: Institute for the Study of Labor (IZA).

Kaestner, Robert. 2009. "The Effects Medicaid Expansions and Welfare Reform on Fertility and the Health of Women and Children." NBER Reporter 2009 Number 4. Cambridge, MA: National Bureau of Economic Research.

Kaestner, Robert, Aaron Racine, and Ted Joyce. 2000. "Did Recent Expansion in Medicaid Narrow Socioeconomic Differences in Hospitalization Rates of Infants?" *Medical Care* 38(2): 195-206.

Kahn, Lisa B. 2010. "The Long-Term Labor Market Consequences of Graduating from College in a Bad Economy." *Labour Economics* 17(2): 303-16.

Kane, Thomas. 1996. "Lessons from the Largest School Voucher Program Ever: Two Decades of Experience with Pell Grants." In *Who chooses? Who loses? Culture, Institutions and the Unequal Effects of School Choice*, edited by Bruce Fuller, Richard F. Elmore, and Gary Orfield. Teachers College Press.

Kane, Thomas J., and Cecilia Rouse. 1993. "Labor Market Returns to Two and Four Year Colleges: Is a Credit a Credit and Do Degrees Matter?" NBER Working Paper 4268. Cambridge, MA: National Bureau of Economic Research.

Kane, Thomas J., et al. 2011. "Identifying Effective Classroom Practices Using Student Achievement Data." *The Journal of Human Resources* 46(3): 587-613.

Kroeger, Teresa, Tanyell Cooke, and Elise Gould. 2016. "The Class of 2016: The Labor Market is Still Far from Ideal for Young Graduates." Report. Washington: Economic Policy Institute.

Krueger, Alan B. 1999. "Experimental Estimates of Education Production Functions." *The Quarterly Journal of Economics* 114(2): 497-532.

LaFortune, Julien, Jesse Rothstein, and Diane Whitmore Schanzenbach. 2016. "School Finance Reform and the Distribution of Student Achievement." NBER Working Paper 22011. Cambridge, MA: National Bureau of Economic Research.

Lavecchia, Adam, Heidi Liu, and Philip Oreopoulos. 2015. "Behavioral Economics of Education: Progress and Possibilities." IZA Discussion Paper 8853. Bonn, Germany: Institute for the Study of Labor (IZA).

LeGower, Michael, and Randall Walsh. 2014. "Promise Scholarship Programs as Place-Making Policy: Evidence from School Enrollment and Housing Prices." NBER Working Paper 20056. Cambridge, MA: National Bureau of Economic Research.

Levine, Phillip B., and David J. Zimmerman. 1995. "The Benefit of Additional High-School Math and Science Classes for Young Men and Women." *Journal of Business & Economic Statistics* 13(2): 137-49.

Liu, Yuen Ting, and Clive Belfield. 2014. "The Labor Market Returns to For-Profit Higher Education: Evidence for Transfer Students." CAPSEE Working Paper. New York: Center for Analysis of Postsecondary Education and Employment.

Lochner, Lance, and Enrico Moretti. 2004. "The Effect of Education on Crime: Evidence from Prison Inmates, Arrests, and Self-Reports." *The American Economic Review* 94(1): 155-89.

Looney, Adam, and Constantine Yannelis. 2015. "A Crisis in Student Loans? How Changes in the Characteristics of Borrowers and in the Institutions they Attended Contributed to Rising Loan Defaults." *Brookings Papers on Economic Activity*. Washington: Brookings Institution.

Luo, Mi, and Simon Mongey. 2016. "Student Debt and Initial Labor Market Decisions: Search, Wages and Job Satisfaction." Working paper. New York University: Department of Economics. (https://wp.nyu.edu/miluo/wp-content/uploads/sites/599/2014/09/Luo_Mongey_StudentDebt_Feb_16.pdf).

Manoli, Dayanand S., and Nicholas Turner. 2014. "Cash-on-Hand & College Enrollment: Evidence from Population Tax Data and Policy Nonlinearities." NBER Working Paper 19836. Cambridge, MA: National Bureau of Economic Research.

Marcotte, Dave E. 2016. "The Returns to Education at Community Colleges: New Evidence from the Education Longitudinal Survey." IZA Discussion Paper 10202. Bonn, Germany: Institute for the Study of Labor (IZA).

Marcotte, Dave E., et al. 2005. "The Returns for Education at Community Colleges: Evidence from the National Educational Longitudinal Survey," *Educational Evaluation and Policy Analysis* 27(2): 157-75.

Martorell, Paco, Brian McCall, and Isaac McFarlin. 2014. "Do Public Tuition Subsidies Promote College Enrollment? Evidence from Community College Taxing Districts in Texas." CES Paper 14-32. Census Bureau, Center for Economic Studies.

Maxfield, Michelle. 2013. "The Effects of the Earned Income Tax Credit on Child Achievement and Long-Term Educational Achievement." Working Paper. Michigan State University: Department of Economics. (https://msu.edu/~maxfiel7/20131114%20Maxfield%20 EITC%20Child%20Education.pdf).

McCrary, Justin, and Heather Royer. 2011. "The Effect of Female Education on Fertility and Infant Health: Evidence from School Entry Policies Using Exact Date of Birth." *American Economic Review* 101(1): 158-95.

MDRC. 2016. "Using Financial Aid to Speed Degree Completion: A Look at MDRC's Research." MDRC Issue Focus. March. New York.

Michelmore, Katherine. 2013. "The Effect of Income on Educational Attainment: Evidence from State Earned Income Tax Credit Expansions." Working Paper. University of Michigan at Ann Arbor and Syracuse University. (http://www.irp.wisc.edu/newsevents/seminars/Presen-tations/2013-2014/Michelmore_Draft_September_2013.pdf).

Miller-Adams, Michelle. 2009. *The Power of a Promise: Education and Economic Renewal in Kalamazoo. Kalamazoo*, MI: W.E. Upjohn Institute for Employment Research.

Mitchell, Michael, Vincent Palacios, and Michael Leachman. 2014. "States Are Still Funding Higher Education Below Pre-Recession Levels." Report. Washington: Center on Budget and Policy Priorities.

Moretti, Enrico. 2004. "Estimating the Social Return to Higher Education: Evidence from Longitudinal and Repeated Cross-Sectional Data." *Journal of Econometrics* 121(1): 175-212.

National Center for Education Statistics. 2015. "Digest of Education Statistics: 2015." Department of Education.

———. 2016. "Digest of Education Statistics: 2016." Department of Education.

Nord, Mark, and Mark Prell. 2011. "Food Security Improved Following the 2009 ARRA Increase in SNAP Benefits." Economic Research Report 116. United States Department of Agriculture.

Oreopoulos, Philip, and Ryan Dunn. 2012. "Information and College Access: Evidence from a Randomized Field Experiment." NBER Working Paper 18551. Cambridge, MA: National Bureau of Economic Research.

Oreopoulos, Philip, and Kjell G. Salvanes. 2011. "Priceless: The Nonpecuniary Benefits of Schooling." *Journal of Economic Perspectives* 25(1): 159-84.

Oreopoulos, Philip, Till von Wachter, and Andrew Heisz. 2012. "Short- and Long-term Career Effects of Graduating in a Recession." *American Economic Journal: Applied Economics* 4(1): 1-29.

Organization for Economic Cooperation and Development (OECD). 2013. "Education Indicators in Focus." Paris.

Ost, Ben, Weixiang Pan, and Doug Webber. 2016. "The Returns to College Persistence for Marginal Students: Regression Discontinuity Evidence from University Dismissal Policies." IZA Discussion Paper 9799. Bonn, Germany: Institute for the Study of Labor (IZA).

Page, Lindsay, and Jennifer E. Iritri. 2016. "On Undermatch and College Cost: A Case Study of the Pittsburgh Promise." In *Matching Students to Opportunity*, edited by Andrew P. Kelley, Jessica S. Howell, and Carolyn Sattin-Bajaj. Cambridge, MA: Harvard Education Press.

Page, Lindsay, and Judith Scott-Clayton. 2015. "Improving College Access in the United States: Barriers and Policy Responses." NBER Working Paper 21781. Cambridge, MA: National Bureau of Economic Research.

Papageorge, Nicholas W., and Kevin Thom. 2016. "Genes, Education, and Labor Market Outcomes: Evidence from the Health and Retirement Study." IZA Discussion Paper 10200. Bonn, Germany: Institute for the Study of Labor (IZA).

Peltzman, Sam. 1973. "The Effect of Government Subsidies-in-Kind on Private Expenditures: The Case of Higher Education." *Journal of Political Economy* 81(1): 1-27.

Reynolds, Arthur J., et al. 2011. "School-Based Early Childhood Education and Age-28 Well-Being: Effects by Timing, Dosage, and Subgroups." Science 333(6040): 360-4.

Ritter, Gary, and Jennifer Ash. 2016. "The Promise of a College Scholarship Transforms a District." *Phi Delta Kappan* 97(5): 13-9.

Rose, Heather, and Julian R. Betts. 2004. "The Effect of High School Courses on Earnings." The *Review of Economics and Statistics* 86(2): 497-513.

Rothstein, Jesse, and Cecilia Rouse. 2011. "Constrained After College: Student Loans and Early-Career Occupation Choices." *Journal of Public Economics* 95(1-2): 149-63.

Rothwell, Jonathan. 2014. "Still Searching: Job Vacancies and STEM Skills." Report. Washington: Brookings Institution.

Ruder, Alex, and Michelle van Noy. 2014. "The Influence of Labor Market Outcomes Data on Major Choice: Evidence from a Survey Experiment." Working Paper. Rutgers University: Heldrich Center for Workforce Development. (http://www.heldrich.rutgers.edu/sites/default/files/products/uploads/Labor_Market_Outcomes_Major_Choice.pdf).

Sargent Jr., John F. 2014. "The U.S. Science and Engineering Workforce: Recent, Current, and Projected Employment, Wages and Unemployment." CRS Report Prepared for Members and Committees of Congress. Congressional Research Service.

Scott-Clayton, Judith, Peter M. Crosta, and Clive R. Belfield. 2014. "Improving the Targeting of Treatment: Evidence from College Remediation." *Educational Evaluation and Policy Analysis* 36(3): 371-93.

Scrivener, Susan, et al. 2015. "Doubling Graduation Rates: Three-Year Effects of CUNY's Accelerated Study in Associate Programs (ASAP) for Developmental Education Students." Report. New York: MDRC.

Seftor, Niel, and Sarah Turner. 2002. "Back to School: Federal Student Aid Policy and Adult College Enrollment." *Journal of Human Resources* 37(2): 336-52.

Stevens, Ann, Michal Kurlaender, and Michel Grosz. 2015. "Career Technical Education and Labor Market Outcomes: Evidence from California Community Colleges." NBER Working Paper 21137. Cambridge, MA: National Bureau of Economic Research.

Sun, Stephen, and Constantine Yannelis. 2016. "Credit Constraints and Demand for Higher Education: Evidence from Financial Deregulation." *The Review of Economics and Statistics* 98(1): 12-24.

Taylor, Eric S., and John H. Tyler. 2012. "The Effect of Evaluation on Teacher Performance." *American Economic Review* 102(7): 3628-51.

Thaler, Richard, and Sendhil Mullainathan. 2008. "Behavioral Economics." In *The Concise Encyclopedia of Economics*, edited by David R. Henderson. Library of Economics and Liberty. (http://www.econlib.org/library/Enc/BehavioralEconomics.html).

Turner, Lesley. 2015. "The Returns to Higher Education for Marginal Students: Evidence from Colorado Welfare Recipients." *Economics of Education Review* 51(1): 169-84.

U.S. Senate. 2012. "For Profit Higher Education: The Failure to Safeguard the Federal Investment and Ensure Student Success." Committee on Health, Education, Labor, and Pensions. 112 Cong. 2 sess. Government Printing Office.

Wiederspan, Mark. 2015. "Denying Loan Access: The Student-Level Consequences When Community Colleges Opt Out of the Stafford Loan Program." CAPSEE Working Paper. New York: Center for Analysis of Postsecondary Education and Employment.

Wiswall, Matthew, and Basit Zafar. 2013. "How Do College Students Respond to Public Information about Earnings?" Federal Reserve Bank of New York Staff Report 516. New York: Federal Reserve Bank of New York.

Wong, Manyee, Thomas D. Cook, and Peter M. Steiner. 2011. "No Child Left Behind: An Interim Evaluation of Its Effects on Learning Using Two Interrupted Time Series Each With Its Own Non-Equivalent Comparison Series." IPR Working Paper 09-11. Evanston, IL: Institute for Policy Research, Northwestern University.

Wozniak, Abigail. 2010. "Are College Graduates More Responsive to Distant Labor Market Opportunities?" *Journal of Human Resources* 45(4): 944-70.

Zimmerman, Seth. 2014. "The Returns to College Admission for Academically Marginal Students." *Journal of Labor Economics* 32(4): 711-54.

CHAPTER 6

Acharya, Viral. V., Deniz Anginer, and A. Joseph Warburton. 2016. "The End of Market Discipline? Investor Expectations of Implicit State Guarantees." Working Paper. (http://pages.stern.nyu.edu/~sternfin/vacharya/public_html/pdfs/End%20of%20Market%20Discipline%20-%20Acharya%20Anginer%20Warburton%202_10_2016.pdf).

Acharya, Viral, Robert Engle, and Matthew Richardson. 2012. "Capital Shortfall: A New Approach to Ranking and Regulating Systemic Risks." *American Economic Review Papers and Proceedings* 102(3): 59-64.

Acharya, Viral V., et al. 2016. "Measuring Systemic Risk." *Review of Financial Studies* published online, forthcoming.

Adams, Robert M., and Jacob Gramlich. 2016. "Where Are All the New Banks? The Role of Regulatory Burden in New Bank Formation." *Review of Industrial Organization* 48(2): 181-208.

Adrian, Tobias, and Markus K. Brunnermeier. 2014. "CoVaR" Federal Reserve Bank of New York Staff Report 348. New York: Federal Reserve Bank of New York.

Balasubramnian, Bhanu, and Ken B. Cyree. 2014. "Has Market Discipline on Banks Improved After the Dodd-Frank Act?" *Journal of Banking and Finance* 41(2014): 155-66.

Basel Committee on Banking Supervision. 2013. "Global Systemically Important Banks: Updated Assessment Methodology and the Higher Loss Absorbency Requirement." Report. Basel, Switzerland: Bank for International Settlements.

Beck, Thorsten, Asli Demirguc-Kunt, and Ross Levine. 2006. "Bank Concentration, Competition, and Crises: First Results." *Journal of Banking and Finance* 30(5): 1581-603.

Bénabou, Roland, and Jean Tirole. 2016. "Bonus Culture: Competitive Pay, Screening, and Multitasking." *Journal of Political Economy* 124(2): 305-70.

Bergstresser, Daniel, John Chalmers, and Peter Tufano. 2009. "Assessing the Costs and Benefits of Brokers in the Mutual Fund Industry." *The Review of Financial Studies* 22(10): 4129-56.

Berk, Jonathan B., and Richard C. Green. 2004. "Mutual Fund Flows and Performance in Rational Markets." *Journal of Political Economy* 112(6): 1269-95.

Bernanke, Ben. 2016. "Ending "too big to fail": What's the right approach?" Blog. May 13. Washington: Brookings Institution. (https://www.brookings.edu/blog/ben-bernanke/2016/05/13/ending-too-big-to-fail-whats-the-right-approach/).

Biais, Bruno, Thierry Foucault, and Sophia Moinas. 2015. "Equilibrium Fast Trading." *Journal of Financial Economics* 116(2): 292-313.

Choi, Dong Beom, and Hyun-Soo Choi. 2016. "The Effect of Monetary Policy on Bank Wholesale Funding." Federal Reserve Bank of New York Staff Report 759. New York: Federal Reserve Bank of New York.

Christoffersen, Susan E.K., Richard Evans, and David K. Musto. 2013. "What Do Consumers' Fund Flows Maximize? Evidence from Their Brokers' Incentives." *Journal of Finance* 68(1): 201-35.

Cochrane, John H. 2013. "Finance: Function Matters, Not Size." *Journal of Economic Perspectives* 27(2): 29-50.

Council of Economic Advisers (CEA). 2015a. "The Effects of Conflicted Investment Advice on Retirement Savings." Report.

_____. 2015b. "Long-Term Interest Rates: A Survey." Report.

_____. 2016. "The Performance of Community Banks Over Time." Issue Brief. August.

Del Guercio, Diane, and Jonathan Reuter. 2014. "Mutual Fund Performance and the Incentive to Generate Alpha." *The Journal of Finance* 69(4): 1673-704.

Department of Treasury. 2016. "General Explanations of the Administration's Fiscal Year 2017 Revenue Proposals." February.

Diamond, Douglas W., and Philip H. Dybvig. 1983. "Bank Runs, Deposit Insurance, and Liquidity." *Journal of Political Economy* 91(3): 401-19.

Engle, Robert. 2012. "European Systemic Risk." Presentation at the Luigi Solari Conference. Geneva: Université de Genève. November 19. (https://www.unige.ch/gsem/iee/files/7613/9574/8572/Solari_2012_slides.pdf).

Fama, Eugene F., and Kenneth R. French. 2010. "Luck versus Skill in the Cross-Section of Mutual Fund Returns." *Journal of Finance* 65 (5): 1915-47.

Federal Reserve Board of Governor (FRB). 2016. "Agencies Announce Determinations and Provide Feedback on Resolution Plans of Eight Systemically Important, Domestic Banking Institutions." Press Release. April 13. (https://www.federalreserve.gov/newsevents/press/bcreg/20160413a.htm).

Financial Crisis Inquiry Commission. 2011. The Financial Crisis Inquiry Report. Government Printing Office.

Financial Stability Board. 2016. "Implementation and Effects of the G20 Financial Regulatory Reforms." 2nd Annual Report. Washington.

General Electric. 2015. "GE To Create Simpler, More Valuable Industrial Company by Selling Most GE Capital Assets; Potential to Return More than $90 Billion to Investors Through 2018 in Dividends, Buyback & Synchrony Exchange." Press Release. April 10. (http://www.genewsroom.com/press-releases/ge-create-simpler-more-valuable-industrial-company-selling-most-ge-capital-assets).

Glasserman, Paul, and Bert Loudis. 2015. "A Comparison of U.S. and International Global Systematically Important Banks." OFR Brief Series 15-07. Treasury Department, Office of Financial Research. August.

Goldstein, Morris, and Nicolas Veron. 2011. "Too Big to Fail: The Transatlantic Debate." Bruegel Working Paper 2011/03. Brussels, Belgium: Bruegel.

Government Accountability Office (GAO). 2014. "Large Bank Holding Companies: Expectations of Government Support." Report to Congressional Requestors. GAO-14-621.

Greenwood, Robin, and David Scharfstein. 2013. "The Growth of Finance." *Journal of Economic Perspectives* 27(2): 3-28.

Holden, Sarah, and Daniel Schrass. 2015. "The Role of IRAs in U.S. Households' Saving for Retirement, 2014." *ICI Research Perspective* 21(1): 1-40.

Huang, Xin, Hao Zhou, and Haibin Zhu. 2011. "Systemic Risk Contributions." Finance and Economics Discussion Series Working Paper. Federal Reserve Board of Governors, Divisions of Research &

Statistics and Monetary Affairs. (https://www.federalreserve.gov/pubs/feds/2011/201108/201108pap.pdf).

Hughes, Joseph P., and Loretta J. Mester. 2013. "Who Said Large Banks Don't Experience Scale Economies? Evidence from a Risk-Return-Driven Cost Function." *Journal of Financial Intermediation* 22(4): 559-85.

International Monetary Fund (IMF). 2014. "Chapter 3: How Big is the Implicit Subsidy for Banks Considered Too Important to Fail?" In *Global Financial Stability Report 2014: Moving from Liquidity- to Growth-Driven Markets*. Washington.

Jorda, Oscar, Moritz Schularick, and Alan M. Taylor. 2016. "The Great Mortgaging: Housing Finance, Crises, and Business Cycles." *Economic Policy* 31(85): 107-52.

Mishkin, Frederic S. 1978. "The Household Balance Sheet and the Great Depression." *Journal of Economic History* 38(4): 918-37.

Philippon, Thomas, and Ariell Reshef. 2012. "Wages and Human Capital in the U.S. Finance Industry: 1909-2006." *Quarterly Journal of Economics* 127(4): 1551-609.

Pozsar, Zoltan, et al. 2012. "Shadow Banking." Federal Reserve Bank of New York Staff Report 458. New York: Federal Reserve Bank of New York.

Sarin, Natasha, and Lawrence H. Summers. 2016. "Have Big Banks Gotten Safer?" BPEA Conference Draft, September 15-16, 2016. *Brookings Papers on Economic Activity*. Washington: Brookings Institution.

Securities and Exchange Commission (SEC). 2011. "Study on Investment Advisers and Broker-Dealers: As Required by Section 913 of the Dodd-Frank Wall Street Reform and Consumer Protection Act."

————. 2014. "Annual Report on Nationally Recognized Statistical Rating Organizations: As Required by Section 6 of the Credit Rating Agency Reform."

Ueda, Kenichi, and Beatrice Weder di Mauro. "Quantifying Structural Subsidy Values for Systemically Important Financial Institutions." *Journal of Banking and Finance* 37(10): 3830-42.

U.S. House of Representatives. 2015. "Dodd-Frank Five Years Later: Accomplishments, Threats, and Next Steps." Democratic Staff Report, 114th Congress. Committee on Financial Services.

Wheelock, David C., and Paul W. Wilson. 2012. "Do Large Banks Have Lower Costs? New Estimates of Returns to Scale for U.S. Banks." *Journal of Money, Credit and Banking* 44(1): 171-99.

Wiggins, Rosalind Z., Thomas Piontek, and Andrew Metrick. 2014. "The Lehman Brothers Bankruptcy A: Overview." Yale Program on Financial Stability Case Study 2014-3A-V1. New Haven: Yale School of Management.

CHAPTER 7

Arrow, Kenneth J., et al. 2013. "Determining Benefits and Costs For Future Generations." *Science* 341(6144): 349-50.

————. 2014. "Should Governments Use a Declining Discount Rate in Project Analysis?" *Review of Environmental Economics and Policy* 8(2): 145-63.

Auffhammer, Maximilian, and Wolfram Schlenker. 2014. "Empirical Studies on Agricultural Impacts and Adaptation." *Energy Economics* 46(C): 555-61.

Bailey, Diane. 2015. "US Approves Five-Year PTC Phase Out." *Wind Power Monthly*. December 18. (http://www.windpowermonthly.com/article/1377405/us-approves-five-year-ptc-phase).

Bakkensen, Laura A., and Robert O. Mendelsohn. 2016. "Risk and Adaptation: Evidence From Global Hurricane Damages and Fatalities." *Journal of the Association of Environmental and Resource Economists* 3(3): 555-87.

Barbose, Galen, and Naïm Darghouth. 2015. "Tracking the Sun VIII: The Installed Price of Residential and Non-Residential Photovoltaic Systems in the United States." Lawrence Berkeley National Laboratory for the Department of Energy.

Barreca, Alan, et al. 2016. "Adapting to Climate Change: The Remarkable Decline in the U.S. Temperature-Mortality Relationship over the 20th Century." *Journal of Political Economy* 124(1): 105-59.

Bergek, Anna, Staffan Jacobsson, and Björn Sandén. 2008. "'Legitimation' and 'Development of Positive Externalities': Two Key Processes in the Formation Phase of Technological Innovation Systems." *Technology Analysis and Strategic Management* 20(5): 575-92.

Bodnar, Paul, and Dave Turk. 2015. "Announcing: 'Mission Innovation.'" White House Blog. November 19. (https://www.whitehouse.gov/blog/2015/11/29/announcing-mission-innovation).

Bolinger, Mark, and Joachim Seel. 2015. "Utility-Scale Solar 2014: An Empirical Analysis of Project Cost, Performance, and Pricing Trends in the United States." Lawrence Berkeley National Laboratory for the Department of Energy.

Brescher Shea, Shannon. 2014. "EV Everywhere: America's Plug-In Electric Vehicle Market Charges Forward." (http://energy.gov/eere/articles/ev-everywhere-america-s-plug-electric-vehicle-market-charges-forward).

Bureau of Land Management (BLM). 2016a. "Discretionary Programmatic Environmental Impact Statement to Modernize the Federal Coal Program." Order 3388. Department of the Interior.

———. 2016b. "Fact Sheet: Modernizing the Federal Coal Program." Department of the Interior.

California Executive Department. 2014. *Executive Order B-29-15*. Executive Department, State of California.

Cavallo, Alfred J., Susan M. Hock, and Don R. Smith. 1993. "Wind Energy: Resources, Systems and Regional Strategies." In *Renewable Energy – Sources for Fuel and Electricity*, edited by Thomas B. Johansson and Laurie Burnham, pp. 157-212. Washington: Island Press.

Christidis, Nikolaos, Gareth S. Jones, and Peter A. Stott. 2015. "Dramatically Increasing Chance of Extremely Hot Summers since the 2003 European Heatwave." *Nature Climate Change* 5(1): 46-50.

Council of Economic Advisers (CEA). 2013. "Chapter 6: Climate Change and the Path toward Sustainable Energy Sources." *Economic Report of the President.*

———. 2014. "The Cost of Delaying Action to Stem Climate Change." Report.

———. 2015a. "Chapter 6: The Energy Revolution: Economic Benefits and the Foundation for a Low-Carbon Energy Future." *Economic Report of the President.*

———. 2015b. "Explaining the U.S. Petroleum Consumption Surprise." Report.

_____. 2016a. "The Economics of Coal Leasing on Federal Lands: Ensuring a Fair Return to Taxpayers." Report.

_____. 2016b. "Incorporating Renewables into the Electric Grid: Expanding Opportunities for Smart Markets and Energy Storage." Report.

_____. 2016c. "A Retrospective Assessment of Clean Energy Investments in the Recovery Act." Report.

Crimmins, Allison, et al. 2016. "The Impacts of Climate Change on Human Health in the United States: A Scientific Assessment." Report. Washington: U.S. Global Change Research Program.

Department of Agriculture (USDA). 2016. "Rural Energy for America Program: Renewable Energy Systems & Energy Efficiency Improvement Loans & Grants." Rural Development. (http://www.rd.usda.gov/programs-services/rural-energy-america-program-renewable-energy-systems-energy-efficiency).

Department of Energy (DOE). 2012. "President Obama Launches EV-Everywhere Challenge as Part of Energy Department's Clean Energy Grand Challenges." (http://energy.gov/articles/president-obama-launches-ev-everywhere-challenge-part-energy-department-s-clean-energy).

_____. 2015. "Revolution…Now: The Future Arrives for Five Clean Energy Technologies – 2015 Update." Report.

_____. 2016a. "Appliance and Equipment Standards Program." Office of Energy Efficiency & Renewable Energy. (http://energy.gov/eere/buildings/appliance-and-equipment-standards-program).

_____. 2016b. "Better Buildings Challenge: Frequently Asked Questions." (https://betterbuildingssolutioncenter.energy.gov/sites/default/files/attachments/Better%20Buildings%20Challenge%20Frequently%20Asked%20Questions.pdf).

_____. 2016c. "Energy Conservation Program for Certain Industrial Equipment: Energy Conservation Standards for Small, Large, and Very Large Air-Cooled Commercial Package Air Conditioning and Heating Equipment and Commercial Warm Air Furnaces" Direct Final Rule.

_____. 2016d. "Moving our Nation Forward, Faster Progress Report 2016." Report.

_____. 2016e. "Recovery Act Smart Grid Programs." (https://www.smart-grid.gov/recovery_act/).

_____. 2016f. "Workplace Charging Challenge: Join the Challenge." (http://energy.gov/eere/vehicles/workplace-charging-challenge-join-challenge).

Department of the Interior (DOI). 2016. "Secretary Jewell Launches Comprehensive Review of Federal Coal Program." (https://www.doi.gov/pressreleases/secretary-jewell-launches-comprehensive-review-federal-coal-program).

Department of State. 2016a. "Overview of the Global Climate Change Initiative: U.S. Climate Finance 2010-2015." Report.

_____. 2016b. "Second Biennial Report of the United States of America." Report for the United Nations Framework Convention on Climate Change.

Department of Transportation (DOT). 2016. "TIGER Discretionary Grants." (https://www.transportation.gov/tiger).

Deschênes, Olivier. 2014. "Temperature, Human Health, and Adaptation: A Review of the Empirical Literature." *Energy Economics* 46(2014): 606-19.

Deschênes, Olivier, and Michael Greenstone. 2011. "Climate Change, Mortality, and Adaptation: Evidence from Annual Fluctuations in Weather in the US." *American Economic Journal: Applied Economics* 3(4): 152-85.

Deschênes, Olivier, and Enrico Moretti. 2009. "Extreme Weather Events, Mortality, and Migration." *Review of Economics and Statistics* 91(4): 659-81.

D'Ippoliti, Daniela, et al. 2010. "The Impact of Heat Waves on Mortality in 9 European Cities: Results from the EuroHEAT Project." *Environmental Health* 9(37).

Electricity Reliability Council of Texas. 2016. "Wind Integration Report: 02/18/2016."

Energy Information Administration (EIA). 2015. "Levelized Cost and Levelized Avoided Cost of New Generation Resources." *Annual Energy Outlook 2015.*

_____. 2016a. *Annual Energy Outlook 2016.*

_____. 2016b. *Monthly Energy Review (MER).* August. Petroleum data. (http://www.eia.gov/totalenergy/data/monthly/pdf/sec3.pdf).

_____. 2016c. *Short Term Energy Outlook (STEO)*. November.

_____. 2016d. "United States Remains the Largest Producer of Petroleum and Natural Gas Hydrocarbons." *Today in Energy*. May 23. (http://www.eia.gov/todayinenergy/detail.php?id=26352).

Environmental Protection Agency (EPA). 2012. "Regulatory Impact Analysis: Final Rulemaking for 2017-2025 Light-Duty Vehicle Greenhouse Gas Emission Standards and Corporate Average Fuel Economy Standards."

_____. 2015a. "Climate Change in the United States: Benefits of Global Action." United States Environmental Protection Agency, Office of Atmospheric Programs, EPA-430-R-15-001.

_____. 2015b. "Fact Sheet: Clean Power Plan by the Numbers." (https://www.epa.gov/cleanpowerplan/fact-sheet-clean-power-plan-numbers).

_____. 2015c. "Regulatory Impact Analysis for the Clean Power Plan Final Rule."

_____. 2015d. "Regulatory Impact Analysis for the Final Standards of Performance for Greenhouse Gas Emissions from New, Modified, and Reconstructed Stationary Sources: Electric Utility Generating Units."

_____. 2016a. "Inventory of U.S. Greenhouse Gas Emissions and Sinks: 1990-2014." Report.

_____. 2016b. "Reducing Hydrofluorocarbon (HFC) Use and Emissions in the Federal Sector." (https://www.epa.gov/snap/reducing-hydrofluorocarbon-hfc-use-and-emissions-federal-sector).

Environmental Protection Agency and National Highway Traffic Safety Administration (EPA and NHTSA). 2016. "Greenhouse Gas Emissions and Fuel Efficiency Standards for Medium- and Heavy-Duty Engines and Vehicles—Phase 2. Regulatory Impact Analysis."

Executive Office of the President (EOP). 2013. "The President's Climate Action Plan." Report. The White House.

_____. 2015. "Executive Order: Planning for Federal Sustainability in the Next Decade." The White House. March 19. (https://www.whitehouse.gov/the-press-office/2015/03/19/executive-order-planning-federal-sustainability-next-decade).

_____. 2016. "Obama Administration Record on an All-of-the-Above Energy Strategy." Report. The White House.

Farmer, E.D., V.G. Newman, and Peter H. Ashmole. 1980. "Economic and Operational Implications of a Complex of Wind-Driven Generators on a Power System." *IEE Proceedings A: Physical Science, Measurement and Instrumentation, Management and Education-Reviews* 127(5): 289-95.

Federal Energy Regulatory Commission. 2016. "Office of Energy Projects, Energy Infrastructure Update." June.

Fishman, Ram Mukul. 2012. "Climate Change, Rainfall Variability, and Adaptation Through Irrigation: Evidence from Indian Agriculture." Working Paper. (https://1b474b80-a-62cb3a1a-s-sites. googlegroups.com/site/ramfishman/RFishman_JMP.pdf?attachauth=ANoY7cqoyLOl2jXcwlfOvyuVEbUMrim5zO0ODs9KYR lEGiIJ0H7CpcNRjDVHWJ5499P54IODZNtjMrsfeZFdx8JVpjV 3a3TfYEW_xHrT32w8hm-Ffz4JqgojoKsvVGRgtkey4qkV_atrP-WfwDQxwxcPcpa_OHtFY0NgNsNn3r56fqqU7tQEk9F2LMjs-JBIoJChBDFZ7TKs8dXmxsA8fSHSerWreJ0FaMA%3D%3D&attre directs=0).

Fowlie, Meredith, et al. 2014. "An Economic Perspective on the EPA's Clean Power Plan." *Science* 346(6211): 815-6.

Gillingham, Kenneth, and James Sweeney. 2012. "Barriers to Implementing Low-Carbon Technologies." *Climate Change Economics* 3(4): 1-21.

Goulder, Lawrence H., and Roberton C. Williams III. 2012. "The Choice of Discount Rate for Climate Change Policy Evaluation." *Climate Change Economics* 3(4).

Government Accountability Office (GAO). 2013. "Coal Leasing: BLM Could Enhance Appraisal Process, More Explicitly Consider Coal Exports, and Provide More Public Information." Report to Congressional Requesters. GAO-14-140.

Graff Zivin, Joshua, and Matthew Neidell. 2012. "The Impact of Pollution on Worker Productivity." *The American Economic Review* 102(7): 3652-73.

_____. 2014. "Temperature and the Allocation of Time: Implications for Climate Change." *Journal of Labor Economics* 32(1): 1-26.

Hsiang, Solomon M., and Daiju Narita. 2012. "Adaptation to Cyclone Risk: Evidence from the Global Cross-Section." *Climate Change Economics* 3(2).

Interagency Working Group on the Social Cost of Carbon (IWG). 2013. "Technical Support Document: Technical Update of the Social Cost of Carbon for Regulatory Impact Analysis - Under Executive Order 12866." The White House.

_____. 2015. "Technical Support Document: Technical Update of the Social Cost of Carbon for Regulatory Impact Analysis Under Executive Order 12866." The White House.

_____. 2016a. "Addendum to Technical Support Document on Social Cost of Carbon for Regulatory Impact Analysis under Executive Order 12866: Application of the Methodology to Estimate the Social Cost of Methane and the Social Cost of Nitrous Oxide." The White House.

_____. 2016b. "Technical Support Document: Technical Update of the Social Cost of Carbon for Regulatory Impact Analysis Under Executive Order 12866." The White House.

Intergovernmental Panel on Climate Change (IPCC). 2013. "Summary for Policymakers." In *Climate Change 2013: The Physical Science Basis. Contribution of Working Group I to the Fifth Assessment Report of the Intergovernmental Panel on Climate Change*, edited by T.F. Stocker, D. Qin, G.-K. Plattner, M. Tignor, S.K. Allen, J. Boschung, A. Nauels, Y. Xia, V. Bex and P.M. Midgley. Cambridge, United Kingdom: Cambridge University Press.

Jaffe, Adam B., and Robert N. Stavins. 1994. "The Energy-Efficiency Gap: What Does It Mean?" *Energy Policy* 22(10): 804-10.

Kaufman, Noah, Michael Obeiter, and Eleanor Krause. 2016. "Putting a Price on Carbon: Reducing Emissions." World Resources Institute Issue Brief. January. Washington: World Resources Institute.

Keohane, Nathaniel O. 2003. "What Did the Market Buy? Cost Savings under the U.S. Tradeable Permits Program for Sulfur Dioxide." Yale School of Management Working Paper ES-33. New Haven: Yale University School of Management.

Leggett, Jane A. 2015. "Climate Change Adaptation by Federal Agencies: An Analysis of Plans and Issues for Congress." CRS Report Prepared for Members and Committees of Congress. Congressional Research Service.

Lenton, Timothy M., et al. 2008. "Tipping Elements in the Earth's Climate System." *Proceedings of the National Academy of Sciences* 105(6): 1786-93.

Millner, Antony. 2013. "On Welfare Frameworks and Catastrophic Climate Risks." *Journal of Environmental Economics and Management* 65(2): 310-25.

Mission Innovation. 2016. "About Mission Innovation." (http://mission-innovation.net/about/).

National Highway Traffic Safety Administration (NHTSA). 2012. "EPA and NHTSA Set Standards to Reduce Greenhouse Gases and Improve Fuel Economy for Model Years 2017-2025 Cars and Light Trucks."

National Oceanic and Atmospheric Administration, National Centers for Environmental Information (NOAA). 2016a. "State of the Climate: Global Analysis for Annual 2015." Report. (https://www.ncdc.noaa.gov/sotc/global/201513).

———. 2016b. "State of the Climate: Global Analysis for August 2016." Report. (https://www.ncdc.noaa.gov/sotc/global/201608).

———. 2016c. "U.S. Billion-Dollar Weather and Climate Disasters." National Centers for Environmental Information. (https://www.ncdc.noaa.gov/billions/).

Newbold, Stephen C., and Adam Daigneault. 2009. "Climate Response Uncertainty and the Benefits of Greenhouse Gas Emission Reductions." *Environmental and Resource Economics* 44(2009): 351-77.

Nordhaus, William D. 2009. "An Analysis of the Dismal Theorem." Cowles Foundation Discussion Paper 1686. New Haven: Cowles Foundation for Research in Economics, Yale University.

———. 2011. "Designing a Friendly Space for Technological Change to Slow Global Warming." *Energy Economics* 33(4): 665-73.

Nykvist, Björn, and Mans Nilsson. 2015. "Rapidly Falling Costs of Battery Packs for Electric Vehicles." *Nature Climate Change* 5(4): 329-32.

Obama, Barack. 2009. "Interview with President Obama on Climate Bill." *The New York Times.* June 28. (http://www.nytimes.com/2009/06/29/us/politics/29climate-text.html?login=email&_r=0&mtrref=undefined).

Office of Management and Budget (OMB). 2016. "Climate Change: The Fiscal Risks Facing the Federal Government, A Preliminary Assessment." Report. The White House.

Popp, David. 2003. "Pollution Control Innovations and the Clean Air Act of 1990." *Journal of Policy Analysis and Management* 22(4): 641-60.

Risky Business Project. 2014. "Risky Business: The Economic Risks of Climate Change in the United States." Report.

Robine, Jean-Marie, et al. 2008. "Death Toll Exceeded 70,000 in Europe During the Summer of 2003." *Comptes Rendus Biologies* 331(2): 171-8.

Schlenker, Wolfram, and Michael J. Roberts. 2009. "Nonlinear Temperature Effects Indicate Severe Damages to U.S. Crop Yields Under Climate Change." *Proceedings of the National Academy of Sciences* 106(37): 15594-8.

Schwietzke, Stefan, et al. 2016. "Upward Revision of Global Fossil Fuel Methane Emissions Based on Isotope Database." *Nature* 538(7623): 88-91.

Slack, Megan. 2012. "Invest in a Clean Energy Future by Ending Fossil Fuels Subsidies." White House Blog. March 26. (https://www.whitehouse.gov/blog/2012/03/26/invest-clean-energy-future-ending-fossil-fuels-subsidies).

Stott, Peter A., Dáithí A. Stone, and Myles R. Allen. 2004. "Human Contribution to the European Heatwave of 2003." *Nature* 432(7017): 610-4.

Turner, Alex J., et al. 2016. "A Large Increase in US Methane Emissions over the Past Decade Inferred from Satellite Data and Surface Observations." *Geophysical Research Letters* 43(5): 2218-24.

United Nations Environment Programme (UNEP). 2016. "Countries Agree to Curb Powerful Greenhouse Gases in Largest Climate Breakthrough Since Paris." October 15. (http://unep.org/newscentre/Default.aspx?DocumentID=27086&ArticleID=36283&l=en).

U.S. Global Change Research Program. 2014. *Climate Change Impacts in the United States: The Third National Climate Assessment.* Edited by Jerry M. Melillo, Terese Richmond, and Gary W. Yohe. Government Printing Office.

Vilsack, Thomas. 2016. "Statement by Thomas Vilsack Secretary of Agriculture Before the Senate Committee on Agriculture." September 21.

Walsh, Bryan. 2010. "Why the Climate Bill Died." *Time*. July 26. (http://science.time.com/2010/07/26/why-the-climate-bill-died/).

Weitzman, Martin L. 2009. "On Modeling and Interpreting the Economics of Catastrophic Climate Change." *Review of Economics and Statistics* 91(1): 1-19.

_____. 2011. "Fat-Tailed Uncertainty in the Economics of Catastrophic Climate Change." *Review of Environmental Economics and Policy* 5(2): 275-92.

_____. 2014. "Fat Tails and the Social Cost of Carbon." *The American Economic Review* 104(5): 544-6.

Wiser, Ryan, and Mark Bolinger. 2014. "2014 Wind Technologies Market Report." Lawrence Berkeley National Laboratory for the Department of Energy.

ZERO. "Consumo de Eletricidade em Portugal Foi Assegurado Durante Mais De 4 Dias Seguidos Por Fontes Renováveis (Portuguese Energy Consumption Was Sustained for More than Four Days by Renewable Energy)." May 15. (http://zero.ong/consumo-de-eletricidade-em-portugal-foi-assegurado-durante-mais-de-4-dias-seguidos-por-fontes-renovaveis/).

APPENDIX A

REPORT TO THE PRESIDENT ON THE ACTIVITIES OF THE COUNCIL OF ECONOMIC ADVISERS DURING 2016

LETTER OF TRANSMITTAL

COUNCIL OF ECONOMIC ADVISERS
Washington, D.C., December 15, 2016

MR. PRESIDENT:

The Council of Economic Advisers submits this report on its activities during calendar year 2016 in accordance with the requirements of the Congress, as set forth in section 10(d) of the Employment Act of 1946 as amended by the Full Employment and Balanced Growth Act of 1978.

Sincerely yours,

Jason Furman, *Chairman*
Sandra E. Black, *Member*
Jay C. Shambaugh, *Member*

Council Members and Their Dates of Service

Name	Position	Oath of office date	Separation date
Edwin G. Nourse	Chairman	August 9, 1946	November 1, 1949
Leon H. Keyserling	Vice Chairman	August 9, 1946	
	Acting Chairman	November 2, 1949	
	Chairman	May 10, 1950	January 20, 1953
John D. Clark	Member	August 9, 1946	
	Vice Chairman	May 10, 1950	February 11, 1953
Roy Blough	Member	June 29, 1950	August 20, 1952
Robert C. Turner	Member	September 8, 1952	January 20, 1953
Arthur F. Burns	Chairman	March 19, 1953	December 1, 1956
Neil H. Jacoby	Member	September 15, 1953	February 9, 1955
Walter W. Stewart	Member	December 2, 1953	April 29, 1955
Raymond J. Saulnier	Member	April 4, 1955	
	Chairman	December 3, 1956	January 20, 1961
Joseph S. Davis	Member	May 2, 1955	October 31, 1958
Paul W. McCracken	Member	December 3, 1956	January 31, 1959
Karl Brandt	Member	November 1, 1958	January 20, 1961
Henry C. Wallich	Member	May 7, 1959	January 20, 1961
Walter W. Heller	Chairman	January 29, 1961	November 15, 1964
James Tobin	Member	January 29, 1961	July 31, 1962
Kermit Gordon	Member	January 29, 1961	December 27, 1962
Gardner Ackley	Member	August 3, 1962	
	Chairman	November 16, 1964	February 15, 1968
John P. Lewis	Member	May 17, 1963	August 31, 1964
Otto Eckstein	Member	September 2, 1964	February 1, 1966
Arthur M. Okun	Member	November 16, 1964	
	Chairman	February 15, 1968	January 20, 1969
James S. Duesenberry	Member	February 2, 1966	June 30, 1968
Merton J. Peck	Member	February 15, 1968	January 20, 1969
Warren L. Smith	Member	July 1, 1968	January 20, 1969
Paul W. McCracken	Chairman	February 4, 1969	December 31, 1971
Hendrik S. Houthakker	Member	February 4, 1969	July 15, 1971
Herbert Stein	Member	February 4, 1969	
	Chairman	January 1, 1972	August 31, 1974
Ezra Solomon	Member	September 9, 1971	March 26, 1973
Marina v.N. Whitman	Member	March 13, 1972	August 15, 1973
Gary L. Seevers	Member	July 23, 1973	April 15, 1975
William J. Fellner	Member	October 31, 1973	February 25, 1975
Alan Greenspan	Chairman	September 4, 1974	January 20, 1977
Paul W. MacAvoy	Member	June 13, 1975	November 15, 1976
Burton G. Malkiel	Member	July 22, 1975	January 20, 1977
Charles L. Schultze	Chairman	January 22, 1977	January 20, 1981
William D. Nordhaus	Member	March 18, 1977	February 4, 1979
Lyle E. Gramley	Member	March 18, 1977	May 27, 1980
George C. Eads	Member	June 6, 1979	January 20, 1981
Stephen M. Goldfeld	Member	August 20, 1980	January 20, 1981
Murray L. Weidenbaum	Chairman	February 27, 1981	August 25, 1982
William A. Niskanen	Member	June 12, 1981	March 30, 1985
Jerry L. Jordan	Member	July 14, 1981	July 31, 1982

COUNCIL MEMBERS AND THEIR DATES OF SERVICE

Name	Position	Oath of office date	Separation date
Martin Feldstein	Chairman	October 14, 1982	July 10, 1984
William Poole	Member	December 10, 1982	January 20, 1985
Beryl W. Sprinkel	Chairman	April 18, 1985	January 20, 1989
Thomas Gale Moore	Member	July 1, 1985	May 1, 1989
Michael L. Mussa	Member	August 18, 1986	September 19, 1988
Michael J. Boskin	Chairman	February 2, 1989	January 12, 1993
John B. Taylor	Member	June 9, 1989	August 2, 1991
Richard L. Schmalensee	Member	October 3, 1989	June 21, 1991
David F. Bradford	Member	November 13, 1991	January 20, 1993
Paul Wonnacott	Member	November 13, 1991	January 20, 1993
Laura D'Andrea Tyson	Chair	February 5, 1993	April 22, 1995
Alan S. Blinder	Member	July 27, 1993	June 26, 1994
Joseph E. Stiglitz	Member	July 27, 1993	
	Chairman	June 28, 1995	February 10, 1997
Martin N. Baily	Member	June 30, 1995	August 30, 1996
Alicia H. Munnell	Member	January 29, 1996	August 1, 1997
Janet L. Yellen	Chair	February 18, 1997	August 3, 1999
Jeffrey A. Frankel	Member	April 23, 1997	March 2, 1999
Rebecca M. Blank	Member	October 22, 1998	July 9, 1999
Martin N. Baily	Chairman	August 12, 1999	January 19, 2001
Robert Z. Lawrence	Member	August 12, 1999	January 12, 2001
Kathryn L. Shaw	Member	May 31, 2000	January 19, 2001
R. Glenn Hubbard	Chairman	May 11, 2001	February 28, 2003
Mark B. McClellan	Member	July 25, 2001	November 13, 2002
Randall S. Kroszner	Member	November 30, 2001	July 1, 2003
N. Gregory Mankiw	Chairman	May 29, 2003	February 18, 2005
Kristin J. Forbes	Member	November 21, 2003	June 3, 2005
Harvey S. Rosen	Member	November 21, 2003	
	Chairman	February 23, 2005	June 10, 2005
Ben S. Bernanke	Chairman	June 21, 2005	January 31, 2006
Katherine Baicker	Member	November 18, 2005	July 11, 2007
Matthew J. Slaughter	Member	November 18, 2005	March 1, 2007
Edward P. Lazear	Chairman	February 27, 2006	January 20, 2009
Donald B. Marron	Member	July 17, 2008	January 20, 2009
Christina D. Romer	Chair	January 29, 2009	September 3, 2010
Austan D. Goolsbee	Member	March 11, 2009	
	Chairman	September 10, 2010	August 5, 2011
Cecilia Elena Rouse	Member	March 11, 2009	February 28, 2011
Katharine G. Abraham	Member	April 19, 2011	April 19, 2013
Carl Shapiro	Member	April 19, 2011	May 4, 2012
Alan B. Krueger	Chairman	November 7, 2011	August 2, 2013
James H. Stock	Member	February 7, 2013	May 19, 2014
Jason Furman	Chairman	August 4, 2013	January 20, 2017
Betsey Stevenson	Member	August 6, 2013	August 7, 2015
Maurice Obstfeld	Member	July 21, 2014	August 28, 2015
Sandra E. Black	Member	August 10, 2015	January 20, 2017
Jay C. Shambaugh	Member	August 31, 2015	January 20, 2017

REPORT TO THE PRESIDENT
ON THE ACTIVITIES OF THE
COUNCIL OF ECONOMIC ADVISERS
DURING 2016

The Council of Economic Advisers was established by the Employment Act of 1946 to provide the President with objective economic analysis and advice on the development and implementation of a wide range of domestic and international economic policy issues. The Council is governed by a Chairman and two Members. The Chairman is appointed by the President and confirmed by the United States Senate. The Members are appointed by the President.

THE CHAIRMAN OF THE COUNCIL

Jason Furman was confirmed by the U.S. Senate on August 1, 2013. Prior to this role, Furman served as Assistant to the President for Economic Policy and the Principal Deputy Director of the National Economic Council.

From 2007 to 2008, Furman was a Senior Fellow in Economic Studies and Director of the Hamilton Project at the Brookings Institution. Previously, he served as a Staff Economist at the Council of Economic Advisers, a Special Assistant to the President for Economic Policy at the National Economic Council under President Clinton, and Senior Adviser to the Chief Economist and Senior Vice President of the World Bank. Furman was the Economic Policy Director for Obama for America. Furman has also served as Visiting Scholar at New York University's Wagner Graduate School of Public Service, a visiting lecturer at Yale and Columbia Universities, and a Senior Fellow at the Center on Budget and Policy Priorities.

THE MEMBERS OF THE COUNCIL

Sandra E. Black was appointed by the President on August 10, 2015. She is on leave from the University of Texas, Austin where she holds the Audre and Bernard Rapoport Centennial Chair in Economics and Public Affairs and is a Professor of Economics. Dr. Black received her B.A. from the

University of California, Berkeley and her Ph.D. in economics from Harvard University.

Jay C. Shambaugh was appointed by the President on August 31, 2015. He is on leave from George Washington University, where he is a Professor of Economics and International Affairs. Dr. Shambaugh received a B.A. from Yale, an M.A.L.D. from The Fletcher School at Tufts University, and a Ph.D. in Economics from the University of California, Berkeley.

AREAS OF ACTIVITIES

A central function of the Council is to advise the President on all economic issues and developments. In the past year, as in previous years, advising the President on policies to spur economic growth and job creation, and evaluating the effects of these policies on the economy, have been priorities.

The Council works closely with various government agencies, including the National Economic Council, the Domestic Policy Council, the Office of Management and Budget, White House senior staff, and other officials to engage in discussions on numerous policy matters. In the area of international economic policy, the Council coordinates with other units of the White House, the Treasury Department, the State Department, the Commerce Department, and the Federal Reserve.

Among the many economic policy areas that received attention in 2016, the Council focused in particular on: income inequality and inclusive growth; the Affordable Care Act and health care costs; labor force participation; criminal justice policies and incarceration; innovation and competition, including in the labor market; the minimum wage and unemployment insurance; trade policies and the Trans Pacific Partnership; international economics; financial system reform; energy and environment policies; and higher education and college affordability.

The Council prepares for the President, the Vice President, and the White House senior staff a daily economic briefing memo analyzing current economic developments, almost-daily memos on key economic data releases, and periodic memos on broader topics. The Council and its staff also presents a monthly briefing on the state of the economy to senior White House officials.

The Council, the Department of Treasury, and the Office of Management and Budget—the Administration's economic "troika"— are responsible for producing the economic forecasts that underlie the Administration's budget proposals. The Council initiates the forecasting process twice each year, consulting with a wide variety of outside sources, including leading private-sector forecasters and other government agencies.

The Council was an active participant in the trade policy process, providing analysis and opinions on a range of trade-related issues involving the enforcement of existing trade agreements, reviews of current U.S. trade policies, and consideration of future policies. The Council also participated on the Trade Promotion Coordinating Committee, helping to examine the ways in which exports may support economic growth in the years to come. In the area of investment and security, the Council participated on the Committee on Foreign Investment in the United States (CFIUS), reviewing individual cases before the committee.

The Council is a leading participant in the Organisation for Economic Co-operation and Development (OECD), an important forum for economic cooperation among high-income industrial economies. The Council coordinated with other agencies to provide information for the OECD's review of the U.S. economy. Chairman Furman is chairman of the OECD's Economic Policy Committee, and Council Members and staff participate actively in working-party meetings on macroeconomic policy and coordination and contribute to the OECD's research agenda.

The Council issued a wide range of reports and issue briefs in 2016. In January, the Council commemorated the seven-year anniversary of the Lilly Ledbetter Fair Pay Act by releasing an issue brief on the gender pay gap and progress made to ensure that women receive equal pay for equal work. In February, the Council released a retrospective assessment of the impact of the clean energy investments made in the American Recovery and Reinvestment Act.

In March, the Council released an issue brief on the digital divide and the economic benefits of broadband access. The brief highlighted the impacts that the Administration's initiatives have had in dramatically expanding access to the Internet for families and students, and reviewed academic research that shows that Internet access leads to better labor market outcomes. The Council also released a March issue brief on patent litigation and its impact on innovation. The brief reviewed recent trends in increasing levels of patent litigation, and the possible negative effect of these suits on entrepreneurship and productivity growth. That same month, the Council released new analysis on the impact of the Affordable Care Act six years after passage. The analysis reviewed the substantial progress made on health care coverage, costs, and quality.

In April, the Council released a report on the economic impacts of incarceration and criminal justice policies. The report applied an economic framework to policy questions related to criminal justice reform and found that some criminal justice policies, such as increased incarceration, fail cost-benefit tests. The report also highlighted that minority communities are disproportionately impacted by interactions with the criminal justice system, and these interactions can have long-run effects on individuals, families, and communities. In addition, the Council released an issue brief on the benefits of competition and indicators of market power. The issue brief highlighted the economic benefits of competition for workers and firms and reviewed several indicators that competition may be decreasing in the U.S. economy.

The Council released a June report on financial inclusion in the United States, which highlighted the lack of access to safe and affordable financial services for many low-income individuals. The report showed that expanding access to traditional banking services for underbanked communities has positive economic impacts. That same month, the Council released an extensive report on the long-term decline in the prime-age male labor force participation rate. The report reviewed trends over the last 50 years of declining labor force participation among working age men, and emphasized the economic impact of this decline for both the macroeconomy as well as individual families. The report reviewed various explanations for these changes, as well as policy responses.

In June, the Council also focused on energy and environment policies, issuing a report on prospects for integrating renewable energy sources into the electric grid. The report emphasized the important transition toward renewable generation in the United States, and the economics of integrating these energy sources into electric grid operation. The Council also released a report on the economics of coal leasing on Federal lands and reforms needed to ensure that taxpayers receive a fair return.

In July, the Council released a report on investments in higher education and the state of student debt. This report highlighted the financial benefits to individuals and the economy from higher education investments, and evaluated recent trends in the level of education-related debt. The report also highlighted the importance of the Administration's policies to make college affordable for American families and to protect students from low-quality academic institutions.

The Council published a report in August on the performance of community banks over time, finding that, across many measures, community banks have remained strong since financial reform legislation was passed in 2010. In October, the Council released an issue brief on the economic progress of the Hispanic community over the past eight years, focusing in particular on rising wages, declining poverty, and increased health insurance coverage.

In October, the Council released a report on labor market monopsony, or wage-setting power, including recent trends and policy responses. The report highlighted the role that firm wage-setting power may have played in the slow wage growth over recent decades and increasing inequality. In November, the Council released an issue brief on trade policy and the industries and jobs at risk if the Trans Pacific Partnership does not pass.

Some of the analysis and findings of these reports can be found throughout this *Economic Report of the President*. Additionally, over the course of 2016, the Council published a series of reports examining the Administration's economic record and quantifying the impact of President Obama's economic policies. These reports included analysis of progress reducing income inequality, economic benefits of health care reform, investments in higher education, the role of financial reform in strengthening the financial system, and actions to address climate change. They are collected and expanded upon in this *Economic Report of the President*.

All of the aforementioned reports can be found on the Council's website, archived at http://www.obamawhitehouse.gov/administration/eop/cea/factsheets-reports.

The Council continued its efforts to improve the public's understanding of economic developments and of the Administration's economic policies through briefings with the economic and financial press, speeches, discussions with outside economists, and regular updates on major data releases and postings of CEA's reports on the White House and CEA blogs. The Chairman and Members also regularly met to exchange views on the economy with the Chairman and Members of the Board of Governors of the Federal Reserve System.

PUBLIC INFORMATION

The Council's annual *Economic Report of the President* is an important vehicle for presenting the Administration's domestic and international economic policies. It is available for purchase through the Government Printing Office, and is viewable on the Internet at www.gpo.gov/erp.

The Council frequently prepared reports and blog posts in 2016, and the Chairman and Members gave numerous public speeches. The reports, posts and texts of speeches are available at the Council's website, archived at www.obamawhitehouse.gov/cea. Finally, the Council published the monthly *Economic Indicators*, which is available online at www.gpo.gov/economicindicators.

THE STAFF OF THE COUNCIL OF ECONOMIC ADVISERS

The staff of the Council consists of the senior staff, senior economists, staff economists, research economists, and the administrative and support staff. The staff at the end of 2016 was:

Senior Staff

Andrea Taverna . . . . Chief of Staff
Matthew Fiedler . . . . Chief Economist
Steven N. Braun . . . . Director of Macroeconomic Forecasting
Tomeka R. Jordan. . . . . Director of Finance and Administration
Adrienne Pilot. . . . . Director of Statistical Office

Senior Economists

Victor Bennett. . . . . Innovation, Industrial Organization, Technology
William J. Congdon . . . . Behavioral Economics, Labor, Welfare
Laura Giuliano . . . . Education, Labor, Welfare
Gregory Leiserson . . . . Budget, Retirement, Tax
Sheila Olmstead . . . . Energy, Environment
Christopher Otrok . . . . Housing, Macroeconomics
Burt Porter. Finance
Katheryn Russ. . . . . International Economics
Aaron Sojourner. . . . . Criminal Justice, Education, Labor

Economists

Emily R. Gee . . . . Health

Staff Economists

James Elwell . . . . Criminal Justice, Labor
Amy Filipek. Housing, Macroeconomics
Conor Foley. International Trade, Macroeconomics
Stephen Harrell. . . . . Labor
Rahul Rekhi. Budget, Health, Tax

Research Economists

David Boddy . . . . Labor
Marie Cases . . . . International Trade, Macroeconomics
Neha Dalal . . . . Education, Labor
Amelia Keyes . . . . Competition, Energy, Environment
Nataliya Langburd . . . . Energy, International Trade,
                                        Macroeconomics
Robert Liu . . . . Finance, Macroeconomics
Ayushi Narayan . . . . Education, Labor
Jana Parsons . . . . Industrial Organization
Wilson Powell III . . . . Health, Labor

Statistical Office

The Statistical Office gathers, administers, and produces statistical information for the Council. Duties include preparing the statistical appendix to the *Economic Report of the President* and the monthly publication *Economic Indicators*. The staff also creates background materials for economic analysis and verifies statistical content in Presidential memoranda. The Office serves as the Council's liaison to the statistical community.

Brian A. Amorosi . . . . Statistical Analyst
Jennifer Vogl . . . . Economic Statistician

Office of the Chairman and Members

Jeff Goldstein . . . . Deputy Chief of Staff and Special
                                        Assistant to the Chairman
Harris R. Eppsteiner . . . . Special Assistant to the Chairman and
                                        Research Economist
Jamie Keene . . . . Special Assistant to the Members

Administrative Office

The Administrative Office provides general support for the Council's activities. This includes financial management, human resource management, travel, operations of facilities, security, information technology, and telecommunications management support.

Doris T. Searles . . . . Operations Manager

Interns

Student interns provide invaluable help with research projects, day-to-day operations, and fact-checking. Interns during the year were: Andres Arguello, Edward Brown, John Patrick Bruno, Arianna Davis, Atticus Francken, Amy Frieder, Samarth Gupta, Kevin Gawora, Joe Jacobson, Joanna Jin, Gloria Li, Stephanie Lu, Karna Malaviya, Victoria Marlin, Brianna E. McClain, Femi Olaleye, Katherine Reinmuth, Andrés Rodríguez Brauer, Kunal Sangani, John Scianimanico, Riley Webster, Stacey Young, Laura Zhang, and Robin Zhang.

DEPARTURES IN 2016

The senior economists who resigned in 2016 (with the institutions to which they returned after leaving the Council in parentheses) were: Kenneth Gillingham (Yale University), Timothy Park (Department of Agriculture), Nirupama Rao (New York University), Claudia Sahm (Federal Reserve), and Robert Seamans (New York University).

The staff economists who departed in 2016 were Martha Gimbel, E. Mallick Hossain, Bryson Rintala, Gabriel Scheffler, Paige Weber, and Emily Weisburst.

The research economists who departed in 2016 were Lydia Cox, Samuel Himel, Emma Rackstraw, and Jason Sockin.

The research assistants who departed in 2016 were William Weber and Samuel Young.

Anna Y. Lee resigned from her position as Director of Finance and Administration. Eric Van Nostrand resigned from his position as Special Assistant to the Chairman and Staff Economist. Jonathan Sheppard resigned from his position as Economic Statistician.

STATISTICAL TABLES RELATING TO INCOME, EMPLOYMENT, AND PRODUCTION

CONTENTS

GOVERNMENT FINANCE, INTEREST RATES, AND MONEY STOCK
—Continued

General Notes

Detail in these tables may not add to totals due to rounding.

Because of the formula used for calculating real gross domestic product (GDP), the chained (2009) dollar estimates for the detailed components do not add to the chained-dollar value of GDP or to any intermediate aggregate. The Department of Commerce (Bureau of Economic Analysis) no longer publishes chained-dollar estimates prior to 1999, except for selected series.

Because of the method used for seasonal adjustment, the sum or average of seasonally adjusted monthly values generally will not equal annual totals based on unadjusted values.

Unless otherwise noted, all dollar figures are in current dollars.

Symbols used:
    p Preliminary.
    ... Not available (also, not applicable).

Data in these tables reflect revisions made by source agencies through December 2, 2016, unless otherwise noted.

Excel versions of these tables are available at *www.gpo.gov/erp*.

GDP, Income, Prices, and Selected Indicators

Table B–1. Percent changes in real gross domestic product, 1965–2016

[Percent change from preceding period; quarterly data at seasonally adjusted annual rates]

Year or quarter	Gross domestic product	Personal consumption expenditures			Gross private domestic investment								Change in private inventories
						Fixed investment							
							Nonresidential					
		Total	Goods	Services	Total	Total	Total	Structures	Equipment	Intellectual property products	Residential		
1965	6.5	6.3	7.1	5.5	13.8	10.4	16.7	15.9	18.2	12.7	−2.6		
1966	6.6	5.7	6.3	4.9	6.2	6.2	12.3	6.8	15.5	13.2	−8.4		
1967	2.7	3.0	2.0	4.1	−3.5	−.9	−.3	−2.5	−1.0	7.8	−2.6		
1968	4.9	5.7	6.2	5.3	6.0	7.0	4.8	1.4	6.1	7.5	13.5		
1969	3.1	3.7	3.1	4.4	5.6	5.9	7.0	5.4	8.3	5.4	3.1		
1970	.2	2.4	.8	3.9	−6.1	−2.1	−.9	.3	−1.8	−.1	−5.2		
1971	3.3	3.8	4.2	3.5	10.3	6.9	.0	−1.6	.8	.4	26.6		
1972	5.2	6.1	6.5	5.8	11.3	11.4	8.7	3.1	12.7	7.0	17.4		
1973	5.6	5.0	5.2	4.7	10.9	8.6	13.2	8.2	18.5	5.0	−.6		
1974	−.5	−.8	−3.6	1.9	−6.6	−5.6	.8	−2.2	2.1	2.9	−19.6		
1975	−.2	2.3	.7	3.8	−16.2	−9.8	−9.0	−10.5	−10.5	.9	−12.1		
1976	5.4	5.6	7.0	4.3	19.1	9.8	5.7	2.4	6.1	10.9	22.1		
1977	4.6	4.2	4.3	4.1	14.3	13.6	10.8	4.1	15.5	6.6	20.5		
1978	5.6	4.4	4.1	4.6	11.6	11.6	13.8	14.4	15.1	7.1	6.7		
1979	3.2	2.4	1.6	3.1	3.5	5.8	10.0	12.7	8.2	11.7	−3.7		
1980	−.2	−.3	−2.5	1.6	−10.1	−5.9	.0	5.9	−4.4	5.0	−20.9		
1981	2.6	1.5	1.2	1.7	8.8	2.7	6.1	8.0	3.7	10.9	−8.2		
1982	−1.9	1.4	.7	2.0	−13.0	−6.7	−3.6	−1.6	−7.6	6.2	−18.1		
1983	4.6	5.7	6.4	5.2	9.3	7.5	−.4	−10.8	4.6	7.9	42.0		
1984	7.3	5.3	7.2	3.9	27.3	16.2	16.7	13.9	19.4	13.7	14.8		
1985	4.2	5.3	5.3	5.3	−.1	5.5	6.6	7.1	5.5	9.0	2.3		
1986	3.5	4.2	5.6	3.2	.2	1.8	−1.7	−11.0	1.1	7.0	12.4		
1987	3.5	3.4	1.8	4.5	2.8	.6	.1	−2.9	.4	3.9	2.0		
1988	4.2	4.2	3.7	4.5	2.5	3.3	5.0	.7	6.6	7.1	−.9		
1989	3.7	2.9	2.5	3.2	4.0	3.2	5.7	2.0	5.3	11.7	−3.2		
1990	1.9	2.1	.6	3.0	−2.6	−1.4	1.1	1.5	−2.1	8.4	−8.5		
1991	−.1	.2	−2.0	1.6	−6.6	−5.1	−3.9	−11.1	−4.6	6.4	−8.9		
1992	3.6	3.7	3.2	4.0	7.3	5.5	2.9	−6.0	5.9	6.0	13.8		
1993	2.7	3.5	4.2	3.1	8.0	7.7	7.5	−.3	12.7	4.2	8.2		
1994	4.0	3.9	5.3	3.1	11.9	8.2	7.9	1.8	12.3	4.0	9.0		
1995	2.7	3.0	3.0	3.0	3.2	6.1	9.7	6.4	12.1	7.3	−3.4		
1996	3.8	3.5	4.5	2.9	8.8	8.9	9.1	5.7	9.5	11.3	8.2		
1997	4.5	3.8	4.8	3.2	11.4	8.6	10.8	7.3	11.1	13.0	2.4		
1998	4.5	5.3	6.7	4.6	9.5	10.2	10.8	5.1	13.1	10.8	8.6		
1999	4.7	5.3	7.9	3.9	8.4	8.8	9.7	.1	12.5	12.4	6.3		
2000	4.1	5.1	5.2	5.0	6.5	6.9	9.1	7.8	9.7	8.9	.7		
2001	1.0	2.6	3.0	2.4	−6.1	−1.6	−2.4	−1.5	−4.3	.5	.9		
2002	1.8	2.6	3.9	1.9	−.6	−3.5	−6.9	−17.7	−5.4	−.5	6.1		
2003	2.8	3.1	4.8	2.2	4.1	4.0	1.9	−3.9	3.2	3.8	9.1		
2004	3.8	3.8	5.1	3.2	8.8	6.7	5.2	−.4	7.7	5.1	10.0		
2005	3.3	3.5	4.1	3.2	6.4	6.8	7.0	1.7	9.6	6.5	6.6		
2006	2.7	3.0	3.6	2.7	2.1	2.0	7.1	7.2	8.6	4.5	−7.6		
2007	1.8	2.2	2.7	2.0	−3.1	−2.0	5.9	12.7	3.2	4.8	−18.8		
2008	−.3	−.3	−2.5	.8	−9.4	−6.8	−.7	6.1	−6.9	3.0	−24.0		
2009	−2.8	−1.6	−3.0	−.9	−21.6	−16.7	−15.6	−18.9	−22.9	−1.4	−21.2		
2010	2.5	1.9	3.4	1.2	12.9	1.5	2.5	−16.4	15.9	1.9	−2.5		
2011	1.6	2.3	3.1	1.8	5.2	6.3	7.7	2.3	13.6	3.6	.5		
2012	2.2	1.5	2.7	.8	10.6	9.8	9.0	12.9	10.8	3.9	13.5		
2013	1.7	1.5	3.1	.6	6.1	5.0	3.5	1.4	4.6	3.4	11.9		
2014	2.4	2.9	3.9	2.3	4.5	5.5	6.0	10.3	5.4	3.9	3.5		
2015	2.6	3.2	4.0	2.8	5.0	4.0	2.1	−4.4	3.5	4.8	11.7		
2013: I	2.8	1.9	5.7	.0	13.8	7.0	5.2	−5.1	8.7	7.6	14.7		
II	.8	.8	1.3	.6	5.0	4.3	2.5	10.4	2.8	−3.2	12.0		
III	3.1	1.9	2.9	1.3	13.4	2.9	2.1	17.1	−5.2	3.6	6.0		
IV	4.0	3.4	4.0	3.1	5.4	6.6	9.5	2.1	19.5	1.1	−4.5		
2014: I	−1.2	1.9	2.4	1.7	−6.6	5.3	7.0	25.1	.3	4.9	−1.4		
II	4.0	3.8	6.7	2.3	11.2	7.2	6.1	7.4	6.5	4.5	11.7		
III	5.0	3.7	4.3	3.4	8.9	7.4	8.3	−2.7	15.2	7.1	3.6		
IV	2.3	4.6	5.1	4.3	2.6	1.3	−1.1	4.1	−8.9	7.8	11.4		
2015: I	2.0	2.4	2.7	2.3	9.9	3.7	1.3	−12.3	9.3	.8	13.3		
II	2.6	2.9	4.3	2.2	1.0	4.3	1.6	−2.7	−.3	8.0	14.9		
III	2.0	2.7	4.2	2.0	2.0	5.7	3.9	−4.3	9.1	2.1	12.6		
IV	.9	2.3	2.1	2.3	−2.3	−.2	−3.3	−15.2	−2.6	4.6	11.5		
2016: I	.8	1.6	1.2	1.9	−3.3	−.9	−3.4	.1	−9.5	3.7	7.8		
II	1.4	4.3	7.1	3.0	−7.9	−1.1	1.0	−2.1	−2.9	9.0	−7.7		
III ᵖ	3.2	2.8	3.4	2.5	2.1	−.9	.1	10.1	−4.8	1.0	−4.4		

See next page for continuation of table.

TABLE B–1. Percent changes in real gross domestic product, 1965–2016—*Continued*

[Percent change from preceding period; quarterly data at seasonally adjusted annual rates]

Year or quarter	Net exports of goods and services			Government consumption expenditures and gross investment					Final sales of domestic product	Gross domestic purchases [1]	Final sales to private domestic purchasers [2]	Gross domestic income (GDI) [3]	Average of GDP and GDI
	Net exports	Exports	Imports	Total	Federal			State and local					
					Total	National defense	Non-defense						
1965		2.8	10.6	3.2	0.8	-1.3	7.9	6.6	5.9	6.9	7.2	6.4	6.4
1966		6.9	14.9	8.7	10.7	12.9	3.6	6.2	6.1	6.9	5.8	6.0	6.3
1967		2.3	7.3	7.9	10.1	12.5	1.9	5.0	3.3	3.0	2.1	3.0	2.9
1968		7.9	14.9	3.4	1.5	1.6	1.3	6.0	5.1	5.2	6.0	5.0	4.9
1969		4.9	5.7	.2	-2.4	-4.1	3.9	3.5	3.2	3.2	4.2	3.3	3.2
1970		10.7	4.3	-2.0	-6.1	-8.2	1.0	2.9	.9	-.1	1.4	-.1	.0
1971		1.7	5.3	-1.8	-6.4	-10.2	5.6	3.1	2.7	3.5	4.4	3.0	3.1
1972		7.8	11.3	-.5	-3.1	-6.9	7.2	2.2	5.2	5.4	7.3	5.5	5.4
1973		18.8	4.6	-.3	-3.6	-5.1	.2	2.8	5.2	4.8	5.8	5.8	5.7
1974		7.9	-2.3	2.3	.7	-1.0	4.6	3.7	-.3	-1.2	-1.9	-.6	-.5
1975		-.6	-11.1	2.2	.5	-1.0	3.9	3.6	1.0	-1.1	-.4	-.5	-.4
1976		4.4	19.5	.5	.2	-.5	1.6	.8	4.0	6.5	6.4	5.1	5.2
1977		2.4	10.9	1.2	2.2	1.0	4.7	.4	4.4	5.3	6.2	4.8	4.7
1978		10.5	8.7	2.9	2.5	.8	6.0	3.3	5.5	5.5	6.0	5.5	5.5
1979		9.9	1.7	1.9	2.3	2.7	1.7	1.5	3.6	2.5	3.2	2.4	2.8
1980		10.8	-6.6	1.9	4.4	3.9	5.4	-.2	.6	-1.9	-1.7	-.1	-.2
1981		1.2	2.6	1.0	4.5	6.2	1.0	-2.0	1.5	2.7	1.8	3.0	2.8
1982		-7.6	-1.3	1.8	3.7	7.2	-3.6	.1	-.6	-1.3	-.5	-1.0	-1.4
1983		-2.6	12.6	3.8	6.5	7.3	4.7	1.3	4.3	5.9	6.1	3.3	4.0
1984		8.2	24.3	3.6	3.3	5.2	-1.4	3.8	5.4	8.7	7.6	7.8	7.5
1985		3.3	6.5	6.8	7.9	8.8	5.7	5.7	5.4	4.5	5.3	4.0	4.1
1986		7.7	8.5	5.4	5.9	6.9	3.1	5.0	3.8	3.7	3.7	3.0	3.3
1987		10.9	5.9	3.0	3.8	5.1	.2	2.2	3.1	3.2	2.8	4.3	3.9
1988		16.2	3.9	1.3	-1.3	-.2	-4.3	3.9	4.4	3.3	4.0	5.1	4.6
1989		11.6	4.4	2.9	1.7	-.2	7.2	4.0	3.5	3.1	3.0	2.5	3.1
1990		8.8	3.6	3.2	2.1	.3	7.3	4.1	2.1	1.5	1.3	1.5	1.7
1991		6.6	-.1	1.2	.0	-1.0	2.4	2.2	.2	-.7	-.9	.0	.0
1992		6.9	7.0	.5	-1.5	-4.5	5.9	2.1	3.3	3.6	4.0	3.3	3.4
1993		3.3	8.6	-.8	-3.5	-5.1	.0	1.2	2.7	3.3	4.3	2.2	2.5
1994		8.8	11.9	.1	-3.5	-4.9	-.8	2.8	3.4	4.4	4.7	4.4	4.2
1995		10.3	8.0	.5	-2.6	-4.0	.0	2.7	3.2	2.6	3.6	3.4	3.1
1996		8.2	8.7	1.0	-1.2	-1.6	-.5	2.4	3.8	3.9	4.6	4.3	4.0
1997		11.9	13.5	1.9	-.8	-2.7	2.8	3.6	4.0	4.7	4.8	5.1	4.8
1998		2.3	11.7	2.1	-.9	-2.1	1.3	3.8	4.5	5.5	6.4	5.3	4.9
1999		2.6	10.1	3.4	2.0	1.5	2.7	4.2	4.7	5.5	6.1	4.4	4.5
2000		8.6	13.0	1.9	.3	-.9	2.3	2.8	4.2	4.8	5.5	4.7	4.4
2001		-5.8	-2.8	3.8	3.9	3.5	4.7	3.7	1.9	1.2	1.7	1.1	1.0
2002		-1.7	3.7	4.4	7.2	7.0	7.4	2.9	1.3	2.3	1.3	1.4	1.6
2003		1.8	4.5	2.2	6.8	8.5	4.1	-.4	2.8	3.1	3.3	2.3	2.5
2004		9.8	11.4	1.6	4.5	6.0	2.0	-.1	3.4	4.3	4.4	3.7	3.8
2005		6.3	6.3	.6	1.7	2.0	1.3	.0	3.4	3.5	4.2	3.6	3.4
2006		9.0	6.3	1.5	2.5	2.0	3.5	.9	2.6	2.6	2.8	4.0	3.3
2007		9.3	2.5	1.6	1.7	2.5	.3	1.5	2.0	1.1	1.3	.1	.9
2008		5.7	-2.6	2.8	6.8	7.5	5.5	.3	.2	-1.3	-1.7	-.8	-.6
2009		-8.8	-13.7	3.2	5.7	5.4	6.2	1.6	-2.0	-3.8	-4.6	-2.6	-2.7
2010		11.9	12.7	.1	4.4	3.2	6.4	-2.7	1.1	2.9	1.9	2.7	2.6
2011		6.9	5.5	-3.0	-2.7	-2.3	-3.4	-3.3	1.7	1.6	2.9	2.2	1.9
2012		3.4	2.2	-1.9	-1.9	-3.4	.9	-1.9	2.1	2.1	2.9	3.3	2.7
2013		3.5	1.1	-2.9	-5.8	-6.8	-4.1	-.8	1.5	1.3	2.1	1.2	1.5
2014		4.3	4.4	-.9	-2.5	-4.1	.1	.2	2.5	2.4	3.4	3.0	2.7
2015		.1	4.6	1.8	.0	-2.1	3.3	2.9	2.4	3.2	3.3	2.5	2.6
2013: I		4.0	1.3	-4.3	-10.5	-12.0	-8.1	.2	1.8	2.4	2.8	-.2	1.3
II		5.0	5.3	-2.0	-5.3	-5.3	-5.2	.3	.6	.9	1.5	2.0	1.4
III		3.1	1.7	-2.0	-5.1	-6.6	-2.6	.1	1.5	2.9	2.1	.8	2.0
IV		11.8	1.6	-2.8	-5.7	-4.2	-8.1	-1.0	4.1	2.6	4.0	2.5	3.2
2014: I		-2.7	4.9	-1.0	-.2	-5.0	8.3	-1.5	.8	.0	2.5	2.1	.4
II		8.7	9.9	.1	-2.8	-3.2	-2.0	2.0	3.3	4.3	4.4	5.4	4.7
III		2.1	-1.2	2.5	3.9	4.0	3.9	1.6	4.7	4.3	4.4	4.5	4.7
IV		4.5	11.2	-.4	-6.0	-11.6	3.5	3.3	2.1	3.4	4.0	4.0	3.1
2015: I		-5.8	5.6	2.6	1.9	-.4	5.4	3.0	1.0	3.6	2.7	1.6	1.8
II		2.9	2.9	3.2	.2	-.5	1.1	5.1	3.2	2.6	3.2	.6	1.6
III		-2.8	1.1	1.9	1.0	-1.2	4.2	2.5	2.6	2.4	3.3	2.5	2.2
IV		-2.7	.7	1.0	3.8	4.4	2.8	-.6	1.2	1.3	1.8	1.5	1.2
2016: I		-.7	-.6	1.6	-1.5	-3.2	.9	3.5	1.2	.8	1.1	.8	.8
II		1.8	.2	-1.7	-.4	-3.2	3.8	-2.5	2.6	1.2	3.2	.7	1.1
III p		10.1	2.1	.2	2.5	2.1	3.0	-1.1	2.7	2.2	2.1	5.2	4.2

[1] Gross domestic product (GDP) less exports of goods and services plus imports of goods and services.
[2] Personal consumption expenditures plus gross private fixed investment.
[3] Gross domestic income is deflated by the implicit price deflator for GDP.

Note: Percent changes based on unrounded GDP quantity indexes.

Source: Department of Commerce (Bureau of Economic Analysis).

TABLE B–2. Gross domestic product, 2000–2016

[Quarterly data at seasonally adjusted annual rates]

Year or quarter	Gross domestic product	Personal consumption expenditures			Gross private domestic investment								
		Total	Goods	Services	Total	Fixed investment						Residential	Change in private inventories
						Total	Nonresidential						
							Total	Structures	Equipment	Intellectual property products			

	Billions of dollars												
2000	10,284.8	6,792.4	2,452.9	4,339.5	2,033.8	1,979.2	1,493.8	318.1	766.1	409.5	485.4		54.5
2001	10,621.8	7,103.1	2,525.2	4,577.9	1,928.6	1,966.9	1,453.9	329.7	711.5	412.6	513.0		−38.3
2002	10,977.5	7,384.1	2,598.6	4,785.5	1,925.0	1,906.5	1,348.9	282.9	659.6	406.4	557.6		18.5
2003	11,510.7	7,765.5	2,721.6	5,044.0	2,027.9	2,008.7	1,371.7	281.8	669.0	420.9	636.9		19.3
2004	12,274.9	8,260.0	2,900.3	5,359.8	2,276.7	2,212.8	1,463.1	301.8	719.2	442.1	749.7		63.9
2005	13,093.7	8,794.1	3,080.3	5,713.8	2,527.1	2,467.5	1,611.5	345.6	790.7	475.1	856.1		59.6
2006	13,855.9	9,304.0	3,235.8	6,068.2	2,680.6	2,613.7	1,776.3	415.6	856.1	504.6	837.4		67.0
2007	14,477.6	9,750.5	3,361.6	6,388.9	2,643.7	2,609.3	1,920.6	496.9	885.8	537.9	688.7		34.5
2008	14,718.6	10,013.6	3,375.7	6,637.9	2,424.8	2,456.8	1,941.0	552.4	825.1	563.4	515.9		−32.0
2009	14,418.7	9,847.0	3,198.4	6,648.5	1,878.1	2,025.7	1,633.4	438.2	644.3	550.9	392.2		−147.6
2010	14,964.4	10,202.2	3,362.8	6,839.4	2,100.8	2,039.3	1,658.2	362.0	731.8	564.3	381.1		61.5
2011	15,517.9	10,689.3	3,596.5	7,092.8	2,239.9	2,198.1	1,812.1	381.6	838.2	592.2	386.0		41.8
2012	16,155.3	11,050.6	3,739.1	7,311.5	2,511.7	2,449.9	2,007.7	448.0	937.9	621.7	442.2		61.8
2013	16,691.5	11,361.2	3,834.5	7,526.7	2,706.3	2,613.9	2,094.4	463.6	982.8	647.9	519.5		92.4
2014	17,393.1	11,863.4	3,970.5	7,892.9	2,886.5	2,821.0	2,251.0	530.7	1,040.7	679.6	570.1		65.4
2015	18,036.6	12,283.7	4,012.1	8,271.6	3,056.6	2,963.2	2,311.3	507.3	1,086.1	717.9	651.9		93.4
2013: I	16,475.4	11,256.7	3,827.6	7,429.0	2,617.6	2,554.0	2,058.3	439.3	974.3	644.7	495.7		63.6
II	16,541.4	11,284.5	3,803.6	7,480.9	2,658.1	2,593.6	2,077.1	454.7	980.4	642.0	516.5		64.5
III	16,749.3	11,379.1	3,834.7	7,544.5	2,750.8	2,625.3	2,094.2	476.1	968.6	649.5	531.1		125.5
IV	16,999.9	11,524.4	3,872.2	7,652.2	2,798.6	2,682.7	2,147.9	484.3	1,008.0	655.6	534.8		115.9
2014: I	17,025.2	11,636.1	3,900.8	7,735.3	2,774.0	2,738.6	2,194.5	518.1	1,011.6	664.7	544.1		35.4
II	17,285.6	11,800.6	3,967.4	7,833.2	2,861.6	2,796.7	2,235.5	531.8	1,031.5	672.2	561.2		64.9
III	17,569.4	11,941.0	3,999.7	7,941.3	2,939.8	2,863.6	2,287.5	532.4	1,070.8	684.4	576.0		76.2
IV	17,692.2	12,075.8	4,014.1	8,061.7	2,970.4	2,885.2	2,286.3	540.4	1,049.0	696.9	598.8		85.3
2015: I	17,783.6	12,098.9	3,956.7	8,142.2	3,044.6	2,915.7	2,297.6	519.8	1,076.6	701.2	618.1		129.0
II	17,998.3	12,240.2	4,010.7	8,229.5	3,049.9	2,944.7	2,304.9	512.9	1,075.7	716.3	639.8		105.2
III	18,141.9	12,356.9	4,043.0	8,313.9	3,072.1	2,995.3	2,331.5	508.5	1,099.7	723.3	663.8		76.8
IV	18,222.8	12,438.8	4,038.1	8,400.6	3,059.9	2,997.2	2,311.3	487.8	1,092.6	730.9	685.9		62.7
2016: I	18,281.6	12,498.0	4,008.7	8,489.3	3,036.8	2,994.8	2,292.4	486.0	1,066.3	740.1	702.4		41.9
II	18,450.1	12,692.7	4,085.4	8,607.3	2,987.5	3,002.5	2,304.7	487.3	1,058.7	758.7	697.8		−15.0
III ᵖ	18,657.9	12,825.3	4,110.6	8,714.8	3,010.0	3,005.8	2,306.9	498.5	1,048.6	759.8	698.9		4.2

	Billions of chained (2009) dollars												
2000	12,559.7	8,170.7	2,588.3	5,599.3	2,375.5	2,316.2	1,647.7	533.5	726.9	426.1	637.9		66.2
2001	12,682.2	8,382.6	2,666.6	5,731.0	2,231.4	2,280.0	1,608.4	525.4	695.7	428.0	643.7		−46.2
2002	12,908.8	8,598.8	2,770.2	5,838.2	2,218.2	2,201.1	1,498.0	432.5	658.0	425.9	682.7		22.5
2003	13,271.1	8,867.6	2,904.5	5,966.9	2,308.7	2,289.5	1,526.1	415.8	679.0	442.2	744.5		22.6
2004	13,773.5	9,208.2	3,051.9	6,156.6	2,511.3	2,443.9	1,605.4	414.1	731.2	464.9	818.9		71.4
2005	14,234.2	9,531.8	3,177.2	6,353.4	2,672.6	2,611.0	1,717.4	421.2	801.6	495.0	872.6		64.3
2006	14,613.8	9,821.7	3,292.5	6,526.6	2,730.0	2,662.5	1,839.6	451.5	870.8	517.5	806.6		71.6
2007	14,873.7	10,041.6	3,381.8	6,656.4	2,644.1	2,609.6	1,948.4	509.0	898.3	542.4	654.8		35.5
2008	14,830.4	10,007.2	3,297.8	6,708.6	2,396.0	2,432.6	1,934.4	540.2	836.1	558.8	497.7		−33.7
2009	14,418.7	9,847.0	3,198.4	6,648.5	1,878.1	2,025.7	1,633.4	438.2	644.3	550.9	392.2		−147.6
2010	14,783.8	10,036.3	3,308.7	6,727.6	2,120.4	2,056.2	1,673.8	366.3	746.7	561.3	382.4		58.2
2011	15,020.6	10,263.5	3,411.8	6,851.4	2,230.4	2,186.7	1,802.3	374.7	847.9	581.3	384.5		37.6
2012	15,354.6	10,413.2	3,504.3	6,908.1	2,465.7	2,400.4	1,964.1	423.1	939.2	603.8	436.5		54.7
2013	15,612.2	10,565.4	3,613.5	6,951.3	2,616.5	2,521.4	2,032.9	428.8	982.3	624.5	488.3		78.7
2014	15,982.3	10,868.9	3,755.4	7,114.2	2,733.6	2,660.6	2,155.6	472.9	1,035.7	648.6	505.4		57.7
2015	16,397.2	11,214.7	3,907.4	7,310.3	2,869.0	2,767.8	2,200.2	452.1	1,072.5	680.0	564.5		84.0
2013: I	15,491.9	10,502.3	3,582.9	6,918.6	2,543.0	2,482.7	2,006.7	412.0	972.7	625.2	475.9		49.6
II	15,521.6	10,523.9	3,594.3	6,929.0	2,574.3	2,508.8	2,019.0	422.3	979.6	620.1	489.5		52.6
III	15,641.3	10,573.1	3,620.5	6,952.2	2,656.8	2,526.7	2,029.6	439.3	966.6	625.5	496.8		109.0
IV	15,793.9	10,662.2	3,656.3	7,005.6	2,692.0	2,567.2	2,076.3	441.6	1,010.5	627.2	491.1		103.6
2014: I	15,747.0	10,712.8	3,678.2	7,034.4	2,646.4	2,600.5	2,111.8	467.0	1,011.3	634.7	489.4		31.7
II	15,900.8	10,813.3	3,738.7	7,075.4	2,717.5	2,646.1	2,143.4	475.4	1,027.4	641.7	503.1		55.2
III	16,094.5	10,912.9	3,778.6	7,135.3	2,776.3	2,693.4	2,186.7	472.2	1,064.4	652.8	507.6		66.8
IV	16,186.7	11,036.4	3,826.2	7,211.4	2,794.1	2,702.3	2,180.6	477.0	1,039.9	665.1	521.4		76.9
2015: I	16,269.0	11,102.4	3,851.5	7,252.4	2,860.8	2,727.2	2,187.9	461.5	1,063.2	666.5	538.0		114.4
II	16,374.2	11,181.3	3,892.1	7,291.8	2,867.7	2,756.0	2,196.6	458.4	1,062.3	679.5	556.9		93.8
III	16,454.9	11,255.9	3,932.6	7,327.2	2,882.2	2,794.5	2,217.5	453.4	1,085.7	683.1	573.7		70.9
IV	16,490.7	11,319.3	3,953.4	7,369.8	2,865.4	2,793.3	2,198.8	435.1	1,078.6	690.7	589.5		56.9
2016: I	16,525.0	11,365.2	3,964.7	7,403.9	2,841.5	2,786.7	2,179.7	435.2	1,052.0	697.1	600.7		40.7
II	16,583.1	11,484.9	4,032.9	7,458.5	2,783.8	2,778.8	2,185.0	432.9	1,044.1	712.2	588.7		−9.5
III ᵖ	16,712.5	11,563.5	4,066.7	7,504.2	2,798.1	2,772.4	2,185.8	443.4	1,031.5	714.0	582.1		7.6

See next page for continuation of table.

[Quarterly data at seasonally adjusted annual rates]

Year or quarter	Net exports of goods and services			Government consumption expenditures and gross investment					Final sales of domestic product	Gross domestic purchases	Final sales to private domestic purchasers [2]	Gross domestic income (GDI) [3]	Average of GDP and GDI
	Net exports	Exports	Imports	Total	Federal			State and local					
					Total	National defense	Non-defense						
				Billions of dollars									
2000	−375.8	1,096.8	1,472.6	1,834.4	632.4	391.7	240.7	1,202.0	10,230.2	10,660.6	8,771.6	10,384.3	10,334.5
2001	−368.7	1,026.7	1,395.4	1,958.8	669.2	412.7	256.5	1,289.5	10,660.1	10,990.5	9,070.0	10,736.8	10,679.3
2002	−426.5	1,002.5	1,429.0	2,094.9	740.6	456.8	283.8	1,354.3	10,959.0	11,404.0	9,290.5	11,050.3	11,013.9
2003	−503.7	1,040.3	1,543.9	2,220.8	824.8	519.9	304.9	1,396.0	11,491.4	12,014.3	9,774.2	11,524.3	11,517.5
2004	−619.2	1,181.5	1,800.7	2,357.4	892.4	570.2	322.1	1,465.0	12,211.1	12,894.1	10,472.8	12,283.5	12,279.2
2005	−721.2	1,308.9	2,030.1	2,493.7	946.3	608.3	338.1	1,547.4	13,034.1	13,814.9	11,261.6	13,129.2	13,111.5
2006	−770.9	1,476.3	2,247.3	2,642.2	1,002.0	642.4	359.6	1,640.2	13,788.9	14,626.8	11,917.7	14,073.2	13,964.5
2007	−718.5	1,664.6	2,383.2	2,801.9	1,049.8	678.7	371.0	1,752.2	14,443.2	15,196.2	12,359.8	14,460.1	14,468.9
2008	−723.1	1,841.9	2,565.0	3,003.2	1,155.6	754.1	401.5	1,847.6	14,750.6	15,441.6	12,470.5	14,619.2	14,668.9
2009	−395.4	1,587.7	1,983.2	3,089.1	1,217.7	788.3	429.4	1,871.4	14,566.3	14,814.2	11,872.7	14,343.4	14,381.1
2010	−512.7	1,852.3	2,365.0	3,174.0	1,303.9	832.8	471.1	1,870.2	14,902.8	15,477.0	12,241.5	14,915.2	14,939.8
2011	−580.0	2,106.4	2,686.4	3,168.7	1,303.5	836.9	466.5	1,865.3	15,476.2	16,097.9	12,887.4	15,556.3	15,537.1
2012	−565.7	2,198.2	2,763.8	3,158.6	1,292.5	817.8	474.7	1,866.1	16,093.5	16,720.9	13,500.5	16,358.5	16,256.9
2013	−492.0	2,276.6	2,768.6	3,116.1	1,229.5	767.0	462.5	1,886.6	16,599.1	17,183.5	13,975.1	16,829.5	16,760.5
2014	−508.8	2,375.3	2,884.1	3,152.1	1,218.9	746.0	472.9	1,933.2	17,327.7	17,901.9	14,684.4	17,651.1	17,522.1
2015	−522.0	2,264.3	2,786.3	3,218.3	1,225.0	732.0	493.0	1,993.3	17,943.3	18,558.6	15,246.9	18,290.3	18,163.5
2013: I	−519.5	2,242.2	2,761.7	3,120.7	1,245.3	779.6	465.7	1,875.4	16,411.8	16,995.0	13,810.6	16,635.8	16,555.6
II	−514.7	2,253.1	2,767.8	3,113.4	1,231.4	770.0	461.5	1,882.0	16,476.8	17,056.1	13,878.1	16,752.6	16,647.0
III	−492.9	2,274.1	2,767.0	3,112.3	1,220.2	759.3	460.9	1,892.1	16,623.8	17,242.3	14,004.4	16,867.8	16,808.6
IV	−440.9	2,337.1	2,777.9	3,117.7	1,220.9	759.0	461.9	1,896.8	16,883.9	17,440.8	14,207.1	17,061.6	17,030.7
2014: I	−508.4	2,339.1	2,847.4	3,123.6	1,218.1	750.0	468.0	1,905.5	16,989.9	17,533.6	14,374.7	17,225.5	17,125.4
II	−515.6	2,388.4	2,904.0	3,139.0	1,214.3	746.0	468.3	1,924.7	17,220.7	17,801.2	14,597.2	17,548.3	17,416.9
III	−485.6	2,394.7	2,880.3	3,174.2	1,230.6	755.5	475.1	1,943.6	17,493.2	18,055.0	14,804.6	17,817.0	17,693.2
IV	−525.5	2,379.0	2,904.6	3,171.4	1,212.5	732.5	480.0	1,958.9	17,606.9	18,217.7	14,961.0	18,013.5	17,852.8
2015: I	−534.7	2,287.8	2,822.4	3,174.7	1,218.8	731.2	487.6	1,955.9	17,654.7	18,318.3	15,014.6	18,084.5	17,934.1
II	−508.9	2,298.6	2,807.5	3,217.2	1,222.1	731.8	490.3	1,995.1	17,893.1	18,507.2	15,184.9	18,211.1	18,104.7
III	−523.4	2,259.1	2,782.5	3,236.3	1,225.0	729.3	495.7	2,011.3	18,065.1	18,665.3	15,352.2	18,378.0	18,260.0
IV	−520.9	2,211.7	2,732.6	3,245.0	1,234.0	735.6	498.4	2,011.0	18,160.1	18,743.7	15,436.0	18,487.6	18,355.2
2016: I	−507.4	2,179.0	2,686.3	3,254.3	1,233.8	731.4	502.4	2,020.5	18,239.7	18,789.0	15,492.8	18,546.0	18,413.8
II	−492.4	2,209.7	2,702.2	3,262.3	1,239.2	729.3	509.9	2,023.1	18,465.0	18,942.5	15,695.2	18,684.0	18,567.0
III p	−459.0	2,277.0	2,736.0	3,281.5	1,251.8	736.0	515.8	2,029.7	18,653.7	19,116.9	15,831.2	18,985.7	18,821.8
				Billions of chained (2009) dollars									
2000	−477.8	1,258.4	1,736.2	2,498.2	817.7	512.3	305.4	1,689.1	12,494.9	13,057.9	10,494.9	12,681.2	12,620.4
2001	−502.1	1,184.9	1,687.0	2,592.4	849.8	530.0	319.7	1,751.5	12,729.6	13,208.5	10,669.0	12,819.5	12,750.9
2002	−584.3	1,164.5	1,748.8	2,705.8	910.8	567.3	343.3	1,802.4	12,888.9	13,518.4	10,805.0	12,994.4	12,951.5
2003	−641.9	1,185.0	1,826.9	2,764.3	973.0	615.4	357.5	1,795.3	13,249.0	13,938.5	11,162.3	13,286.8	13,278.9
2004	−734.8	1,300.6	2,035.3	2,808.2	1,017.1	652.7	364.5	1,792.8	13,702.2	14,531.7	11,657.9	13,783.1	13,778.3
2005	−782.3	1,381.9	2,164.2	2,826.2	1,034.8	665.5	369.4	1,792.3	14,168.8	15,040.3	12,149.9	14,272.7	14,253.5
2006	−794.3	1,506.8	2,301.0	2,869.3	1,060.9	678.8	382.1	1,808.8	14,542.3	15,431.6	12,490.8	14,842.9	14,728.4
2007	−712.6	1,646.4	2,359.0	2,914.4	1,078.7	695.6	383.1	1,836.1	14,836.2	15,606.8	12,655.0	14,855.8	14,864.8
2008	−557.8	1,740.8	2,298.6	2,994.8	1,152.3	748.1	404.2	1,842.4	14,865.7	15,399.9	12,441.1	14,730.2	14,780.3
2009	−395.4	1,587.7	1,983.2	3,089.1	1,217.7	788.3	429.4	1,871.4	14,566.3	14,814.2	11,872.7	14,343.4	14,381.1
2010	−458.8	1,776.6	2,235.4	3,091.4	1,270.7	813.5	457.1	1,820.8	14,722.2	15,244.9	12,092.5	14,735.2	14,759.5
2011	−459.4	1,898.3	2,357.7	2,997.4	1,236.4	795.0	441.4	1,761.0	14,979.0	15,483.9	12,448.1	15,057.7	15,039.1
2012	−447.1	1,963.2	2,410.2	2,941.6	1,213.5	768.2	445.3	1,728.1	15,292.3	15,804.3	12,806.0	15,547.8	15,451.2
2013	−404.9	2,031.5	2,436.4	2,857.6	1,142.8	715.7	427.0	1,714.1	15,521.1	16,016.9	13,076.3	15,741.2	15,676.7
2014	−425.7	2,118.3	2,544.0	2,833.0	1,113.8	686.3	427.3	1,718.1	15,912.9	16,408.9	13,516.9	16,219.3	16,100.8
2015	−540.0	2,120.6	2,660.5	2,883.7	1,113.8	672.0	441.3	1,768.2	16,300.6	16,937.8	13,969.1	16,627.8	16,512.5
2013: I	−414.4	1,991.1	2,405.5	2,880.6	1,166.1	731.1	435.0	1,714.1	15,434.3	15,906.2	12,975.3	15,642.7	15,567.3
II	−421.1	2,015.5	2,436.6	2,866.2	1,150.5	721.2	429.2	1,715.2	15,459.1	15,943.5	13,022.4	15,719.8	15,620.7
III	−416.1	2,031.0	2,447.1	2,852.0	1,135.5	709.0	426.4	1,715.7	15,516.6	16,057.8	13,089.4	15,752.0	15,696.7
IV	−368.1	2,088.6	2,456.6	2,831.5	1,119.1	701.5	417.5	1,711.5	15,674.3	16,160.2	13,218.3	15,851.3	15,822.6
2014: I	−412.0	2,074.1	2,486.1	2,824.3	1,118.6	692.5	425.9	1,704.8	15,703.8	16,159.6	13,301.5	15,932.3	15,839.7
II	−427.5	2,118.0	2,545.5	2,825.1	1,110.8	686.8	423.8	1,713.2	15,833.0	16,329.7	13,447.0	16,142.4	16,021.6
III	−409.4	2,128.7	2,538.1	2,842.6	1,121.5	693.5	427.8	1,720.1	16,015.6	16,504.1	13,593.2	16,321.2	16,207.8
IV	−454.0	2,152.3	2,606.2	2,840.0	1,104.4	672.5	431.6	1,734.1	16,099.3	16,642.1	13,725.8	16,480.7	16,333.7
2015: I	−521.2	2,120.6	2,641.8	2,858.0	1,109.6	671.8	437.3	1,746.9	16,140.9	16,791.3	13,816.5	16,544.3	16,406.6
II	−524.9	2,135.5	2,660.5	2,880.7	1,110.1	671.0	438.6	1,768.9	16,267.5	16,900.1	13,924.1	16,567.8	16,471.0
III	−547.1	2,120.4	2,667.6	2,894.4	1,112.7	669.0	443.1	1,779.9	16,371.7	17,002.6	14,036.7	16,669.0	16,561.9
IV	−566.6	2,105.8	2,672.4	2,901.7	1,123.0	676.3	446.2	1,777.1	16,422.4	17,057.2	14,099.1	16,730.3	16,610.5
2016: I	−566.3	2,102.0	2,668.2	2,913.2	1,118.7	670.9	447.2	1,792.6	16,473.5	17,091.5	14,138.7	16,763.9	16,644.5
II	−558.5	2,111.3	2,669.7	2,900.9	1,117.7	665.5	451.4	1,781.4	16,579.5	17,142.6	14,251.0	16,793.4	16,688.3
III p	−521.0	2,162.9	2,683.9	2,902.7	1,124.5	668.9	454.8	1,776.6	16,688.9	17,236.9	14,323.7	17,006.1	16,859.3

[1] Gross domestic product (GDP) less exports of goods and services plus imports of goods and services.
[2] Personal consumption expenditures plus gross private fixed investment.
[3] For chained dollar measures, gross domestic income is deflated by the implicit price deflator for GDP.

Source: Department of Commerce (Bureau of Economic Analysis).

Table B–3. Quantity and price indexes for gross domestic product, and percent changes, 1965–2016

[Quarterly data are seasonally adjusted]

Year or quarter	Index numbers, 2009=100						Percent change from preceding period [1]					
	Gross domestic product (GDP)			Personal consumption expenditures (PCE)		Gross domestic purchases price index	Gross domestic product (GDP)			Personal consumption expenditures (PCE)		Gross domestic purchases price index
	Real GDP (chain-type quantity index)	GDP chain-type price index	GDP implicit price deflator	PCE chain-type price index	PCE less food and energy price index		Real GDP (chain-type quantity index)	GDP chain-type price index	GDP implicit price deflator	PCE chain-type price index	PCE less food and energy price index	
1965	27.580	18.744	18.702	18.681	19.325	18.321	6.5	1.8	1.8	1.4	1.3	1.7
1966	29.399	19.271	19.227	19.155	19.762	18.830	6.6	2.8	2.8	2.5	2.3	2.8
1967	30.205	19.831	19.786	19.637	20.367	19.346	2.7	2.9	2.9	2.5	3.1	2.7
1968	31.688	20.674	20.627	20.402	21.240	20.164	4.9	4.3	4.3	3.9	4.3	4.2
1969	32.683	21.691	21.642	21.326	22.238	21.149	3.1	4.9	4.9	4.5	4.7	4.9
1970	32.749	22.836	22.784	22.325	23.281	22.287	.2	5.3	5.3	4.7	4.7	5.4
1971	33.833	23.996	23.941	23.274	24.377	23.450	3.3	5.1	5.1	4.3	4.7	5.2
1972	35.609	25.035	24.978	24.070	25.165	24.498	5.2	4.3	4.3	3.4	3.2	4.5
1973	37.618	26.396	26.337	25.368	26.126	25.888	5.6	5.4	5.4	5.4	3.8	5.7
1974	37.424	28.760	28.703	28.009	28.196	28.511	–.5	9.0	9.0	10.4	7.9	10.1
1975	37.350	31.431	31.361	30.348	30.558	31.116	–.2	9.3	9.3	8.4	8.4	9.1
1976	39.361	33.157	33.083	32.013	32.415	32.821	5.4	5.5	5.5	5.5	6.1	5.5
1977	41.175	35.209	35.135	34.091	34.495	34.977	4.6	6.2	6.2	6.5	6.4	6.6
1978	43.466	37.680	37.602	36.479	36.802	37.459	5.6	7.0	7.0	7.0	6.7	7.1
1979	44.846	40.790	40.706	39.714	39.479	40.730	3.2	8.3	8.3	8.9	7.3	8.7
1980	44.736	44.480	44.377	43.978	43.093	44.963	–.2	9.0	9.0	10.7	9.2	10.4
1981	45.897	48.658	48.520	47.908	46.857	49.088	2.6	9.4	9.3	8.9	8.7	9.2
1982	45.020	51.624	51.530	50.553	49.881	51.876	–1.9	6.1	6.2	5.5	6.5	5.7
1983	47.105	53.658	53.565	52.729	52.466	53.697	4.6	3.9	3.9	4.3	5.2	3.5
1984	50.525	55.564	55.466	54.724	54.645	55.483	7.3	3.6	3.5	3.8	4.2	3.3
1985	52.666	57.341	57.240	56.661	56.898	57.151	4.2	3.2	3.2	3.5	4.1	3.0
1986	54.516	58.504	58.395	57.887	58.850	58.345	3.5	2.0	2.0	2.2	3.4	2.1
1987	56.403	59.935	59.885	59.650	60.719	59.985	3.5	2.4	2.6	3.0	3.2	2.8
1988	58.774	62.036	61.982	61.974	63.290	62.092	4.2	3.5	3.5	3.9	4.2	3.5
1989	60.937	64.448	64.392	64.641	65.869	64.516	3.7	3.9	3.9	4.3	4.1	3.9
1990	62.107	66.841	66.773	67.440	68.492	67.040	1.9	3.7	3.7	4.3	4.0	3.9
1991	62.061	69.057	68.996	69.652	70.886	69.112	–.1	3.3	3.3	3.3	3.5	3.1
1992	64.267	70.632	70.569	71.494	73.021	70.720	3.6	2.3	2.3	2.6	3.0	2.3
1993	66.032	72.315	72.248	73.279	75.008	72.324	2.7	2.4	2.4	2.5	2.7	2.3
1994	68.698	73.851	73.785	74.803	76.680	73.835	4.0	2.1	2.1	2.1	2.2	2.1
1995	70.566	75.393	75.324	76.356	78.324	75.421	2.7	2.1	2.1	2.1	2.1	2.1
1996	73.245	76.767	76.699	77.981	79.801	76.729	3.8	1.8	1.8	2.1	1.9	1.7
1997	76.531	78.088	78.012	79.327	81.196	77.852	4.5	1.7	1.7	1.7	1.7	1.5
1998	79.937	78.935	78.859	79.936	82.200	78.359	4.5	1.1	1.1	.8	1.2	.7
1999	83.682	80.065	80.065	81.110	83.291	79.579	4.7	1.4	1.5	1.5	1.3	1.6
2000	87.107	81.890	81.887	83.131	84.747	81.644	4.1	2.3	2.3	2.5	1.7	2.6
2001	87.957	83.755	83.754	84.736	86.281	83.209	1.0	2.3	2.3	1.9	1.8	1.9
2002	89.528	85.040	85.039	85.873	87.750	84.360	1.8	1.5	1.5	1.3	1.7	1.4
2003	92.041	86.735	86.735	87.572	89.047	86.196	2.8	2.0	2.0	2.0	1.5	2.2
2004	95.525	89.118	89.120	89.703	90.751	88.729	3.8	2.7	2.7	2.4	1.9	2.9
2005	98.720	91.985	91.988	92.261	92.711	91.851	3.3	3.2	3.2	2.9	2.2	3.5
2006	101.353	94.812	94.814	94.729	94.786	94.783	2.7	3.1	3.1	2.7	2.2	3.2
2007	103.156	97.340	97.337	97.102	96.832	97.372	1.8	2.7	2.7	2.5	2.2	2.7
2008	102.855	99.218	99.246	100.065	98.827	100.244	–.3	1.9	2.0	3.1	2.1	2.9
2009	100.000	100.000	100.000	100.000	100.000	100.000	–2.8	.8	.8	–.1	1.2	–.2
2010	102.532	101.226	101.221	101.653	101.286	101.527	2.5	1.2	1.2	1.7	1.3	1.5
2011	104.174	103.315	103.311	104.149	102.800	103.970	1.6	2.1	2.1	2.5	1.5	2.4
2012	106.491	105.220	105.214	106.121	104.741	105.805	2.2	1.8	1.8	1.9	1.9	1.8
2013	108.277	106.917	106.913	107.532	106.323	107.287	1.7	1.6	1.6	1.3	1.5	1.4
2014	110.844	108.838	108.828	109.150	108.048	109.109	2.4	1.8	1.8	1.5	1.6	1.7
2015	113.721	109.999	109.998	109.532	109.540	109.569	2.6	1.1	1.1	.3	1.4	.4
2013: I	107.443	106.318	106.349	107.184	105.796	106.813	2.8	1.4	1.6	1.4	1.7	1.4
II	107.649	106.565	106.570	107.229	106.097	106.972	.8	.9	.8	.2	1.1	.6
III	108.479	107.112	107.084	107.625	106.465	107.403	3.1	2.1	1.9	1.5	1.4	1.6
IV	109.538	107.674	107.636	108.089	106.934	107.961	4.0	2.1	2.1	1.7	1.8	2.1
2014: I	109.212	108.140	108.117	108.621	107.365	108.525	–1.2	1.7	1.8	2.0	1.6	2.1
II	110.279	108.714	108.709	109.133	107.910	109.015	4.0	2.1	2.2	1.9	2.0	1.8
III	111.622	109.178	109.165	109.425	108.308	109.411	5.0	1.7	1.7	1.1	1.5	1.5
IV	112.262	109.321	109.300	109.422	108.608	109.487	2.3	.5	.5	.0	1.1	.3
2015: I	112.832	109.307	109.310	108.979	108.908	109.090	2.0	–.1	.0	–1.6	1.1	–1.4
II	113.562	109.922	109.919	109.472	109.385	109.512	2.6	2.3	2.2	1.8	1.8	1.6
III	114.121	110.268	110.253	109.784	109.770	109.793	2.0	1.3	1.2	1.1	1.4	1.0
IV	114.370	110.498	110.504	109.892	109.881	109.881	.9	.8	.9	.4	1.2	.3
2016: I	114.608	110.635	110.630	109.969	110.657	109.936	.8	.5	.5	.3	2.1	.2
II	115.011	111.268	111.258	110.519	111.150	110.509	1.4	2.3	2.3	2.0	1.8	2.1
III p	115.908	111.656	111.640	110.914	111.619	110.922	3.2	1.4	1.4	1.4	1.7	1.5

[1] Quarterly percent changes are at annual rates.

Source: Department of Commerce (Bureau of Economic Analysis).

Table B–4. Growth rates in real gross domestic product by area and country, 1998–2017

[Percent change]

Area and country	1998–2007 annual average	2008	2009	2010	2011	2012	2013	2014	2015	2016[1]	2017[1]
World	4.2	3.0	−.1	5.4	4.2	3.5	3.3	3.4	3.2	3.1	3.4
Advanced economies	2.8	.1	−3.4	3.1	1.7	1.2	1.2	1.9	2.1	1.6	1.8
Of which:											
United States	3.0	−.3	−2.8	2.5	1.6	2.2	1.7	2.4	2.6	1.6	2.2
Euro area[2]	2.4	.4	−4.5	2.1	1.5	−.9	−.3	1.1	2.0	1.7	1.5
Germany	1.7	.8	−5.6	4.0	3.7	.7	.6	1.6	1.5	1.7	1.4
France	2.4	.2	−2.9	2.0	2.1	.2	.6	.6	1.3	1.3	1.3
Italy	1.5	−1.1	−5.5	1.7	.6	−2.8	−1.7	−.3	.8	.8	.9
Spain	3.9	1.1	−3.6	.0	−1.0	−2.6	−1.7	1.4	3.2	3.1	2.2
Japan	1.0	−1.0	−5.5	4.7	−.5	1.7	1.4	.0	.5	.5	.6
United Kingdom	2.9	−.6	−4.3	1.9	1.5	1.3	1.9	3.1	2.2	1.8	1.1
Canada	3.2	1.0	−2.9	3.1	3.1	1.7	2.2	2.5	1.1	1.2	1.9
Other advanced economies	4.0	1.7	−.9	5.9	3.4	2.1	2.3	2.8	2.0	2.0	2.3
Emerging market and developing economies	5.8	5.8	2.9	7.5	6.3	5.3	5.0	4.6	4.0	4.2	4.6
Regional groups:											
Commonwealth of Independent States[3]	6.2	5.3	−6.3	4.7	4.7	3.5	2.1	1.1	−2.8	−.3	1.4
Russia	5.8	5.2	−7.8	4.5	4.0	3.5	1.3	.7	−3.7	−.8	1.1
Excluding Russia	7.5	5.6	−2.4	5.1	6.2	3.6	4.3	2.0	−.5	.9	2.3
Emerging and Developing Asia	7.6	7.2	7.5	9.6	7.9	7.0	7.0	6.8	6.6	6.5	6.3
China	9.9	9.6	9.2	10.6	9.5	7.9	7.8	7.3	6.9	6.6	6.2
India[4]	7.1	3.9	8.5	10.3	6.6	5.6	6.6	7.2	7.6	7.6	7.6
ASEAN-5[5]	3.7	5.4	2.4	6.9	4.7	6.2	5.1	4.6	4.8	4.8	5.1
Emerging and Developing Europe	4.2	3.1	−3.0	4.7	5.4	1.2	2.8	2.8	3.6	3.3	3.1
Latin America and the Caribbean	3.1	4.0	−1.8	6.1	4.6	3.0	2.9	1.0	.0	−.6	1.6
Brazil	3.0	5.1	−.1	7.5	3.9	1.9	3.0	.1	−3.8	−3.3	.5
Mexico	2.9	1.4	−4.7	5.1	4.0	4.0	1.4	2.2	2.5	2.1	2.3
Middle East, North Africa, Afghanistan, and Pakistan ..	5.3	4.8	1.5	4.9	4.5	5.0	2.4	2.7	2.3	3.4	3.4
Saudi Arabia	2.9	6.2	−2.1	4.8	10.0	5.4	2.7	3.6	3.5	1.2	2.0
Sub-Saharan Africa	5.2	5.9	3.9	7.0	5.0	4.3	5.2	5.1	3.4	1.4	2.9
Nigeria	7.0	7.2	8.4	11.3	4.9	4.3	5.4	6.3	2.7	−1.7	.6
South Africa	3.7	3.2	−1.5	3.0	3.3	2.2	2.3	1.6	1.3	.1	.8

[1] All figures are forecasts as published by the International Monetary Fund.
[2] For 2017, includes data for: Austria, Belgium, Cyprus, Estonia, Finland, France, Germany, Greece, Ireland, Italy, Latvia, Lithuania, Luxembourg, Malta, Netherlands, Portugal, Slovak Republic, Slovenia, and Spain.
[3] Includes Georgia, Turkmenistan, and Ukraine, which are not members of the Commonwealth of Independent States but are included for reasons of geography and similarity in economic structure.
[4] Data and forecasts are presented on a fiscal year basis and output growth is based on GDP at market prices.
[5] Consists of Indonesia, Malaysia, Philippines, Thailand, and Vietnam.

Note: For details on data shown in this table, see *World Economic Outlook*, October 2016, published by the International Monetary Fund.

Source: International Monetary Fund.

TABLE B–5. Real exports and imports of goods and services, 1999–2016

[Billions of chained (2009) dollars; quarterly data at seasonally adjusted annual rates]

Year or quarter	Exports of goods and services					Imports of goods and services				
	Total	Goods [1]			Services [1]	Total	Goods [1]			Services [1]
		Total	Durable goods	Nondurable goods			Total	Durable goods	Nondurable goods	
1999	1,159.1	819.4	533.8	288.0	338.6	1,536.2	1,286.9	724.4	572.8	245.4
2000	1,258.4	902.2	599.3	301.9	354.3	1,736.2	1,455.4	834.4	624.4	276.4
2001	1,184.9	846.7	549.5	300.1	336.6	1,687.0	1,408.4	782.2	641.1	274.6
2002	1,164.5	817.8	518.7	305.7	345.7	1,748.8	1,461.1	815.3	659.3	283.6
2003	1,185.0	833.1	528.0	312.0	350.8	1,826.9	1,533.0	850.4	698.9	289.6
2004	1,300.6	904.5	586.0	323.4	395.4	2,035.3	1,704.1	969.3	745.7	326.4
2005	1,381.9	970.6	641.0	333.2	410.3	2,164.2	1,817.9	1,051.6	774.8	341.1
2006	1,506.8	1,062.0	710.1	355.2	443.5	2,301.0	1,925.4	1,145.2	787.7	370.5
2007	1,646.4	1,141.5	770.8	373.9	504.1	2,359.0	1,960.9	1,174.5	794.2	393.5
2008	1,740.8	1,211.5	810.2	404.2	528.3	2,298.6	1,887.9	1,129.0	766.1	408.2
2009	1,587.7	1,065.1	671.6	393.5	522.6	1,983.2	1,590.3	893.8	696.5	392.9
2010	1,776.6	1,218.3	784.8	434.0	558.0	2,235.4	1,826.7	1,095.2	735.8	407.8
2011	1,898.3	1,297.6	852.0	448.2	600.6	2,357.7	1,932.1	1,197.9	745.9	424.2
2012	1,963.2	1,344.2	890.8	457.5	618.7	2,410.2	1,972.2	1,283.3	715.1	437.1
2013	2,031.5	1,385.7	911.3	477.4	645.7	2,436.4	1,995.4	1,332.1	698.1	439.9
2014	2,118.3	1,447.3	948.2	501.7	670.9	2,544.0	2,090.8	1,433.8	702.7	451.4
2015	2,120.6	1,438.1	922.5	516.4	681.9	2,660.5	2,194.1	1,509.6	733.4	464.4
2013: I	1,991.1	1,350.5	894.2	460.4	640.7	2,405.2	1,968.0	1,301.8	697.5	436.5
II	2,015.5	1,372.3	916.6	461.2	643.1	2,436.6	1,996.1	1,326.4	703.0	439.3
III	2,031.0	1,384.2	908.2	478.7	646.6	2,447.1	2,004.7	1,340.7	699.5	441.2
IV	2,088.6	1,435.7	926.3	509.5	652.6	2,456.6	2,012.8	1,359.3	692.3	442.6
2014: I	2,074.1	1,408.8	926.8	485.3	665.0	2,486.1	2,040.7	1,376.3	703.3	443.9
II	2,118.0	1,445.0	945.8	501.7	672.8	2,545.5	2,093.0	1,435.5	703.5	450.7
III	2,128.7	1,460.7	959.1	504.5	667.9	2,538.1	2,085.6	1,437.2	695.8	450.7
IV	2,152.3	1,474.5	961.1	515.4	677.7	2,606.2	2,144.0	1,486.0	708.3	460.4
2015: I	2,120.6	1,435.8	928.1	508.9	684.0	2,641.8	2,179.6	1,501.5	727.3	460.2
II	2,135.5	1,452.0	929.8	523.0	683.2	2,660.5	2,198.1	1,507.2	739.4	460.4
III	2,120.4	1,440.7	921.5	520.0	679.3	2,667.6	2,197.4	1,512.7	733.5	468.2
IV	2,105.8	1,423.8	910.7	513.8	681.1	2,672.4	2,201.4	1,517.0	733.3	469.0
2016: I	2,102.0	1,424.1	899.3	526.2	677.3	2,668.2	2,194.1	1,497.0	745.4	471.9
II	2,111.3	1,430.1	900.4	531.3	680.5	2,669.7	2,194.3	1,493.1	749.4	473.2
III ᵖ	2,162.9	1,478.3	911.1	569.7	685.4	2,683.9	2,198.1	1,508.5	738.5	483.1

[1] Certain goods, primarily military equipment purchased and sold by the Federal Government, are included in services. Repairs and alterations of equipment are also included in services.

Source: Department of Commerce (Bureau of Economic Analysis).

Table B–6. Corporate profits by industry, 1965–2016

[Billions of dollars; quarterly data at seasonally adjusted annual rates]

Year or quarter	Total	Domestic industries Total	Financial Total	Financial Federal Reserve banks	Financial Other	Nonfinancial Total	Manufacturing	Transportation [1]	Utilities	Wholesale trade	Retail trade	Information	Other	Rest of the world
SIC: [2]														
1965	81.9	77.2	9.3	1.3	8.0	67.9	42.1	11.4	....	3.8	4.9	....	5.7	4.7
1966	88.3	83.7	10.7	1.7	9.1	73.0	45.3	12.6	....	4.0	4.9	....	6.3	4.5
1967	86.1	81.3	11.2	2.0	9.2	70.1	42.4	11.4	....	4.1	5.7	....	6.6	4.8
1968	94.3	88.6	12.9	2.5	10.4	75.7	45.8	11.4	....	4.7	6.4	....	7.4	5.6
1969	90.8	84.2	13.6	3.1	10.6	70.6	41.6	11.1	....	4.9	6.4	....	6.5	6.6
1970	79.7	72.6	15.5	3.5	12.0	57.1	32.0	8.8	....	4.6	6.1	....	5.8	7.1
1971	94.7	86.8	17.9	3.3	14.6	69.0	40.0	9.6	....	5.4	7.3	....	6.7	7.9
1972	109.3	99.7	19.5	3.3	16.1	80.3	47.6	10.4	....	7.2	7.5	....	7.6	9.5
1973	126.6	111.7	21.1	4.5	16.6	90.6	55.0	10.2	....	8.8	7.0	....	9.6	14.9
1974	123.3	105.8	20.8	5.7	15.1	85.1	51.0	9.1	....	12.2	2.8	....	10.0	17.5
1975	144.2	129.6	20.4	5.6	14.8	109.2	63.0	11.7	....	14.3	8.4	....	11.8	14.6
1976	182.1	165.6	25.6	5.9	19.7	140.0	82.5	17.5	....	13.7	10.9	....	15.3	16.5
1977	212.8	193.7	32.6	6.1	26.5	161.1	91.5	21.2	....	16.4	12.8	....	19.2	19.1
1978	246.7	223.8	40.8	7.6	33.1	183.1	105.8	25.5	....	16.7	13.1	....	22.0	22.9
1979	261.0	226.4	41.8	9.4	32.3	184.6	107.1	21.6	....	20.0	10.7	....	25.2	34.6
1980	240.6	205.2	35.2	11.8	23.5	169.9	97.6	22.2	....	18.5	7.0	....	24.6	35.5
1981	252.0	222.3	30.3	14.4	15.9	192.0	112.5	25.1	....	23.7	10.7	....	20.1	29.7
1982	224.8	192.2	27.2	15.2	12.0	165.0	89.6	28.1	....	20.7	14.3	....	12.3	32.6
1983	256.4	221.4	36.2	14.6	21.6	185.2	97.3	34.3	....	21.9	19.3	....	12.3	35.1
1984	294.3	257.7	34.7	16.4	18.3	223.0	114.2	44.7	....	30.4	21.5	....	12.1	36.6
1985	289.7	251.6	46.5	16.3	30.2	205.1	107.1	39.1	....	24.6	22.8	....	11.4	38.1
1986	273.3	233.8	56.4	15.5	40.8	177.4	75.6	39.3	....	24.4	23.4	....	14.7	39.5
1987	314.6	266.5	60.3	16.2	44.1	206.2	101.8	42.0	....	18.9	23.3	....	20.3	48.0
1988	366.2	309.2	66.9	18.1	48.8	242.3	132.8	46.8	....	20.4	19.8	....	22.5	57.0
1989	373.1	305.9	78.3	20.6	57.6	227.6	122.3	41.9	....	22.0	20.9	....	20.5	67.1
1990	391.2	315.1	89.6	21.8	67.8	225.5	120.9	43.5	....	19.4	20.3	....	21.3	76.1
1991	434.2	357.8	120.4	20.7	99.7	237.3	109.3	54.5	....	22.3	26.9	....	24.3	76.5
1992	459.7	386.6	132.4	18.3	114.1	254.2	109.8	57.7	....	25.3	28.1	....	33.4	73.1
1993	501.9	425.0	119.9	16.7	103.2	305.1	122.9	70.1	....	26.5	39.7	....	45.8	76.9
1994	589.3	511.3	125.9	18.5	107.4	385.4	162.6	83.9	....	31.4	46.3	....	61.2	78.0
1995	667.0	574.0	140.3	22.9	117.3	433.7	199.8	89.0	....	28.0	43.9	....	73.1	92.9
1996	741.8	639.8	147.9	22.5	125.3	492.0	220.4	91.2	....	39.9	52.0	....	88.5	102.0
1997	811.0	703.4	162.2	24.3	137.9	541.2	248.5	81.0	....	48.1	63.4	....	100.3	107.6
1998	743.8	641.1	138.9	25.6	113.3	502.1	220.4	72.6	....	50.6	72.3	....	86.3	102.8
1999	762.2	640.2	154.6	26.7	127.9	485.6	219.4	49.3	....	46.8	72.5	....	97.6	122.0
2000	730.3	584.1	149.7	31.2	118.5	434.4	205.9	33.8	....	50.4	68.9	....	75.4	146.2
NAICS: [2]														
1998	743.8	641.1	138.9	25.6	113.3	502.1	193.5	12.8	33.3	57.3	62.5	33.1	109.7	102.8
1999	762.2	640.2	154.6	26.7	127.9	485.6	184.5	7.2	34.4	55.6	59.5	20.8	123.5	122.0
2000	730.3	584.1	149.7	31.2	118.5	434.4	175.6	9.5	24.3	59.5	51.3	–11.9	126.1	146.2
2001	698.7	528.3	195.0	28.9	166.1	333.3	75.1	–.7	22.5	51.1	71.3	–26.4	140.2	170.4
2002	795.1	636.3	270.7	23.5	247.2	365.6	75.1	–6.0	11.1	55.8	83.7	–3.1	149.0	158.8
2003	959.9	793.3	306.5	20.1	286.5	486.7	125.3	4.8	13.5	59.3	90.5	16.3	177.1	166.6
2004	1,215.2	1,010.1	349.4	20.0	329.4	660.7	182.7	12.0	20.5	74.7	93.2	52.7	224.9	205.0
2005	1,621.2	1,382.1	409.7	26.6	383.1	972.4	277.7	27.7	30.8	96.2	121.7	91.3	327.2	239.1
2006	1,815.7	1,559.6	415.1	33.8	381.3	1,144.4	349.7	41.2	55.1	105.9	132.5	107.0	353.1	256.2
2007	1,708.9	1,355.5	301.5	36.0	265.5	1,054.0	321.9	23.9	49.5	103.2	119.0	108.4	328.2	353.4
2008	1,345.5	938.8	95.4	35.1	60.4	843.4	240.6	28.8	30.1	90.6	80.3	92.2	280.8	406.7
2009	1,479.2	1,122.0	362.9	47.3	315.5	759.2	171.4	22.4	23.8	89.3	108.7	81.2	262.3	357.2
2010	1,799.7	1,404.5	406.3	71.6	334.8	998.2	287.6	44.7	30.3	102.4	118.6	95.1	319.5	395.2
2011	1,738.5	1,316.6	375.9	75.9	300.0	940.7	298.1	30.4	9.8	94.4	114.3	83.8	309.9	421.9
2012	2,116.6	1,706.3	479.0	71.7	407.3	1,227.2	395.7	53.8	12.5	135.3	154.1	100.6	375.2	410.3
2013	2,159.4	1,747.6	429.4	79.6	349.8	1,318.2	429.6	50.6	26.9	142.7	154.5	125.4	388.5	411.8
2014	2,265.9	1,854.9	480.3	103.5	376.8	1,374.7	449.8	59.4	33.3	146.5	167.8	117.4	400.4	411.0
2015	2,192.4	1,806.6	493.2	100.7	392.5	1,313.4	412.7	68.1	6.7	150.0	178.7	120.1	377.0	385.8
2014: I	2,135.5	1,722.9	469.2	98.5	370.7	1,253.7	384.7	53.1	40.3	121.7	152.2	115.0	386.6	413.7
II	2,287.0	1,885.5	515.7	104.7	411.0	1,369.8	474.6	63.5	28.9	139.4	164.0	118.5	380.9	401.5
III	2,308.9	1,886.5	446.7	106.2	340.4	1,439.8	464.4	67.1	31.1	170.1	169.2	115.7	422.2	422.4
IV	2,331.2	1,924.9	489.4	104.3	385.1	1,435.4	475.4	54.0	33.0	155.1	185.7	120.2	412.1	406.3
2015: I	2,284.5	1,895.0	507.9	99.5	408.3	1,387.1	456.6	69.4	24.1	148.3	188.7	118.1	381.9	389.5
II	2,214.9	1,832.3	504.2	100.7	403.5	1,328.1	436.4	63.8	9.4	142.6	173.5	120.8	381.6	382.6
III	2,200.5	1,826.0	489.1	103.7	385.4	1,336.9	447.0	71.0	4.7	150.3	177.3	115.3	371.4	374.5
IV	2,069.8	1,673.3	471.8	99.0	372.8	1,201.5	310.8	68.1	–11.2	158.7	175.5	126.3	373.3	396.5
2016: I	2,139.2	1,769.6	479.1	115.2	364.0	1,290.5	394.4	68.5	4.1	153.9	185.3	126.9	357.4	369.6
II	2,127.1	1,719.5	484.6	110.0	374.6	1,234.9	384.0	63.8	2.5	116.1	181.5	129.8	357.3	407.6
III [p]	2,256.8	1,842.8	534.8	108.4	426.3	1,308.1	....	....	....	....	....	....	....	414.0

[1] Data on Standard Industrial Classification (SIC) basis include transportation and public utilities. Those on North American Industry Classification System (NAICS) basis include transporation and warehousing. Utilities classified separately in NAICS (as shown beginning 1998).
[2] SIC-based industry data use the 1987 SIC for data beginning in 1987 and the 1972 SIC for prior data. NAICS-based data use 2002 NAICS.

Note: Industry data on SIC basis and NAICS basis are not necessarily the same and are not strictly comparable.

Source: Department of Commerce (Bureau of Economic Analysis).

TABLE B–7. Real farm income, 1952–2016

[Billions of chained (2009) dollars]

Year	Income of farm operators from farming [1]							
	Gross farm income					Direct Federal Government payments	Production expenses	Net farm income
	Total	Value of agricultural sector production			Farm-related income [4]			
		Total	Crops [2,3]	Animals and animal products [3]				
1952	251.7	249.9	102.2	135.7	12.0	1.8	152.0	99.8
1953	226.8	225.4	93.1	120.1	12.2	1.4	141.3	85.4
1954	222.7	221.1	94.0	115.3	11.8	1.7	142.1	80.6
1955	215.1	213.6	91.6	110.0	12.0	1.5	142.4	72.6
1956	210.9	207.5	89.7	106.2	11.6	3.4	141.0	69.9
1957	208.8	202.7	81.9	109.0	11.7	6.1	142.2	66.5
1958	228.5	222.1	88.0	121.9	12.2	6.4	151.3	77.2
1959	219.3	215.4	85.5	116.8	13.1	3.9	157.3	62.0
1960	220.3	216.3	89.5	113.5	13.4	4.0	156.3	64.0
1961	229.0	220.5	89.3	117.4	13.8	8.4	161.4	67.5
1962	236.2	226.5	92.9	119.5	14.0	9.7	168.9	67.3
1963	239.2	229.9	98.9	116.4	14.6	9.4	174.3	64.9
1964	229.8	218.0	91.7	111.2	15.1	11.8	172.8	57.0
1965	248.3	235.2	101.5	118.4	15.3	13.1	179.5	68.8
1966	261.9	244.9	95.0	134.2	15.6	17.0	189.4	72.4
1967	254.8	239.2	96.9	126.0	16.3	15.5	192.5	62.2
1968	250.8	234.0	91.5	126.3	16.2	16.7	191.2	59.6
1969	260.1	242.6	90.7	135.2	16.6	17.5	194.2	65.9
1970	257.6	241.3	89.9	134.7	16.7	16.3	194.7	62.9
1971	258.9	245.8	97.6	131.1	17.0	13.1	196.3	62.6
1972	284.2	268.4	103.7	147.4	17.3	15.8	206.5	77.7
1973	374.7	364.8	163.1	183.2	18.5	9.9	244.6	130.2
1974	341.6	339.8	170.9	148.9	20.0	1.8	246.8	94.8
1975	319.9	317.4	160.4	136.8	20.2	2.6	238.8	81.2
1976	310.4	308.2	145.9	140.6	21.7	2.2	249.5	60.8
1977	308.9	303.7	145.3	134.4	24.1	5.2	252.4	56.5
1978	340.9	332.8	150.2	156.2	26.4	8.0	274.0	66.9
1979	369.5	366.1	163.4	174.5	28.2	3.4	302.3	67.2
1980	335.6	332.7	144.7	158.1	29.9	2.9	299.3	36.3
1981	341.8	337.8	162.2	144.7	31.0	4.0	286.6	55.2
1982	318.0	311.2	139.1	136.6	35.5	6.8	271.8	46.2
1983	286.7	269.4	106.0	130.5	32.9	17.3	260.2	26.6
1984	302.3	287.1	139.9	129.6	17.6	15.2	255.6	46.7
1985	280.9	267.5	128.5	120.3	18.7	13.4	231.2	49.7
1986	266.9	246.7	108.2	120.9	17.5	20.2	213.7	53.2
1987	281.0	253.0	107.6	126.4	19.1	27.9	217.6	63.4
1988	286.8	263.5	111.7	126.8	25.0	23.3	222.9	63.9
1989	297.3	280.4	126.4	129.5	24.5	16.9	225.2	72.1
1990	295.9	282.0	124.5	134.7	22.8	13.9	226.7	69.2
1991	278.1	266.2	117.6	126.3	22.3	11.9	219.8	58.3
1992	283.9	271.0	126.1	123.4	21.5	13.0	212.9	71.0
1993	283.5	265.0	114.3	127.2	23.5	18.5	218.9	64.6
1994	292.6	282.0	136.1	121.5	24.4	10.7	221.4	71.2
1995	279.6	270.0	127.2	116.4	26.4	9.7	226.9	52.8
1996	307.2	297.6	150.7	119.9	27.0	9.6	230.4	76.8
1997	304.8	295.2	144.1	123.3	27.8	9.6	239.1	65.7
1998	294.7	279.0	129.4	119.3	30.3	15.7	235.0	59.7
1999	293.4	266.6	115.9	118.9	31.8	26.9	233.9	59.6
2000	295.1	266.8	116.0	121.0	29.8	28.4	233.2	61.9
2001	298.4	271.6	113.5	127.0	31.1	26.8	232.8	65.5
2002	271.1	256.5	115.1	109.9	31.5	14.6	225.1	46.0
2003	298.3	279.2	125.2	121.1	33.0	19.1	228.0	70.3
2004	330.9	316.3	140.4	139.4	36.5	14.6	232.8	98.1
2005	324.5	298.0	124.3	137.5	36.1	26.5	238.9	85.6
2006	306.0	289.4	125.2	125.9	38.3	16.7	245.5	60.6
2007	348.8	336.6	155.2	142.2	39.2	12.2	276.9	71.9
2008	367.5	355.1	175.2	140.5	39.4	12.3	288.7	78.7
2009	336.5	324.4	164.7	119.5	40.2	12.2	274.4	62.2
2010	352.2	339.9	166.1	138.5	35.3	12.2	276.0	76.2
2011	406.9	396.8	192.9	158.4	45.4	10.1	297.0	109.9
2012	427.5	417.4	202.3	160.7	54.3	10.1	335.8	91.7
2013	452.4	442.1	218.5	169.2	54.4	10.3	336.7	115.7
2014	444.4	435.4	189.5	197.3	48.6	9.0	359.2	85.2
2015	400.2	390.4	166.4	177.1	46.9	9.8	326.6	73.6
2016 P	374.0	362.5	166.3	151.4	44.8	11.6	313.9	60.1

[1] The GDP chain-type price index is used to convert the current-dollar statistics to 2009=100 equivalents.
[2] Crop receipts include proceeds received from commodities placed under Commodity Credit Corporation loans.
[3] The value of production equates to the sum of cash receipts, home consumption, and the value of the change in inventories.
[4] Includes income from forest products sold, the gross imputed rental value of farm dwellings, machine hire and custom work, and other sources of farm income such as commodity insurance indemnities.

Note: Data for 2016 are forecasts.

Source: Department of Agriculture (Economic Research Service).

Table B-8. New private housing units started, authorized, and completed and houses sold, 1972–2016

[Thousands; monthly data at seasonally adjusted annual rates]

Year or month	New housing units started — Total	1 unit	2 to 4 units [2]	5 units or more	New housing units authorized [1] — Total	1 unit	2 to 4 units	5 units or more	New housing units completed	New houses sold
1972	2,356.6	1,309.2	141.2	906.2	2,218.9	1,033.1	148.6	1,037.2	2,003.9	718
1973	2,045.3	1,132.0	118.2	795.0	1,819.5	882.1	117.0	820.5	2,100.5	634
1974	1,337.7	888.1	68.0	381.6	1,074.4	643.8	64.4	366.2	1,728.5	519
1975	1,160.4	892.2	64.0	204.3	939.2	675.5	63.8	199.8	1,317.2	549
1976	1,537.5	1,162.4	85.8	289.2	1,296.2	893.6	93.1	309.5	1,377.2	646
1977	1,987.1	1,450.9	121.7	414.4	1,690.0	1,126.1	121.3	442.7	1,657.1	819
1978	2,020.3	1,433.3	125.1	462.0	1,800.5	1,182.6	130.6	487.3	1,867.5	817
1979	1,745.1	1,194.1	122.0	429.0	1,551.8	981.5	125.4	444.8	1,870.8	709
1980	1,292.2	852.2	109.5	330.5	1,190.6	710.4	114.5	365.7	1,501.6	545
1981	1,084.2	705.4	91.2	287.7	985.5	564.3	101.8	319.4	1,265.7	436
1982	1,062.2	662.6	80.1	319.6	1,000.5	546.4	88.3	365.8	1,005.5	412
1983	1,703.0	1,067.6	113.5	522.0	1,605.2	901.5	133.7	570.1	1,390.3	623
1984	1,749.5	1,084.2	121.4	543.9	1,681.8	922.4	142.6	616.8	1,652.2	639
1985	1,741.8	1,072.4	93.5	576.0	1,733.3	956.6	120.1	656.6	1,703.3	688
1986	1,805.4	1,179.4	84.0	542.0	1,769.4	1,077.6	108.4	583.5	1,756.4	750
1987	1,620.5	1,146.4	65.1	408.7	1,534.8	1,024.4	89.3	421.1	1,668.8	671
1988	1,488.1	1,081.3	58.7	348.0	1,455.6	993.8	75.7	386.1	1,529.8	676
1989	1,376.1	1,003.3	55.3	317.6	1,338.4	931.7	66.9	339.8	1,422.8	650
1990	1,192.7	894.8	37.6	260.4	1,110.8	793.9	54.3	262.6	1,308.0	534
1991	1,013.9	840.4	35.6	137.9	948.8	753.5	43.1	152.1	1,090.8	509
1992	1,199.7	1,029.9	30.9	139.0	1,094.9	910.7	45.8	138.4	1,157.5	610
1993	1,287.6	1,125.7	29.4	132.6	1,199.1	986.5	52.4	160.2	1,192.7	666
1994	1,457.0	1,198.4	35.2	223.5	1,371.6	1,068.5	62.2	241.0	1,346.9	670
1995	1,354.1	1,076.2	33.8	244.1	1,332.5	997.3	63.8	271.5	1,312.6	667
1996	1,476.8	1,160.9	45.3	270.8	1,425.6	1,069.5	65.8	290.3	1,412.9	757
1997	1,474.0	1,133.7	44.5	295.8	1,441.1	1,062.4	68.4	310.3	1,400.5	804
1998	1,616.9	1,271.4	42.6	302.9	1,612.3	1,187.6	69.2	355.5	1,474.2	886
1999	1,640.9	1,302.4	31.9	306.6	1,663.5	1,246.7	65.8	351.1	1,604.9	880
2000	1,568.7	1,230.9	38.7	299.1	1,592.3	1,198.1	64.9	329.3	1,573.7	877
2001	1,602.7	1,273.3	36.6	292.8	1,636.7	1,235.6	66.0	335.2	1,570.8	908
2002	1,704.9	1,358.6	38.5	307.9	1,747.7	1,332.6	73.7	341.4	1,648.4	973
2003	1,847.7	1,499.0	33.5	315.2	1,889.2	1,460.9	82.5	345.8	1,678.7	1,086
2004	1,955.8	1,610.5	42.3	303.0	2,070.1	1,613.4	90.4	366.2	1,841.9	1,203
2005	2,068.3	1,715.8	41.1	311.4	2,155.3	1,682.0	84.0	389.3	1,931.4	1,283
2006	1,800.9	1,465.4	42.7	292.8	1,838.9	1,378.2	76.6	384.1	1,979.4	1,051
2007	1,355.0	1,046.0	31.7	277.3	1,398.4	979.9	59.6	359.0	1,502.8	776
2008	905.5	622.0	17.5	266.0	905.4	575.6	34.4	295.4	1,119.7	485
2009	554.0	445.1	11.6	97.3	583.0	441.1	20.7	121.1	794.4	375
2010	586.9	471.2	11.4	104.3	604.6	447.3	22.0	135.3	651.7	323
2011	608.8	430.6	10.9	167.3	624.1	418.5	21.6	184.0	584.9	306
2012	780.6	535.3	11.4	233.9	829.7	518.7	25.9	285.1	649.2	368
2013	924.9	617.6	13.6	293.7	990.8	620.8	29.0	341.1	764.4	429
2014	1,003.3	647.9	13.7	341.7	1,052.1	640.3	29.9	382.0	883.8	437
2015	1,111.8	714.5	11.5	385.8	1,182.6	696.0	32.1	454.5	968.2	501
2015: Jan	1,101	712	....	383	1,073	669	28	376	964	524
Feb	893	591	....	294	1,114	636	30	448	876	549
Mar	964	626	....	318	1,071	656	27	388	798	490
Apr	1,192	746	....	428	1,178	679	33	466	1,008	500
May	1,063	694	....	360	1,266	693	34	539	1,024	507
June	1,213	686	....	513	1,334	702	34	598	966	472
July	1,147	760	....	376	1,142	694	30	418	994	498
Aug	1,132	731	....	394	1,166	710	30	426	963	505
Sept	1,189	743	....	435	1,129	708	38	383	1,010	457
Oct	1,073	714	....	347	1,175	725	35	415	984	478
Nov	1,171	786	....	379	1,286	735	29	522	973	508
Dec	1,160	765	....	378	1,201	738	35	428	1,033	538
2016: Jan	1,128	775	....	335	1,188	727	35	426	1,056	526
Feb	1,213	845	....	356	1,162	733	33	396	1,025	525
Mar	1,113	751	....	353	1,077	725	34	318	1,063	537
Apr	1,155	764	....	378	1,130	741	32	357	952	570
May	1,128	737	....	386	1,136	731	28	377	1,015	566
June	1,195	763	....	414	1,153	738	29	386	1,129	558
July	1,218	769	....	442	1,144	711	29	404	1,070	622
Aug	1,164	724	....	422	1,152	736	33	383	1,034	567
Sept p	1,054	785	....	255	1,225	742	36	447	1,000	574
Oct p	1,323	869	....	445	1,260	774	30	456	1,055	563

[1] Authorized by issuance of local building permits in permit-issuing places: 20,100 places beginning with 2014; 19,300 for 2004–2013; 19,000 for 1994–2003; 17,000 for 1984–93; 16,000 for 1978–83; and 14,000 for 1972–77.
[2] Monthly data do not meet publication standards because tests for identifiable and stable seasonality do not meet reliability standards.

Note: One-unit estimates prior to 1999, for new housing units started and completed and for new houses sold, include an upward adjustment of 3.3 percent to account for structures in permit-issuing areas that did not have permit authorization.

Source: Department of Commerce (Bureau of the Census).

TABLE B–9. Median money income (in 2015 dollars) and poverty status of families and people, by race, 2007-2015

Race, Hispanic origin, and year	Families[1]						People below poverty level[2]		Median money income (in 2015 dollars) of people 15 years old and over with income[3]			
	Number (millions)	Median money income (in 2015 dollars)[3]	Below poverty level[2]				Number (millions)	Percent	Males		Females	
			Total		Female householder, no husband present				All people	Year-round full-time workers	All people	Year-round full-time workers
			Number (millions)	Percent	Number (millions)	Percent						
TOTAL (all races)[4]												
2007	77.9	$70,137	7.6	9.8	4.1	28.3	37.3	12.5	$37,948	$52,840	$23,917	$41,344
2008	78.9	67,726	8.1	10.3	4.2	28.7	39.8	13.2	36,505	52,598	22,972	40,388
2009	78.9	66,379	8.8	11.1	4.4	29.9	43.6	14.3	35,554	54,311	23,151	41,132
2010[5]	79.6	65,483	9.4	11.8	4.8	31.7	46.3	15.1	35,010	54,519	22,585	41,787
2011	80.5	64,259	9.5	11.8	4.9	31.2	46.2	15.0	34,763	53,027	22,239	40,769
2012	80.9	64,252	9.5	11.8	4.8	30.9	46.5	15.0	35,000	52,321	22,215	41,312
2013[6]	81.2	64,934	9.1	11.2	4.6	30.6	45.3	14.5	35,846	51,836	22,450	41,309
2013[7]	82.3	66,619	9.6	11.7	5.2	32.2	46.3	14.8	36,255	52,320	22,514	41,413
2014	81.7	66,709	9.5	11.6	4.8	30.6	46.7	14.8	36,344	51,515	22,266	40,844
2015	82.2	70,697	8.6	10.4	4.4	28.2	43.1	13.5	37,138	52,247	23,769	41,754
WHITE, non-Hispanic[8]												
2007	53.9	79,948	3.2	5.9	1.5	20.7	16.0	8.2	42,723	58,832	24,791	44,214
2008	54.5	77,137	3.4	6.2	1.5	20.7	17.0	8.6	41,182	57,625	23,942	43,451
2009	54.5	74,391	3.8	7.0	1.7	23.3	18.5	9.4	40,636	57,962	24,236	44,481
2010[5]	53.8	74,905	3.9	7.2	1.7	24.1	19.3	9.9	40,390	59,414	23,607	44,932
2011	54.2	73,591	4.0	7.3	1.8	23.4	19.2	9.8	40,203	58,767	23,423	43,602
2012	54.0	73,788	3.8	7.1	1.7	23.4	18.9	9.7	40,003	58,065	23,642	43,534
2013[6]	53.8	73,897	3.7	6.9	1.6	22.6	18.8	9.6	40,825	57,446	24,197	43,534
2013[7]	54.7	75,941	4.0	7.3	1.9	25.8	19.6	10.0	41,572	59,907	24,149	43,832
2014	53.8	76,746	3.9	7.3	1.7	23.7	19.7	10.1	41,119	58,780	24,033	44,287
2015	53.8	80,527	3.5	6.4	1.6	21.7	17.8	9.1	42,207	60,750	25,629	45,694
BLACK[8]												
2007	9.3	45,889	2.0	22.1	1.5	37.3	9.2	24.5	29,518	41,994	22,579	36,113
2008	9.4	43,901	2.1	22.0	1.5	37.2	9.4	24.7	27,801	42,506	22,234	35,432
2009	9.4	42,430	2.1	22.7	1.5	36.7	9.9	25.8	26,223	43,483	21,508	35,869
2010[5]	9.6	41,956	2.3	24.1	1.7	38.7	10.7	27.4	25,325	41,010	21,357	37,008
2011	9.7	42,677	2.3	24.2	1.7	39.0	10.9	27.6	24,740	42,443	20,819	37,039
2012	9.8	41,826	2.3	23.7	1.6	37.8	10.9	27.2	25,728	41,103	20,668	36,224
2013[6]	9.9	42,317	2.3	22.8	1.6	38.5	11.0	27.2	25,291	42,360	20,395	36,001
2013[7]	9.9	42,624	2.2	22.4	1.7	36.7	10.2	25.2	25,560	41,146	21,437	35,248
2014	9.9	43,201	2.3	22.9	1.6	37.2	10.8	26.2	26,600	41,339	20,990	35,370
2015	9.8	45,781	2.1	21.1	1.5	33.9	10.0	24.1	27,404	41,710	21,613	37,110
ASIAN[8]												
2007	3.3	88,174	.3	7.9	.1	16.1	1.3	10.2	42,517	58,544	27,841	47,229
2008	3.5	80,999	.3	9.8	.1	16.7	1.6	11.8	40,299	57,008	25,440	48,667
2009	3.6	82,882	.3	9.4	.1	16.9	1.7	12.5	41,238	59,022	26,892	49,299
2010[5]	3.9	81,769	.4	9.3	.1	21.1	1.9	12.2	38,943	57,078	25,615	45,571
2011	4.2	76,929	.4	9.7	.1	19.1	2.0	12.3	38,291	59,315	23,226	43,642
2012	4.1	80,380	.4	9.4	.1	19.2	1.9	11.7	41,527	62,200	24,089	47,869
2013[6]	4.4	77,742	.4	8.7	.1	14.9	1.8	10.5	40,857	61,209	25,276	45,866
2013[7]	4.4	84,245	.4	10.2	.1	25.7	2.3	13.1	43,539	62,291	26,296	48,047
2014	4.5	82,827	.4	8.9	.1	18.9	2.1	12.0	40,948	60,368	25,420	48,602
2015	4.7	90,847	.4	8.0	.1	16.2	2.1	11.4	43,705	64,740	26,532	50,118
HISPANIC (any race)[8]												
2007	10.4	46,373	2.0	19.7	1.0	38.4	9.9	21.5	27,951	34,813	19,145	31,041
2008	10.5	44,547	2.2	21.3	1.0	39.2	11.0	23.2	26,424	34,368	18,073	30,209
2009	10.4	43,890	2.4	22.7	1.1	38.8	12.4	25.3	24,586	34,950	17,907	30,802
2010[5]	11.3	42,723	2.7	24.3	1.3	42.6	13.5	26.5	24,373	34,617	17,711	31,630
2011	11.6	42,219	2.7	22.9	1.3	41.2	13.2	25.3	25,009	33,817	17,736	31,724
2012	12.0	42,081	2.8	23.5	1.3	40.7	13.6	25.6	25,387	33,567	17,265	30,462
2013[6]	12.1	43,010	2.6	21.6	1.3	40.4	12.7	23.5	25,857	33,527	18,073	31,339
2013[7]	12.4	41,657	2.9	23.1	1.4	40.5	13.4	24.7	24,625	32,933	17,249	31,717
2014	12.5	45,166	2.7	21.5	1.3	37.9	13.1	23.6	26,706	35,154	17,605	30,864
2015	12.8	47,328	2.5	19.6	1.2	35.5	12.1	21.4	28,110	35,973	18,905	31,657

[1] The term "family" refers to a group of two or more persons related by birth, marriage, or adoption and residing together. Every family must include a reference person.
[2] Poverty thresholds are updated each year to reflect changes in the consumer price index for all urban consumers (CPI-U).
[3] Adjusted by consumer price index research series (CPI-U-RS).
[4] Data for American Indians and Alaska natives, native Hawaiians and other Pacific Islanders, and those reporting two or more races are included in the total but not shown separately.
[5] Reflects implementation of Census 2010-based population controls comparable to succeeding years.
[6] The 2014 Current Population Survey (CPS) Annual Social and Economic Supplement (ASEC) included redesigned income questions, which were implemented to a subsample of the 98,000 addresses using a probability split panel design. These 2013 data are based on the 2014 ASEC sample of 68,000 addresses that received income questions similar to those used in the 2013 ASEC and are consistent with data in earlier years.
[7] These 2013 data are based on the 2014 ASEC sample of 30,000 addresses that received redesigned income questions and are consistent with data in later years.
[8] The CPS allows respondents to choose more than one race. Data shown are for "white alone, non-Hispanic," "black alone," and "Asian alone" race categories. ("Black" is also "black or African American.") Family race and Hispanic origin are based on the reference person.

Note: For details see *Income and Poverty in the United States* in publication Series P–60 on the CPS ASEC.

Source: Department of Commerce (Bureau of the Census).

TABLE B–10. Changes in consumer price indexes, 1947–2015

[For all urban consumers; percent change]

December to December	All items	All items less food and energy					Food			Energy [4]		C-CPI-U [5]
		Total [1]	Shelter [2]	Medical care [3]	Apparel	New vehicles	Total [1]	At home	Away from home	Total [1,3]	Gasoline	
1947	8.8	....	....	6.9	8.2	....	11.3				16.4	....
1948	3.0	....	....	5.8	5.1	11.5	−.8	−1.1			6.2	....
1949	−2.1	....	....	1.4	−7.4	4.0	−3.9	−3.7			1.6	....
1950	5.9	....	....	3.4	5.3	.2	9.8	9.5			1.6	....
1951	6.0	....	....	5.8	5.7	9.7	7.1	7.6			2.1	....
1952	.8	....	....	4.3	−2.9	4.4	−1.0	−1.3			.5	....
1953	.7		3.2	3.5	.7	−1.7	−1.1	−1.6			10.1	....
1954	−.7		1.8	2.3	−.7	1.3	−1.8	−2.3	0.9		−1.4	....
1955	.4		.9	3.3	.5	−2.3	−.7	−1.0	1.4		4.2	....
1956	3.0		2.6	3.2	2.5	7.8	2.9	2.7	2.7		3.1	....
1957	2.9		3.4	4.7	.9	2.0	2.8	3.0	3.9		2.2	....
1958	1.8	1.7	.8	4.5	.2	6.1	2.4	1.9	2.1	−0.9	−3.8	....
1959	1.7	2.0	2.0	3.8	1.3	−.2	−1.0	−1.3	3.3	4.7	7.0	....
1960	1.4	1.0	1.6	3.2	1.5	−3.0	3.1	3.2	2.4	1.3	1.2	....
1961	.7	1.3	.8	3.1	.4	.2	−.7	−1.6	2.3	−1.3	−3.2	....
1962	1.3	1.3	.8	2.2	.6	−1.0	1.3	1.3	3.0	2.2	3.8	....
1963	1.6	1.6	1.9	2.5	1.7	−.4	2.0	1.6	1.8	−.9	−2.4	....
1964	1.0	1.2	1.5	2.1	.4	−.6	1.3	1.5	1.4	.0	.0	....
1965	1.9	1.5	2.2	2.8	1.3	−2.9	3.5	3.6	3.2	1.8	4.1	....
1966	3.5	3.3	4.0	6.7	3.9	.0	4.0	3.2	5.5	1.7	3.2	....
1967	3.0	3.8	2.8	6.3	4.2	2.8	1.2	.3	4.6	1.7	1.5	....
1968	4.7	5.1	6.5	6.2	6.3	1.4	4.4	4.0	5.6	1.7	1.5	....
1969	6.2	6.2	8.7	6.2	5.2	2.1	7.0	7.1	7.4	2.9	3.4	....
1970	5.6	6.6	8.9	7.4	3.9	6.6	2.3	1.3	6.1	4.8	2.5	....
1971	3.3	3.1	2.7	4.6	2.1	−3.2	4.3	4.3	4.4	3.1	−.4	....
1972	3.4	3.0	4.0	3.3	2.6	.2	4.6	5.1	4.2	2.6	2.8	....
1973	8.7	4.7	7.1	5.3	4.4	1.3	20.3	22.0	12.7	17.0	19.6	....
1974	12.3	11.1	11.4	12.6	8.7	11.4	12.0	12.4	11.3	21.6	20.7	....
1975	6.9	6.7	7.2	9.8	2.4	7.3	6.6	6.2	7.4	11.4	11.0	....
1976	4.9	6.1	4.2	10.0	4.6	4.8	.5	−.8	6.0	7.1	2.8	....
1977	6.7	6.5	8.8	8.9	4.3	7.2	8.1	7.9	7.9	7.2	4.8	....
1978	9.0	8.5	11.4	8.8	3.1	6.2	11.8	12.5	10.4	7.9	8.6	....
1979	13.3	11.3	17.5	10.1	5.5	7.4	10.2	9.7	11.4	37.5	52.1	....
1980	12.5	12.2	15.0	9.9	6.8	7.4	10.2	10.5	9.6	18.0	18.9	....
1981	8.9	9.5	9.9	12.5	3.5	6.8	4.3	2.9	7.1	11.9	9.4	....
1982	3.8	4.5	2.4	11.0	1.6	1.4	3.1	2.3	5.1	1.3	−6.7	....
1983	3.8	4.8	4.7	6.4	2.9	3.3	2.7	1.8	4.1	−.5	−1.6	....
1984	3.9	4.7	5.2	6.1	2.0	2.5	3.8	3.6	4.2	.2	−2.5	....
1985	3.8	4.3	6.0	6.8	2.8	3.6	2.6	2.0	3.8	1.8	3.0	....
1986	1.1	3.8	4.6	7.7	.9	5.6	3.8	3.7	4.3	−19.7	−30.7	....
1987	4.4	4.2	4.8	5.8	4.8	1.8	3.5	3.5	3.7	8.2	18.6	....
1988	4.4	4.7	4.5	6.9	4.7	2.2	5.2	5.6	4.4	.5	−1.8	....
1989	4.6	4.4	4.9	8.5	1.0	2.4	5.6	6.2	4.6	5.1	6.5	....
1990	6.1	5.2	5.2	9.6	5.1	2.0	5.3	5.8	4.5	18.1	36.8	....
1991	3.1	4.4	3.9	7.9	3.4	3.2	1.9	1.3	2.9	−7.4	−16.2	....
1992	2.9	3.3	2.9	6.6	1.4	2.3	1.5	1.5	1.4	2.0	2.0	....
1993	2.7	3.2	3.0	5.4	.9	3.3	2.9	3.5	1.9	−1.4	−5.9	....
1994	2.7	2.6	3.0	4.9	−1.6	3.3	2.9	3.5	1.9	2.2	6.4	....
1995	2.5	3.0	3.5	3.9	.1	1.9	2.1	2.0	2.2	−1.3	−4.2	....
1996	3.3	2.6	2.9	3.0	−.2	1.8	4.3	4.9	3.1	8.6	12.4	....
1997	1.7	2.2	3.4	2.8	1.0	−.9	1.5	1.0	2.6	−3.4	−6.1	....
1998	1.6	2.4	3.3	3.4	−.7	.0	2.3	2.1	2.5	−8.8	−15.4	....
1999	2.7	1.9	2.5	3.7	−.5	−.3	1.9	1.7	2.3	13.4	30.1	....
2000	3.4	2.6	3.4	4.2	−1.8	.0	2.8	2.9	2.4	14.2	13.9	2.6
2001	1.6	2.7	4.2	4.7	−3.2	−.1	2.8	2.6	3.0	−13.0	−24.9	1.3
2002	2.4	1.9	3.1	5.0	−1.8	−2.0	1.5	.8	2.3	10.7	24.8	2.0
2003	1.9	1.1	2.2	3.7	−2.1	−1.8	3.6	4.5	2.3	6.9	6.8	1.7
2004	3.3	2.2	2.7	4.2	−.2	.6	2.7	2.4	3.0	16.6	26.1	3.2
2005	3.4	2.2	2.6	4.3	−1.1	−.4	2.3	1.7	3.2	17.1	16.1	2.9
2006	2.5	2.6	4.2	3.6	.9	−.9	2.1	1.4	3.2	2.9	6.4	2.3
2007	4.1	2.4	3.1	5.2	−.3	−.3	4.9	5.6	4.0	17.4	29.6	3.7
2008	.1	1.8	1.9	2.6	−1.0	−3.2	5.9	6.6	5.0	−21.3	−43.1	.2
2009	2.7	1.8	.3	3.4	1.9	4.9	−.5	−2.4	1.9	18.2	53.5	2.5
2010	1.5	.8	.4	3.3	−1.1	−.2	1.5	1.7	1.3	7.7	13.8	1.3
2011	3.0	2.2	1.9	3.5	4.6	3.2	4.7	6.0	2.9	6.6	9.9	2.9
2012	1.7	1.9	2.2	3.2	1.8	1.6	1.8	1.3	2.5	.5	1.7	1.5
2013	1.5	1.7	2.5	2.0	.6	.4	1.1	.4	2.1	.5	−1.0	1.3
2014	.8	1.6	2.9	3.0	−2.0	.5	3.4	3.7	3.0	−10.6	−21.0	.5
2015	.7	2.1	3.2	2.6	−.9	.2	.8	−.4	2.6	−12.6	−19.7	.4

[1] Includes other items not shown separately.
[2] Data beginning with 1983 incorporate a rental equivalence measure for homeowners' costs.
[3] Commodities and services.
[4] Household energy--electricity, utility (piped) gas service, fuel oil, etc.--and motor fuel.
[5] Chained consumer price index (C-CPI-U) introduced in 2002. Reflects the effect of substitution that consumers make across item categories in response to changes in relative prices.

Note: Changes from December to December are based on unadjusted indexes.

Source: Department of Labor (Bureau of Labor Statistics).

TABLE B–11. Civilian labor force, 1929–2016

[Monthly data seasonally adjusted, except as noted]

Year or month	Civilian noninstitutional population [1]	Civilian labor force					Not in labor force	Civilian labor force participation rate [2]	Civilian employment/population ratio [3]	Unemployment rate, civilian workers [4]
		Total	Employment			Unemployment				
			Total	Agricultural	Nonagricultural					
		Thousands of persons 14 years of age and over							Percent	
1929	....	49,180	47,630	10,450	37,180	1,550	....	....	....	3.2
1930	....	49,820	45,480	10,340	35,140	4,340	....	....	....	8.7
1931	....	50,420	42,400	10,290	32,110	8,020	....	....	....	15.9
1932	....	51,000	38,940	10,170	28,770	12,060	....	....	....	23.6
1933	....	51,590	38,760	10,090	28,670	12,830	....	....	....	24.9
1934	....	52,230	40,890	9,900	30,990	11,340	....	....	....	21.7
1935	....	52,870	42,260	10,110	32,150	10,610	....	....	....	20.1
1936	....	53,440	44,410	10,000	34,410	9,030	....	....	....	16.9
1937	....	54,000	46,300	9,820	36,480	7,700	....	....	....	14.3
1938	....	54,610	44,220	9,690	34,530	10,390	....	....	....	19.0
1939	....	55,230	45,750	9,610	36,140	9,480	....	....	....	17.2
1940	99,840	55,640	47,520	9,540	37,980	8,120	44,200	55.7	47.6	14.6
1941	99,900	55,910	50,350	9,100	41,250	5,560	43,990	56.0	50.4	9.9
1942	98,640	56,410	53,750	9,250	44,500	2,660	42,230	57.2	54.5	4.7
1943	94,640	55,540	54,470	9,080	45,390	1,070	39,100	58.7	57.6	1.9
1944	93,220	54,630	53,960	8,950	45,010	670	38,590	58.6	57.9	1.2
1945	94,090	53,860	52,820	8,580	44,240	1,040	40,230	57.2	56.1	1.9
1946	103,070	57,520	55,250	8,320	46,930	2,270	45,550	55.8	53.6	3.9
1947	106,018	60,168	57,812	8,256	49,557	2,356	45,850	56.8	54.5	3.9
		Thousands of persons 16 years of age and over								
1947	101,827	59,350	57,038	7,890	49,148	2,311	42,477	58.3	56.0	3.9
1948	103,068	60,621	58,343	7,629	50,714	2,276	42,447	58.8	56.6	3.8
1949	103,994	61,286	57,651	7,658	49,993	3,637	42,708	58.9	55.4	5.9
1950	104,995	62,208	58,918	7,160	51,758	3,288	42,787	59.2	56.1	5.3
1951	104,621	62,017	59,961	6,726	53,235	2,055	42,604	59.2	57.3	3.3
1952	105,231	62,138	60,250	6,500	53,749	1,883	43,093	59.0	57.3	3.0
1953	107,056	63,015	61,179	6,260	54,919	1,834	44,041	58.9	57.1	2.9
1954	108,321	63,643	60,109	6,205	53,904	3,532	44,678	58.8	55.5	5.5
1955	109,683	65,023	62,170	6,450	55,722	2,852	44,660	59.3	56.7	4.4
1956	110,954	66,552	63,799	6,283	57,514	2,750	44,402	60.0	57.5	4.1
1957	112,265	66,929	64,071	5,947	58,123	2,859	45,336	59.6	57.1	4.3
1958	113,727	67,639	63,036	5,586	57,450	4,602	46,088	59.5	55.4	6.8
1959	115,329	68,369	64,630	5,565	59,065	3,740	46,960	59.3	56.0	5.5
1960	117,245	69,628	65,778	5,458	60,318	3,852	47,617	59.4	56.1	5.5
1961	118,771	70,459	65,746	5,200	60,546	4,714	48,312	59.3	55.4	6.7
1962	120,153	70,614	66,702	4,944	61,759	3,911	49,539	58.8	55.5	5.5
1963	122,416	71,833	67,762	4,687	63,076	4,070	50,583	58.7	55.4	5.7
1964	124,485	73,091	69,305	4,523	64,782	3,786	51,394	58.7	55.7	5.2
1965	126,513	74,455	71,088	4,361	66,726	3,366	52,058	58.9	56.2	4.5
1966	128,058	75,770	72,895	3,979	68,915	2,875	52,288	59.2	56.9	3.8
1967	129,874	77,347	74,372	3,844	70,527	2,975	52,527	59.6	57.3	3.8
1968	132,028	78,737	75,920	3,817	72,103	2,817	53,291	59.6	57.5	3.6
1969	134,335	80,734	77,902	3,606	74,296	2,832	53,602	60.1	58.0	3.5
1970	137,085	82,771	78,678	3,463	75,215	4,093	54,315	60.4	57.4	4.9
1971	140,216	84,382	79,367	3,394	75,972	5,016	55,834	60.2	56.6	5.9
1972	144,126	87,034	82,153	3,484	78,669	4,882	57,091	60.4	57.0	5.6
1973	147,096	89,429	85,064	3,470	81,594	4,365	57,667	60.8	57.8	4.9
1974	150,120	91,949	86,794	3,515	83,279	5,156	58,171	61.3	57.8	5.6
1975	153,153	93,775	85,846	3,408	82,438	7,929	59,377	61.2	56.1	8.5
1976	156,150	96,158	88,752	3,331	85,421	7,406	59,991	61.6	56.8	7.7
1977	159,033	99,009	92,017	3,283	88,734	6,991	60,025	62.3	57.9	7.1
1978	161,910	102,251	96,048	3,387	92,661	6,202	59,659	63.2	59.3	6.1
1979	164,863	104,962	98,824	3,347	95,477	6,137	59,900	63.7	59.9	5.8
1980	167,745	106,940	99,303	3,364	95,938	7,637	60,806	63.8	59.2	7.1
1981	170,130	108,670	100,397	3,368	97,030	8,273	61,460	63.9	59.0	7.6
1982	172,271	110,204	99,526	3,401	96,125	10,678	62,067	64.0	57.8	9.7
1983	174,215	111,550	100,834	3,383	97,450	10,717	62,665	64.0	57.9	9.6
1984	176,383	113,544	105,005	3,321	101,685	8,539	62,839	64.4	59.5	7.5
1985	178,206	115,461	107,150	3,179	103,971	8,312	62,744	64.8	60.1	7.2
1986	180,587	117,834	109,597	3,163	106,434	8,237	62,752	65.3	60.7	7.0
1987	182,753	119,865	112,440	3,208	109,232	7,425	62,888	65.6	61.5	6.2
1988	184,613	121,669	114,968	3,169	111,800	6,701	62,944	65.9	62.3	5.5
1989	186,393	123,869	117,342	3,199	114,142	6,528	62,523	66.5	63.0	5.3

[1] Not seasonally adjusted.
[2] Civilian labor force as percent of civilian noninstitutional population.
[3] Civilian employment as percent of civilian noninstitutional population.
[4] Unemployed as percent of civilian labor force.

See next page for continuation of table.

TABLE B–11. Civilian labor force, 1929–2016—*Continued*

[Monthly data seasonally adjusted, except as noted]

Year or month	Civilian noninstitutional population [1]	Civilian labor force					Not in labor force	Civilian labor force participation rate [2]	Civilian employment/ population ratio [3]	Unemployment rate, civilian workers [4]
		Total	Employment			Unemployment				
			Total	Agricultural	Nonagricultural					
	Thousands of persons 16 years of age and over							Percent		
1990	189,164	125,840	118,793	3,223	115,570	7,047	63,324	66.5	62.8	5.6
1991	190,925	126,346	117,718	3,269	114,449	8,628	64,578	66.2	61.7	6.8
1992	192,805	128,105	118,492	3,247	115,245	9,613	64,700	66.4	61.5	7.5
1993	194,838	129,200	120,259	3,115	117,144	8,940	65,638	66.3	61.7	6.9
1994	196,814	131,056	123,060	3,409	119,651	7,996	65,758	66.6	62.5	6.1
1995	198,584	132,304	124,900	3,440	121,460	7,404	66,280	66.6	62.9	5.6
1996	200,591	133,943	126,708	3,443	123,264	7,236	66,647	66.8	63.2	5.4
1997	203,133	136,297	129,558	3,399	126,159	6,739	66,837	67.1	63.8	4.9
1998	205,220	137,673	131,463	3,378	128,085	6,210	67,547	67.1	64.1	4.5
1999	207,753	139,368	133,488	3,281	130,207	5,880	68,385	67.1	64.3	4.2
2000 [5]	212,577	142,583	136,891	2,464	134,427	5,692	69,994	67.1	64.4	4.0
2001	215,092	143,734	136,933	2,299	134,635	6,801	71,359	66.8	63.7	4.7
2002	217,570	144,863	136,485	2,311	134,174	8,378	72,707	66.6	62.7	5.8
2003	221,168	146,510	137,736	2,275	135,461	8,774	74,658	66.2	62.3	6.0
2004	223,357	147,401	139,252	2,232	137,020	8,149	75,956	66.0	62.3	5.5
2005	226,082	149,320	141,730	2,197	139,532	7,591	76,762	66.0	62.7	5.1
2006	228,815	151,428	144,427	2,206	142,221	7,001	77,387	66.2	63.1	4.6
2007	231,867	153,124	146,047	2,095	143,952	7,078	78,743	66.0	63.0	4.6
2008	233,788	154,287	145,362	2,168	143,194	8,924	79,501	66.0	62.2	5.8
2009	235,801	154,142	139,877	2,103	137,775	14,265	81,659	65.4	59.3	9.3
2010	237,830	153,889	139,064	2,206	136,858	14,825	83,941	64.7	58.5	9.6
2011	239,618	153,617	139,869	2,254	137,615	13,747	86,001	64.1	58.4	8.9
2012	243,284	154,975	142,469	2,186	140,283	12,506	88,310	63.7	58.6	8.1
2013	245,679	155,389	143,929	2,130	141,799	11,460	90,290	63.2	58.6	7.4
2014	247,947	155,922	146,305	2,237	144,068	9,617	92,025	62.9	59.0	6.2
2015	250,801	157,130	148,834	2,422	146,411	8,296	93,671	62.7	59.3	5.3
2014: Jan	246,915	155,285	145,092	2,161	142,922	10,192	91,630	62.9	58.8	6.6
Feb	247,085	155,560	145,185	2,137	143,098	10,375	91,526	63.0	58.8	6.7
Mar	247,258	156,187	145,772	2,133	143,544	10,415	91,071	63.2	59.0	6.7
Apr	247,439	155,376	145,677	2,162	143,504	9,699	92,063	62.8	58.9	6.2
May	247,622	155,511	145,792	2,057	143,737	9,719	92,111	62.8	58.9	6.2
June	247,814	155,684	146,214	2,158	144,090	9,470	92,130	62.8	59.0	6.1
July	248,023	156,090	146,438	2,180	144,213	9,651	91,934	62.9	59.0	6.2
Aug	248,229	156,080	146,464	2,288	144,128	9,617	92,149	62.9	59.0	6.2
Sept	248,446	156,129	146,834	2,384	144,420	9,296	92,317	62.8	59.1	6.0
Oct	248,657	156,363	147,374	2,402	145,057	8,989	92,294	62.9	59.3	5.7
Nov	248,844	156,442	147,389	2,399	145,042	9,053	92,402	62.9	59.2	5.8
Dec	249,027	156,142	147,439	2,355	145,132	8,704	92,885	62.7	59.2	5.6
2015: Jan	249,723	157,025	148,104	2,417	145,683	8,920	92,699	62.9	59.3	5.7
Feb	249,899	156,878	148,231	2,424	145,801	8,646	93,022	62.8	59.3	5.5
Mar	250,080	156,890	148,333	2,556	145,681	8,557	93,190	62.7	59.3	5.5
Apr	250,266	157,032	148,509	2,419	146,065	8,523	93,234	62.7	59.3	5.4
May	250,455	157,367	148,748	2,395	146,336	8,619	93,089	62.8	59.4	5.5
June	250,663	156,984	148,722	2,548	146,198	8,262	93,679	62.6	59.3	5.3
July	250,876	157,115	148,866	2,369	146,444	8,249	93,761	62.6	59.3	5.3
Aug	251,096	157,061	149,043	2,350	146,666	8,018	94,035	62.6	59.4	5.1
Sept	251,325	156,867	148,942	2,368	146,535	7,925	94,458	62.4	59.3	5.1
Oct	251,541	157,096	149,197	2,394	146,864	7,899	94,446	62.5	59.3	5.0
Nov	251,747	157,367	149,444	2,424	147,110	7,924	94,380	62.5	59.4	5.0
Dec	251,936	157,833	149,929	2,411	147,587	7,904	94,103	62.6	59.5	5.0
2016: Jan	252,397	158,335	150,544	2,385	148,115	7,791	94,062	62.7	59.6	4.9
Feb	252,577	158,890	151,074	2,456	148,620	7,815	93,688	62.9	59.8	4.9
Mar	252,768	159,286	151,320	2,623	148,704	7,966	93,482	63.0	59.9	5.0
Apr	252,969	158,924	151,004	2,592	148,377	7,920	94,044	62.8	59.7	5.0
May	253,174	158,466	151,030	2,585	148,429	7,436	94,708	62.6	59.7	4.7
June	253,397	158,880	151,097	2,516	148,640	7,783	94,517	62.7	59.6	4.9
July	253,620	159,287	151,517	2,388	149,155	7,770	94,333	62.8	59.7	4.9
Aug	253,854	159,463	151,614	2,520	149,118	7,849	94,391	62.8	59.7	4.9
Sept	254,091	159,907	151,968	2,441	149,560	7,939	94,184	62.9	59.8	5.0
Oct	254,321	159,712	151,925	2,321	149,637	7,787	94,609	62.8	59.7	4.9
Nov	254,540	159,486	152,085	2,438	149,772	7,400	95,055	62.7	59.7	4.6

[5] Beginning in 2000, data for agricultural employment are for agricultural and related industries; data for this series and for nonagricultural employment are not strictly comparable with data for earlier years. Because of independent seasonal adjustment for these two series, monthly data will not add to total civilian employment.

Note: Labor force data in Tables B–11 through B–13 are based on household interviews and usually relate to the calendar week that includes the 12th of the month. Historical comparability is affected by revisions to population controls, changes in occupational and industry classification, and other changes to the survey. In recent years, updated population controls have been introduced annually with the release of January data, so data are not strictly comparable with earlier periods. Particularly notable changes were introduced for data in the years 1953, 1960, 1962, 1972, 1973, 1978, 1980, 1990, 1994, 1997, 1998, 2000, 2003, 2008 and 2012. For definitions of terms, area samples used, historical comparability of the data, comparability with other series, etc., see *Employment and Earnings* or concepts and methodology of the CPS at http://www.bls.gov/cps/documentation.htm#concepts.

Source: Department of Labor (Bureau of Labor Statistics).

TABLE B-12. Civilian unemployment rate, 1972–2016

[Percent [1]; monthly data seasonally adjusted, except as noted]

Year or month	All civilian workers	Males Total	Males 16–19 years	Males 20 years and over	Females Total	Females 16–19 years	Females 20 years and over	Both sexes 16–19 years	White [2]	Black or African American [2]	Asian [2]	Hispanic or Latino ethnicity [3]	Married men, spouse present	Women who maintain families [4]
1972	5.6	5.0	15.9	4.0	6.6	16.7	5.4	16.2	5.1	10.4	....	....	2.8	7.2
1973	4.9	4.2	13.9	3.3	6.0	15.3	4.9	14.5	4.3	9.4	....	7.5	2.3	7.1
1974	5.6	4.9	15.6	3.8	6.7	16.6	5.5	16.0	5.0	10.5	....	8.1	2.7	7.0
1975	8.5	7.9	20.1	6.8	9.3	19.7	8.0	19.9	7.8	14.8	....	12.2	5.1	10.0
1976	7.7	7.1	19.2	5.9	8.6	18.7	7.4	19.0	7.0	14.0	....	11.5	4.2	10.1
1977	7.1	6.3	17.3	5.2	8.2	18.3	7.0	17.8	6.2	14.0	....	10.1	3.6	9.4
1978	6.1	5.3	15.8	4.3	7.2	17.1	6.0	16.4	5.2	12.8	....	9.1	2.8	8.5
1979	5.8	5.1	15.9	4.2	6.8	16.4	5.7	16.1	5.1	12.3	....	8.3	2.8	8.3
1980	7.1	6.9	18.3	5.9	7.4	17.2	6.4	17.8	6.3	14.3	....	10.1	4.2	9.2
1981	7.6	7.4	20.1	6.3	7.9	19.0	6.8	19.6	6.7	15.6	....	10.4	4.3	10.4
1982	9.7	9.9	24.4	8.8	9.4	21.9	8.3	23.2	8.6	18.9	....	13.8	6.5	11.7
1983	9.6	9.9	23.3	8.9	9.2	21.3	8.1	22.4	8.4	19.5	....	13.7	6.5	12.2
1984	7.5	7.4	19.6	6.6	7.6	18.0	6.8	18.9	6.5	15.9	....	10.7	4.6	10.3
1985	7.2	7.0	19.5	6.2	7.4	17.6	6.6	18.6	6.2	15.1	....	10.5	4.3	10.4
1986	7.0	6.9	19.0	6.1	7.1	17.6	6.2	18.3	6.0	14.5	....	10.6	4.4	9.8
1987	6.2	6.2	17.8	5.4	6.2	15.9	5.4	16.9	5.3	13.0	....	8.8	3.9	9.2
1988	5.5	5.5	16.0	4.8	5.6	14.4	4.9	15.3	4.7	11.7	....	8.2	3.3	8.1
1989	5.3	5.2	15.9	4.5	5.4	14.0	4.7	15.0	4.5	11.4	....	8.0	3.0	8.1
1990	5.6	5.7	16.3	5.0	5.5	14.7	4.9	15.5	4.8	11.4	....	8.2	3.4	8.3
1991	6.8	7.2	19.8	6.4	6.4	17.5	5.7	18.7	6.1	12.5	....	10.0	4.4	9.3
1992	7.5	7.9	21.5	7.1	7.0	18.6	6.3	20.1	6.6	14.2	....	11.6	5.1	10.0
1993	6.9	7.2	20.4	6.4	6.6	17.5	5.9	19.0	6.1	13.0	....	10.8	4.4	9.7
1994	6.1	6.2	19.0	5.4	6.0	16.2	5.4	17.6	5.3	11.5	....	9.9	3.7	8.9
1995	5.6	5.6	18.4	4.8	5.6	16.1	4.9	17.3	4.9	10.4	....	9.3	3.3	8.0
1996	5.4	5.4	18.1	4.6	5.4	15.2	4.8	16.7	4.7	10.5	....	8.9	3.0	8.2
1997	4.9	4.9	16.9	4.2	5.0	15.0	4.4	16.0	4.2	10.0	....	7.7	2.7	8.1
1998	4.5	4.4	16.2	3.7	4.6	12.9	4.1	14.6	3.9	8.9	....	7.2	2.4	7.2
1999	4.2	4.1	14.7	3.5	4.3	13.2	3.8	13.9	3.7	8.0	....	6.4	2.2	6.4
2000	4.0	3.9	14.0	3.3	4.1	12.1	3.6	13.1	3.5	7.6	3.6	5.7	2.0	5.9
2001	4.7	4.8	16.0	4.2	4.7	13.4	4.1	14.7	4.2	8.6	4.5	6.6	2.7	6.6
2002	5.8	5.9	18.1	5.3	5.6	14.9	5.1	16.5	5.1	10.2	5.9	7.5	3.6	8.0
2003	6.0	6.3	19.3	5.6	5.7	15.6	5.1	17.5	5.2	10.8	6.0	7.7	3.8	8.5
2004	5.5	5.6	18.4	5.0	5.4	15.5	4.9	17.0	4.8	10.4	4.4	7.0	3.1	8.0
2005	5.1	5.1	18.6	4.4	5.1	14.5	4.6	16.6	4.4	10.0	4.0	6.0	2.8	7.8
2006	4.6	4.6	16.9	4.0	4.6	13.8	4.1	15.4	4.0	8.9	3.0	5.2	2.4	7.1
2007	4.6	4.7	17.6	4.1	4.5	13.8	4.0	15.7	4.1	8.3	3.2	5.6	2.5	6.5
2008	5.8	6.1	21.2	5.4	5.4	16.2	4.9	18.7	5.2	10.1	4.0	7.6	3.4	8.0
2009	9.3	10.3	27.8	9.6	8.1	20.7	7.5	24.3	8.5	14.8	7.3	12.1	6.6	11.5
2010	9.6	10.5	28.8	9.8	8.6	22.8	8.0	25.9	8.7	16.0	7.5	12.5	6.8	12.3
2011	8.9	9.4	27.2	8.7	8.5	21.7	7.9	24.4	7.9	15.8	7.0	11.5	5.8	12.4
2012	8.1	8.2	26.8	7.5	7.9	21.1	7.3	24.0	7.2	13.8	5.9	10.3	4.9	11.4
2013	7.4	7.6	25.5	7.0	7.1	20.3	6.5	22.9	6.5	13.1	5.2	9.1	4.3	10.2
2014	6.2	6.3	21.4	5.7	6.1	17.7	5.6	19.6	5.3	11.3	5.0	7.4	3.4	8.6
2015	5.3	5.4	18.4	4.9	5.2	15.5	4.8	16.9	4.6	9.6	3.8	6.6	2.8	7.4
2015: Jan	5.7	5.8	20.0	5.3	5.5	17.8	5.0	18.9	4.9	10.3	4.0	6.7	2.9	8.1
Feb	5.5	5.6	17.7	5.2	5.4	16.3	4.9	17.0	4.7	10.3	4.0	6.7	3.0	7.7
Mar	5.5	5.6	19.8	5.1	5.3	15.3	4.9	17.6	4.7	10.0	3.2	6.8	2.8	8.1
Apr	5.4	5.5	17.8	5.0	5.4	16.3	4.9	17.1	4.7	9.6	4.4	6.9	3.0	7.0
May	5.5	5.5	20.4	5.0	5.4	15.2	5.0	17.8	4.7	10.2	4.1	6.7	2.9	6.8
June	5.3	5.3	20.1	4.8	5.2	15.8	4.7	17.9	4.6	9.5	3.8	6.6	2.8	7.8
July	5.3	5.2	17.6	4.8	5.3	14.9	4.9	16.3	4.6	9.1	4.0	6.8	2.8	8.0
Aug	5.1	5.1	17.6	4.7	5.1	15.9	4.7	16.8	4.4	9.4	3.5	6.6	2.8	8.1
Sept	5.1	5.1	16.8	4.7	5.0	15.6	4.5	16.2	4.4	9.2	3.7	6.4	2.8	7.1
Oct	5.0	5.1	16.7	4.7	4.9	14.9	4.5	15.8	4.4	9.2	3.5	6.4	2.8	7.5
Nov	5.0	5.2	18.1	4.7	4.9	13.0	4.6	15.6	4.4	9.4	3.9	6.4	2.7	6.9
Dec	5.0	5.2	17.7	4.7	4.8	14.4	4.4	16.1	4.5	8.3	4.0	6.3	2.7	5.8
2016: Jan	4.9	4.9	17.4	4.5	4.9	14.5	4.5	16.0	4.3	8.8	3.7	5.9	2.6	7.1
Feb	4.9	4.9	16.8	4.5	4.9	14.3	4.5	15.6	4.3	8.8	3.8	5.4	2.6	7.0
Mar	5.0	5.0	17.0	4.5	5.0	14.6	4.6	15.9	4.3	9.0	4.0	5.6	2.9	6.8
Apr	5.0	5.0	16.4	4.6	5.0	15.7	4.5	16.0	4.3	8.8	3.8	6.1	2.7	6.7
May	4.7	4.7	16.2	4.3	4.7	15.9	4.2	16.0	4.1	8.2	4.1	5.6	2.6	6.6
June	4.9	4.9	17.1	4.5	4.9	14.8	4.5	16.0	4.4	8.6	3.5	5.8	2.6	7.3
July	4.9	5.0	16.5	4.6	4.7	14.8	4.3	15.6	4.3	8.4	3.8	5.4	2.6	7.2
Aug	4.9	5.0	17.5	4.5	4.9	13.7	4.5	15.7	4.4	8.1	4.2	5.6	2.7	7.9
Sept	5.0	5.1	16.5	4.7	4.8	15.0	4.4	15.8	4.4	8.3	3.9	6.4	2.9	6.4
Oct	4.9	5.1	17.9	4.6	4.7	13.3	4.3	15.6	4.3	8.6	3.4	5.7	2.8	6.1
Nov	4.6	4.7	18.0	4.3	4.5	12.1	4.2	15.2	4.2	8.1	3.0	5.7	2.7	6.2

[1] Unemployed as percent of civilian labor force in group specified.
[2] Beginning in 2003, persons who selected this race group only. Prior to 2003, persons who selected more than one race were included in the group they identified as the main race. Data for "black or African American" were for "black" prior to 2003. See *Employment and Earnings* or concepts and methodology of the CPS at http://www.bls.gov/cps/documentation.htm#concepts for details.
[3] Persons whose ethnicity is identified as Hispanic or Latino may be of any race.
[4] Not seasonally adjusted.

Note: Data relate to persons 16 years of age and over.
See Note, Table B–11.

Source: Department of Labor (Bureau of Labor Statistics).

TABLE B–13. Unemployment by duration and reason, 1972–2016

[Thousands of persons, except as noted; monthly data seasonally adjusted [1]]

Year or month	Un-employ-ment	Duration of unemployment						Reason for unemployment					
		Less than 5 weeks	5–14 weeks	15–26 weeks	27 weeks and over	Average (mean) duration (weeks) [2]	Median duration (weeks)	Job losers [3]			Job leavers	Re-entrants	New entrants
								Total	On layoff	Other			
1972	4,882	2,242	1,472	601	566	12.0	6.2	2,108	582	1,526	641	1,456	677
1973	4,365	2,224	1,314	483	343	10.0	5.2	1,694	472	1,221	683	1,340	649
1974	5,156	2,604	1,597	574	381	9.8	5.2	2,242	746	1,495	768	1,463	681
1975	7,929	2,940	2,484	1,303	1,203	14.2	8.4	4,386	1,671	2,714	827	1,892	823
1976	7,406	2,844	2,196	1,018	1,348	15.8	8.2	3,679	1,050	2,628	903	1,928	895
1977	6,991	2,919	2,132	913	1,028	14.3	7.0	3,166	865	2,300	909	1,963	953
1978	6,202	2,865	1,923	766	648	11.9	5.9	2,585	712	1,873	874	1,857	885
1979	6,137	2,950	1,946	706	535	10.8	5.4	2,635	851	1,784	880	1,806	817
1980	7,637	3,295	2,470	1,052	820	11.9	6.5	3,947	1,488	2,459	891	1,927	872
1981	8,273	3,449	2,539	1,122	1,162	13.7	6.9	4,267	1,430	2,837	923	2,102	981
1982	10,678	3,883	3,311	1,708	1,776	15.6	8.7	6,268	2,127	4,141	840	2,384	1,185
1983	10,717	3,570	2,937	1,652	2,559	20.0	10.1	6,258	1,780	4,478	830	2,412	1,216
1984	8,539	3,350	2,451	1,104	1,634	18.2	7.9	4,421	1,171	3,250	823	2,184	1,110
1985	8,312	3,498	2,509	1,025	1,280	15.6	6.8	4,139	1,157	2,982	877	2,256	1,039
1986	8,237	3,448	2,557	1,045	1,187	15.0	6.9	4,033	1,090	2,943	1,015	2,160	1,029
1987	7,425	3,246	2,196	943	1,040	14.5	6.5	3,566	943	2,623	965	1,974	920
1988	6,701	3,084	2,007	801	809	13.5	5.9	3,092	851	2,241	983	1,809	816
1989	6,528	3,174	1,978	730	646	11.9	4.8	2,983	850	2,133	1,024	1,843	677
1990	7,047	3,265	2,257	822	703	12.0	5.3	3,387	1,028	2,359	1,041	1,930	688
1991	8,628	3,480	2,791	1,246	1,111	13.7	6.8	4,694	1,292	3,402	1,004	2,139	792
1992	9,613	3,376	2,830	1,453	1,954	17.7	8.7	5,389	1,260	4,129	1,002	2,285	937
1993	8,940	3,262	2,584	1,297	1,798	18.0	8.3	4,848	1,115	3,733	976	2,198	919
1994	7,996	2,728	2,408	1,237	1,623	18.8	9.2	3,815	977	2,838	791	2,786	604
1995	7,404	2,700	2,342	1,085	1,278	16.6	8.3	3,476	1,030	2,446	824	2,525	579
1996	7,236	2,633	2,287	1,053	1,262	16.7	8.3	3,370	1,021	2,349	774	2,512	580
1997	6,739	2,538	2,138	995	1,067	15.8	8.0	3,037	931	2,106	795	2,338	569
1998	6,210	2,622	1,950	763	875	14.5	6.7	2,822	866	1,957	734	2,132	520
1999	5,880	2,568	1,832	755	725	13.4	6.4	2,622	848	1,774	783	2,005	469
2000	5,692	2,558	1,815	669	649	12.6	5.9	2,517	852	1,664	780	1,961	434
2001	6,801	2,853	2,196	951	801	13.1	6.8	3,476	1,067	2,409	835	2,031	459
2002	8,378	2,893	2,580	1,369	1,535	16.6	9.1	4,607	1,124	3,483	866	2,368	536
2003	8,774	2,785	2,612	1,442	1,936	19.2	10.1	4,838	1,121	3,717	818	2,477	641
2004	8,149	2,696	2,382	1,293	1,779	19.6	9.8	4,197	998	3,199	858	2,408	686
2005	7,591	2,667	2,304	1,130	1,490	18.4	8.9	3,667	933	2,734	872	2,386	666
2006	7,001	2,614	2,121	1,031	1,235	16.8	8.3	3,321	921	2,400	827	2,237	616
2007	7,078	2,542	2,232	1,061	1,243	16.8	8.5	3,515	976	2,539	793	2,142	627
2008	8,924	2,932	2,804	1,427	1,761	17.9	9.4	4,789	1,176	3,614	896	2,472	766
2009	14,265	3,165	3,828	2,775	4,496	24.4	15.1	9,160	1,630	7,530	882	3,187	1,035
2010	14,825	2,771	3,267	2,371	6,415	33.0	21.4	9,250	1,431	7,819	889	3,466	1,220
2011	13,747	2,677	2,993	2,061	6,016	39.3	21.4	8,106	1,230	6,876	956	3,401	1,284
2012	12,506	2,644	2,866	1,859	5,136	39.4	19.3	6,877	1,183	5,694	967	3,345	1,316
2013	11,460	2,584	2,759	1,807	4,310	36.5	17.0	6,073	1,136	4,937	932	3,207	1,247
2014	9,617	2,471	2,432	1,497	3,218	33.7	14.0	4,878	1,007	3,871	824	2,829	1,086
2015	8,296	2,399	2,302	1,267	2,328	29.2	11.6	4,063	974	3,089	819	2,535	879
2015: Jan	8,920	2,390	2,332	1,371	2,776	32.0	13.4	4,246	919	3,327	851	2,836	1,026
Feb	8,646	2,432	2,251	1,317	2,677	31.4	13.0	4,177	1,027	3,150	880	2,632	949
Mar	8,557	2,488	2,330	1,255	2,547	30.4	12.1	4,194	1,004	3,190	870	2,666	812
Apr	8,523	2,707	2,339	1,162	2,503	30.5	11.6	4,130	959	3,171	824	2,649	867
May	8,619	2,397	2,507	1,286	2,491	30.5	11.6	4,263	1,041	3,222	823	2,584	963
June	8,262	2,347	2,350	1,385	2,128	28.1	11.4	4,060	1,040	3,019	767	2,488	931
July	8,249	2,471	2,249	1,182	2,190	28.3	11.4	4,116	989	3,127	844	2,441	827
Aug	8,018	2,106	2,354	1,254	2,189	28.3	12.1	4,014	968	3,046	787	2,344	846
Sept	7,925	2,373	2,211	1,228	2,109	26.3	11.3	3,883	901	2,982	778	2,443	832
Oct	7,899	2,339	2,295	1,227	2,132	28.0	11.1	3,944	936	3,007	790	2,435	812
Nov	7,924	2,412	2,253	1,270	2,054	27.9	10.7	3,873	939	2,934	800	2,449	847
Dec	7,904	2,405	2,192	1,235	2,085	27.6	10.5	3,796	937	2,859	821	2,476	858
2016: Jan	7,791	2,249	2,282	1,135	2,089	28.9	10.9	3,664	923	2,741	766	2,468	827
Feb	7,815	2,297	2,236	1,132	2,165	29.0	11.2	3,749	960	2,790	760	2,467	833
Mar	7,966	2,412	2,205	1,178	2,213	28.4	11.4	3,835	921	2,914	833	2,495	778
Apr	7,920	2,545	2,131	1,304	2,063	27.7	11.4	3,855	841	3,014	851	2,357	839
May	7,436	2,207	2,239	1,173	1,885	26.7	10.7	3,573	829	2,744	796	2,209	865
June	7,783	2,418	2,140	1,129	1,979	27.7	10.3	3,776	1,097	2,679	828	2,268	902
July	7,770	2,160	2,266	1,150	2,020	28.1	11.6	3,739	997	2,743	824	2,298	826
Aug	7,849	2,290	2,329	1,056	2,006	27.6	11.2	3,791	998	2,792	885	2,271	861
Sept	7,939	2,574	2,234	1,157	1,974	27.5	10.3	3,967	1,075	2,892	893	2,333	805
Oct	7,787	2,397	2,296	1,165	1,979	27.2	10.2	3,749	994	2,755	949	2,354	793
Nov	7,400	2,421	2,136	1,077	1,856	26.3	10.1	3,555	904	2,651	934	2,274	729

[1] Because of independent seasonal adjustment of the various series, detail will not sum to totals.
[2] Beginning with 2011, includes unemployment durations of up to 5 years; prior data are for up to 2 years.
[3] Beginning with 1994, job losers and persons who completed temporary jobs.

Note: Data relate to persons 16 years of age and over.
See Note, Table B–11.

Source: Department of Labor (Bureau of Labor Statistics).

[Thousands of jobs; monthly data seasonally adjusted]

Year or month	Total non-agricultural employment	Private industries									
		Total private	Goods-producing industries						Private service-providing industries		
			Total	Mining and logging	Construction	Manufacturing			Total	Trade, transportation, and utilities [1]	
						Total	Durable goods	Non-durable goods		Total	Retail trade
1972	73,798	60,333	22,299	672	3,957	17,669	10,630	7,039	38,034	14,788	8,038
1973	76,912	63,050	23,450	693	4,167	18,589	11,414	7,176	39,600	15,349	8,371
1974	78,389	64,086	23,364	755	4,095	18,514	11,432	7,082	40,721	15,693	8,536
1975	77,069	62,250	21,318	802	3,608	16,909	10,266	6,643	40,932	15,606	8,600
1976	79,502	64,501	22,025	832	3,662	17,531	10,640	6,891	42,476	16,128	8,966
1977	82,593	67,334	22,972	865	3,940	18,167	11,132	7,035	44,362	16,765	9,359
1978	86,826	71,014	24,156	902	4,322	18,932	11,770	7,162	46,858	17,658	9,879
1979	89,933	73,865	24,997	1,008	4,562	19,426	12,220	7,206	48,869	18,303	10,180
1980	90,533	74,158	24,263	1,077	4,454	18,733	11,679	7,054	49,895	18,413	10,244
1981	91,297	75,117	24,118	1,180	4,304	18,634	11,611	7,023	50,999	18,604	10,364
1982	89,689	73,706	22,550	1,163	4,024	17,363	10,610	6,753	51,156	18,457	10,372
1983	90,295	74,284	22,110	997	4,065	17,048	10,326	6,722	52,174	18,668	10,635
1984	94,548	78,389	23,435	1,014	4,501	17,920	11,050	6,870	54,954	19,653	11,223
1985	97,532	81,000	23,585	974	4,793	17,819	11,034	6,784	57,415	20,379	11,733
1986	99,500	82,661	23,318	829	4,937	17,552	10,795	6,757	59,343	20,795	12,078
1987	102,116	84,960	23,470	771	5,090	17,609	10,767	6,842	61,490	21,302	12,419
1988	105,378	87,838	23,909	770	5,233	17,906	10,969	6,938	63,929	21,974	12,808
1989	108,051	90,124	24,045	750	5,309	17,985	11,004	6,981	66,079	22,510	13,108
1990	109,527	91,112	23,723	765	5,263	17,695	10,737	6,958	67,389	22,666	13,182
1991	108,427	89,881	22,588	739	4,780	17,068	10,220	6,848	67,293	22,281	12,896
1992	108,802	90,015	22,095	689	4,608	16,799	9,946	6,853	67,921	22,125	12,828
1993	110,935	91,946	22,219	666	4,779	16,774	9,901	6,872	69,727	22,378	13,021
1994	114,398	95,124	22,774	659	5,095	17,020	10,132	6,889	72,350	23,128	13,491
1995	117,407	97,975	23,156	641	5,274	17,241	10,373	6,868	74,819	23,834	13,897
1996	119,836	100,297	23,409	637	5,536	17,237	10,486	6,751	76,888	24,239	14,143
1997	122,951	103,287	23,886	654	5,813	17,419	10,705	6,714	79,401	24,700	14,389
1998	126,157	106,248	24,354	645	6,149	17,560	10,911	6,649	81,894	25,186	14,609
1999	129,240	108,933	24,465	598	6,545	17,322	10,831	6,491	84,468	25,771	14,970
2000	132,024	111,235	24,649	599	6,787	17,263	10,877	6,386	86,585	26,225	15,280
2001	132,087	110,969	23,873	606	6,826	16,441	10,336	6,105	87,096	25,983	15,239
2002	130,649	109,136	22,557	583	6,716	15,259	9,485	5,774	86,579	25,497	15,025
2003	130,347	108,764	21,816	572	6,735	14,509	8,964	5,546	86,948	25,287	14,917
2004	131,787	110,166	21,882	591	6,976	14,315	8,925	5,390	88,284	25,533	15,058
2005	134,051	112,247	22,190	628	7,336	14,227	8,956	5,271	90,057	25,959	15,280
2006	136,453	114,479	22,530	684	7,691	14,155	8,981	5,174	91,949	26,276	15,353
2007	137,999	115,781	22,233	724	7,630	13,879	8,808	5,071	93,548	26,630	15,520
2008	137,242	114,732	21,335	767	7,162	13,406	8,463	4,943	93,398	26,293	15,283
2009	131,313	108,758	18,558	694	6,016	11,847	7,284	4,564	90,201	24,906	14,522
2010	130,361	107,871	17,751	705	5,518	11,528	7,064	4,464	90,120	24,636	14,440
2011	131,932	109,845	18,047	788	5,533	11,726	7,273	4,453	91,798	25,065	14,668
2012	134,175	112,255	18,420	848	5,646	11,927	7,470	4,457	93,834	25,476	14,841
2013	136,381	114,529	18,738	863	5,856	12,020	7,548	4,472	95,791	25,862	15,079
2014	138,958	117,076	19,226	891	6,151	12,185	7,674	4,512	97,850	26,383	15,357
2015	141,865	119,859	19,584	820	6,446	12,318	7,756	4,562	100,275	26,920	15,641
2015: Jan	140,623	118,669	19,552	890	6,351	12,311	7,764	4,547	99,117	26,698	15,510
Feb	140,888	118,921	19,568	875	6,378	12,315	7,769	4,546	99,353	26,750	15,539
Mar	140,972	119,011	19,548	859	6,371	12,318	7,769	4,549	99,463	26,788	15,564
Apr	141,223	119,252	19,569	844	6,409	12,316	7,765	4,551	99,683	26,815	15,578
May	141,496	119,508	19,574	824	6,426	12,324	7,767	4,557	99,934	26,861	15,605
June	141,724	119,734	19,571	820	6,426	12,325	7,765	4,560	100,163	26,909	15,640
July	142,001	119,979	19,585	812	6,437	12,336	7,762	4,574	100,394	26,963	15,671
Aug	142,151	120,102	19,562	803	6,441	12,318	7,756	4,562	100,540	26,978	15,675
Sept	142,300	120,264	19,550	790	6,451	12,309	7,749	4,560	100,714	26,987	15,681
Oct	142,595	120,568	19,581	786	6,484	12,311	7,745	4,566	100,987	27,011	15,702
Nov	142,875	120,847	19,634	771	6,549	12,314	7,733	4,581	101,213	27,087	15,754
Dec	143,146	121,106	19,678	761	6,597	12,320	7,731	4,589	101,428	27,114	15,761
2016: Jan	143,314	121,261	19,702	749	6,615	12,338	7,742	4,596	101,559	27,173	15,827
Feb	143,547	121,483	19,682	732	6,628	12,322	7,728	4,594	101,801	27,229	15,879
Mar	143,733	121,650	19,675	717	6,665	12,293	7,703	4,590	101,975	27,280	15,922
Apr	143,877	121,797	19,663	706	6,659	12,298	7,706	4,592	102,134	27,296	15,920
May	143,901	121,796	19,618	696	6,641	12,281	7,686	4,595	102,178	27,292	15,920
June	144,172	122,034	19,613	689	6,635	12,289	7,681	4,608	102,421	27,311	15,942
July	144,424	122,255	19,627	685	6,651	12,291	7,685	4,606	102,628	27,340	15,955
Aug	144,600	122,387	19,601	681	6,645	12,275	7,669	4,606	102,786	27,378	15,972
Sept	144,808	122,592	19,622	682	6,671	12,269	7,663	4,606	102,970	27,409	15,994
Oct [p]	144,950	122,727	19,629	680	6,685	12,264	7,662	4,602	103,098	27,421	15,985
Nov [p]	145,128	122,883	19,646	682	6,704	12,260	7,656	4,604	103,237	27,424	15,977

[1] Includes wholesale trade, transportation and warehousing, and utilities, not shown separately.

Note: Data in Tables B–14 and B–15 are based on reports from employing establishments and relate to full- and part-time wage and salary workers in nonagricultural establishments who received pay for any part of the pay period that includes the 12th of the month. Not comparable with labor force data (Tables B–11 through B–13), which include proprietors, self-employed persons, unpaid family workers, and private household workers; which count persons as

See next page for continuation of table.

[Thousands of jobs; monthly data seasonally adjusted]

Year or month	Private industries—Continued						Government			
	Private service-providing industries—Continued									
	Information	Financial activities	Professional and business services	Education and health services	Leisure and hospitality	Other services	Total	Federal	State	Local
1972	2,056	3,784	5,523	4,863	5,121	1,900	13,465	2,815	2,859	7,790
1973	2,135	3,920	5,774	5,092	5,341	1,990	13,862	2,794	2,923	8,146
1974	2,160	4,023	5,974	5,322	5,471	2,078	14,303	2,858	3,039	8,407
1975	2,061	4,047	6,034	5,497	5,544	2,144	14,820	2,882	3,179	8,758
1976	2,111	4,155	6,287	5,756	5,794	2,244	15,001	2,863	3,273	8,865
1977	2,185	4,348	6,587	6,052	6,065	2,359	15,258	2,859	3,377	9,023
1978	2,287	4,599	6,972	6,427	6,411	2,505	15,812	2,893	3,474	9,446
1979	2,375	4,843	7,312	6,768	6,631	2,637	16,068	2,894	3,541	9,633
1980	2,361	5,025	7,544	7,077	6,721	2,755	16,375	3,000	3,610	9,765
1981	2,382	5,163	7,782	7,364	6,840	2,865	16,180	2,922	3,640	9,619
1982	2,317	5,209	7,848	7,526	6,874	2,924	15,982	2,884	3,640	9,458
1983	2,253	5,334	8,039	7,781	7,078	3,021	16,011	2,915	3,662	9,434
1984	2,398	5,553	8,464	8,211	7,489	3,186	16,159	2,943	3,734	9,482
1985	2,437	5,815	8,871	8,679	7,869	3,366	16,533	3,014	3,832	9,687
1986	2,445	6,128	9,211	9,086	8,156	3,523	16,838	3,044	3,893	9,901
1987	2,507	6,385	9,608	9,543	8,446	3,699	17,156	3,089	3,967	10,100
1988	2,585	6,500	10,090	10,096	8,778	3,907	17,540	3,124	4,076	10,339
1989	2,622	6,562	10,555	10,652	9,062	4,116	17,927	3,136	4,182	10,609
1990	2,688	6,614	10,848	11,024	9,288	4,261	18,415	3,196	4,305	10,914
1991	2,677	6,561	10,714	11,556	9,256	4,249	18,545	3,110	4,355	11,081
1992	2,641	6,559	10,970	11,948	9,437	4,240	18,787	3,111	4,408	11,267
1993	2,668	6,742	11,495	12,362	9,732	4,350	18,989	3,063	4,488	11,438
1994	2,738	6,910	12,174	12,872	10,100	4,428	19,275	3,018	4,576	11,682
1995	2,843	6,866	12,844	13,360	10,501	4,572	19,432	2,949	4,635	11,849
1996	2,940	7,018	13,462	13,761	10,777	4,690	19,539	2,877	4,606	12,056
1997	3,084	7,255	14,335	14,185	11,018	4,825	19,664	2,806	4,582	12,276
1998	3,218	7,565	15,147	14,570	11,232	4,976	19,909	2,772	4,612	12,525
1999	3,419	7,753	15,957	14,939	11,543	5,087	20,307	2,769	4,709	12,829
2000	3,630	7,783	16,666	15,252	11,862	5,168	20,790	2,865	4,786	13,139
2001	3,629	7,900	16,476	15,814	12,036	5,258	21,118	2,764	4,905	13,449
2002	3,395	7,956	15,976	16,398	11,986	5,372	21,513	2,766	5,029	13,718
2003	3,188	8,078	15,987	16,835	12,173	5,401	21,583	2,761	5,002	13,820
2004	3,118	8,105	16,394	17,230	12,493	5,409	21,621	2,730	4,982	13,909
2005	3,061	8,197	16,954	17,676	12,816	5,395	21,804	2,732	5,032	14,041
2006	3,038	8,367	17,566	18,154	13,110	5,438	21,974	2,732	5,075	14,167
2007	3,032	8,348	17,942	18,676	13,427	5,494	22,218	2,734	5,122	14,362
2008	2,984	8,206	17,735	19,228	13,436	5,515	22,509	2,762	5,177	14,571
2009	2,804	7,838	16,579	19,630	13,077	5,367	22,555	2,832	5,169	14,554
2010	2,707	7,695	16,728	19,975	13,049	5,331	22,490	2,977	5,137	14,376
2011	2,674	7,697	17,332	20,318	13,353	5,360	22,086	2,859	5,078	14,150
2012	2,676	7,784	17,932	20,769	13,768	5,430	21,920	2,820	5,055	14,045
2013	2,706	7,886	18,515	21,086	14,254	5,483	21,853	2,769	5,046	14,037
2014	2,726	7,977	19,062	21,439	14,696	5,567	21,882	2,733	5,064	14,084
2015	2,750	8,124	19,672	22,055	15,128	5,625	22,007	2,754	5,103	14,149
2015: Jan	2,734	8,061	19,370	21,731	14,924	5,599	21,954	2,743	5,092	14,119
Feb	2,738	8,070	19,409	21,790	14,989	5,607	21,967	2,747	5,096	14,124
Mar	2,735	8,082	19,436	21,828	14,989	5,605	21,961	2,747	5,094	14,120
Apr	2,745	8,089	19,505	21,905	15,010	5,614	21,971	2,750	5,096	14,125
May	2,747	8,098	19,585	21,962	15,059	5,622	21,988	2,752	5,096	14,140
June	2,751	8,117	19,661	22,017	15,089	5,619	21,990	2,752	5,099	14,139
July	2,756	8,137	19,707	22,075	15,125	5,631	22,022	2,751	5,098	14,173
Aug	2,753	8,150	19,742	22,137	15,158	5,622	22,049	2,753	5,106	14,190
Sept	2,766	8,153	19,782	22,192	15,208	5,626	22,036	2,754	5,113	14,169
Oct	2,771	8,164	19,873	22,270	15,261	5,637	22,027	2,752	5,114	14,161
Nov	2,753	8,182	19,921	22,315	15,307	5,648	22,028	2,758	5,110	14,160
Dec	2,763	8,190	19,981	22,378	15,342	5,660	22,040	2,768	5,108	14,164
2016: Jan	2,763	8,207	19,979	22,404	15,376	5,657	22,053	2,763	5,107	14,183
Feb	2,774	8,215	20,014	22,481	15,413	5,675	22,064	2,765	5,108	14,191
Mar	2,782	8,229	20,045	22,527	15,431	5,681	22,083	2,771	5,111	14,201
Apr	2,782	8,250	20,102	22,574	15,446	5,684	22,080	2,767	5,109	14,204
May	2,741	8,266	20,134	22,620	15,449	5,676	22,105	2,783	5,104	14,218
June	2,782	8,283	20,182	22,672	15,502	5,689	22,138	2,787	5,115	14,236
July	2,777	8,300	20,266	22,714	15,538	5,693	22,169	2,790	5,110	14,269
Aug	2,776	8,318	20,294	22,770	15,548	5,702	22,213	2,797	5,116	14,300
Sept	2,781	8,320	20,381	22,808	15,556	5,715	22,216	2,800	5,120	14,296
Oct p	2,778	8,329	20,429	22,852	15,571	5,718	22,223	2,808	5,112	14,303
Nov p	2,768	8,335	20,492	22,896	15,600	5,722	22,245	2,811	5,117	14,317

Note (cont'd): employed when they are not at work because of industrial disputes, bad weather, etc., even if they are not paid for the time off; which are based on a sample of the working-age population; and which count persons only once—as employed, unemployed, or not in the labor force. In the data shown here, persons who work at more than one job are counted each time they appear on a payroll.
Establishment data for employment, hours, and earnings are classified based on the 2012 North American Industry Classification System (NAICS). For further description and details see *Employment and Earnings.*

Source: Department of Labor (Bureau of Labor Statistics).

[Monthly data seasonally adjusted]

| Year or month | All employees | | | | | | | Production and nonsupervisory employees [1] | | | | | | |
| | Average weekly hours | Average hourly earnings | | Average weekly earnings Level | | Average weekly earnings Percent change from year earlier | | Average weekly hours | Average hourly earnings | | Average weekly earnings Level | | Average weekly earnings Percent change from year earlier | |
		Current dollars	1982–84 dollars [2]	Current dollars	1982–84 dollars [2]	Current dollars	1982–84 dollars [2]		Current dollars	1982–84 dollars [3]	Current dollars	1982–84 dollars [3]	Current dollars	1982–84 dollars [3]
1972								36.9	$3.90	$9.26	$143.87	$341.73	8.0	4.4
1973								36.9	4.14	9.26	152.59	341.36	6.1	−.1
1974								36.4	4.43	8.93	161.61	325.83	5.9	−4.5
1975								36.0	4.73	8.74	170.29	314.77	5.4	−3.4
1976								36.1	5.06	8.85	182.65	319.32	7.3	1.4
1977								35.9	5.44	8.93	195.58	321.15	7.1	.6
1978								35.8	5.88	8.96	210.29	320.56	7.5	−.2
1979								35.6	6.34	8.67	225.69	308.74	7.3	−3.7
1980								35.2	6.85	8.26	241.07	290.80	6.8	−5.8
1981								35.2	7.44	8.14	261.53	286.14	8.5	−1.6
1982								34.7	7.87	8.12	273.10	281.84	4.4	−1.5
1983								34.9	8.20	8.22	286.43	287.00	4.9	1.8
1984								35.1	8.49	8.22	298.26	288.73	4.1	.6
1985								34.9	8.74	8.18	304.62	284.96	2.1	−1.3
1986								34.7	8.93	8.22	309.78	285.25	1.7	.1
1987								34.7	9.14	8.12	317.39	282.12	2.5	−1.1
1988								34.6	9.44	8.07	326.48	279.04	2.9	−1.1
1989								34.5	9.80	7.99	338.34	275.97	3.6	−1.1
1990								34.3	10.20	7.91	349.63	271.03	3.3	−1.8
1991								34.1	10.51	7.83	358.46	266.91	2.5	−1.5
1992								34.2	10.77	7.79	368.20	266.43	2.7	−.2
1993								34.3	11.05	7.78	378.89	266.64	2.9	.1
1994								34.5	11.34	7.79	391.17	268.66	3.2	.8
1995								34.3	11.65	7.78	400.04	267.05	2.3	−.6
1996								34.3	12.04	7.81	413.25	268.17	3.3	.4
1997								34.5	12.51	7.94	431.86	274.02	4.5	2.2
1998								34.5	13.01	8.15	448.59	280.90	3.9	2.5
1999								34.3	13.49	8.27	463.15	283.79	3.2	1.0
2000								34.3	14.02	8.30	480.99	284.78	3.9	.3
2001								34.0	14.54	8.38	493.74	284.58	2.7	−.1
2002								33.9	14.96	8.50	506.54	287.97	2.6	1.2
2003								33.7	15.37	8.55	517.76	287.96	2.2	.0
2004								33.7	15.68	8.50	528.81	286.62	2.1	−.5
2005								33.8	16.12	8.44	544.20	284.82	2.9	−.6
2006								33.9	16.75	8.50	567.06	287.70	4.2	1.0
2007	34.4	$20.92	$10.09	$719.88	$347.19			33.8	17.42	8.59	589.18	290.57	3.9	1.0
2008	34.3	21.56	10.01	739.05	343.26	2.7	−1.1	33.6	18.06	8.56	607.42	287.80	3.1	−1.0
2009	33.8	22.18	10.34	750.09	349.63	1.5	1.9	33.1	18.61	8.88	615.96	293.83	1.4	2.1
2010	34.1	22.56	10.35	769.66	352.96	2.6	1.0	33.4	19.05	8.90	636.19	297.33	3.3	1.2
2011	34.3	23.03	10.24	791.07	351.68	2.8	−.4	33.6	19.44	8.77	652.89	294.66	2.6	−.9
2012	34.5	23.50	10.24	809.83	352.72	2.4	.3	33.7	19.74	8.73	665.65	294.24	2.0	−.1
2013	34.4	23.96	10.29	825.37	354.30	1.9	.4	33.7	20.13	8.78	677.73	295.53	1.8	.4
2014	34.5	24.47	10.34	845.00	356.94	2.4	.7	33.7	20.61	8.85	694.91	298.54	2.5	1.0
2015	34.5	25.03	10.56	864.59	364.78	2.3	2.2	33.7	21.04	9.08	709.13	305.91	2.0	2.5
2015: Jan	34.6	24.76	10.54	856.70	364.62	2.8	3.0	33.8	20.81	9.06	703.38	306.13	2.9	3.9
Feb	34.6	24.80	10.53	858.08	364.50	2.8	2.9	33.8	20.83	9.05	704.05	305.73	2.8	3.6
Mar	34.5	24.87	10.54	858.02	363.79	1.9	1.9	33.7	20.89	9.05	703.99	305.05	2.0	2.5
Apr	34.5	24.91	10.55	859.40	363.85	2.3	2.5	33.7	20.93	9.06	705.34	305.26	2.0	2.8
May	34.5	24.97	10.54	861.47	363.68	2.3	2.3	33.6	20.99	9.05	705.26	304.24	1.8	2.3
June	34.5	24.96	10.51	861.12	362.69	2.0	1.8	33.6	21.00	9.04	705.60	303.70	1.7	2.0
July	34.6	25.03	10.53	866.04	364.29	2.5	2.3	33.7	21.05	9.05	709.39	304.91	2.0	2.3
Aug	34.6	25.12	10.57	869.15	365.65	2.6	2.4	33.7	21.11	9.08	711.41	305.91	1.8	2.1
Sept	34.5	25.14	10.59	867.33	365.21	2.4	2.4	33.7	21.12	9.10	711.74	306.62	2.1	2.8
Oct	34.5	25.21	10.59	866.75	365.52	2.6	2.4	33.7	21.21	9.12	714.78	307.34	2.4	2.9
Nov	34.5	25.27	10.60	871.82	365.85	2.1	1.7	33.7	21.23	9.11	715.45	307.16	2.0	2.0
Dec	34.5	25.26	10.61	871.47	366.10	2.3	1.7	33.8	21.26	9.14	718.59	307.70	2.6	2.2
2016: Jan	34.6	25.38	10.66	878.15	368.80	2.5	1.1	33.7	21.33	9.18	718.82	309.26	2.2	1.0
Feb	34.4	25.39	10.68	873.42	367.44	1.8	.8	33.7	21.35	9.21	719.50	310.54	2.2	1.6
Mar	34.4	25.45	10.70	875.48	367.97	2.0	1.1	33.6	21.40	9.22	719.04	309.94	2.1	1.6
Apr	34.4	25.53	10.69	878.23	367.63	2.2	1.0	33.6	21.46	9.21	721.06	309.42	2.2	1.4
May	34.4	25.59	10.69	880.30	367.71	2.2	1.1	33.6	21.48	9.20	721.73	309.08	2.3	1.6
June	34.4	25.62	10.68	881.33	367.36	2.3	1.3	33.6	21.52	9.20	723.07	309.01	2.5	1.7
July	34.4	25.71	10.72	884.42	368.80	2.1	1.2	33.7	21.59	9.24	727.58	311.22	2.6	2.1
Aug	34.3	25.74	10.71	882.88	367.41	1.6	.5	33.6	21.62	9.23	726.43	310.18	2.1	1.4
Sept	34.4	25.81	10.71	887.86	368.40	2.4	.9	33.6	21.67	9.22	728.11	309.85	2.3	1.1
Oct [p]	34.4	25.92	10.72	891.65	368.66	2.5	.9	33.6	21.71	9.20	729.46	309.17	2.1	.6
Nov [p]	34.4	25.89		890.62		2.2		33.6	21.73		730.13		2.1	

[1] Production employees in goods-producing industries and nonsupervisory employees in service-providing industries. These groups account for four-fifths of the total employment on private nonfarm payrolls.

[2] Current dollars divided by the consumer price index for all urban consumers (CPI-U) on a 1982–84=100 base.

[3] Current dollars divided by the consumer price index for urban wage earners and clerical workers (CPI-W) on a 1982–84=100 base.

Note: See Note, Table B–14.

Source: Department of Labor (Bureau of Labor Statistics).

TABLE B–16. Productivity and related data, business and nonfarm business sectors, 1967–2016

[Index numbers, 2009=100; quarterly data seasonally adjusted]

Year or quarter	Labor productivity (output per hour) Business sector	Labor productivity (output per hour) Nonfarm business sector	Output [1] Business sector	Output [1] Nonfarm business sector	Hours of all persons [2] Business sector	Hours of all persons [2] Nonfarm business sector	Compensation per hour [3] Business sector	Compensation per hour [3] Nonfarm business sector	Real compensation per hour [4] Business sector	Real compensation per hour [4] Nonfarm business sector	Unit labor costs Business sector	Unit labor costs Nonfarm business sector	Implicit price deflator [5] Business sector	Implicit price deflator [5] Nonfarm business sector
1967	42.1	43.8	27.3	27.3	64.9	62.3	10.4	10.6	61.0	62.2	24.7	24.2	23.0	22.5
1968	43.5	45.4	28.7	28.8	65.9	63.4	11.2	11.4	63.1	64.2	25.7	25.1	23.9	23.4
1969	43.8	45.5	29.6	29.7	67.5	65.2	12.0	12.2	64.0	65.0	27.4	26.8	25.0	24.4
1970	44.6	46.1	29.5	29.6	66.2	64.2	12.9	13.0	65.1	65.8	28.9	28.3	26.1	25.5
1971	46.4	47.9	30.7	30.7	66.0	64.1	13.7	13.8	66.1	66.9	29.4	28.9	27.2	26.6
1972	48.0	49.6	32.7	32.8	68.1	66.1	14.5	14.7	68.0	69.0	30.3	29.7	28.1	27.4
1973	49.4	51.1	34.9	35.2	70.7	68.8	15.7	15.8	69.1	69.9	31.7	31.0	29.6	28.4
1974	48.5	50.2	34.4	34.6	70.8	68.9	17.1	17.3	68.1	68.9	35.3	34.5	32.5	31.4
1975	50.3	51.6	34.0	34.1	67.7	66.0	19.0	19.2	69.1	69.8	37.8	37.2	35.6	34.7
1976	51.9	53.4	36.3	36.5	70.0	68.3	20.5	20.7	70.5	71.1	39.5	38.7	37.5	36.6
1977	52.8	54.3	38.4	38.6	72.7	71.0	22.1	22.4	71.5	72.2	41.9	41.2	39.7	38.9
1978	53.4	55.0	40.8	41.1	76.4	74.7	24.0	24.3	72.4	73.3	44.9	44.1	42.5	41.5
1979	53.5	54.9	42.3	42.5	79.0	77.4	26.3	26.6	72.6	73.3	49.2	48.5	46.1	45.0
1980	53.5	54.8	41.9	42.1	78.3	76.8	29.1	29.5	72.3	73.0	54.5	53.7	50.2	49.3
1981	54.7	55.7	43.1	43.1	78.8	77.3	31.9	32.3	72.3	73.1	58.4	58.0	54.8	54.0
1982	54.2	55.1	41.8	41.7	77.1	75.6	34.2	34.6	73.1	74.0	63.1	62.8	58.0	57.4
1983	56.2	57.6	44.1	44.4	78.4	77.1	35.8	36.2	73.3	74.2	63.7	62.9	60.0	59.2
1984	57.8	58.8	48.0	48.1	83.0	81.8	37.4	37.8	73.5	74.3	64.7	64.2	61.7	60.9
1985	59.1	59.8	50.2	50.2	84.9	84.0	39.3	39.6	74.7	75.3	66.5	66.3	63.5	62.9
1986	60.8	61.6	52.0	52.1	85.6	84.6	41.5	41.9	77.5	78.3	68.3	68.0	64.3	63.8
1987	61.1	61.9	53.9	54.0	88.2	87.2	43.1	43.5	77.8	78.6	70.5	70.2	65.6	65.1
1988	62.0	62.9	56.2	56.4	90.6	89.7	45.3	45.7	79.0	79.7	73.1	72.7	67.7	67.1
1989	62.7	63.5	58.3	58.5	93.0	92.1	46.7	47.0	78.1	78.6	74.5	74.1	70.2	69.5
1990	64.1	64.7	59.3	59.4	92.4	91.8	49.7	50.0	79.2	79.6	77.6	77.2	72.5	71.8
1991	65.3	65.9	58.9	59.0	90.3	89.6	52.2	52.5	80.2	80.6	79.9	79.6	74.5	74.1
1992	68.2	68.8	61.4	61.4	90.1	89.3	55.3	55.6	82.8	83.3	81.0	80.9	75.7	75.3
1993	68.3	68.8	63.2	63.3	92.5	92.0	56.1	56.3	82.0	82.3	82.1	81.8	77.5	77.0
1994	68.8	69.5	66.2	66.3	96.2	95.4	56.6	57.0	81.1	81.6	82.2	82.0	78.9	78.5
1995	69.1	70.0	68.3	68.6	98.9	98.0	57.7	58.1	80.7	81.3	83.6	83.1	80.2	79.8
1996	71.2	71.9	71.5	71.7	100.5	99.7	60.1	60.5	81.9	82.4	84.5	84.2	81.5	80.9
1997	72.5	73.0	75.3	75.4	103.9	103.2	62.3	62.6	83.1	83.5	85.9	85.7	82.7	82.3
1998	74.7	75.3	79.2	79.4	105.9	105.5	66.0	66.2	86.8	87.1	88.3	88.0	83.1	82.8
1999	77.3	77.7	83.6	83.8	108.0	107.8	68.9	69.0	88.7	88.9	89.1	88.8	83.7	83.6
2000	80.0	80.3	87.3	87.5	109.2	108.9	73.9	74.1	92.1	92.3	92.5	92.3	85.3	85.2
2001	82.2	82.5	87.9	88.1	106.9	106.8	77.3	77.4	93.7	93.7	94.1	93.8	86.8	86.6
2002	85.7	86.1	89.5	89.7	104.4	104.2	79.0	79.1	94.3	94.4	92.2	91.9	87.4	87.3
2003	89.0	89.2	92.3	92.5	103.7	103.6	82.0	82.1	95.7	95.7	92.2	92.0	88.6	88.5
2004	91.9	92.0	96.5	96.6	105.0	105.0	85.8	85.8	97.5	97.5	93.4	93.3	90.7	90.3
2005	93.8	93.9	100.1	100.2	106.8	106.8	88.9	88.9	97.7	97.7	94.8	94.7	93.5	93.4
2006	94.7	94.7	103.3	103.4	109.1	109.2	92.4	92.4	98.3	98.3	97.6	97.5	96.0	96.0
2007	96.1	96.3	105.5	105.8	109.7	109.9	96.5	96.4	99.9	99.7	100.4	100.1	98.2	97.9
2008	96.9	97.0	104.2	104.4	107.6	107.7	99.0	99.0	98.7	98.6	102.2	102.1	99.8	99.4
2009	100.0	100.0	100.0	100.0	100.0	100.0	100.0	100.0	100.0	100.0	100.0	100.0	100.0	100.0
2010	103.3	103.3	103.2	103.2	99.9	99.9	101.8	101.9	100.2	100.3	98.6	98.7	101.1	101.0
2011	103.3	103.4	105.3	105.5	102.0	102.0	104.0	104.1	99.2	99.4	100.7	100.7	103.3	102.8
2012	104.0	104.3	108.4	108.8	104.2	104.2	106.9	106.9	99.9	99.9	102.7	102.5	105.3	104.7
2013	104.8	104.7	110.8	110.9	105.8	106.0	108.3	108.2	99.8	99.6	103.4	103.3	106.9	106.3
2014	105.4	105.5	114.1	114.3	108.2	108.3	111.1	111.2	100.7	100.8	105.4	105.4	108.5	108.1
2015	106.2	106.5	117.6	117.8	110.7	110.6	114.3	114.5	103.4	103.6	107.5	107.5	109.3	109.2
2013: I	104.3	104.3	109.7	109.9	105.1	105.3	106.9	106.8	98.8	98.6	102.5	102.3	106.4	105.6
II	104.3	104.1	110.0	110.1	105.4	105.7	108.4	108.2	100.3	100.1	104.0	103.9	106.6	105.9
III	104.7	104.6	111.1	111.1	106.1	106.2	108.6	108.6	99.9	99.9	103.7	103.8	107.1	106.5
IV	105.7	105.6	112.6	112.6	106.5	106.6	109.1	109.1	100.0	99.9	103.3	103.3	107.5	107.1
2014: I	104.8	104.7	112.0	112.1	106.9	107.1	109.9	110.8	101.0	100.9	105.8	105.8	107.9	107.5
II	105.2	105.2	113.4	113.5	107.7	107.9	110.4	110.3	100.0	100.0	104.9	104.9	108.5	108.0
III	106.1	106.3	115.1	115.3	108.5	108.5	111.2	111.4	100.6	100.7	104.8	104.8	108.9	108.5
IV	105.6	105.9	115.9	116.1	109.7	109.7	112.1	112.4	101.5	101.7	106.1	106.1	108.9	108.5
2015: I	105.8	106.1	116.6	116.8	110.2	110.1	112.6	112.9	102.6	102.9	106.4	106.3	108.7	108.6
II	106.2	106.4	117.5	117.7	110.6	110.6	114.0	114.2	103.3	103.4	107.3	107.3	109.3	109.1
III	106.8	107.0	118.1	118.2	110.6	110.5	114.8	115.0	103.7	103.8	107.5	107.5	109.5	109.4
IV	106.1	106.3	118.3	118.5	111.5	111.4	115.6	115.9	104.2	104.4	108.9	109.0	109.6	109.5
2016: I	106.0	106.2	118.6	118.7	111.9	111.8	115.3	115.6	104.0	104.3	108.8	108.9	109.7	109.7
II	105.9	106.1	119.1	119.1	112.5	112.3	116.3	116.7	104.2	104.6	109.8	109.9	110.3	110.3
III p	106.7	106.9	120.1	120.1	112.5	112.4	117.3	117.6	104.7	105.0	109.9	110.0	110.5	110.7

[1] Output refers to real gross domestic product in the sector.
[2] Hours at work of all persons engaged in sector, including hours of employees, proprietors, and unpaid family workers. Estimates based primarily on establishment data.
[3] Wages and salaries of employees plus employers' contributions for social insurance and private benefit plans. Also includes an estimate of wages, salaries, and supplemental payments for the self-employed.
[4] Hourly compensation divided by consumer price series. The trend for 1978-2015 is based on the consumer price index research series (CPI-U-RS). The change for prior years and recent quarters is based on the consumer price index for all urban consumers (CPI-U).
[5] Current dollar output divided by the output index.

Source: Department of Labor (Bureau of Labor Statistics).

TABLE B–17. Federal receipts, outlays, surplus or deficit, and debt, fiscal years 1952–2017

[Billions of dollars; fiscal years]

Fiscal year or period	Total			On-budget			Off-budget			Federal debt (end of period)		Addendum: Gross domestic product
	Receipts	Outlays	Surplus or deficit (−)	Receipts	Outlays	Surplus or deficit (−)	Receipts	Outlays	Surplus or deficit (−)	Gross Federal	Held by the public	
1952	66.2	67.7	−1.5	62.6	66.0	−3.4	3.6	1.7	1.9	259.1	214.8	357.5
1953	69.6	76.1	−6.5	65.5	73.8	−8.3	4.1	2.3	1.8	266.0	218.4	382.5
1954	69.7	70.9	−1.2	65.1	67.9	−2.8	4.6	2.9	1.7	270.8	224.5	387.7
1955	65.5	68.4	−3.0	60.4	64.5	−4.1	5.1	4.0	1.1	274.4	226.6	407.0
1956	74.6	70.6	3.9	68.2	65.7	2.5	6.4	5.0	1.5	272.7	222.2	439.0
1957	80.0	76.6	3.4	73.2	70.6	2.6	6.8	6.0	.8	272.3	219.3	464.2
1958	79.6	82.4	−2.8	71.6	74.9	−3.3	8.0	7.5	.5	279.7	226.3	474.3
1959	79.2	92.1	−12.8	71.0	83.1	−12.1	8.3	9.0	−.7	287.5	234.7	505.6
1960	92.5	92.2	.3	81.9	81.3	.5	10.6	10.9	−.2	290.5	236.8	535.1
1961	94.4	97.7	−3.3	82.3	86.0	−3.8	12.1	11.7	.4	292.6	238.4	547.6
1962	99.7	106.8	−7.1	87.4	93.3	−5.9	12.3	13.5	−1.3	302.9	248.0	586.9
1963	106.6	111.3	−4.8	92.4	96.4	−4.0	14.2	15.0	−.8	310.3	254.0	619.3
1964	112.6	118.5	−5.9	96.2	102.8	−6.5	16.4	15.7	.6	316.1	256.8	662.9
1965	116.8	118.2	−1.4	100.1	101.7	−1.6	16.7	16.5	.2	322.3	260.8	710.7
1966	130.8	134.5	−3.7	111.7	114.8	−3.1	19.1	19.7	−.6	328.5	263.7	781.9
1967	148.8	157.5	−8.6	124.4	137.0	−12.6	24.4	20.4	4.0	340.4	266.6	838.2
1968	153.0	178.1	−25.2	128.1	155.8	−27.7	24.9	22.3	2.6	368.7	289.5	899.3
1969	186.9	183.6	3.2	157.9	158.4	−.5	29.0	25.2	3.7	365.8	278.1	982.3
1970	192.8	195.6	−2.8	159.3	168.0	−8.7	33.5	27.6	5.9	380.9	283.2	1,049.1
1971	187.1	210.2	−23.0	151.3	177.3	−26.1	35.8	32.8	3.0	408.2	303.0	1,119.3
1972	207.3	230.7	−23.4	167.4	193.5	−26.1	39.9	37.2	2.7	435.9	322.4	1,219.5
1973	230.8	245.7	−14.9	184.7	200.0	−15.2	46.1	45.7	.3	466.3	340.9	1,356.0
1974	263.2	269.4	−6.1	209.3	216.5	−7.2	53.9	52.9	1.1	483.9	343.7	1,486.2
1975	279.1	332.3	−53.2	216.6	270.8	−54.1	62.5	61.6	.9	541.9	394.7	1,610.6
1976	298.1	371.8	−73.7	231.7	301.1	−69.4	66.4	70.7	−4.3	629.0	477.4	1,790.3
Transition quarter	81.2	96.0	−14.7	63.2	77.3	−14.1	18.0	18.7	−.7	643.6	495.5	472.6
1977	355.6	409.2	−53.7	278.7	328.7	−49.9	76.8	80.5	−3.7	706.4	549.1	2,028.4
1978	399.6	458.7	−59.2	314.2	369.6	−55.4	85.4	89.2	−3.8	776.6	607.1	2,278.2
1979	463.3	504.0	−40.7	365.3	404.9	−39.6	98.0	99.1	−1.1	829.5	640.3	2,570.0
1980	517.1	590.9	−73.8	403.9	477.0	−73.1	113.2	113.9	−.7	909.0	711.9	2,796.8
1981	599.3	678.2	−79.0	469.1	543.0	−73.9	130.2	135.3	−5.1	994.8	789.4	3,138.4
1982	617.8	745.7	−128.0	474.3	594.9	−120.6	143.5	150.9	−7.4	1,137.3	924.6	3,313.9
1983	600.6	808.4	−207.8	453.2	660.9	−207.7	147.3	147.4	−.1	1,371.7	1,137.3	3,541.1
1984	666.4	851.8	−185.4	500.4	685.6	−185.3	166.1	166.2	−.1	1,564.6	1,307.0	3,952.8
1985	734.0	946.3	−212.3	547.9	769.4	−221.5	186.2	176.9	9.2	1,817.4	1,507.3	4,270.4
1986	769.2	990.4	−221.2	568.9	806.8	−237.9	200.2	183.5	16.7	2,120.5	1,740.6	4,536.1
1987	854.3	1,004.0	−149.7	640.9	809.2	−168.4	213.4	194.8	18.6	2,346.0	1,889.8	4,781.9
1988	909.2	1,064.4	−155.2	667.7	860.0	−192.3	241.5	204.4	37.1	2,601.1	2,051.6	5,155.1
1989	991.1	1,143.7	−152.6	727.4	932.8	−205.4	263.7	210.9	52.8	2,867.8	2,190.7	5,570.0
1990	1,032.0	1,253.0	−221.0	750.3	1,027.9	−277.6	281.7	225.1	56.6	3,206.3	2,411.6	5,914.6
1991	1,055.0	1,324.2	−269.2	761.1	1,082.5	−321.4	293.9	241.7	52.2	3,598.2	2,689.0	6,110.1
1992	1,091.2	1,381.5	−290.3	788.8	1,129.2	−340.4	302.4	252.3	50.1	4,001.8	2,999.7	6,434.7
1993	1,154.3	1,409.4	−255.1	842.4	1,142.8	−300.4	311.9	266.6	45.3	4,351.0	3,248.4	6,794.9
1994	1,258.6	1,461.8	−203.2	923.5	1,182.4	−258.8	335.0	279.4	55.7	4,643.3	3,433.1	7,197.8
1995	1,351.8	1,515.7	−164.0	1,000.7	1,227.1	−226.4	351.1	288.7	62.4	4,920.6	3,604.4	7,583.4
1996	1,453.1	1,560.5	−107.4	1,085.6	1,259.6	−174.0	367.5	300.9	66.6	5,181.5	3,734.1	7,978.3
1997	1,579.2	1,601.1	−21.9	1,187.2	1,290.5	−103.2	392.0	310.6	81.4	5,369.2	3,772.3	8,483.2
1998	1,721.7	1,652.5	69.3	1,305.9	1,335.9	−29.9	415.8	316.6	99.2	5,478.2	3,721.1	8,954.8
1999	1,827.5	1,701.8	125.6	1,383.0	1,381.1	1.9	444.5	320.8	123.7	5,605.5	3,632.4	9,510.5
2000	2,025.2	1,789.0	236.2	1,544.6	1,458.2	86.4	480.6	330.8	149.8	5,628.7	3,409.8	10,148.2
2001	1,991.1	1,862.8	128.2	1,483.6	1,516.0	−32.4	507.5	346.8	160.7	5,769.9	3,319.6	10,564.6
2002	1,853.1	2,010.9	−157.8	1,337.8	1,655.2	−317.4	515.3	355.7	159.7	6,198.4	3,540.4	10,876.9
2003	1,782.3	2,159.9	−377.6	1,258.5	1,796.9	−538.4	523.8	363.0	160.8	6,760.0	3,913.4	11,332.4
2004	1,880.1	2,292.8	−412.7	1,345.4	1,913.3	−568.0	534.7	379.5	155.2	7,354.7	4,295.5	12,088.6
2005	2,153.6	2,472.0	−318.3	1,576.1	2,069.7	−493.6	577.5	402.2	175.3	7,905.3	4,592.2	12,888.9
2006	2,406.9	2,655.1	−248.2	1,798.5	2,233.0	−434.5	608.4	422.1	186.3	8,451.4	4,829.0	13,684.7
2007	2,568.0	2,728.7	−160.7	1,932.9	2,275.0	−342.2	635.1	453.6	181.5	8,950.7	5,035.1	14,322.9
2008	2,524.0	2,982.5	−458.6	1,865.9	2,507.8	−641.8	658.0	474.8	183.3	9,986.1	5,803.1	14,752.4
2009	2,105.0	3,517.7	−1,412.7	1,451.0	3,000.7	−1,549.7	654.0	517.0	137.0	11,875.9	7,544.7	14,414.6
2010	2,162.7	3,457.1	−1,294.4	1,531.0	2,902.4	−1,371.4	631.7	554.7	77.0	13,528.8	9,018.9	14,798.5
2011	2,303.5	3,603.1	−1,299.6	1,737.7	3,104.5	−1,366.8	565.8	498.6	67.2	14,764.2	10,128.2	15,379.2
2012	2,450.0	3,537.0	−1,087.0	1,880.5	3,029.4	−1,148.9	569.5	507.6	61.9	16,050.9	11,281.1	16,027.2
2013	2,775.1	3,454.6	−679.5	2,101.8	2,820.8	−719.0	673.3	633.8	39.5	16,719.4	11,982.7	16,498.1
2014	3,021.5	3,506.1	−484.6	2,285.9	2,800.1	−514.1	735.6	706.1	29.5	17,794.5	12,779.9	17,183.5
2015	3,249.9	3,688.3	−438.4	2,479.5	2,945.2	−465.7	770.4	743.1	27.3	18,120.1	13,116.7	17,809.8
2016 (estimates)[1]	3,276.2	3,876.0	−599.8	2,466.0	3,099.9	−633.9	810.2	776.1	34.1	19,451.8	14,127.7	18,348.6
2017 (estimates)[1]	3,632.2	4,073.2	−440.9	2,791.4	3,259.6	−468.2	840.9	813.5	27.3	20,143.6	14,699.8	19,063.2

[1] Estimates from *Mid-Session Review*, Budget of the U.S. Government, Fiscal Year 2017, issued July 2016.

Note: Fiscal years through 1976 were on a July 1–June 30 basis; beginning with October 1976 (fiscal year 1977), the fiscal year is on an October 1–September 30 basis. The transition quarter is the three-month period from July 1, 1976 through September 30, 1976.
See *Budget of the United States Government, Fiscal Year 2017*, for additional information.

Sources: Department of Commerce (Bureau of Economic Analysis), Department of the Treasury, and Office of Management and Budget.

TABLE B–18. Federal receipts, outlays, surplus or deficit, and debt, as percent of gross domestic product, fiscal years 1945–2017

[Percent; fiscal years]

Fiscal year or period	Receipts	Outlays		Surplus or deficit (−)	Federal debt (end of period)	
		Total	National defense		Gross Federal	Held by public
1945	19.9	41.0	36.6	−21.0	114.9	103.9
1946	17.2	24.2	18.7	−7.0	118.9	106.1
1947	16.1	14.4	5.4	1.7	107.6	93.9
1948	15.8	11.3	3.5	4.5	96.0	82.4
1949	14.2	14.0	4.8	.2	91.3	77.4
1950	14.1	15.3	4.9	−1.1	92.1	78.5
1951	15.8	13.9	7.2	1.9	78.0	65.5
1952	18.5	18.9	12.9	−.4	72.5	60.1
1953	18.2	19.9	13.8	−1.7	69.5	57.1
1954	18.0	18.3	12.7	−.3	69.9	57.9
1955	16.1	16.8	10.5	−.7	67.4	55.7
1956	17.0	16.1	9.7	.9	62.1	50.6
1957	17.2	16.5	9.8	.7	58.6	47.2
1958	16.8	17.4	9.9	−.6	59.0	47.7
1959	15.7	18.2	9.7	−2.5	56.9	46.4
1960	17.3	17.2	9.0	.1	54.3	44.3
1961	17.2	17.8	9.1	−.6	53.4	43.5
1962	17.0	18.2	8.9	−1.2	51.6	42.3
1963	17.2	18.0	8.6	−.8	50.1	41.0
1964	17.0	17.9	8.3	−.9	47.7	38.7
1965	16.4	16.6	7.1	−.2	45.4	36.7
1966	16.7	17.2	7.4	−.5	42.0	33.7
1967	17.8	18.8	8.5	−1.0	40.6	31.8
1968	17.0	19.8	9.1	−2.8	41.0	32.2
1969	19.0	18.7	8.4	.3	37.2	28.3
1970	18.4	18.6	7.8	−.3	36.3	27.0
1971	16.7	18.8	7.0	−2.1	36.5	27.1
1972	17.0	18.9	6.5	−1.9	35.7	26.4
1973	17.0	18.1	5.7	−1.1	34.4	25.1
1974	17.7	18.1	5.3	−.4	32.6	23.1
1975	17.3	20.6	5.4	−3.3	33.6	24.5
1976	16.6	20.8	5.0	−4.1	35.1	26.7
Transition quarter	17.2	20.3	4.7	−3.1	34.0	26.2
1977	17.5	20.2	4.8	−2.6	34.8	27.1
1978	17.5	20.1	4.6	−2.6	34.1	26.6
1979	18.0	19.6	4.5	−1.6	32.3	24.9
1980	18.5	21.1	4.8	−2.6	32.5	25.5
1981	19.1	21.6	5.0	−2.5	31.7	25.2
1982	18.6	22.5	5.6	−3.9	34.3	27.9
1983	17.0	22.8	5.9	−5.9	38.7	32.1
1984	16.9	21.5	5.8	−4.7	39.6	33.1
1985	17.2	22.2	5.9	−5.0	42.6	35.3
1986	17.0	21.8	6.0	−4.9	46.7	38.4
1987	17.9	21.0	5.9	−3.1	49.1	39.5
1988	17.6	20.6	5.6	−3.0	50.5	39.8
1989	17.8	20.5	5.4	−2.7	51.5	39.3
1990	17.4	21.2	5.1	−3.7	54.2	40.8
1991	17.3	21.7	4.5	−4.4	58.9	44.0
1992	17.0	21.5	4.6	−4.5	62.2	46.6
1993	17.0	20.7	4.3	−3.8	64.0	47.8
1994	17.5	20.3	3.9	−2.8	64.5	47.7
1995	17.8	20.0	3.6	−2.2	64.9	47.5
1996	18.2	19.6	3.3	−1.3	64.9	46.8
1997	18.6	18.9	3.2	−.3	63.3	44.5
1998	19.2	18.5	3.0	.8	61.2	41.6
1999	19.2	17.9	2.9	1.3	58.9	38.2
2000	20.0	17.6	2.9	2.3	55.5	33.6
2001	18.8	17.6	2.9	1.2	54.6	31.4
2002	17.0	18.5	3.2	−1.5	57.0	32.5
2003	15.7	19.1	3.6	−3.3	59.7	34.5
2004	15.6	19.0	3.8	−3.4	60.8	35.5
2005	16.7	19.2	3.8	−2.5	61.3	35.6
2006	17.6	19.4	3.8	−1.8	61.8	35.3
2007	17.9	19.1	3.8	−1.1	62.5	35.2
2008	17.1	20.2	4.2	−3.1	67.7	39.3
2009	14.6	24.4	4.6	−9.8	82.4	52.3
2010	14.6	23.4	4.7	−8.7	91.4	60.9
2011	15.0	23.4	4.6	−8.5	96.0	65.9
2012	15.3	22.1	4.2	−6.8	100.1	70.4
2013	16.8	20.9	3.8	−4.1	101.3	72.6
2014	17.6	20.4	3.5	−2.8	103.6	74.4
2015	18.2	20.7	3.3	−2.5	101.7	73.6
2016 (estimates)	17.9	21.1	3.2	−3.3	106.0	77.0
2017 (estimates)	19.1	21.4	3.2	−2.3	105.7	77.1

Note: See footnote 1 and Note, Table B–17.

Sources: Department of the Treasury and Office of Management and Budget.

TABLE B–19. Federal receipts and outlays, by major category, and surplus or deficit, fiscal years 1952–2017

[Billions of dollars; fiscal years]

Fiscal year or period	Receipts (on-budget and off-budget)					Outlays (on-budget and off-budget)										Surplus or deficit (−) (on-budget and off-budget)
	Total	Individual income taxes	Corporation income taxes	Social insurance and retirement receipts	Other	Total	National defense Total	Department of Defense, military	International affairs	Health	Medicare	Income security	Social security	Net interest	Other	
1952	66.2	27.9	21.2	6.4	10.6	67.7	46.1	....	2.7	0.3	....	3.7	2.1	4.7	8.1	−1.5
1953	69.6	29.8	21.2	6.8	11.7	76.1	52.8	....	2.1	.3	....	3.8	2.7	5.2	9.1	−6.5
1954	69.7	29.5	21.1	7.2	11.9	70.9	49.3	....	1.6	.3	....	4.4	3.4	4.8	7.1	−1.2
1955	65.5	28.7	17.9	7.9	11.0	68.4	42.7	....	2.2	.3	....	5.1	4.4	4.9	8.9	−3.0
1956	74.6	32.2	20.9	9.3	12.2	70.6	42.5	....	2.4	.4	....	4.7	5.5	5.1	10.1	3.9
1957	80.0	35.6	21.2	10.0	13.2	76.6	45.4	....	3.1	.5	....	5.4	6.7	5.4	10.1	3.4
1958	79.6	34.7	20.1	11.2	13.6	82.4	46.8	....	3.4	.5	....	7.5	8.2	5.6	10.3	−2.8
1959	79.2	36.7	17.3	11.7	13.5	92.1	49.0	....	3.1	.7	....	8.2	9.7	5.8	15.5	−12.8
1960	92.5	40.7	21.5	14.7	15.6	92.2	48.1	....	3.0	.8	....	7.4	11.6	6.9	14.4	.3
1961	94.4	41.3	21.0	16.4	15.7	97.7	49.6	....	3.2	.9	....	9.7	12.5	6.7	15.2	−3.3
1962	99.7	45.6	20.5	17.0	16.5	106.8	52.3	50.1	5.6	1.2	....	9.2	14.4	6.9	17.2	−7.1
1963	106.6	47.6	21.6	19.8	17.6	111.3	53.4	51.1	5.3	1.5	....	9.3	15.8	7.7	18.3	−4.8
1964	112.6	48.7	23.5	22.0	18.5	118.5	54.8	52.6	4.9	1.8	....	9.7	16.6	8.2	22.6	−5.9
1965	116.8	48.8	25.5	22.2	20.3	118.2	50.6	48.8	5.3	1.8	....	9.5	17.5	8.6	25.0	−1.4
1966	130.8	55.4	30.1	25.5	19.8	134.5	58.1	56.6	5.6	2.5	0.1	9.7	20.7	9.4	28.5	−3.7
1967	148.8	61.5	34.0	32.6	20.7	157.5	71.4	70.1	5.6	3.4	2.7	10.3	21.7	10.3	32.1	−8.6
1968	153.0	68.7	28.7	33.9	21.7	178.1	81.9	80.4	5.3	4.4	4.6	11.8	23.9	11.1	35.1	−25.2
1969	186.9	87.2	36.7	39.0	23.9	183.6	82.5	80.8	4.6	5.2	5.7	13.1	27.3	12.7	32.6	3.2
1970	192.8	90.4	32.8	44.4	25.2	195.6	81.7	80.1	4.3	5.9	6.2	15.7	30.3	14.4	37.2	−2.8
1971	187.1	86.2	26.8	47.3	26.8	210.2	78.9	77.5	4.2	6.8	6.6	22.9	35.9	14.8	40.0	−23.0
1972	207.3	94.7	32.2	52.6	27.8	230.7	79.2	77.6	4.8	8.7	7.5	27.7	40.2	15.5	47.3	−23.4
1973	230.8	103.2	36.2	63.1	28.3	245.7	76.7	75.0	4.1	9.4	8.1	28.3	49.1	17.3	52.8	−14.9
1974	263.2	119.0	38.6	75.1	30.6	269.4	79.3	77.9	5.7	10.7	9.6	33.7	55.9	21.4	52.9	−6.1
1975	279.1	122.4	40.6	84.5	31.5	332.3	86.5	84.9	7.1	12.9	12.9	50.2	64.7	23.2	74.8	−53.2
1976	298.1	131.6	41.4	90.8	34.3	371.8	89.6	87.9	6.4	15.7	15.8	60.8	73.9	26.7	82.7	−73.7
Transition quarter	81.2	38.8	8.5	25.2	8.8	96.0	22.3	21.8	2.5	3.9	4.3	15.0	19.8	6.9	21.4	−14.7
1977	355.6	157.6	54.9	106.5	36.6	409.2	97.2	95.1	6.4	17.3	19.3	61.1	85.1	29.9	93.0	−53.7
1978	399.6	181.0	60.0	121.0	37.7	458.7	104.5	102.3	7.5	18.5	22.8	61.5	93.9	35.5	114.6	−59.2
1979	463.3	217.8	65.7	138.9	40.8	504.0	116.3	113.6	7.5	20.5	26.5	66.4	104.1	42.6	120.2	−40.7
1980	517.1	244.1	64.6	157.8	50.6	590.9	134.0	130.9	12.7	23.2	32.1	86.6	118.5	52.5	131.3	−73.8
1981	599.3	285.9	61.1	182.7	69.5	678.2	157.5	153.9	13.1	26.9	39.1	100.3	139.6	68.8	133.0	−79.0
1982	617.8	297.7	49.2	201.5	69.3	745.7	185.3	180.7	12.3	27.4	46.6	108.2	156.0	85.0	125.0	−128.0
1983	600.6	288.9	37.0	209.0	65.6	808.4	209.9	204.4	11.8	28.6	52.6	123.0	170.7	89.8	121.8	−207.8
1984	666.4	298.4	56.9	239.4	71.8	851.8	227.4	220.9	15.9	30.4	57.5	113.4	178.2	111.1	117.8	−185.4
1985	734.0	334.5	61.3	265.2	73.0	946.3	252.7	245.1	16.2	33.5	65.8	129.0	188.6	129.5	130.9	−212.3
1986	769.2	349.0	63.1	283.9	73.2	990.4	273.4	265.4	14.1	35.9	70.2	120.7	198.8	136.0	141.3	−221.2
1987	854.3	392.6	83.9	303.3	74.5	1,004.0	282.0	273.9	11.6	40.0	75.1	124.1	207.4	138.6	125.2	−149.7
1988	909.2	401.2	94.5	334.3	79.2	1,064.4	290.4	281.9	10.5	44.5	78.9	130.4	219.3	151.8	138.7	−155.2
1989	991.1	445.7	103.3	359.4	82.7	1,143.7	303.6	294.8	9.6	48.4	85.0	137.6	232.5	169.0	158.1	−152.6
1990	1,032.0	466.9	93.5	380.0	91.5	1,253.0	299.3	289.7	13.8	57.7	98.1	148.8	248.6	184.3	202.3	−221.0
1991	1,055.0	467.8	98.1	396.0	93.1	1,324.2	273.3	262.3	15.8	71.2	104.5	172.6	269.0	194.4	223.3	−269.2
1992	1,091.2	476.0	100.3	413.7	101.3	1,381.5	298.3	286.8	16.1	89.5	119.0	199.7	287.6	199.3	171.9	−290.3
1993	1,154.3	509.7	117.5	428.3	98.8	1,409.4	291.1	278.5	17.2	99.4	130.6	210.1	304.6	198.7	157.7	−255.1
1994	1,258.6	543.1	140.4	461.5	113.7	1,461.8	281.6	268.6	17.1	107.1	144.7	217.3	319.6	202.9	171.4	−203.2
1995	1,351.8	590.2	157.0	484.5	120.1	1,515.7	272.1	259.4	16.4	115.4	159.9	223.8	335.8	232.1	160.2	−164.0
1996	1,453.1	656.4	171.8	509.4	115.4	1,560.5	265.7	253.1	13.5	119.4	174.2	229.7	349.7	241.1	167.2	−107.4
1997	1,579.2	737.5	182.3	539.4	120.1	1,601.1	270.5	258.3	15.2	123.8	190.0	235.0	365.3	244.0	157.3	−21.9
1998	1,721.7	828.6	188.7	571.8	132.6	1,652.5	268.2	255.8	13.1	131.4	192.8	237.8	379.2	241.1	188.9	69.3
1999	1,827.5	879.5	184.7	611.8	151.5	1,701.8	274.8	261.2	15.2	141.0	190.4	242.5	390.0	229.8	218.1	125.6
2000	2,025.2	1,004.5	207.3	652.9	160.6	1,789.0	294.4	281.0	17.2	154.5	197.1	253.7	409.4	222.9	239.7	236.2
2001	1,991.1	994.3	151.1	694.0	151.7	1,862.8	304.7	290.2	16.5	172.2	217.4	269.8	433.0	206.2	243.1	128.2
2002	1,853.1	858.3	148.0	700.8	146.0	2,010.9	348.5	331.8	22.3	196.5	230.9	312.7	456.0	170.9	273.1	−157.8
2003	1,782.3	793.7	131.8	713.0	143.9	2,159.9	404.7	387.1	21.2	219.5	249.4	334.6	474.7	153.1	302.6	−377.6
2004	1,880.1	809.0	189.4	733.4	148.4	2,292.8	455.8	436.4	26.9	240.1	269.4	333.1	495.5	160.2	311.8	−412.7
2005	2,153.6	927.2	278.3	794.1	154.0	2,472.0	495.3	474.1	34.6	250.5	298.6	345.8	523.3	184.0	339.8	−318.3
2006	2,406.9	1,043.9	353.9	837.8	171.2	2,655.1	521.8	499.3	29.5	252.7	329.9	352.5	548.5	226.6	393.5	−248.2
2007	2,568.0	1,163.5	370.2	869.6	164.7	2,728.7	551.3	528.5	28.5	266.4	375.4	366.0	586.2	237.1	317.9	−160.7
2008	2,524.0	1,145.7	304.3	900.2	173.7	2,982.5	616.1	594.6	28.9	280.6	390.8	431.3	617.0	252.8	365.2	−458.6
2009	2,105.0	915.3	138.2	890.9	160.5	3,517.7	661.0	636.7	37.5	334.3	430.1	533.2	683.0	186.9	651.6	−1,412.7
2010	2,162.7	898.5	191.4	864.8	207.9	3,457.1	693.5	666.7	45.2	369.1	451.6	622.2	706.7	196.2	372.6	−1,294.4
2011	2,303.5	1,091.5	181.1	818.8	212.1	3,603.1	705.6	678.1	45.7	372.5	485.7	597.3	730.8	230.0	435.5	−1,299.6
2012	2,450.0	1,132.2	242.3	845.3	230.2	3,537.0	677.9	650.9	47.2	346.7	471.8	541.3	773.3	220.4	458.3	−1,087.0
2013	2,775.1	1,316.4	273.5	947.8	237.4	3,454.6	633.4	607.8	46.2	358.3	497.8	536.5	813.6	220.9	347.9	−679.5
2014	3,021.5	1,394.6	320.7	1,023.5	282.7	3,506.1	603.5	577.9	46.7	409.4	511.7	513.6	850.5	229.0	341.7	−484.6
2015	3,249.9	1,540.8	343.8	1,065.3	300.0	3,688.3	589.6	562.5	48.6	482.2	546.2	508.8	887.8	223.2	402.0	−438.4
2016 (estimates)[1]	3,266.7	1,546.1	299.6	1,115.1	306.0	3,854.1	595.3	565.4	45.3	511.3	594.5	514.6	916.1	240.7	436.3	−587.4
2017 (estimates)[2]	3,632.2	1,746.6	409.9	1,158.5	317.2	4,073.2	618.6	588.0	57.0	552.3	598.4	533.0	954.1	265.8	494.1	−440.9

[1] Estimates from *Final Monthly Treasury Statement*, issued October 2016.
[2] Estimates from *Mid-Session Review*, Budget of the U.S. Government, Fiscal Year 2017, issued July 2016.

Note: See Note, Table B–17.

Sources: Department of the Treasury and Office of Management and Budget.

TABLE B–20. Federal receipts, outlays, surplus or deficit, and debt, fiscal years 2011–2016

[Millions of dollars; fiscal years]

Description	Actual					Estimates [1]
	2011	2012	2013	2014	2015	2016
RECEIPTS, OUTLAYS, AND SURPLUS OR DEFICIT						
Total:						
Receipts	2,303,466	2,449,988	2,775,103	3,021,487	3,249,886	3,266,688
Outlays	3,603,056	3,536,951	3,454,647	3,506,114	3,688,292	3,854,100
Surplus or deficit (–)	–1,299,590	–1,086,963	–679,544	–484,627	–438,406	–587,412
On-budget:						
Receipts	1,737,678	1,880,487	2,101,829	2,285,922	2,479,514	2,456,509
Outlays	3,104,450	3,029,363	2,820,836	2,800,061	2,945,215	3,077,747
Surplus or deficit (–)	–1,366,772	–1,148,876	–719,007	–514,139	–465,701	–621,239
Off-budget:						
Receipts	565,788	569,501	673,274	735,565	770,372	810,180
Outlays	498,606	507,588	633,811	706,053	743,077	776,353
Surplus or deficit (–)	67,182	61,913	39,463	29,512	27,295	33,827
OUTSTANDING DEBT, END OF PERIOD						
Gross Federal debt	14,764,222	16,050,921	16,719,434	17,794,483	18,120,106	19,537,417
Held by Federal Government accounts	4,636,035	4,769,790	4,736,721	5,014,584	5,003,414	5,368,993
Held by the public	10,128,187	11,281,131	11,982,713	12,779,899	13,116,692	14,168,425
Federal Reserve System	1,664,660	1,645,285	2,072,283	2,451,743	2,461,947	
Other	8,463,527	9,635,846	9,910,430	10,328,156	10,654,745	
RECEIPTS BY SOURCE						
Total: On-budget and off-budget	2,303,466	2,449,988	2,775,103	3,021,487	3,249,886	3,266,688
Individual income taxes	1,091,473	1,132,206	1,316,405	1,394,568	1,540,802	1,546,075
Corporation income taxes	181,085	242,289	273,506	320,731	343,797	299,571
Social insurance and retirement receipts	818,792	845,314	947,820	1,023,458	1,065,257	1,115,063
On-budget	253,004	275,813	274,546	287,893	294,885	
Off-budget	565,788	569,501	673,274	735,565	770,372	
Excise taxes	72,381	79,061	84,007	93,368	98,279	95,045
Estate and gift taxes	7,399	13,973	18,912	19,300	19,232	21,354
Customs duties and fees	29,519	30,307	31,815	33,926	35,041	34,837
Miscellaneous receipts	102,817	106,838	102,638	136,136	147,478	154,743
Deposits of earnings by Federal Reserve System	82,546	81,957	75,767	99,235	96,468	
All other	20,271	24,881	26,871	36,901	51,010	
OUTLAYS BY FUNCTION						
Total: On-budget and off-budget	3,603,056	3,536,951	3,454,647	3,506,114	3,688,292	3,854,100
National defense	705,554	677,852	633,446	603,457	589,564	595,303
International affairs	45,685	47,184	46,231	46,686	48,576	45,304
General science, space, and technology	29,466	29,060	28,908	28,570	29,412	30,230
Energy	12,174	14,858	11,042	5,270	6,838	3,749
Natural resources and environment	45,473	41,631	38,145	36,171	36,034	37,792
Agriculture	20,662	17,791	29,678	24,386	18,500	20,175
Commerce and housing credit	–12,573	40,647	–83,199	–94,861	–37,905	–32,789
On-budget	–13,381	37,977	–81,286	–92,330	–36,195	
Off-budget	808	2,670	–1,913	–2,531	–1,710	
Transportation	92,966	93,019	91,673	91,938	89,533	92,941
Community and regional development	23,883	25,132	32,336	20,670	20,670	21,052
Education, training, employment, and social services	101,233	90,823	72,808	90,615	122,061	108,058
Health	372,504	346,742	358,315	409,449	482,223	511,320
Medicare	485,653	471,793	497,826	511,688	546,202	594,535
Income security	597,349	541,344	536,511	513,644	508,843	514,583
Social security	730,811	773,290	813,551	850,533	887,753	916,078
On-budget	101,933	140,387	56,009	25,946	30,990	
Off-budget	628,878	632,903	757,542	824,587	856,763	
Veterans benefits and services	127,189	124,595	138,938	149,616	159,738	174,515
Administration of justice	56,056	56,277	52,601	50,457	51,903	57,144
General government	27,476	28,041	27,737	26,913	20,969	18,640
Net interest	229,962	220,408	220,885	228,956	223,181	240,722
On-budget	345,943	332,801	326,535	329,222	319,149	
Off-budget	–115,981	–112,393	–105,650	–100,266	–95,968	
Allowances						
Undistributed offsetting receipts	–88,467	–103,536	–92,785	–88,044	–115,803	–95,251
On-budget	–73,368	–87,944	–76,617	–72,307	–99,795	
Off-budget	–15,099	–15,592	–16,168	–15,737	–16,008	

[1] Estimates from *Final Monthly Treasury Statement*, issued October 2016.

Note: See Note, Table B–17.

Sources: Department of the Treasury and Office of Management and Budget.

Table B–21. Federal and State and local government current receipts and expenditures, national income and product accounts (NIPA) basis, 1965–2016

[Billions of dollars; quarterly data at seasonally adjusted annual rates]

Year or quarter	Total government			Federal Government			State and local government			Addendum: Grants-in-aid to State and local governments
	Current receipts	Current expenditures	Net government saving (NIPA)	Current receipts	Current expenditures	Net Federal Government saving (NIPA)	Current receipts	Current expenditures	Net State and local government saving (NIPA)	
1965	179.7	181.0	–1.4	120.4	125.9	–5.5	65.8	61.7	4.1	6.6
1966	202.1	203.9	–1.8	137.4	144.3	–7.0	74.1	68.9	5.2	9.4
1967	216.9	231.7	–14.8	146.3	165.7	–19.5	81.6	76.9	4.7	10.9
1968	251.2	260.7	–9.5	170.6	184.3	–13.7	92.5	88.2	4.3	11.8
1969	282.5	283.5	–1.0	191.8	196.9	–5.1	104.3	100.2	4.1	13.7
1970	285.7	317.5	–31.8	185.1	219.9	–34.8	118.9	115.9	3.0	18.3
1971	302.1	352.4	–50.2	190.7	241.5	–50.8	133.6	133.0	.6	22.1
1972	345.4	385.9	–40.5	219.0	267.9	–48.9	156.9	148.5	8.4	30.5
1973	388.5	416.6	–28.0	249.2	286.9	–37.7	172.8	163.1	9.6	33.5
1974	430.0	468.3	–38.3	278.5	319.1	–40.6	186.4	184.1	2.3	34.9
1975	440.9	543.5	–102.5	276.8	373.8	–97.0	207.7	213.3	–5.6	43.6
1976	505.4	582.4	–77.1	322.6	402.4	–79.9	231.9	229.1	2.8	49.1
1977	567.0	630.5	–63.5	363.9	435.8	–71.9	257.9	249.5	8.4	54.8
1978	645.7	692.0	–46.4	423.8	483.7	–59.8	285.3	271.9	13.4	63.5
1979	728.8	765.1	–36.3	487.0	531.5	–44.5	305.8	297.6	8.2	64.0
1980	799.3	880.2	–80.9	533.7	619.9	–86.3	335.3	329.9	5.4	69.7
1981	918.7	1,000.3	–81.7	621.1	706.9	–85.8	367.0	362.9	4.1	69.4
1982	940.5	1,110.3	–169.7	618.7	783.3	–164.6	388.1	393.2	–5.1	66.3
1983	1,001.7	1,205.4	–203.7	644.8	849.8	–205.0	424.8	423.6	1.3	67.9
1984	1,114.4	1,285.9	–171.4	711.2	903.5	–192.3	475.6	454.7	20.9	72.3
1985	1,216.5	1,391.8	–175.4	775.7	971.3	–195.6	516.9	496.7	20.3	76.2
1986	1,292.3	1,484.5	–192.2	817.9	1,030.6	–212.7	556.8	536.4	20.4	82.4
1987	1,406.1	1,557.2	–151.1	899.5	1,062.7	–163.2	585.0	572.9	12.1	78.4
1988	1,506.5	1,646.9	–140.4	962.4	1,119.8	–157.3	629.9	612.9	17.0	85.7
1989	1,631.4	1,780.6	–149.2	1,042.5	1,199.1	–156.6	680.8	673.4	7.4	91.8
1990	1,712.9	1,920.2	–207.4	1,087.6	1,288.5	–200.9	729.6	736.0	–6.5	104.4
1991	1,763.3	2,034.6	–271.3	1,107.8	1,354.0	–246.2	779.5	804.6	–25.1	124.0
1992	1,848.2	2,218.4	–370.2	1,154.4	1,487.0	–332.7	835.6	873.1	–37.5	141.7
1993	1,952.3	2,301.4	–349.0	1,231.0	1,542.8	–311.8	877.1	914.3	–37.2	155.7
1994	2,096.5	2,377.2	–280.7	1,329.3	1,583.0	–253.7	934.1	961.0	–27.0	166.8
1995	2,222.8	2,495.1	–272.4	1,417.4	1,658.2	–240.8	979.8	1,011.4	–31.5	174.5
1996	2,387.4	2,578.3	–191.0	1,536.3	1,714.8	–178.5	1,032.6	1,045.0	–12.5	181.5
1997	2,565.0	2,654.5	–89.5	1,667.3	1,758.5	–91.2	1,085.8	1,084.1	1.7	188.1
1998	2,737.7	2,719.6	18.1	1,789.8	1,787.0	2.7	1,148.7	1,133.3	15.4	200.8
1999	2,908.1	2,832.2	75.9	1,905.4	1,838.8	66.6	1,221.8	1,212.6	9.2	219.2
2000	3,138.2	2,971.8	166.4	2,068.2	1,911.7	156.5	1,303.1	1,293.2	9.9	233.1
2001	3,123.2	3,174.0	–50.8	2,031.8	2,017.4	14.5	1,352.6	1,417.9	–65.3	261.3
2002	2,971.9	3,363.3	–391.4	1,870.6	2,141.1	–270.5	1,388.4	1,509.4	–120.9	287.2
2003	3,048.0	3,572.2	–524.3	1,895.1	2,297.9	–402.9	1,474.6	1,596.0	–121.4	321.7
2004	3,270.3	3,777.9	–507.6	2,027.4	2,426.6	–399.2	1,575.1	1,683.4	–108.4	332.2
2005	3,669.0	4,040.3	–371.3	2,303.5	2,608.2	–304.7	1,708.8	1,775.4	–66.6	343.4
2006	4,007.9	4,274.3	–266.4	2,537.7	2,764.8	–227.0	1,810.9	1,850.3	–39.4	340.8
2007	4,208.8	4,547.2	–338.4	2,667.2	2,932.8	–265.7	1,900.6	1,973.3	–72.7	359.0
2008	4,117.5	4,916.6	–799.0	2,579.5	3,213.5	–634.0	1,909.1	2,074.1	–165.1	371.0
2009	3,699.5	5,220.3	–1,520.8	2,238.4	3,487.2	–1,248.8	1,919.2	2,191.2	–271.9	458.1
2010	3,936.5	5,502.5	–1,566.0	2,443.3	3,772.0	–1,328.7	1,998.5	2,235.8	–237.3	505.3
2011	4,132.2	5,592.2	–1,460.1	2,574.1	3,818.3	–1,244.1	2,030.5	2,246.4	–215.9	472.5
2012	4,312.3	5,623.1	–1,310.8	2,699.1	3,789.1	–1,090.1	2,057.2	2,277.9	–220.8	440.0
2013	4,825.2	5,659.5	–834.4	3,138.4	3,782.2	–643.8	2,136.8	2,327.3	–190.5	450.0
2014	5,021.4	5,804.1	–782.7	3,288.4	3,901.3	–612.9	2,227.7	2,397.6	–169.8	494.8
2015	5,253.5	5,984.5	–731.0	3,453.3	4,022.9	–569.7	2,331.5	2,492.8	–161.3	531.2
2013: I	4,657.9	5,633.9	–976.0	2,972.8	3,764.6	–791.8	2,123.5	2,307.6	–184.1	438.3
II	4,941.7	5,651.5	–709.7	3,250.8	3,781.7	–530.9	2,144.3	2,323.1	–178.8	453.4
III	4,763.5	5,673.3	–909.8	3,083.2	3,792.9	–709.7	2,138.2	2,338.3	–200.1	457.9
IV	4,937.5	5,679.4	–741.9	3,246.8	3,789.8	–542.9	2,141.1	2,340.1	–199.0	450.4
2014: I	4,960.5	5,731.5	–771.0	3,254.1	3,846.2	–592.1	2,173.6	2,352.4	–178.9	467.1
II	5,017.0	5,784.9	–767.9	3,290.7	3,893.9	–603.2	2,214.8	2,379.5	–164.7	488.5
III	5,050.7	5,847.6	–796.9	3,309.5	3,942.6	–633.1	2,255.4	2,419.2	–163.8	514.2
IV	5,057.4	5,852.5	–795.1	3,299.4	3,922.5	–623.1	2,267.2	2,439.1	–172.0	509.2
2015: I	5,177.3	5,868.9	–691.6	3,410.0	3,944.5	–534.5	2,291.9	2,449.0	–157.1	524.6
II	5,219.3	5,987.2	–767.9	3,439.4	4,018.2	–578.9	2,301.1	2,490.2	–189.0	521.2
III	5,234.9	6,045.2	–810.3	3,447.8	4,070.2	–622.3	2,322.7	2,510.7	–187.9	535.6
IV	5,382.6	6,036.7	–654.2	3,515.9	4,058.9	–543.1	2,410.3	2,521.4	–111.1	543.6
2016: I	5,255.4	6,097.3	–841.9	3,442.5	4,110.8	–668.3	2,354.1	2,527.7	–173.6	541.2
II	5,288.0	6,145.8	–857.8	3,484.7	4,137.1	–652.4	2,342.9	2,548.2	–205.3	539.6
III ᵖ	5,363.9	6,206.9	–843.0	3,537.1	4,187.5	–650.4	2,387.4	2,580.0	–192.6	560.6

Note: Federal grants-in-aid to State and local governments are reflected in Federal current expenditures and State and local current receipts. Total government current receipts and expenditures have been adjusted to eliminate this duplication.

Source: Department of Commerce (Bureau of Economic Analysis).

State and local government revenues and expenditures, fiscal years 1954–2013

[Millions of dollars]

Fiscal year [1]	General revenues by source [2]							General expenditures by function [2]				
	Total	Property taxes	Sales and gross receipts taxes	Individual income taxes	Corporation net income taxes	Revenue from Federal Government	All other [3]	Total [4]	Education	Highways	Public welfare [4]	All other [4,5]
1954	29,012	9,967	7,276	1,127	778	2,966	6,898	30,701	10,557	5,527	3,060	11,557
1955	31,073	10,735	7,643	1,237	744	3,131	7,583	33,724	11,907	6,452	3,168	12,197
1956	34,670	11,749	8,691	1,538	890	3,335	8,467	36,715	13,224	6,953	3,139	13,399
1957	38,164	12,864	9,467	1,754	984	3,843	9,252	40,375	14,134	7,816	3,485	14,940
1958	41,219	14,047	9,829	1,759	1,018	4,865	9,701	44,851	15,919	8,567	3,818	16,547
1959	45,306	14,983	10,437	1,994	1,001	6,377	10,514	48,887	17,283	9,592	4,136	17,876
1960	50,505	16,405	11,849	2,463	1,180	6,974	11,634	51,876	18,719	9,428	4,404	19,325
1961	54,037	18,002	12,463	2,613	1,266	7,131	12,562	56,201	20,574	9,844	4,720	21,063
1962	58,252	19,054	13,494	3,037	1,308	7,871	13,488	60,206	22,216	10,357	5,084	22,549
1963	62,891	20,089	14,456	3,269	1,505	8,722	14,850	64,815	23,776	11,135	5,481	24,423
1963–64	68,443	21,241	15,762	3,791	1,695	10,002	15,952	69,302	26,286	11,664	5,766	25,586
1964–65	74,000	22,583	17,118	4,090	1,929	11,029	17,251	74,678	28,563	12,221	6,315	27,579
1965–66	83,036	24,670	19,085	4,760	2,038	13,214	19,269	82,843	33,287	12,770	6,757	30,029
1966–67	91,197	26,047	20,530	5,825	2,227	15,370	21,198	93,350	37,919	13,932	8,218	33,281
1967–68	101,264	27,747	22,911	7,308	2,518	17,181	23,599	102,411	41,158	14,481	9,857	36,915
1968–69	114,550	30,673	26,519	8,908	3,180	19,153	26,117	116,728	47,238	15,417	12,110	41,963
1969–70	130,756	34,054	30,322	10,812	3,738	21,857	29,973	131,332	52,718	16,427	14,679	47,508
1970–71	144,927	37,852	33,233	11,900	3,424	26,146	32,372	150,674	59,413	18,095	18,226	54,940
1971–72	167,535	42,877	37,518	15,227	4,416	31,342	36,156	168,549	65,813	19,021	21,117	62,598
1972–73	190,222	45,283	42,047	17,994	5,425	39,264	40,210	181,357	69,713	18,615	23,582	69,447
1973–74	207,670	47,705	46,098	19,491	6,015	41,820	46,542	199,222	75,833	19,946	25,085	78,358
1974–75	228,171	51,491	49,815	21,454	6,642	47,034	51,735	230,722	87,858	22,528	28,156	92,180
1975–76	256,176	57,001	54,547	24,575	7,273	55,589	57,191	256,731	97,216	23,907	32,604	103,004
1976–77	285,157	62,527	60,641	29,246	9,174	62,444	61,125	274,215	102,780	23,058	35,906	112,472
1977–78	315,960	66,422	67,596	33,176	10,738	69,592	68,435	296,984	110,758	24,609	39,140	122,478
1978–79	343,236	64,944	74,247	36,932	12,128	75,164	79,822	327,517	119,448	28,440	41,898	137,731
1979–80	382,322	68,499	79,927	42,080	13,321	83,029	95,467	369,086	133,211	33,311	47,288	155,276
1980–81	423,404	74,969	85,971	46,426	14,143	90,294	111,599	407,449	145,784	34,603	54,105	172,957
1981–82	457,654	82,067	93,613	50,738	15,028	87,282	128,925	436,733	154,282	34,520	57,996	189,935
1982–83	486,753	89,105	100,247	55,129	14,258	90,007	138,008	466,516	163,876	36,655	60,906	205,080
1983–84	542,730	96,457	114,097	64,871	16,798	96,935	153,571	505,008	176,108	39,419	66,414	223,068
1984–85	598,121	103,757	126,376	70,361	19,152	106,158	172,317	553,899	192,686	44,989	71,479	244,745
1985–86	641,486	111,709	135,005	74,365	19,994	113,099	187,314	605,623	210,819	49,368	75,868	269,568
1986–87	686,860	121,203	144,091	83,935	22,425	114,857	200,350	657,134	226,619	52,355	82,650	295,510
1987–88	726,762	132,212	156,452	88,350	23,663	117,602	208,482	704,921	242,683	55,621	89,090	317,527
1988–89	786,129	142,400	166,336	97,806	25,926	125,824	227,838	762,360	263,898	58,105	97,879	342,479
1989–90	849,502	155,613	177,885	105,640	23,566	136,802	249,996	834,818	288,148	61,057	110,518	375,094
1990–91	902,207	167,999	185,570	109,341	22,242	154,099	262,955	908,108	309,302	64,937	130,402	403,467
1991–92	979,137	180,337	197,731	115,638	23,880	179,174	282,376	981,253	324,652	67,351	158,723	430,526
1992–93	1,041,643	189,744	209,649	123,235	26,417	198,663	293,935	1,030,434	342,287	68,370	170,705	449,072
1993–94	1,100,490	197,141	223,628	128,810	28,320	215,492	307,099	1,077,665	353,287	72,067	183,394	468,916
1994–95	1,169,505	203,451	237,268	137,931	31,406	228,771	330,677	1,149,863	378,273	77,109	196,703	497,779
1995–96	1,222,821	209,440	248,993	146,844	32,009	234,891	350,645	1,193,276	398,859	79,092	197,354	517,971
1996–97	1,289,237	218,877	261,418	159,042	33,820	244,847	371,233	1,249,984	418,416	82,062	203,779	545,727
1997–98	1,365,762	230,150	274,883	175,630	34,412	255,048	395,639	1,318,042	450,365	87,214	208,120	572,343
1998–99	1,434,029	239,672	290,993	189,309	33,922	270,628	409,505	1,402,369	483,259	93,018	218,957	607,134
1999–2000	1,541,322	249,178	309,290	211,661	36,059	291,950	443,186	1,506,797	521,612	101,336	237,336	646,512
2000–01	1,647,161	263,689	320,217	226,334	35,296	324,033	477,592	1,626,063	563,572	107,235	261,622	693,634
2001–02	1,684,879	279,191	324,123	202,832	28,152	360,546	490,035	1,736,866	594,694	115,295	285,464	741,413
2002–03	1,763,212	296,683	337,787	199,407	31,369	389,264	508,702	1,821,917	621,335	117,696	310,783	772,102
2003–04	1,887,397	317,941	361,027	215,215	33,716	423,112	536,386	1,908,543	655,182	117,215	340,523	795,622
2004–05	2,026,034	335,779	384,266	242,273	43,256	438,558	581,902	2,012,110	688,314	126,350	365,295	832,151
2005–06	2,197,475	364,559	417,735	268,667	53,081	452,975	640,458	2,123,663	728,917	136,502	373,846	884,398
2006–07	2,330,611	388,905	440,470	290,278	60,955	464,914	685,089	2,264,035	774,170	145,011	389,259	955,595
2007–08	2,421,977	409,540	449,945	304,902	57,231	477,441	722,919	2,406,183	826,061	153,831	408,920	1,017,372
2008–09	2,429,672	434,818	434,128	270,942	46,280	537,949	705,555	2,500,796	851,689	154,338	437,184	1,057,586
2009–10	2,510,846	443,947	435,571	261,510	44,108	623,801	701,909	2,542,231	860,118	155,912	460,230	1,065,971
2010–11	2,618,037	445,771	463,979	285,293	48,422	647,606	726,966	2,583,805	862,271	153,895	494,682	1,072,957
2011–12	2,598,906	447,120	476,544	307,256	48,934	585,128	733,924	2,593,180	869,223	160,327	489,430	1,074,200
2012–13	2,690,427	455,442	496,439	338,471	53,039	584,652	762,383	2,643,122	876,566	158,745	516,389	1,091,421

[1] Fiscal years not the same for all governments. See Note.
[2] Excludes revenues or expenditures of publicly owned utilities and liquor stores and of insurance-trust activities. Intergovernmental receipts and payments between State and local governments are also excluded.
[3] Includes motor vehicle license taxes, other taxes, and charges and miscellaneous revenues.
[4] Includes intergovernmental payments to the Federal Government.
[5] Includes expenditures for libraries, hospitals, health, employment security administration, veterans' services, air transportation, sea and inland port facilities, parking facilities, police protection, fire protection, correction, protective inspection and regulation, sewerage, natural resources, parks and recreation, housing and community development, solid waste management, financial administration, judicial and legal, general public buildings, other government administration, interest on general debt, and other general expenditures, not elsewhere classified.

Note: Except for States listed, data for fiscal years listed from 1963–64 to 2012–13 are the aggregation of data for government fiscal years that ended in the 12-month period from July 1 to June 30 of those years; Texas used August and Alabama and Michigan used September as end dates. Data for 1963 and earlier years include data for government fiscal years ending during that particular calendar year.

Source: Department of Commerce (Bureau of the Census).

[Billions of dollars]

End of fiscal year or month	Total Treasury securities outstanding [1]	Marketable							Nonmarketable				
		Total [2]	Treasury bills	Treasury notes	Treasury bonds	Treasury inflation-protected securities			Total	U.S. savings securities [3]	Foreign series [4]	Government account series	Other [5]
						Total	Notes	Bonds					
1977	697.8	443.5	156.1	241.7	45.7				254.3	75.6	21.8	140.1	16.8
1978	767.2	485.2	160.9	267.9	56.4				282.0	79.9	21.7	153.3	27.1
1979	819.1	506.7	161.4	274.2	71.1				312.4	80.6	28.1	176.4	27.4
1980	906.8	594.5	199.8	310.9	83.8				312.3	73.0	25.2	189.8	24.2
1981	996.8	683.2	223.4	363.6	96.2				313.6	68.3	20.5	201.1	23.7
1982	1,141.2	824.4	277.9	442.9	103.6				316.8	67.6	14.6	210.5	24.1
1983	1,376.3	1,024.0	340.7	557.5	125.7				352.3	70.6	11.5	234.7	35.6
1984	1,560.4	1,176.6	356.8	661.7	158.1				383.8	73.7	8.8	259.5	41.8
1985	1,822.3	1,360.2	384.2	776.4	199.5				462.1	78.2	6.6	313.9	63.3
1986	2,124.9	1,564.3	410.7	896.9	241.7				560.5	87.8	4.1	365.9	102.8
1987	2,349.4	1,676.0	378.3	1,005.1	277.6				673.4	98.5	4.4	440.7	129.8
1988	2,601.4	1,802.9	398.5	1,089.6	299.9				798.5	107.8	6.3	536.5	148.0
1989	2,837.9	1,892.8	406.6	1,133.2	338.0				945.2	115.7	6.8	663.7	159.0
1990	3,212.7	2,092.8	482.5	1,218.1	377.2				1,119.9	123.9	36.0	779.4	180.6
1991	3,664.5	2,390.7	564.6	1,387.7	423.4				1,273.9	135.4	41.6	908.4	188.5
1992	4,063.8	2,677.5	634.3	1,566.3	461.8				1,386.3	150.3	37.0	1,011.0	188.0
1993	4,410.7	2,904.9	658.4	1,734.2	497.4				1,505.8	169.1	42.5	1,114.3	179.9
1994	4,691.7	3,091.6	697.3	1,867.5	511.8				1,600.1	178.6	42.0	1,211.7	167.8
1995	4,953.0	3,260.4	742.5	1,980.3	522.6				1,692.6	183.5	41.0	1,324.3	143.8
1996	5,220.8	3,418.4	761.2	2,098.7	543.5				1,802.4	184.1	37.5	1,454.7	126.1
1997	5,407.6	3,439.6	701.9	2,122.2	576.2	24.4	24.4		1,968.0	182.7	34.9	1,608.5	141.9
1998	5,518.7	3,331.0	637.6	2,009.1	610.4	58.8	41.9	17.0	2,187.6	180.8	35.1	1,777.3	194.4
1999	5,647.3	3,233.0	653.2	1,828.8	643.7	92.4	67.6	24.8	2,414.3	180.0	31.0	2,005.2	198.1
2000	5,622.1	2,992.8	616.2	1,611.3	635.3	115.0	81.6	33.4	2,629.4	177.7	25.4	2,242.9	183.3
2001 [1]	5,807.5	2,930.7	734.9	1,433.0	613.0	134.9	95.1	39.7	2,876.7	186.5	18.3	2,492.1	179.9
2002	6,228.2	3,136.7	868.3	1,521.6	593.0	138.9	93.7	45.1	3,091.5	193.3	12.5	2,707.3	178.4
2003	6,783.2	3,460.7	918.2	1,799.5	576.9	166.1	120.0	46.1	3,322.5	201.6	11.0	2,912.2	197.7
2004	7,379.1	3,846.1	961.5	2,109.6	552.0	223.0	164.5	58.5	3,533.0	204.2	5.9	3,130.0	192.9
2005	7,932.7	4,084.9	914.3	2,328.8	520.7	307.1	229.1	78.0	3,847.8	203.6	3.1	3,380.6	260.5
2006	8,507.0	4,303.0	911.5	2,447.2	534.7	395.6	293.9	101.7	4,203.9	203.7	3.0	3,722.7	274.5
2007	9,007.7	4,448.1	958.1	2,458.0	561.1	456.9	335.7	121.2	4,559.5	197.1	3.0	4,026.8	332.6
2008	10,024.7	5,236.0	1,489.8	2,624.8	582.9	524.5	380.2	144.3	4,788.7	194.3	3.0	4,297.7	293.8
2009	11,909.8	7,009.7	1,992.5	3,773.8	679.8	551.7	396.2	155.5	4,900.1	192.5	4.9	4,454.3	248.4
2010	13,561.6	8,498.3	1,788.5	5,255.9	849.9	593.8	421.1	172.7	5,063.3	188.7	4.2	4,645.3	225.1
2011	14,790.3	9,624.5	1,477.5	6,412.5	1,020.4	705.7	509.4	196.3	5,165.8	185.1	3.0	4,793.9	183.8
2012	16,066.2	10,749.7	1,616.0	7,120.7	1,198.2	807.7	584.7	223.0	5,316.5	183.8	3.0	4,939.3	190.4
2013	16,738.2	11,596.2	1,530.0	7,758.0	1,366.2	936.4	685.5	250.8	5,142.0	180.0	3.0	4,803.1	156.0
2014	17,824.1	12,294.2	1,411.0	8,167.8	1,534.1	1,044.7	765.2	279.5	5,529.9	176.7	3.0	5,212.5	137.7
2015	18,150.6	12,853.8	1,358.0	8,372.7	1,688.3	1,135.4	832.1	303.3	5,296.9	172.8	.3	5,013.5	110.3
2016	19,573.4	13,660.6	1,647.0	8,631.0	1,825.5	1,210.0	881.6	328.3	5,912.8	167.5	.3	5,604.1	141.0
2015: Jan	18,082.3	12,483.3	1,412.9	8,239.9	1,589.2	1,063.7	779.5	284.2	5,599.0	175.6	.3	5,277.4	145.8
Feb	18,155.9	12,570.3	1,472.9	8,230.1	1,594.6	1,067.1	775.5	291.6	5,585.5	175.3	.3	5,265.2	144.8
Mar	18,152.1	12,643.8	1,477.9	8,264.4	1,607.6	1,075.2	785.0	290.2	5,508.3	174.9	.3	5,183.1	150.0
Apr	18,152.6	12,645.5	1,432.9	8,284.0	1,620.6	1,074.2	782.9	291.3	5,507.1	174.6	.3	5,182.7	149.5
May	18,153.3	12,688.4	1,447.0	8,264.6	1,637.0	1,093.2	800.1	293.0	5,464.8	174.3	.3	5,147.5	142.7
June	18,152.0	12,711.1	1,395.0	8,305.4	1,650.0	1,102.4	801.7	300.7	5,440.9	173.9	.3	5,134.9	131.8
July	18,151.3	12,813.4	1,440.0	8,335.1	1,663.0	1,101.9	799.7	302.2	5,337.9	173.6	.3	5,043.0	121.1
Aug	18,151.2	12,846.5	1,424.0	8,338.8	1,675.3	1,122.1	818.9	303.3	5,304.6	173.2	.3	5,017.9	113.2
Sept	18,150.6	12,853.8	1,358.0	8,372.7	1,688.3	1,135.4	832.1	303.3	5,296.9	172.8	.3	5,013.5	110.3
Oct	18,153.0	12,803.0	1,273.0	8,385.7	1,701.3	1,141.0	831.0	310.0	5,350.0	172.5	.3	5,070.5	106.7
Nov	18,827.3	13,122.6	1,506.0	8,422.6	1,711.8	1,152.2	842.7	309.5	5,704.7	172.1	.3	5,426.3	106.0
Dec	18,922.2	13,206.6	1,514.0	8,456.8	1,724.8	1,167.9	858.6	309.4	5,715.6	171.6	.3	5,436.8	107.0
2016: Jan	19,012.8	13,189.0	1,477.9	8,469.8	1,737.8	1,160.4	851.6	308.8	5,823.9	171.1	.3	5,547.4	105.1
Feb	19,125.5	13,312.7	1,551.9	8,515.9	1,748.5	1,166.0	849.0	317.0	5,812.7	170.8	.3	5,534.3	107.4
Mar	19,264.9	13,446.1	1,618.0	8,543.2	1,760.5	1,181.1	863.6	317.5	5,818.8	170.3	.3	5,533.7	114.6
Apr	19,187.4	13,355.2	1,527.0	8,555.5	1,772.6	1,156.8	839.1	317.8	5,832.2	169.9	.3	5,540.3	121.7
May	19,265.4	13,393.5	1,524.0	8,587.7	1,772.2	1,175.4	856.3	319.1	5,871.9	169.5	.3	5,574.9	127.3
June	19,381.6	13,430.8	1,507.9	8,606.6	1,784.2	1,186.7	860.3	326.4	5,950.8	169.0	.3	5,648.0	133.5
July	19,427.8	13,494.4	1,549.9	8,621.5	1,797.0	1,180.7	853.0	327.7	5,933.5	168.6	.3	5,631.0	133.6
Aug	19,510.3	13,599.1	1,632.9	8,619.2	1,813.5	1,200.0	871.2	328.8	5,911.2	168.0	.3	5,608.2	134.7
Sept	19,573.4	13,660.6	1,647.0	8,631.0	1,825.5	1,210.0	881.6	328.3	5,912.8	167.5	.3	5,604.1	141.0
Oct	19,805.7	13,770.1	1,752.9	8,641.2	1,837.5	1,216.3	882.3	334.0	6,035.6	166.8	.3	5,723.5	145.0

[1] Data beginning with January 2001 are interest-bearing and non-interest-bearing securities; prior data are interest-bearing securities only.

[2] Data from 1986 to 2002 and 2005 forward include Federal Financing Bank securities, not shown separately. Beginning with data for January 2014, includes Floating Rate Notes, not shown separately.

[3] Through 1996, series is U.S. savings bonds. Beginning 1997, includes U.S. retirement plan bonds, U.S. individual retirement bonds, and U.S. savings notes previously included in "other" nonmarketable securities.

[4] Nonmarketable certificates of indebtedness, notes, bonds, and bills in the Treasury foreign series of dollar-denominated and foreign-currency-denominated issues.

[5] Includes depository bonds; retirement plan bonds through 1996; Rural Electrification Administration bonds; State and local bonds; special issues held only by U.S. Government agencies and trust funds and the Federal home loan banks; for the period July 2003 through February 2004, depositary compensation securities; and for the period August 2008 through April 2016, Hope bonds for the HOPE For Homeowners Program.

Note: The fiscal year is on an October 1–September 30 basis.

Source: Department of the Treasury.

Table B–24. Estimated ownership of U.S. Treasury securities, 2003–2016

[Billions of dollars]

End of month	Total public debt [1]	Federal Reserve and Intra-governmental holdings [2]	Held by private investors									
			Total privately held	Depository institutions [3]	U.S. savings bonds [4]	Pension funds		Insurance companies	Mutual funds [6]	State and local governments	Foreign and international [7]	Other investors [8]
						Private [5]	State and local governments					
2003: Mar	6,460.8	3,390.8	3,070.0	162.6	196.9	111.6	162.1	163.5	282.7	350.0	1,275.2	365.3
June	6,670.1	3,505.4	3,164.7	155.0	199.2	115.4	161.3	166.0	285.4	347.9	1,371.9	362.7
Sept	6,783.2	3,515.3	3,267.9	158.0	201.6	112.1	155.5	168.5	271.0	356.2	1,443.3	401.8
Dec	6,998.0	3,620.1	3,377.9	165.3	203.9	116.9	148.6	166.4	271.2	361.8	1,523.1	420.7
2004: Mar	7,131.1	3,628.3	3,502.8	172.7	204.5	114.0	143.6	172.4	275.2	372.8	1,670.0	377.6
June	7,274.3	3,742.8	3,531.5	167.8	204.6	115.4	134.9	174.6	252.3	390.1	1,735.4	356.4
Sept	7,379.1	3,772.0	3,607.1	146.3	204.2	113.6	140.1	182.9	249.4	393.0	1,794.5	383.1
Dec	7,596.1	3,905.6	3,690.5	133.4	204.5	113.0	149.4	188.5	256.1	404.9	1,849.3	391.6
2005: Mar	7,776.9	3,921.6	3,855.3	149.4	204.2	114.4	157.2	193.3	264.3	429.3	1,952.2	391.0
June	7,836.5	4,033.5	3,803.0	135.9	204.2	115.4	165.9	195.0	248.6	461.1	1,877.5	399.4
Sept	7,932.7	4,067.8	3,864.9	134.0	203.6	116.7	161.1	200.7	246.6	493.6	1,929.6	378.9
Dec	8,170.4	4,199.8	3,970.6	129.4	205.2	116.5	154.2	202.3	254.1	512.2	2,033.9	362.7
2006: Mar	8,371.2	4,257.2	4,114.0	113.0	206.0	116.8	152.9	200.3	254.2	515.7	2,082.1	473.0
June	8,420.0	4,389.2	4,030.8	119.5	205.2	117.7	149.6	196.1	243.4	531.6	1,977.8	490.1
Sept	8,507.0	4,432.8	4,074.2	113.6	203.7	125.8	149.3	196.8	234.2	542.3	2,025.3	483.2
Dec	8,680.2	4,558.1	4,122.1	114.8	202.4	139.8	153.4	197.9	248.2	570.5	2,103.1	392.0
2007: Mar	8,849.7	4,576.6	4,273.1	119.8	200.3	139.7	156.3	185.4	263.2	608.3	2,194.8	405.2
June	8,867.7	4,715.1	4,152.6	110.4	198.6	139.9	162.3	168.9	257.6	637.8	2,192.0	285.1
Sept	9,007.7	4,738.0	4,269.7	119.7	197.1	140.5	153.2	155.1	292.7	643.1	2,235.3	332.9
Dec	9,229.2	4,833.5	4,395.7	129.8	196.5	141.0	144.2	141.9	343.5	647.8	2,353.2	297.8
2008: Mar	9,437.6	4,694.7	4,742.9	120.5	195.4	143.7	135.4	152.1	466.7	646.4	2,506.3	371.9
June	9,492.0	4,685.8	4,806.2	112.7	195.0	145.0	135.5	159.4	440.3	635.1	2,587.4	395.9
Sept	10,024.7	4,692.7	5,332.0	130.0	194.3	147.0	136.7	163.4	631.4	614.0	2,802.4	512.9
Dec	10,699.8	4,806.4	5,893.4	105.0	194.1	147.4	129.9	171.4	758.2	601.4	3,077.2	708.9
2009: Mar	11,126.9	4,785.2	6,341.7	125.7	194.0	155.4	137.0	191.0	721.1	588.2	3,265.7	963.7
June	11,545.3	5,026.8	6,518.5	140.8	193.6	164.1	144.6	200.0	711.8	588.5	3,460.8	914.2
Sept	11,909.8	5,127.1	6,782.7	198.2	192.5	167.2	145.6	210.2	668.5	583.6	3,570.6	1,046.3
Dec	12,311.3	5,276.9	7,034.4	202.5	191.3	175.6	151.4	222.0	668.8	585.6	3,685.1	1,152.1
2010: Mar	12,773.1	5,259.8	7,513.3	269.3	190.2	183.0	153.6	225.7	678.5	585.0	3,877.9	1,350.1
June	13,201.8	5,345.1	7,856.7	266.1	189.6	190.8	150.1	231.8	676.8	584.4	4,070.0	1,497.1
Sept	13,561.6	5,350.5	8,211.1	322.8	188.7	198.2	145.2	240.6	671.0	586.0	4,324.2	1,534.4
Dec	14,025.2	5,656.2	8,368.9	319.3	187.9	206.8	153.7	248.4	721.7	595.7	4,435.6	1,499.9
2011: Mar	14,270.0	5,958.9	8,311.1	321.0	186.7	215.8	157.9	253.5	749.4	583.5	4,481.4	1,360.1
June	14,343.1	6,220.4	8,122.7	279.4	186.0	251.8	158.0	254.8	753.7	572.2	4,690.6	976.1
Sept	14,790.3	6,328.0	8,462.4	293.8	185.1	373.6	155.7	259.6	788.7	557.9	4,912.1	935.8
Dec	15,222.8	6,439.6	8,783.3	279.7	185.2	391.9	160.7	271.8	927.9	562.2	5,006.9	997.0
2012: Mar	15,582.3	6,397.2	9,185.1	317.0	184.8	406.6	169.4	271.5	1,015.4	567.2	5,145.1	1,108.1
June	15,855.5	6,475.8	9,379.7	303.2	184.7	427.4	171.2	268.6	997.8	585.1	5,310.9	1,130.8
Sept	16,066.2	6,446.8	9,619.4	338.2	183.8	447.0	171.4	269.5	1,080.7	593.7	5,476.1	1,058.9
Dec	16,432.7	6,523.7	9,909.1	347.7	182.5	467.5	172.9	270.6	1,031.8	606.7	5,573.8	1,255.6
2013: Mar	16,771.6	6,656.8	10,114.8	338.9	181.7	464.6	173.9	266.6	1,066.7	610.7	5,725.0	1,286.7
June	16,738.2	6,773.3	9,964.9	300.2	180.9	454.0	178.7	262.6	1,000.1	608.7	5,595.0	1,384.6
Sept	16,738.2	6,834.2	9,904.0	293.2	180.0	358.6	182.8	262.3	976.2	584.1	5,652.8	1,414.1
Dec	17,352.0	7,205.3	10,146.6	321.1	179.2	478.1	188.3	264.7	975.3	586.7	5,792.6	1,360.6
2014: Mar	17,601.2	7,301.5	10,299.7	368.3	178.3	480.1	189.0	266.7	1,050.1	586.7	5,948.3	1,232.2
June	17,632.6	7,461.0	10,171.6	407.2	177.6	481.1	189.3	273.6	977.9	605.9	6,018.7	1,040.3
Sept	17,824.1	7,490.8	10,333.2	470.9	176.7	485.5	187.1	280.0	1,067.6	602.6	6,069.2	993.5
Dec	18,141.4	7,578.9	10,562.6	513.7	175.9	492.1	181.3	285.4	1,108.3	623.1	6,157.7	1,025.1
2015: Mar	18,152.1	7,521.3	10,630.8	511.7	174.9	442.8	176.4	292.7	1,156.8	640.6	6,172.6	1,062.4
June	18,152.0	7,536.5	10,615.5	515.4	173.9	382.9	178.0	293.2	1,135.9	630.8	6,163.1	1,142.2
Sept	18,150.6	7,488.7	10,661.9	513.6	172.8	318.8	173.5	297.8	1,186.6	643.6	6,105.9	1,249.3
Dec	18,922.2	7,711.2	11,211.0	546.8	171.6	529.2	174.8	298.3	1,315.3	666.4	6,146.3	1,362.3
2016: Mar	19,264.9	7,801.4	11,463.6	555.3	170.3	538.0	175.6	301.5	1,390.7	680.1	6,285.9	1,366.2
June	19,381.6	7,911.2	11,470.4	570.3	169.0	544.4	173.9	304.1	1,378.9	700.0	6,280.0	1,349.8
Sept	19,573.4	7,863.5	11,709.9	....	167.5	....	....	....	....	....	6,154.7	....

[1] Face value.
[2] Federal Reserve holdings exclude Treasury securities held under repurchase agreements.
[3] Includes U.S. chartered depository institutions, foreign banking offices in U.S., banks in U.S. affiliated areas, credit unions, and bank holding companies.
[4] Current accrual value includes myRA.
[5] Includes Treasury securities held by the Federal Employees Retirement System Thrift Savings Plan "G Fund."
[6] Includes money market mutual funds, mutual funds, and closed-end investment companies.
[7] Includes nonmarketable foreign series, Treasury securities, and Treasury deposit funds. Excludes Treasury securities held under repurchase agreements in custody accounts at the Federal Reserve Bank of New York. Estimates reflect benchmarks to this series at differing intervals; for further detail, see *Treasury Bulletin* and http://www.treasury.gov/resource-center/data-chart-center/tic/pages/index.aspx.
[8] Includes individuals, Government-sponsored enterprises, brokers and dealers, bank personal trusts and estates, corporate and noncorporate businesses, and other investors.

Note: Data shown in this table are as of November 25, 2016.

Source: Department of the Treasury.

TABLE B–25. Bond yields and interest rates, 1947–2016

[Percent per annum]

Year and month	U.S. Treasury securities Bills (at auction)[1] 3-month	6-month	Constant maturities[2] 3-year	10-year	30-year	Corporate bonds (Moody's) Aaa[3]	Baa	High-grade municipal bonds (Standard & Poor's)	New-home mortgage yields[4]	Prime rate charged by banks[5]	Discount window (Federal Reserve Bank of New York)[5,6] Primary credit	Adjustment credit	Federal funds rate[7]
1947	0.594	....	....	....	....	2.61	3.24	2.01	....	1.50–1.75	....	1.00	....
1948	1.040	....	....	....	....	2.82	3.47	2.40	....	1.75–2.00	....	1.34	....
1949	1.102	....	....	....	....	2.66	3.42	2.21	....	2.00	....	1.50	....
1950	1.218	....	....	....	....	2.62	3.24	1.98	....	2.07	....	1.59	....
1951	1.552	....	....	....	....	2.86	3.41	2.00	....	2.56	....	1.75	....
1952	1.766	....	....	....	....	2.96	3.52	2.19	....	3.00	....	1.75	....
1953	1.931	....	2.47	2.85	....	3.20	3.74	2.72	....	3.17	....	1.99	....
1954	.953	....	1.63	2.40	....	2.90	3.51	2.37	....	3.05	....	1.60	....
1955	1.753	....	2.47	2.82	....	3.06	3.53	2.53	....	3.16	....	1.89	1.79
1956	2.658	....	3.19	3.18	....	3.36	3.88	2.93	....	3.77	....	2.77	2.73
1957	3.267	....	3.98	3.65	....	3.89	4.71	3.60	....	4.20	....	3.12	3.11
1958	1.839	....	2.84	3.32	....	3.79	4.73	3.56	....	3.83	....	2.15	1.57
1959	3.405	3.832	4.46	4.33	....	4.38	5.05	3.95	....	4.48	....	3.36	3.31
1960	2.93	3.25	3.98	4.12	....	4.41	5.19	3.73	....	4.82	....	3.53	3.21
1961	2.38	2.61	3.54	3.88	....	4.35	5.08	3.46	....	4.50	....	3.00	1.95
1962	2.78	2.91	3.47	3.95	....	4.33	5.02	3.18	....	4.50	....	3.00	2.71
1963	3.16	3.25	3.67	4.00	....	4.26	4.86	3.23	5.89	4.50	....	3.23	3.18
1964	3.56	3.69	4.03	4.19	....	4.40	4.83	3.22	5.83	4.50	....	3.55	3.50
1965	3.95	4.05	4.22	4.28	....	4.49	4.87	3.27	5.81	4.54	....	4.04	4.07
1966	4.88	5.08	5.23	4.93	....	5.13	5.67	3.82	6.25	5.63	....	4.50	5.11
1967	4.32	4.63	5.03	5.07	....	5.51	6.23	3.98	6.46	5.63	....	4.19	4.22
1968	5.34	5.47	5.68	5.64	....	6.18	6.94	4.51	6.97	6.31	....	5.17	5.66
1969	6.68	6.85	7.02	6.67	....	7.03	7.81	5.81	7.81	7.96	....	5.87	8.21
1970	6.43	6.53	7.29	7.35	....	8.04	9.11	6.51	8.45	7.91	....	5.95	7.17
1971	4.35	4.51	5.66	6.16	....	7.39	8.56	5.70	7.74	5.73	....	4.88	4.67
1972	4.07	4.47	5.72	6.21	....	7.21	8.16	5.27	7.60	5.25	....	4.50	4.44
1973	7.04	7.18	6.96	6.85	....	7.44	8.24	5.18	7.96	8.03	....	6.45	8.74
1974	7.89	7.93	7.84	7.56	....	8.57	9.50	6.09	8.92	10.81	....	7.83	10.51
1975	5.84	6.12	7.50	7.99	....	8.83	10.61	6.89	9.00	7.86	....	6.25	5.82
1976	4.99	5.27	6.77	7.61	....	8.43	9.75	6.49	9.00	6.84	....	5.50	5.05
1977	5.27	5.52	6.68	7.42	7.75	8.02	8.97	5.56	9.02	6.83	....	5.46	5.54
1978	7.22	7.58	8.29	8.41	8.49	8.73	9.49	5.90	9.56	9.06	....	7.46	7.94
1979	10.05	10.02	9.70	9.43	9.28	9.63	10.69	6.39	10.78	12.67	....	10.29	11.20
1980	11.51	11.37	11.51	11.43	11.27	11.94	13.67	8.51	12.66	15.26	....	11.77	13.35
1981	14.03	13.78	14.46	13.92	13.45	14.17	16.04	11.23	14.70	18.87	....	13.42	16.39
1982	10.69	11.08	12.93	13.01	12.76	13.79	16.11	11.57	15.14	14.85	....	11.01	12.24
1983	8.63	8.75	10.45	11.10	11.18	12.04	13.55	9.47	12.57	10.79	....	8.50	9.09
1984	9.53	9.77	11.92	12.46	12.41	12.71	14.19	10.15	12.38	12.04	....	8.80	10.23
1985	7.47	7.64	9.64	10.62	10.79	11.37	12.72	9.18	11.55	9.93	....	7.69	8.10
1986	5.98	6.03	7.06	7.67	7.78	9.02	10.39	7.38	10.17	8.33	....	6.32	6.80
1987	5.82	6.05	7.68	8.39	8.59	9.38	10.58	7.73	9.31	8.21	....	5.66	6.66
1988	6.69	6.92	8.26	8.85	8.96	9.71	10.83	7.76	9.19	9.32	....	6.20	7.57
1989	8.12	8.04	8.55	8.49	8.45	9.26	10.18	7.24	10.13	10.87	....	6.93	9.21
1990	7.51	7.47	8.26	8.55	8.61	9.32	10.36	7.25	10.05	10.01	....	6.98	8.10
1991	5.42	5.49	6.82	7.86	8.14	8.77	9.80	6.89	9.32	8.46	....	5.45	5.69
1992	3.45	3.57	5.30	7.01	7.67	8.14	8.98	6.41	8.24	6.25	....	3.25	3.52
1993	3.02	3.14	4.44	5.87	6.59	7.22	7.93	5.63	7.20	6.00	....	3.00	3.02
1994	4.29	4.66	6.27	7.09	7.37	7.96	8.62	6.19	7.49	7.15	....	3.60	4.21
1995	5.51	5.59	6.25	6.57	6.88	7.59	8.20	5.95	7.87	8.83	....	5.21	5.83
1996	5.02	5.09	5.99	6.44	6.71	7.37	8.05	5.75	7.80	8.27	....	5.02	5.30
1997	5.07	5.18	6.10	6.35	6.61	7.26	7.86	5.55	7.71	8.44	....	5.00	5.46
1998	4.81	4.85	5.14	5.26	5.58	6.53	7.22	5.12	7.07	8.35	....	4.92	5.35
1999	4.66	4.76	5.49	5.65	5.87	7.04	7.87	5.43	7.04	8.00	....	4.62	4.97
2000	5.85	5.92	6.22	6.03	5.94	7.62	8.36	5.77	7.52	9.23	....	5.73	6.24
2001	3.44	3.39	4.09	5.02	5.49	7.08	7.95	5.19	7.00	6.91	....	3.40	3.88
2002	1.62	1.69	3.10	4.61	5.43	6.49	7.80	5.05	6.43	4.67	....	1.17	1.67
2003	1.01	1.06	2.10	4.01	....	5.67	6.77	4.73	5.80	4.12	2.12	....	1.13
2004	1.38	1.57	2.78	4.27	....	5.63	6.39	4.63	5.77	4.34	2.34	....	1.35
2005	3.16	3.40	3.93	4.29	....	5.24	6.06	4.29	5.94	6.19	4.19	....	3.22
2006	4.73	4.80	4.77	4.80	4.91	5.59	6.48	4.42	6.63	7.96	5.96	....	4.97
2007	4.41	4.48	4.35	4.63	4.84	5.56	6.48	4.42	6.41	8.05	5.86	....	5.02
2008	1.48	1.71	2.24	3.66	4.28	5.63	7.45	4.80	6.05	5.09	2.39	....	1.92
2009	.16	.29	1.43	3.26	4.08	5.31	7.30	4.64	5.14	3.25	.50	....	.16
2010	.14	.20	1.11	3.22	4.25	4.94	6.04	4.16	4.80	3.25	.72	....	.18
2011	.06	.10	.75	2.78	3.91	4.64	5.66	4.29	4.56	3.25	.75	....	.10
2012	.09	.13	.38	1.80	2.92	3.67	4.94	3.14	3.69	3.25	.75	....	.14
2013	.06	.09	.54	2.35	3.45	4.24	5.10	3.96	4.00	3.25	.75	....	.11
2014	.03	.06	.90	2.54	3.34	4.16	4.85	3.78	4.22	3.25	.75	....	.09
2015	.06	.17	1.02	2.14	2.84	3.89	5.00	3.48	4.01	3.26	.76	....	.13

[1] High bill rate at auction, issue date within period, bank-discount basis. On or after October 28, 1998, data are stop yields from uniform-price auctions. Before that date, they are weighted average yields from multiple-price auctions.

See next page for continuation of table.

Table B–25. Bond yields and interest rates, 1947–2016—*Continued*

[Percent per annum]

Year and month	U.S. Treasury securities					Corporate bonds (Moody's)		High-grade municipal bonds (Standard & Poor's)[3]	New-home mortgage yields[4]	Prime rate charged by banks[5]	Discount window (Federal Reserve Bank of New York)[5,6]		Federal funds rate[7]
	Bills (at auction)[1]		Constant maturities[2]										
	3-month	6-month	3-year	10-year	30-year	Aaa[3]	Baa				Primary credit	Adjustment credit	
											High-low	High-low	High-low
2012: Jan	0.02	0.06	0.36	1.97	3.03	3.85	5.23	3.43	4.09	3.25–3.25	0.75–0.75	....	0.08
Feb	.08	.11	.38	1.97	3.11	3.85	5.14	3.25	4.01	3.25–3.25	0.75–0.75	....	.10
Mar	.09	.14	.51	2.17	3.28	3.99	5.23	3.51	3.72	3.25–3.25	0.75–0.75	....	.13
Apr	.08	.14	.43	2.05	3.18	3.96	5.19	3.47	3.93	3.25–3.25	0.75–0.75	....	.14
May	.09	.14	.39	1.80	2.93	3.80	5.07	3.21	3.88	3.25–3.25	0.75–0.75	....	.16
June	.09	.14	.39	1.62	2.70	3.64	5.02	3.30	3.80	3.25–3.25	0.75–0.75	....	.16
July	.10	.14	.33	1.53	2.59	3.40	4.87	3.14	3.76	3.25–3.25	0.75–0.75	....	.16
Aug	.11	.14	.37	1.68	2.77	3.48	4.91	3.07	3.67	3.25–3.25	0.75–0.75	....	.13
Sept	.10	.13	.34	1.72	2.88	3.49	4.84	3.02	3.62	3.25–3.25	0.75–0.75	....	.14
Oct	.10	.15	.37	1.75	2.90	3.47	4.58	2.89	3.58	3.25–3.25	0.75–0.75	....	.16
Nov	.11	.15	.36	1.65	2.80	3.50	4.51	2.68	3.46	3.25–3.25	0.75–0.75	....	.16
Dec	.08	.12	.35	1.72	2.88	3.65	4.63	2.73	3.40	3.25–3.25	0.75–0.75	....	.16
2013: Jan	.07	.11	.39	1.91	3.08	3.80	4.73	2.93	3.41	3.25–3.25	0.75–0.75	....	.14
Feb	.10	.12	.40	1.98	3.17	3.90	4.85	3.09	3.49	3.25–3.25	0.75–0.75	....	.15
Mar	.09	.11	.39	1.96	3.16	3.93	4.85	3.27	3.61	3.25–3.25	0.75–0.75	....	.14
Apr	.06	.09	.34	1.76	2.93	3.73	4.59	3.22	3.66	3.25–3.25	0.75–0.75	....	.15
May	.05	.08	.40	1.93	3.11	3.89	4.73	3.39	3.55	3.25–3.25	0.75–0.75	....	.11
June	.05	.09	.58	2.30	3.40	4.27	5.19	4.02	3.64	3.25–3.25	0.75–0.75	....	.09
July	.04	.08	.64	2.58	3.61	4.34	5.32	4.51	4.07	3.25–3.25	0.75–0.75	....	.09
Aug	.04	.07	.70	2.74	3.76	4.54	5.42	4.77	4.33	3.25–3.25	0.75–0.75	....	.08
Sept	.02	.04	.78	2.81	3.79	4.64	5.47	4.74	4.44	3.25–3.25	0.75–0.75	....	.08
Oct	.05	.08	.63	2.62	3.68	4.53	5.31	4.50	4.47	3.25–3.25	0.75–0.75	....	.09
Nov	.07	.10	.58	2.72	3.80	4.63	5.38	4.51	4.39	3.25–3.25	0.75–0.75	....	.08
Dec	.07	.09	.69	2.90	3.89	4.62	5.38	4.55	4.37	3.25–3.25	0.75–0.75	....	.09
2014: Jan	.05	.07	.78	2.86	3.77	4.49	5.19	4.38	4.45	3.25–3.25	0.75–0.75	....	.07
Feb	.06	.08	.69	2.71	3.66	4.45	5.10	4.25	4.04	3.25–3.25	0.75–0.75	....	.07
Mar	.05	.08	.82	2.72	3.62	4.38	5.06	4.16	4.35	3.25–3.25	0.75–0.75	....	.08
Apr	.04	.05	.88	2.71	3.52	4.24	4.90	4.02	4.33	3.25–3.25	0.75–0.75	....	.09
May	.03	.05	.83	2.56	3.39	4.16	4.76	3.80	4.01	3.25–3.25	0.75–0.75	....	.09
June	.03	.06	.90	2.60	3.42	4.25	4.80	3.72	4.27	3.25–3.25	0.75–0.75	....	.10
July	.03	.06	.97	2.54	3.33	4.16	4.73	3.75	4.25	3.25–3.25	0.75–0.75	....	.09
Aug	.03	.05	.93	2.42	3.20	4.08	4.69	3.53	4.25	3.25–3.25	0.75–0.75	....	.09
Sept	.02	.05	1.05	2.53	3.26	4.11	4.80	3.55	4.23	3.25–3.25	0.75–0.75	....	.09
Oct	.02	.05	.88	2.30	3.04	3.92	4.69	3.35	4.23	3.25–3.25	0.75–0.75	....	.09
Nov	.02	.07	.96	2.33	3.04	3.92	4.79	3.49	4.16	3.25–3.25	0.75–0.75	....	.09
Dec	.04	.11	1.06	2.21	2.83	3.79	4.74	3.39	4.14	3.25–3.25	0.75–0.75	....	.12
2015: Jan	.03	.10	.90	1.88	2.46	3.46	4.45	3.16	4.05	3.25–3.25	0.75–0.75	....	.11
Feb	.02	.07	.99	1.98	2.57	3.61	4.51	3.26	3.91	3.25–3.25	0.75–0.75	....	.11
Mar	.02	.11	1.02	2.04	2.63	3.64	4.54	3.29	3.93	3.25–3.25	0.75–0.75	....	.11
Apr	.03	.10	.87	1.94	2.59	3.52	4.48	3.40	3.92	3.25–3.25	0.75–0.75	....	.12
May	.02	.08	.98	2.20	2.96	3.98	4.89	3.77	3.89	3.25–3.25	0.75–0.75	....	.12
June	.01	.08	1.07	2.36	3.11	4.19	5.13	3.76	3.98	3.25–3.25	0.75–0.75	....	.13
July	.03	.12	1.03	2.32	3.07	4.15	5.20	3.73	4.10	3.25–3.25	0.75–0.75	....	.13
Aug	.09	.21	1.03	2.17	2.86	4.04	5.19	3.57	4.12	3.25–3.25	0.75–0.75	....	.14
Sept	.06	.23	1.01	2.17	2.95	4.07	5.34	3.56	4.09	3.25–3.25	0.75–0.75	....	.14
Oct	.01	.10	.93	2.07	2.89	3.95	5.34	3.48	4.02	3.25–3.25	0.75–0.75	....	.12
Nov	.13	.33	1.20	2.26	3.03	4.06	5.46	3.50	4.00	3.25–3.25	0.75–0.75	....	.12
Dec	.26	.52	1.28	2.24	2.97	3.97	5.46	3.23	4.03	3.50–3.25	1.00–0.75	....	.24
2016: Jan	.25	.44	1.14	2.09	2.86	4.00	5.45	3.01	4.04	3.50–3.50	1.00–1.00	....	.34
Feb	.32	.44	.90	1.78	2.62	3.96	5.34	3.21	4.01	3.50–3.50	1.00–1.00	....	.38
Mar	.32	.48	1.04	1.89	2.68	3.82	5.13	3.28	3.92	3.50–3.50	1.00–1.00	....	.36
Apr	.23	.37	.92	1.81	2.62	3.62	4.79	3.04	3.86	3.50–3.50	1.00–1.00	....	.37
May	.27	.41	.97	1.81	2.63	3.65	4.68	2.95	3.82	3.50–3.50	1.00–1.00	....	.37
June	.29	.41	.86	1.64	2.45	3.50	4.53	2.84	3.81	3.50–3.50	1.00–1.00	....	.38
July	.31	.40	.79	1.50	2.23	3.28	4.22	2.57	3.74	3.50–3.50	1.00–1.00	....	.39
Aug	.30	.43	.85	1.56	2.26	3.32	4.24	2.77	3.68	3.50–3.50	1.00–1.00	....	.40
Sept	.32	.48	.90	1.63	2.35	3.41	4.31	2.86	3.58	3.50–3.50	1.00–1.00	....	.40
Oct	.34	.48	.99	1.76	2.50	3.51	4.38	3.13	3.57	3.50–3.50	1.00–1.00	....	.40
Nov	.44	.57	1.22	2.14	2.86	3.86	4.71	3.36	....	3.50–3.50	1.00–1.00	....	.41

[2] Yields on the more actively traded issues adjusted to constant maturities by the Department of the Treasury. The 30-year Treasury constant maturity series was discontinued on February 18, 2002, and reintroduced on February 9, 2006.

[3] Beginning with December 7, 2001, data for corporate Aaa series are industrial bonds only.

[4] Effective rate (in the primary market) on conventional mortgages, reflecting fees and charges as well as contract rate and assuming, on the average, repayment at end of 10 years. Rates beginning with January 1973 not strictly comparable with prior rates.

[5] For monthly data, high and low for the period. Prime rate for 1947–1948 are ranges of the rate in effect during the period.

[6] Primary credit replaced adjustment credit as the Federal Reserve's principal discount window lending program effective January 9, 2003.

[7] Beginning March 1, 2016, the daily effective federal funds rate is a volume-weighted median of transaction-level data collected from depository institutions in the Report of Selected Money Market Rates (FR 2420). Between July 21, 1975 and February 29, 2016, the daily effective rate was a volume-weighted mean of rates on brokered trades. Prior to that, the daily effective rate was the rate considered most representative of the day's transactions, usually the one at which most transactions occurred.

Sources: Department of the Treasury, Board of Governors of the Federal Reserve System, Federal Housing Finance Agency, Moody's Investors Service, Bloomberg, and Standard & Poor's.

TABLE B-26. Money stock and debt measures, 1975–2016

[Averages of daily figures, except debt end-of-period basis; billions of dollars, seasonally adjusted]

Year and month	M1 Sum of currency, demand deposits, travelers checks, and other checkable deposits	M2 M1 plus savings deposits, retail MMMF balances, and small time deposits [1]	Debt Debt of domestic nonfinancial sectors [2]	Percent change		
				From year or 6 months earlier [3]		From previous period [4]
				M1	M2	Debt
December:						
1975	287.1	1,016.2	2,311.0	4.7	12.6	9.3
1976	306.2	1,152.0	2,562.9	6.7	13.4	11.0
1977	330.9	1,270.3	2,892.8	8.1	10.3	12.9
1978	357.3	1,366.0	3,286.7	8.0	7.5	13.8
1979	381.8	1,473.7	3,682.2	6.9	7.9	12.0
1980	408.5	1,599.8	4,045.1	7.0	8.6	9.6
1981	436.7	1,755.5	4,459.4	6.9	9.7	10.2
1982	474.8	1,905.9	4,895.6	8.7	8.6	10.5
1983	521.4	2,123.5	5,492.1	9.8	11.4	12.1
1984	551.6	2,306.4	6,302.3	5.8	8.6	14.8
1985	619.8	2,492.1	7,334.6	12.4	8.1	16.1
1986	724.7	2,728.0	8,212.6	16.9	9.5	12.0
1987	750.2	2,826.4	8,930.6	3.5	3.6	9.0
1988	786.7	2,989.3	9,747.9	4.9	5.8	9.2
1989	792.9	3,154.0	10,482.9	.8	5.5	7.4
1990	824.7	3,272.7	11,198.6	4.0	3.8	6.6
1991	897.0	3,372.2	11,722.5	8.8	3.0	4.7
1992	1,024.9	3,424.1	12,278.2	14.3	1.5	4.7
1993	1,129.6	3,473.6	13,020.0	10.2	1.4	5.9
1994	1,150.7	3,483.8	13,701.9	1.9	.3	5.2
1995	1,127.5	3,626.4	14,382.8	−2.0	4.1	4.9
1996	1,081.3	3,805.3	15,135.7	−4.1	4.9	5.2
1997	1,072.3	4,018.0	15,973.9	−.8	5.6	5.6
1998	1,095.0	4,358.5	17,021.7	2.1	8.5	6.6
1999	1,122.2	4,619.0	18,179.6	2.5	6.0	6.6
2000	1,088.5	4,905.0	19,064.4	−3.0	6.2	4.8
2001	1,183.1	5,408.4	20,150.5	8.7	10.3	5.8
2002	1,219.9	5,744.2	21,503.1	3.1	6.2	6.7
2003	1,305.8	6,037.4	23,198.2	7.0	5.1	7.7
2004	1,375.8	6,387.4	26,116.5	5.4	5.8	9.2
2005	1,374.9	6,651.2	28,365.2	−.1	4.1	8.7
2006	1,368.2	7,041.4	30,800.3	−.5	5.9	8.4
2007	1,376.5	7,444.2	33,276.6	.6	5.7	8.1
2008	1,606.8	8,166.6	35,065.4	16.7	9.7	5.8
2009	1,698.5	8,471.0	35,918.6	5.7	3.7	3.5
2010	1,842.5	8,775.2	37,232.9	8.5	3.6	4.4
2011	2,169.8	9,636.2	38,386.5	17.8	9.8	3.5
2012	2,461.4	10,428.7	40,133.1	13.4	8.2	5.0
2013	2,660.3	10,994.7	41,564.0	8.1	5.4	3.8
2014	2,930.2	11,646.9	43,324.4	10.1	5.9	4.3
2015	3,079.7	12,313.5	45,204.4	5.1	5.7	4.5
2015: Jan	2,930.7	11,706.7		6.6	5.2	
Feb	2,984.8	11,803.3		12.6	6.2	
Mar	2,990.7	11,839.2	43,603.6	8.5	6.2	2.7
Apr	2,994.8	11,890.9		8.3	6.1	
May	2,988.6	11,927.8		7.1	6.1	
June	3,015.0	11,975.2	44,073.7	5.8	5.6	4.4
July	3,034.2	12,036.1		7.1	5.6	
Aug	3,041.2	12,100.4		3.8	5.0	
Sept	3,055.5	12,157.7	44,360.5	4.3	5.4	2.7
Oct	3,031.8	12,180.7		2.5	4.9	
Nov	3,083.4	12,266.3		6.3	5.7	
Dec	3,079.7	12,313.5	45,204.4	4.3	5.7	7.7
2016: Jan	3,091.0	12,436.5		3.7	6.7	
Feb	3,104.0	12,485.2		4.1	6.4	
Mar	3,144.5	12,572.7	45,810.6	5.8	6.8	5.4
Apr	3,176.8	12,652.4		9.6	7.7	
May	3,224.6	12,728.9		9.2	7.5	
June	3,231.1	12,803.7	46,300.8	9.8	8.0	4.4
July	3,225.1	12,878.1		8.7	7.1	
Aug	3,312.4	12,987.0		13.4	8.0	
Sept	3,318.0	13,061.0		11.0	7.8	
Oct	3,340.5	13,137.9		10.3	7.7	

[1] Money market mutual fund (MMMF). Savings deposits include money market deposit accounts.

[2] Consists of outstanding debt securities and loans of the U.S. Government, State and local governments, and private nonfinancial sectors. Quarterly data shown in last month of quarter. End-of-year data are for fourth quarter.

[3] Annual changes are from December to December; monthly changes are from six months earlier at a simple annual rate.

[4] Debt growth of domestic nonfinancial sectors is the seasonally adjusted borrowing flow divided by the seasonally adjusted level of debt outstanding in the previous period. Annual changes are from fourth quarter to fourth quarter; quarterly changes are from the previous quarter at an annual rate.

Note: For further information on M1 and M2, see the H.6 release.
For further information on the debt of domestic nonfinancial sectors and the derivation of debt growth, see the Z.1 release.

Source: Board of Governors of the Federal Reserve System.